FRENCH
ENGLISH

DICTIONARY • DICTIONNAIRE

ANGLAIS
FRANÇAIS

Berlitz Dictionaries

Dansk	Engelsk, Fransk, Italiensk, Spansk, Tysk
Deutsch	Dänisch, Englisch, Finnisch, Französisch, Italienisch, Niederländisch, Norwegisch, Portugiesisch, Schwedish, Spanisch
English	Danish, Dutch, Finnish, French, German, Italian, Norwegian, Portuguese, Spanish, Swedish, Turkish
Español	Alemán, Danés, Finlandés, Francés, Holandés, Inglés, Noruego, Sueco
Français	Allemand, Anglais, Danois, Espagnol, Finnois, Italien, Néerlandais, Norvégien, Portugais, Suédois
Italiano	Danese, Finlandese, Francese, Inglese, Norvegese, Olandese, Svedese, Tedesco
Nederlands	Duits, Engels, Frans, Italiaans, Portugees, Spaans
Norsk	Engelsk, Fransk, Italiensk, Spansk, Tysk
Português	Alemão, Francês, Holandês, Inglês, Sueco
Suomi	Englanti, Espanja, Italia, Ranska, Ruotsi, Saksa
Svenska	Engelska, Finska, Franska, Italienska, Portugisiska, Spanska, Tyska

FRENCH ENGLISH

DICTIONARY • DICTIONNAIRE

ANGLAIS FRANÇAIS

with mini grammar section
avec section de mini-grammaire

Copyright © 1994, 1979, 1974, Berlitz Publishing Company, Ltd.
Peterley Road, Oxford OX4 2TX, U.K.

All rights reserved. No part of this book may be reproduced or transmitted
in any form or by any means, electronic or mechanical, including photo-
copying, recording or by any information storage and retrieval system, without permission in writing from the publisher.

Library of Congress Catalog Card Number: 78-78078

2nd revised edition — 1st printing 1994
Printed in The Netherlands

Berlitz Trademark Reg. U.S. Patent Office
and other countries—Marca Registrada.

Contents

Table des matières

Preface

In selecting the 12.500 word-concepts in each language for this dictionary, the editors have had the traveller's needs foremost in mind. This book will prove invaluable to all the millions of travellers, tourists and business people who appreciate the reassurance a small and practical dictionary can provide. It offers them—as it does beginners and students—all the basic vocabulary they are going to encounter and to have to use, giving the key words and expressions to allow them to cope in everyday situations.

Like our successful phrase books and travel guides, these dictionaries—created with the help of a computer data bank—are designed to slip into pocket or purse, and thus have a role as handy companions at all times.

Besides just about everything you normally find in dictionaries, there are these Berlitz bonuses:

● imitated pronunciation next to each foreign-word entry, making it easy to read and enunciate words whose spelling may look forbidding

● a unique, practical glossary to simplify reading a foreign restaurant menu and to take the mystery out of complicated dishes and indecipherable names on bills of fare

● useful information on how to tell the time and how to count, on conjugating irregular verbs, commonly seen abbreviations and converting to the metric system, in addition to basic phrases.

While no dictionary of this size can pretend to completeness, we expect the user of this book will feel well armed to affront foreign travel with confidence. We should, however, be very pleased to receive comments, criticism and suggestions that you think may be of help in preparing future editions.

Préface

En choisissant 12 500 mots-concepts dans chacune des langues de ce dictionnaire, nos rédacteurs se sont souciés des besoins essentiels du voyageur. Cet ouvrage s'avérera indispensable aux millions de touristes, globe-trotters, hommes ou femmes d'affaires qui apprécient l'appoint qu'apporte un dictionnaire pratique et de format réduit. Il leur offre, ainsi qu'aux débutants et aux étudiants, tout le vocabulaire qu'ils seront amenés à rencontrer et à utiliser; il leur propose des mots-clés et des expressions leur permettant de faire face aux situations courantes.

A l'instar de nos manuels de conversation et de nos guides de voyage déjà fort appréciés, nos dictionnaires – réalisés grâce à une banque de données sur ordinateur – sont conçus pour se glisser dans une poche ou dans un sac, assumant ainsi leur rôle de compagnons à tout moment.

Outre tous les éléments contenus dans n'importe quel dictionnaire, nos ouvrages proposent:

- une transcription phonétique à côté de chaque entrée afin d'en faciliter la lecture, apport non négligeable lorsque le mot étranger semble à priori imprononçable

- un lexique pratique visant à simplifier la lecture du menu dans un restaurant et révélant tous les mystères de plats jusqu'alors inconnus

- des informations précieuses sur la façon d'exprimer le temps, de compter, sur les verbes irréguliers, sur les abréviations courantes, en plus des expressions usuelles.

Aucun dictionnaire de ce format ne peut prétendre être exhaustif, mais le but de cet ouvrage est de permettre à son utilisateur d'affronter avec confiance un voyage à l'étranger. Nous n'en serions pas moins très heureux de recevoir de nos lecteurs tous commentaires, critiques et suggestions qui nous permettraient de compléter nos futures rééditions.

french-english
français-anglais

Introduction

The dictionary has been designed to take account of your practical needs. Unnecessary linguistic information has been avoided. The entries are listed in alphabetical order, regardless of whether the entry word is printed in a single word, contains an apostrophe, or is in two or more separate words. As the only exception to this rule, a few idiomatic expressions are listed alphabetically as main entries, according to the most significant word of the expression. When an entry is followed by sub-entries such as expressions and locutions, these, too, have been listed in alphabetical order.

Each main-entry word is followed by a phonetic transcription (see Guide to pronunciation). Following the transcription is the part of speech of the entry word whenever applicable. When an entry word may be used as more than one part of speech, the translations are grouped together after the respective part of speech.

The feminine or plural forms of French adjectives have been supplied whenever they diverge from the standard rule for the word-ending in question. Similarly, the plural forms of nouns are given when not in accordance with the rules for the particular word-ending.

Whenever an entry word is repeated in irregular forms, or in sub-entries, a tilde (~) is used to represent the full entry word.

In irregular feminine and plural forms, a hyphen is used to represent the part of the main-entry word that precedes the relevant word-ending.

An asterisk (*) in front of a verb indicates that the verb is irregular. For details, refer to the lists of irregular verbs.

Abbreviations

adj	adjective	*num*	numeral
adv	adverb	*p*	past tense
Am	American	*pl*	plural
art	article	*plAm*	plural (American)
conj	conjunction	*pp*	past participle
f	feminine	*pr*	present tense
fpl	feminine plural	*pref*	prefix
m	masculine	*prep*	preposition
mpl	masculine plural	*pron*	pronoun
n	noun	*v*	verb
nAm	noun (American)	*vAm*	verb (American)

Guide to Pronunciation

Each main entry in this part of the dictionary is followed by a phonetic transcription which shows you how to pronounce the words. This transcription should be read as if it were English. It is based on Standard British pronunciation, though we have tried to take account of General American pronunciation also. Below, only those letters and symbols are explained which we consider likely to be ambiguous or not immediately understood.

The syllables are separated by hyphens, and stressed syllables are printed in *italics*.

Of course, the sounds of any two languages are never exactly the same, but if you follow carefully our indications, you should be able to pronounce the foreign words in such a way that you'll be understood. To make your task easier, our transcriptions occasionally simplify slightly the sound system of the language while still reflecting the essential sound differences.

Consonants

g	always hard, as in go
ñ	as in Spanish señor, or like ni in onion
r	pronounced in the back of the mouth
s	always hard, as in so
zh	a soft, voiced sh, like s in pleasure

The sign (') indicates a so-called aspirate h. It means that no liaison (*les huttes*—lay 'ewt) nor elision (*la hutte*—lah 'ewt) should be made.

Vowels and Diphthongs

aa	long **a,** as in car
ah	a short version of **aa**; between **a** in cat and **u** in cut
ai	like **air**, without any **r**-sound
eh	like **e** in get
er	as in other, without any **r**-sound
ew	a "rounded ee-sound". Say the vowel sound **ee** (as in see), and while saying it, round your lips as for **oo** (as in soon), without moving your tongue; when your lips are in the **oo** position, but your tongue in the **ee** position, you should be pronouncing the correct sound

igh   as in s**igh**

o   always as in h**o**t (British pronunciation)

ur   as in f**ur**, but with rounded lips and no **r**-sound

1) A bar over a vowel symbol (e.g. **ēw**) shows that this sound is long.

2) Raised letters (e.g. **oo**ᵉᵉ, ʸ**ur**) should be pronounced only fleetingly.

3) French contains nasal vowels, which we transcribe with a vowel symbol plus **ng** (e.g. **ahng**). This **ng** should *not* be pronounced, and serves solely to indicate nasal quality of the preceding vowel. A nasal vowel is pronounced simultaneously through the mouth and the nose.

4) French vowels (i.e. not diphthongs) are relatively short and pure. Therefore, you should try to read a transcription like **oa** without moving tongue or lips while pronouncing the sound.

A

à (ah) *prep* to; at, on

abandonner (ah-bahng-do-*nay*) *v* desert

abat-jour (ah-bah-*zhoor*) *m* lampshade

*abattre (ah-*bahtr*) *v* knock down; kill; dishearten

abbaye (ah-bay-*ee*) *f* abbey

abcès (ah-*psay*) *m* abscess

abeille (ah-*bay*) *f* bee

aberration (ah-beh-rah-*s^yawng*) *f* aberration

abîme (ah-*beem*) *m* abyss

abîmer (ah-bee-*may*) *v* *spoil

abolir (ah-bo-*leer*) *v* abolish

abondance (ah-bawng-*dahngss*) *f* abundance; plenty

abondant (ah-bawng-*dahng*) *adj* abundant; plentiful

abonné (ah-bo-*nay*) *m* subscriber

abonnement (ah-bon-*mahng*) *m* subscription

d'abord (dah-*bawr*) at first

abordage (ah-bor-*daazh*) *m* collision

aboutir à (ah-boo-*teer*) end at; result in

aboyer (ah-bwah-*^yay*) *v* bark, bay

abréviation (ah-bray-v^yah-*s^yawng*) *f* abbreviation

abri (ah-*bree*) *m* shelter; cover

abricot (ah-bree-*koa*) *m* apricot

abriter (ah-bree-*tay*) *v* shelter

abrupt (ah-*brewpt*) *adj* steep

absence (ah-*psahngss*) *f* absence

absent (ah-*psahng*) *adj* absent

absolu (ah-pso-*lew*) *adj* total, sheer

absolument (ah-pso-lew-*mahng*) *adv* absolutely

absorber (ah-psor-*bay*) *v* absorb

s'*abstenir de (ahp-ster-*neer*) abstain from

abstraction faite de (ahp-strahk-*s^yawng* feht der) apart from

abstrait (ahp-*stray*) *adj* abstract

absurde (ah-*psewrd*) *adj* absurd; foolish

abus (ah-*bew*) *m* abuse, misuse

académie (ah-kah-day-*mee*) *f* academy; ~ **des beaux-arts** art school

accélérateur (ahk-say-lay-rah-*tūrr*) *m* accelerator

accélérer (ahk-say-lay-*ray*) *v* accelerate

accent (ahk-*sahng*) *m* accent, stress

accepter (ahk-sehp-*tay*) *v* accept

accès (ahk-*say*) *m* access; approach, entrance, admittance

accessible (ahk-say-*seebl*) *adj* accessible; attainable

accessoire (ahk-say-*swaar*) *adj* additional

accessoires (ahk-say-*swaar*) *mpl* accessories *pl*

accident (ahk-see-*dahng*) *m* accident; ~ **d'avion** plane crash

accidenté (ahk-see-dahng-*tay*) *adj* hilly; uneven

accidentel (ahk-see-dahng-*tehl*) *adj* accidental

acclamer (ah-klah-*may*) *v* cheer

accommodation (ah-ko-mo-dah-s*Yawng*) *f* accommodation

accompagner (ah-kawng-pah-*ñay*) *v* accompany; conduct

accomplir (ah-kawng-*pleer*) *v* accomplish; perform, achieve

accomplissement (ah-kawng-plee-*smahng*) *m* feat

accord (ah-*kawr*) *m* settlement, agreement; approval; **d'accord!** all right!; okay!; *être d'accord agree; *être d'accord avec approve of

accorder (ah-kor-*day*) *v* grant; extend; tune in; **s'accorder avec** match

accoster (ah-ko-*stay*) *v* dock

accouchement (ah-koosh-*mahng*) *m* childbirth, delivery

accoutumé (ah-koo-tew-*may*) *adj* accustomed

s'accrocher (ah-kro-*shay*) *hold on

accueil (ah-*kuree*) *m* reception; welcome

*accueillir** (ah-kur-*Yeer*) *v* welcome

accumulateur (ah-kew-mew-lah-*tūrr*) *m* battery

s'accumuler (ah-kew-mew-*lay*) increase

accusation (ah-kew-zah-s*Yawng*) *f* charge

accuser (ah-kew-*zay*) *v* accuse; charge

achat (ah-*shah*) *m* purchase; ~ **à tempérament** hire-purchase; *faire des achats shop

acheter (ahsh-*tay*) *v* *buy, purchase

acheteur (ahsh-*tūrr*) *m* buyer, pur-

chaser

achever (ahsh-*vay*) *v* finish; complete, accomplish

acide (ah-*seed*) *m* acid

acier (ah-s*Yay*) *m* steel; ~ **inoxydable** stainless steel

acné (ahk-*nay*) *f* acne

acompte (ah-*kawngt*) *m* down payment

à-coup (ah-*koo*) *m* tug

*acquérir** (ah-kay-*reer*) *v* acquire; *buy

acquisition (ah-kee-zee-s*Yawng*) *f* acquisition, purchase

acquittement (ah-keet-*mahng*) *m* acquittal

acte (ahkt) *m* act, deed

acteur (ahk-*tūrr*) *m* actor

actif (ahk-*teef*) *adj* active

action (ahk-s*Yawng*) *f* action, deed; share; **actions** stocks and shares

activité (ahk-tee-vee-*tay*) *f* activity; work

actrice (ahk-*treess*) *f* actress

actualité (ahk-twah-lee-*tay*) *f* current events; **actualités** news; newsreel

actuel (ahk-*twehl*) *adj* present; topical

actuellement (ahk-twehl-*mahng*) *adv* nowadays

adapter (ah-dahp-*tay*) *v* adapt; ~ **à** suit

addition (ah-dee-s*Yawng*) *f* addition; bill

additionner (ah-dee-s*Yo*-*nay*) *v* add; count

adéquat (ah-day-*kwah*) *adj* adequate; appropriate, proper; sufficient

adhérer à (ah-day-*ray*) join

adieu (ah-d*Yur*) *m* parting

adjectif (ah-jehk-*teef*) *m* adjective

*admettre** (ahd-*mehtr*) *v* acknowledge, admit; **en admettant que** supposing that

administratif (ahd-mee-nee-strah-*teef*)

adj administrative

administration (ahd-mee-nee-strah-s*y*awng) *f* administration; direction

administrer (ahd-mee-nee-stray) *v* direct; administer

admiration (ahd-mee-rah-s*y*awng) *f* admiration

admirer (ahd-mee-ray) *v* admire

admission (ahd-mee-s*y*awng) *f* admission; entry

adolescent (ah-do-leh-sahng) *m* teenager

adopter (ah-dop-tay) *v* adopt

adorable (ah-do-rahbl) *adj* adorable

adorer (ah-do-ray) *v* worship

adoucir (ah-doo-seer) *v* soften

adoucisseur d'eau (ah-doo-see-sürr doa) water-softener

adresse (ah-drehss) *f* address

adresser (ah-dray-say) *v* address; **s'adresser à** address

adroit (ah-drwah) *adj* skilful; smart

adulte (ah-dewlt) *m* adult, grown-up; *adj* adult, grown-up

adverbe (ahd-vehrb) *m* adverb

adversaire (ahd-vehr-sair) *m* opponent

aération (ah-ay-rah-s*y*awng) *f* ventilation

aérer (ah-ay-ray) *v* ventilate, air; **aéré** airy

aéroport (ah-ay-ro-pawr) *m* airport

aérosol (ah-ay-ro-sol) *m* atomizer

affaire (ah-fair) *f* business, matter, case; affair, concern; deal; ~ **de cœur** affair

affairé (ah-fay-ray) *adj* busy

affaires (ah-fair) *fpl* business; belongings *pl*; **chiffre d'affaires** turnover; **faire des ~ avec **deal with

affamé (ah-fah-may) *adj* hungry

affecter (ah-fehk-tay) *v* affect

affection (ah-fehk-s*y*awng) *f* affection; ailment

affectueux (ah-fehk-twur) *adj* affec-tionate

affiche (ah-feesh) *f* placard, poster

affiler (ah-fee-lay) *v* sharpen

affiliation (ah-fee-l*y*ah-s*y*awng) *f* membership

s'affilier à (ah-fee-l*y*ay) join

affirmatif (ah-feer-mah-teef) *adj* affirmative

affirmer (ah-feer-may) *v* affirm; state

affliction (ah-fleek-s*y*awng) *f* grief, affliction

affligé (ah-flee-zhay) *adj* sad

affluent (ah-flew-ahng) *m* tributary

affranchir (ah-frahng-sheer) *v* stamp

affreux (ah-frur) *adj* dreadful, frightful

affronter (ah-frawng-tay) *v* face

afin de (ah-fang der) to, in order to; **afin que** so that

Africain (ah-free-kang) *m* African

africain (ah-free-kang) *adj* African

Afrique (ah-freek) *f* Africa; ~ **du Sud** South Africa

after-shave (ahf-terr-shehv) *m* after-shave lotion

agacer (ah-gah-say) *v* irritate, annoy

âge (aazh) *m* age

âgé (ah-zhay) *adj* aged, elderly; **le plus ~** eldest; **plus ~** elder

agence (ah-zhahngss) *f* agency

agenda (ah-zhang-dah) *m* diary

s'agenouiller (ahzh-noo-*y*ay) **kneel

agent (ah-zhahng) *m* agent; ~ **de police** policeman; ~ **de voyages** travel agent; ~ **immobilier** house agent

agir (ah-zheer) *v* act

agitation (ah-zhee-tah-s*y*awng) *f* excitement, fuss; disturbance, unrest

agiter (ah-zhee-tay) *v* agitate; stir; **agité** restless

agneau (ah-ñoa) *m* lamb

agrafe (ah-grahf) *f* staple

agraire (ah-grair) *adj* agrarian

agrandir (ah-grahng-deer) *v* extend;

enlarge

agrandissement (ah-grahng-dee-smahng) *m* enlargement; extension

agréable (ah-gray-*ahbl*) *adj* pleasing, pleasant, agreeable; enjoyable

agréer (ah-gray-*ay*) *v* accept

agrément (ah-gray-*mahng*) *m* pleasure

agressif (ah-gray-*seef*) *adj* aggressive

agricole (ah-gree-*kol*) *adj* agricultural

agriculteur (ah-gree-kewl-*tūrr*) *m* farmer

agriculture (ah-gree-kewl-*tewr*) *f* agriculture

aide (ehd) *f* help, assistance, aid; *m* helper

aider (ay-*day*) *v* help, aid

aigle (aigl) *m* eagle

aiglefin (ehgl-*fang*) *m* haddock

aigre (aigr) *adj* sour

aigu (ay-*gew*) *adj* (f -guë) acute; sharp; keen

aiguille (ay-*gweeʸ*) *f* needle; spire; **travail à l'aiguille** needlework

aiguiser (ay-gee-*zay*) *v* sharpen

ail (igh) *m* (pl ails, aulx) garlic

aile (ehl) *f* wing

ailleurs (ah-ʸūrr) *adv* elsewhere; **d'ailleurs** moreover, besides

aimable (ay-*mahbl*) *adj* kind

aimer (ay-*may*) *v* like, *be fond of, love; fancy; **aimé** beloved; ~ **mieux** prefer

aine (ehn) *f* groin

aîné (ay-*nay*) *adj* elder

ainsi (ang-*see*) *adv* so, thus

air (air) *m* air; sky; tune; *avoir l'air** look

aisance (eh-*zahngss*) *f* ease

aise (aiz) *f* leisure, ease

aisé (ay-*zay*) *adj* well-to-do

ajournement (ah-zhoor-ner-*mahng*) *m* delay

ajourner (ah-zhoor-*nay*) *v* adjourn, *put off, postpone

ajouter (ah-zhoo-*tay*) *v* add

ajuster (ah-zhew-*stay*) *v* adjust

alarmer (ah-lahr-*may*) *v* alarm

album (ahl-*bom*) *m* album; ~ **de collage** scrap-book

alcool (ahl-*kol*) *m* alcohol; ~ **à brûler** methylated spirits; **réchaud à ~** spirit stove

alcoolique (ahl-ko-*leek*) *adj* alcoholic

alentours (ah-lahng-*tōōr*) *mpl* surroundings *pl*; vicinity

alerte (ah-*lehrt*) *f* alarm; *adj* smart

algèbre (ahl-*zhaibr*) *f* algebra

Algérie (ahl-zhay-*ree*) *f* Algeria

Algérien (ahl-zhay-rʸ*ang*) *m* Algerian

algérien (ahl-zhay-rʸ*ang*) *adj* Algerian

alimentation (ah-lee-mahng-tah-sʸ*awng*) *f* nourishment

alimenter (ah-lee-mahng-*tay*) *v* *feed

aliments (ah-lee-*mahng*) *mpl* foodstuffs *pl*; ~ **surgelés** frozen food

allaiter (ah-lay-*tay*) *v* nurse

allée (ah-*lay*) *f* avenue

Allemagne (ahl-*mahñ*) *f* Germany

Allemand (ahl-*mahng*) *m* German

allemand (ahl-*mahng*) *adj* German

***aller** (ah-*lay*) *v* *go; ~ **chercher** collect, pick up; **aller et retour** round trip *Am*; ~ **prendre** *get; **bien ~** suit; *become; **s'en ~** *go away; depart

allergie (ah-lehr-*zhee*) *f* allergy

alliance (ah-lʸ*ahngss*) *f* alliance; wedding-ring

allié (ah-lʸ*ay*) *m* associate; **Alliés** Allies *pl*

s'allier (ah-lʸ*ay*) ally

allocation (ah-lo-kah-sʸ*awng*) *f* allowance

allocution (ah-lo-kew-sʸ*awng*) *f* speech

allonger (ah-lawng-*zhay*) *v* lengthen; dilute

allumage (ah-lew-*maazh*) *m* ignition

allumer (ah-lew-*may*) *v* *light; switch on, turn on

allumette (ah-lew-*meht*) *f* match

allure (ah-*lēwr*) *f* pace, gait

almanach (ahl-mah-*nahk*) *m* almanac

alors (ah-*lawr*) *adv* then

alouette (ah-*lweht*) *f* lark

alphabet (ahl-fah-*bay*) *m* alphabet

alpinisme (ahl-pee-*neezm*) *m* mountaineering

alternatif (ahl-tehr-nah-*teef*) *adj* alternate

alternative (ahl-tehr-nah-*teev*) *f* alternative

altitude (ahl-tee-*tewd*) *f* altitude

aluminium (ah-lew-mee-*nʸom*) *m* aluminium

amande (ah-*mahngd*) *f* almond

amant (ah-*mahng*) *m* lover

amateur (ah-mah-*tūr*) *m* amateur

ambassade (ahng-bah-*sahd*) *f* embassy

ambassadeur (ahng-bah-sah-*dūr*) *m* ambassador

ambiance (ahng-*bʸahngss*) *f* atmosphere

ambigu (ahng-bee-*gew*) *adj* (f -guë) ambiguous

ambitieux (ahng-bee-*sʸur*) *adj* ambitious

ambre (ahngbr) *m* amber

ambulance (ahng-bew-*lahngss*) *f* ambulance

ambulant (ahng-bew-*lahng*) *adj* itinerant

âme (aam) *f* soul

amélioration (ah-may-lʸo-rah-*sʸawng*) *f* improvement

améliorer (ah-may-lʸo-*ray*) *v* improve

amende (ah-*mahngd*) *f* fine, penalty

amener (ahm-*nay*) *v* *bring; lower, *strike

amer (ah-*mair*) *adj* bitter

Américain (ah-may-ree-*kang*) *m* American

américain (ah-may-ree-*kang*) *adj* American

Amérique (ah-may-*reek*) *f* America; ~ **latine** Latin America

améthyste (ah-may-*teest*) *f* amethyst

ami (ah-*mee*) *m* friend

amiante (ah-*mʸahngt*) *m* asbestos

amical (ah-mee-*kahl*) *adj* friendly

amidon (ah-mee-*dawng*) *m* starch

amidonner (ah-mee-do-*nay*) *v* starch

amie (ah-*mee*) *f* friend

amiral (ah-mee-*rahl*) *m* admiral

amitié (ah-mee-*tʸay*) *f* friendship

ammoniaque (ah-mo-*nʸahk*) *f* ammonia

amnistie (ahm-nee-*stee*) *f* amnesty

amoncellement (ah-mawng-sehl-*mahng*) *m* heap

en amont (ahng-nah-*mawng*) upstream

amorce (ah-*mors*) *f* bait

amortir (ah-mor-*teer*) *v* *pay off

amortisseur (ah-mor-tee-*sūr*) *m* shock absorber

amour (ah-*mōōr*) *m* love; **mon ~** sweetheart

amoureux (ah-moo-*rur*) *adj* in love

ample (ahngpl) *adj* detailed; full

ampoule (ahng-*pool*) *f* blister; light bulb; ~ **de flash** flash-bulb

amulette (ah-mew-*leht*) *f* charm

amusant (ah-mew-*zahng*) *adj* funny, entertaining

amuse-gueule (ah-mewz-*gurl*) *m* appetizer

amusement (ah-mewz-*mahng*) *m* entertainment, amusement

amuser (ah-mew-*zay*) *v* entertain, amuse

amygdales (ah-mee-*dahl*) *fpl* tonsils *pl*

amygdalite (ah-mee-dah-*leet*) *f* tonsilitis

an (ahng) *m* year

analogue (ah-nah-*log*) *adj* similar

analyse (ah-nah-*leez*) *f* analysis

analyser (ah-nah-lee-*zay*) *v* analyse; *break down

analyste (ah-nah-*leest*) *m* analyst

ananas (ah-nah-*nah*) *m* pineapple

anarchie (ah-nahr-*shee*) *f* anarchy

anatomie (ah-nah-to-*mee*) *f* anatomy

ancêtre (ahng-*saitr*) *m* ancestor

anchois (ahng-*shwah*) *m* anchovy

ancien (ahng-*sʸang*) *adj* ancient; former

ancre (ahngkr) *f* anchor

andouiller (ahng-doo-*ʸay*) *m* antlers *pl*

âne (aan) *m* ass, donkey

anéantissement (ah-nay-ahng-tee-*smahng*) *m* destruction

anémie (ah-nay-*mee*) *f* anaemia

anesthésie (ah-neh-stay-*zee*) *f* anaesthesia

anesthésique (ah-neh-stay-*zeek*) *m* anaesthetic

ange (ahngzh) *m* angel

Anglais (ahng-*glay*) *m* Englishman; Briton

anglais (ahng-*glay*) *adj* English

angle (ahnggl) *m* angle

Angleterre (ahng-gler-*tair*) *f* England; Britain

angoisse (ahng-*gwahss*) *f* anguish

anguille (ahng-*geey*) *f* eel

animal (ah-nee-*mahl*) *m* animal; ~ **familier** pet

animateur (ah-nee-mah-*tūrr*) *m* entertainer

animer (ah-nee-*may*) *v* enliven; **animé** busy, active, crowded

anneau (ah-*noa*) *m* ring

année (ah-*nay*) *f* year; ~ **bissextile** leap-year; **par** ~ per annum

annexe (ah-*nehks*) *f* annex

annexer (ah-nehk-*say*) *v* annex

anniversaire (ah-nee-vehr-*sair*) *m* anniversary, birthday; jubilee

annonce (ah-*nawngss*) *f* announcement; advertisement; ~ **publicitaire** commercial

annoncer (ah-nawng-*say*) *v* announce

annuaire (ah-*nwair*) *m* annual; ~ **téléphonique** telephone directory; telephone book *Am*

annuel (ah-*nwehl*) *adj* yearly, annual

annulation (ah-new-lah-*sʸawng*) *f* cancellation

annuler (ah-new-*lay*) *v* cancel

anonyme (ah-no-*neem*) *adj* anonymous

anormal (ah-nor-*mahl*) *adj* abnormal

antenne (ahng-*tehn*) *f* aerial

antérieur (ahng-tay-*rʸūrr*) *adj* prior, previous

antérieurement (ahng-tay-rʸurr-*mahng*) *adv* formerly

anthologie (ahng-to-lo-*zhee*) *f* anthology

antialcoolique (ahng-tee-ahl-ko-*leek*) *m* teetotaller

antibiotique (ahng-tee-bʸo-*teek*) *m* antibiotic

anticiper (ahng-tee-see-*pay*) *v* anticipate

antigel (ahng-tee-*zhehl*) *m* antifreeze

antipathie (ahng-tee-pah-*tee*) *f* dislike, antipathy

antipathique (ahng-tee-pah-*teek*) *adj* nasty; unpleasant

antiquaire (ahng-tee-*kair*) *m* antique dealer

antique (ahng-*teek*) *adj* antique, ancient

antiquité (ahng-tee-kee-*tay*) *f* antique; **Antiquité** antiquity; **antiquités** antiquities *pl*

antiseptique (ahng-tee-sehp-*teek*) *m* antiseptic

anxiété (ahng-ksʸay-*tay*) *f* anxiety

août (oo) August

*__apercevoir__ (ah-pehr-ser-*vwaar*) v perceive

aperçu (ah-pehr-*sew*) m glimpse

apéritif (ah-pay-ree-*teef*) m drink, aperitif

apeuré (ah-pur-*ray*) adj afraid

apogée (ah-po-*zhay*) m height, zenith; peak

*__apparaître__ (ah-pah-*raitr*) v appear

appareil (ah-pah-*ray*) m appliance, apparatus, machine; aircraft; ~ **à jetons** slot-machine; ~ **de chauffage** heater; ~ **photographique** camera

apparemment (ah-pah-rah-*mahng*) adv apparently

apparence (ah-pah-*rahngss*) f appearance; semblance, look

apparent (ah-pah-*rahng*) adj apparent

apparenté (ah-pah-rahng-*tay*) adj related

apparition (ah-pah-ree-s*Yawng*) f apparition

appartement (ah-pahr-ter-*mahng*) m flat; apartment nAm, suite

*__appartenir__ (ah-pahr-ter-*neer*) v belong

appel (ah-*pehl*) m call, cry; appeal; ~ **interurbain** trunk-call; ~ **téléphonique** telephone call

appeler (ah-*play*) v call, cry; s'**appeler** *be called

appendice (ah-pang-*deess*) m appendix

appendicite (ah-pang-dee-*seet*) f appendicitis

appétissant (ah-pay-tee-*sahng*) adj appetizing

appétit (ah-pay-*tee*) m appetite

applaudir (ah-ploa-*deer*) v clap

applaudissements (ah-ploa-dee-*smahng*) mpl applause

application (ah-plee-kah-s*Yawng*) f application; diligence

appliquer (ah-plee-*kay*) v apply; s'**appliquer à** apply

apporter (ah-por-*tay*) v *bring; fetch

appréciation (ah-pray-s*Yah*-s*Yawng*) f appreciation

apprécier (ah-pray-s*Yay*) v appreciate; judge

*__apprendre__ (ah-*prahngdr*) v *learn; *teach; ~ **par cœur** memorize

apprivoiser (ah-pree-vwah-*zay*) v tame; **apprivoisé** tame

approbation (ah-pro-bah-s*Yawng*) f approval

approche (ah-*prosh*) f approach

approcher (ah-pro-*shay*) v approach

approprié (ah-pro-pree-*ay*) adj appropriate, adequate, convenient; proper, suitable

approuver (ah-proo-*vay*) v approve; consent

approvisionner en (ah-pro-vee-z*Yo*-*nay*) furnish with

approximatif (ah-prok-see-mah-*teef*) adj approximate

approximativement (ah-prok-see-mah-teev-*mahng*) adv approximately

appuyer (ah-pwee-*Yay*) v press; s'**appuyer** *lean

âpre (aapr) adj harsh

après (ah-*pray*) adv afterwards; prep after; ~ **que** after; **d'après** according to

après-midi (ah-pray-mee-*dee*) m/f afternoon

apte (ahpt) adj apt

aptitude (ahp-tee-*tewd*) f faculty

aquarelle (ah-kwah-*rehl*) f water-colour

Arabe (ah-*rahb*) m Arab

arabe (ah-*rahb*) adj Arab

Arabie Séoudite (ah-rah-bee say-oo-*deet*) Saudi Arabia

araignée (ah-ray-*ñay*) f spider; **toile d'araignée** spider's web

arbitraire (ahr-bee-*trair*) *adj* arbitrary

arbitre (ahr-*beetr*) *m* umpire

arbre (ahrbr) *m* tree; ~ **à cames** camshaft

arbuste (ahr-*bewst*) *m* shrub

arc (ahrk) *m* bow

arcade (ahr-*kahd*) *f* arcade

arc-en-ciel (ahr-kahng-*sᵛehl*) *m* rainbow

arche (ahrsh) *f* arch

archéologie (ahr-kay-o-lo-*zhee*) *f* archaeology

archéologue (ahr-kay-o-*log*) *m* archaeologist

archevêque (ahr-sher-*vehk*) *m* archbishop

architecte (ahr-shee-*tehkt*) *m* architect

architecture (ahr-shee-tehk-*tewr*) *f* architecture

archives (ahr-*sheev*) *fpl* archives *pl*

ardoise (ahr-*dwaaz*) *f* slate

arène (ah-*rehn*) *f* bullring

arête (ah-*reht*) *f* ridge; fishbone, bone

argent (ahr-*zhahng*) *m* silver; money; ~ **comptant** cash; ~ **liquide** cash; **en** ~ silver

argenterie (ahr-zhahng-*tree*) *f* silverware

Argentin (ahr-zhahng-*tang*) *m* Argentinian

argentin (ahr-zhahng-*tang*) *adj* Argentinian

Argentine (ahr-zhahng-*teen*) *f* Argentina

argile (ahr-*zheel*) *f* clay

argument (ahr-gew-*mahng*) *m* argument

argumenter (ahr-gew-mahng-*tay*) *v* argue

aride (ah-*reed*) *adj* arid

arithmétique (ah-reet-may-*teek*) *f* arithmetic

armateur (ahr-mah-*tūr*) *m* shipowner

arme (ahrm) *f* weapon, arm

armée (ahr-*may*) *f* army

armer (ahr-*may*) *v* arm

armoire (ahr-*mwaar*) *f* cupboard

armure (ahr-*mewr*) *f* armour

arôme (ah-*roam*) *m* aroma

arqué (ahr-*kay*) *adj* arched

arracher (ah-rah-*shay*) *v* extract

arrangement (ah-rahngzh-*mahng*) *m* settlement

arranger (ah-rahng-*zhay*) *v* arrange; settle

arrestation (ah-reh-stah-*sᵛawng*) *f* arrest

arrêt (ah-*reh*) *m* stop

arrêter (ah-ray-*tay*) *v* stop; arrest; **s'arrêter** halt; pull up

arriéré (ah-rᵛay-*ray*) *adj* overdue

arrière (ah-*rᵛair*) *m* rear; **en** ~ backwards, back; behind

arrivée (ah-ree-*vay*) *f* coming, arrival

arriver (ah-ree-*vay*) *v* arrive; happen

arrondi (ah-rawng-*dee*) *adj* rounded

art (aar) *m* art; **arts et métiers** arts and crafts

artère (ahr-*tair*) *f* artery; thoroughfare

artichaut (ahr-tee-*shoa*) *m* artichoke

article (ahr-*teekl*) *m* article; item; **articles d'épicerie** groceries *pl*; **articles de toilette** toiletry

articulation (ahr-tee-kew-lah-*sᵛawng*) *f* joint

artificiel (ahr-tee-fee-*sᵛehl*) *adj* artificial

artisan (ahr-tee-*zahng*) *m* craftsman

artisanat (ahr-tee-zah-*nah*) *m* handicraft

artiste (ahr-*teest*) *m/f* artist

artistique (ahr-tee-*steek*) *adj* artistic

ascenseur (ah-sahng-*sūr*) *m* lift; elevator *nAm*

ascension (ah-sahng-*sᵛawng*) *f* climb; ***faire l'ascension de** ascend

Asiatique (ah-zᵛah-*teek*) *m* Asian

asiatique (ah-zᵛah-*teek*) *adj* Asian

Asie (ah-*zee*) f Asia

asile (ah-*zeel*) m asylum

aspect (ah-*spay*) m aspect; appearance, look

asperge (ah-*spehrzh*) f asparagus

asphalte (ah-*sfahlt*) m asphalt

aspirateur (ah-spee-rah-*tūr*) m vacuum cleaner; **passer l'aspirateur** hoover; vacuum *vAm*

aspirer (ah-spee-*ray*) v aspire; ~ **à** pursue, aim at

aspirine (ah-spee-*reen*) f aspirin

assaisonner (ah-say-zo-*nay*) v flavour

assassinat (ah-sah-see-*nah*) m assassination, murder

assassiner (ah-sah-see-*nay*) v murder

assécher (ah-say-*shay*) v drain

assemblée (ah-sahng-*blay*) f assembly, meeting

assembler (ah-sahng-*blay*) v assemble; join

assentiment (ah-sahng-tee-*mahng*) m consent

s'*asseoir (ah-*swaar*) *sit down

assez (ah-*say*) adv enough; fairly, pretty, rather, quite

assidu (ah-see-*dew*) adj diligent

assiette (ah-*s^yeht*) f plate, dish; ~ **à soupe** soup-plate

assigner (ah-see-*ñay*) v allot; ~ **à** assign to

assistance (ah-see-*stahngss*) f assistance; attendance

assistant (ah-see-*stahng*) m assistant

assister (ah-see-*stay*) v assist, aid; ~ **à** attend, assist at

association (ah-so-s^yah-s^y*awng*) f society, club, association

associé (ah-so-s^y*ay*) m associate, partner

associer (ah-so-s^y*ay*) v associate

assoiffé (ah-swah-*fay*) adj thirsty

assortiment (ah-sor-tee-*mahng*) m assortment

assurance (ah-sew-*rahngss*) f insurance; **assurance-vie** f life insurance; **assurance-voyages** f travel insurance

assurer (ah-sew-*ray*) v insure, assure; **s'assurer de** ascertain; secure

asthme (ahsm) m asthma

astronomie (ah-stro-no-*mee*) f astronomy

astucieux (ah-stew-s^y*ur*) adj clever

atelier (ah-ter-*l^yay*) m workshop

athée (ah-*tay*) m atheist

athlète (ah-*tleht*) m athlete

athlétisme (ah-tlay-*teezm*) m athletics pl

atmosphère (aht-mo-*sfair*) f atmosphere

atome (ah-*tom*) m atom

atomique (ah-to-*meek*) adj atomic

atroce (ah-*tross*) adj horrible

attacher (ah-tah-*shay*) v fasten, attach; tie; **attaché à** attached to

attaque (ah-*tahk*) f fit, attack; hold-up; stroke

attaquer (ah-tah-*kay*) v attack, assault

***atteindre** (ah-*tangdr*) *attain, reach

attendre (ah-*tahngdr*) v wait; expect, await; **en attendant** in the meantime

attente (ah-*tahngt*) f waiting; expectation

attentif (ah-tahng-*teef*) adj attentive, careful

attention (ah-tahng-s^y*awng*) f attention, consideration; notice; ***faire ~** *pay attention, look out; beware; ***faire ~ à** attend to, mind; **prêter ~ à** mind

atterrir (ah-tay-*reer*) v land

attestation (ah-teh-stah-s^y*awng*) f certificate

attirer (ah-tee-*ray*) v attract

attitude (ah-tee-*tewd*) f attitude; position

attouchement (ah-toosh-*mahng*) *m* touch

attraction (ah-trahk-*s^{y}awng*) *f* attraction

attrait (ah-*tray*) *m* attraction; **attraits** charm

attraper (ah-trah-*pay*) *v* *catch; contract

attribuer à (ah-tree-*bway*) assign to

aube (ōab) *f* dawn

auberge (oa-*behrzh*) *f* inn, hostel; roadhouse; roadside restaurant; ~ **de jeunesse** youth hostel

aubergine (oa-behr-*zheen*) *f* eggplant

aubergiste (oa-behr-*zheest*) *m* innkeeper

aucun (oa-*kurng*) *adj* no; *pron* none

aucunement (oa-kewn-*mahng*) *adv* by no means

audace (oa-*dahss*) *f* nerve

audacieux (oa-dah-*s^{y}ur*) *adj* bold

au-dessous (oa-der-*soo*) *adv* beneath; ~ **de** below

au-dessus (oa-der-*sew*) *adv* over; ~ **de** above; over

audible (oa-*deebl*) *adj* audible

auditeur (oa-dee-*tūrr*) *m* auditor, listener

auditorium (oa-dee-to-*r^{y}om*) *m* auditorium

augmentation (oag-mahng-tah-*s^{y}awng*) *f* increase, rise; ~ **de salaire** rise; raise *nAm*

augmenter (oag-mahng-*tay*) *v* increase

aujourd'hui (oa-zhoor-*dwee*) *adv* today

auparavant (oa-pah-rah-*vahng*) *adv* formerly

auprès de (oa-*pray* der) near

auriculaire (oa-ree-kew-*lair*) *m* little finger

aurore (oa-*rawr*) *f* dawn

aussi (oa-*see*) *adv* too, also; as; ~

bien as well; ~ **bien que** as well as; both ... and

aussitôt (oa-see-*toa*) *adv* at once; ~ **que** as soon as

Australie (oa-strah-*lee*) *f* Australia

Australien (oa-strah-*l^{y}ang*) *m* Australian

australien (oa-strah-*l^{y}ang*) *adj* Australian

autant (oa-*tahng*) *adv* as much

autel (oa-*tehl*) *m* altar

auteur (oa-*tūrr*) *m* author

authentique (oa-tahng-*teek*) *adj* authentic, original, genuine

auto (oa-*toa*) *f* automobile

autobus (oa-toa-*bewss*) *m* bus

autocar (oa-toa-*kaar*) *m* coach

automatique (oa-toa-mah-*teek*) *adj* automatic

automatisation (oa-toa-mah-tee-zah-*s^{y}awng*) *f* automation

automne (oa-*ton*) *m* autumn; fall *nAm*

automobile (oa-toa-mo-*beel*) *f* motorcar

automobilisme (oa-toa-mo-bee-*leesm*) *m* motoring

automobiliste (oa-toa-mo-bee-*leest*) *m* motorist

autonome (oa-to-*nom*) *adj* autonomous; independent

autonomie (oa-to-no-*mee*) *f* self-government

autopsie (oa-to-*psee*) *f* autopsy

autorisation (oa-to-ree-zah-*s^{y}awng*) *f* authorization; permission

autoriser (oa-to-ree-*zay*) *v* allow; license; ~ **à** allow to

autoritaire (oa-to-ree-*tair*) *adj* authoritarian

autorité (oa-to-ree-*tay*) *f* authority

autoroute (oa-toa-*root*) *f* motorway; highway *nAm*

auto-stoppeur (oa-toa-sto-*pūrr*) *m*

hitchhiker; *faire de l'auto-stop hitchhike

autour (oa-*tōōr*) *adv* about; around; ~ **de** around, about; round

autre (ōatr) *adj* other; different; **entre autres** among other things

autrefois (oa-trer-*fwah*) *adv* formerly

autrement (oa-trer-*mahng*) *adv* otherwise, else

Autriche (oa-*treesh*) *f* Austria

Autrichien (oa-tree-sh*Yang*) *m* Austrian

autrichien (oa-tree-sh*Yang*) *adj* Austrian

autruche (oa-*trewsh*) *f* ostrich

en aval (ahng-nah-*vahl*) downstream

avalanche (ah-vah-*lahngsh*) *f* avalanche

avaler (ah-vah-*lay*) *v* swallow

avance (ah-*vahngss*) *f* lead; advance; **à l'avance** in advance; **d'avance** before; in advance

avancement (ah-vahng-*smahng*) *m* advance

avancer (ah-vahng-*say*) *v* advance

avant (ah-*vahng*) *prep* before; *adv* before; ~ **que** before; **en** ~ forward; ahead, onwards

avantage (ah-vahng-*taazh*) *m* profit, advantage, benefit

avantageux (ah-vahng-tah-*zhur*) *adj* advantageous; cheap

avant-hier (ah-vahng-*t*Y*air*) *adv* the day before yesterday

avare (ah-*vaar*) *adj* avaricious

avec (ah-*vehk*) *prep* with

avenir (ah-*vneer*) *m* future

aventure (ah-vahng-*tewr*) *f* adventure

avenue (ah-*vnew*) *f* avenue

averse (ah-*vehrs*) *f* shower; downpour

aversion (ah-vehr-s*Yawng*) *f* aversion, dislike

avertir (ah-vehr-*teer*) *v* warn, caution; notify

avertissement (ah-vehr-tee-*smahng*) *m* warning

aveugle (ah-*vurgl*) *adj* blind

aveugler (ah-vur-*glay*) *v* blind

aviation (ah-v*Y*ah-s*Yawng*) *f* aviation

avion (ah-v*Yawng*) *m* aeroplane; plane, aircraft; airplane *nAm*; ~ **à réaction** jet

avis (ah-*vee*) *m* advice; notice

avocat (ah-vo-*kah*) *m* solicitor, attorney, lawyer, barrister

avoine (ah-*vwahn*) *f* oats *pl*

*avoir (ah-*vwaar*) *v* *have

avoisinant (ah-vwah-zee-*nahng*) *adj* neighbouring

avortement (ah-vort-*mahng*) *m* abortion

avoué (ah-voo-*ay*) *m* solicitor

avouer (ah-voo-*ay*) *v* admit

avril (ah-*vreel*) April

azote (ah-*zot*) *m* nitrogen

B

bâbord (bah-*bawr*) *m* port

bâche (baash) *f* tarpaulin

bactérie (bahk-tay-*ree*) *f* bacterium

bagage (bah-*gaazh*) *m* baggage; luggage; ~ **à main** hand luggage; hand baggage *Am*

bague (bahg) *f* ring; ~ **de fiançailles** engagement ring

baie (bay) *f* berry; bay, creek

se baigner (bay-*ñay*) bathe

bail (bigh) *m* (pl baux) lease

bâiller (bah-*Yay*) *v* yawn

bain (bang) *m* bath; ~ **turc** Turkish bath; **bonnet de** ~ bathing-cap; **caleçon de** ~ bathing-trunks

baiser (bay-*zay*) *m* kiss

baisse (behss) *f* drop, decline

baisser (bay-*say*) *v* lower

bal (bahl) *m* (pl ~s) ball

balai (bah-*lay*) *m* broom

balance (bah-*lahngss*) *f* scales *pl*

balancer (bah-lahng-*say*) *v* *swing; rock

balançoire (bah-lahng-*swaar*) *f* swing; seesaw

balayer (bah-lay-*Yay*) *v* *sweep

balbutier (bahl-bew-s*Yay*) *v* falter

balcon (bahl-*kawng*) *m* balcony; circle

baleine (bah-*lehn*) *f* whale

balle (bahl) *f* ball; bullet

ballet (bah-*lay*) *m* ballet

ballon (bah-*lawng*) *m* football, ball; balloon

balustrade (bah-lew-*strahd*) *f* rail

bambin (bahng-*bang*) *m* tot, toddler

bambou (bahng-*boo*) *m* bamboo

banane (bah-*nahn*) *f* banana

banc (bahng) *m* bench; ~ **d'école** desk

bande (bahngd) *f* bunch, gang; tape, strip; **bandes dessinées** comics *pl*

bandit (bahng-*dee*) *m* bandit

banlieue (bahng-*lYur*) *f* suburb

bannière (bah-n*Yair*) *f* banner

banque (bahngk) *f* bank

banquet (bahng-*kay*) *m* banquet

baptême (bah-*tehm*) *m* christening, baptism

baptiser (bah-tee-*zay*) *v* christen, baptize

bar (baar) *m* bar

baratiner (bah-rah-tee-*nay*) *v* talk rubbish

barbe (bahrb) *f* beard

barbue (bahr-*bew*) *f* brill

baril (bah-*ree*) *m* cask, barrel; keg

bariton (bah-ree-*tawng*) *m* baritone

barmaid (bahr-*mehd*) *f* barmaid

barman (bahr-*mahn*) *m* barman; bartender

baromètre (bah-ro-*mehtr*) *m* barom-eter

baroque (bah-*rok*) *adj* baroque

barque (bahrk) *f* boat

barrage (bah-*raazh*) *m* dam

barre (baar) *f* rod, bar, rail; helm; counter

barreau (bah-*roa*) *m* bar

barrière (bah-r*Yair*) *f* barrier; fence

bas[1] (bah) *adj* (f ~se) low; **en** ~ down; downstairs; **en** ~ **de** under, below; **vers le** ~ downwards, down

bas[2] (bah) *m* stocking; ~ **élastiques** support hose

bas-côté (bah-koa-*tay*) *m* aisle

bascule (bah-*skewl*) *f* weighing-machine

base (bahz) *f* basis, base

baser (bah-*zay*) *v* base

basilique (bah-zee-*leek*) *f* basilica

basse (bahss) *f* bass

bassin (bah-*sang*) *m* pelvis, basin

bataille (bah-*tigh*) *f* battle

bateau (bah-*toa*) *m* boat; ~ **à moteur** launch; ~ **à rames** rowing-boat; ~ **à vapeur** steamer; ~ **à voiles** sailing-boat; **bateau-citerne** *m* tanker

bâtiment (bah-tee-*mahng*) *m* building; building trade

bâtir (bah-*teer*) *v* *build; construct

bâton (bah-*tawng*) *m* stick; **bâtons de ski** ski sticks; ski poles *Am*

*battre (bahtr) *v* slap; *beat; shuffle; **se** ~ *fight

bavard (bah-*vaar*) *adj* talkative

bavardage (bah-vahr-*daazh*) *m* chat

bavarder (bah-vahr-*day*) *v* chat

beau (boa) *adj* (bel; f belle) beautiful; fair, pretty, lovely, handsome

beaucoup (boa-*koo*) *adv* much; far; ~ **de** much; many; **de** ~ by far

beau-fils (boa-*feess*) *m* son-in-law

beau-frère (boa-*frair*) *m* brother-in-law

beau-père (boa-*pair*) *m* father-in-law; stepfather

beauté (boa-*tay*) *f* beauty; **produits de ~** cosmetics *pl*

beaux-arts (boa-*zaar*) *mpl* fine arts

beaux-parents (boa-pah-*rahng*) *mpl* parents-in-law *pl*

bébé (bay-*bay*) *m* baby

bec (behk) *m* beak; nozzle

bec-de-corbin (behk-der-kor-*bang*) *m* crowbar

bêche (behsh) *f* spade

beige (baizh) *adj* beige

Belge (behlzh) *m* Belgian

belge (behlzh) *adj* Belgian

Belgique (behl-*zheek*) *f* Belgium

belle-fille (behl-*feey*) *f* daughter-in-law

belle-mère (behl-*mair*) *f* mother-in-law; stepmother

belle-sœur (behl-*sūrr*) *f* sister-in-law

bénédiction (bay-nay-deek-s^y*awng*) *f* blessing

bénéfice (bay-nay-*feess*) *m* profit, benefit

bénéficiaire (bay-nay-fee-s^y*air*) *m* payee

bénéficier de (bay-nay-fee-s^y*ay*) profit by

bénir (bay-*neer*) *v* bless

béquille (bay-*keey*) *f* crutch

berceau (behr-*soa*) *m* cradle; **~ de voyage** carry-cot

béret (bay-*ray*) *m* beret

berge (behrzh) *f* embankment

berger (behr-*zhay*) *m* shepherd

besogne (ber-*zoñ*) *f* work

besoin (ber-*zwang*) *m* need; want; ***avoir ~** need

bétail (bay-*tigh*) *m* cattle *pl*

bête (beht) *f* beast; *adj* silly, dumb; **~ de proie** beast of prey

béton (bay-*tawng*) *m* concrete

betterave (beh-*traav*) *f* beetroot, beet

beurre (burr) *m* butter

Bible (beebl) *f* bible

bibliothèque (bee-blee-o-*tehk*) *f* library

bicyclette (bee-see-*kleht*) *f* cycle, bicycle

bien (b^yang) *adv* well; **bien!** well!; all right!; **~ que** though, although; **biens** *mpl* goods *pl*, possessions

bien-être (b^yang-*naitr*) *m* welfare; comfort

bientôt (b^yang-*toa*) *adv* soon; shortly

bienveillance (b^yang-vay-*y*ahngss) *f* goodwill

bienvenu (b^yang-*vnew*) *adj* welcome

bière (b^yair) *f* beer; ale

bifteck (beef-*tehk*) *m* steak

bifurcation (bee-fewr-kah-s^y*awng*) *f* fork, road fork

bifurquer (bee-fewr-*kay*) *v* fork

bigorneau (bee-gor-*noa*) *m* winkle

bigoudi (bee-goo-*dee*) *m* curler

bijou (bee-*zhoo*) *m* (pl ~x) jewel; gem; **bijoux** jewellery

bijoutier (bee-zhoo-*t*^yay) *m* jeweller

bilan (bee-*lahng*) *m* balance

bile (beel) *f* gall, bile

bilingue (bee-*langg*) *adj* bilingual

billard (bee-*y*aar) *m* billiards *pl*

bille (beey) *f* marble

billet (bee-*y*ay) *m* ticket; **~ de banque** banknote; **~ de quai** platform ticket; **~ gratuit** free ticket

biologie (bee-o-lo-*zhee*) *f* biology

biscuit (bee-*skwee*) *m* biscuit; cookie *nAm*; cracker *nAm*

bistrot (bee-*stroa*) *m* pub

bizarre (bee-*zaar*) *adj* funny, odd, strange

blague (blahg) *f* joke; **~ à tabac** tobacco pouch

blaireau (bleh-*roa*) *m* shaving-brush

blâme (blaam) *m* blame

blâmer (blah-*may*) *v* blame

blanc (blah*ng*) *adj* (f blanche) white; blank

blanchaille (blah*ng*-*shigh*) f whitebait

blanchisserie (blah*ng*-shee-*sree*) f laundry

blé (blay) *m* corn; wheat; grain

blesser (blay-*say*) *v* injure, *hurt, wound; offend

blessure (blay-se͞wr) f wound; injury

bleu (blur) *adj* (pl bleus) blue; *m* bruise

bloc (blok) *m* block

bloc-notes (blok-*not*) *m* pad, writing-pad

blond (blaw*ng*) *adj* fair

blonde (blaw*ng*d) f blonde

bloquer (blo-*kay*) *v* block

bobine (bo-*been*) f spool; ~ **d'allumage** ignition coil

bœuf (burf) *m* ox; beef

bohémien (bo-ay-m*Yang*) *m* gipsy

*boire (bwaar) *v* *drink

bois (blur) *m* wood; forest; ~ **d'œuvre** timber; **en** ~ wooden

boisé (bwah-*zay*) *adj* wooded

boisson (bwah-*saw*ng) f drink, beverage; ~ **non alcoolisée** soft drink; **boissons alcoolisées** spirits

boîte (bwaht) f box; can, tin; ~ **à ordures** dustbin; trash can *Am*; ~ **à outils** tool kit; ~ **aux lettres** letterbox; mailbox *nAm*; ~ **d'allumettes** match-box; ~ **de couleurs** paint-box; ~ **de nuit** nightclub; ~ **de vitesse** gear-box

boiter (bwah-*tay*) *v* limp

boiteux (bwah-*tur*) *adj* lame

bol (bol) *m* basin; bowl

Bolivie (bo-lee-*vee*) f Bolivia

Bolivien (bo-lee-v*Yang*) *m* Bolivian

bolivien (bo-lee-v*Yang*) *adj* Bolivian

bombarder (baw*ng*-bahr-*day*) *v* bomb

bombe (baw*ng*b) f bomb

bon¹ (baw*ng*) *adj* good; enjoyable, nice; kind

bon² (baw*ng*) *m* voucher; ~ **de commande** order-form

bonbon (baw*ng*-*baw*ng) *m* sweet; candy *nAm*

bond (baw*ng*) *m* jump

bondé (baw*ng*-*day*) *adj* crowded

bondir (baw*ng*-*deer*) *v* *leap

bonheur (bo-*nūr*) *m* happiness

bonjour! (baw*ng*-zho͞or) hello!

bonne (bon) f maid; housemaid; ~ **d'enfants** nurse

bonne-maman (bon-mah-*mah*ng) f grandmother

bonneterie (bo-neh-*tree*) f hosiery

bon-papa (baw*ng*-pah-*pah*) *m* grandfather

bonsoir! (baw*ng*-*swaar*) good evening!

bonté (baw*ng*-*tay*) f kindness

bord (bawr) *m* edge; brim, verge, border; **à** ~ aboard; ~ **de la mer** seaside, seashore; ~ **de la rivière** riverside; ~ **de la route** roadside; wayside; ~ **du trottoir** curb

bordel (bor-*dehl*) *m* brothel

borne routière (born roo-t*Yair*) milestone

borné (bor-*nay*) *adj* narrow-minded

bosquet (bo-*skay*) *m* grove

bosse (boss) f dent, lump

botanique (bo-tah-*neek*) f botany

botte (bot) f boot

bottin (bo-*tang*) *m* telephone directory

bouc (book) *m* goat; ~ **émissaire** scapegoat

bouche (boosh) f mouth

bouchée (boo-*shay*) f bite

boucher¹ (boo-*shay*) *m* butcher

boucher² (boo-*shay*) *v* stop up

boucherie (boo-*shree*) f butcher's shop

bouchon (boo-*shaw*ng) *m* cork; stopper

boucle (book l) f buckle; curl; loop; ~ **d'oreille** earring

boucler (boo-*klay*) v curl; **bouclé** curly

boue (boo) f mud; slush

bouée (boo-*ay*) f buoy; ~ **de sauvetage** lifebelt

boueux (boo-*ur*) adj muddy

bouger (boo-*zhay*) v move; stir

bougie (boo-*zhee*) f candle; ~ **d'allumage** sparking-plug

***bouillir** (boo-*Yeer*) v boil

bouilloire (boo-*Ywaar*) f kettle

bouillotte (boo-*Yot*) f hot-water bottle

boulanger (boo-lahng-*zhay*) m baker

boulangerie (boo-lahng-*zhree*) f bakery

boule (bool) f ball

bouleau (boo-*loa*) m birch

bouleversé (bool-vehr-*say*) adj upset

boulon (boo-*lawng*) m bolt

boulot (boo-*loa*) m job

bouquet (boo-*kay*) m bunch, bouquet

bourg (bōōr) m town

bourgeois (boor-*zhwah*) adj bourgeois, middle-class

bourgeon (boor-*zhawng*) m bud

bourré (boo-*ray*) adj chock-full

bourreau (boo-*roa*) m executioner

bourse (boors) f purse; ~ **des valeurs** stock exchange; ~ **d'études** scholarship

boussole (boo-*sol*) f compass

bout (boo) m end; tip

bouteille (boo-*tay*) f bottle

boutique (boo-*teek*) f boutique; shop

bouton (boo-*tawng*) m button, knob; ~ **de col** collar stud; **boutons de manchettes** cuff-links pl

boutonner (boo-to-*nay*) v button

boutonnière (boo-to-*n'air*) f buttonhole

bowling (boa-*leeng*) m bowling; bowling alley

boxer (bok-*say*) v box

bracelet (brah-*slay*) m bracelet; bangle; **bracelet-montre** m wristwatch; ~ **pour montre** watch-strap

braconner (brah-ko-*nay*) v poach

braguette (brah-*geht*) f fly

branche (brahngsh) f branch; bough

brancher (brahng-*shay*) v connect; plug in

branchie (brahng-*shee*) f gill

branlant (brahng-*lahng*) adj unsteady

bras (brah) m arm; **bras-dessus bras-dessous** arm-in-arm

brasse (brahss) f breaststroke; ~ **papillon** butterfly stroke

brasser (brah-*say*) v brew

brasserie (brah-*sree*) f brewery

brave (brahv) adj brave, courageous; good

brèche (brehsh) f breach; gap

bref (brehf) adj (f **brève**) brief

brème (brehm) f bream

Brésil (bray-*zeel*) m Brazil

Brésilien (bray-zee-*l'Yang*) m Brazilian

brésilien (bray-zee-*l'Yang*) adj Brazilian

bretelles (brer-*tehl*) fpl braces pl; suspenders plAm

brevet (brer-*vay*) m patent

bridge (breej) m bridge

brillant (bree-*Yahng*) adj bright; brilliant

briller (bree-*Yay*) v *shine; glow

brin d'herbe (brang dehrb) blade of grass

brindille (brang-*deey*) f twig

brioche (bree-*osh*) f bun

brique (breek) f brick

briquet (bree-*kay*) m cigarette-lighter, lighter

brise (breez) f breeze

briser (bree-*zay*) v *break; **brisé** broken

Britannique (bree-tah-*neek*) m Briton

britannique (bree-tah-*neek*) *adj* British

broche (brosh) *f* brooch; spit

brochet (bro-*shay*) *m* pike

brochure (bro-*shewr*) *f* brochure

broder (bro-*day*) *v* embroider

broderie (bro-*dree*) *f* embroidery

bronchite (brawng-*sheet*) *f* bronchitis

bronze (brawngz) *m* bronze; **en ~** bronze

brosse (bross) *f* brush; **~ à cheveux** hairbrush; **~ à dents** toothbrush; **~ à habits** clothes-brush; **~ à ongles** nailbrush

brosser (bro-*say*) *v* brush

brouette (broo-*eht*) *f* wheelbarrow

brouillard (broo-*Yaar*) *m* fog, mist

brouiller (broo-*Yay*) *v* mix; mix up; *sow discord

bruit (brwee) *m* noise

brûler (brew-*lay*) *v* *burn

brûlure (brew-*lewr*) *f* burn; **brûlures d'estomac** heartburn

brume (brewm) *f* mist; haze

brumeux (brew-*mur*) *adj* misty, hazy, foggy

brun (brurng) *adj* brown

brunette (brew-*neht*) *f* brunette

brusque (brewsk) *adj* sudden; rude

brut (brewt) *adj* gross

brutal (brew-*tahl*) *adj* brutal

bruyant (brwee-*yahng*) *adj* noisy

bruyère (brwee-*Yair*) *f* heather; moor

bûche (bewsh) *f* log

bûcher (bew-*shay*) *v* labour

budget (bew-*jay*) *m* budget

buffet (bew-*fay*) *m* buffet

buisson (bwee-*sawng*) *m* bush, scrub

bulbe (bewlb) *m* bulb

Bulgare (bewl-*gaar*) *m* Bulgarian

bulgare (bewl-*gaar*) *adj* Bulgarian

Bulgarie (bewl-gah-*ree*) *f* Bulgaria

bulle (bewl) *f* bubble

bulletin météorologique (bewl-tang may-tay-o-ro-lo-*zheek*) weather forecast

bureau (bew-*roa*) *m* office; bureau; desk, agency; **~ de change** exchange office; **~ de l'emploi** employment exchange; **~ de poste** post-office; **~ de renseignements** information bureau; **~ des objets trouvés** lost property office; **~ de tabac** cigar shop; **~ de voyages** travel agency; **employé de ~** clerk; **heures de ~** business hours

bureaucratie (bew-roa-krah-*see*) *f* bureaucracy

burin (bew-*rang*) *m* chisel

buste (bewst) *m* bust

but (bew) *m* purpose, aim; goal

butte (bewt) *f* mound

C

ça (sah) *pron* that

cabane (kah-*bahn*) *f* cabin

cabaret (kah-bah-*ray*) *m* cabaret

cabine (kah-*been*) *f* cabin, booth; **~ de pont** deck cabin; **~ d'essayage** fitting room; **~ téléphonique** telephone booth

cabinet (kah-bee-*nay*) *m* lavatory; cabinet; study; **~ de consultations** surgery

câble (kahbl) *m* cable

cacahuète (kah-kah-*weht*) *f* peanut

cachemire (kahsh-*meer*) *m* cashmere

cacher (kah-*shay*) *v* *hide

cachet (kah-*shay*) *m* stamp; capsule

cadavre (kah-*daavr*) *m* corpse

cadeau (kah-*doa*) *m* present, gift

cadenas (kahd-*nah*) *m* padlock

cadet (kah-*day*) *adj* junior

cadre (kaadr) *m* frame; setting; cadre

café (kah-*fay*) *m* coffee; café, public house, saloon

caféine (kah-fay-*een*) *f* caffeine

cafétéria (kah-fay-tay-r*Y*ah) *f* cafeteria

cage (kaazh) *f* cage

cahier (kah-*Y*ay) *m* notebook; ~ **de croquis** sketch-book

cahoteux (kah-o-*tur*) *adj* bumpy

caille (kigh) *f* quail

caillou (kah-*Y*oo) *m* (pl ~x) pebble

caisse (kehss) *f* crate; pay-desk; ~ **d'épargne** savings bank

caissier (kay-s*Y*ay) *m* cashier

caissière (kay-s*Y*air) *f* cashier

cal (kahl) *m* callus

calamité (kah-lah-mee-*tay*) *f* calamity, disaster

calcium (kahl-s*Y*om) *m* calcium

calcul (kahl-*kewl*) *m* calculation; ~ **biliaire** gallstone

calculatrice (kahl-kew-lah-*treess*) *f* calculator

calculer (kahl-kew-*lay*) *v* reckon; calculate

cale (kahl) *f* wedge, hold

caleçon (kahl-*sawng*) *m* drawers; briefs *pl*, shorts *plAm*, pants *pl*; underpants *plAm*; ~ **de bain** swimming-trunks

calendrier (kah-lahng-dree-*ay*) *m* calendar

câliner (kah-lee-*nay*) *v* cuddle

calmant (kahl-*mahng*) *m* tranquillizer

calme (kahlm) *adj* calm, quiet

calmer (kahl-*may*) *v* calm down

calomnie (kah-lom-*nee*) *f* slander

calorie (kah-lo-*ree*) *f* calorie

camarade (kah-mah-*rahd*) *m* comrade; ~ **de classe** class-mate

cambrioler (kahng-bree-o-*lay*) *v* burgle

cambrioleur (kahng-bree-o-*lurr*) *m* burglar

camée (kah-*may*) *m* cameo

caméra (kah-may-*rah*) *f* camera; ~

vidéo video camera

camion (kah-m*Y*awng) *m* lorry; truck *nAm*; ~ **de livraison** delivery van

camionnette (kah-m*Y*o-*neht*) *f* pick-up van

camp (kahng) *m* camp; ~ **de vacances** holiday camp

campagne (kahng-*pahñ*) *f* countryside, country; campaign

camper (kahng-*pay*) *v* camp

campeur (kahng-*purr*) *m* camper

camping (kahng-*peeng*) *m* camping; **terrain de ~** camping site

Canada (kah-nah-*dah*) *m* Canada

Canadien (kah-nah-d*Y*ang) *m* Canadian

canadien (kah-nah-d*Y*ang) *adj* Canadian

canal (kah-*nahl*) *m* canal; channel

canapé (kah-nah-*pay*) *m* sofa, couch

canard (kah-*naar*) *m* duck

canari (kah-nah-*ree*) *m* canary

cancer (kahng-*sair*) *m* cancer

candélabre (kahng-day-*laabr*) *m* candelabrum

candidat (kahng-dee-*dah*) *m* candidate

candidature (kahng-dee-dah-*tewr*) *f* application

canif (kah-*neef*) *m* penknife

caniveau (kah-nee-*voa*) *m* gutter

canne (kahn) *f* cane; walking-stick; ~ **à pêche** fishing rod

cannelle (kah-*nehl*) *f* cinnamon

canon (kah-*nawng*) *m* gun

canot (kah-*noa*) *m* canoe; dinghy; ~ **automobile** motor-boat

cantine (kahng-*teen*) *f* canteen

caoutchouc (kah-oo-*choo*) *m* rubber; ~ **mousse** foam-rubber

cap (kahp) *m* cape; course

capable (kah-*pahbl*) *adj* capable; able; *°être ~ de °be able to

capacité (kah-pah-see-*tay*) *f* ability;

capacity

cape (kahp) f cape

capitaine (kah-pee-*tehn*) m captain

capital (kah-pee-*tahl*) m capital; adj capital

capitale (kah-pee-*tahl*) f capital

capitalisme (kah-pee-tah-*leesm*) m capitalism

capitonner (kah-pee-to-*nay*) v upholster

capitulation (kah-pee-tew-lah-sʸawng) f capitulation

capot (kah-*poa*) m bonnet; hood nAm

caprice (kah-*preess*) m fancy; whim

capsule (kah-*psewl*) f capsule

capture (kahp-*tewr*) f capture

capturer (kahp-tew-*ray*) v capture

capuchon (kah-pew-*shawng*) m hood

car[1] (kaar) conj for

car[2] (kaar) m coach

caractère (kah-rahk-*tair*) m character

caractériser (kah-rahk-tay-ree-*zay*) v characterize; mark

caractéristique (kah-rahk-tay-ree-*steek*) f feature, characteristic, quality; adj characteristic, typical

carafe (kah-*rahf*) f carafe

caramel (kah-rah-*mehl*) m caramel; toffee

carat (kah-*rah*) m carat

caravane (kah-rah-*vahn*) f caravan; trailer nAm

carburateur (kahr-bew-rah-*tūrr*) m carburettor

cardigan (kahr-dee-*gahng*) m cardigan

cardinal (kahr-dee-*nahl*) m cardinal; adj cardinal

carence (kah-*rahngss*) f shortage; want

cargaison (kahr-gay-*zawng*) f cargo

carillon (kah-ree-ʸawng) m chimes pl

carnaval (kahr-nah-*vahl*) m (pl ~s) carnival

carnet (kahr-*nay*) m notebook; ~ de chèques cheque-book; check-book nAm

carotte (kah-*rot*) f carrot

carpe (kahrp) f carp

carré (kah-*ray*) m square; adj square

carreau (kah-*roa*) m tile; pane; à carreaux chequered

carrefour (kahr-*fōōr*) m junction; crossroads

carrière (kah-rʸair) f career; quarry

carrosse (kah-*ross*) m carriage; coach

carrosserie (kah-ro-*sree*) f coachwork; motor body Am

cartable (kahr-*tahbl*) m satchel

carte (kahrt) f card; map; menu; ~ d'abonnement season-ticket; ~ de crédit credit card; charge plate Am; ~ de jeu playing-card; ~ des vins wine-list; ~ de visite visiting-card; ~ d'identité identity card; ~ marine chart; ~ postale card, picture postcard, postcard; ~ routière road map; ~ verte green card

carter (kahr-*tair*) m crankcase

cartilage (kahr-tee-*laazh*) m cartilage

carton (kahr-*tawng*) m cardboard; carton; en ~ cardboard

cartouche (kahr-*toosh*) f cartridge; carton

cas (kah) m case; instance, event; au ~ où in case; ~ d'urgence emergency; en aucun ~ by no means; en ~ de in case of

cascade (kah-*skahd*) f waterfall

case (kaaz) f section

caserne (kah-*zehrn*) f barracks pl

casino (kah-zee-*noa*) m casino

casque (kahsk) m helmet

casquette (kah-*skeht*) f cap

casse-croûte (kah-*skroot*) m snack

casse-noix (kah-*snwah*) m nutcrackers pl

casser (kah-*say*) v *break; **cassé** broken

casserole (kah-*srol*) f pan

casse-tête (kah-*steht*) m puzzle

cassis (kah-*seess*) m black-currant

castor (kah-*stawr*) m beaver

catacombe (kah-tah-*kawngb*) f catacomb

catalogue (kah-tah-*log*) m catalogue

catarrhe (kah-*taar*) m catarrh

catastrophe (kah-tah-*strof*) f calamity, disaster

catégorie (kah-tay-go-*ree*) f category; sort

cathédrale (kah-tay-*drahl*) f cathedral

catholique (kah-to-*leek*) adj catholic; Roman Catholic

cause (kōaz) f cause, reason; **à ~ de** because of; for, on account of

causer (koa-*zay*) v cause; chat

causette (koa-*zeht*) f chat

caution (koa-s*yawng*) f bail, security, guarantee; **sujet à ~** untrustworthy

cavalier (kah-vah-*lyay*) m horseman; rider

cave (kahv) f cellar; wine-cellar

caverne (kah-*vehrn*) f cavern

caviar (kah-v*yaar*) m caviar

cavité (kah-vee-*tay*) f cavity

ce (ser) adj (cet; f cette, pl ces) that; this

ceci (ser-*see*) pron this

céder (say-*day*) v *give in; indulge

ceinture (sang-*tewr*) f belt; **~ de sécurité** safety-belt; seat-belt

cela (ser-*lah*) pron that

célébration (say-lay-brah-s*yawng*) f celebration

célèbre (say-*lehbr*) adj famous

célébrer (say-lay-*bray*) v celebrate

célébrité (say-lay-bree-*tay*) f fame, celebrity

céleri (sehl-*ree*) m celery

célibat (say-lee-*bah*) m celibacy

célibataire (say-lee-bah-*tair*) m bachelor; adj single

cellophane (seh-lo-*fahn*) f cellophane

cellule (seh-*lewl*) f cell

celui-là (ser-lwee-*lah*) pron (f celle-là, pl ceux-là, celles-là) that

cendre (sahngdr) f ash

cendrier (sahng-dree-*ay*) m ashtray

censure (sahng-*sewr*) f censorship

cent (sahng) num hundred; **pour ~** percent

centigrade (sahng-tee-*grahd*) adj centigrade

centimètre (sahng-tee-*mehtr*) m centimetre; tape-measure

central (sahng-*trahl*) adj central; **~ téléphonique** telephone exchange

centrale (sahng-*trahl*) f power-station

centraliser (sahng-trah-lee-*zay*) v centralize

centre (sahngtr) m centre; **~ commercial** shopping centre; **~ de la ville** town centre; **~ de loisirs** recreation centre

cependant (ser-pahng-*dahng*) conj however; but, yet, only

céramique (say-rah-*meek*) f ceramics pl

cercle (sehrkl) m circle, ring; club

céréale (say-ray-*ahl*) f grain; corn

cérémonie (say-ray-mo-*nee*) f ceremony

cérémonieux (say-ray-mo-n*yur*) adj formal

cerise (ser-*reez*) f cherry

certain (sehr-*tang*) adj certain; **certains** pron some

certificat (sehr-tee-fee-*kah*) m certificate; **~ médical** health certificate

cerveau (sehr-*voa*) m brain

ces (say) adj these; those

cesser (say-*say*) v cease; discontinue, quit, stop

ceux-là (sur-*lah*) pron (f celles-là) those

chacun (shah-*kurng*) *pron* everyone; anyone

chagrin (shah-*grang*) *m* sorrow; grief

chaîne (shehn) *f* chain; ~ **de montagnes** mountain range

chair (shair) *f* flesh; ~ **de poule** goose-flesh

chaire (shair) *f* pulpit

chaise (shaiz) *f* chair; ~ **longue** deck chair

châle (shaal) *m* shawl

chalet (shah-*lay*) *m* chalet

chaleur (shah-*lūrr*) *f* heat; warmth

chambre (shahngbr) *f* room; ~ **à air** inner tube; ~ **à coucher** bedroom; ~ **d'ami** spare room, guest-room; ~ **d'enfants** nursery; ~ **et petit déjeuner** bed and breakfast; ~ **forte** vault

chameau (shah-*moa*) *m* camel

champ (shahng) *m* field; ~ **de blé** cornfield; ~ **de courses** racecourse; **sur-le-champ** immediately

champagne (shahng-*pahñ*) *m* champagne

champignon (shahng-pee-*ñawng*) *m* mushroom, toadstool

champion (shahng-*p*ʸ*awng*) *m* champion

chance (shahngss) *f* luck; fortune; chance

chanceux (shahng-*sur*) *adj* lucky

chandail (shahng-*digh*) *m* jersey, jumper, sweater

change (shahngzh) *m* change; **bureau de** ~ money exchange

changement (shahngzh-*mahng*) *m* change; variation, alteration

changer (shahng-*zhay*) *v* vary, change, alter; exchange, switch; ~ **de vitesse** change gear; ~ **en** turn into; **se** ~ change

chanson (shahng-*sawng*) *f* song; ~ **populaire** folk song

chant (shahng) *m* song, singing

chantage (shahng-*taazh*) *m* blackmail

chanter (shahng-*tay*) *v* *sing; ***faire** ~ blackmail

chanteur (shahng-*tūrr*) *m* singer; vocalist

chanteuse (shahng-*tūrz*) *f* singer

chantier naval (shahng-tʸay nah-*vahl*) shipyard

chanvre (shahngvr) *m* hemp

chaos (kah-*oa*) *m* chaos

chaotique (kah-o-*teek*) *adj* chaotic

chapeau (shah-*poa*) *m* hat

chapelain (shah-*plang*) *m* chaplain

chapelet (shah-*play*) *m* beads *pl*

chapelle (shah-*pehl*) *f* chapel

chapitre (shah-*peetr*) *m* chapter

chaque (shahk) *adj* each; every

charbon (shahr-*bawng*) *m* coal; ~ **de bois** charcoal

charcuterie (shahr-kew-*tree*) *f* delicatessen; butcher's shop

chardon (shahr-*dawng*) *m* thistle

charge (shahrzh) *f* charge

chargement (shahr-zher-*mahng*) *m* cargo, load, charge, freight

charger (shahr-*zhay*) *v* charge; load; **chargé de** in charge of; **se** ~ **de** *take charge of

charité (shah-ree-*tay*) *f* charity

charlatan (shahr-lah-*tahng*) *m* quack

charmant (shahr-*mahng*) *adj* graceful; glamorous

charme (shahrm) *m* charm, glamour

charmer (shahr-*may*) *v* charm, enchant

charnière (shahr-*nʸair*) *f* hinge

charrette (shah-*reht*) *f* cart

charrue (shah-*rew*) *f* plough

chasse (shahss) *f* chase; hunt

chasser (shah-*say*) *v* chase; hunt

chasseur (shah-*sūrr*) *m* hunter; bell-boy

châssis (shah-*see*) *m* chassis

chaste (shahst) *adj* chaste

chat (shah) *m* cat

châtain (shah-*tang*) *adj* auburn

château (shah-*toa*) *m* castle

chatouiller (shah-too-*ʸay*) *v* tickle

chaud (shoa) *adj* hot; warm

chaudière (shoa-*dʸair*) *f* boiler

chauffage (shoa-*faazh*) *m* heating; ~ **central** central heating

chauffer (shoa-*fay*) *v* heat; warm

chauffeur (shoa-*fūrr*) *m* chauffeur; ~ **de taxi** cab-driver

chaussée (shoa-*say*) *f* causeway; carriageway; roadway *nAm*

chaussette (shoa-*seht*) *f* sock

chaussure (shoa-*sewr*) *f* shoe; **chaussures** footwear; **chaussures de basket** plimsolls *pl*; **chaussures de gymnastique** gym shoes; sneakers *plAm*; **chaussures de ski** ski boots; **chaussures de tennis** tennis shoes

chauve (shōav) *adj* bald

chaux (shoa) *f* lime

chef (shehf) *m* chief; manager, boss; chieftain; ~ **cuisinier** chef; ~ **de gare** station-master; ~ **d'Etat** head of state; ~ **d'orchestre** conductor

chef-d'œuvre (sheh-*dūrvr*) *m* masterpiece

chemin (sher-*mang*) *m* lane; **à mi-chemin** halfway; ~ **de fer** railroad *nAm*; railway; ~ **du retour** way back

chemineau (sher-mee-*noa*) *m* tramp

cheminée (sher-mee-*nay*) *f* chimney; fireplace; hearth

chemise (sher-*meez*) *f* shirt; vest; ~ **de nuit** nightdress

chemisier (sher-mee-*zʸay*) *m* blouse

chêne (shehn) *m* oak

chenil (sher-*nee*) *m* kennel

chèque (shehk) *m* cheque; check *nAm*; ~ **de voyage** traveller's cheque

cher (shair) *adj* dear; expensive

chercher (shehr-*shay*) *v* *seek, search; hunt for, look up, look for; *aller ~ fetch

chère (shair) *f* fare

chéri (shay-*ree*) *m* darling, sweetheart

cheval (sher-*vahl*) *m* horse; ~ **de course** race-horse; **cheval-vapeur** *m* horsepower; **chevaux de bois** merry-go-round; **monter à ~** *ride

chevalier (sher-vah-*lʸay*) *m* knight

chevelu (sher-*vlew*) *adj* hairy

cheveu (sher-*vur*) *m* hair; **coupe de cheveux** haircut

cheville (sher-*veey*) *f* ankle

chèvre (shaivr) *f* goat

chevreau (sher-*vroa*) *m* kid

chez (shay) *prep* at; to; with; ~ **soi** home

chic (sheek) *adj* (f ~) smart

chichi (shee-*shee*) *m* fuss

chien (shʸang) *m* dog; ~ **d'aveugle** guide-dog

chienne (shʸehn) *f* bitch

chiffon (shee-*fawng*) *m* cloth; rag

chiffre (sheefr) *m* figure; digit, number

Chili (shee-*lee*) *m* Chile

Chilien (shee-*lʸang*) *m* Chilean

chilien (shee-*lʸang*) *adj* Chilean

chimie (shee-*mee*) *f* chemistry

chimique (shee-*meek*) *adj* chemical

Chine (sheen) *f* China

Chinois (shee-*nwah*) *m* Chinese

chinois (shee-*nwah*) *adj* Chinese

chirurgien (shee-rewr-*zhʸang*) *m* surgeon

chlore (klawr) *m* chlorine

choc (shok) *m* shock

chocolat (sho-kô-*lah*) *m* chocolate

chœur (kūrr) *m* choir

choisir (shwah-*zeer*) *v* *choose; pick, select; **choisi** select

choix (shwah) *m* choice; pick, selection

chômage (shoa-*maazh*) *m* unemployment; **en ~** unemployed

chômeur (shoa-*mūrr*) *m* unemployed worker

chope (shop) *f* mug

choquer (sho-*kay*) *v* shock

chose (shōāz) *f* thing; **quelque ~** something

chou (shoo) *m* (pl ~x) cabbage; **chou-fleur** cauliflower; **choux de Bruxelles** sprouts *pl*

chouchou (shoo-*shoo*) *m* pet

chrétien (kray-t*Y*ang) *m* Christian; *adj* Christian

Christ (kreest) *m* Christ

chrome (krom) *m* chromium

chronique (kro-*neek*) *adj* chronic

chronologique (kro-no-lo-*zheek*) *adj* chronological

chuchotement (shew-shot-*mahng*) *m* whisper

chuchoter (shew-sho-*tay*) *v* whisper

chute (shewt) *f* fall

cible (seebl) *f* target; mark

ciboulette (see-boo-*leht*) *f* chives *pl*

cicatrice (see-kah-*treess*) *f* scar

ciel (s*Y*ehl) *m* (pl cieux) heaven; sky

cigare (see-*gaar*) *m* cigar

cigarette (see-gah-*reht*) *f* cigarette

cigogne (see-*goñ*) *f* stork

cil (seel) *m* eyelash

ciment (see-*mahng*) *m* cement

cimetière (seem-t*Y*air) *f* graveyard, cemetery, churchyard

cinéma (see-nay-*mah*) *m* cinema; pictures; movie theater *Am*, movies *Am*

cinq (sangk) *num* five

cinquante (sang-*kahngt*) *num* fifty

cinquième (sang-*k*Y*ehm*) *num* fifth

cintre (sangtr) *m* coat-hanger, hanger

cirage (see-*raazh*) *m* shoe polish

circonstance (seer-kawng-*stahngss*) *f* circumstance; condition

circuit (seer-*kwee*) *m* circumference; circuit

circulation (seer-kew-lah-s*Y*awng) *f* circulation; traffic

cire (seer) *f* wax; **musée des figures de ~** waxworks *pl*

cirque (seerk) *m* circus

ciseaux (see-*zoa*) *mpl* scissors *pl*; **~ à ongles** nail-scissors *pl*

citation (see-tah-s*Y*awng) *f* quotation

cité (see-*tay*) *f* city

citer (see-*tay*) *v* quote

citoyen (see-twah-*Y*ang) *m* citizen

citoyenneté (see-twah-*Y*ehn-*tay*) *f* citizenship

citron (see-*trawng*) *m* lemon

civil (see-*veel*) *m* civilian; *adj* civilian, civil

civilisation (see-vee-lee-zah-s*Y*awng) *f* civilization

civilisé (see-vee-lee-*zay*) *adj* civilized

civique (see-*veek*) *adj* civic

clair (klair) *adj* clear; plain, light, serene

clairière (kleh-r*Y*air) *f* clearing

claque (klahk) *f* slap; smack, blow; **donner une ~** smack

claquer (klah-*kay*) *v* slam

clarifier (klah-ree-f*Y*ay) *v* clarify

clarté (klahr-*tay*) *f* light, clearness

classe (klahss) *f* class; form; **~ moyenne** middle class; **~ touriste** tourist class

classer (klah-*say*) *v* classify; assort, grade, arrange, sort

classique (klah-*seek*) *adj* classical

clause (klōāz) *f* clause

clavecin (klahv-*sang*) *m* harpsichord

clavicule (klah-vee-*kewl*) *f* collarbone

clé (klay) *f* key; wrench; **~ à écrous** spanner; **~ de la maison** latchkey

clémence (klay-*mahngss*) *f* mercy;

grace

client (klee-*ahng*) *m* client; customer

clientèle (klee-ahng-*tehl*) *f* customers *pl*

clignotant (klee-ño-*tahng*) *m* indicator

climat (klee-*mah*) *m* climate

climatisation (klee-mah-tee-zah-*s*ʸ*awng*) *f* air-conditioning

climatisé (klee-mah-tee-*zay*) *adj* air-conditioned

clinique (klee-*neek*) *f* clinic

cloche (klosh) *f* bell

clocher (klo-*shay*) *m* steeple

cloison (klwah-*zawng*) *f* partition; wall

cloître (klwaatr) *m* cloister

cloque (klok) *f* blister

clos (kloa) *adj* closed; shut

clôture (kloa-*te͞wr*) *f* fence

clou (kloo) *m* nail

clown (kloon) *m* clown

club (klurb) *m* club; ~ **automobile** automobile club; ~ **de golf** golf-club

coaguler (koa-ah-gew-*lay*) *v* coagulate

cocaïne (ko-kah-*een*) *f* cocaine

cochon (ko-*shawng*) *m* pig; ~ **de lait** piglet; ~ **d'Inde** guinea-pig

cocktail (kok-*tehl*) *m* cocktail

cocotte à pression (ko-kot ah preh-*s*ʸ*awng*) pressure-cooker

code (kod) *m* code; ~ **postal** zip code *Am*

cœur (ku͞rr) *m* heart; core; **par** ~ by heart

coffre (kofr) *m* chest; boot; trunk *nAm*; **coffre-fort** safe

cognac (ko-*ñahk*) *m* cognac

cogner (ko-*ñay*) *v* bump; ~ **contre** knock against

cohérence (koa-ay-*rahngss*) *f* coherence

coiffeur (kwah-*fu͞rr*) *m* hairdresser; barber

coiffeuse (kwah-*fu͞rz*) *f* dressing-table

coiffure (kwah-*fe͞wr*) *f* hair-do

coin (kwang) *m* corner

coïncidence (koa-ang-see-*dahngss*) *f* concurrence

coïncider (koa-ang-see-*day*) *v* coincide

col (kol) *m* collar; mountain pass

coléoptère (ko-lay-op-*tair*) *m* bug

colère (ko-*lair*) *f* anger; temper, passion; **en** ~ angry

coléreux (ko-lay-*rur*) *adj* hot-tempered

colis (ko-*lee*) *m* parcel, package

collaboration (ko-lah-borah-*s*ʸ*awng*) *f* co-operation

collants (ko-*lahng*) *mpl* tights *pl*; panty-hose

colle (kol) *f* glue, gum

collectif (ko-lehk-*teef*) *adj* collective

collection (ko-lehk-*s*ʸ*awng*) *f* collection; ~ **d'art** art collection

collectionner (ko-lehk-s*ʸ*o-*nay*) *v* gather

collectionneur (ko-lehk-s*ʸ*o-*nu͞rr*) *m* collector

collège (ko-*laizh*) *m* college

collègue (ko-*lehg*) *m* colleague

coller (ko-*lay*) *v* paste; *stick

collier (ko-*l*ʸ*ay*) *m* necklace; collar; beads *pl*

colline (ko-*leen*) *f* hill

collision (ko-lee-z*ʸ*awng) *f* collision; crash; **entrer en** ~ collide, crash

Colombie (ko-lawng-*bee*) *f* Colombia

Colombien (ko-lawng-*b*ʸ*ang*) *m* Colombian

colombien (ko-lawng-*b*ʸ*ang*) *adj* Colombian

colonel (ko-lo-*nehl*) *m* colonel

colonie (ko-lo-*nee*) *f* colony

colonne (ko-*lon*) *f* column; pillar; ~ **de direction** steering-column

colorant (ko-lo-*rahng*) *m* colourant

coloré (ko-lo-*ray*) *adj* colourful

coma (ko-*mah*) *m* coma

combat (kawng-*bah*) *m* struggle; fight, combat, contest, battle

*__combattre__ (kawng-*bahtr*) *v* *fight; combat, battle

combien (kawng-*byang*) *adv* how much; how many

combinaison (kawng-bee-nay-*zawng*) *f* combination; slip

combiner (kawng-bee-*nay*) *v* combine

comble (kawngbl) *m* roof; height; *adj* full

combler (kawng-*blay*) *v* fill up; overload

combustible (kawng-bew-*steebl*) *m* fuel

comédie (ko-may-*dee*) *f* comedy; ~ **musicale** musical

comédien (ko-may-*dyang*) *m* comedian

comestible (ko-meh-*steebl*) *adj* edible

comique (ko-*meek*) *m* comedian; *adj* comic, humorous

comité (ko-mee-*tay*) *m* committee

commandant (ko-mahng-*dahng*) *m* commander; captain

commande (ko-*mahngd*) *f* order; **fait sur** ~ made to order

commandement (ko-mahngd-*mahng*) *m* order

commander (ko-mahng-*day*) *v* command; order

comme (kom) *conj* as; like, like; since; ~ **si** as if

commémoration (ko-may-mo-rah-*syawng*) *f* commemoration

commencement (ko-mahng-*smahng*) *m* beginning

commencer (ko-mahng-*say*) *v* *begin; commence, start

comment (ko-*mahng*) *adv* how; **n'importe** ~ anyhow; any way

commentaire (ko-mahng-*tair*) *m* comment

commenter (ko-mahng-*tay*) *v* comment

commerçant (ko-mehr-*sahng*) *m* merchant; trader, shopkeeper

commerce (ko-*mehrs*) *m* commerce; business, trade; ~ **de détail** retail trade; *__faire du__ ~ trade

commercial (ko-mehr-*syahl*) *adj* commercial

*__commettre__ (ko-*mehtr*) *v* commit

commission (ko-mee-*syawng*) *f* committee, commission; errand, message

commode (ko-*mod*) *f* chest of drawers; bureau *nAm*; *adj* convenient, easy, handy

commodité (ko-mo-dee-*tay*) *f* comfort

commotion (ko-moa-*syawng*) *f* concussion

commun (ko-*murng*) *adj* common; ordinary

communauté (ko-mew-noa-*tay*) *f* community; congregation

communication (ko-mew-nee-kah-*syawng*) *f* communication; information; connection; ~ **locale** local call; *__mettre en__ ~ connect

communiqué (ko-mew-nee-*kay*) *m* communiqué

communiquer (ko-mew-nee-*kay*) *v* communicate; inform

communisme (ko-mew-*neesm*) *m* communism

commutateur (ko-mew-tah-*tūr*) *m* switch

compact (kawng-*pahkt*) *adj* compact

compact disc (kawng-*pahkt* deesk) *m* compact disc; **lecteur de** ~ compact disc player

compagnie (kawng-pah-*ñee*) *f* company; society; ~ **de navigation** shipping line

compagnon (kawng-pah-*ñawng*) *m* companion

comparaison (kawng-pah-ray-*zawng*) *f*

comparison

comparer (kawng-pah-*ray*) *v* compare

compartiment (kawng-pahr-tee-*mahng*) *m* compartment; ~ **fumeurs** smoking-compartment

compassion (kawng-pah-*s^yawng*) *f* sympathy

compatir (kawng-pah-*teer*) *v* pity

compatissant (kawng-pah-tee-*sahng*) *adj* sympathetic

compatriote (kawng-pah-tree-*ot*) *m* countryman

compensation (kawng-pahng-sah-*s^yawng*) *f* compensation

compenser (kawng-pahng-*say*) *v* compensate; *make good

compétence (kawng-pay-*tahngss*) *f* capacity

compétent (kawng-pay-*tahng*) *adj* qualified; expert

compétition (kawng-pay-tee-*s^yawng*) *f* competition

compiler (kawng-pee-*lay*) *v* compile

complémentaire (kawng-play-mahng-*tair*) *adj* further

complet¹ (kawng-*play*) *adj* (f -plète) whole, complete; total, utter; full up

complet² (kawng-*play*) *m* suit

complètement (kawng-pleht-*mahng*) *adv* completely

complexe (kawng-*plehks*) *m* complex; *adj* complex

complice (kawng-*pleess*) *m* accessary

compliment (kawng-plee-*mahng*) *m* compliment

complimenter (kawng-plee-mahng-*tay*) *v* compliment

compliqué (kawng-plee-*kay*) *adj* complicated

complot (kawng-*ploa*) *m* plot

comportement (kawng-por-ter-*mahng*) *m* behaviour

comporter (kawng-por-*tay*) *v* imply;

se ~ behave

composer (kawng-poa-*zay*) *v* compose

compositeur (kawng-po-zee-*tūrr*) *m* composer

composition (kawng-po-zee-*s^yawng*) *f* composition; essay

compréhension (kawng-pray-ahng-*s^yawng*) *f* understanding; insight

***comprendre** (kawng-*prahngdr*) *v* *understand; *take, *see; *conceive; comprise, include, contain

comprimé (kawng-pree-*may*) *m* tablet

compris (kawng-*pree*) *adj* inclusive; **tout ~** all in

compromis (kawng-pro-*mee*) *m* compromise

comptable (kawng-*tahbl*) *m* bookkeeper

compte (kawngt) *m* account; ~ **en banque** bank account; ~ **rendu** report; minutes; **en fin de ~** at last; **rendre ~ de** account for; **se rendre ~** realize; *see

compter (kawng-*tay*) *v* count; ~ **sur** rely on

compteur (kawng-*tūrr*) *m* meter

comptoir (kawng-*twaar*) *m* counter

comte (kawngt) *m* count; earl

comté (kawng-*tay*) *m* county

comtesse (kawng-*tehss*) *f* countess

concéder (kawng-say-*day*) *v* grant

concentration (kawng-sahng-trah-*s^yawng*) *f* concentration

concentrer (kawng-sahng-*tray*) *v* concentrate

concept (kawng-*sehpt*) *m* idea

conception (kawng-seh-*ps^yawng*) *f* conception

concernant (kawng-sehr-*nahng*) *prep* concerning; as regards, about, regarding

concerner (kawng-sehr-*nay*) *v* concern; **en ce qui concerne** as regards, regarding

concert (kawng-*sair*) *m* concert

concession (kawng-seh-s*ʸawng*) *f* concession

concessionnaire (kawng-seh-s*ʸo*-*nair*) *m* distributor

***concevoir** (kawng-*svvaar*) *v* conceive; devise, *take

concierge (kawng-s*ʸehrzh*) *m* concierge; janitor

concis (kawng-*see*) *adj* concise

***conclure** (kawng-*klew*-z*ʸawng*) *v* finish; conclude

conclusion (kawng-klew-z*ʸawng*) *f* conclusion, end; issue

concombre (kawng-*kawngbr*) *m* cucumber

concorder (kawng-kor-*day*) *v* agree

***concourir** (kawng-koo-*reer*) *v* compete

concours (kawng-*kōōr*) *m* contest

concret (kawng-*kray*) *adj* (f -crète) concrete

concupiscence (kawng-kew-pee-*sahngss*) *f* lust

concurrence (kawng-kew-*rahngss*) *f* rivalry

concurrent (kawng-kew-*rahng*) *m* competitor; rival

condamnation (kawng-dah-nah-s*ʸawng*) *f* conviction

condamné (kawng-dah-*nay*) *m* convict

condamner (kawng-dah-*nay*) *v* sentence

condition (kawng-dee-s*ʸawng*) *f* condition; term

conditionnel (kawng-dee-s*ʸo*-*nehl*) *adj* conditional

conducteur (kawng-dewk-*tūrr*) *m* driver; conductor

***conduire** (kawng-*dweer*) *v* conduct, guide; *drive; carry, *take; **se ~** act

conduite (kawng-*dweet*) *f* conduct; lead

confédération (kawng-fay-day-rah-s*ʸawng*) *f* federation; union

conférence (kawng-fay-*rahngss*) *f* conference; lecture; **~ de presse** press conference

confesser (kawng-fay-*say*) *v* confess

confession (kawng-feh-s*ʸawng*) *f* confession

confiance (kawng-f*ʸahngss*) *f* confidence; faith, trust; **digne de ~** reliable, trustworthy; ***faire ~** trust

confiant (kawng-f*ʸahng*) *adj* confident

confidentiel (kawng-fee-dahng-s*ʸehl*) *adj* confidential

confier (kawng-f*ʸay*) *v* commit

confirmation (kawng-feer-mah-s*ʸawng*) *f* confirmation

confirmer (kawng-feer-*may*) *v* confirm; acknowledge

confiserie (kawng-fee-*zree*) *f* sweetshop; candy *nAm*; candy store *Am*

confiseur (kawng-fee-*zūrr*) *m* confectioner

confisquer (kawng-fee-*skay*) *v* confiscate; impound

confiture (kawng-fee-*tewr*) *f* jam

conflit (kawng-*flee*) *m* conflict

confondre (kawng-*fawngdr*) *v* confuse; *mistake

***être conforme** (aitr kawng-*form*) correspond

conformément à (kawng-for-may-*mahng*) in accordance with, according to

confort (kawng-*fawr*) *m* comfort

confortable (kawng-for-*tahbl*) *adj* comfortable; cosy

confus (kawng-*few*) *adj* confused; obscure; embarrassed

confusion (kawng-few-z*ʸawng*) *f* confusion; disorder, muddle

congé (kawng-*zhay*) *m* vacation

congélateur (kawng-zhay-lah-*tūrr*) *m* deep-freeze

congelé (kawng-*zhlay*) *adj* frozen

congratuler (kawng-grah-tew-*lay*) *v* congratulate

congrégation (kawng-gray-gah-*s^yawng*) *f* congregation

congrès (kawng-*gray*) *m* congress

conifère (ko-nee-*fair*) *m* fir-tree

conjecture (kawng-zhehk-*tewr*) *f* guess

conjoint (kawng-*zhwang*) *adj* joint

conjointement (kawng-zhwangt-*mahng*) *adv* jointly

connaissance (ko-nay-*sahngss*) *f* knowledge; acquaintance

connaisseur (ko-nay-*sürr*) *m* connoisseur

*****connaître** (ko-*naitr*) *v* *know; **connu** well-known

connotation (ko-no-tah-*s^yawng*) *f* connotation

conquérant (kawng-kay-*rahng*) *m* conqueror

*****conquérir** (kawng-kay-*reer*) *v* conquer

conquête (kawng-*keht*) *f* conquest

consacrer (kawng-sah-*kray*) *v* devote

conscience (kawng-*s^yahngss*) *f* conscience; consciousness

conscient (kawng-*s^yahng*) *adj* conscious; aware

conscrit (kawng-*skree*) *m* conscript

conseil (kawng-*say*) *m* advice; counsel, council; board; **donner des conseils** advise

conseiller (kawng-say-*^yay*) *v* advise; recommend; *m* councillor; counsellor

consentement (kawng-sahngt-*mahng*) *m* consent, approval

*****consentir** (kawng-sahng-*teer*) *v* consent, agree

conséquence (kawng-say-*kahngss*) *f* consequence; issue

par conséquent (pahr kawng-say-*kahng*) consequently

conservateur (kawng-sehr-vah-*türr*) *adj* conservative

conservation (kawng-sehr-vah-*s^yawng*) *f* preservation

conservatoire (kawng-sehr-vah-*twaar*) *m* music academy

conserver (kawng-sehr-*vay*) *v* preserve

conserves (kawng-*sehrv*) *fpl* tinned food; *****mettre en conserve** preserve

considérable (kawng-see-day-*rahbl*) *adj* considerable; extensive

considération (kawng-see-day-rah-*s^yawng*) *f* consideration; respect

considérer (kawng-see-day-*ray*) *v* consider; count, regard

consigne (kawng-*seeñ*) *f* deposit; left luggage office; baggage deposit office *Am*

consister en (kawng-see-*stay*) consist of

consoler (kawng-so-*lay*) *v* comfort

consommateur (kawng-so-mah-*türr*) *m* consumer

consommation (kawng-so-mah-*s^yawng*) *f* consumption; drink

consommer (kawng-so-*may*) *v* consume

conspiration (kawng-spee-rah-*s^yawng*) *f* plot

conspirer (kawng-spee-*ray*) *v* conspire

constant (kawng-*stahng*) *adj* constant; even

constater (kawng-stah-*tay*) *v* ascertain; diagnose, note

constipation (kawng-stee-pah-*s^yawng*) *f* constipation

constipé (kawng-stee-*pay*) *adj* constipated

constituer (kawng-stee-*tway*) *v* constitute

constitution (kawng-stee-tew-*s^yawng*) *f* constitution

construction (kawng-strewk-*s^yawng*) *f*

construction; building

`**construire** (kawng-*strweer*) v construct

consul (kawng-*sewl*) m consul

consulat (kawng-sew-*lah*) m consulate

consultation (kawng-sewl-tah-s^y*awng*) f consultation

consulter (kawng-sewl-*tay*) v consult

contact (kawng-*tahkt*) m contact; touch

contacter (kawng-tahk-*tay*) v contact

contagieux (kawng-tah-zh^y*ur*) adj contagious

conte (kawngt) m tale; ~ **de fées** fairytale

contempler (kawng-tahng-*play*) v view

contemporain (kawng-tahng-po-*rang*) m contemporary; adj contemporary

conteneur (kawngt-*nūrr*) m container

`**contenir** (kawngt-*neer*) v contain; restrain

content (kawng-*tahng*) adj glad; pleased, joyful, happy

contenu (kawngt-*new*) m contents pl

contester (kawng-teh-*stay*) v dispute

contigu (kawng-tee-*gew*) adj (f -guë) neighbouring

continent (kawng-tee-*nahng*) m continent

continental (kawng-tee-nahng-*tahl*) adj continental

continu (kawng-tee-*new*) adj continuous

continuel (kawng-tee-*nwehl*) adj continual; continuous

continuellement (kawng-tee-nwehl-*mahng*) adv all the time, continually

continuer (kawng-tee-*nway*) v continue; carry on, *keep on, *keep, *go on, *go ahead

contour (kawng-*tōōr*) m outline, contour

contourner (kawng-toor-*nay*) v by-

pass

contraceptif (kawng-trah-sehp-*teef*) m contraceptive

contradictoire (kawng-trah-deek-*twaar*) adj contradictory

`**contraindre** (kawng-*trangdr*) v compel

contraire (kawng-*trair*) adj opposite; m reverse, contrary; **au ~** on the contrary

contralto (kawng-trahl-*toa*) m alto

contraste (kawng-*trahst*) m contrast

contrat (kawng-*trah*) m agreement, contract

contravention (kawng-trah-vahng-s^y*awng*) f ticket

contre (kawngtr) prep against; versus

à contrecœur (ah kawng-trer-*kūrr*) unwilling

`**contredire** (kawng-trer-*deer*) v contradict

`**contrefaire** (kawng-trer-*fair*) v counterfeit

contrefait (kawng-trer-*fay*) adj deformed

contremaître (kawng-trer-*maitr*) m foreman

contribution (kawng-tree-bew-s^y*awng*) f contribution

contrôle (kawng-*trōāl*) m control; inspection; ~ **des passeports** passport control

contrôler (kawng-troa-*lay*) v control; check

contrôleur (kawng-troa-*lūrr*) m ticket collector

controversé (kawng-troa-vehr-*say*) adj controversial

contusion (kawng-tew-z^y*awng*) f bruise

contusionner (kawng-tew-z^yo-*nay*) v bruise

`**convaincre** (kawng-*vangkr*) v convince; persuade

convenable (kawng-*vnahbl*) *adj* proper; fit

***convenir** (kawng-*vneer*) *v* fit, suit

conversation (kawng-vehr-sah-*s*ʸ*awng*) *f* conversation; discussion, talk

convertir (kawng-vehr-*teer*) *v* convert

conviction (kawng-veek-*s*ʸ*awng*) *f* conviction; persuasion

convocation (kawng-vo-kah-*s*ʸ*awng*) *f* summons

convulsion (kawng-vewl-*s*ʸ*awng*) *f* convulsion

coopérant (koa-o-pay-*rahng*) *adj* co-operative

coopératif (koa-o-pay-rah-*teef*) *adj* co-operative

coopération (koa-o-pay-rah-*s*ʸ*awng*) *f* co-operation

coopérative (koa-o-pay-rah-*teev*) *f* co-operative

coordination (koa-or-dee-nah-*s*ʸ*awng*) *f* co-ordination

coordonner (koa-or-do-*nay*) *v* co-ordinate

copain (ko-*pang*) *m* pal

copie (ko-*pee*) *f* copy; carbon copy

copier (ko-*p*ʸ*ay*) *v* copy

coq (kok) *m* cock; ~ **de bruyère** grouse

coquelicot (ko-klee-*koa*) *m* poppy

coquetier (kok-*t*ʸ*ay*) *m* egg-cup

coquillage (ko-kee-*ʸaazh*) *m* sea-shell

coquille (ko-*keey*) *f* shell; ~ **de noix** nutshell

coquin (ko-*kang*) *m* rascal

cor (kawr) *m* horn; ~ **au pied** corn

corail (ko-*righ*) *m* (pl coraux) coral

corbeau (kor-*boa*) *m* raven

corbeille à papier (kor-bay ah pah-*p*ʸ*ay*) wastepaper-basket

corde (kord) *f* rope; cord; string

cordial (kor-*d*ʸ*ahl*) *adj* hearty, cordial; sympathetic

cordon (kor-*dawng*) *m* cord; tape

cordonnier (kor-do-*n*ʸ*ay*) *m* shoemaker

coriace (ko-*r*ʸ*ahss*) *adj* tough

corne (korn) *f* horn

corneille (kor-*nay*) *f* crow

corps (kawr) *m* body

corpulent (kor-pew-*lahng*) *adj* corpulent; stout

correct (ko-*rehkt*) *adj* correct; right

correction (ko-rehk-*s*ʸ*awng*) *f* correction

correspondance (ko-reh-spawng-*dahngss*) *f* correspondence; connection

correspondant (ko-reh-spawng-*dahng*) *m* correspondent

correspondre (ko-reh-*spawngdr*) *v* correspond

corrida (ko-ree-*dah*) *f* bullfight

corridor (ko-ree-*dawr*) *m* corridor

corriger (ko-ree-*zhay*) *v* correct

***corrompre** (ko-*rawngpr*) *v* corrupt; bribe; **corrompu** corrupt

corruption (ko-rew-*ps*ʸ*awng*) *f* corruption; bribery

corset (kor-*say*) *m* corset

cortège (kor-*taizh*) *m* procession

cosmétiques (ko-smay-*teek*) *mpl* cosmetics *pl*

costume (ko-*stewm*) *m* suit; costume; ~ **national** national dress

côte (kōat) *f* coast; rib; chop

côté (koa-*tay*) *m* side; way; **à** ~ next-door; **à** ~ **de** next to, beside; **de** ~ aside, sideways; **de l'autre** ~ **de** across; **passer à** ~ pass by

coteau (ko-*toa*) *m* hillside

côtelette (ko-*tleht*) *f* chop, cutlet

coton (ko-*tawng*) *m* cotton; **en** ~ cotton

cou (koo) *m* neck

couche (koosh) *f* layer; nappy; diaper *nAm*; **fausse** ~ miscarriage

se coucher (koo-*shay*) **lie down

couchette (koo-*sheht*) f bunk, berth

coucou (koo-*koo*) m cuckoo

coude (kood) m elbow

*__coudre__ (koodr) v sew

couler (koo-*lay*) v flow, stream

couleur (koo-*lūr*) f colour; ~ **à l'eau** water-colour; **de** ~ coloured

couloir (koo-*lwaar*) m corridor

coup (koo) m blow; bump, tap, push, knock; ~ **de feu** shot; ~ **d'envoi** kick-off; ~ **de pied** kick; ~ **de poing** punch; ~ **de téléphone** call; **jeter un** ~ **d'œil** glance

coupable (koo-*pahbl*) adj guilty; **déclarer** ~ convict

coupe (koop) f cup

coupe-papier (koop-pah-*p*y*ay*) m paper-knife

couper (koo-*pay*) v *cut; *cut off

couple (koopl) m couple; ~ **marié** married couple

coupon (koo-*pawng*) m coupon

coupure (koo-*pēwr*) f cut

cour (kōor) f court; yard

courage (koo-*raazh*) m courage

courageux (koo-rah-*zhur*) adj courageous; plucky, brave

couramment (koo-rah-*mahng*) adv fluent

courant (koo-*rahng*) m current, stream; undercurrent; adj frequent, current; ~ **alternatif** alternating current; ~ **continu** direct current; ~ **d'air** draught; *__mettre au__ ~ inform

courbe (koorb) f bend, curve; adj bent, curved, crooked

courbé (koor-*bay*) adj curved

courber (koor-*bay*) v *bend; bow

*__courir__ (koo-*reer*) v *run

couronne (koo-*ron*) f crown

couronner (koo-ro-*nay*) v crown

courrier (koo-*r*y*ay*) m mail

courroie (koo-*rwah*) f strap; ~ **de**

ventilateur fan belt

cours (kōor) m course; lecture; ~ **accéléré** intensive course; ~ **du change** exchange rate, rate of exchange

course (koors) f race; ride; ~ **de chevaux** horserace

court (kōor) adj short; ~ **de tennis** tennis-court

court-circuit (koor-seer-*kwee*) m short circuit

courtepointe (koort-*pwangt*) f quilt

courtier (koor-*t*y*ay*) m broker

courtois (koor-*twah*) adj courteous

cousin (koo-*zang*) m cousin

cousine (koo-*zeen*) f cousin

coussin (koo-*sang*) m cushion

coussinet (koo-see-*nay*) m pad

coût (koo) m cost

couteau (koo-*toa*) m knife; ~ **de poche** pocket-knife

coûter (koo-*tay*) v *cost

coûteux (koo-*tur*) adj expensive

coutume (koo-*tewm*) f custom

coutumier (koo-tew-*m*y*ay*) adj customary

couture (koo-*tēwr*) f seam; **sans** ~ seamless

couturière (koo-tew-*r*y*air*) f dressmaker

couvent (koo-*vahng*) m convent; nunnery

couvercle (koo-*vehrkl*) m top, lid, cover

couvert (koo-*vair*) m cutlery; cover charge; adj cloudy

couverture (koo-vehr-*tēwr*) f blanket; cover

couvre-lit (koo-vrer-*lee*) m counterpane

*__couvrir__ (koo-*vreer*) v cover

crabe (krahb) m crab

crachat (krah-*shah*) m spit

cracher (krah-*shay*) v *spit

crachin (krah-*shang*) m drizzle

craie (kray) f chalk

*craindre (krangdr) v fear, dread

crainte (krangt) f fear, dread

cramoisi (krah-mwah-zee) adj crimson

crampe (krahngp) f cramp

crampon (krahng-pawng) m clamp

cran (krahng) m guts

crâne (kraan) m skull

crapaud (krah-poa) m toad

craquement (krahk-mahng) m crack

craquer (krah-kay) v crack

cratère (krah-tair) m crater

cravate (krah-vaht) f necktie, tie

crawl (krōal) m crawl

crayon (kreh-Yawng) m pencil; **~ à bille** Biro; **~ pour les yeux** eye-pencil

création (kray-ah-sYawng) f creation

créature (kray-ah-tēwr) f creature

crèche (krehsh) f nursery

crédit (kray-dee) m credit

créditer (kray-dee-tay) v credit

créditeur (kray-dee-tūrr) m creditor

crédule (kray-dewl) adj credulous

créer (kray-ay) v create; design

crémation (kray-mah-sYawng) f cremation

crème (krehm) f cream; adj cream; **~ à raser** shaving-cream; **~ capillaire** hair cream; **~ de beauté** face-cream; skin cream; **~ de nuit** night-cream; **~ fraîche** cream; **~ glacée** ice-cream; **~ hydratante** moisturizing cream

crémeux (kray-mur) adj creamy

crépi (kray-pee) m plaster

crépuscule (kray-pew-skewl) m dusk, twilight

cresson (kreh-sawng) m watercress

creuser (krur-zay) v *dig

creux (krur) adj hollow

crevaison (krer-vay-zawng) f puncture; blow-out

crevasse (krer-vahss) f chasm; cave

crever (krer-vay) v *burst; die; **crevé** punctured

crevette (krer-veht) f shrimp; prawn; **~ rose** prawn

cri (kree) m shout, yell, scream, cry; **pousser des cris** shriek

cric (kreek) m jack

cricket (kree-keht) m cricket

crier (kree-ay) v cry; shout, scream

crime (kreem) m crime

criminalité (kree-mee-nah-lee-tay) f criminality

criminel (kree-mee-nehl) m criminal; adj criminal

crique (kreek) f inlet, creek

crise (kreez) f crisis; **~ cardiaque** heart attack

cristal (kree-stahl) m crystal; **en ~** crystal

critique (kree-teek) f criticism; review; m critic; adj critical

critiquer (kree-tee-kay) v criticize

crochet (kro-shay) m hook; ***faire du ~** crochet

crocodile (kro-ko-deel) m crocodile

*croire (krwaar) v believe; guess

croisade (krwah-zahd) f crusade

croisement (krwahz-mahng) m crossing

croisière (krwah-zYair) f cruise

croissance (krwah-sahngss) f growth

*croître (krwaatr) v increase

croix (krwah) f cross

croulant (kroo-lahng) adj ramshackle

croustillant (kroo-stee-Yahng) adj crisp

croûte (kroot) f crust

croyable (krwah-Yaabl) adj credible

croyance (krwah-Yahngss) f belief

cru (krew) adj raw

cruche (krewsh) f pitcher; jug

crucifier (krew-see-fYay) v crucify

crucifix (krew-see-fee) m crucifix

crucifixion (krew-see-fee-ksYawng) f

crucifixion

cruel (krew-*ehl*) *adj* cruel; harsh

crustacé (krew-stah-*say*) *m* shellfish

Cuba (kew-*bah*) *m* Cuba

Cubain (kew-*bang*) *m* Cuban

cubain (kew-*bang*) *adj* Cuban

cube (kewb) *m* cube

*cueillir (kur-*Yeer*) *v* pick

cuillère (kwee-*Yair*) *f* spoon; tablespoon; ~ **à soupe** soup-spoon; ~ **à thé** teaspoon

cuillerée (kwee-Yer-*ray*) *f* spoonful

cuir (kweer) *m* leather; **en** ~ leather

*cuire (kweer) *v* cook; ~ **au four** bake

cuisine (kwee-*zeen*) *f* kitchen

cuisinier (kwee-zee-n*Yay*) *m* cook

cuisinière (kwee-zee-n*Yair*) *f* cooker; stove; ~ **à gaz** gas cooker

cuisse (kwees) *f* thigh

cuivre (kweevr) *m* brass, copper; **cuivres** brassware

cul-de-sac (kewd-*sahk*) *m* cul-de-sac

culotte (kew-*lot*) *f* panties *pl*; ~ **de gymnastique** trunks *pl*

culpabilité (kewl-pah-bee-lee-*tay*) *f* guilt

culte (kewlt) *m* worship

cultiver (kewl-tee-*vay*) *v* cultivate; **grow, raise; **cultivé** cultured

culture (kewl-*tewr*) *f* culture

cupide (kew-*peed*) *adj* greedy

cupidité (kew-pee-dee-*tay*) *f* greed

cure (kewr) *f* cure

cure-dent (kewr-*dahng*) *m* toothpick

cure-pipe (kewr-*peep*) *m* pipe cleaner

curieux (kew-r*Yur*) *adj* inquisitive, curious

curiosité (kew-r*Yo*-zee-*tay*) *f* curiosity; curio; sight

curry (kur-*ree*) *m* curry

cycle (seekl) *m* cycle

cycliste (see-*kleest*) *m* cyclist

cygne (seeñ) *m* swan

cylindre (see-*langdr*) *m* cylinder; **tête de** ~ cylinder head

cystite (see-*steet*) *f* cystitis

D

dactylo (dahk-tee-*loa*) *f* typist

dactylographier (dahk-tee-loa-grah-f*Yay*) *v* type

dada (dah-*dah*) *m* hobby-horse

daim (dang) *m* deer; suede

daltonien (dahl-to-n*Yang*) *adj* colourblind

dame (dahm) *f* lady

damier (dah-m*Yay*) *m* draught-board; check; **à damiers** chequered

Danemark (dahn-*mahrk*) *m* Denmark

danger (dahng-*zhay*) *m* risk, danger

dangereux (dahng-*zhrur*) *adj* dangerous; risky; unsafe

Danois (dah-*nwah*) *m* Dane

danois (dah-*nwah*) *adj* Danish

dans (dahng) *prep* into, inside, in, within

danse (dahngss) *f* dance; ~ **folklorique** folk-dance

danser (dahng-*say*) *v* dance

date (daht) *f* date

datte (daht) *f* date

davantage (dah-vahng-*taazh*) *adv* more

de (der) *prep* of; out of, from, off; about; with

dé (day) *m* thimble

déballer (day-bah-*lay*) *v* unwrap, unpack

débarquer (day-bahr-*kay*) *v* disembark, land

se débarrasser de (day-bah-rah-*say*) discard

débat (day-*bah*) *m* debate; discussion

*débattre (day-*bahtr*) *v* discuss

débit (day-*bee*) *m* debit

déboucher (day-boo-*shay*) *v* uncork

debout (der-*boo*) *adv* upright; erect

déboutonner (day-boo-to-*nay*) *v* un-button

débrancher (day-brahng-*shay*) *v* disconnect

se débrouiller avec (day-broo-*Yay*) *make do with

début (day-*bew*) *m* start, beginning; **au ~** at first

débutant (day-bew-*tahng*) *m* learner, beginner

débuter (day-bew-*tay*) *v* *begin

décaféiné (day-kah-fay-ee-*nay*) *adj* decaffeinated

décédé (day-say-*day*) *adj* dead

décembre (day-*sahngbr*) December

décence (day-*sahngss*) *f* decency

décent (day-*sahng*) *adj* decent

déception (day-seh-*psYawng*) *f* disappointment

décerner (day-sehr-*nay*) *v* award

décevoir (day-*svwaar*) *v* disappoint

déchaînement (day-shehn-*mahng*) *m* outbreak

décharger (day-shahr-*zhay*) *v* discharge; unload

déchets (day-*shay*) *mpl* trash

déchirer (day-shee-*ray*) *v* rip, *tear

déchirure (day-shee-*rēwr*) *f* tear

décider (day-see-*day*) *v* decide

décision (day-see-*zYawng*) *f* decision

déclaration (day-klah-rah-*sYawng*) *f* declaration, statement

déclarer (day-klah-*ray*) *v* declare, state

décliner (day-klee-*nay*) *v* slope

décollage (day-ko-*laazh*) *m* take-off

décoller (day-ko-*lay*) *v* *take off

décolorer (day-ko-lo-*ray*) *v* discolour; bleach

déconcerter (day-kawng-sehr-*tay*) *v* embarrass; overwhelm

décontracté (day-kawng-trahk-*tay*) *adj* easy-going

décoration (day-ko-rah-*sYawng*) *f* decoration

décorer (day-ko-*ray*) *v* decorate

découper (day-koo-*pay*) *v* carve; *cut off

décourager (day-koo-rah-*zhay*) *v* discourage

découverte (day-koo-*vehrt*) *f* discovery

découvrir (day-koo-*vreer*) *v* discover; uncover

décrire (day-*kreer*) *v* describe

dédain (day-*dang*) *m* contempt; scorn

dedans (der-*dahng*) *adv* in; inside

dédier (day-*dYay*) *v* dedicate

dédommagement (day-do-mahzh-*mahng*) *m* indemnity

déduire (day-*dweer*) *v* infer, deduce; deduct

déesse (day-*ehss*) *f* goddess

défaillant (day-fah-*Yahng*) *adj* faint

défaire (day-*fair*) *v* *undo

défaite (day-*feht*) *f* defeat

défaut (day-*foa*) *m* fault

défavorable (day-fah-vo-*rahbl*) *adj* unfavourable

défectueux (day-fehk-*twur*) *adj* faulty, defective

défendre (day-*fahngdr*) *v* defend

défense (day-*fahngss*) *f* defence; **~ de doubler** no overtaking; no passing *Am*; **~ de fumer** no smoking; **~ d'entrer** no entry

défi (day-*fee*) *m* challenge

défiance (day-*fYahngss*) *f* suspicion

déficience (day-fee-*sYahngss*) *f* deficiency

déficit (day-fee-*seet*) *m* deficit

défier (day-*fYay*) *v* challenge, dare

définir (day-fee-*neer*) *v* determine, define

définition (day-fee-nee-*sYawng*) *f* definition

dégel (day-_zhehl_) _m_ thaw

dégeler (day-_zhlay_) _v_ thaw

dégoût (day-_goo_) _m_ disgust

dégoûtant (day-goo-_tahng_) _adj_ disgusting, revolting

dégoûté (day-goo-_tay_) _adj_ fed up with

degré (der-_gray_) _m_ degree

déguisement (day-geez-_mahng_) _m_ disguise

se déguiser (day-gee-_zay_) disguise

dehors (der-_awr_) _adv_ outside, outdoors, out; **en ~ de** out of

déjà (day-_zhah_) _adv_ already

déjeuner (day-zhur-_nay_) _m_ dinner; luncheon, lunch; **petit ~** breakfast

au delà de (oa der-_lah_ der) past, beyond

délabré (day-lah-_bray_) _adj_ dilapidated

délai (day-_lay_) _m_ set term; delay

délégation (day-lay-gah-s_y_awng) _f_ delegation

délégué (day-lay-_gay_) _m_ delegate

délibération (day-lee-bay-rah-s_y_awng) _f_ deliberation; discussion

délibérer (day-lee-bay-_ray_) _v_ deliberate; **délibéré** deliberate

délicat (day-lee-_kah_) _adj_ tender, delicate; gentle; critical

délicatesse (day-lee-kah-_tehss_) _f_ delicacy

délice (day-_leess_) _m_ delight

délicieux (day-lee-s_y_ur) _adj_ delightful, delicious, wonderful, lovely

délinquant (day-lang-_kahng_) _m_ criminal

délivrance (day-lee-_vrahngss_) _f_ delivery

délivrer (day-lee-_vray_) _v_ deliver, redeem

demain (der-_mang_) _adv_ tomorrow

demande (der-_mahngd_) _f_ demand; application, request

demander (der-mahng-_day_) _v_ ask, beg; charge; **se ~** wonder

démangeaison (day-mahng-zhay-_zawng_) _f_ itch

démanger (day-mahng-_zhay_) _v_ itch

démarche (day-_mahrsh_) _f_ walk, pace, gait

démarreur (day-mah-_rurr_) _m_ starter motor

déménagement (day-may-nahzh-_mahng_) _m_ move

déménager (day-may-nah-_zhay_) _v_ move

démence (day-_mahngss_) _f_ madness

dément (day-_mahng_) _adj_ mad

demeure (der-_murr_) _f_ home

demeurer (der-mur-_ray_) _v_ stay; live

demi (der-_mee_) _adj_ half

démission (day-mee-s_y_awng) _f_ resignation

démissionner (day-mee-s_y_o-_nay_) _v_ resign

démocratie (day-mo-krah-_see_) _f_ democracy

démocratique (day-mo-krah-_teek_) _adj_ democratic

démodé (day-mo-_day_) _adj_ out of date, old-fashioned, ancient

demoiselle (der-mwah-_zehl_) _f_ miss

démolir (day-mo-_leer_) _v_ demolish

démolition (day-mo-lee-s_y_awng) _f_ demolition

démonstration (day-mawng-strah-s_y_awng) _f_ demonstration

démontrer (day-mawng-_tray_) _v_ *show, demonstrate, prove

dénier (day-n_y_ay) _v_ deny

dénomination (day-no-mee-nah-s_y_awng) _f_ denomination

dénouer (day-_nway_) _v_ untie

dense (dahngss) _adj_ dense

dent (dahng) _f_ tooth

dentelle (dahng-_tehl_) _f_ lace

dentier (dahng-t_y_ay) _m_ false teeth, denture

dentiste (dahng-_teest_) _m_ dentist

dénudé (day-new-*day*) *adj* naked

dénutrition (day-new-tree-s*y*awng) *f* malnutrition

départ (day-*paar*) *m* departure

département (day-pahr-ter-*mahng*) *m* division, department

dépasser (day-pah-*say*) *v* *overtake; pass

se dépêcher (day-pay-shay) hurry

dépendant (day-pahng-*dahng*) *adj* dependent

dépendre de (day-*pahngdr*) depend on

dépense (day-*pahngss*) *f* expense, expenditure

dépenser (day-pahng-*say*) *v* *spend

en dépit de (ahng day-*pee* der) in spite of

déplacement (day-plah-*smahng*) *m* removal

déplacer (day-plah-*say*) *v* move

*déplaire (day-*plair*) *v* displease

déplaisant (day-play-*zahng*) *adj* unpleasant

déplier (day-plee-*ay*) *v* unfold

déployer (day-plwah-*Yay*) *v* expand

déposer (day-poa-*zay*) *v* deposit, bank

dépôt (day-*poa*) *m* deposit; warehouse, depot

dépression (day-preh-s*y*awng) *f* depression

déprimer (day-pree-*may*) *v* depress; **déprimé** down; blue; low

depuis (der-*pwee*) *prep* since; *adv* since; ~ **que** since

député (day-pew-*tay*) *m* deputy; Member of Parliament

déraisonnable (day-ray-zo-*nahbl*) *adj* unreasonable

dérangement (day-rahngzh-*mahng*) *m* trouble; disturbance; **en** ~ broken, out of order

déranger (day-rahng-*zhay*) *v* disturb, upset, trouble

déraper (day-rah-*pay*) *v* slip, skid

dernier (dehr-n*y*ay) *adj* last; past

dernièrement (dehr-n*y*ehr-*mahng*) *adv* lately

derrière (deh-r*y*air) *prep* after, behind; *m* bottom

dès que (day ker) as soon as

*être en désaccord (aitr ahng day-zah-*kawr*) disagree

désagréable (day-zah-gray-*ahbl*) *adj* nasty, disagreeable, unpleasant, unkind

désagrément (day-zah-gray-*mahng*) *m* inconvenience

*désapprendre (day-zah-*prahngdr*) *v* unlearn

désapprouver (day-zah-proo-*vay*) *v* disapprove

désastre (day-*zahstr*) *m* disaster

désastreux (day-zah-*strur*) *adj* disastrous

désavantage (day-zah-vahng-*taazh*) *m* disadvantage

descendance (day-sahng-*dahngss*) *f* origin

descendant (day-sahng-*dahng*) *m* descendant

descendre (day-*sahngdr*) *v* descend; *get off

descente (day-*sahngt*) *f* descent

description (day-skree-ps*y*awng) *f* description

désenchanter (day-zahng-shahng-*tay*) *v* *let down

désert (day-*zair*) *m* desert; *adj* desert

déserter (day-zehr-*tay*) *v* desert

désespérer (day-zeh-spay-*ray*) *v* despair; **désespéré** desperate; hopeless

désespoir (day-zeh-*spwaar*) *m* despair

se déshabiller (day-zah-bee-*Yay*) undress

déshonneur (day-zo-*nurr*) *m* disgrace, shame

désigner (day-zee-*ñay*) *v* designate;

appoint

désinfectant (day-zang-fehk-*tahng*) *m* disinfectant

désinfecter (day-zang-fehk-*tay*) *v* disinfect

désintéressé (day-zang-tay-ray-*say*) *adj* unselfish

désir (day-*zeer*) *m* desire, wish

désirable (day-zee-*rahbl*) *adj* desirable

désirer (day-zee-*ray*) *v* want, desire, wish, long for

désireux (day-zee-*rur*) *adj* eager, anxious

désobligeant (day-zo-blee-*zhahng*) *adj* unfriendly, offensive

désodorisant (day-zo-do-ree-*zahng*) *m* deodorant

désoler (day-zo-*lay*) *v* grieve; **désolé** sorry

désordonné (day-zor-do-*nay*) *adj* sloppy, untidy

désordre (day-*zordr*) *m* disorder, mess

désosser (day-zo-*say*) *v* bone

dessein (day-*sang*) *m* design

desserrer (day-say-*ray*) *v* loosen

dessert (day-*sair*) *m* dessert, sweet

dessin (day-*sang*) *m* sketch, drawing; pattern; **dessins animés** cartoon

dessiner (day-see-*nay*) *v* sketch, *draw

dessous (der-*soo*) *adv* underneath; **en** ~ below; **en** ~ **de** beneath

dessus (der-*sew*) *m* top; **au-dessus de** on top of; **sens** ~ **dessous** upside-down

destin (day-*stang*) *m* destiny; fate

destinataire (day-stee-nah-*tair*) *m* addressee

destination (day-stee-nah-*s*ʸ*awng*) *f* destination

destiner (day-stee-*nay*) *v* destine

destruction (day-strewk-*s*ʸ*awng*) *f* destruction

détachant (day-tah-*shahng*) *m* clean-

ing fluid, stain remover

détacher (day-tah-*shay*) *v* unfasten, detach

détail (day-*tigh*) *m* detail; **commerce de** ~ retail trade

détaillant (day-tah-ʸ*ahng*) *m* retailer

détaillé (day-tah-ʸ*ay*) *adj* detailed

détailler (day-tah-ʸ*ay*) *v* retail

détecter (day-tehk-*tay*) *v* detect

détective (day-tehk-*teev*) *m* detective

*déteindre** (day-*tangdr*) *v* fade

se détendre (day-*tahngdr*) relax

détente (day-*tahngt*) *f* relaxation

détention (day-tahng-*s*ʸ*awng*) *f* custody

détenu (dayt-*new*) *m* prisoner

détergent (day-tehr-*zhahng*) *m* detergent

déterminer (day-tehr-mee-*nay*) *v* determine, define; **déterminé** *adj* definite; resolute

détester (day-tehs-*tay*) *v* dislike, hate

détour (day-*toor*) *m* detour

détourner (day-toor-*nay*) *v* avert; hijack

détresse (day-*trehss*) *f* distress; misery

détritus (day-tree-*tewss*) *m* litter, garbage, rubbish

*détruire** (day-*trweer*) *v* destroy, wreck

dette (deht) *f* debt

deuil (durᵉᵉ) *m* mourning

deux (dur) *num* two; **les** ~ either, both

deuxième (dur-zʸ*ehm*) *num* second

deux-pièces (dur-pʸ*ehss*) *m* two-piece

dévaluation (day-vah-lwah-*s*ʸ*awng*) *f* devaluation

dévaluer (day-vah-*lway*) *v* devalue

devant (der-*vahng*) *prep* in front of, ahead of, before

dévaster (day-vah-*stay*) *v* destroy

développement (day-vlop-*mahng*) *m*

development

développer (day-vlo-*pay*) *v* develop

*****devenir** (der-*vneer*) *v* *grow, *go, *get, *become

déviation (day-v^yah-s^y*awng*) *f* diversion, detour

dévier (day-v^y*ay*) *v* deviate

deviner (der-vee-*nay*) *v* guess

devise (der-*veez*) *f* slogan, motto

dévisser (day-vee-*say*) *v* unscrew

devoir (der-*vwaar*) *m* duty

*****devoir** (der-*vwaar*) *v* *be obliged to, *be bound to, *have to; need to, *should, *ought to, *shall; owe

dévorer (day-vo-*ray*) *v* devour

dévouement (day-voo-*mahng*) *m* devotion

diabète (d^yah-*beht*) *m* diabetes

diabétique (d^yah-bay-*teek*) *m* diabetic

diable (d^yaabl) *m* devil

diagnostic (d^yahg-no-*steek*) *m* diagnosis

diagnostiquer (d^yahg-no-stee-*kay*) *v* diagnose

diagonale (d^yah-go-*nahl*) *f* diagonal; *adj* diagonal

diagramme (d^yah-*grahm*) *m* graph, diagram

dialecte (d^yah-*lehkt*) *m* dialect

diamant (d^yah-*mahng*) *m* diamond

diapositive (d^yah-po-zee-*teev*) *f* slide

diarrhée (d^yah-*ray*) *f* diarrhoea

dictaphone (deek-tah-*fon*) *m* dictaphone

dictateur (deek-tah-*turr*) *m* dictator

dictée (deek-*tay*) *f* dictation

dicter (deek-*tay*) *v* dictate

dictionnaire (deek-s^yo-*nair*) *m* dictionary

diesel (d^yay-*zehl*) *m* diesel

dieu (d^yur) *m* god

différence (dee-fay-*rahngss*) *f* distinction, difference, contrast

différent (dee-fay-*rahng*) *adj* different; unlike

différer (dee-fay-*ray*) *v* delay; vary, differ

difficile (dee-fee-*seel*) *adj* difficult, hard

difficulté (dee-fee-kewl-*tay*) *f* difficulty

difforme (dee-*form*) *adj* deformed

digérer (dee-zhay-*ray*) *v* digest

digestible (dee-zheh-*steebl*) *adj* digestible

digestion (dee-zheh-st^y*awng*) *f* digestion

digne (deeñ) *adj* dignified; ~ **de** worthy of

digue (deeg) *f* dike, dam

diluer (dee-*lway*) *v* dissolve, dilute

dimanche (dee-*mahngsh*) *m* Sunday

dimension (dee-mahng-s^y*awng*) *f* size, extent

diminuer (dee-mee-*nway*) *v* decrease, lessen, reduce

diminution (dee-mee-new-s^y*awng*) *f* decrease

dinde (dangd) *f* turkey

dîner (dee-*nay*) *v* dine, *eat; *m* dinner

diphtérie (deef-tay-*ree*) *f* diphtheria

diplomate (dee-plo-*maht*) *m* diplomat

diplôme (dee-*plōam*) *m* certificate, diploma

*****dire** (deer) *v* *tell, *say

direct (dee-*rehkt*) *adj* direct

directement (dee-rehk-ter-*mahng*) *adv* straight away, straight

directeur (dee-rehk-*turr*) *m* manager, director; ~ **d'école** headmaster, head teacher

direction (dee-rehk-s^y*awng*) *f* management, direction, leadership; way; **indicateur de** ~ trafficator; directional signal *Am*

directive (dee-rehk-*teev*) *f* directive

dirigeant (dee-ree-*zhahng*) *m* leader, ruler

diriger (dee-ree-*zhay*) v direct; head, conduct, *lead; manage

discerner (dee-sehr-*nay*) v distinguish

discipline (dee-see-*pleen*) f discipline

discours (dee-*skōōr*) m speech

discret (dee-*skray*) adj (f -crète) inconspicuous

discussion (dee-skew-*s*ʸ*awng*) f discussion, argument, deliberation; dispute

discuter (dee-skew-*tay*) v discuss, argue, deliberate

***disjoindre** (deess-*zhwangdr*) v disconnect

disloqué (dee-slo-*kay*) adj dislocated

***disparaître** (dee-spah-*raitr*) v vanish, disappear

disparu (dee-spah-*rew*) adj lost; m missing person

dispensaire (dee-spahng-*sair*) m health centre

dispenser (dee-spahng-*say*) v exempt; ~ **de** discharge of

disperser (dee-spehr-*say*) v scatter

disponible (dee-spo-*neebl*) adj available; obtainable; spare

disposé (dee-spoa-*zay*) adj inclined, willing

disposer de (dee-spoa-*zay*) dispose of

dispositif (dee-spoa-zee-*teef*) m apparatus

disposition (dee-spoa-zee-*s*ʸ*awng*) f disposal

dispute (dee-*spewt*) f argument

disputer (dee-spew-*tay*) v argue; se ~ dispute, quarrel

disque (deesk) m disc; record

dissertation (dee-sehr-tah-*s*ʸ*awng*) f essay

dissimuler (dee-see-mew-*lay*) v *hide, conceal

***dissoudre** (dee-*soodr*) v dissolve; se ~ dissolve

dissuader (dee-swah-*day*) v dissuade

from

distance (dee-*stahngss*) f way, distance, space

distinct (dee-*stang*) adj distinct, separate

distinction (dee-stangk-*s*ʸ*awng*) f distinction, difference

distinguer (dee-stang-*gay*) v distinguish

distraction (dee-strahk-*s*ʸ*awng*) f diversion; inadvertence

distrait (dee-*stray*) adj absent-minded

distribuer (dee-stree-*bway*) v distribute, *deal; issue

distributeur (dee-stree-bew-*tūrr*) m distributor; ~ **de billets** ticket machine; ~ **d'essence** fuel pump Am; ~ **de timbres** stamp machine; ~ **automatique** cash dispenser, ATM

distribution (dee-stree-bew-*s*ʸ*awng*) f distribution

district (dee-*stree*) m district

divers (dee-*vair*) adj various, several; miscellaneous

diversion (dee-vehr-*s*ʸ*awng*) f diversion

divertir (dee-vehr-*teer*) v entertain, amuse

divertissant (dee-vehr-tee-*sahng*) adj entertaining

divertissement (dee-vehr-tee-*smahng*) m pleasure, fun, entertainment, amusement

divin (dee-*vang*) adj divine

diviser (dee-vee-*zay*) v divide; ~ **en deux** halve

division (dee-vee-*z*ʸ*awng*) f division; department

divorce (dee-*vors*) m divorce

divorcer (dee-vor-*say*) v divorce

dix (deess) num ten

dix-huit (dee-*zweet*) num eighteen

dix-huitième (dee-zwee-*t*ʸ*ehm*) num eighteenth

dixième (dee-z^yehm) *num* tenth

dix-neuf (deez-*nurf*) *num* nineteen

dix-neuvième (deez-nur-v^yehm) *num* nineteenth

dix-sept (dee-*seht*) *num* seventeen

dix-septième (dee-seh-t^yehm) *num* seventeenth

dock (dok) *m* dock

docteur (dok-*turr*) *m* doctor

document (do-kew-*mahng*) *m* document, certificate

doigt (dwah) *m* finger

domaine (do-*mehn*) *m* field

dôme (dōam) *m* dome

domestique (do-meh-*steek*) *adj* domestic; *m* domestic, servant

domestiqué (do-meh-stee-*kay*) *adj* tame

domicile (do-mee-*seel*) *m* domicile

domicilié (do-mee-see-*l^yay*) *adj* resident

domination (do-mee-nah-s^y*awng*) *f* domination

dominer (do-mee-*nay*) *v* dominate; prevail; **dominant** leading

dommage (do-*maazh*) *m* mischief, damage; **dommage!** what a pity!

don (dawng) *m* faculty, talent; donation, gift

donateur (do-nah-*turr*) *m* donor

donation (do-nah-s^y*awng*) *f* donation

donc (dawngk) *conj* therefore; so

donnée (do-*nay*) *f* data *pl*

donner (do-*nay*) *v* *give; donate; **étant donné que** because

dont (dawng) *pron* of which; of whom

doré (do-*ray*) *adj* gilt

dorénavant (do-ray-nah-*vahng*) *adv* henceforth

*dormir (dor-*meer*) *v* *sleep; ~ **trop longtemps** *oversleep

dortoir (dor-*twaar*) *m* dormitory

dos (doa) *m* back

dose (dōaz) *f* dose

dossier (do-s^y*ay*) *m* file, record

douane (dwahn) *f* Customs *pl*; **droit de ~** Customs duty

douanier (dwah-n^y*ay*) *m* Customs officer

double (dōobl) *adj* double

doubler (doo-*blay*) *v pass vAm*

doublure (doo-*blewr*) *f* lining

douceurs (doo-*surr*) *fpl* sweets

douche (doosh) *f* shower

doué (doo-*ay*) *adj* talented, gifted

douille (doo^{ee}) *f* socket

douleur (doo-*lurr*) *f* ache, pain; sore; sorrow, grief; **douleurs** labour; **sans ~** painless

douloureux (doo-loo-*rur*) *adj* sore, painful

doute (doot) *m* doubt; ***mettre en ~** query; **sans ~** undoubtedly, without doubt

douter (doo-*tay*) *v* doubt; ~ **de** doubt

douteux (doo-*tur*) *adj* doubtful; unreliable

douve (dōov) *f* moat

doux (doo) *adj* (f douce) mild; smooth, gentle

douzaine (doo-*zehn*) *f* dozen

douze (dōoz) *num* twelve

douzième (doo-z^yehm) *num* twelfth

dragon (drah-*gawng*) *m* dragon

drainer (dray-*nay*) *v* drain

dramatique (drah-mah-*teek*) *adj* dramatic

dramaturge (drah-mah-*tewrzh*) *m* dramatist; playwright

drame (drahm) *m* drama

drap (drah) *m* sheet

drapeau (drah-*poa*) *m* flag

drapier (drah-p^y*ay*) *m* draper

dresser (dray-*say*) *v* *make up; train

drogue (drog) *f* drug

droguerie (dro-*gree*) *f* pharmacy, chemist's; drugstore *nAm*

droit (drwah) *m* right, law, justice; *adj* right, straight; erect, upright; ~ **administratif** administrative law; ~ **civil** civil law; ~ **commercial** commercial law; ~ **de douane** Customs duty; ~ **de stationnement** parking fee; ~ **de vote** suffrage; ~ **d'importation** duty; ~ **pénal** criminal law; **droits** dues *pl*; **tout** ~ straight ahead

de droite (der drwaht) right-hand

drôle (drōāl) *adj* humorous, funny, queer

dû (dew) *adj* (f due; pl dus, dues) due

duc (dewk) *m* duke

duchesse (dew-shehss) *f* duchess

dune (dewn) *f* dune

dupe (dewp) *f* victim

duper (dew-pay) *v* cheat

dur (dewr) *adj* hard

durable (dew-rahbl) *adj* permanent, lasting

durant (dew-rahng) *prep* during

durée (dew-ray) *f* duration

durer (dew-ray) *v* continue, last

durillon (dew-ree-ʸawng) *m* corn

duvet (dew-vay) *m* down

dynamo (dee-nah-moa) *f* dynamo

dysenterie (dee-sahng-tree) *f* dysentery

E

eau (oa) *f* water; ~ **courante** running water; ~ **de mer** sea-water; ~ **dentifrice** mouthwash; ~ **de Seltz** soda-water; ~ **douce** fresh water; ~ **gazeuse** soda-water; ~ **glacée** iced water; ~ **minérale** mineral water; ~ **oxygénée** peroxide; ~ **potable** drinking-water

eau-forte (oa-fort) *f* etching

ébène (ay-behn) *f* ebony

éblouissant (ay-bloo-ee-sahng) *adj* glaring

éblouissement (ay-bloo-ee-smahng) *m* glare

ébrécher (ay-bray-shay) *v* chip

écaille (ay-kigh) *f* scale

écarlate (ay-kahr-laht) *adj* scarlet

écarter (ay-kahr-tay) *v* *spread, part; remove; **écarté** out of the way

ecclésiastique (ay-klay-zʸah-steek) *m* clergyman

échafaudage (ay-shah-foa-daazh) *m* scaffolding

échange (ay-shahngzh) *m* exchange

échanger (ay-shahng-zhay) *v* exchange

échantillon (ay-shahng-tee-ʸawng) *m* sample

échappement (ay-shahp-mahng) *m* exhaust

échapper (ay-shah-pay) *v* escape; **s'échapper** slip

écharde (ay-shahrd) *f* splinter

écharpe (ay-shahrp) *f* scarf

échec (ay-shehk) *m* failure; **échec!** check!; **échecs** chess

échelle (ay-shehl) *f* ladder; scale

échiquier (ay-shee-kʸay) *m* checkerboard *nAm*

écho (ay-koa) *m* echo

échoppe (ay-shop) *f* booth

échouer (ay-shway) *v* fail

éclabousser (ay-klah-boo-say) *v* splash

éclair (ay-klair) *m* flash; lightning

éclairage (ay-kleh-raazh) *m* lighting

éclaircir (ay-klehr-seer) *v* clarify

éclaircissement (ay-klehr-see-smahng) *m* explanation

éclairer (ay-klay-ray) *v* illuminate

éclat (ay-klah) *m* glow; glare; chip

éclatant (ay-klah-tahng) *adj* gay

éclater (ay-klah-tay) *v* *burst

éclipse (ay-kleeps) *f* eclipse

éclisse (ay-kleess) *f* splint

écluse (ay-klewz) f sluice, lock

écœurant (ay-kur-rahng) adj repellent

école (ay-kol) f school; ~ **maternelle** kindergarten; ~ **secondaire** secondary school; *faire l'école buissonnière play truant

écolier (ay-ko-lYay) m schoolboy

écolière (ay-ko-lYair) f schoolgirl

économe (ay-ko-nom) adj economical

économie (ay-ko-no-mee) f economy; **économies** savings pl

économique (ay-ko-no-meek) adj economic

économiser (ay-ko-no-mee-zay) v economize

économiste (ay-ko-no-meest) m economist

écorce (ay-kors) f bark

Ecossais (ay-ko-say) m Scot

écossais (ay-ko-say) adj Scotch; Scottish

Ecosse (ay-koss) f Scotland

s'écouler (ay-koo-lay) flow

écouter (ay-koo-tay) v listen

écouteur (ay-koo-tūrr) m receiver

écran (ay-krahng) m screen

écraser (ay-krah-zay) v mash; overwhelm; **s'écraser** crash

*écrire (ay-kreer) v *write; **par écrit** in writing, written

écriture (ay-kree-tewr) f handwriting

écrivain (ay-kree-vang) m writer

écrou (ay-kroo) m nut

s'écrouler (ay-kroo-lay) collapse

Ecuadorien (ay-kwah-do-rYang) m Ecuadorian

écume (ay-kewm) f froth, foam

écureuil (ay-kew-ruree) m squirrel

eczéma (ehg-zay-mah) m eczema

édification (ay-dee-fee-kah-sYawng) f construction

édifice (ay-dee-feess) m construction

édifier (ay-dee-fYay) v construct

éditeur (ay-dee-tūrr) m publisher

édition (ay-dee-sYawng) f issue, edition; ~ **du matin** morning edition

édredon (ay-drer-dawng) m eiderdown

éducation (ehr-tsee-oong) f education

éduquer (ay-dew-kay) v educate

effacer (ay-fah-say) v wipe out

effectif (ay-fehk-teef) adj effective

effectivement (ay-fehk-teev-mahng) adv as a matter of fact

effectuer (ay-fehk-tway) v effect

effet (ay-fay) m result; consequence, effect; **en** ~ indeed

efficace (ay-fee-kahss) adj effective; efficient

s'effilocher (ay-fee-lo-shay) fray

effondrement (ay-fawng-drer-mahng) m ruination

s'effondrer (ay-fawng-dray) collapse

s'efforcer (ay-for-say) try; bother

effort (ay-fawr) m effort, strain

effrayé (ay-fray-Yay) adj frightened, afraid

effrayer (ay-fray-Yay) v frighten; scare

effronté (ay-frawng-tay) adj bold; impertinent

égal (ay-gahl) adj even, level, equal

également (ay-gahl-mahng) adv as well, likewise, equally, also

égaler (ay-gah-lay) v equal

égaliser (ay-gah-lee-zay) v level, equalize

égalité (ay-gah-lee-tay) f equality

égard (ay-gaar) m consideration

égarer (ay-gah-ray) v *mislay

égayer (ay-gay-Yay) v cheer up

église (ay-gleez) f chapel, church

égocentrique (ay-go-sahng-treek) adj self-centred

égoïsme (ay-go-eesm) m selfishness

égoïste (ay-go-eest) adj egoistic, selfish

égout (ay-goo) m drain, sewer

égratignure (ay-grah-tee-ñewr) f graze, scratch

Egypte (ay-*zheept*) f Egypt

Egyptien (ay-zhee-*ps*ʸ*ang*) m Egyptian

égyptien (ay-zhee-*ps*ʸ*ang*) adj Egyptian

élaborer (ay-lah-bo-*ray*) v elaborate

élan (ay-*lahng*) m diligence; moose

élargir (ay-lahr-*zheer*) v widen

élasticité (ay-lah-stee-see-*tay*) f elasticity

élastique (ay-lah-*steek*) adj elastic; m elastic, rubber band

électeur (ay-lehk-*tūrr*) m voter

élection (ay-lehk-*s*ʸ*awng*) f election

électricien (ay-lehk-tree-*s*ʸ*ang*) m electrician

électricité (ay-lehk-tree-see-*tay*) f electricity

électrique (ay-lehk-*treek*) adj electric

électronique (ay-lehk-tro-*neek*) adj electronic

élégance (ay-lay-*gahngss*) f elegance

élégant (ay-lay-*gahng*) adj smart, elegant

élément (ay-lay-*mahng*) m element

élémentaire (ay-lay-mahng-*tair*) adj primary

éléphant (ay-lay-*fahng*) m elephant

élevage (ehl-*vaazh*) m stock-farming

élévation (ay-lay-vah-*s*ʸ*awng*) f rise

élève (ay-*laiv*) m pupil, scholar

élever (ehl-*vay*) v *bring up, rear, raise; *breed

elfe (ehlf) m elf

éliminer (ay-lee-mee-*nay*) v eliminate

***élire** (ehl-*vay*) v elect

elle (ehl) pron she

elle-même (ehl-*mehm*) pron herself

éloge (ay-*lozh*) m praise

éloigner (ay-lwah-*ñay*) v remove; **éloigné** distant, far-away, remote

élucider (ay-lew-see-*day*) v elucidate

émail (ay-*migh*) m (pl émaux) enamel

émaillé (ay-mah-*ʸay*) adj enamelled

émancipation (ay-mahng-see-pah-*s*ʸ*awng*) f emancipation

emballage (ahng-bah-*laazh*) m packing

emballer (ahng-bah-*lay*) v pack up, pack

embargo (ahng-bahr-*goa*) m embargo

embarquement (ahng-bahr-ker-*mahng*) m embarkation

embarquer (ahng-bahr-*kay*) v embark

embarras (ahng-bah-*rah*) m fuss

embarrassant (ahng-bah-rah-*sahng*) adj awkward, embarrassing; puzzling

embarrasser (ahng-bah-rah-*say*) v embarrass

emblème (ahng-*blehm*) m emblem

embouchure (ahng-boo-*shewr*) f mouth

embouteillage (ahng-boo-teh-ʸ*aazh*) m traffic jam, jam

embrasser (ahng-brah-*say*) v kiss

embrayage (ahng-breh-ʸ*aazh*) m clutch

embrouiller (ahng-broo-ʸ*ay*) v muddle

embuscade (ahng-bew-*skahd*) f ambush

émeraude (aym-*road*) f emerald

s'émerveiller (ay-mehr-vay-ʸ*ay*) marvel

émetteur (ay-meh-*tūrr*) m transmitter

***émettre** (ay-*mehtr*) v utter; transmit, *broadcast

émeute (ay-*mūrt*) f riot

émigrant (ay-mee-*grahng*) m emigrant

émigration (ay-mee-grah-*s*ʸ*awng*) f emigration

émigrer (ay-mee-*gray*) v emigrate

éminent (ay-mee-*nahng*) adj outstanding

émission (ay-mee-*s*ʸ*awng*) f issue; transmission, broadcast

emmagasinage (ahng-mah-gah-zee-*naazh*) m storage

emmagasiner (ahng-mah-gah-zee-*nay*) v store

emmener (ahng-mer-*nay*) v *take along

émoi (ay-*mwah*) m emotion

émotion (ay-moa-s^y*awng*) f emotion

émoussé (ay-moo-*say*) adj dull, blunt

***émouvoir** (ay-moo-*vwaar*) v move

empêcher (ahng-pay-*shay*) v prevent

empereur (ahng-*prūr*) m emperor

empiéter (ahng-p^yay-*tay*) v trespass

empire (ahng-*peer*) m empire

emploi (ahng-*plwah*) m use; job, employment; **solliciter un ~** apply

employé (ahng-plwah-*Yay*) m employee; **~ de bureau** clerk

employer (ahng-plwah-*Yay*) v use; employ

employeur (ahng-plwah-*Yūrr*) m employer

empoisonner (ahng-pwah-zo-*nay*) v poison

emporter (ahng-por-*tay*) v *take away

empreinte digitale (ahng-prangt dee-zhee-*tahl*) fingerprint

emprisonnement (ahng-pree-zon-*mahng*) m imprisonment

emprisonner (ahng-pree-zo-*nay*) v imprison

emprunt (ahng-*prurng*) m loan

emprunter (ahng-prurng-*tay*) v borrow

en (ahng) prep in; by; pron of it

encaisser (ahng-kay-*say*) v cash

enceinte (ahng-*sangt*) adj pregnant

encens (ahng-*sahng*) m incense

encercler (ahng-sehr-*klay*) v circle, encircle

enchantement (ahng-shahngt-*mahng*) m spell

enchanter (ahng-shahng-*tay*) v delight; bewitch

enchanteur (ahng-shahng-*tūrr*) adj (f teresse) glamorous

enclin (ahng-*klang*) adj inclined

encore (ahng-*kawr*) adv again; still, yet; **~ que** though; **~ un** another; **~ un peu** some more

encourager (ahng-koo-rah-*zhay*) v encourage

encre (ahngkr) f ink

encyclopédie (ahng-see-klo-pay-*dee*) f encyclopaedia

endommager (ahng-do-mah-*zhay*) v damage

endormi (ahng-dor-*mee*) adj asleep

endosser (ahng-do-*say*) v endorse

endroit (ahng-*drwah*) m spot

endurance (ahng-dew-*rahngss*) f stamina

endurer (ahng-dew-*ray*) v endure, sustain; *go through

énergie (ay-nehr-*zhee*) f energy; power; **~ nucléaire** nuclear energy

énergique (ay-nehr-*zheek*) adj energetic

énerver (ay-nehr-*vay*) v *get on someone's nerves; **s'énerver** *lose one's nerve

enfance (ahng-*fahngss*) f childhood

enfant (ahng-*fahng*) m child, kid

enfer (ahng-*fair*) m hell

enfermer (ahng-fehr-*may*) v lock up, *shut in

enfiler (ahng-fee-*lay*) v thread

enfin (ahng-*fang*) adv at last

enfler (ahng-*flay*) v *swell

enflure (ahng-*flewr*) f swelling

s'enfoncer (ahng-fawng-*say*) *sink

engagement (ahng-gahzh-*mahng*) m engagement

engager (ahng-gah-*zhay*) v engage; **s'engager** engage

engelure (ahng-*zhlewr*) f chilblain

engourdi (ahng-goor-*dee*) adj numb

engrais (ahng-*gray*) m fertilizer

énigme (ay-*neegm*) f mystery, riddle, puzzle, enigma

enjeu (ahng-*zhur*) *m* bet

enlacement (ahng-lah-*smah*) *m* embrace

enlever (ahngl-*vay*) *v* remove; *take away

ennemi (ehn-*mee*) *m* enemy

ennui (ahng-*nwee*) *m* annoyance, trouble; nuisance

ennuyer (ahng-nwee-*Yay*) *v* annoy, bore

ennuyeux (ahng-nwee-*Yur*) *adj* annoying; dull, unpleasant, boring

énorme (ay-*norm*) *adj* tremendous, immense, huge, enormous

enquête (ahng-*keht*) *f* inquiry; enquiry

enquêter (ahng-kay-*tay*) *v* investigate, enquire

enragé (ahng-rah-*zhay*) *adj* mad

enregistrement (ahngr-zhee-strer-*mahng*) *m* recording

enregistrer (ahngr-zhee-*stray*) *v* book; record

s'enrhumer (ahng-rew-*may*) catch a cold

enroué (ahng-roo-*ay*) *adj* hoarse

enrouler (ahng-roo-*lay*) *v* *wind

enseignement (ahng-sehn-*mahng*) *m* tuition; **enseignements** teachings *pl*

enseigner (ahng-say-*ñay*) *v* *teach

ensemble (ahng-*sahngbl*) *adv* together; *m* whole

ensoleillé (ahng-so-lay-*Yay*) *adj* sunny

ensorceler (ahng-sor-ser-*lay*) *v* bewitch

ensuite (ahng-*sweet*) *adv* then, afterwards

entailler (ahng-tah-*Yay*) *v* carve

entasser (ahng-tah-*say*) *v* pile

entendre (ahng-*tahngdr*) *v* *hear

entente (ahng-*tahngt*) *f* agreement

enterrement (ahng-tehr-*mahng*) *m* burial

enterrer (ahng-tay-*ray*) *v* bury

enthousiasme (ahng-too-*zYahsm*) *m* enthusiasm

enthousiaste (ahng-too-*zYahst*) *adj* enthusiastic

entier (ahng-*tYay*) *adj* whole, complete, entire

entièrement (ahng-tYehr-*mahng*) *adv* wholly, completely, entirely, altogether, quite

entonnoir (ahng-to-*nwaar*) *m* funnel

entourer (ahng-too-*ray*) *v* encircle; circle, surround

entracte (ahng *trahkt*) *m* interval, intermission

entrailles (ahng-*trigh*) *fpl* insides

entrain (ahng-*trang*) *m* zest

entraînement (ahng-trehn-*mahng*) *m* training

entraîner (ahng-tray-*nay*) *v* drill

entraîneur (ahng-treh-*nūrr*) *m* coach

entrave (ahng-*traav*) *f* impediment

entraver (ahng-trah-*vay*) *v* impede

entre (ahngtr) *prep* between, among, amid

entrée (ahng-*tray*) *f* way in, entry, entrance; appearance; ~ **interdite** no admittance

entrepôt (ahng-trer-*poa*) *m* depository

*__entreprendre__ (ahng-trer-*prahngdr*) *v* *undertake

entrepreneur (ahng-trer-prer-*nūrr*) *m* contractor

entreprise (ahng-trer-*preez*) *f* enterprise; business, concern, company, undertaking

entrer (ahng-*tray*) *v* enter, *go in

entresol (ahng-trer-*sol*) *m* mezzanine

entre-temps (ahng-trer-*tahng*) *adv* meanwhile, in the meantime

*__entretenir__ (ahng-trer-*tneer*) *v* maintain; support

entretien (ahng-trer-*tYang*) *m* upkeep, maintenance; conversation

*entrevoir (ahng-trer-*vwaar*) v glimpse

entrevue (ahng-trer-*vew*) f interview

envahir (ahng-vah-*eer*) v invade

enveloppe (ahng-*vlop*) f envelope

envelopper (ahng-vlo-*pay*) v wrap

envers (ahng-*vair*) prep towards; **à l'envers** inside out

envie (ahng-*vee*) f longing, desire; envy; ***avoir ~ de** *feel like; fancy, desire

envier (ahng-v*Y*ay) v grudge, envy

envieux (ahng-v*Y*ur) adj envious

environ (ahng-vee-*rawng*) adv about

environnant (ahng-vee-ro-*nahng*) adj surrounding

environnement (ahng-vee-ron-*mahng*) m environment

environs (ahng-vee-*rawng*) mpl environment

envisager (ahng-vee-zah-*zhay*) v consider

envoyé (ahng-vwah-*Y*ay) m envoy

*envoyer (ahng-vwah-*Y*ay) v *send; dispatch

épais (ay-*pay*) adj (f ~se) thick

épaisseur (ay-peh-*surr*) f thickness

épaissir (ay-pay-*seer*) v thicken

épargner (ay-pahr-*ñay*) v save

épaule (ay-*pōal*) f shoulder

épave (ay-*paav*) f wreck

épée (ay-*pay*) f sword

épeler (eh-*play*) v *spell

épice (ay-*peess*) f spice

épicé (ay-pee-*say*) adj spicy, spiced

épicerie (ay-pee-*sree*) f grocer's; **~ fine** delicatessen

épicier (ay-pee-s*Y*ay) m grocer

épidémie (ay-pee-day-*mee*) f epidemic

épier (ay-p*Y*ay) v peep

épilepsie (ay-pee-leh-*psee*) f epilepsy

épilogue (ay-pee-*log*) m epilogue

épinards (ay-pee-*naar*) mpl spinach

épine (ay-*peen*) f thorn; **~ dorsale** backbone, spine

épingle (ay-*panggl*) f pin; **~ à cheveux** hairpin; **~ de sûreté** safety-pin

épingler (ay-pang-*glay*) v pin

épique (ay-*peek*) adj epic

épisode (ay-pee-*zod*) m episode

éponge (ay-*pawngzh*) f sponge

époque (ay-*pok*) f period; **de l'époque** contemporary

épouse (ay-*pōoz*) f wife

épouser (ay-poo-*zay*) v marry

épouvantable (ay-poo-vahng-*tahbl*) adj terrible

épouvante (ay-poo-*vahngt*) f horror

époux (ay-*poo*) m husband

épreuve (ay-*prūrv*) f test, experiment; print

éprouver (ay-proo-*vay*) v experience; test

épuiser (ay-pwee-*zay*) v exhaust; use up; **épuisé** sold out

Equateur (ay-kwah-*tūrr*) m Ecuador

équateur (ay-kwah-*tūrr*) m equator

équilibre (ay-kee-*leebr*) m balance

équipage (ay-kee-*paazh*) m crew

équipe (ay-*keep*) f shift, team, gang; soccer team

équipement (ay-keep-*mahng*) m outfit, gear, equipment

équiper (ay-kee-*pay*) v equip

équitable (ay-kee-*tahbl*) adj right; reasonable

équitation (ay-kee-tah-s*Y*awng) f riding

équivalent (ay-kee-vah-*lahng*) adj equivalent

équivoque (ay-kee-*vok*) adj ambiguous

érable (ay-*rahbl*) m maple

érafler (ay-rah-*flay*) v scratch

ériger (ay-ree-*zhay*) v erect

errer (ay-*ray*) v err; wander

erreur (eh-*rūrr*) f error; mistake

erroné (eh-ro-*nay*) adj mistaken

érudit (ay-rew-*dee*) *m* scholar

éruption (ay-rew-ps^y*awng*) *f* rash

escadrille (eh-skah-*dreey*) *f* squadron

escalier (eh-skah-l^y*ay*) *m* staircase; stairs *pl*; ~ **de secours** fire-escape; ~ **roulant** escalator

escargot (eh-skahr-*goa*) *m* snail

escarpé (eh-skahr-*pay*) *adj* steep

esclave (eh-*sklaav*) *m* slave

escorte (eh-*skort*) *f* escort

escorter (eh-skor-*tay*) *v* escort

*faire de l'escrime (fair der leh-*skreem*) fence

escroc (eh-*skroa*) *m* swindler

escroquer (eh-skro-*kay*) *v* swindle

escroquerie (eh-skro-*kree*) *f* swindle

espace (eh-*spahss*) *m* space; room

espacer (eh-spah-*say*) *v* space

Espagne (eh-*spahñ*) *f* Spain

Espagnol (eh-spah-*ñol*) *m* Spaniard

espagnol (eh-spah-*ñol*) *adj* Spanish

espèce (eh-*spehss*) *f* species; breed

espérance (eh-spay-*rahngss*) *f* expectation

espérer (eh-spay-*ray*) *v* hope

espièglerie (eh-sp^yeh-gler-*ree*) *f* mischief

espion (eh-sp^y*awng*) *m* spy

esplanade (eh-splah-*nahd*) *f* esplanade

espoir (eh-*spwaar*) *m* hope

esprit (eh-*spree*) *m* spirit; soul, mind; ghost

esquisse (eh-*skeess*) *f* sketch

esquisser (eh-skee-*say*) *v* sketch

essai (ay-*say*) *m* trial, essay; **à l'essai** on approval

essayer (ay-say-^y*ay*) *v* try; attempt, test; try on

essence (ay-*sahngss*) *f* essence; petrol, fuel; gasoline *nAm*, gas *nAm*

essentiel (ay-sahng-s^y*ehl*) *adj* capital, essential

essentiellement (ay-sahng-s^yehl-*mahng*) *adv* essentially

essieu (ay-s^y*ur*) *m* axle

essor (ay-*sawr*) *m* rise .

essuie-glace (ay-swee-*glahss*) *m* windscreen wiper; windshield wiper *Am*

essuyer (ay-swee-^y*ay*) *v* wipe; dry

est (ehst) *m* east

estampe (eh-*stahngp*) *f* print; engraving

estimation (eh-stee-mah-s^y*awng*) *f* estimate

estime (eh-*steem*) *f* esteem; respect

estimer (eh-stee-*may*) *v* consider, esteem, reckon; value, estimate

estomac (eh-sto-*mah*) *m* stomach

estropié (eh-stro-p^y*ay*) *adj* crippled

estuaire (eh-*stwair*) *m* estuary

et (ay) *conj* and

étable (ay-*tahbl*) *f* stable

établir (ay-tah-*bleer*) *v* establish; found; **s'établir** settle down

étage (ay-*taazh*) *m* floor, storey; apartment *nAm*

étagère (ay-tah-*zhair*) *f* shelf

étain (ay-*tang*) *m* pewter, tin

étal (ay-*tahl*) *m* stall

étalage (ay-tah-*laazh*) *m* shop-window

étaler (ay-tah-*lay*) *v* display

étang (ay-*tahng*) *m* pond

étape (ay-*tahp*) *f* stage

Etat (ay-*tah*) *m* state; **Etats-Unis** United States; the States

état (ay-*tah*) *m* state; condition; ~ **d'urgence** emergency

et cætera (eht-say-tay-*rah*) etcetera

été (ay-*tay*) *m* summer; **plein ~** midsummer

*éteindre (ay-*tangdr*) *v* *put out; switch off; extinguish

étendre (ay-*tahngdr*) *v* expand, *spread, enlarge; extend

étendu (ay-tahng-*dew*) *adj* broad, extensive; comprehensive

éternel (ay-tehr-*nehl*) *adj* eternal

éternité (ay-tehr-nee-*tay*) *f* eternity

éternuer (ay-tehr-*nway*) *v* sneeze

éther (ay-*tair*) *m* ether

Ethiopie (ay-t*y*o-*pee*) *f* Ethiopia

Ethiopien (ay-t*y*o-*py*ang) *m* Ethiopian

éthiopien (ay-t*y*o-*py*ang) *adj* Ethiopian

étincelle (ay-tang-*sehl*) *f* spark

étiqueter (ay-teek-*tay*) *v* label

étiquette (ay-tee-*keht*) *f* tag, label

étoffes (ay-*tof*) *fpl* drapery

étoile (ay-*twahl*) *f* star

étole (ay-*tol*) *f* stole

étonnant (ay-to-*nahng*) *adj* astonishing

étonnement (ay-ton-*mahng*) *m* astonishment, wonder, amazement

étonner (ay-to-*nay*) *v* amaze; astonish

étouffant (ay-too-*fahng*) *adj* stuffy

étouffer (ay-too-*fay*) *v* choke

étourdi (ay-toor-*dee*) *adj* dizzy, giddy

étourneau (ay-toor-*noa*) *m* starling

étrange (ay-*trahngzh*) *adj* strange; quaint, curious, queer

étranger (ay-trahng-*zhay*) *m* foreigner, alien, stranger; *adj* foreign, alien; **à l'étranger** abroad

étrangler (ay-trahng-*glay*) *v* choke, strangle

être (aitr) *m* being; creature; ~ **humain** human being

* **être** (aitr) *v* *be

* **étreindre** (ay-*trangdr*) *v* hug, embrace

étreinte (ay-*trangt*) *f* grip; hug

étrier (ay-tree-*ay*) *m* stirrup

étroit (ay-*trwah*) *adj* narrow, tight

étude (ay-*tewd*) *f* study

étudiant (ay-tew-d*y*ahng) *m* student

étudiante (ay-tew-d*y*ahngt) *f* student

étudier (ay-tew-d*y*ay) *v* study

étui (ay-*twee*) *m* case; ~ **à cigarettes** cigarette-case

Europe (ur-*rop*) *f* Europe

Européen (ur-ro-pay-*ang*) *m* European

pean

européen (ur-ro-pay-*ang*) *adj* European

eux (ur) *pron* them; **eux-mêmes** *pron* themselves

évacuer (ay-vah-*kway*) *v* vacate, evacuate

évaluer (ay-vah-*lway*) *v* evaluate; appreciate, estimate

évangile (ay-vahng-*zheel*) *m* gospel

s'évanouir (ay-vah-*nweer*) faint

évaporer (ay-vah-po-*ray*) *v* evaporate

évasion (ay-vah-*zy*awng) *f* escape

éveillé (ay-vay-*y*ay) *adj* clever

s'éveiller (ay-vay-*y*ay) wake up

événement (ay-vehn-*mahng*) *m* event; occurrence, happening

éventail (ay-vahng-*tigh*) *m* fan

éventuel (ay-vahng-*twehl*) *adj* possible, eventual

évêque (ay-*vehk*) *m* bishop

évidemment (ay-vee-dah-*mahng*) *adv* of course

évident (ay-vee-*dahng*) *adj* obvious, evident; self-evident

évier (ay-v*y*ay) *m* sink

éviter (ay-vee-*tay*) *v* avoid

évolution (ay-vo-lew-s*y*awng) *f* evolution

évoquer (ay-vo-*kay*) *v* call to mind; evoke

exact (ehg-*zahkt*) *adj* just, precise, exact

exactement (ehg-zahk-ter-*mahng*) *adv* exactly

exactitude (ehg-zahk-tee-*tewd*) *f* correctness

exagérer (ehg-zah-zhay-*ray*) *v* exaggerate

examen (ehg-zah-*mang*) *m* examination; check-up

examiner (ehg-zah-mee-*nay*) *v* examine

excavation (ehk-skah-vah-s*y*awng) *f*

excavation
excéder (ehk-say-*day*) v exceed
excellent (ehk-seh-*lahng*) adj excellent
exceller (ehk-say-*lay*) v excel
excentrique (ehk-sahng-*treek*) adj eccentric
excepté (ehk-sehp-*tay*) prep except
exception (ehk-sehp-s*Yawng*) f exception
exceptionnel (ehk-sehp-s*Yo-nehl*) adj exceptional
excès (ehk-*say*) m excess; ~ **de vitesse** speeding
excessif (ehk-say-*seef*) adj excessive
excitation (ehk-see-tah-s*Yawng*) f excitement
exciter (ehk-see-*tay*) v excite
exclamation (ehk-sklah-mah-s*Yawng*) f exclamation
exclamer (ehk-sklah-*may*) v exclaim
*exclure** (ehk-*sklewr*) v exclude
exclusif (ehk-sklew-*zeef*) adj exclusive
exclusivement (ehk-sklew-zeev-*mahng*) adv solely, exclusively
excursion (ehk-skewr-s*Yawng*) f trip, excursion; day trip; tour
excuse (ehk-*skewz*) f excuse, apology
excuser (ehk-skew-*zay*) v excuse; **excusez-moi!** sorry!; **s'excuser** apologize
exécuter (ehg-zay-kew-*tay*) v execute
exécutif (ehg-zay-kew-*teef*) m executive; adj executive
exécution (ehg-zay-kew-s*Yawng*) f execution
exemplaire (ehg-zahng-*plair*) m copy
exemple (ehg-*zahngpl*) m instance, example; **par** ~ for instance, for example
exempt (ehg-*zahng*) adj exempt; ~ **de droits** duty-free; ~ **d'impôts** tax-free
exempter (ehg-zahng-*tay*) v exempt
exemption (ehg-zahng-ps*Yawng*) f exemption

exercer (ehg-zehr-*say*) v exercise; **s'exercer** practise
exercice (ehg-zehr-*seess*) m exercise
exhiber (ehg-zee-*bay*) v exhibit
exhibition (ehg-zee-bee-s*Yawng*) f exhibition
exhorter (ehg-zor-*tay*) v urge
exigeant (ehg-zee-*zhahng*) adj particular
exigence (ehg-zee-*zhahngss*) f requirement
exiger (ehg-zee-*zhay*) v demand, require
exile (ehg-*zeel*) m exile
exilé (ehg-zee-*lay*) m exile
existence (ehg-zee-*stahngss*) f existence
exister (ehg-zee-*stay*) v exist
exotique (ehg-zo-*teek*) adj exotic
expédier (ehk-spay-d*Yay*) v dispatch, despatch, *send off, *send; ship
expédition (ehk-spay-dee-s*Yawng*) f expedition; consignment
expérience (ehk-spay-r*Yahngss*) f experience; experiment; *faire l'**expérience de** experience
expérimenter (ehk-spay-ree-mahng-*tay*) v experiment; **expérimenté** experienced
expert (ehk-*spair*) adj skilled; m expert
expiration (ehk-spee-rah-s*Yawng*) f expiry
expirer (ehk-spee-*ray*) v expire, exhale
explicable (ehk-splee-*kahbl*) adj accountable
explication (ehk-splee-kah-s*Yawng*) f explanation
explicite (ehk-splee-*seet*) adj definite; express, explicit
expliquer (ehk-splee-*kay*) v explain
exploitation (ehk-splwah-tah-s*Yawng*) f exploitation; enterprise; ~ **minière**

mining
exploiter (ehk-splwah-*tay*) v exploit
explorer (ehk-splo-*ray*) v explore
exploser (ehk-sploa-*zay*) v explode
explosif (ehk-sploa-*zeef*) m explosive; *adj* explosive
explosion (ehk-sploa-*zⁱawng*) f explosion, blast
exportation (ehk-spor-tah-*sⁱawng*) f exports *pl*, exportation, export
exporter (ehk-spor-*tay*) v export
exposer (ehk-spoa-*zay*) v exhibit, *show
exposition (ehk-spoa-zee-*sⁱawng*) f display, exposition, exhibition, show; exposure; ~ **d'art** art exhibition
exprès¹ (ehk-*spray*) adv on purpose
exprès² (ehk-*sprehss*) adj express; special delivery
expression (ehk-spreh-*sⁱawng*) f expression
exprimer (ehk-spree-*may*) v express
expulser (ehk-spewl-*say*) v chase; expel
exquis (ehk-*skee*) adj delicious; exquisite; select
extase (ehk-*staaz*) m ecstasy
exténuer (ehk-stay-*nway*) v exhaust
extérieur (ehk-stay-*rⁱūr*) m exterior, outside; *adj* external, exterior; **vers l'extérieur** outwards
externe (ehk-*stehrn*) adj outward
extincteur (ehk-stangk-*tūrr*) m fire-extinguisher
extorquer (ehk-stor-*kay*) v extort
extorsion (ehk-stor-*sⁱawng*) f extortion
extrader (ehk-strah-*day*) v extradite
***extraire** (ehk-*strair*) v extract
extrait (ehk-*stray*) m excerpt
extraordinaire (ehk-strah-or-dee-*nair*) adj extraordinary, exceptional
extravagant (ehk-strah-vah-*gahng*) adj

extravagant
extrême (ehk-*strehm*) adj extreme, utmost; very; m extreme
exubérant (ehg-zew-bay-*rahng*) adj exuberant

F

fable (fahbl) f fable
fabricant (fah-bree-*kahng*) m manufacturer
fabriquer (fah-bree-*kay*) v manufacture
façade (fah-*sahd*) f façade
face (fahss) f front; **en ~ de** facing, opposite
fâcher (fah-*shay*) v annoy; **fâché** cross
facile (fah-*seel*) adj easy
facilité (fah-see-lee-*tay*) f facility
façon (fah-*sawng*) f way; **de la même ~** alike; **de toute ~** anyway; at any rate
façonner (fah-so-*nay*) v model
facteur (fahk-*tūrr*) m factor; postman
facture (fahk-*tēwr*) f invoice, bill
facturer (fahk-tew-*ray*) v bill
facultatif (fah-kewl-tah-*teef*) adj optional
faculté (fah-kewl-*tay*) f faculty
faible (fehbl) adj feeble, weak; small, slight; faint
faiblesse (feh-*blehss*) f weakness
faïence (fah-ⁱahngss) f faience; crockery
en faillite (ahng fah-*ⁱeet*) bankrupt
faim (fang) f hunger
***faire** (fair) v *do; *make; cause to, *have
faisable (fer-*zahbl*) adj feasible, attainable
faisan (fer-*zahng*) m pheasant

fait (fay) *m* fact; **de ~** in fact; **en ~** as a matter of fact, in effect

falaise (fah-*laiz*) *f* cliff

*****falloir** (fah-*lwaar*) *v* need, *must

falsification (fahl-see-fee-kah-*s*ʸ*awng*) *f* fake

falsifier (fahl-see-*f*ʸ*ay*) *v* forge

fameux (fah-*mur*) *adj* famous

familial (fah-mee-*l*ʸ*ahl*) *adj* of the family

familiariser (fah-mee-l*ʸ*ah-ree-*zay*) *v* accustom

familier (fah-mee-l*ʸ*ay) *adj* familiar

famille (fah-*meey*) *f* family

fan (fahn) *m* fan

fanatique (fah-nah-*teek*) *adj* fanatical

se faner (fah-*nay*) fade

fanfare (fahng-*faar*) *f* brass band

fantaisie (fahng-tay-*zee*) *f* fantasy

fantastique (fahng-tah-*steek*) *adj* fantastic

fantôme (fahng-*tōam*) *m* phantom, ghost; spook

faon (fahng) *m* fawn

farce (fahrs) *f* farce; filling, stuffing

farci (fahr-*see*) *adj* stuffed

fardeau (fahr-*doa*) *m* burden, load

farine (fah-*reen*) *f* flour

farouche (fah-*roosh*) *adj* shy

fasciner (fah-see-*nay*) *v* fascinate

fascisme (fah-*sheesm*) *m* fascism

fasciste (fah-*sheest*) *m* fascist; *adj* fascist

fastidieux (fah-stee-d*ʸur*) *adj* annoying; difficult

fatal (fah-*tahl*) *adj* (*pl* ~s) fatal, mortal

fatigant (fah-tee-*gahng*) *adj* tiring

fatigue (fah-*teeg*) *f* fatigue

fatiguer (fah-tee-*gay*) *v* tire; **fatigué** weary

faubourg (foa-*bōor*) *m* outskirts *pl*, suburb

fauché (foa-*shay*) *adj* broke

faucon (foa-*kawng*) *m* hawk

faute (fōat) *f* mistake, error; fault; **donner la ~ à** blame; **sans ~** without fail

fauteuil (foa-*tur*ee) *m* armchair, easy chair; **~ d'orchestre** orchestra seat *Am*; **~ roulant** wheelchair

faux (foa) *adj* (f fausse) false; untrue

faveur (fah-*vūrr*) *f* favour; **en ~ de** on behalf of

favorable (fah-vo-*rahbl*) *adj* favourable

favori (fah-vo-*ree*) *m* (f -rite) favourite; *adj* pet; **favoris** whiskers *pl*, sideburns *pl*

favoriser (fah-vo-ree-*zay*) *v* favour

fax (fahks) *m* fax; **envoyer un ~** send a fax

fédéral (fay-day-*rahl*) *adj* federal

fédération (fay-day-rah-s*ʸawng*) *f* federation

fée (fay) *f* fairy

*****feindre** (fangdr) *v* pretend

félicitation (fay-lee-see-tah-s*ʸawng*) *f* congratulation

féliciter (fay-lee-see-*tay*) *v* congratulate, compliment

femelle (fer-*mehl*) *f* female

féminin (fay-mee-*nang*) *adj* feminine, female

femme (fahm) *f* woman, wife; **~ de chambre** chambermaid

fendre (fahngdr) *v* *split; crack

fenêtre (fer-*naitr*) *f* window

fente (fahngt) *f* slot, cleft

fer (fair) *m* iron; **~ à** iron; **~ à cheval** horseshoe; **~ à friser** curling-tongs *pl*; **~ à repasser** iron; **~ à souder** soldering-iron

ferme (fehrm) *f* farmhouse, farm; *adj* firm, steady; steadfast

fermenter (fehr-mahng-*tay*) *v* ferment

fermer (fehr-*may*) *v* close, *shut; fasten; turn off; **fermé** closed shut; ~ **à clé** lock

fermeture (fehrm-*tewr*) f fastener; ~ **éclair** zipper, zip

fermier (fehr-*m^yay*) m farmer

fermière (fehr-*m^yair*) f farmer's wife

féroce (fay-*ross*) adj fierce, wild

ferraille (feh-*righ*) f scrap-iron

ferry-boat (feh-ree-*boat*) m ferry-boat; train ferry

fertile (fehr-*teel*) adj fertile

fesse (fehss) f buttock

fessée (fay-*say*) f spanking

festival (feh-stee-*vahl*) m (pl ~s) festival

fête (feht) f feast

feu (fur) m fire; ~ **arrière** tail-light, rear-light; ~ **de circulation** traffic light; ~ **de position** parking light

feuille (fur^{ee}) f leaf; sheet

feuilleton (fur^{ee}-*tawng*) m serial

feutre (fūrtr) m felt

février (fay-vree-*ay*) February

fiançailles (f^yahng-*sigh*) fpl engagement

fiancé (f^yahng-*say*) m fiancé; adj engaged

fiancée (f^yahng-*say*) f fiancée, bride

fibre (feebr) f fibre

ficelle (fee-*sehl*) f twine, string

fiche (feesh) f plug

fiction (feek-*s^yawng*) f fiction

fidèle (fee-*dehl*) adj faithful, true

fier (f^yair) adj proud

fièvre (f^yaivr) f fever

fiévreux (f^yay-vrur) adj feverish

figue (feeg) f fig

se figurer (fee-gew-*ray*) imagine

fil (feel) m thread; line, yarn; ~ **de fer** wire; ~ **électrique** flex; electric cord

file (feel) f file

filer (fee-*lay*) v *spin

filet (fee-*lay*) m net; ~ **à bagage** luggage rack; ~ **de pêche** fishing net

fille (feey) f girl; daughter; **vieille** ~ spinster

film (feelm) m film, movie; ~ **en couleurs** colour film

filmer (feel-*may*) v film

fils (feess) m son

filtre (feeltr) m filter; ~ **à air** air-filter; ~ **à huile** oil filter

filtrer (feel-*tray*) v strain

fin (fang) f finish, ending, end; issue; adj fine; sheer

final (fee-*nahl*) adj (pl ~s) final; eventual

financer (fee-nahng-*say*) v finance

finances (fee-*nahngss*) fpl finances pl

financier (fee-nahng-*s^yay*) adj financial

finir (fee-*neer*) v finish, end; **fini** finished, over

Finlandais (fang-lahng-*day*) m Finn

finlandais (fang-lahng-*day*) adj Finnish

Finlande (fang-*lahngd*) f Finland

firme (feerm) f firm

fissure (fee-*sewr*) f chink, crack

fixateur (feek-sah-*tūr*) m setting lotion

fixe (feeks) adj fixed; permanent

fixer (feek-*say*) v attach; gaze, stare; ~ **le prix** price

fjord (f^yor) m fjord

flacon (flah-*kawng*) m flask

flamant (flah-*mahng*) m flamingo

flamme (flahm) f flame

flanelle (flah-*nehl*) f flannel

flâner (flah-*nay*) v stroll

flaque (flahk) f puddle

flasque (flahsk) adj limp

fléau (flay-*oa*) m plague

flèche (flehsh) f arrow

flétan (flay-*tahng*) m halibut

fleur (flūrr) f flower

fleuriste (flur-*reest*) m flower-shop, florist

fleuve (flŭrv) m river

flexible (flehk-seebl) adj flexible, elastic, supple

flotte (flot) f fleet

flotter (flo-tay) v float

flotteur (flo-tŭrr) m float

fluide (flew-eed) adj fluid

flûte (flewt) f flute

foi (fwah) f faith

foie (fwah) m liver

foin (fwang) m hay

foire (fwaar) f fair

fois (fwah) f time; prep times; **à la ~** at the same time; **deux ~** twice; **une ~** once; some time; **une ~ de plus** once more

folie (fo-lee) f lunacy

folklore (folk-klawr) m folklore

foncé (fawng-say) adj dark

foncer (fawng-say) v *speed

fonction (fawngk-sʸawng) f function; office

fonctionnaire (fawngk-sʸo-nair) m civil servant

fonctionnement (fawngk-sʸon-mahng) m working, operation

fonctionner (fawngk-sʸo-nay) v work, operate

fond (fawng) m ground, bottom; essence; background; **à ~** thoroughly; **au ~** fundamentally; **~ de teint** foundation cream

fondamental (fawng-dah-mahng-tahl) adj fundamental, basic, essential

fondation (fawng-dah-sʸawng) f foundation

fondement (fawngd-mahng) m base

fonder (fawng-day) v found; **bien fondé** well-founded

fonderie (fawng-dree) f ironworks

fondre (fawngdr) v melt; thaw

fonds (fawng) mpl fund

fontaine (fawng-tehn) f fountain

fonte (fawngt) f cast iron

football (foot-bol) m soccer

force (fors) f force, power, strength; **~ armée** military force; **~ motrice** driving force

forcément (for-say-mahng) adv by force

forcer (for-say) v force; strain

forer (fo-ray) v drill, bore

forestier (fo-reh-stʸay) m forester

forêt (fo-ray) f forest

foreuse (fo-rŭz) f drill

forgeron (for-zher-rawng) m smith, blacksmith

formalité (for-mah-lee-tay) f formality

format (for-mah) m size

formation (for-mah-sʸawng) f background

forme (form) f shape, form; figure; condition

formel (for-mehl) adj explicit

former (for-may) v shape, form; train, educate

formidable (for-mee-dahbl) adj fine, swell; terrific

formulaire (for-mew-lair) m form; **~ d'inscription** registration form

formule (for-mewl) f formula

fort (fawr) adj powerful, strong; loud; m fort

fortement (for-ter-mahng) adv tight

forteresse (for-ter-rehss) f fortress

fortuit (for-twee) adj casual, incidental

fortune (for-tewn) f fortune

fosse (foass) f pit

fossé (foa-say) m ditch

fou[1] (foo) adj (fol; f folle) crazy, mad; insane, lunatic

fou[2] (foo) m fool

foudre (foodr) f lightning

fouet (fway) m whip

fouetter (fway-tay) v whip

fouille (fooee) f search

fouiller (foo-ʸay) v search; *dig

foulard (foo-*laar*) m scarf

foule (fool) f crowd

fouler (foo-*lay*) v sprain

foulure (foo-*lewr*) f sprain

four (foor) m oven; **~ à micro-ondes** microwave oven

fourbe (foorb) adj hypocritical

fourchette (foor-*sheht*) f fork

fourgon (foor-*gawng*) m luggage van; van

fourmi (foor-*mee*) f ant

fournaise (foor-*naiz*) f furnace

fourneau (foor-*noa*) m stove; **~ à gaz** gas stove

fournir (foor-*neer*) v provide, furnish, supply

fourniture (foor-nee-*tewr*) f supply

fourreur (foo-*rūrr*) m furrier

fourrure (foo-*rewr*) f fur

foyer (fwah-*Yay*) m foyer, lounge; home; focus

fracas (frah-*kah*) m noise

fraction (frahk-s*Yawng*) f fraction

fracture (frahk-*tewr*) f break, fracture

fracturer (frahk-tew-*ray*) v fracture

fragile (frah-*zheel*) adj fragile

fragment (frahg-*mahng*) m extract, fragment

frais¹ (fray) adj (f fraîche) fresh; chilly, cool

frais² (fray) mpl expenses pl, expenditure; **~ de voyage** travelling expenses

fraise (fraiz) f strawberry

framboise (frahng-*bwaaz*) f raspberry

franc (frahng) adj (f franche) open

Français (frahng-*say*) m Frenchman

français (frahng-*say*) adj French

France (frahngss) f France

franchir (frahng-*sheer*) v cross

franc-tireur (frahng-tee-*rūrr*) m sniper

frange (frahngzh) f fringe

frappant (frah-*pahng*) adj striking

frappé (frah-*pay*) m milk-shake

frapper (frah-*pay*) v *beat; *hit, bump, tap, knock, *strike

fraternité (frah-tehr-nee-*tay*) f fraternity

fraude (froad) f fraud

frayeur (freh-*Yūrr*) f fright

fredonner (frer-do-*nay*) v hum

frein (frang) m brake; **~ à main** hand-brake; **~ à pédale** foot-brake

freiner (fray-*nay*) v slow down, curb

fréquemment (fray-kah-*mahng*) adv frequently

fréquence (fray-*kahngss*) f frequency

fréquent (fray-*kahng*) adj frequent

fréquenter (fray-kahng-*tay*) v associate with, mix with

frère (frair) m brother

fret (fray) m freight

en friche (ahng freesh) waste

friction (freek-s*Yawng*) f friction

frigidaire (free-zhee-*dair*) m refrigerator

frigo (free-*goa*) m fridge

fripon (free-*pawng*) m rascal

*frire (freer) v fry

friser (free-*zay*) v curl

frisson (free-*sawng*) m shudder, chill, shiver

frissonnant (free-so-*nahng*) adj shivery

frissonner (free-so-*nay*) v tremble, shiver

froid (frwah) m cold; adj cold

froisser (frwah-*say*) v crease

fromage (fro-*maazh*) m cheese

front (frawng) m forehead

frontière (frawng-t*Yair*) f border; frontier, boundary

frotter (fro-*tay*) v rub, scrub

fruit (frwee) m fruit

fugitif (few-zhee-*teef*) m runaway

*fuir (fweer) v escape; leak

fuite (fweet) f flight; leak

fume-cigarettes (fewm-see-gah-*reht*)

m cigarette-holder

fumée (few-*may*) *f* smoke

fumer (few-*may*) *v* smoke

fumeur (few-*mūrr*) *m* smoker; **compartiment fumeurs** smoker

fumier (few-*mᵞay*) *m* manure; dung; **tas de ~** dunghill

fumoir (few-*mwaar*) *m* smoking-room

funérailles (few-nay-*righ*) *fpl* funeral

fureur (few-*rūrr*) *f* anger, rage

furibond (few-ree-*bawng*) *adj* furious

furieux (few-*rᵞur*) *adj* furious

furoncle (few-*rawngkl*) *m* boil

fusée (few-*zay*) *f* rocket

fusible (few-*zeebl*) *m* fuse

fusil (few-*zee*) *m* rifle, gun

fusion (few-*zᵞawng*) *f* merger

futile (few-*teel*) *adj* petty, insignificant, idle

futur (few-*tēwr*) *adj* future

G

gâcher (gah-*shay*) *v* mess up

gâchette (gah-*sheht*) *f* trigger

gâchis (gah-*shee*) *m* mess

gadget (gah-*jeht*) *m* gadget

gadoue (gah-*doo*) *f* muck

gages (gaazh) *mpl* wages *pl*; **donner en gage** pawn

gagner (gah-*ñay*) *v* *win; *make, earn, gain

gai (gay) *adj* jolly, cheerful, gay

gain (gang) *m* gain; **gains** earnings *pl*; winnings *pl*

gaine (gehn) *f* girdle

gaîté (gay-*tay*) *f* gaiety

galerie (gahl-*ree*) *f* gallery; **~ d'art** art gallery

galet (gah-*lay*) *m* pebble

galop (gah-*loa*) *m* gallop

gamin (gah-*mang*) *m* boy

gamme (gahm) *f* scale; range

gant (gahng) *m* glove

garage (gah-*raazh*) *m* garage

garagiste (gah-rah-*zheest*) *m* garage proprietor

garant (gah-*rahng*) *m* guarantor

garantie (gah-rahng-*tee*) *f* guarantee

garantir (gah-rahng-*teer*) *v* guarantee

garçon (gahr-*sawng*) *m* boy; lad; waiter

garde (gahrd) *m* guard; *f* custody; **~ du corps** bodyguard; ***prendre ~** watch out

garde-boue (gahrd-*boo*) *m* mud-guard

garde-manger (gahrd-mahng-*zhay*) *m* larder

garder (gahr-*day*) *v* *keep; *hold

garde-robe (gahr-*drob*) *f* wardrobe; closet *nAm*

gardien (gahr-*dᵞang*) *m* attendant, warden; custodian; caretaker; **~ de but** goalkeeper

gardon (gahr-*dawng*) *m* roach

gare (gaar) *f* station; depot *nAm*

garer (gah-*ray*) *v* garage; **se ~** park

se gargariser (gahr-gah-ree-*zay*) gargle

gars (gah) *m* fellow

gaspillage (gah-spee-*ᵞaazh*) *m* waste

gaspiller (gah-spee-*ᵞay*) *v* waste

gaspilleur (gah-spee-*ᵞūrr*) *adj* wasteful

gastrique (gah-*streek*) *adj* gastric

gâteau (gah-*toa*) *m* cake

gâter (gah-*tay*) *v* *spoil

gauche (gōash) *adj* left; **de ~** left-hand

gaucher (goa-*shay*) *adj* left-handed

gaufre (gōafr) *f* waffle

gaufrette (goa-*freht*) *f* wafer

gaz (gaaz) *m* gas; **~ d'échappement** exhaust gases

gaze (gaaz) *f* gauze

gazon (gah-*zawng*) *m* lawn

géant (zhay-*ahng*) *m* giant

gel (zhehl) *m* frost

gelée (zher-*lay*) *f* jelly

geler (zher-*lay*) *v* *freeze

gémir (zhay-*meer*) *v* groan, moan

gênant (zheh-*nahng*) *adj* inconvenient, troublesome

gencive (zhahng-*seev*) *f* gum

gendre (zhahngdr) *m* son-in-law

gêner (zhay-*nay*) *v* hinder; embarrass, bother; **se ~** *be embarrassed

général (zhay-nay-*rahl*) *m* general; *adj* universal, public, general; **en ~** as a rule, in general

généralement (zhay-nay-rahl-*mahng*) *adv* as a rule

générateur (zhay-nay-rah-*tūrr*) *m* generator

génération (zhay-nay-rah-*sʸawng*) *f* generation

généreux (zhay-nay-*rur*) *adj* liberal, generous

générosité (zhay-nay-ro-zee-*tay*) *f* generosity

génie (zhay-*nee*) *m* genius

génital (zhay-nee-*tahl*) *adj* genital

genou (zher-*noo*) *m* (pl ~x) knee

genre (zhahngr) *m* kind; gender

gens (zhahng) *mpl/fpl* people *pl*

gentil (zhahng-*tee*) *adj* friendly, kind; nice; sweet

géographie (zhay-o-grah-*fee*) *f* geography

geôlier (zhoa-*lʸay*) *m* jailer

géologie (zhay-o-lo-*zhee*) *f* geology

géométrie (zhay-o-may-*tree*) *f* geometry

germe (zhehrm) *m* germ

geste (zhehst) *m* sign

gesticuler (zheh-stee-kew-*lay*) *v* gesticulate

gestion (zheh-*stʸawng*) *f* management, administration

gibet (zhee-*bay*) *m* gallows *pl*

gibier (zhee-*bʸay*) *m* game

gigantesque (zhee-gahng-*tehsk*) *adj* gigantic, enormous

gilet (zhee-*lay*) *m* waistcoat; vest *nAm*

gingembre (zhang-*zhahngbr*) *m* ginger

glace (glahss) *f* ice; ice-cream

glacial (glah-*sʸahl*) *adj* freezing

glacier (glah-*sʸay*) *m* glacier

gland (glahng) *m* acorn

glande (glahngd) *f* gland

glissade (glee-*sahd*) *f* slide

glissant (glee-*sahng*) *adj* slippery

glisser (glee-*say*) *v* *slide, glide; slip

global (glo-*bahl*) *adj* broad

globe (glob) *m* globe

gloire (glwaar) *f* glory

glousser (gloo-*say*) *v* chuckle; giggle

gluant (glew-*ahng*) *adj* sticky

gobelet (go-*blay*) *m* mug, tumbler

goéland (go-ay-*lahng*) *m* seagull

golf (golf) *m* golf; **terrain de ~** golf-links

golfe (golf) *m* gulf

gomme (gom) *f* gum; rubber, eraser

gondole (gawng-*dol*) *f* gondola

gonflable (gawng-*flahbl*) *adj* inflatable

gonfler (gawng-*flay*) *v* inflate

gorge (gorzh) *f* throat; gorge, glen

gorgée (gor-*zhay*) *f* sip

gosse (goss) *m* kid, boy

goudron (goo-*drawng*) *m* tar

goulot d'étranglement (goo-lo day-trahng-gler-*mahng*) bottleneck

gourdin (goor-*dang*) *m* club, cudgel

gourmand (goor-*mahng*) *adj* greedy

gourmet (goor-*may*) *m* gourmet

goût (goo) *m* taste; ***avoir ~ de** taste

goûter (goo-*tay*) *v* taste

goutte (goot) *f* drop; gout

gouvernail (goo-vehr-*nigh*) *m* rudder

gouvernante (goo-vehr-*nahngt*) *f* governess; housekeeper

gouvernement (goo-vehr-ner-*mahng*) *m* rule, government

gouverner (goo-vehr-*nay*) *v* rule, gov-

ern
gouverneur (goo-vehr-*nūrr*) *m* governor

grâce (graass) *f* grace; pardon; ~ **à** thanks to

gracieux (grah-*s*ʸ*ur*) *adj* graceful; **à titre** ~ free of charge

grade (grahd) *m* grade; degree, rank

graduel (grah-*dwehl*) *adj* gradual

graduellement (grah-dwehl-*mahng*) *adv* gradually

grain (grang) *m* corn, grain

graisse (grehss) *f* grease, fat

graisser (gray-*say*) *v* grease

graisseux (greh-*sur*) *adj* greasy

grammaire (grah-*mair*) *f* grammar

grammatical (grah-mah-tee-*kahl*) *adj* grammatical

gramme (grahm) *m* gram

grand (grahng) *adj* great; tall, big, major

Grande-Bretagne (grahngd-brer-*tahñ*) *f* Great Britain

grandeur (grahng-*dūrr*) *f* size

grandiose (grahng-d*ʸōāz*) *adj* superb, magnificent

grandir (grahng-*deer*) *v* *grow

grand-mère (grahng-*mair*) *f* grandmother

grand-papa (grahng-pah-*pah*) *m* granddad

grand-père (grahng-*pair*) *m* grandfather

grands-parents (grahng-pah-*rahng*) *mpl* grandparents *pl*

grange (grahngzh) *f* barn

granit (grah-*neet*) *m* granite

graphique (grah-*feek*) *adj* graphic; *m* diagram; chart

gras (grah) *adj* (f ~se) fatty, fat

gratitude (grah-tee-*tewd*) *f* gratitude

gratte-ciel (grah-ts*ʸehl*) *m* skyscraper

gratter (grah-*tay*) *v* scratch

gratuit (grah-*twee*) *adj* gratis, free of

charge, free

grave (graav) *adj* grave; bad, severe

graver (grah-*vay*) *v* engrave

graveur (grah-*vūrr*) *m* engraver

gravier (grah-v*ʸay*) *m* gravel

gravillon (grah-vee-ʸ*awng*) *m* grit

gravité (grah-vee-*tay*) *f* gravity

gravure (grah-*vewr*) *f* engraving; picture; carving

Grec (grehk) *m* Greek

grec (grehk) *adj* (f grecque) Greek

Grèce (grehss) *f* Greece

greffier (gray-f*ʸay*) *m* clerk

grêle (grehl) *f* hail

grenier (grer-n*ʸay*) *m* attic

grenouille (grer-*noo*ᵉᵉ) *f* frog

grève (graiv) *f* strike; *faire ~ *strike

gréviste (gray-*veest*) *m* striker

griffe (greef) *f* claw

grill (greel) *m* grill

grille (greey) *f* gate; grate

griller (gree-ʸ*ay*) *v* roast; grill

grillon (gree-ʸ*awng*) *m* cricket

grimper (grang-*pay*) *v* climb

grincer (grang-*say*) *v* creak

grippe (greep) *f* flu, influenza

gris (gree) *adj* grey

grive (greev) *f* thrush

grogner (gro-*ñay*) *v* grumble, growl

grondement (grawngd-*mahng*) *m* roar

gronder (grawng-*day*) *v* thunder; scold

gros (groa) *adj* (f ~se) big; thick, fat, corpulent, stout

groseille (groa-*zay*) *f* currant; ~ **à maquereau** gooseberry

grosse (grōāss) *f* gross

grossier (groa-s*ʸay*) *adj* coarse, gross, rude

grossir (gro-*seer*) *v* increase; *put on weight

grossiste (groa-*seest*) *m* wholesale dealer

grotesque (gro-*tehsk*) *adj* ludicrous

grotte (grot) f cave; grotto

groupe (groop) m group; party, set

grouper (groo-pay) v group

grue (grew) f crane

grumeau (grew-moa) m lump

grumeleux (grewm-lur) adj lumpy

gué (gay) m ford

guêpe (gehp) f wasp

ne ... guère (ner ... gair) f scarcely

guérir (gay-reer) v cure; heal, recover

guérison (gay-ree-zawng) f recovery, cure

guérisseur (gay-ree-sūrr) m quack

guerre (gair) f war; **d'avant-guerre** pre-war; ~ **mondiale** world war

guetter (gay-tay) v watch for

gueule (gurl) f mouth; ~ **de bois** hangover

guichet (gee-shay) m box-office; ~ **de location** box-office

guide (geed) m guide; guidebook

guider (gee-day) v *lead

guillemets (geey-may) mpl quotation marks

guitare (gee-taar) f guitar

gymnase (zheem-naaz) m gymnasium

gymnaste (zheem-nahst) m gymnast

gymnastique (zheem-nah-steek) f gymnastics pl

gynécologue (zhee-nay-ko-log) m gynaecologist

H

habile (ah-beel) adj skilful; skilled

habileté (ah-beel-tay) f skill, art

habiller (ah-bee-ʸay) v dress

habitable (ah-bee-tahbl) adj inhabitable, habitable

habitant (ah-bee-tahng) m inhabitant

habitation (ah-bee-tah-sʸawng) f house

habiter (ah-bee-tay) v inhabit, live

habits (ah-bee) mpl clothes pl

habitude (ah-bee-tewd) f habit; custom; ***avoir l'habitude de** would; **d'habitude** usually

habitué (ah-bee-tway) adj accustomed; ***être ~ à** *be used to

habituel (ah-bee-twehl) adj common, habitual, ordinary

habituellement (ah-bee-twehl-mahng) adv usually

s'habituer *get accustomed

hache ('ahsh) f axe

hacher ('ah-shay) v chop, mince

haie ('ay) f hedge

haine ('ehn) f hatred, hate

*haïr ('ah-eer) v hate

hâlé ('ah-lay) adj tanned

haleter ('ahl-tay) v pant

hamac ('ah-mahk) m hammock

hameau ('ah-moa) m hamlet

hameçon (ahm-sawng) m fishing hook

hanche ('ahngsh) f hip

handicapé ('ahng-dee-kah-pay) adj disabled

hardi ('ahr-dee) adj bold

hareng ('ah-rahng) m herring

haricot ('ah-ree-koa) m bean

harmonie (ahr-mo-nee) f harmony

harmonieux (ahr-mo-nʸur) adj tuneful

harpe ('ahrp) f harp

hasard ('ah-zaar) m chance, luck; hazard; **par ~** by chance

hâte ('aat) f hurry, speed, haste

se hâter ('ah-tay) hasten

hausse ('ōass) f rise

haut ('oa) m top side; adj high, tall; **en ~** upstairs, above, overhead; up; **vers le ~** upwards

hautain ('oa-tang) adj haughty

hauteur ('oa-tūrr) f height; ***être à la ~ de** *keep up with

haut-parleur ('oa-pahr-lūrr) m loud-speaker

havresac ('ah-vrer-*sahk*) m haversack; knapsack

hebdomadaire (ehb-do-mah-*dair*) adj weekly

hébreu (ay-*brur*) m Hebrew

hélas ('ay-*laass*) adv unfortunately

hélice (ay-*leess*) f propeller

hémorragie (ay-mo-rah-*zhee*) f haemorrhage

hémorroïdes (ay-mo-ro-*eed*) fpl piles pl, haemorrhoids pl

herbe (ehrb) f grass; herb; **mauvaise** ~ weed

héréditaire (ay-ray-dee-*tair*) adj hereditary

hérisson ('ay-ree-*sawng*) m hedgehog

héritage (ay-ree-*taazh*) m inheritance

hériter (ay-ree-*tay*) v inherit

hermétique (ehr-may-*teek*) adj airtight

hernie ('ehr-*nee*) f hernia; slipped disc

héron ('ay-*rawng*) m heron

héros (ay-*roa*) m hero

hésiter (ay-zee-*tay*) v hesitate

hétérosexuel (ay-tay-ro-sehk-*swehl*) adj heterosexual

hêtre ('aitr) m beech

heure (ūrr) f hour; **à ... heures** at ... o'clock; ~ **d'arrivée** time of arrival; ~ **de départ** time of departure; ~ **de pointe** rush-hour; ~ **d'été** summer time; **heures de bureau** office hours; **heures de consultation** consultation hours; **heures de visite** visiting hours; **heures d'ouverture** business hours; **tout à l'heure** presently; **toutes les heures** hourly

heureux (ur-*rur*) adj fortunate, happy

heurter ('urr-*tay*) v knock

hibou ('ee-*boo*) m (pl ~x) owl

hideux ('ee-*dur*) adj hideous

hier ('ʸair) adv yesterday

hiérarchie ('ʸay-rahr-*shee*) f hierarchy

hippodrome (ee-po-*drom*) m racecourse

hirondelle (ee-rawng-*dehl*) f swallow

hisser ('ee-*say*) v hoist

histoire (ee-*stwaar*) f history; story; ~ **d'amour** love-story; ~ **de l'art** art history

historien (ee-sto-*rʸang*) m historian

historique (ee-sto-*reek*) adj historic; historical

hiver (ee-*vair*) m winter

hobby ('o-*bee*) m hobby

hockey ('o-*kay*) m hockey

Hollandais ('o-lahng-*day*) m Dutchman

hollandais ('o-lahng-*day*) adj Dutch

Hollande ('o-*lahngd*) f Holland

homard ('o-*maar*) m lobster

hommage (o-*maazh*) m homage, tribute; **rendre** ~ honour

homme (om) m man; ~ **d'affaires** businessman; ~ **d'Etat** statesman

homosexuel (o-mo-sehk-*swehl*) adj homosexual

Hongrie ('awng-*gree*) f Hungary

Hongrois ('awng-*grwah*) m Hungarian

hongrois ('awng-*grwah*) adj Hungarian

honnête (o-*neht*) adj honourable, honest; fair

honnêteté (o-neht-*tay*) f honesty

honneur (o-*nūrr*) m honour, glory

honorable (o-no-*rahbl*) adj honourable, respectable

honoraires (o-no-*rair*) mpl fee

honorer (o-no-*ray*) v honour

honte ('awngt) f shame; ***avoir** ~ *be ashamed; **quelle honte!** shame!

honteux ('awng-*tur*) adj ashamed

hôpital (o-pee-*tahl*) m hospital

hoquet ('o-*kay*) m hiccup

horaire (o-*rair*) m timetable, schedule

horizon (o-ree-*zawng*) *m* horizon

horizontal (o-ree-zawng-*tahl*) *adj* horizontal

horloge (or-*lawzh*) *f* clock

horloger (or-lo-*zhay*) *m* watch-maker

horreur (o-*rūrr*) *f* horror

horrible (o-*reebl*) *adj* horrible

horrifiant (o-ree-f*Y*ahng) *adj* horrible

hors ('awr) *adv* out; ~ **de** outside

hors-d'œuvre ('or-*dūrvr*) *m* hors-d'œuvre

horticulture (or-tee-kewl-*tūr*) *f* horticulture

hospice (o-*speess*) *m* asylum

hospitalier (o-spee-tah-l*Y*ay) *adj* hospitable

hospitalité (o-spee-tah-lee-*tay*) *f* hospitality

hostile (o-*steel*) *adj* hostile

hôte (ōat) *m* host; guest

hôtel (oa-*tehl*) *m* hotel; ~ **de ville** town hall

hôtesse (oa-*tehss*) *f* hostess; receptionist; ~ **de l'air** stewardess

houblon ('oo-*blawng*) *m* hop

houppette ('oo-*peht*) *f* powder-puff

housse ('ooss) *f* sleeve

hublot ('ew-*bloa*) *m* porthole

huile (weel) *f* oil; ~ **capillaire** hair-oil; ~ **de table** salad-oil; ~ **d'olive** olive oil; ~ **solaire** suntan oil

huiler (wee-*lay*) *v* lubricate

huileux (wee-*lur*) *adj* oily

huissier (wee-s*Y*ay) *m* bailiff

huit ('weet) *num* eight

huitième ('wee-t*Y*ehm) *num* eighth

huître (weetr) *f* oyster

humain (ew-*mang*) *adj* human

humanité (ew-mah-nee-*tay*) *f* mankind, humanity

humble (urngbl) *adj* humble

humecter (ew-mehk-*tay*) *v* moisten

humeur (ew-*mūrr*) *f* mood, spirit

humide (ew-*meed*) *adj* humid; wet, damp

humidifier (ew-mee-dee-f*Y*ay) *v* damp

humidité (ew-mee-dee-*tay*) *f* humidity, moisture, damp

humour ('ew-*mōōr*) *m* humour

hurler ('ewr-*lay*) *v* yell, scream

hutte ('ewt) *f* hut

hydrogène (ee-dro-*zhehn*) *m* hydrogen

hygiène (ee-zh*Y*ehn) *f* hygiene

hygiénique (ee-zh*Y*ay-*neek*) *adj* hygienic

hymne (eemn) *m* hymn; ~ **national** national anthem

hypocrisie (ee-po-kree-*zee*) *f* hypocrisy

hypocrite (ee-po-*kreet*) *m* hypocrite; *adj* hypocritical

hypothèque (ee-po-*tehk*) *f* mortgage

hystérique (ee-stay-*reek*) *adj* hysterical

I

ici (ee-*see*) *adv* here

icône (ee-*kōan*) *f* icon

idéal[1] (ee-day-*ahl*) *adj* (pl -aux) ideal

idéal[2] (ee-day-*ahl*) *m* (pl ~s, -aux) ideal

idée (ee-*day*) *f* idea; opinion; ~ **lumineuse** brain-wave

identification (ee-dahng-tee-fee-kah-s*Y*awng) *f* identification

identifier (ee-dahng-tee-f*Y*ay) *v* identify

identique (ee-dahng-*teek*) *adj* identical

identité (ee-dahng-tee-*tay*) *f* identity

idiomatique (ee-d*Y*o-mah-*teek*) *adj* idiomatic

idiome (ee-d*Y*ōam) *m* idiom

idiot (ee-d*Y*oa) *m* fool, idiot; *adj* idiotic

idole (ee-*dol*) f idol

idylle (ee-*deel*) f romance

ignifuge (eeg-nee-*fewzh*) adj fireproof

ignorant (ee-ño-*rahng*) adj ignorant; uneducated

ignorer (ee-ño-*ray*) v ignore; overlook

il (eel) *pron* he

île (eel) f island

illégal (ee-lay-*gahl*) adj illegal

illettré (ee-leh-*tray*) m illiterate

illicite (ee-lee-*seet*) adj unlawful, unauthorized

illimité (ee-lee-mee-*tay*) adj unlimited

illisible (ee-lee-*zeebl*) adj illegible

illumination (ee-lew-mee-nah-sʸ*awng*) f illumination

illuminer (ee-lew-mee-*nay*) v illuminate

illusion (ee-lew-zʸ*awng*) f illusion

illustration (ee-lew-strah-sʸ*awng*) f illustration; picture

illustre (ee-*lewstr*) adj noted

illustré (ee-lew-*stray*) m magazine

illustrer (ee-lew-*stray*) v illustrate

ils (eel) *pron* they

image (ee-*maazh*) f picture, image

imaginaire (ee-mah-zhee-*nair*) adj imaginary

imagination (ee-mah-zhee-nah-sʸ*awng*) f fancy, imagination

imaginer (ee-mah-zhee-*nay*) v fancy, imagine; **s'imaginer** fancy, imagine

imitation (ee-mee-tah-sʸ*awng*) f imitation

imiter (ee-mee-*tay*) v imitate, copy

immaculé (ee-mah-kew-*lay*) adj stainless, spotless

immangeable (ang-mahng-*zhahbl*) adj inedible

immédiat (ee-may-dʸ*ah*) adj immediate

immédiatement (ee-may-dʸaht-*mahng*) adv at once, instantly, immediately

immense (ee-*mahngss*) adj immense; vast, huge

immérité (ee-may-ree-*tay*) adj unearned

immeuble (ee-*murbl*) m house; ~ **d'habitation** block of flats; apartment house *Am*

immigrant (ee-mee-*grahng*) m immigrant

immigration (ee-mee-grah-sʸ*awng*) f immigration

immigrer (ee-mee-*gray*) v immigrate

immobile (ee-mo-*beel*) adj motionless

immodeste (ee-mo-*dehst*) adj immodest

immondices (ee-mawng-*deess*) fpl litter

immuniser (ee-mew-nee-*zay*) v immunize

immunité (ee-mew-nee-*tay*) f immunity

impair (ang-*pair*) adj odd

imparfait (ang-pahr-*fay*) adj imperfect; faulty

impartial (ang-pahr-sʸ*ahl*) adj impartial

impatient (ang-pah-sʸ*ahng*) adj impatient; eager

impeccable (ang-peh-*kahbl*) adj faultless

impératrice (ang-pay-rah-*treess*) f empress

imperfection (ang-pehr-fehk-sʸ*awng*) f shortcoming; fault

impérial (ang-pay-rʸ*ahl*) adj imperial

imperméable (ang-pehr-may-*ahbl*) m mackintosh, raincoat; adj waterproof, rainproof

impersonnel (ang-pehr-so-*nehl*) adj impersonal

impertinence (ang-pehr-tee-*nahngss*) f impertinence

impertinent (ang-pehr-tee-*nahng*) adj

impertinent

impétueux (ang-pay-*twur*) *adj* rash

impliquer (ang-plee-*kay*) *v* involve, imply

impoli (ang-po-*lee*) *adj* impolite

impopulaire (ang-po-pew-*lair*) *adj* unpopular

importance (ang-por-*tahngss*) *f* importance; ***avoir de l'importance** matter; **sans** ~ insignificant

important (ang-por-*tahng*) *adj* important; considerable, big

importateur (ang-por-tah-*türr*) *m* importer

importation (ang-por-tah-*syawng*) *f* import; **taxe d'importation** import duty

importer (ang-por-*tay*) *v* import

imposable (ang-poa-*zahbl*) *adj* dutiable

imposant (ang-poa-*zahng*) *adj* imposing

imposer (ang-poa-*zay*) *v* tax

impossible (ang-po-*seebl*) *adj* impossible

impôt (ang-*poa*) *m* tax; ~ **sur le chiffre d'affaires** turnover tax; ~ **sur le revenu** income-tax

impotence (ang-po-*tahngss*) *f* impotence

impotent (ang-po-*tahng*) *adj* impotent

impraticable (ang-prah-tee-*kahbl*) *adj* impassable

impression (ang-preh-*syawng*) *f* impression; sensation; ***faire** ~ **sur** impress

impressionnant (ang-preh-syo-*nahng*) *adj* impressive

impressionner (ang-preh-syo-*nay*) *v* impress

imprévu (ang-pray-*vew*) *adj* unexpected

imprimé (ang-pree-*may*) *m* printed matter

imprimer (ang-pree-*may*) *v* print

imprimerie (ang-preem-*ree*) *f* printing office

improbable (ang-pro-*bahbl*) *adj* improbable, unlikely

impropre (ang-*propr*) *adj* improper, unfit; wrong

improviser (ang-pro-vee-*zay*) *v* improvise

imprudent (ang-prew-*dahng*) *adj* unwise

impuissant (ang-pwee-*sahng*) *adj* powerless

impulsif (ang-pewl-*seef*) *adj* impulsive

impulsion (ang-pewl-*syawng*) *f* urge, impulse

inabordable (ee-nah-bor-*dahbl*) *adj* prohibitive

inacceptable (ee-nahk-sehp-*tahbl*) *adj* unacceptable

inaccessible (ee-nahk-say-*seebl*) *adj* inaccessible

inadéquat (ee-nah-day-*kwah*) *adj* inadequate, unsuitable

inadvertance (ee-nahd-vehr-*tahngss*) *f* oversight

inattendu (ee-nah-tahng-*dew*) *adj* unexpected

inattentif (ee-nah-tahng-*teef*) *adj* careless

incapable (ang-kah-*pahbl*) *adj* incapable, unable

incassable (ang-kah-*sahbl*) *adj* unbreakable

incendie (ang-sahng-*dee*) *m* fire; **alarme d'incendie** fire-alarm

incertain (ang-sehr-*tang*) *adj* doubtful, uncertain

incident (ang-see-*dahng*) *m* incident

incinérer (ang-see-nay-*ray*) *v* cremate

incision (ang-see-*zyawng*) *f* cut

inciter (ang-see-*tay*) *v* incite

inclinaison (ang-klee-neh-*zawng*) *f* gradient

inclination (ang-klee-nah-s^yawng) f
tendency; ~ **de la tête** nod

incliné (ang-klee-nay) adj slanting

s'incliner (ang-klee-nay) slant

*****inclure** (ang-klewr) v include, enclose; comprise, count

incompétent (ang-kawng-pay-tahng)
adj incompetent, unqualified

incomplet (ang-kawng-play) adj (f - plète) incomplete

inconcevable (ang-kawng-svahbl) adj
inconceivable

inconditionnel (ang-kawng-dee-s^yo-nehl) adj unconditional

inconfortable (ang-kawng-for-tahbl)
adj uncomfortable

inconnu (ang-ko-new) adj unknown,
unfamiliar; m stranger

inconscient (ang-kawng-s^yahng) adj
unconscious; unaware

inconsidéré (ang-kawng-see-day-ray)
adj rash

inconvénient (ang-kawng-vay-n^yahng)
m inconvenience

incorrect (ang-ko-rehkt) adj incorrect,
inaccurate, wrong

incroyable (ang-krwah-^yahbl) adj incredible

inculte (ang-kewlt) adj uncultivated

incurable (ang-kew-rahbl) adj incurable

Inde (angd) f India

indécent (ang-day-sahng) adj indecent

indéfini (ang-day-fee-nee) adj indefinite

indemne (ang-dehmn) adj unhurt

indemnité (ang-dehm-nee-tay) f compensation, indemnity

indépendance (ang-day-pahng-dahngss) f independence

indépendant (ang-day-pahng-dahng)
adj independent; self-employed

indésirable (ang-day-zee-rahbl) adj
undesirable

index (ang-dehks) m index finger; index

indicatif (ang-dee-kah-teef) m area
code

indication (ang-dee-kah-s^yawng) f indication

Indien (ang-d^yang) m Indian

indien (ang-d^yang) adj Indian

indifférent (ang-dee-fay-rahng) adj indifferent

indigène (ang-dee-zhehn) m native;
adj native

indigent (ang-dee-zhahng) adj poor

indigestion (ang-dee-zheh-st^yawng) f
indigestion

indignation (ang-dee-ñah-s^yawng) f
indignation

indiquer (ang-dee-kay) v point out, indicate; declare

indirect (ang-dee-rehkt) adj indirect

indispensable (ang-dee-spahng-sahbl)
adj essential

indisposé (ang-dee-spoa-zay) adj unwell

indistinct (ang-dee-stang) adj dim

individu (ang-dee-vee-dew) m individual

individuel (ang-dee-vee-dwehl) adj individual

Indonésie (ang-do-nay-zee) f Indonesia

Indonésien (ang-do-nay-z^yang) m Indonesian

indonésien (ang-do-nay-z^yang) adj Indonesian

industrie (ang-dew-stree) f industry

industriel (ang-dew-stree-ehl) adj industrial

industrieux (ang-dew-stree-ur) adj industrious

inefficace (ee-nay-fee-kahss) adj inefficient

inégal (ee-nay-gahl) adj uneven, unequal

inéquitable (ee-nay-kee-*tahbl*) *adj* unfair

inestimable (ee-neh-stee-*mahbl*) *adj* priceless

inévitable (ee-nay-vee-*tahbl*) *adj* inevitable, unavoidable

inexact (ee-nehg-*zahkt*) *adj* false, incorrect

inexpérimenté (ee-nehk-spay-ree-mahng-*tay*) *adj* inexperienced

inexplicable (ee-nehk-splee-*kahbl*) *adj* unaccountable

infâme (ang-*faam*) *adj* foul

infanterie (ang-fahng-*tree*) *f* infantry

infecter (ang-fehk-*tay*) *v* infect; **s'infecter** *become septic

infectieux (ang-fehk-*s*ʸ*ur*) *adj* infectious

infection (ang-fehk-*s*ʸ*awng*) *f* infection

inférieur (ang-fay-*r*ʸ*urr*) *adj* inferior, bottom

infidèle (ang-fee-*dehl*) *adj* unfaithful

infini (ang-fee-*nee*) *adj* infinite, endless

infinitif (ang-fee-nee-*teef*) *m* infinitive

infirme (ang-*feerm*) *m* invalid; *adj* invalid

infirmerie (ang-feer-mer-*ree*) *f* infirmary

infirmière (ang-feer-*m*ʸ*air*) *f* nurse

inflammable (ang-flah-*mahbl*) *adj* inflammable

inflammation (ang-flah-mah-*s*ʸ*awng*) *f* inflammation

inflation (ang-flah-*s*ʸ*awng*) *f* inflation

influence (ang-flew-*ahngss*) *f* influence

influencer (ang-flew-ahng-*say*) *v* influence

influent (ang-flew-*ahng*) *adj* influential

information (ang-for-mah-*s*ʸ*awng*) *f* information; enquiry

informer (ang-for-*may*) *v* inform; **s'informer** inquire, enquire, query

infortune (ang-for-*tewn*) *f* misfortune

infortuné (ang-for-tew-*nay*) *adj* unlucky

infraction (ang-frahk-*s*ʸ*awng*) *f* offence

infrarouge (ang-frah-*roozh*) *adj* infrared

infructueux (ang-frewk-*twur*) *adj* unsuccessful

ingénieur (ang-zhay-*n*ʸ*urr*) *m* engineer

ingénu (ang-zhay-*new*) *adj* simple

ingérence (ang-zhay-*rahngss*) *f* interference

ingrat (ang-*grah*) *adj* ungrateful

ingrédient (ang-gray-*d*ʸ*ahng*) *m* ingredient

inhabitable (ee-nah-bee-*tahbl*) *adj* uninhabitable

inhabité (ee-nah-bee-*tay*) *adj* uninhabited

inhabitué (ee-nah-bee-*tway*) *adj* unaccustomed

inhabituel (ee-nah-bee-*twehl*) *adj* unusual, uncommon

inhaler (ee-nah-*lay*) *v* inhale

ininterrompu (ee-nang-teh-rawng-*pew*) *adj* continuous

initial (ee-nee-*s*ʸ*ahl*) *adj* initial

initiale (ee-nee-*s*ʸ*ahl*) *f* initial

initiative (ee-nee-s*ʸ*ah-*teev*) *f* initiative

injecter (ang-zhehk-*tay*) *v* inject

injection (ang-zhehk-*s*ʸ*awng*) *f* injection

injurier (ang-zhew-*r*ʸ*ay*) *v* call names

injuste (ang-*zhewst*) *adj* unjust, unfair

injustice (ang-zhew-*steess*) *f* injustice

inné (ee-*nay*) *adj* natural

innocence (ee-no-*sahngss*) *f* innocence

innocent (ee-no-*sahng*) *adj* innocent

inoculation (ee-no-kew-lah-*s*ʸ*awng*) *f*

inoculation
inoculer (ee-no-kew-*lay*) *v* inoculate
inoffensif (ee-no-fahng-*seef*) *adj* harmless
inondation (ee-nawng-dah-*s^y awng*) *f* flood
inopportun (ee-no-por-*turng*) *adj* inconvenient, misplaced
inquiet (ang-*k^y ay*) *adj* (f -ète) anxious; restless
inquiétant (ang-k^y ay-*tahng*) *adj* scary
s'inquiéter (ang-k^y ay-*tay*) worry
inquiétude (ang-k^y ay-*tewd*) *f* worry; unrest
insatisfaisant (ang-sah-teess-fer-*zahng*) *adj* unsatisfactory
insatisfait (ang-sah-tee-*sfay*) *adj* dissatisfied
inscription (ang-skree-*ps^y awng*) *f* inscription; registration; entry
***inscrire** (ang-*skreer*) *v* enter, book; list; **s'*inscrire** check in, register
insecte (ang-*sehkt*) *m* insect; bug *nAm*
insecticide (ang-sehk-tee-*seed*) *m* insecticide
insectifuge (ang-sehk-tee-*fewzh*) *m* insect repellent
insensé (ang-sahng-*say*) *adj* crazy, senseless, mad
insensible (ang-sahng-*seebl*) *adj* insensitive; heartless
insérer (ang-say-*ray*) *v* insert
insignifiant (ang-see-ñee-*f^y ahng*) *adj* petty, insignificant, unimportant
insipide (ang-see-*peed*) *adj* tasteless
insister (ang-see-*stay*) *v* insist
insolation (ang-so-lah-*s^y awng*) *f* sunstroke
insolence (ang-so-*lahngss*) *f* insolence
insolent (ang-so-*lahng*) *adj* insolent, impudent, impertinent
insolite (ang-so-*leet*) *adj* unusual
insomnie (ang-som-*nee*) *f* insomnia
insonorisé (ang-so-noa-ree-*zay*) *adj* soundproof
insouciant (ang-soo-*s^y ahng*) *adj* carefree
inspecter (ang-spehk-*tay*) *v* inspect
inspecteur (ang-spehk-*tūrr*) *m* inspector
inspection (ang-spehk-*s^y awng*) *f* inspection
inspirer (ang-spee-*ray*) *v* inspire
instable (ang-*stahbl*) *adj* unsteady, unstable
installation (ang-stah-lah-*s^y awng*) *f* installation
installer (ang-stah-*lay*) *v* install; furnish
instant (ang-*stahng*) *m* instant, moment; second
instantané (ang-stahng-tah-*nay*) *m* snapshot; *adj* prompt
instantanément (ang-stahng-tah-nay-*mahng*) *adv* instantly
instinct (ang-*stang*) *m* instinct
instituer (ang-stee-*tway*) *v* institute
institut (ang-stee-*tew*) *m* institute; ~ **de beauté** beauty parlour
instituteur (ang-stee-tew-*tūrr*) *m* master, teacher, schoolteacher, schoolmaster
institution (ang-stee-tew-*s^y awng*) *f* institution; institute
instructeur (ang-strewk-*tūrr*) *m* instructor
instructif (ang-strewk-*teef*) *adj* instructive
instruction (ang-strewk-*s^y awng*) *f* instruction, direction
***instruire** (ang-*strweer*) *v* instruct
instrument (ang-strew-*mahng*) *m* instrument; tool, implement; ~ **de musique** musical instrument
insuffisant (ang-sew-fee-*zahng*) *adj* insufficient
insulte (ang-*sewlt*) *f* insult

insulter (ang-sewl-*tay*) v insult; scold

insupportable (ang-sew-por-*tahbl*) adj unbearable

insurrection (ang-sew-rehk-s^y*awng*) f rising

intact (ang-*tahkt*) adj whole, intact, unbroken

intellect (ang-teh-*lehkt*) m intellect

intellectuel (ang-teh-lehk-*twehl*) adj intellectual

intelligence (ang-teh-lee-*zhahngss*) f intelligence, intellect, brain

intelligent (ang-teh-lee-*zhahng*) adj intelligent, bright, clever

intense (ang-*tahngss*) adj intense; violent

intention (ang-tahng-s^y*awng*) f intention, purpose; *avoir l'intention de** intend

intentionnel (ang-tahng-s^yo-*nehl*) adj intentional, on purpose

interdiction (ang-tehr-deek-s^y*awng*) f prohibition

***interdire** (ang-tehr-*deer*) v *forbid, prohibit

interdit (ang-tehr-*dee*) adj prohibited; ~ aux piétons no pedestrians

intéressant (ang-tay-reh-*sahng*) adj interesting

intéresser (ang-tay-ray-*say*) v interest

intérêt (ang-tay-*ray*) m interest

intérieur (ang-tay-r^y*ūūr*) m interior, inside; adj internal, inside, inner; indoor; domestic; à l'intérieur inside; indoors, within; à l'intérieur de inside; vers l'intérieur inwards

intérim (ang-tay-*reem*) m interim

interloqué (ang-tehr-lo-*kay*) adj speechless

interlude (ang-tehr-*lewd*) m interlude

intermédiaire (ang-tehr-may-d^y*air*) m intermediary; *servir d'intermédiaire** mediate

internat (ang-tehr-*nah*) m boarding-school

international (ang-tehr-nah-s^yo-*nahl*) adj international

interne (ang-*tehrn*) adj internal, resident

interprète (ang-tehr-*preht*) m interpreter

interpréter (ang-tehr-pray-*tay*) v interpret

interrogatif (ang-tehr-ro-gah-*teef*) adj interrogative

interrogatoire (ang-teh-ro-gah-*twaar*) m interrogation, examination

interroger (ang-teh-ro-*zhay*) v interrogate

***interrompre** (ang-teh-*rawng*pr) v interrupt; s'*interrompre** pause

interruption (ang-teh-rew-ps^y*awng*) f interruption

intersection (ang-tehr-sehk-s^y*awng*) f intersection

intervalle (ang-tehr-*vahl*) m interval; space

***intervenir** (ang-tehr-ver-*neer*) v intervene, interfere

intervertir (ang-tehr-vehr-*teer*) v invert

intestin (ang-teh-*stang*) m intestine, gut; intestins bowels pl

intime (ang-*teem*) adj intimate, cosy

intimité (ang-tee-mee-*tay*) f privacy

intolérable (ang-to-lay-*rahbl*) adj intolerable

intoxication alimentaire (ang-tok-see-kah-s^yawng ah-lee-mahng-*tair*) food poisoning

intrigue (ang-*treeg*) f intrigue; plot

introduction (ang-tro-dewk-s^y*awng*) f introduction

***introduire** (ang-tro-*dweer*) v introduce

intrus (ang-*trew*) m trespasser

inutile (ee-new-*teel*) adj useless

inutilement (ee-new-teel-*mahng*) adv in vain

invalide (ang-vah-*leed*) *adj* disabled

invasion (ang-vah-*z*Ŷ*awng*) *f* invasion

inventaire (ang-vahng-*tair*) *m* inventory

inventer (ang-vahng-*tay*) *v* invent

inventeur (ang-vahng-*tūrr*) *m* inventor

inventif (ang-vahng-*teef*) *adj* inventive

invention (ang-vahng-*s*Ŷ*awng*) *f* invention

inverse (ang-*vehrs*) *adj* reverse

investigation (ang-veh-stee-gah-*s*Ŷ*awng*) *f* investigation, enquiry

investir (ang-veh-*steer*) *v* invest

investissement (ang-veh-stee-*smahng*) *m* investment

investisseur (ang-veh-stee-*sūrr*) *m* investor

invisible (ang-vee-*zeebl*) *adj* invisible

invitation (ang-vee-tah-*s*Ŷ*awng*) *f* invitation

invité (ang-vee-*tay*) *m* guest

inviter (ang-vee-*tay*) *v* invite

involontaire (ang-vo-lawng-*tair*) *adj* unintentional

iode (Ŷ*od*) *m* iodine

Irak (ee-*rahk*) *m* Iraq

Irakien (ee-rah-*k*Ŷ*ang*) *m* Iraqi

irakien (ee-rah-*k*Ŷ*ang*) *adj* Iraqi

Iran (ee-*rahng*) *m* Iran

Iranien (ee-rah-*n*Ŷ*ang*) *m* Iranian

iranien (ee-rah-*n*Ŷ*ang*) *adj* Iranian

irascible (ee-rah-*seebl*) *adj* irascible, quick-tempered

Irlandais (eer-lahng-*day*) *m* Irishman

irlandais (eer-lahng-*day*) *adj* Irish

Irlande (eer-*lahngd*) *f* Ireland

ironie (ee-ro-*nee*) *f* irony

ironique (ee-ro-*neek*) *adj* ironical

irréel (ee-ray-*ehl*) *adj* unreal

irrégulier (ee-ray-gew-*l*Ŷ*ay*) *adj* irregular, uneven

irréparable (ee-ray-pah-*rahbl*) *adj* irreparable

irrétrécissable (ee-ray-tray-see-*sahbl*) *adj* shrinkproof

irrévocable (ee-ray-vo-*kahbl*) *adj* irrevocable

irritable (ee-ree-*tahbl*) *adj* irritable

irrité (ee-ree-*tay*) *adj* cross

irriter (ee-ree-*tay*) *v* irritate

Islandais (ee-slahng-*day*) *m* Icelander

islandais (ee-slahng-*day*) *adj* Icelandic

Islande (ee-*slahngd*) *f* Iceland

isolateur (ee-zo-lah-*tūrr*) *m* insulator

isolation (ee-zo-lah-*s*Ŷ*awng*) *f* isolation, insulation

isolement (ee-zol-*mahng*) *m* isolation

isoler (ee-zo-*lay*) *v* isolate, insulate

Israël (ee-srah-*ehl*) *m* Israel

Israélien (ee-srah-ay-*l*Ŷ*ang*) *m* Israeli

israélien (ee-srah-ay-*l*Ŷ*ang*) *adj* Israeli

issue (ee-*sew*) *f* issue

isthme (*eesm*) *m* isthmus

Italie (ee-tah-*lee*) *f* Italy

Italien (ee-tah-*l*Ŷ*ang*) *m* Italian

italien (ee-tah-*l*Ŷ*ang*) *adj* Italian

italiques (ee-tah-*leek*) *mpl* italics *pl*

itinéraire (ee-tee-nay-*rair*) *m* itinerary

ivoire (ee-*vwaar*) *m* ivory

ivre (*eevr*) *adj* drunk; intoxicated

J

jade (*zhahd*) *m* jade

jadis (zhah-*deess*) *adv* formerly

jalon (zhah-*lawng*) *m* landmark

jalousie (zhah-loo-*zee*) *f* jealousy

jaloux (zhah-*loo*) *adj* jealous, envious

jamais (zhah-*may*) *adv* ever; **ne ... ~** never

jambe (*zhahngb*) *f* leg

jambon (zhahng-*bawng*) *m* ham

jante (*zhahngt*) *f* rim

janvier (zhahng-*v*Ŷ*ay*) January

Japon (zhah-*pawng*) *m* Japan

Japonais (zhah-po-*nay*) *m* Japanese

japonais (zhah-po-*nay*) *adj* Japanese

jaquette (zhah-*keht*) *f* jacket

jardin (zhahr-*dang*) *m* garden; **~ potager** kitchen garden; **~ public** public garden; **~ zoologique** zoological gardens

jardinier (zhahr-dee-*n*ᵞ*ay*) *m* gardener

jarre (zhaar) *f* jar

jauge (zhōāzh) *f* gauge

jaune (zhōān) *adj* yellow; **~ d'œuf** yolk, egg-yolk

jaunisse (zhoa-*neess*) *f* jaundice

je (zher) *pron* I

jersey (zhehr-*zay*) *m* jersey

jet (zhay) *m* cast; jet, squirt, spout

jetée (zher-*tay*) *f* jetty, pier

jeter (zher-*tay*) *v* *cast, *throw; **à ~** disposable

jeton (zher-*tawng*) *m* token, chip

jeu (zhur) *m* play, game; set; **carte de ~** playing-card; **~ concours** quiz; **~ de dames** draughts; checkers *plAm*; **~ de quilles** bowling; **terrain de jeux** playground

jeudi (zhur-*dee*) *m* Thursday

jeune (zhurn) *adj* young

jeunesse (zhur-*nehss*) *f* youth

joaillerie (zhwigh-*ree*) *f* jewellery

jockey (zho-*kay*) *m* jockey

joie (zhwah) *f* joy, gladness

***joindre** (zhwa*ng*dr) *v* join, connect; attach, enclose

jointure (zhwa*ng*-*tewr*) *f* knuckle

joli (zho-*lee*) *adj* fine, nice, pretty, good-looking

jonc (zhaw*ng*) *m* rush

jonction (zhaw*ng*k-s*ᵞawng*) *f* junction

jonquille (zhaw*ng*-*keey*) *f* daffodil

Jordanie (zhor-dah-*nee*) *f* Jordan

Jordanien (zhor-dah-*n*ᵞ*ang*) *m* Jordanian

jordanien (zhor-dah-*n*ᵞ*ang*) *adj* Jordanian

joue (zhoo) *f* cheek

jouer (zhoo-*ay*) *v* play; act

jouet (zhoo-*ay*) *m* toy

joueur (zhoo-*ūīr*) *m* player

joug (zhoo) *m* yoke

jouir de (zhoo-*eer*) enjoy

jour (zhōōr) *m* day; **de ~** by day; **~ de fête** holiday; **~ de la semaine** weekday; **~ ouvrable** working day; **l'autre ~** recently; **par ~** per day; **un ~ ou l'autre** some day

journal (zhoor-*nahl*) *m* newspaper, paper; diary; **~ du matin** morning paper

journalier (zhoor-nah-*l*ᵞ*ay*) *adj* daily

journalisme (zhoor-nah-*leesm*) *m* journalism

journaliste (zhoor-nah-*leest*) *m* journalist

journée (zhoor-*nay*) *f* day

joyau (zhwah-ᵞ*oa*) *m* gem

joyeux (zhwah-ᵞ*ur*) *adj* joyful, cheerful, merry, glad

juge (zhe*wzh*) *m* judge

jugement (zhewzh-*mahng*) *m* judgment; sentence

juger (zhew-*zhay*) *v* judge

juif (zhweef) *adj* Jewish; *m* Jew

juillet (zhwee-ᵞ*ay*) July

juin (zhwa*ng*) June

jumeaux (zhew-*moa*) *mpl* twins *pl*

jumelles (zhew-*mehl*) *fpl* field glasses, binoculars *pl*

jument (zhew-*mahng*) *f* mare

jungle (zhaw*ng*gl) *f* jungle

jupe (zhewp) *f* skirt

jupon (zhew-*pawng*) *m* underskirt

jurer (zhew-*ray*) *v* vow, *swear; curse

juridique (zhew-ree-*deek*) *adj* legal

juriste (zhew-*reest*) *m* lawyer

juron (zhew-*rawng*) *m* curse

jury (zhew-*ree*) *m* jury

jus (zhew) *m* juice; gravy; **~ de fruits** squash

jusque (zhewsk) *prep* to; **jusqu'à**

prep till; until; **jusqu'à ce que** till

juste (zhewst) *adj* just, righteous, right, fair; appropriate, proper, correct, exact; tight; *adv* just

justement (zhew-ster-*mahng*) *adv* rightly

justice (zhew-*steess*) *f* justice

justifier (zhew-stee-f*Y*ay) *v* justify

juteux (zhew-*tur*) *adj* juicy

juvénile (zhew-vay-*neel*) *adj* juvenile

K

kaki (kah-*kee*) *m* khaki

kangourou (kahng-goo-*roo*) *m* kangaroo

Kenya (kay-n*Y*ah) *m* Kenya

kilo (kee-*loa*) *m* kilogram

kilométrage (kee-lo-may-*traazh*) *m* distance in kilometres

kilomètre (kee-lo-*mehtr*) *m* kilometre

kiosque (k*Y*osk) *m* kiosk; ~ **à journaux** newsstand

klaxon (klahk-*sawng*) *m* hooter; horn

klaxonner (klahk-so-*nay*) *v* hoot; toot *vAm*, honk *vAm*

L

la (lah) *art* the; *pron* her

là (lah) *adv* there

là-bas (lah-*bah*) *adv* over there

labeur (lah-*būrr*) *m* labour

laboratoire (lah-bo-rah-*twaar*) *m* laboratory; ~ **de langues** language laboratory

labourer (lah-boo-*ray*) *v* plough

labyrinthe (lah-bee-*rangt*) *m* maze, labyrinth

lac (lahk) *m* lake

lacet (lah-*say*) *m* shoe-lace, lace

lâche (laash) *m* coward; *adj* cowardly; loose

lâcher (lah-*shay*) *v* *let go

lagune (lah-*gewn*) *f* lagoon

laid (lay) *adj* ugly

laine (lehn) *f* wool; **en** ~ woollen; ~ **à repriser** darning wool; ~ **peignée** worsted

laisse (lehss) *f* leash, lead

laisser (lay-*say*) *v* *let, *leave; *leave behind

lait (lay) *m* milk

laitance (lay-*tahngss*) *f* roe

laiterie (leh-*tree*) *f* dairy

laiteux (lay-*tur*) *adj* milky

laitier (lay-t*Y*ay) *m* milkman

laiton (lay-*tawng*) *m* brass

laitue (lay-*tew*) *f* lettuce

lambrissage (lahng-bree-*saazh*) *m* panelling

lame (lahm) *f* blade; ~ **de rasoir** razor-blade

lamentable (lah-mahng-*tahbl*) *adj* lamentable

lampadaire (lahng-pah-*dair*) *m* lamp-post

lampe (lahngp) *f* lamp; ~ **de poche** torch; ~ **de travail** reading-lamp; **lampe-tempête** *f* hurricane lamp

lance (lahngss) *f* spear

lancement (lahng-*smahng*) *m* throw; launching

lancer (lahng-*say*) *v* *cast, toss, *throw; launch

lande (lahngd) *f* heath, moor

langage (lahng-*gaazh*) *m* speech

langue (lahngg) *f* tongue; language; ~ **maternelle** native language, mother tongue

lanterne (lahng-*tehrn*) *f* lantern

lapin (lah-*pang*) *m* rabbit

laque (lahk) *f* varnish; ~ **capillaire** hair-spray

lard (laar) *m* bacon

large (lahrzh) *adj* wide, broad; generous, liberal

largeur (lahr-*zhŭrr*) *f* width, breadth

larme (lahrm) *f* tear

laryngite (lah-rang-*zheet*) *f* laryngitis

las (lah) *adj* (f ~se) weary; ~ **de** tired of

latitude (lah-tee-*tewd*) *f* latitude

lavable (lah-*vahbl*) *adj* washable, fast-dyed

lavabo (lah-vah-*boa*) *m* wash-stand, wash-basin

lavage (lah-*vaazh*) *m* washing

laver (lah-*vay*) *v* wash

laverie automatique (lah-vree oa-toa-mah-*teek*) launderette

laxatif (lahk-sah-*teef*) *m* laxative

le[1] (ler) *art* (f la, pl les) the

le[2] (ler) *pron* (f la) him; it

leader (lee-*dair*) *m* leader

lécher (lay-*shay*) *v* lick

leçon (ler-*sawng*) *f* lesson

lecteur (lehk-*tŭrr*) *m* reader

lecture (lehk-*tewr*) *f* reading

légal (lay-*gahl*) *adj* legal, lawful

légalisation (lay-gah-lee-zah-*sawng*) *f* legalization

légation (lay-gah-*sawng*) *f* legation

léger (lay-*zhay*) *adj* (f légère) slight, light; weak, gentle

légitime (lay-zhee-*teem*) *adj* legitimate, legal; just

legs (lay) *m* legacy

légume (lay-*gewm*) *m* vegetable

lendemain (lahngd-*mang*) *m* next day

lent (lahng) *adj* slow; slack

lentille (lahng-*teey*) *f* lens

lèpre (lehpr) *f* leprosy

lequel (ler-*kehl*) *pron* (f laquelle; pl lesquels, lesquelles) which

les (lay) *art* the; *pron* them

lésion (lay-z*Yawng*) *f* injury

lessive (lay-*seev*) *f* washing, laundry

lettre (lehtr) *f* letter; **boîte aux lettres** pillar-box; ~ **de crédit** letter of credit; ~ **de recommandation** letter of recommendation; ~ **recommandée** registered letter

leur (lŭrr) *adj* their; *pron* them

levée (ler-*vay*) *f* collection

lever (ler-*vay*) *v* lift; ~ **du jour** daybreak; **se** ~ *rise, *get up

levier (ler-v*Yay*) *m* lever; ~ **de vitesse** gear lever

lèvre (laivr) *f* lip

lévrier (lay-vr*Yay*) *m* greyhound

levure (ler-*vewr*) *f* yeast

liaison (l*Yay*-*zawng*) *f* affair

Liban (lee-*bahng*) *m* Lebanon

Libanais (lee-bah-*nay*) *m* Lebanese

libanais (lee-bah-*nay*) *adj* Lebanese

libéral (lee-bay-*rahl*) *adj* liberal

libération (lee-bay-rah-s*Yawng*) *f* liberation

libérer (lee-bay-*ray*) *v* release; liberate

Libéria (lee-bay-r*Yah*) *m* Liberia

Libérien (lee-bay-r*Yang*) *m* Liberian

libérien (lee-bay-r*Yang*) *adj* Liberian

liberté (lee-behr-*tay*) *f* freedom, liberty

libraire (lee-*brair*) *m* bookseller

librairie (lee-bray-*ree*) *f* bookstore

libre (leebr) *adj* free

libre-service (leebr-sehr-*veess*) *m* self-service

licence (lee-*sahngss*) *f* permission, licence

licencier (lee-sahng-s*Yay*) *v* fire

lien (l*Yang*) *m* band; link

lier (lee-*ay*) *v* *bind

lierre (l*Yair*) *m* ivy

lieu (l*Yur*) *m* spot; **au** ~ **de** instead of; *avoir ~ *take place; ~ **de naissance** place of birth; ~ **de rencontre** meeting-place

lièvre (l*Yaivr*) *m* hare

ligne (leeñ) *f* line; ~ **aérienne** airline; ~ **d'arrivée** finish; ~ **de pêche** fishing line; ~ **intérieure** extension; ~ **principale** main line

ligue (leeg) f union, league

lime (leem) f file; ~ **à ongles** nail-file

limette (lee-*meht*) f lime

limite (lee-*meet*) f limit, boundary, bound; ~ **de vitesse** speed limit

limiter (lee-mee-*tay*) v limit

limonade (lee-mo-*nahd*) f lemonade

linge (langzh) m linen

lingerie (lang-*zhree*) f lingerie

lion (lYawng) m lion

liqueur (lee *kūr*) f liqueur

liquide (lee-*keed*) m fluid; adj liquid

***lire** (leer) v *read

lis (leess) m lily

lisible (lee-*zeebl*) adj legible

lisse (leess) adj smooth, level, even

liste (leest) f list; ~ **d'attente** waiting-list

lit (lee) m bed; ~ **de camp** campbed; cot nAm; **lits jumeaux** twin beds

literie (lee-*tree*) f bedding

litige (lee-*teezh*) m dispute

litre (leetr) m litre

littéraire (lee-tay-*rair*) adj literary

littérature (lee-tay-rah-*tēwr*) f literature

littoral (lee-to-*rahl*) m sea-coast

livraison (lee-vreh-*zawng*) f delivery

livre¹ (leevr) m book; ~ **de cuisine** cookery-book; cookbook nAm; ~ **de poche** paperback

livre² (leevr) f pound

livrer (lee-*vray*) v deliver

local (lo-*kahl*) adj local

localiser (lo-kah-lee-*zay*) v locate

localité (lo-kah-lee-*tay*) f locality

locataire (lo-kah-*tair*) m tenant

location (lo-kah-*sYawng*) f lease; **donner en** ~ lease; ~ **de voitures** car hire; car rental Am

locomotive (lo-ko-mo-*teev*) f locomotive, engine

locution (lo-kew-*sYawng*) f phrase

loge (lozh) f dressing-room

logement (lozh-*mahng*) m lodgings pl, accommodation

loger (lo-*zhay*) v accommodate; lodge

logeur (lo-*zhūr*) m landlord

logeuse (lo-*zhūz*) f landlady

logique (lo-*zheek*) f logic; adj logical

loi (lwah) f law

loin (lwang) adv away, far; **plus** ~ further

lointain (lwang-*tang*) adj far-off, remote

loisir (lwah-*zeer*) m leisure

long (lawng) adj (f longue) long; **en** ~ lengthways; **le** ~ **de** past, along

longitude (lawng-zhee-*tewd*) f longitude

longtemps (lawng-*tahng*) adv long

longueur (lawng-*gūr*) f length; ~ **d'onde** wave-length

lopin (lo-*pang*) m plot

lors de (lor der) at the time of

lorsque (lorsk) conj when

lot (loa) m batch

loterie (lo-*tree*) f lottery

lotion (lo-*sYawng*) f lotion

louange (loo-*ahngzh*) f glory

louche (loosh) adj cross-eyed

louer (loo-*ay*) v hire, rent, lease; *let; engage; praise; **à** ~ for hire

loup (loo) m wolf

lourd (lōōr) adj heavy

loyal (lwah-*Yahl*) adj true, loyal

loyer (lwah-*Yay*) m rent

lubie (lew-*bee*) f whim, fad

lubrifiant (lew-bree-*fYahng*) m lubrication oil

lubrification (lew-bree-fee-kah-*sYawng*) f lubrication

lubrifier (lew-bree-*fYay*) v lubricate

lueur (lwūr) f gleam

luge (lewzh) *f* sleigh, sledge
lugubre (lew-*gewbr*) *adj* creepy
lui (lwee) *pron* him; her; **lui-même** *pron* himself
luisant (lwee-*zahng*) *adj* glossy
lumbago (lawng-bah-*goa*) *m* lumbago
lumière (lew-*m*y*air*) *f* light; ~ **du jour** daylight; ~ **du soleil** sunlight; ~ **latérale** sidelight
lumineux (lew-mee-*nur*) *adj* luminous
lundi (lurng-*dee*) *m* Monday
lune (lewn) *f* moon; **clair de ~** moonlight; ~ **de miel** honeymoon
lunettes (lew-*neht*) *fpl* spectacles, glasses; ~ **de plongée** goggles *pl*; ~ **de soleil** sun-glasses *pl*
lustre (lewstr) *m* gloss
lustrer (lew-*stray*) *v* brush
lutte (lewt) *f* strife; fight, combat, battle, struggle
lutter (lew-*tay*) *v* struggle; combat
luxe (lewks) *m* luxury
luxueux (lewk-*swur*) *adj* luxurious

M

mâcher (mah-*shay*) *v* chew
machine (mah-*sheen*) *f* engine, machine; ~ **à coudre** sewing-machine; ~ **à écrire** typewriter; ~ **à laver** washing-machine
machinerie (mah-sheen-*ree*) *f* machinery
mâchoire (mah-*shwaar*) *f* jaw
maçon (mah-*sawng*) *m* bricklayer
madame (mah-*dahm*) madam
mademoiselle (mahd-mwah-*zehl*) miss
magasin (mah-gah-*zang*) *m* store; warehouse, store-house; **grand ~** department store; ~ **de chaussures** shoe-shop; ~ **de jouets** toyshop; ~ **de spiritueux** off-licence
magie (mah-*zhee*) *f* magic

magique (mah-*zheek*) *adj* magic
magistrat (mah-zhee-*strah*) *m* magistrate
magnétique (mah-ñay-*teek*) *adj* magnetic
magnéto (mah-ñay-*toa*) *f* magneto
magnétophone (mah-ñay-to-*fon*) *m* tape-recorder
magnétoscope (mah-ñay-to-*skop*) *m* video recorder
magnifique (mah-ñee-*feek*) *adj* splendid, gorgeous, magnificent
mai (may) May
maigre (maigr) *adj* thin, lean
maigrir (meh-*greer*) *v* slim
maille (migh) *f* mesh
maillet (mah-y*ay*) *m* mallet
maillon (mah-y*awng*) *m* link
maillot de bain (mah-y*oa* der bang) bathing-suit, swim-suit
main (mang) *f* hand; **fait à la ~** hand-made
main-d'œuvre (mang-*dūīvr*) *f* manpower
maintenant (mangt-*nahng*) *adv* now; **jusqu'à ~** so far
*****maintenir** (mangt-*neer*) *v* maintain
maire (mair) *m* mayor
mairie (may-*ree*) *f* town hall
mais (may) *conj* but
maïs (mah-*eess*) *m* maize; ~ **en épi** corn on the cob
maison (may-*zawng*) *f* house; home; **à la ~** at home; **fait à la ~** homemade; **maison-bateau** houseboat; ~ **de campagne** country house; ~ **de repos** rest-home
maître (maitr) *m* master; ~ **d'école** teacher, schoolmaster; ~ **d'hôtel** head-waiter
maîtresse (meh-*trehss*) *f* mistress; ~ **de maison** mistress
maîtriser (meh-tree-*zay*) *v* master
majeur (mah-*zhūr*) *adj* major; su-

perior, main; of age

majorité (mah-zho-ree-*tay*) *f* bulk, majority

majuscule (mah-zhew-*skewl*) *f* capital letter

mal (mahl) *m* (pl maux) evil, harm; mischief; **faire du ~* harm; **faire ~ à* ache; **hurt; ~ à l'aise* uneasy; *~ au cœur* sickness; *~ au dos* backache; *~ au ventre* stomachache; *~ aux dents* toothache; *~ de gorge* sore throat; *~ de l'air* airsickness; *~ de mer* seasickness; *~ d'estomac* stomach-ache; *~ de tête* headache; *~ d'oreille* earache; *~ du pays* homesickness

malade (mah-*lahd*) *adj* sick, ill

maladie (mah-lah-*dee*) *f* sickness, illness, disease, ailment; *~ vénérienne* venereal disease

maladroit (mah-lah-*drwah*) *adj* clumsy, awkward

Malais (mah-*lay*) *m* Malay

malaisien (mah-lay-z*Yang*) *adj* Malaysian

malaria (mah-lah-*rYah*) *f* malaria

malchance (mahl-*shahngss*) *f* bad luck

mâle (maal) *adj* male

malentendu (mah-lahng-tahng-*dew*) *m* misunderstanding

malgré (mahl-*gray*) *prep* in spite of, despite

malheur (mah-*lūrr*) *m* misfortune

malheureusement (mah-lur-rurz-*mahng*) *adv* unfortunately

malheureux (mah-lur-*rur*) *adj* unhappy, unfortunate; miserable, sad

malhonnête (mah-lo-*neht*) *adj* dishonest, crooked

malice (mah-*leess*) *f* mischief

malicieux (mah-lee-s*Yur*) *adj* mischievous

malin (mah-*lang*) *adj* (f maligne) malignant; sly; bright

malle (mahl) *f* trunk

mallette (mah-*leht*) *f* grip *nAm*

malodorant (mah-lo-do-*rahng*) *adj* smelly

malpropre (mahl-*propr*) *adj* foul, unclean

malsain (mahl-*sang*) *adj* unsound, unhealthy

malveillant (mahl-veh-*Yahng*) *adj* spiteful; malicious

maman (mah-*mahng*) *f* mum

mammifère (mah-mee-*fair*) *m* mammal

mammouth (mah-*moot*) *m* mammoth

manche (mahngsh) *m* handle; *f* sleeve; *La Manche* English Channel

manchette (mahng-*sheht*) *f* cuff; headline

mandarine (mahng-dah-*reen*) *f* tangerine, mandarin

mandat (mahng-*dah*) *m* mandate

mandat-poste (mahng-dah-*post*) *m* money order, postal order; mail order *Am*

manège (mah-*naizh*) *m* riding-school

mangeoire (mahng-*zhwaar*) *f* manger

manger (mahng-*zhay*) *v* *eat; *m* food

maniable (mah-*nYahbl*) *adj* manageable

manier (mah-*nYay*) *v* handle

manière (mah-*nYair*) *f* way, manner; *de la même ~* likewise; *de ~ que* so that

manifestation (mah-nee-feh-stah-s*Yawng*) *f* demonstration

manifestement (mah-nee-feh-ster-*mahng*) *adv* apparently

manifester (mah-nee-feh-*stay*) *v* express; demonstrate

manipuler (mah-nee-pew-*lay*) *v* handle

mannequin (mahn-*kang*) *m* model, mannequin

manoir (mah-*nwaar*) *m* mansion,

manor-house

manquant (mahng-*kahng*) *adj* missing

manque (mahngk) *m* want, shortage, lack

manquer (mahng-*kay*) *v* fail, lack; miss

manteau (mahng-*toa*) *m* coat, cloak; ~ **de fourrure** fur coat

manucure (mah-new-*kewr*) *f* manicure

manuel (mah-*nwehl*) *m* textbook, handbook; *adj* manual; ~ **de conversation** phrase-book

manuscrit (mah-new-*skree*) *m* manuscript

maquereau (mah-*kroa*) *m* mackerel

maquillage (mah-kee-*Yaazh*) *m* make-up

marais (mah-*ray*) *m* marsh, swamp, bog

marbre (mahrbr) *m* marble

marchand (mahr-*shahng*) *m* merchant; tradesman, dealer; ~ **de journaux** newsagent; ~ **de légumes** greengrocer; vegetable merchant; ~ **de volaille** poulterer

marchander (mahr-shahng-*day*) *v* bargain

marchandise (mahr-shahng-*deez*) *f* merchandise; wares *pl*, goods *pl*

marche (mahrsh) *f* march; step; **faire ~ arrière* reverse

marché (mahr-*shay*) *m* market; **bon ~** cheap; inexpensive; ~ **des valeurs** stock market; ~ **noir** black market; **place du ~** market-place

marcher (mahr-*shay*) *v* walk, step, **go*; march; **faire ~* fool

mardi (mahr-*dee*) *m* Tuesday

marécageux (mah-ray-kah-*zhur*) *adj* marshy

marée (mah-*ray*) *f* tide; ~ **basse** low tide; ~ **haute** flood; high tide

margarine (mahr-gah-*reen*) *f* margarine

marge (mahrzh) *f* margin

mari (mah-*ree*) *m* husband

mariage (mah-*rYaazh*) *m* matrimony, marriage; wedding

marié (mah-*rYay*) *m* bridegroom

se marier (mah-*rYay*) marry

marin (mah-*rang*) *m* sailor; seaman

marinade (mah-ree-*nahd*) *f* pickles *pl*

marine (mah-*reen*) *f* navy; seascape

maritime (mah-ree-*teem*) *adj* maritime

marmelade (mahr-mer-*lahd*) *f* marmalade

marmite (mahr-*meet*) *f* pot

Maroc (mah-*rok*) *m* Morocco

Marocain (mah-ro-*kang*) *m* Moroccan

marocain (mah-ro-*kang*) *adj* Moroccan

marque (mahrk) *f* mark; sign, brand; tick; ~ **de fabrique** trademark

marquer (mahr-*kay*) *v* mark

marquise (mahr-*keez*) *f* awning

marron (mah-*rawng*) *m* chestnut

mars (mahrs) March

marteau (mahr-*toa*) *m* hammer

marteler (mahr-ter-*lay*) *v* thump

martyr (mahr-*teer*) *m* martyr

masculin (mah-skew-*lang*) *adj* masculine

masque (mahsk) *m* mask; ~ **de beauté** face-pack

massage (mah-*saazh*) *m* massage; ~ **facial** face massage

masse (mahss) *f* mass; bulk; crowd

masser (mah-*say*) *v* massage

masseur (mah-*surr*) *m* masseur

massif (mah-*seef*) *adj* massive, solid

massue (mah-*sew*) *f* club

mat (maht) *adj* mat, dull, dim

mât (mah) *m* mast

match (mahch) *m* match; ~ **de boxe** boxing match; ~ **de football** football match

matelas (mah-*tlah*) *m* mattress

matériau (mah-tay-*rYoa*) *m* material

matériel (mah-tay-r^yehl) m material; adj material; substantial

maternel (mah-tehr-nehl) adj motherly

mathématique (mah-tay-mah-teek) adj mathematical

mathématiques (mah-tay-mah-teek) fpl mathematics

matière (mah-t^yair) f matter; ~ première raw material

matin (mah-tang) m morning; ce ~ this morning

matinée (mah-tee-nay) f morning

matrimonial (mah-tree-mo-n^yahl) adj matrimonial

maturité (mah-tew-ree-tay) f maturity

***maudire** (moa-deer) v curse

mausolée (moa-zo-lay) m mausoleum

mauvais (moa-vay) adj bad; wicked, ill, evil; le plus ~ worst

mauve (mōav) adj mauve

maximum (mahk-see-mom) m maximum; au ~ at most

mazout (mah-zoot) m fuel oil

me (mer) pron me; myself

mécanicien (may-kah-nee-s^yang) m mechanic

mécanique (may-kah-neek) adj mechanical

mécanisme (may-kah-neesm) m mechanism, machinery

méchant (may-shahng) adj evil; naughty, nasty, ill

mèche (mehsh) f fuse

mécontent (may-kawng-tahng) adj discontented

médaille (may-digh) f medal

médecin (may-dsang) m physician, doctor; ~ généraliste general practitioner

médecine (may-dseen) f medicine

médiateur (may-d^yah-tūrr) m mediator

médical (may-dee-kahl) adj medical

médicament (may-dee-kah-mahng) m medicine, drug

médiéval (may-d^yay-vahl) adj mediaeval

méditer (may-dee-tay) v meditate

Méditerranée (may-dee-tay-rah-nay) f Mediterranean

méduse (may-dewz) f jelly-fish

méfiance (may-f^yahngss) f suspicion

méfiant (may-f^yahng) adj suspicious

se méfier de (may-f^yay) mistrust

meilleur (meh-^yūrr) adj better; le ~ best

mélancolie (may lahng ko lcc) f melancholy

mélancolique (may-lahng-ko-leek) adj sad

mélange (may-lahngzh) m mixture

mélanger (may-lahng-zhay) v mix

mêler (may-lay) v mix; se ~ de interfere with

mélo (may-loa) m tear-jerker

mélodie (may-lo-dee) f melody

mélodrame (may-lo-drahm) m melodrama

melon (mer-lawng) m melon

membrane (mahng-brahn) f diaphragm

membre (mahngbr) m member, associate; limb

mémé (may-may) f grandmother

même (mehm) adj same; adv even; de ~ also

mémoire (may-mwaar) f memory

mémorable (may-mo-rahbl) adj memorable

mémorandum (may-mo-rahng-dom) m memo

mémorial (may-mo-r^yahl) m memorial

menaçant (mer-nah-sahng) adj threatening

menace (mer-nahss) f threat

menacer (mer-nah-say) v threaten

ménage (may-naazh) m housekeeping,

household

ménagère (may-nah-*zhair*) f housewife

mendiant (mahng-*d*ᵞ*ahng*) m beggar

mendier (mahng-*d*ᵞ*ay*) v beg

mener (mer-*nay*) v *take, *lead

menottes (mer-*not*) fpl handcuffs pl

mensonge (mahng-*sawngzh*) m lie

menstruation (mahng-strew-ah-*s*ᵞ*awng*) f menstruation

mensuel (mahng-*swehl*) adj monthly

mental (mahng-*tahl*) adj mental; **aliéné ~** lunatic

menthe (mahngt) f peppermint, mint

mention (mahng-*s*ᵞ*awng*) f mention

mentionner (mahng-sᵞo-*nay*) v mention

***mentir** (mahng-*teer*) v lie

menton (mahng-*tawng*) m chin

menu[1] (mer-*new*) m menu; **~ fixe** set menu

menu[2] (mer-*new*) adj minor

menuisier (mer-nwee-zᵞ*ay*) m carpenter

mépris (may-*pree*) m contempt, scorn

méprise (may-*preez*) f mistake

mépriser (may-pree-*zay*) v despise, scorn

mer (mair) f sea

mercerie (mehr-ser-*ree*) f haberdashery

merci (mehr-*see*) thank you

mercredi (mehr-krer-*dee*) m Wednesday

mercure (mehr-*ke̅w̅r*) m mercury

mère (mair) f mother

méridional (may-ree-dᵞo-*nahl*) adj southern, southerly

mérite (may-*reet*) m merit

mériter (may-ree-*tay*) v merit, deserve

merlan (mehr-*lahng*) m whiting

merle (mehrl) m blackbird

merveille (mehr-*vay*) f marvel

merveilleux (mehr-veh-ᵞ*ur*) adj marvellous; fine, wonderful

mesquin (meh-*skang*) adj mean, stingy

message (meh-*saazh*) m message

messager (meh-sah-*zhay*) m messenger

messe (mehss) f Mass

mesure (mer-*ze̅w̅r*) f measure; size; **en ~ able**; **fait sur ~** tailor-made

mesurer (mer-zew-*ray*) v measure

métal (may-*tahl*) m metal

métallique (may-tah-*leek*) adj metal

méthode (may-*tod*) f method

méthodique (may-to-*deek*) adj methodical

méticuleux (may-tee-kew-*lur*) adj precise

métier (may-tᵞ*ay*) m trade, profession

mètre (mehtr) m metre

métrique (may-*treek*) adj metric

métro (may-*troa*) m underground; subway *nAm*

***mettre** (mehtr) v *put; *put on

meuble (murbl) m piece of furniture; **meubles** furniture

meubler (mur-*blay*) v furnish; **non meublé** unfurnished

meunier (mur-nᵞ*ay*) m miller

meurtrier (murr-tree-*ay*) m murderer

Mexicain (mehk-see-*kang*) m Mexican

mexicain (mehk-see-*kang*) adj Mexican

Mexique (mehk-*seek*) m Mexico

miche (meesh) f loaf

microbe (mee-*krob*) m germ

microphone (mee-kro-*fon*) m microphone

microsillon (mee-kro-see-ᵞ*awng*) m long-playing record

midi (mee-*dee*) m midday, noon

miel (mᵞehl) m honey

le mien (ler mᵞ*ang*) mine

miette (mᵞeht) f crumb

mieux (mᵞur) adv better

migraine (mee-*grehn*) f migraine

milieu (mee-*l*Yur) *m* middle, midst; milieu; **au ~ de** among, amid; **du ~** middle

militaire (mee-lee-*tair*) *adj* military

mille (meel) *num* thousand; *m* mile

million (mee-*l*Yawng) *m* million

millionnaire (mee-*l*Yo-*nair*) *m* millionaire

mince (mangss) *adj* slim, thin

mine¹ (meen) *f* pit, mine; **~ d'or** goldmine

mine² (meen) *f* look

minerai (meen-*ray*) *m* ore

minéral (mee-nay-*rahl*) *m* mineral

minet (mee-*nay*) *m* pussy-cat

mineur (mee-*nūr*) *m* miner; minor; *adj* minor; under age

miniature (mee-n*Y*ah-*tewr*) *f* miniature

minimum (mee-nee-*mom*) *m* minimum

ministère (mee-nee-*stair*) *m* ministry

ministre (mee-*neestr*) *m* minister; **premier ~** Prime Minister

minorité (mee-no-ree-*tay*) *f* minority

minuit (mee-*nwee*) midnight

minuscule (mee-new-*skewl*) *adj* tiny, minute

minute (mee-*newt*) *f* minute

minutieux (mee-new-s*Y*ur) *adj* thorough

miracle (mee-*raakl*) *m* miracle, wonder

miraculeux (mee-rah-kew-*lur*) *adj* miraculous

miroir (mee-*rwaar*) *m* looking-glass, mirror

misaine (mee-*zehn*) *f* foresail

misérable (mee-zay-*rahbl*) *adj* miserable

misère (mee-*zair*) *f* misery

miséricorde (mee-zay-ree-*kord*) *f* mercy

miséricordieux (mee-zay-ree-kor-d*Y*ur) *adj* merciful

mite (meet) *f* moth

mi-temps (mee-*tahng*) *f* half-time

mixeur (meek-*sūr*) *m* mixer

mobile (mo-*beel*) *adj* mobile; movable

mode¹ (mod) *f* fashion; **à la ~** fashionable

mode² (mod) *m* fashion, manner; **~ d'emploi** directions for use

modèle (mo-*dehl*) *m* model

modeler (mo-*dlay*) *v* model

modéré (mo-day-*ray*) *adj* moderate

moderne (mo-*dehrn*) *adj* modern

modeste (mo-*dehst*) *adj* modest

modestie (mo-deh-*stee*) *f* modesty

modification (mo-dee-fee-kah-s*Y*awng) *f* change, alteration

modifier (mo-dee-f*Y*ay) *v* change, modify, alter

modiste (mo-*deest*) *f* milliner

moelle (mwahl) *f* marrow

moelleux (mwah-*lur*) *adj* mellow

mœurs (murrs) *fpl* morals

mohair (mo-*air*) *m* mohair

moi (mwah) *pron* me; **moi-même** *pron* myself

moindre (mwangdr) *adj* least; inferior

moine (mwahn) *m* monk

moineau (mwah-*noa*) *m* sparrow

moins (mwang) *adv* less; *prep* minus; **à ~ que** unless; **au ~** at least

mois (mwah) *m* month

moisi (mwah-*zee*) *adj* mouldy

moisissure (mwah-zee-*sewr*) *f* mildew

moisson (mwah-*sawng*) *f* harvest

moite (mwaht) *adj* moist; damp

moitié (mwah-t*Y*ay) *f* half; **à ~** half

molaire (mo-*lair*) *f* molar

mollet (mo-*lay*) *m* calf

moment (mo-*mahng*) *m* moment; while

momentané (mo-mahng-tah-*nay*) *adj* momentary

mon (mawng) *adj* (f ma, pl mes) my

monarchie (mo-nahr-*shee*) *f* monarchy

monarque (mo-*nahrk*) *m* monarch, ruler

monastère (mo-nah-*stair*) *m* monastery

monde (mawngd) *m* world; **tout le ~** everyone

mondial (mawng-*d*ʸ*ahl*) *adj* worldwide; global

monétaire (mo-nay-*tair*) *adj* monetary

monnaie (mo-*nay*) *f* currency; **~ étrangère** foreign currency; **petite ~** petty cash, change; **pièce de ~** coin

monopole (mo-no-*pol*) *m* monopoly

monotone (mo-no-*ton*) *adj* monotonous

monsieur (mer-s*ʸur*) *m* (pl messieurs) gentleman; mister; sir

mont (mawng) *m* mount

montagne (mawng-*tahñ*) *f* mountain

montagneux (mawng-tah-*ñur*) *adj* mountainous

montant (mawng-*tahng*) *m* amount

montée (mawng-*tay*) *f* rise; ascent

monter (mawng-*tay*) *v* *rise; ascend; *get on; assemble; mount; **se ~ à** amount to

monteur (mawng-*tūrr*) *m* mechanic

monticule (mawng-tee-*kewl*) *m* hillock

montre (mawngtr) *f* watch; **~ de gousset** pocket-watch; **~ à affichage numérique** digital watch

montrer (mawng-*tray*) *v* *show; display; **~ du doigt** point

monture (mawng-*tēwr*) *f* frame

monument (mo-new-*mahng*) *m* monument

se moquer de (mo-*kay*) mock

moquerie (mo-*kree*) *f* mockery

moral (mo-*rahl*) *adj* moral; *m* spirits

morale (mo-*rahl*) *f* moral

moralité (mo-rah-lee-*tay*) *f* morality

morceau (mor-*soa*) *m* piece, part; morsel, fragment, scrap, bit, lump; **~ de sucre** lump of sugar

mordache (mor-*dahsh*) *f* clamp

mordre (mordr) *v* *bite

morphine (mor-*feen*) *f* morphine, morphia

morsure (mor-*sēwr*) *f* bite

mort (mawr) *f* death; *adj* dead

mortel (mor-*tehl*) *adj* fatal; mortal

morue (mo-*rew*) *f* cod

mosaïque (mo-zah-*eek*) *f* mosaic

mosquée (mo-*skay*) *f* mosque

mot (moa) *m* word; **~ de passe** password

motel (mo-*tehl*) *m* motel

moteur (mo-*tūrr*) *m* motor, engine

motif (mo-*teef*) *m* cause, motive, occasion; pattern

motion (mo-s*ʸawng*) *f* motion

motocyclette (mo-to-see-*kleht*) *f* motor-cycle

mou (moo) *adj* (f molle) soft

mouche (moosh) *f* fly

mouchoir (moo-*shwaar*) *m* handkerchief; **~ de papier** tissue

***moudre** (moodr) *v* *grind

mouette (mweht) *f* gull; seagull

moufles (moofl) *fpl* mittens *pl*

mouiller (moo-*ʸay*) *v* wet; **mouillé** wet, moist

moule (mool) *f* mussel

moulin (moo-*lang*) *m* mill; **~ à paroles** chatterbox; **~ à vent** windmill

***mourir** (moo-*reer*) *v* die

mousse (mooss) *f* foam; moss

mousseline (moo-*sleen*) *f* muslin

mousser (moo-*say*) *v* foam

mousseux (moo-*sur*) *adj* sparkling

moustache (moo-*stahsh*) *f* moustache

moustiquaire (moo-stee-*kair*) *f* mosquito-net

moustique (moo-*steek*) *m* mosquito

moutarde (moo-*tahrd*) f mustard

mouton (moo-*tawng*) m sheep; mutton

mouvement (moov-*mahng*) m motion, movement

se *mouvoir (moo-*vwaar*) move

moyen (mwah-*Yang*) m means; adj medium, average

moyen-âge (mwah-*Yeh-naazh*) m Middle Ages

moyenne (mwah-*Yehn*) f mean, average; **en ~** on the average

muet (mway) adj dumb, mute

mugir (mew-*zheer*) v roar

mule (mewl) f mule

mulet (mew-*lay*) m mule; mullet

multiplication (mewl-tee-plee-kah-*sYawng*) f multiplication

multiplier (mewl-tee-plee-*ay*) v multiply

municipal (mew-nee-see-*pahl*) adj municipal

municipalité (mew-nee-see-pah-lee-*tay*) f municipality

munir de (mew-*neer*) provide with

mur (mēwr) m wall

mûr (mēwr) adj mature, ripe

mûre (mēwr) f blackberry; mulberry

muscade (mew-*skahd*) f nutmeg

muscle (mewskl) m muscle

musclé (mew-*sklay*) adj muscular

museau (mew-*zoa*) m snout

musée (mew-*zay*) m museum

musical (mew-zee-*kahl*) adj musical

musicien (mew-zee-*sYang*) m musician

musique (mew-*zeek*) f music; **~ pop** pop music

mutinerie (mew-teen-*ree*) f mutiny

mutuel (mew-*twehl*) adj mutual

myope (mYop) adj short-sighted

mystère (mee-*stair*) m mystery

mystérieux (mee-stay-*rYur*) adj mysterious

mythe (meet) m myth

N

nacre (nahkr) f mother-of-pearl

nager (nah-*zhay*) v *swim

nageur (nah-*zhūūr*) m swimmer

naïf (nah-*eef*) adj naïve

nain (nang) m dwarf

naissance (nay-*sahngss*) f birth

*naître (naitr) v *be born

nappe (nahp) f table-cloth

narcose (nahr-*kōāz*) f narcosis

narcotique (nahr-ko-*teek*) m narcotic

narine (nah-*reen*) f nostril

natation (nah-tah-*sYawng*) f swimming

nation (nah-*sYawng*) f nation

national (nah-sYo-*nahl*) adj national

nationaliser (nah-sYo-nah-lee-*zay*) v nationalize

nationalité (nah-sYo-nah-lee-*tay*) f nationality

nature (nah-*tēwr*) f nature; essence

naturel (nah-tew-*rehl*) adj natural

naturellement (nah-tew-rehl-*mahng*) adv naturally

naufrage (noa-*fraazh*) m shipwreck

nausée (noa-*zay*) f nausea

naval (nah-*vahl*) adj (pl ~s) naval

navetteur (nah-veh-*tūūr*) m commuter

navigable (nah-vee-*gahbl*) adj navigable

navigation (nah-vee-gah-*sYawng*) f navigation

naviguer (nah-vee-*gay*) v navigate; sail

navire (nah-*veer*) m ship; boat; **~ de guerre** man-of-war

né (nay) adj born

néanmoins (nay-ahng-*mwang*) adv nevertheless

nébuleux (nay-bew-*lur*) *adj* hazy

nécessaire (nay-say-*sair*) *adj* necessary; ~ **de toilette** toilet case

nécessité (nay-say-see-*tay*) *f* need, necessity

nécessiter (nay-say-see-*tay*) *v* demand

Néerlandais (nay-ehr-lah<del>ng</del>-*day*) *m* Dutchman

néerlandais (nay-ehr-lah<del>ng</del>-*day*) *adj* Dutch

néfaste (nay-*fahst*) *adj* fatal

négatif (nay-gah-*teef*) *m* negative; *adj* negative

négligé (nay-glee-*zhay*) *m* negligee

négligence (nay-glee-*zhah<del>ng</del>ss*) *f* neglect

négligent (nay-glee-*zhah<del>ng</del>*) *adj* careless, neglectful

négliger (nay-glee-*zhay*) *v* neglect

négociant (nay-go-s^y*ah<del>ng</del>*) *m* dealer; ~ **en vins** wine-merchant

négociation (nay-go-s^yah-s^y*aw<del>ng</del>*) *f* negotiation

négocier (nay-go-s^y*ay*) *v* negotiate

neige (naizh) *f* snow

neiger (nay-*zhay*) *v* snow

neigeux (neh-*zhur*) *adj* snowy

néon (nay-*aw<del>ng</del>*) *m* neon

nerf (nair) *m* nerve

nerveux (nehr-*vur*) *adj* nervous

net (neht) *adj* distinct; net

nettoyage (neh-twah-^y*aazh*) *m* cleaning

nettoyer (neh-twah-^y*ay*) *v* clean; ~ **à sec** dry-clean

neuf[1] (nurf) *adj* (f neuve) new

neuf[2] (nurf) *num* nine

neutre (nūrtr) *adj* neuter; neutral

neuvième (nur-v^y*ehm*) *num* ninth

neveu (ner-*vur*) *m* nephew

névralgie (nay-vrahl-*zhee*) *f* neuralgia

névrose (nay-*vrōaz*) *f* neurosis

nez (nay) *m* nose; **saignement de** ~ nosebleed

ni ... ni (nee) neither ... nor

nickel (nee-*kehl*) *m* nickel

nicotine (nee-ko-*teen*) *f* nicotine

nid (nee) *m* nest

nièce (n^yehss) *f* niece

nier (nee-*ay*) *v* deny

Nigeria (nee-zhay-r^y*ah*) *m* Nigeria

Nigérien (nee-zhay-r^y*ang*) *m* Nigerian

nigérien (nee-zhay-r^y*ang*) *adj* Nigerian

niveau (nee-*voa*) *m* level; ~ **de vie** standard of living; **passage à** ~ level crossing

niveler (nee-*vlay*) *v* level

noble (nobl) *adj* noble

noblesse (no-*blehss*) *f* nobility

nocturne (nok-*tewrn*) *adj* nightly

Noël (no-*ehl*) Christmas, Xmas

nœud (nur) *m* knot; ~ **papillon** bow tie

noir (nwaar) *adj* black; *m* Negro

noisette (nwah-*zeht*) *f* hazelnut

noix (nwah) *f* nut; walnut; ~ **de coco** coconut

nom (naw<del>ng</del>) *m* name; noun; denomination; **au** ~ **de** in the name of, on behalf of; ~ **de famille** family name, surname; ~ **de jeune fille** maiden name

nombre (naw<del>ng</del>br) *m* number; quantity; numeral

nombre de milles mileage

nombreux (naw<del>ng</del>-*brur*) *adj* numerous

nombril (naw<del>ng</del>-*bree*) *m* navel

nominal (no-mee-*nahl*) *adj* nominal

nomination (no-mee-nah-s^y*aw<del>ng</del>*) *f* nomination, appointment

nommer (no-*may*) *v* name; nominate, appoint

non (naw<del>ng</del>) no

nord (nawr) *m* north

nord-est (no-*rehst*) *m* north-east

nord-ouest (no-*rwehst*) *m* north-west

normal (nor-*mahl*) *adj* normal, regular

norme (norm) f standard

Norvège (nor-vaizh) f Norway

Norvégien (nor-vay-zhᵛang) m Norwegian

norvégien (nor-vay-zhᵛang) adj Norwegian

notaire (no-tair) m notary

notamment (no-tah-mahng) adv namely

note (not) f note; mark; bill; check nAm

noter (no-tay) v note, *write down; notice

notifier (no-tee-fᵛay) v notify

notion (noa-sᵛawng) f notion; idea

notoire (no-twaar) adj notorious

notre (notr) adj our

nouer (noo-ay) v tie, knot

nougat (noo-gah) m nougat

nourrir (noo-reer) v *feed; **nourrissant** nourishing

nourrisson (noo-ree-sawng) m infant

nourriture (noo-ree-tewr) f food; fare

nous (noo) pron we; ourselves, us; **nous-mêmes** pron ourselves

nouveau (noo-voa) adj (nouvel; f nouvelle) new; **de ~** again; **Nouvel An** New Year

nouvelle (noo-vehl) f notice; **nouvelles** news, tidings pl

Nouvelle-Zélande (noo-vehl-zay-lahngd) f New Zealand

novembre (no-vahngbr) November

noyau (nwah-ᵛoa) m stone; nucleus

noyer (nwah-ᵛay) v drown; **se ~** *be drowned

nu (new) adj naked, nude; bare; m nude

nuage (nwaazh) m cloud; **nuages** clouds

nuageux (nwah-zhur) adj cloudy, overcast

nuance (nwahngss) f nuance; shade

nucléaire (new-klay-air) adj atomic, nuclear

*nuire (nweer) v harm

nuisible (nwee-zeebl) adj hurtful, harmful

nuit (nwee) f night; **boîte de ~** cabaret; **cette ~** tonight; **de ~** by night, overnight; **tarif de ~** night rate

nul (newl) adj (f nulle) invalid, void

numéro (new-may-roa) m number; act; **~ d'immatriculation** registration number; licence number Am

nuque (newk) f nape of the neck

nutritif (new-tree-teef) adj nutritious

nylon (nee-lawng) m nylon

O

oasis (oa-ah-zeess) f oasis

obéir (o-bay-eer) v obey

obéissance (o-bay-ee-sahngss) f obedience

obéissant (o-bay-ee-sahng) adj obedient

obèse (o-baiz) adj stout, corpulent

obésité (o-bay-zee-tay) f fatness

objecter (ob-zhehk-tay) v object

objectif (ob-zhehk-teef) m target, objective, object, goal; adj objective

objection (ob-zhehk-sᵛawng) f objection; ***faire ~ à** object to; mind

objet (ob-zhay) m object; **objets de valeur** valuables pl; **objets trouvés** lost and found

obligation (o-blee-gah-sᵛawng) f bond

obligatoire (o-blee-gah-twaar) adj compulsory, obligatory

obligeant (o-blee-zhahng) adj obliging

obliger (o-blee-zhay) v oblige; force

oblique (o-bleek) adj slanting

oblong (o-blawng) adj (f oblongue) oblong

obscène (o-*psehn*) *adj* obscene

obscur (op-*skewr*) *adj* obscure; dim, dark

obscurité (op-skew-ree-*tay*) *f* dark

observation (o-psehr-vah-s*Yawng*) *f* observation

observatoire (o-psehr-vah-*twaar*) *m* observatory

observer (o-psehr-*vay*) *v* watch, observe; notice, note

obsession (o-pseh-s*Yawng*) *f* obsession

obstacle (op-*stahkl*) *m* obstacle

obstiné (op-stee-*nay*) *adj* pig-headed, obstinate; dogged

obstruer (op-strew-*ay*) *v* block

***obtenir** (op-ter-*neer*) *v* *get; obtain

occasion (o-kah-z*Yawng*) *f* chance, opportunity; occasion; **d'occasion** second-hand

occident (ok-see-*dahng*) *m* west

occidental (ok-see-dahng-*tahl*) *adj* western, westerly

occupant (o-kew-*pahng*) *m* occupant

occupation (o-kew-pah-s*Yawng*) *f* occupation; business

occuper (o-kew-*pay*) *v* occupy; *take up; **occupé** busy, engaged, occupied; **s'occuper de** attend to, look after; *take care of, see to, *deal with

océan (o-say-*ahng*) *m* ocean; **Océan Atlantique** Atlantic; **Océan Pacifique** Pacific Ocean

octobre (ok-*tobr*) October

oculiste (o-kew-*leest*) *m* oculist

odeur (o-*dūr*) *f* smell, odour

œil (ur*ee*) *m* (pl yeux) eye; **coup d'œil** look; glance; glimpse

œuf (urf) *m* egg; **œufs de poisson** roe

œuvre (ūrvr) *m* work; ~ **d'art** work of art

offense (o-*fahngss*) *f* offence

offenser (o-fahng-*say*) *v* injure, *hurt, wound, offend; **s'offenser de** resent

offensif (o-fahng-*seef*) *adj* offensive

offensive (o-fahng-*seev*) *f* offensive

officiel (o-fee-s*Yehl*) *adj* official

officier (o-fee-s*Yay*) *m* officer

officieux (o-fee-s*Yur*) *adj* unofficial

offre (ofr) *f* offer; supply

***offrir** (o-*freer*) *v* offer

oie (wah) *f* goose

oignon (o-*ñawng*) *m* onion; bulb

oiseau (wah-*zoa*) *m* bird; ~ **de mer** sea-bird

oisif (wah-*zeef*) *adj* idle

olive (o-*leev*) *f* olive

ombragé (awng-brah-*zhay*) *adj* shady

ombre (awngbr) *f* shadow, shade; ~ **à paupières** eye-shadow

omelette (om-*leht*) *f* omelette

***omettre** (o-*mehtr*) *v* *leave out, omit; fail

omnibus (om-nee-*bewss*) *m* stopping train

omnipotent (om-nee-po-*tahng*) *adj* omnipotent

on (awng) *pron* one

oncle (awngkl) *m* uncle

ondulation (awng-dew-lah-s*Yawng*) *f* wave

ondulé (awng-dew-*lay*) *adj* wavy, undulating

ongle (awnggl) *m* nail

onguent (awng-*gahng*) *m* ointment, salve

onyx (o-*neeks*) *m* onyx

onze (awngz) *num* eleven

onzième (awng-z*Yehm*) *num* eleventh

opale (o-*pahl*) *f* opal

opéra (o-pay-*rah*) *m* opera; opera house

opération (o-pay-rah-s*Yawng*) *f* operation, surgery

opérer (o-pay-*ray*) *v* operate

opérette (o-pay-*reht*) *f* operetta

opiniâtre (o-pee-n^yaatr) *adj* obstinate

opinion (o-pee-n^yawng) *f* view, opinion

opposé (o-poa-zay) *adj* contrary, opposite; averse

s'opposer (o-poa-zay) *v* oppose

opposition (o-poa-zee-s^yawng) *f* opposition

oppresser (o-pray-say) *v* oppress

opprimer (o-pree-may) *v* oppress

opticien (op-tee-s^yang) *m* optician

optimisme (op-tee-meesm) *m* optimism

optimiste (op-tee-meest) *m* optimist; *adj* optimistic

or (awr) *m* gold; **en ~** golden; **~ en feuille** gold leaf

orage (o-raazh) *m* thunderstorm

orageux (o-rah-zhur) *adj* thundery, stormy

oral (o-rahl) *adj* oral

orange (o-rahngzh) *f* orange; *adj* orange

orchestre (or-kehstr) *m* orchestra; band; **fauteuil d'orchestre** stall

ordinaire (or-dee-nair) *adj* plain, simple, usual, regular, customary; common, vulgar

ordinateur (or-dee-nah-tūrr) *n* computer; **~ portable** lap-top computer

ordonner (or-do-nay) *v* arrange; order; **ordonné** *adj* tidy

ordre (ordr) *m* order; method; command; **~ du jour** agenda

ordures (or-dewr) *fpl* garbage

oreille (o-ray) *f* ear

oreiller (o-ray-y^yay) *m* pillow; **taie d'oreiller** pillow-case

oreillons (o-reh-y^yawng) *mpl* mumps

orfèvre (or-faivr) *m* goldsmith; silversmith

organe (or-gahn) *m* organ

organique (or-gah-neek) *adj* organic

organisation (or-gah-nee-zah-s^yawng) *f* organization

organiser (or-gah-nee-zay) *v* organize

orgue (org) *m* (pl *f*) organ; **~ de Barbarie** street-organ

orgueil (or-gur^{ee}) *m* pride

orgueilleux (or-gur-^yur) *adj* proud

orient (o-r^yahng) *m* Orient

oriental (o-r^yahng-tahl) *adj* oriental; eastern, easterly

s'orienter (o-r^yahng-tay) orientate

originairement (o-ree-zhee-nehr-mahng) *adv* originally

original (o-ree-zhee-nahl) *adj* original

origine (o-ree-zheen) *f* origin

orme (orm) *m* elm

ornement (or-ner-mahng) *m* ornament

ornemental (or-ner-mahng-tahl) *adj* ornamental

orphelin (or-fer-lang) *m* orphan

orteil (or-tay) *m* toe

orthodoxe (or-to-doks) *adj* orthodox

orthographe (or-to-grahf) *f* spelling

os (oss) *m* (pl ~) bone

oser (oa-zay) *v* dare

otage (o-taazh) *m* hostage

ôter (oa-tay) *v* *take out; wipe

ou (oo) *conj* or; **~ ... ou** either ... or

où (oo) *adv* where; *pron* where; **n'importe ~** anywhere

ouate (waht) *f* cotton-wool

oublier (oo-blee-ay) *v* *forget

oublieux (oo-blee-ur) *adj* forgetful

ouest (wehst) *m* west

oui (wee) yes

ouïe (oo-ee) *f* hearing

ouragan (oo-rah-gahng) *m* hurricane

ourlet (oor-lay) *m* hem

ours (oors) *m* bear

oursin (oor-sang) *m* sea-urchin

outil (oo-tee) *m* tool, utensil, implement

outrage (oo-traazh) *m* outrage; offence

outrager (oo-trah-*zhay*) v offend

outre (ootr) prep beyond, besides; **d'outre-mer** overseas; **en** ~ furthermore, besides

ouvert (oo-*vair*) adj open

ouverture (oo-vehr-*tēwr*) f opening; overture

ouvrage (oo-*vraazh*) m work

ouvre-boîte (oo-vrer-*bwaht*) m tin-opener; can opener

ouvre-bouteille (oo-vrer-boo-*tay*) m bottle opener

ouvreur (oo-*vrūr*) m usher

ouvreuse (oo-*vrūz*) f usherette

ouvrier (oo-vree-*ay*) m workman, worker

*ouvrir** (oo-*vreer*) v open; unlock; turn on

ovale (o-*vahl*) adj oval

oxygène (ok-see-*zhehn*) m oxygen

P

pacifisme (pah-see-*feesm*) m pacifism

pacifiste (pah-see-*feest*) m pacifist; adj pacifist

pagaie (pah-*gay*) f paddle

pagaille (pah-*gigh*) f muddle

page (paazh) f page; m page-boy

paie (pay) f salary

paiement (pay-*mahng*) m payment; ~ **à tempérament** instalment

païen (pah-*Yang*) m pagan, heathen; adj pagan, heathen

paille (pigh) f straw

pain (pang) m bread; ~ **complet** wholemeal bread; **petit** ~ roll

pair (pair) adj even

paire (pair) f pair

paisible (pay-*zeebl*) adj peaceful, quiet

*paître** (paitr) v graze

paix (pay) f peace

Pakistan (pah-kee-*stahng*) m Pakistan

Pakistanais (pah-kee-stah-*nay*) m Pakistani

pakistanais (pah-kee-stah-*nay*) adj Pakistani

palais (pah-*lay*) m palace; palate

pâle (paal) adj pale

palme (pahlm) f palm

palpable (pahl-*pahbl*) adj palpable

palper (pahl-*pay*) v *feel

palpitation (pahl-pee-tah-s*Yawng*) f palpitation

pamplemousse (pahng-pler-*mooss*) m grapefruit

panier (pah-*nYay*) m hamper, basket

panique (pah-*neek*) f panic; scare

panne (pahn) f breakdown; **tomber en** ~ *break down

panneau (pah-*noa*) m panel

pansement (pahng-*smahng*) m bandage

panser (pahng-*say*) v dress

pantalon (pahng-tah-*lawng*) m trousers pl, slacks pl; pants plAm; **ensemble-pantalon** pant-suit; ~ **de ski** ski pants

pantoufle (pahng-*toofl*) f slipper

paon (pahng) m peacock

papa (pah-*pah*) m daddy

pape (pahp) m pope

papeterie (pah-peh-*tree*) f stationer's; stationery

papier (pah-*pYay*) m paper; **en** ~ paper; ~ **à écrire** notepaper; ~ **à lettres** notepaper, writing-paper; ~ **à machine** typing paper; ~ **buvard** blotting paper; ~ **carbone** carbon paper; ~ **d'emballage** wrapping paper; ~ **d'étain** tinfoil; ~ **de verre** sandpaper; ~ **hygiénique** toilet-paper; ~ **peint** wallpaper

papillon (pah-pee-*Yawng*) m butterfly

paquebot (pahk-*boa*) m liner

Pâques (paak) Easter

paquet (pah-*kay*) *m* parcel, packet; bundle

par (pahr) *prep* by; for

parade (pah-*rahd*) *f* parade

paragraphe (pah-rah-*grahf*) *m* paragraph

***paraître** (pah-*raitr*) *v* seem, appear

parallèle (pah-rah-*lehl*) *m* parallel; *adj* parallel

paralyser (pah-rah-lee-*zay*) *v* paralise; **paralysé** lame

parapher (pah-rah-*fay*) *v* initial

parapluie (pah-rah-*plwee*) *m* umbrella

parasol (pah-rah-*sol*) *m* sunshade

parc (pahrk) *m* park; ~ **de stationnement** car park; ~ **national** national park

parce que (pahr-sker) as, because

parcimonieux (pahr-see-mo-*n*^y*ur*) *adj* economical, thrifty

parcomètre (pahr-ko-*mehtr*) *m* parking meter

***parcourir** (pahr-koo-*reer*) *v* *go through; cover

parcours (pahr-*koor*) *m* stretch

par-dessus (pahr-der-*sew*) *prep* over

pardessus (pahr-der-*sew*) *m* coat, overcoat; topcoat

pardon (pahr-*dawng*) *m* pardon; **pardon!** sorry!

pardonner (pahr-do-*nay*) *v* *forgive

pare-brise (pahr-*breez*) *m* windscreen; windshield *nAm*

pare-choc (pahr-*shok*) *m* bumper, fender

pareil (pah-*ray*) *adj* alike, like; **sans** ~ unsurpassed

parent (pah-*rahng*) *m* relative, relation; **parents** parents *pl*; **parents nourriciers** foster-parents *pl*

paresseux (pah-reh-*sur*) *adj* lazy

parfait (pahr-*fay*) *adj* perfect; faultless

parfois (pahr-*fwah*) *adv* sometimes

parfum (pahr-*furng*) *m* scent; perfume

parfumerie (pahr-fewm-*ree*) *f* perfumery

pari (pah-*ree*) *m* bet

parier (pah-r^y*ay*) *v* *bet

parking (pahr-*keeng*) *m* parking lot *Am*

parlement (pahr-ler-*mahng*) *m* parliament

parlementaire (pahr-ler-mahng-*tair*) *adj* parliamentary

parler (pahr-*lay*) *v* talk, *speak

parmi (pahr-*mee*) *prep* among, amid

paroisse (pah-*rwahss*) *f* parish

parole (pah-*rol*) *f* speech

parrain (pah-*rang*) *m* godfather

part (paar) *f* part, share; **à** ~ separately, apart; aside; **nulle** ~ nowhere; **quelque** ~ somewhere

partager (pahr-tah-*zhay*) *v* share

partenaire (pahr-ter-*nair*) *m* associate, partner

parti (pahr-*tee*) *m* party; side

partial (pahr-s^y*ahl*) *adj* partial

participant (pahr-tee-see-*pahng*) *m* participant

participer (pahr-tee-see-*pay*) *v* participate

particularité (pahr-tee-kew-lah-ree-*tay*) *f* peculiarity; detail

particulier (pahr-tee-kew-l^y*ay*) *adj* particular, special; individual, private; peculiar; **en** ~ in particular

particulièrement (pahr-tee-kew-l^y*ehr*-*mahng*) *adv* specially

partie (pahr-*tee*) *f* part; **en** ~ partly

partiel (pahr-s^y*ehl*) *adj* partial

partiellement (pahr-s^yehl-*mahng*) *adv* partly

***partir** (pahr-*teer*) *v* *leave, *go away; *set out, depart, pull out; check out; **à partir de** as from, from; **parti** gone

partisan (pahr-tee-*zahng*) *m* advocate

partout (pahr-*too*) *adv* throughout,

everywhere; ~ **où** wherever

*__parvenir à__ (pahr-ver-*neer*) achieve

pas (pah) *m* step; pace, move; **faux ~** slip; **ne ... ~** not

passablement (pah-sah-bler-*mahng*) *adv* pretty, rather, quite

passage (pah-*saazh*) *m* passage; crossing; aisle; **~ à niveau** crossing; **~ clouté** pedestrian crossing; **~ pour piétons** crosswalk *nAm*

passager (pah-sah-*zhay*) *m* passenger

passant (pah-*sahng*) *m* passer-by

passé (pah-*say*) *m* past; *adj* past; *prep* over

passeport (pah-*spawr*) *m* passport

passer (pah-*say*) *v* pass; *give; **en passant** casual; **~ à côté** pass by; **~ en contrebande** smuggle; **se ~** occur; **se ~ de** spare

passerelle (pah-*srehl*) *f* gangway

passe-temps (pah-*stahng*) *m* hobby

passif (pah-*seef*) *adj* passive

passion (pah-s*yawng*) *f* passion

passionnant (pah-s*y*o-*nahng*) *adj* exciting

passionné (pah-s*y*o-*nay*) *adj* passionate; keen

passoire (pah-*swaar*) *f* sieve; strainer

pastèque (pah-*stehk*) *f* watermelon

pasteur (pah-*stūr*) *m* clergyman; parson, minister, rector

patauger (pah-toa-*zhay*) *v* wade

pâte (paat) *f* paste; dough, batter; **~ dentifrice** toothpaste

patère (pah-*tair*) *f* peg

paternel (pah-tehr-*nehl*) *adj* fatherly

patience (pah-s*yahngss*) *f* patience

patient (pah-s*yahng*) *m* patient; *adj* patient

patin (pah-*tang*) *m* skate

patinage (pah-tee-*naazh*) *m* skating; **~ à roulettes** roller-skating

patiner (pah-tee-*nay*) *v* skate

patinette (pah-tee-*neht*) *f* scooter

patinoire (pah-tee-*nwaar*) *f* skating-rink

pâtisserie (pah-tee-*sree*) *f* cake, pastry; pastry shop

patrie (pah-*tree*) *f* fatherland, native country

patriote (pah-tree-*ot*) *m* patriot

patron (pah-*trawng*) *m* master, boss

patronne (pah-*tron*) *f* mistress

patrouille (pah-*troo*ee) *f* patrol

patrouiller (pah-troo-*Yay*) *v* patrol

patte (paht) *f* paw

pâture (pah-*tewr*) *f* pasture

paume (pōam) *f* palm

paupière (poa-p*Yair*) *f* eyelid

pause (pōaz) *f* pause; break

pauvre (pōavr) *adj* poor

pauvreté (poa-vrer-*tay*) *f* poverty

pavage (pah-*vaazh*) *m* pavement

paver (pah-*vay*) *v* pave

pavillon (pah-vee-*Yawng*) *m* pavilion; **~ de chasse** lodge

pavot (pah-*voa*) *m* poppy

payable (pay-*Yahbl*) *adj* due

paye (pay) *f* pay

payer (pay-*Yay*) *v* *pay; **~ à tempérament** *pay on account

pays (pay-*ee*) *m* country, land; **~ boisé** woodland; **~ natal** native country

paysage (pay-ee-*zaazh*) *m* landscape, scenery

paysan (pay-ee-*zahng*) *m* peasant

Pays-Bas (pay-ee-*bah*) *mpl* the Netherlands

péage (pay-*aazh*) *m* toll

peau (poa) *f* skin; hide; **~ de porc** pigskin; **~ de vache** cow-hide

péché (pay-*shay*) *m* sin

pêche¹ (pehsh) *f* peach

pêche² (pehsh) *f* fishing industry; **attirail de ~** fishing tackle, fishing gear

pêcher (pay-*shay*) *v* fish; **~ à la ligne**

angle

pêcheur (peh-*shūrr*) *m* fisherman

pédale (pay-*dahl*) *f* pedal

pédicure (pay-dee-*kewr*) *m* pedicure, chiropodist

peigne (pehñ) *m* comb; ~ **de poche** pocket-comb

peigner (pay-*ñay*) *v* comb

peignoir (peh-*ñwaar*) *m* bathrobe

***peindre** (pangdr) *v* paint

peine (pehn) *f* trouble, pains, difficulty; penalty; **à** ~ hardly; just, barely, scarcely; ***avoir de la** ~ grieve; ~ **de mort** death penalty

peiner (pay-*nay*) *v* labour

peintre (pangtr) *m* painter

peinture (pang-*tewr*) *f* paint; picture, painting; ~ **à l'huile** oil-painting

pelage (per-*laazh*) *m* furs

peler (per-*lay*) *v* peel

pèlerin (pehl-*rang*) *m* pilgrim

pèlerinage (pehl-ree-*naazh*) *m* pilgrimage

pélican (pay-lee-*kahng*) *m* pelican

pelle (pehl) *f* spade, shovel

pellicule (peh-lee-*kewl*) *f* film; **pellicules** dandruff

pelouse (per-*looz*) *f* lawn

pelure (per-*lewr*) *f* peel

penchant (pahng-*shahng*) *m* inclination

se pencher (pahng-*shay*) *bend down

pendant (pahng-*dahng*) *prep* for, during; ~ **que** while

pendentif (pahng-dahng-*teef*) *m* pendant

pendre (pahngdr) *v* *hang

pénétrer (pay-nay-*tray*) *v* penetrate

pénible (pay-*neebl*) *adj* laborious; painful

pénicilline (pay-nee-see-*leen*) *f* penicillin

péninsule (pay-nang-*sewl*) *f* peninsula

pensée (pahng-*say*) *f* thought; idea

penser (pahng-*say*) *v* *think; ~ **à** *think of

penseur (pahng-*sūrr*) *m* thinker

pensif (pahng-*seef*) *adj* thoughtful

pension (pahng-*s*ʸ*awng*) *f* guesthouse, pension, boarding-house; board; ~ **alimentaire** alimony; ~ **complète** room and board, full board, bed and board, board and lodging

pensionnaire (pahng-s*ʸ*o-*nair*) *m* boarder

pente (pahngt) *f* incline; ramp; **en** ~ sloping, slanting

Pentecôte (pahngt-*kōat*) *f* Whitsun

pénurie (pay-new-*ree*) *f* scarcity

pépé (pay-*pay*) *m* grandfather

pépin (pay-*pang*) *m* pip

pépinière (pay-pee-*n*ʸ*air*) *f* nursery

perceptible (pehr-sehp-*teebl*) *adj* noticeable, perceptible

perception (pehr-seh-*ps*ʸ*awng*) *f* perception

percer (pehr-*say*) *v* pierce

***percevoir** (pehr-ser-*vwaar*) *v* perceive; sense

perche (pehrsh) *f* perch, bass

percolateur (pehr-ko-lah-*tūrr*) *m* percolator

perdre (pehrdr) *v* *lose

perdrix (pehr-*dree*) *f* partridge

père (pair) *m* father; dad

perfection (pehr-fehk-*s*ʸ*awng*) *f* perfection

performance (pehr-for-*mahngss*) *f* achievement; performance

péril (pay-*reel*) *m* peril

périlleux (pay-ree-ʸ*ur*) *adj* perilous

périmé (pay-ree-*may*) *adj* expired

période (pay-*r*ʸ*od*) *f* period; term

périodique (pay-r*ʸ*o-*deek*) *adj* periodical; *m* journal, periodical

périr (pay-*reer*) *v* perish

périssable (pay-ree-*sahbl*) *adj* perishable

perle (pehrl) f pearl; bead

permanent (pehr-mah-*nahng*) adj permanent

permanente (pehr-mah-*nahngt*) f permanent wave

*__permettre__ (pehr-*mehtr*) v permit, allow; enable; **se ~** afford

permis (pehr-*mee*) m permit; permission, licence; **~ de conduire** driving licence; **~ de pêche** fishing licence; **~ de séjour** residence permit; **~ de travail** work permit; labor permit *Am*

permission (pehr-mee-*s^yawng*) f authorization, permission; leave

perpendiculaire (pehr-pahng-dee-kew-*lair*) adj perpendicular

perroquet (pehr-ro-*kay*) m parrot

perruche (peh-*rewsh*) f parakeet

perruque (peh-*rewk*) f wig

Persan (pehr-*sahng*) m Persian

persan (pehr-*sahng*) adj Persian

Perse (pehrs) f Persia

persévérer (pehr-say-vay-*ray*) v *keep up

persienne (pehr-s^y*ehn*) f blind; shutter

persil (pehr-*see*) m parsley

persister (pehr-see-*stay*) v insist

personnalité (pehr-so-nah-lee-*tay*) f personality

personne (pehr-*son*) f person; **ne ... personne** nobody, no one; **par ~** per person

personnel (pehr-so-*nehl*) m personnel, staff; adj personal, private

perspective (pehr-spehk-*teev*) f perspective, prospect

persuader (pehr-swah-*day*) v persuade

perte (pehrt) f loss

pertinent (pehr-tee-*nahng*) adj proper

peser (per-*zay*) v weigh

pessimisme (peh-see-*meesm*) m pessimism

pessimiste (peh-see-*meest*) m pessimist; adj pessimistic

pétale (pay-*tahl*) m petal

pétillement (pay-teey-*mahng*) m fizz

petit (per-*tee*) adj small, little; petty, short, minor

petite-fille (per-teet-*feey*) f granddaughter

petit-fils (per-tee-*feess*) m grandson

pétition (pay-tee-s^y*awng*) f petition

pétrole (pay-*trol*) m petroleum, oil; kerosene, paraffin; **gisement de ~** oil-well

peu (pur) adj little; m bit; **à ~ près** approximately, about; almost; **~ de** few; **quelque ~** somewhat; **sous ~** soon, shortly; **un ~** some

peuple (purpl) m people; nation; folk

peur (pūrr) f fear, fright; *__avoir ~__ *be afraid

peut-être (pur-*taitr*) adv maybe, perhaps

phare (faar) m lighthouse; headlight, headlamp; **~ anti-brouillard** fog-lamp

pharmacie (fahr-mah-*see*) f pharmacy, chemist's; drugstore *nAm*

pharmacien (fahr-mah-s^y*ang*) m chemist

pharmacologie (fahr-mah-ko-lo-*zhee*) f pharmacology

phase (faaz) f phase, stage

Philippin (fee-lee-*pang*) m Filipino

philippin (fee-lee-*pang*) adj Philippine

Philippines (fee-lee-*peen*) fpl Philippines pl

philosophe (fee-lo-*zof*) m philosopher

philosophie (fee-lo-zo-*fee*) f philosophy

phonétique (fo-nay-*teek*) adj phonetic

phonographe (fo-no-*grahf*) m gramophone

phoque (fok) m seal

photo 102 **placement**

photo (fo-*toa*) f photo; ~ **d'identité** passport photograph

photocopie (fo-to-ko-*pee*) f photocopy

photographe (fo-to-*grahf*) m photographer

photographie (fo-to-grah-*fee*) f photography; photograph

photographier (fo-to-grah-f^yay) v photograph

photomètre (fo-to-*mehtr*) m exposure meter

phrase (fraaz) f sentence

physicien (fee-zee-s^yang) m physicist

physiologie (fee-z^yo-lo-zhee) f physiology

physique (fee-*zeek*) f physics; adj physical; material

pianiste (p^yah-neest) m pianist

piano (p^yah-*noa*) m piano; ~ **à queue** grand piano

pie (pee) f magpie

pièce (p^yehss) f piece; room, chamber; ~ **de monnaie** coin; ~ **de rechange** spare part; ~ **de séjour** living-room; ~ **détachée** spare part; ~ **de théâtre** play

pied (p^yay) m foot; leg; **à** ~ walking, on foot

piège (p^yaizh) m trap

pierre (p^yair) f stone; **en** ~ stone; ~ **à briquet** flint; ~ **ponce** pumice stone; ~ **précieuse** gem; stone; ~ **tombale** tombstone, gravestone

piétiner (p^yay-tee-*nay*) v stamp

piéton (p^yay-*tawng*) m pedestrian

piètre (p^yehtr) adj poor

pieuvre (p^yūrvr) f octopus

pieux (p^yur) adj pious

pigeon (pee-*zhawng*) m pigeon

pignon (pee-*ñawng*) m gable

pile (peel) f stack; battery

pilier (pee-l^yay) m pillar

pilote (pee-*lot*) m pilot

pilule (pee-*lewl*) f pill

pin (pang) m pine

pince (pangss) f pliers pl, tongs pl; tweezers pl; ~ **à cheveux** hairgrip; bobby pin Am

pinceau (pang-*soa*) m brush; paintbrush

pincer (pang-*say*) v pinch

pincettes (pang-*seht*) fpl tweezers pl

pingouin (pang-*gwang*) m penguin

ping-pong (peeng-*pong*) m table tennis

pinson (pang-*sawng*) m finch

pioche (p^yosh) f pick-axe

pion (p^yawng) m pawn

pionnier (p^yo-n^yay) m pioneer

pipe (peep) f pipe

piquant (pee-*kahng*) adj savoury

pique-nique (peek-*neek*) m picnic

pique-niquer (peek-nee-*kay*) v picnic

piquer (pee-*kay*) v *sting, prick

piqûre (pee-*kēwr*) f shot; sting, bite

pirate (pee-*raht*) m pirate

pire (peer) adj worse; **le** ~ worst

pis (pee) adv worse; **tant pis!** never mind!

piscine (pee-*seen*) f swimming pool

pissenlit (pee-sahng-*lee*) m dandelion

piste (peest) f trail; track; ring; ~ **de courses** race-track; ~ **de décollage** runway

pistolet (pee-sto-*lay*) m pistol

piston (pee-*stawng*) m piston; **segment de** ~ piston ring; **tige de** ~ piston-rod

pitié (pee-t^yay) f pity; *avoir ~ **de** pity

pittoresque (pee-to-*rehsk*) adj picturesque, scenic

placard (plah-*kaar*) m closet, cupboard

place (plahss) f place; seat; room; square; ~ **forte** stronghold

placement (plah-*smahng*) m investment

placer (plah-*say*) v place; *put, *lay; invest

plafond (plah-*fawng*) m ceiling

plage (plaazh) f beach; ~ **pour nudistes** nudist beach

plaider (play-*day*) v plead

plaidoyer (pleh-dwah-*Yay*) m plea

plaie (play) f wound

se *plaindre (plangdr) complain

plaine (plehn) f plain, lowlands pl

plainte (plangt) f complaint

*plaire (plair) v please; **s'il vous plaît** please

plaisant (pleh-*zahng*) adj pleasant; nice, enjoyable, amusing

plaisanter (pleh-zahng-*tay*) v joke

plaisanterie (play-zahng-*tree*) f joke

plaisir (play-*zeer*) m pleasure; joy, delight, fun, enjoyment; **avec ~** gladly; ***prendre ~** enjoy

plan (plahng) m plan, project; map; scheme; adj flat, level, even; **premier ~** foreground

planche (plahngsh) f plank, board

plancher (plahng-*shay*) m floor

planétarium (plah-nay-tah-*rYom*) m planetarium

planète (plah-*neht*) f planet

planeur (plah-*nūr*) m glider

planifier (plah-nee-*fYay*) v plan

plantation (plahng-tah-*sYawng*) f plantation

plante (plahngt) f plant

planter (plahng-*tay*) v plant

plaque (plahk) f plate; sheet; ~ **d'immatriculation** registration plate; licence plate Am

plastique (plah-*steek*) adj plastic; m plastic

plat (plah) m dish; course; adj flat, plane, smooth, level

plateau (plah-*toa*) m plateau; tray

plate-bande (plaht-*bahngd*) f flowerbed

platine (plah-*teen*) m platinum

plâtre (plaatr) m plaster

plein (plang) adj full; ***faire le ~** fill up; **pleine saison** high season

pleurer (plur-*ray*) v *weep, cry

*pleuvoir (plur-*vwaar*) v rain

pli (plee) m fold; crease; ~ **permanent** permanent press

plie (plee) f plaice

plier (plee-*ay*) v fold

plomb (plawng) m lead; **sans ~** unleaded

plombage (plawng-*baazh*) m filling

plombier (plawng-*bYay*) m plumber

plonger (plawng-*zhay*) v dive

pluie (plwee) f rain

plume (plewm) f feather; pen

(la) plupart (plew-*paar*) most

pluriel (plew-*rYehl*) m plural

plus (plewss) adj more; prep plus; **de ~** moreover; **le ~** most; **ne ... ~** no longer; **~ ... plus** the ... the

plusieurs (plew-*zYūrr*) adj several

plutôt (plew-*toa*) adv fairly, pretty, rather, quite; sooner

pluvieux (plew-*vYur*) adj rainy

pneu (pnur) m (pl ~s) tyre; tire; ~ **crevé** flat tyre; ~ **de rechange** spare tyre

pneumatique (pnur-mah-*teek*) adj pneumatic

pneumonie (pnur-mo-*nee*) f pneumonia

poche (posh) f pocket; **lampe de ~** flash-light

pochette (po-*sheht*) f pouch

poêle (pwahl) f saucepan; m stove; ~ **à frire** frying-pan

poème (po-*ehm*) m poem; ~ **épique** epic

poésie (po-ay-*zee*) f poetry

poète (po-*eht*) m poet

poids (pwah) m weight

poignée (pwah-*ñay*) f handle; handful; ~ **de main** handshake

poignet (pwah-*ñay*) *m* wrist

poil (pwahl) *m* hair

poing (pwang) *m* fist

point (pwang) *m* point; item; period, full stop; stitch; ~ **de congélation** freezing-point; ~ **de départ** starting-point; ~ **de repère** landmark; ~ **de vue** view, outlook; ~ **d'interrogation** question mark; **point-virgule** *m* semi-colon

pointe (pwangt) *f* point; **heure de ~** peak hour

pointer (pwang-*tay*) *v* tick off

pointu (pwang-*tew*) *adj* pointed

poire (pwaar) *f* pear

poireau (pwah-*roa*) *m* leek

pois (pwah) *m* pea

poison (pwah-*zawng*) *m* poison

poisson (pwah-*sawng*) *m* fish

poissonnerie (pwah-son-*ree*) *f* fish shop

poitrine (pwah-*treen*) *f* chest; bosom

poivre (pwaavr) *m* pepper

pôle nord (poal nawr) North Pole

pôle sud (poal sewd) South Pole

poli (po-*lee*) *adj* polite; civil

police (po-*leess*) *f* police *pl*; policy; **commissariat de ~** police-station; ~ **d'assurance** insurance policy

policier (po-lee-*s*ʸ*ay*) *m* policeman

poliomyélite (po-lʸo-mʸay-*leet*) *f* polio

polir (po-*leer*) *v* polish

polisson (po-lee-*sawng*) *adj* naughty

politicien (po-lee-tee-*s*ʸ*ang*) *m* politician

politique (po-lee-*teek*) *f* politics; policy; *adj* political

pollution (po-lew-*s*ʸ*awng*) *f* pollution

Pologne (po-*loñ*) *f* Poland

Polonais (po-lo-*nay*) *m* Pole

polonais (po-lo-*nay*) *adj* Polish

pomme (pom) *f* apple; ~ **de terre** potato; **pommes frites** chips

pommette (po-*meht*) *f* cheek-bone

pompe (pawngp) *f* pump; ~ **à eau** water pump; ~ **à essence** petrol pump; gas pump *Am*

pomper (pawng-*pay*) *v* pump

pompier (pawng-*p*ʸ*ay*) *m* fireman; **pompiers** fire-brigade

ponctuel (pawngk-*twehl*) *adj* punctual

pondéré (pawng-day-*ray*) *adj* sober

pondre (pawngdr) *v* *lay

poney (po-*nay*) *m* pony

pont (pawng) *m* bridge; deck; **pont-levis** *m* drawbridge; ~ **principal** main deck; ~ **suspendu** suspension bridge

popeline (po-*pleen*) *f* poplin

populaire (po-pew-*lair*) *adj* popular

population (po-pew-lah-*s*ʸ*awng*) *f* population

populeux (po-pew-*lur*) *adj* populous

porc (pawr) *m* pork

porcelaine (por-ser-*lehn*) *f* porcelain; china

porc-épic (por-kay-*peek*) *m* porcupine

port[1] (pawr) *m* port, harbour; ~ **de mer** seaport

port[2] (pawr) *m* postage; ~ **payé** postage paid, post-paid

portatif (por-tah-*teef*) *adj* portable

porte (port) *f* door; gate; ~ **coulissante** sliding door; ~ **tournante** revolving door

porte-bagages (port-bah-*gaazh*) *m* luggage rack

porte-bonheur (port-bo-*nürr*) *m* lucky charm

porte-documents (port-do-kew-*mahng*) *m* attaché case

portée (por-*tay*) *f* reach; litter

portefeuille (por-ter-*fur*ᵉᵉ) *m* pocketbook, wallet

porte-jarretelles (port-zhahr-*tehl*) *m* suspender belt; garter belt *Am*

porte-manteau (port-mahng-*toa*) *m*

hat rack

porte-monnaie (port-mo-*nay*) *m* purse

porter (por-*tay*) *v* carry, *bear; *wear; ~ **sur** concern; **se ~ bien** *be in good health

porteur (por-*tŭrr*) *m* bearer; porter

portier (por-*t*ʸ*ay*) *m* porter, doorman, door-keeper

portion (por-s*ʸawng*) *f* helping, portion

portrait (por-*tray*) *m* portrait

Portugais (por-tew-*gay*) *m* Portuguese

portugais (por-tew-*gay*) *adj* Portuguese

Portugal (por-tew-*gahl*) *m* Portugal

poser (poa-*zay*) *v* place; *put, *lay, *set

positif (poa-zee-*teef*) *m* positive; *adj* positive

position (poa-zee-s*ʸawng*) *f* position; site

posséder (po-say-*day*) *v* possess, own

possession (po-seh-s*ʸawng*) *f* possession

possibilité (po-see-bee-lee-*tay*) *f* possibility

possible (po-*seebl*) *adj* possible

poste¹ (post) *f* post; ***mettre à la ~** mail; ~ **aérienne** airmail; ~ **restante** poste restante

poste² (post) *m* station; post; ~ **de secours** first-aid post; ~ **d'essence** petrol station

poster (po-*stay*) *v* post

postérieur (po-stay-r*ʸŭrr*) *m* bottom; *adj* subsequent

postiche (po-*steesh*) *m* hair piece

pot (poa) *m* pot

potable (po-*tahbl*) *adj* for drinking

potage (po-*taazh*) *m* soup

poteau (po-*toa*) *m* post, pole; ~ **indicateur** milepost, signpost

potelé (po-*tlay*) *adj* plump

poterie (po-*tree*) *f* pottery, earthen-

ware, crockery

pou (poo) *m* (pl ~x) louse

poubelle (poo-*behl*) *f* rubbish-bin

pouce (pooss) *m* thumb

poudre (poodr) *f* powder; ~ **à canon** gunpowder; ~ **dentifrice** tooth-powder; ~ **de riz** face-powder; ~ **pour les pieds** foot powder; **savon en** ~ soap powder

poudrier (poo-dree-*ay*) *m* powder compact

poule (pool) *f* hen

poulet (poo-*lay*) *m* chicken

poulie (poo-*lee*) *f* pulley

pouls (poo) *m* pulse

poumon (poo-*mawng*) *m* lung

poupée (poo-*pay*) *f* doll

pour (poōr) *prep* for, to; ~ **que** so that

pourboire (poor-*bwaar*) *m* tip, gratuity

pourcentage (poor-sahng-*taazh*) *m* percentage

pourchasser (poor-shah-*say*) *v* chase

pourpre (poorpr) *adj* purple

pourquoi (poor-*kwah*) *adv* why; what for

pourrir (poo-*reer*) *v* rot; **pourri** rotten

*poursuivre (poor-*sweevr*) *v* carry on, continue, pursue

pourtant (poor-*tahng*) *adv* however, yet; though

pourvu que (poor-vew ker) provided that

poussée (poo-*say*) *f* push

pousser (poo-*say*) *v* push

poussette (poo-*seht*) *f* baby carriage *Am*

poussière (poo-s*ʸair*) *f* dust

poussiéreux (poo-s*ʸay*-rur) *adj* dusty

poussoir (poo-*swaar*) *m* push-button

poutre (pootr) *f* beam

pouvoir (poo-*vwaar*) *m* power; authority; ~ **exécutif** executive

*pouvoir (poo-*vwaar*) *v* *can, *be able

to; *might, *may

praline (prah-*leen*) f chocolate

pratique (prah-*teek*) f practice; adj practical, convenient

pratiquer (prah-tee-*kay*) v practise

pré (pray) m meadow

préalable (pray-ah-*lahbl*) adj previous

précaire (pray-*kair*) adj precarious, critical

précaution (pray-koa-sᵞawng) f precaution

précédemment (pray-say-dah-*mahng*) adv before

précédent (pray-say-*dahng*) adj preceding, previous, last; former

précéder (pray-say-*day*) v precede

précepteur (pray-sehp-*tūrr*) m tutor

prêcher (pray-*shay*) v preach

précieux (pray-sᵞur) adj valuable; precious

précipice (pray-see-*peess*) m precipice

précipitation (pray-see-pee-tah-sᵞawng) f precipitation

précipité (pray-see-pee-*tay*) adj hasty

se précipiter (pray-see-pee-*tay*) dash

précis (pray-*see*) adj precise; accurate, very

préciser (pray-see-*zay*) v specify

précision (pray-see-zᵞawng) f precision; **précisions** particulars pl

prédécesseur (pray-day-seh-*sūrr*) m predecessor

*prédire (pray-*deer*) v predict

préférable (pray-fay-*rahbl*) adj preferable

préférence (pray-fay-*rahngss*) f preference

préférer (pray-fay-*ray*) v prefer; **préféré** favourite

préfixe (pray-*feeks*) m prefix

préjudiciable (pray-zhew-dee-sᵞahbl) adj harmful

préjugé (pray-zhew-*zhay*) m prejudice

prélever (prayl-*vay*) v raise

préliminaire (pray-lee-mee-*nair*) adj preliminary

prématuré (pray-mah-tew-*ray*) adj premature

premier (prer-mᵞay) num first; adj foremost, primary; ~ **ministre** premier

*prendre (prahngdr) v *take; collect; v *catch; capture; ~ **garde** look out, beware; ~ **soin de** look after

prénom (pray-*nawng*) m first name, Christian name

préparation (pray-pah-rah-sᵞawng) f preparation

préparer (pray-pah-*ray*) v prepare; arrange; cook

préposition (pray-poa-zee-sᵞawng) f preposition

près (pray) adv near; **à peu** ~ about; ~ **de** by, near

prescription (preh-skree-psᵞawng) f prescription

*prescrire (preh-*skreer*) v prescribe

présence (pray-*zahngss*) f presence

présent (pray-*zahng*) m present; adj present; **jusqu'à** ~ so far

présentation (pray-zahng-tah-sᵞawng) f introduction

présenter (pray-zahng-*tay*) v present; introduce; **se** ~ appear; report

préservatif (pray-sehr-vah-*teef*) m condom

président (pray-zee-*dahng*) m president, chairman

présomptueux (pray-zawngp-*twur*) adj presumptuous

presque (prehsk) adv nearly, almost

pressant (preh-*sahng*) adj pressing

presse (prehss) f press

presser (pray-*say*) v press; **se** ~ hurry, rush

pression (preh-sᵞawng) f pressure; ~ **atmosphérique** atmospheric pressure; ~ **des pneus** tyre pressure; ~

d'huile oil pressure

prestidigitateur (preh-stee-dee-zhee-tah-tūrr) m magician

prestige (preh-steezh) m prestige

présumer (pray-zew-may) v assume

prêt (pray) m loan; adj ready; prepared

prétendre (pray-tahngdr) v claim, pretend

prétentieux (pray-tahng-sʸur) adj conceited

prétention (pray-tahng-sʸawng) f claim

prêter (pray-tay) v *lend; ~ attention à attend to, mind

prêteur sur gage (preh-turr sewr gaazh) pawnbroker

prétexte (pray-tehkst) m pretence, pretext

prêtre (praitr) m priest

preuve (prūrv) f proof, evidence; token

prévenant (preh-vnahng) adj considerate, thoughtful

***prévenir** (preh-vneer) v warn; prevent, anticipate

préventif (preh-vahng-teef) adj preventive

prévenu (pray-vnew) m accused

prévision (pray-vee-zʸawng) f forecast, outlook

***prévoir** (pray-vwaar) v forecast; anticipate

prier (pree-ay) v pray; ask

prière (pree-air) f prayer

primaire (pree-mair) adj primary

prime (preem) f premium

primordial (pree-mor-dʸahl) adj primary

prince (prangss) m prince

princesse (prang-sehss) f princess

principal (prang-see-pahl) adj principal; cardinal, chief, leading, main

principalement (prang-see-pahl-mahng) adv especially, mainly

principe (prang-seep) m principle

printemps (prang-tahng) m spring; springtime

priorité (pree-o-ree-tay) f priority; ~ de passage right of way

prise (preez) f grip, clutch, grasp; capture; ~ de vue shot

prison (pree-zawng) f prison; jail, gaol

prisonnier (pree-zo-nʸay) m prisoner; *faire ~ capture; ~ de guerre prisoner of war

privation (pree-vah-sʸawng) f exposure

privé (pree-vay) adj private

priver de (pree-vay) deprive of

privilège (pree-vee-laizh) m privilege

prix (pree) m price-list; charge, cost; award, prize; prix-courant m price list; ~ d'achat purchase price; ~ de consolation consolation prize; ~ d'entrée entrance-fee; ~ du voyage fare

probable (pro-bahbl) adj probable; presumable, likely

probablement (pro-bah-bler-mahng) adv probably

problème (pro-blehm) m problem; question

procédé (pro-say-day) m process

procéder (pro-say-day) v proceed

procédure (pro-say-dewr) f procedure

procès (pro-say) m process; trial, lawsuit

procession (pro-seh-sʸawng) f procession

processus (pro-say-sewss) m process

prochain (pro-shang) adj following, next

prochainement (pro-shehn-mahng) adv soon, shortly

proche (prosh) adj close, near; nearby; oncoming

proclamer (pro-klah-may) v proclaim

procurer (pro-kew-ray) v furnish; **se ~** obtain

prodigue (pro-deeg) adj lavish

producteur (pro-dewk-tūrr) m producer

production (pro-dewk-syawng) f production; output; **~ en série** mass production

*produire (pro-dweer) v produce; generate; **se ~** occur, happen

produit (pro-dwee) m product; produce

profane (pro-fahn) m layman

professer (pro-fay-say) v confess

professeur (pro-feh-sūrr) m teacher; professor, master

profession (pro-feh-syawng) f profession

professionnel (pro-feh-syo-nehl) adj professional

profit (pro-fee) m profit, benefit

profitable (pro-fee-tahbl) adj profitable

profiter (pro-fee-tay) v profit, benefit

profond (pro-fawng) adj deep; low; profound

profondeur (pro-fawng-dūrr) f depth

programme (pro-grahm) m programme

progrès (pro-gray) m progress

progresser (pro-gray-say) v *get on

progressif (pro-gray-seef) adj progressive

progressiste (pro-gray-seest) adj progressive

projecteur (pro-zhehk-tūrr) m spotlight; searchlight

projet (pro-zhay) m project; scheme

prolongation (pro-lawng-gah-syawng) f extension

prolonger (pro-lawng-zhay) v renew

promenade (prom-nahd) f walk, stroll; promenade; **~ en voiture** drive

se promener (prom-nay) walk

promeneur (prom-nūrr) m walker

promesse (pro-mehss) f promise

*promettre (pro-mehtr) v promise

promontoire (pro-mawng-twaar) m headland

promotion (pro-mo-syawng) f promotion

*promouvoir (pro-moo-vwaar) v promote

prompt (prawng) adj prompt; fast

promptitude (prawng-tee-tewd) f haste

pronom (pro-nawng) m pronoun

prononcer (pro-nawng-say) v pronounce

prononciation (pro-nawng-syah-syawng) f pronunciation

propagande (pro-pah-gahngd) f propaganda

prophète (pro-feht) m prophet

proportion (pro-por-syawng) f proportion

proportionnel (pro-por-syo-nehl) adj proportional

propos (pro-poa) m intention; **à ~** by the way; **à ~ de** regarding

proposer (pro-poa-zay) v propose

proposition (pro-poa-zee-syawng) f proposition, proposal

propre (propr) adj clean; own

propriétaire (pro-pree-ay-tair) m owner, proprietor; landlord

propriété (pro-pree-ay-tay) f property; estate

propulser (pro-pewl-say) v propel

prospectus (pro-spehk-tewss) m prospectus

prospère (pro-spair) adj prosperous

prospérité (pro-spay-ree-tay) f prosperity

prostituée (pro-stee-tway) f prostitute

protection (pro-tehk-syawng) f protection

protéger (pro-tay-*zhay*) v protect

protéine (pro-tay-*een*) f protein

protestant (pro-teh-*stahng*) adj Protestant

protestation (pro-teh-stah-*s^yawng*) f protest

protester (pro-teh-*stay*) v protest

prouver (proo-*vay*) v prove

provenance (pro-vnah*ngss*) f origin

***provenir de** (pro-*vneer*) *come from

proverbe (pro-*vehrb*) m proverb

province (pro-*vangss*) f province

provincial (pro-vang-*s^yahl*) adj provincial

proviseur (pro-vee-*zūrr*) m principal

provision (pro-vee-*z^yawng*) f store; provisions pl

provisoire (pro-vee-*zwaar*) adj temporary, provisional

provoquer (pro-vo-*kay*) v cause

prudence (prew-*dahngss*) f caution

prudent (prew-*dahng*) adj careful; cautious, wary

prune (prewn) f plum

pruneau (prew-*noa*) m prune

prurit (prew-*reet*) m itch

psychanalyste (psee-kah-nah-*leest*) m psychoanalyst, analyst

psychiatre (psee-*k^yaatr*) m psychiatrist

psychique (psee-*sheek*) adj psychic

psychologie (psee-ko-lo-*zhee*) f psychology

psychologique (psee-ko-lo-*zheek*) adj psychological

psychologue (psee-ko-*log*) m psychologist

public (pew-*bleek*) m audience, public; adj public

publication (pew-blee-kah-*s^yawng*) f publication

publicité (pew-blee-see-*tay*) f advertising, publicity; advertisement

publier (pew-blee-*ay*) v publish

puer (pway) v *stink

puis (pwee) adv then

puisque (pweesk) conj as

puissance (pwee-*sahngss*) f might, force; power, energy; capacity

puissant (pwee-*sahng*) adj powerful, mighty; strong

puits (pwee) m well; ~ **de pétrole** oil-well

pull-over (pew-lo-*vair*) m pullover

pulvérisateur (pewl-vay-ree-zah-*tūrr*) m atomizer

pulvériser (pewl-vay-ree-*zay*) v *grind

punaise (pew-*naiz*) f bug; drawing-pin; thumbtack nAm

punir (pew-*neer*) v punish

punition (pew-nee-*s^yawng*) f punishment

pupitre (pew-*peetr*) m desk; pulpit

pur (pewr) adj pure; clean; sheer, neat

pus (pew) m pus

pustule (pew-*stewl*) f pimple

putain (pew-*tang*) f whore

puzzle (purzl) m jigsaw puzzle

pyjama (pee-zhah-*mah*) m pyjamas pl

Q

quai (kay) m wharf, dock, quay; platform

qualification (kah-lee-fee-kah-*s^yawng*) f qualification

qualifié (kah-lee-*f^yay*) adj qualified; *être ~ qualify; non ~ unskilled

qualité (kah-lee-*tay*) f quality; de première ~ first-class; first-rate

quand (kahng) adv when; conj when; n'importe ~ whenever

quant à (kahng-*tah*) as regards

quantité (kahng-tee-*tay*) f quantity, amount; lot

quarantaine (kah-rahng-tehn) f quarantine

quarante (kah-rahngt) num forty

quart (kaar) m quarter; ~ **d'heure** quarter of an hour

quartier (kahr-t^yay) m district, quarter; **bas** ~ slum; ~ **général** headquarters pl

quatorze (kah-torz) num fourteen

quatorzième (kah-tor-z^yehm) num fourteenth

quatre (kahtr) num four

quatre-vingt-dix (kah-trer-vang-deess) num ninety

quatre-vingts (kah-trer-vang) num eighty

quatrième (kah-tr^yehm) num fourth

que (ker) conj that; as, than; adv how; **ce** ~ what

quel (kehl) pron which; **n'importe** ~ any; whichever

quelquefois (kehl-ker-fwah) adv sometimes

quelques (kehlk) adj some, some

quelqu'un (kehl-kurng) pron someone, somebody

querelle (ker-rehl) f dispute, row, quarrel

se quereller (ker-ray-lay) quarrel

question (keh-st^yawng) f question; inquiry, query; matter, issue, problem

quêter (kay-tay) v collect

quêteur (keh-turr) m collector

queue (kur) f tail; queue; ***faire la** ~ queue; stand in line Am

qui (kee) pron who; which, that; **à** ~ whom; **n'importe** ~ anybody

quiconque (kee-kawngk) pron whoever

quille (keey) f keel

quincaillerie (kang-kigh-ree) f hardware; hardware store

quinine (kee-neen) f quinine

quinze (kangz) num fifteen; ~ **jours**

fortnight

quinzième (kang-z^yehm) num fifteenth

quitter (kee-tay) v *leave

quoi (kwah) pron what; **n'importe** ~ anything

quoique (kwahk) conj though, although; **quoiqu'il en soit** at any rate

quote-part (kot-paar) f quota

quotidien (ko-tee-d^yang) adj everyday, daily; m daily

R

rabais (rah-bay) m discount, reduction, rebate

raccourcir (rah-koor-seer) v shorten

race (rahss) f race; breed

racial (rah-s^yahl) adj racial

racine (rah-seen) f root

racler (rah-klay) v scrape

raconter (rah-kawng-tay) v *tell

radeau (rah-doa) m raft

radiateur (rah-d^yah-turr) m radiator

radical (rah-dee-kahl) adj radical

radio (rah-d^yoa) f wireless, radio

radiographie (rah-d^yoa-grah-fee) f X-ray

radiographier (rah-d^yoa-grah-f^yay) v X-ray

radis (rah-dee) m radish

radotage (rah-do-taazh) m rubbish

rafale (rah-fahl) f gust; ~ **de pluie** cloud-burst

raffinerie (rah-feen-ree) f refinery; ~ **de pétrole** oil-refinery

rafraîchir (rah-fray-sheer) v refresh

rafraîchissement (rah-freh-shee-smahng) m refreshment

rage (raazh) f rabies; rage; craze

rager (rah-zhay) v rage

raide (rehd) *adj* stiff

raie (ray) *f* stripe; parting

raifort (ray-*fawr*) *m* horseradish

rail (righ) *m* rail

raisin (ray-*zang*) *m* grapes *pl*; ~ **sec** currant, raisin

raison (ray-*zawng*) *f* reason; cause; wits *pl*, sense; ***avoir** ~ * be right; **en** ~ **de** for, owing to, because of

raisonnable (ray-zo-*nahbl*) *adj* reasonable; sensible

raisonner (ray-zo-*nay*) *v* reason

ralentir (rah-lahng-*teer*) *v* slow down

rallonge (rah-*lawngzh*) *f* extension cord

ramasser (rah-mah-*say*) *v* pick up

rame (rahm) *f* oar

ramener (rahm-*nay*) *v* *bring back

ramer (rah-*may*) *v* row

rampe (rahngp) *f* banisters *pl*; railing

ramper (rahng-*pay*) *v* *creep, crawl

rance (rahngss) *adj* rancid

rançon (rahng-*sawng*) *f* ransom

rang (rahng) *m* row, rank

rangée (rahng-*zhay*) *f* line

ranger (rahng-*zhay*) *v* sort; tidy up, *put away

râpe (raap) *f* grater

râper (rah-*pay*) *v* grate

rapide (rah-*peed*) *adj* quick; fast, swift, rapid; *m* rapids *pl*

rapidement (rah-peed-*mahng*) *adv* soon

rapidité (rah-pee-dee-*tay*) *f* speed

rapiécer (rah-pᵞay-*say*) *v* patch

rappeler (rah-*play*) *v* remind; recall; **se** ~ remember, recall

rapport (rah-*pawr*) *m* report; connection, relation, reference; intercourse

rapporter (rah-por-*tay*) *v* *bring back; report

rapprocher (rah-pro-*shay*) *v* *bring closer

raquette (rah-*keht*) *f* racquet

rare (raar) *adj* rare; uncommon, scarce

rarement (rahr-*mahng*) *adv* seldom, rarely

se raser (rah-*zay*) shave

raseur (rah-*zūrr*) *m* bore

rasoir (rah-*zwaar*) *m* safety-razor, razor; ~ **électrique** electric razor; shaver

rassemblement (rah-sahng-bler-*mahng*) *m* rally

rassembler (rah-sahng-*blay*) *v* assemble; collect

rassis (rah-*see*) *adj* stale

rassurer (rah-sew-*ray*) *v* reassure

rat (rah) *m* rat

râteau (rah-*toa*) *m* rake

ration (rah-sᵞ*awng*) *f* ration

rauque (rōak) *adj* hoarse

ravissant (rah-vee-*sahng*) *adj* lovely, delightful, enchanting

rayé (ray-ᵞay) *adj* striped

rayon (ray-ᵞ*awng*) *m* beam, ray; radius; spoke

rayonne (ray-ᵞon) *f* rayon

rayure (ray-ᵞe͞wr) *f* scratch

réaction (ray-ahk-sᵞ*awng*) *f* reaction

réalisable (ray-ah-lee-*zahbl*) *adj* realizable

réalisation (ray-ah-lee-zah-sᵞ*awng*) *f* realization; direction

réaliser (ray-ah-lee-*zay*) *v* realize; carry out, implement

réaliste (ray-ah-*leest*) *adj* matter-of-fact

réalité (ray-ah-lee-*tay*) *f* reality; **en** ~ actually; really

rébellion (ray-beh-lᵞ*awng*) *f* revolt, rebellion

rebord (rer-*bawr*) *m* edge, rim; ~ **de fenêtre** window-sill

rebut (rer-*bew*) *m* junk, refuse

récemment (ray-sah-*mahng*) *adv* lately, recently

récent (ray-*sahng*) *adj* recent

réception (ray-seh-*ps*Yawng) *f* receipt; reception; reception office

récession (ray-seh-sYawng) *f* recession

recette (rer-*seht*) *f* recipe; **recettes** revenue

*recevoir (rer-*svwaar*) *v* receive; entertain

recharge (rer-*shahrzh*) *f* refill

réchauffer (ray-shoa-*fay*) *v* warm up

recherche (rer-*shehrsh*) *f* research

rechercher (rer-shehr-*shay*) *v* aim at

récif (ray-*seef*) *m* reef

récipient (ray-see-*p*Yahng) *m* container, vessel

réciproque (ray-see-*prok*) *adj* mutual

récit (ray-*see*) *m* tale; account

récital (ray-see-*tahl*) *m* (pl ~s) recital

réclamation (ray-klah-mah-sYawng) *f* claim

réclame (ray-*klahm*) *f* publicity

réclamer (ray-klah-*may*) *v* claim

récolte (ray-*kolt*) *f* crop

recommandation (rer-ko-mahng-dah-sYawng) *f* recommendation

recommander (rer-ko-mahng-*day*) *v* recommend; register

recommencer (rer-ko-mahng-*say*) *v* recommence

récompense (ray-kawng-*pahngss*) *f* reward, prize

récompenser (ray-kawng-pahng-*say*) *v* reward

réconciliation (ray-kawng-see-lYah-sYawng) *f* reconciliation

réconfort (ray-kawng-*fawr*) *m* comfort

reconnaissance (rer-ko-nay-*sahngss*) *f* recognition

reconnaissant (rer-ko-nay-*sahng*) *adj* thankful, grateful

*reconnaître (rer-ko-*naitr*) *v* recognize; acknowledge; admit, confess

record (rer-*kawr*) *m* record

*recouvrir (rer-koo-*vreer*) *v* upholster

récréation (ray-kray-ah-sYawng) *f* recreation

recrue (rer-*krew*) *f* recruit

rectangle (rehk-*tahng*gl) *m* rectangle; oblong

rectangulaire (rehk-tahng-gew-*lair*) *adj* rectangular

rectification (rehk-tee-fee-kah-sYawng) *f* correction

rectum (rehk-*tom*) *m* rectum

reçu (rer-*sew*) *m* receipt; voucher

*recueillir (rer-kur-*Yeer*) *v* gather

reculer (rer-kew-*lay*) *v* step back; back up

récupérer (ray-kew-pay-*ray*) *v* recover

rédacteur (ray-dahk-*tūr*) *m* editor

reddition (reh-dee-sYawng) *f* surrender

rédiger (ray-dee-*zhay*) *v* *draw up

redouter (rer-doo-*tay*) *v* fear

réduction (ray-dewk-sYawng) *f* discount, reduction, rebate

*réduire (ray-*dweer*) *v* reduce; decrease, *cut

réduit (ray-*dwee*) *m* shed

rééducation (ray-ay-dew-kah-sYawng) *f* rehabilitation

réel (ray-*ehl*) *adj* real; true, factual, actual, substantial

réellement (ray-ehl-*mahng*) *adv* really

référence (ray-fay-*rahngss*) *f* reference

réfléchir (ray-flay-*sheer*) *v* *think; *think over

réflecteur (ray-flehk-*tūr*) *m* reflector

reflet (rer-*flay*) *m* reflection

refléter (rer-flay-*tay*) *v* reflect

réforme (ray-*form*) *f* reformation

réfrigérateur (ray-free-zhay-rah-*tūr*) *m* fridge, refrigerator

refroidir (rer-frwah-*deer*) *v* cool off

refuge (rer-*fewzh*) *m* refuge

réfugié (ray-few-zh*Y*ay) *m* refugee

refus (rer-*few*) *m* refusal

refuser (rer-few-*zay*) *v* refuse; deny, reject

regard (rer-*gaar*) m look

regarder (rer-gahr-*day*) v look; watch, look at; concern

régate (ray-*gaht*) f regatta

régime (ray-*zheem*) m régime; rule, government; diet

région (ray-zh^y*awng*) f region; district, area, zone, country

régional (ray-zh^yo-*nahl*) adj regional

règle (raigl) f rule; ruler; **en ~** in order

règlement (reh-gler-*mahng*) m regulation; arrangement, settlement

régler (ray-*glay*) v regulate; settle

réglisse (ray-*gleess*) f liquorice

règne (rehñ) m reign; dominion, rule

régner (ray-*ñay*) v reign; rule

regret (rer-*gray*) m regret

regretter (rer-gray-*tay*) v regret

régulier (ray-gew-l^y*ay*) adj regular

rein (rang) m kidney

reine (rehn) f queen

rejeter (rerzh-*tay*) v reject; turn down

***rejoindre** (rer-zhwang*dr*) v rejoin

relater (rer-lah-*tay*) v relate; report

relatif (rer-lah-*teef*) adj relative; comparative; **~ à** with reference to, concerning

relation (rer-lah-s^y*awng*) f connection; relation

relayer (rer-lay-*^yay*) v relieve

relèvement (rer-lehv-*mahng*) m increase

relever (rerl-*vay*) v raise

relief (rer-l^y*ehf*) m relief

relier (rer-l^y*ay*) v link; bundle

religieuse (rer-lee-zh^y*ūrz*) f nun

religieux (rer-lee-zh^y*ur*) adj religious

religion (rer-lee-zh^y*awng*) f religion

relique (rer-*leek*) f relic

reliure (rer-l^y*ēwr*) f binding

remarquable (rer-mahr-*kahbl*) adj remarkable; noticeable, striking

remarque (rer-*mahrk*) f remark

remarquer (rer-mahr-*kay*) v notice; remark

remboursement (rahng-boor-ser-*mahng*) m repayment, refund

rembourser (rahng-boor-*say*) v *repay, reimburse, refund

remède (rer-*mehd*) m remedy

remerciement (rer-mehr-see-*mahng*) m thanks pl

remercier (rer-mehr-s^y*ay*) v thank

***remettre** (rer-*mehtr*) v deliver; commit, hand; remit; **se ~** recover

remise (rer-*meez*) f delivery

remonter (rer-mawng-*tay*) v *wind

remorque (rer-*mork*) f trailer

remorquer (rer-mor-*kay*) v tow, tug

remorqueur (rer-mor-*kūrr*) m tug

remplacer (rahng-plah-*say*) v replace

remplir (rahng-*pleer*) v fill; fill in; fill out Am

remue-ménage (rer-mew-may-*naazh*) m bustle

remuer (rer-*mway*) v stir

rémunération (ray-mew-nay-rah-s^y*awng*) f remuneration

rémunérer (ray-mew-nay-*ray*) v remunerate

renard (rer-*naar*) m fox

rencontre (rahng-*kawng*tr) f meeting, encounter; **venant à la ~** oncoming

rencontrer (rahng-kawng-*tray*) v *meet; *come across, run into, encounter

rendement (rahng-der-*mahng*) m profit

rendez-vous (rahng-day-*voo*) m appointment, date

rendre (rahng*dr*) v refund; *make; **~ compte de** account for; **~ visite à** call on; **se ~** surrender; *go; **se ~ compte** realize

renne (rehn) m reindeer

renom (rer-*nawng*) m reputation

renommée (rer-no-*may*) f fame

renoncer (rer-nawng-*say*) v *give up

renouveler (rer-noo-*vlay*) v renew

renseignement (rahng-sehñ-*mahng*) m information; **bureau de renseignements** inquiry office

se renseigner (rahng-say-*ñay*) inquire

rentable (rahng-*tahbl*) adj paying

rentrer (rahng-*tray*) v *go home; gather

renverser (rahng-vehr-*say*) v knock down

****renvoyer** (rahng-vwah-*Yay*) v *send back; dismiss; ~ à refer to; postpone

répandre (ray-*pahngdr*) v *shed; *spill

réparation (ray-pah-rah-s*Yawng*) f reparation, repair

réparer (ray-pah-*ray*) v repair; mend, fix

répartir (ray-pahr-*teer*) v divide

repas (rer-*pah*) m meal

repasser (rer-pah-*say*) v press, iron; **repassage permanent** drip-dry

repentir (rer-pahng-*teer*) m repentance

répertoire (ray-pehr-*twaar*) m repertory

répéter (ray-pay-*tay*) v repeat; rehearse

répétition (ray-pay-tee-s*Yawng*) f repetition; rehearsal

répit (ray-*pee*) m respite

répondre (ray-*pawngdr*) v reply, answer

réponse (ray-*pawngss*) f reply, answer; **en ~** in reply; **sans ~** unanswered

reporter (rer-por-*tay*) m reporter

repos (rer-*poa*) m rest

reposant (rer-poa-*zahng*) adj restful

se reposer (rer-poa-*zay*) rest

repousser (rer-poo-*say*) v turn down; repel; **repoussant** repulsive

****reprendre** (rer-*prahngdr*) v resume;

*take over

représentant (rer-pray-zahng-*tahng*) m agent

représentatif (rer-pray-zahng-tah-*teef*) adj representative

représentation (rer-pray-zahng-tah-s*Yawng*) f show; representation

représenter (rer-pray-zahng-*tay*) v represent

réprimander (ray-pree-mahng-*day*) v reprimand

réprimer (ray-pree-*may*) v suppress

reprise (rer-*preez*) f revival; round

repriser (rer-pree-*zay*) v darn

reproche (rer-*prosh*) m reproach

reprocher (rer-pro-*shay*) v reproach

reproduction (rer-pro-dewk-s*Yawng*) f reproduction

****reproduire** (rer-pro-*dweer*) v reproduce

reptile (rehp-*teel*) m reptile

républicain (ray-pew-blee-*kang*) adj republican

république (ray-pew-*bleek*) f republic

répugnance (ray-pew-*ñahngss*) f dislike

répugnant (ray-pew-*ñahng*) adj repellent; filthy, disgusting, revolting

réputation (ray-pew-tah-s*Yawng*) f fame, reputation

****requérir** (rer-kay-*reer*) v request

requête (rer-*keht*) f request

requin (rer-*kang*) m shark

requis (rer-*kee*) adj requisite

réseau (ray-*zoa*) m network; ~ **routier** road system

réservation (ray-zehr-vah-s*Yawng*) f reservation; booking

réserve (ray-*zehrv*) f reserve; qualification; **de ~** spare; ~ **zoologique** game reserve

réserver (ray-zehr-*vay*) v reserve; book

réservoir (ray-zehr-*vwaar*) m reservoir;

tank; ~ **d'essence** petrol tank

résidence (ray-zee-*dahngss*) f residence

résident (ray-zee-*dahng*) m resident

résider (ray-zee-*day*) v reside

résille (ray-*zeey*) f hair-net

résine (ray-*zeen*) f resin

résistance (ray-zee-*stahngss*) f resistance

résister (ray-zee-*stay*) v resist

résolu (ray-zo-*lew*) adj determined, resolute

*****résoudre** (ray-*zoodr*) v solve

respect (reh-*spay*) m respect; esteem, regard

respectable (reh-spehk-*tahbl*) adj respectable

respecter (reh-spehk-*tay*) v respect

respectif (reh-spehk-*teef*) adj respective

respectueux (reh-spehk-*twur*) adj respectful

respiration (reh-spee-rah-*sᵞawng*) f breathing, respiration

respirer (reh-spee-*ray*) v breathe

resplendir (reh-splahng-*deer*) v *shine

responsabilité (reh-spawng-sah-bee-lee-*tay*) f responsibility; liability

responsable (reh-spawng-*sahbl*) adj responsible; liable

ressemblance (rer-sahng-*blahngss*) f resemblance

ressembler à (rer-sahng-*blay*) resemble

resserrer (rer-say-*ray*) v tighten; **se ~** tighten

ressort (rer-*sawr*) m spring

ressource (rer-*soors*) f expedient; **ressources** resources pl; means pl

restant (reh-*stahng*) adj remaining; m remnant, remainder

restaurant (reh-stoa-*rahng*) m restaurant; ~ **libre service** self-service restaurant

reste (rehst) m rest; remnant, remainder

rester (reh-*stay*) v stay; remain

restituer (reh-stee-*tway*) v reimburse

restriction (reh-streek-*sᵞawng*) f restriction; qualification

résultat (ray-zewl-*tah*) m result; issue, effect, outcome

résulter (ray-zewl-*tay*) v result

résumé (ray-zew-*may*) m résumé, summary

retard (rer-*taar*) m delay; **en ~** overdue, late

retarder (rer-tahr-*day*) v delay

*****retenir** (rert-*neer*) v reserve, book; remember; restrain

rétine (ray-*teen*) f retina

retirer (rer-tee-*ray*) v *withdraw; *draw

retour (rer-*tōōr*) m return; **voyage de ~** return journey

retourner (rer-toor-*nay*) v *get back; return, turn back, *go back; turn over, turn, turn round; **se ~** turn round

retracer (rer-trah-*say*) v trace

retraite (rer-*treht*) f retirement; pension

retraité (rer-tray-*tay*) adj retired

rétrécir (ray-tray-*seer*) v *shrink

réunion (ray-ew-*nᵞawng*) f meeting, assembly

réunir (ray-ew-*neer*) v join; reunite; **se ~** gather

réussir (ray-ew-*seer*) v manage, succeed; pass, *make; **réussi** successful

rêve (raiv) m dream

réveil (ray-*vay*) m alarm-clock

réveiller (ray-vay-*ᵞay*) v *awake, *wake; **réveillé** awake; **se ~** wake up

révélation (ray-vay-lah-*sᵞawng*) f revelation

révéler (ray-vay-*lay*) v reveal; *give away; **se ~** prove

revendeur (rer-vahng-*durr*) m retailer

revendication (rer-vahng-dee-kah-s^yawng) f claim

revendiquer (rer-vahng-dee-*kay*) v claim

***revenir** (rer-*vneer*) v return

revenu (rer-*vnew*) m earnings pl, income, revenue

rêver (ray-*vay*) v *dream

revers (rer-*vair*) m reverse; lapel

revirement (rer-veer-*mahng*) m reverse, turn

reviser (rer-vee-*zay*) v revise; overhaul

révision (ray-vee-z^yawng) f revision

***revoir** (rer-*vwaar*) v *see again; review; **au revoir!** good-bye!

révoltant (ray-vol-*tahng*) adj revolting

révolte (ray-*volt*) f revolt, rebellion

se révolter (ray-vol-*tay*) revolt

révolution (ray-vo-lew-s^yawng) f revolution

révolutionnaire (ray-vo-lew-s^yo-*nair*) adj revolutionary

revolver (ray-vol-*vair*) m gun, revolver

révoquer (ray-vo-*kay*) v recall

revue (rer-*vew*) f revue; review, magazine; **~ mensuelle** monthly magazine

rez-de-chaussée (reh-dshoa-*say*) m ground floor

rhinocéros (ree-no-say-*ross*) m rhinoceros

rhubarbe (rew-*bahrb*) f rhubarb

rhumatisme (rew-mah-*teesm*) m rheumatism

rhume (rewm) m cold; **~ des foins** hay fever

riche (reesh) adj rich; wealthy

richesse (ree-*shehss*) f wealth; riches pl

ride (reed) f wrinkle

rideau (ree-*doa*) m curtain

ridicule (ree-dee-*kewl*) adj ridiculous; ludicrous

ridiculiser (ree-dee-kew-lee-*zay*) v ridicule

rien (r^yang) pron nothing; nil; **ne ... ~** nothing; **~ que** only

rime (reem) f rhyme

rinçage (rang-*saazh*) m rinse

rincer (rang-*say*) v rinse

rire (reer) m laughter, laugh

***rire** (reer) v laugh

risque (reesk) m risk; chance

risquer (ree-*skay*) v venture, risk; **risqué** risky

rivage (ree-*vaazh*) m shore

rival (ree-*vahl*) m rival

rivaliser (ree-vah-lee-*zay*) v rival

rivalité (ree-vah-lee-*tay*) f rivalry

rive (reev) f bank, shore

rivière (ree-v^yair) f river

riz (ree) m rice

robe (rob) f dress; robe, frock, gown; **~ de chambre** dressing-gown

robinet (ro-bee-*nay*) m tap; faucet nAm

robuste (ro-*bewst*) adj solid, robust

rocher (ro-*shay*) m rock, boulder

rocheux (ro-*shur*) adj rocky

roi (rwah) m king

rôle (roal) m role

roman (ro-*mahng*) m novel; **~ policier** detective story

romancier (ro-mahng-s^yay) m novelist

romantique (ro-mahng-*teek*) adj romantic

rompre (rawngpr) v *break

rond (rawng) adj round

rond-point (rawng-*pwang*) m roundabout

ronfler (rawng-*flay*) v snore

rosaire (roa-*zair*) m rosary

rose (roaz) f rose; adj pink, rose

roseau (roa-*zoa*) m reed

rosée (roa-*zay*) f dew

rossignol (ro-see-ñol) *m* nightingale

rotation (ro-tah-sʸawng) *f* revolution

rotin (ro-tang) *m* rattan

rôtir (roa-teer) *v* roast

rôtisserie (ro-tee-sree) *f* grill-room

rotule (ro-tewl) *f* kneecap

roue (roo) *f* wheel; ~ **de secours** spare wheel

rouge (roozh) *adj* red; *m* rouge; ~ **à lèvres** lipstick

rouge-gorge (roozh-gorzh) *m* robin

rougeole (roo-zhol) *f* measles

rougir (roo-zheer) *v* blush

rouille (rooᵉᵉ) *f* rust

rouillé (roo-ʸay) *adj* rusty

rouleau (roo-loa) *m* roll

rouler (roo-lay) *v* roll; *ride

roulette (roo-leht) *f* roulette

roulotte (roo-lot) *f* caravan

Roumain (roo-mang) *m* Rumanian

roumain (roo-mang) *adj* Rumanian

Roumanie (roo-mah-nee) *f* Rumania

route (root) *f* drive, road; route; **en ~ pour** bound for; ~ **à péage** turnpike *nAm*; ~ **d'évitement** by-pass; ~ **en réfection** road up; ~ **principale** highway, thoroughfare, main road

routine (roo-teen) *f* routine

royal (rwah-ʸahl) *adj* royal

royaume (rwah-ʸōam) *m* kingdom

ruban (rew-bahng) *m* ribbon; ~ **adhésif** adhesive tape, scotch tape

rubis (rew-bee) *m* ruby

rubrique (rew-breek) *f* column

ruche (rewsh) *f* beehive

rude (rewd) *adj* bleak

rue (rew) *f* street; road; ~ **principale** main street; ~ **transversale** side-street

ruelle (rwehl) *f* alley, lane

rugir (rew-zheer) *v* roar

rugissement (rew-zhee-smahng) *m* roar

rugueux (rew-gur) *adj* rough

ruine (rween) *f* ruins; ruin

ruiner (rwee-nay) *v* ruin

ruisseau (rwee-soa) *m* brook, stream

rumeur (rew-mūr) *f* rumour

rural (rew-rahl) *adj* rural

ruse (rēwz) *f* ruse, artifice

rusé (rew-zay) *adj* cunning

Russe (rewss) *m* Russian

russe (rewss) *adj* Russian

Russie (rew-see) *f* Russia

rustique (rew-steek) *adj* rustic

rythme (reetm) *m* rhythm; pace

S

sable (sahbl) *m* sand

sableux (sah-blur) *adj* sandy

sabot (sah-boa) *m* wooden shoe; hoof

sac (sahk) *m* bag; sack; ~ **à dos** rucksack; ~ **à glace** ice-bag; ~ **à main** bag, handbag; ~ **à provisions** shopping bag; ~ **de couchage** sleeping-bag; ~ **en papier** paper bag

saccharine (sah-kah-reen) *f* saccharin

sacré (sah-kray) *adj* holy, sacred

sacrifice (sah-kree-feess) *m* sacrifice

sacrifier (sah-kree-fʸay) *v* sacrifice

sacrilège (sah-kree-laizh) *m* sacrilege

sacristain (sah-kree-stang) *m* sexton

sage (saazh) *adj* wise; good

sage-femme (sahzh-fahm) *f* midwife

sagesse (sah-zhehss) *f* wisdom

saigner (say-ñay) *v* *bleed

sain (sang) *adj* healthy; wholesome, well

saint (sang) *m* saint

saisir (say-zeer) *v* seize; *catch, grip, *take, grasp

saison (seh-zawng) *f* season; **hors ~** off season; **morte-saison** *f* low season; **pleine ~** peak season

salade (sah-*lahd*) f salad

salaire (sah-*lair*) m salary, pay

salaud (sah-*loa*) m bastard

sale (sahl) adj dirty; filthy

salé (sah-*lay*) adj salty

saleté (sahl-*tay*) f dirt

salière (sah-*l^yair*) f salt-cellar

salir (sah-*leer*) v soil

salive (sah-*leev*) f spit

salle (sahl) f hall; **~ à manger** dining-room; **~ d'attente** waiting-room; **~ de bain** bathroom; **~ de bal** ballroom; **~ de banquet** banqueting-hall; **~ de classe** classroom; **~ de concert** concert hall; **~ de lecture** reading-room; **~ de séjour** living-room; **~ d'exposition** showroom

salon (sah-*lawng*) m sitting-room; drawing-room, salon; **~ de beauté** beauty salon; **~ de thé** tea-shop

salopette (sah-lo-*peht*) f overalls pl

saluer (sah-*lway*) v greet; salute

salut (sah-*lew*) m welfare

salutation (sah-lew-tah-*s^yawng*) f greeting

samedi (sahm-*dee*) m Saturday

sanatorium (sah-nah-to-*r^yom*) m sanatorium

sanctuaire (sahngk-*twair*) m shrine

sandale (sahng-*dahl*) f sandal

sandwich (sahng-*dweech*) m sandwich

sang (sahng) m blood; **pur ~** thoroughbred

sanitaire (sah-nee-*tair*) adj sanitary

sans (sahng) prep without

santé (sahng-*tay*) f health

saphir (sah-*feer*) m sapphire

sapin (sah-*pang*) m fir-tree

sardine (sahr-*deen*) f sardine

satellite (sah-tay-*leet*) m satellite

satin (sah-*tang*) m satin

satisfaction (sah-teess-fahk-*s^yawng*) f satisfaction

*satisfaire (sah-tee-*sfair*) v satisfy; **satisfait** satisfied; content

sauce (sōass) f sauce

saucisse (soa-*seess*) f sausage

sauf (soaf) prep but

saumon (soa-*mawng*) m salmon

sauna (soa-*nah*) m sauna

saut (soa) m jump; hop, leap; **~ à ski** ski-jump

sauter (soa-*tay*) v jump; skip; *faire ~** fry

sauterelle (soa-*trehl*) f grasshopper

sautiller (soa tēē-*^yay*) v hop, skip

sauvage (soa-*vaazh*) adj savage; wild, fierce, desert

sauver (soa-*vay*) v rescue, save

sauvetage (soav-*taazh*) m rescue

sauveur (soa-*vūr*) m saviour

savant (sah-*vahng*) m scientist

saveur (sah-*vūr*) f flavour

*savoir (sah-*vwaar*) v *know; *be able to

savon (sah-*vawng*) m soap; **~ à barbe** shaving-soap; **~ en poudre** washing-powder

savoureux (sah-voo-*rur*) adj tasty, savoury

scandale (skahng-*dahl*) m scandal

Scandinave (skahng-dee-*naav*) m Scandinavian

scandinave (skahng-dee-*naav*) adj Scandinavian

Scandinavie (skahng-dee-nah-*vee*) f Scandinavia

scarabée (skah-rah-*bay*) m beetle

sceau (soa) m seal

scélérat (say-lay-*rah*) m villain

scène (sehn) f scene; stage; **metteur en ~** director; ***mettre en ~** direct

schéma (shay-*mah*) m diagram

scie (see) f saw

science (s^yahngss) f science

scientifique (s^yahng-tee-*feek*) *adj* scientific

scierie (see-*ree*) f saw-mill

scintillant (sang-tee-^y*ahng*) *adj* sparkling

sciure (see-*ewr*) f sawdust

scolaire (sko-*lair*) *adj* school-

scooter (skoo-*tair*) m scooter

scout (skoot) m scout; boy scout

sculpteur (skewl-*tūrr*) m sculptor

sculpture (skewl-*tewr*) f sculpture; ~ **sur bois** wood-carving

se (ser) *pron* himself; herself; themselves

séance (say-*ahngss*) f session

seau (soa) m bucket, pail

sec (sehk) *adj* (f sèche) dry

sèche-cheveux (sehsh-sher-*vur*) m hair-dryer

sécher (say-*shay*) v dry

sécheresse (say-*shrehss*) f drought

séchoir (say-*shwaar*) m dryer

second (ser-*gawng*) *adj* second

secondaire (ser-gawng-*dair*) *adj* secondary; subordinate

seconde (ser-*gawngd*) f second

secouer (ser-*kway*) v *shake

secours (ser-*kōōr*) m assistance; **premier** ~ first-aid

secousse (ser-*kooss*) f wrench

secret¹ (ser-*kray*) m secret

secret² (ser-*kray*) *adj* (f secrète) secret

secrétaire (ser-kray-*tair*) m clerk, secretary

section (sehk-s^y*awng*) f section; stretch

sécurité (say-kew-ree-*tay*) f safety, security; **glissière de** ~ crash barrier

sédatif (say-dah-*teef*) m sedative

sédiment (say-dee-*mahng*) m deposit

*séduire (say-*dweer*) v seduce

séduisant (say-dwee-*zahng*) *adj* attractive, charming

sein (sang) m breast; bosom

seize (saiz) *num* sixteen

seizième (seh-z^y*ehm*) *num* sixteenth

séjour (say-*zhōōr*) m stay

séjourner (say-zhoor-*nay*) v stay

sel (sehl) m salt; **sels de bain** bath salts

sélection (say-lehk-s^y*awng*) f choice, selection

sélectionner (say-lehk-s^yo-*nay*) v select

selle (sehl) f saddle

selon (ser-*lawng*) *prep* according to

semaine (ser-*mehn*) f week

semblable (sahng-*blahbl*) *adj* alike

sembler (sahng-*blay*) v seem; look, appear

semelle (ser-*mehl*) f sole

semence (ser-*mahngss*) f seed

semer (ser-*may*) v *sow

semi- (ser-*mee*) semi-

sénat (say-*nah*) m senate

sénateur (say-nah-*tūrr*) m senator

sénile (say-*neel*) *adj* senile

sens (sahngss) m sense; reason; **bon** ~ sense; **en** ~ **inverse** the other way round; ~ **unique** one-way traffic

sensation (sahng-sah-s^y*awng*) f sensation; feeling

sensationnel (sahng-sah-s^yo-*nehl*) *adj* sensational

sensible (sahng-*seebl*) *adj* sensitive; considerable

sentence (sahng-*tahngss*) f verdict

sentier (sahng-t^y*ay*) m path; trail; ~ **pour piétons** footpath

sentimental (sahng-tee-mahng-*tahl*) *adj* sentimental

*sentir (sahng-*teer*) v *feel; *smell; ~ **mauvais** *smell

séparation (say-pah-rah-s^y*awng*) f division

séparé (say-pah-*ray*) *adj* separate

séparément (say-pah-ray-*mahng*) *adv*
apart

séparer (say-pah-*ray*) *v* separate; divide, part

sept (seht) *num* seven

septembre (sehp-*tahngbr*) September

septentrional (sehp-tahng-tree-o-*nahl*)
adj northern, north

septicémie (sehp-tee-say-*mee*) *f*
blood-poisoning

septième (seh-*t Yehm*) *num* seventh

septique (sehp-*teek*) *adj* septic

sépulture (say-pewl-*tewr*) *f* burial

serein (ser-*rang*) *adj* serene

série (say-*ree*) *f* sequence; series

sérieux (say-*r Yur*) *adj* serious; *m* seriousness

seringue (ser-*rangg*) *f* syringe

serment (sehr-*mahng*) *m* vow, oath;
faux ~ perjury

sermon (sehr-*mawng*) *m* sermon

serpent (sehr-*pahng*) *m* snake

serpentant (sehr-pahng-*tahng*) *adj*
winding

serpenter (sehr-pahng-*tay*) *v* *wind

serre (sair) *f* greenhouse

serrer (say-*ray*) *v* tighten; **serré** tight,
narrow

serrure (say-*rewr*) *f* lock; **trou de la
~** keyhole

sérum (say-*rom*) *m* serum

serveuse (sehr-*vurz*) *f* waitress

serviable (sehr-*v Yahbl*) *adj* helpful

service (sehr-*veess*) *m* service; service
charge; section; **~ à thé** tea-set; **~
de table** dinner-service; **~ d'étage**
room service; **services postaux**
postal service

serviette (sehr-*v Yeht*) *f* towel; napkin,
serviette; briefcase; **~ de bain** bath
towel; **~ de papier** paper napkin;
~ hygiénique sanitary towel

***servir** (sehr-*veer*) *v* serve; attend on,
wait on; *be of use; **se ~ de** apply

serviteur (sehr-vee-*turr*) *m* boy

seuil (sur[ee]) *m* threshold

seul (surl) *adv* alone; *adj* single, only

seulement (surl-*mahng*) *adv* only;
merely

sévère (say-*vair*) *adj* strict; harsh; severe

sévir (say-*veer*) *v* rage

sexe (sehks) *m* sex

sexualité (sehk-swah-lee-*tay*) *f* sexuality

sexuel (sehk-*swehl*) *adj* sexual

shampooing (shahng-*pwang*) *m*
shampoo

si (see) *conj* if; whether; *adv* so; **si
... ou** whether ... or

Siam (s Yahm) *m* Siam

Siamois (s Yah-*mwah*) *m* Siamese

siamois (s Yah-*mwah*) *adj* Siamese

siècle (s Yehkl) *m* century

siège (s Yaizh) *m* chair, seat; siege

le sien (ler s Yang) his

siffler (see-*flay*) *v* whistle

sifflet (see-*flay*) *m* whistle

signal (see-*ñahl*) *m* signal; **~ de détresse** distress signal

signalement (see-ñahl-*mahng*) *m* description

signaler (see-ñah-*lay*) *v* signal; indicate

signature (see-ñah-*tewr*) *f* signature

signe (seeñ) *m* sign; token, signal, indication; ***faire ~** wave

signer (see-*ñay*) *v* sign

significatif (see-ñee-fee-kah-*teef*) *adj*
significant

signification (see-ñee-fee-kah-*s Yawng*)
f meaning, sense

signifier (see-ñee-*f Yay*) *v* *mean

silence (see-*lahngss*) *m* silence; quiet,
stillness

silencieux (see-lahng-*s Yur*) *adj* silent;
m silencer; muffler *nAm*

sillon (see-*Yawng*) *m* groove

similaire (see-mee-*lair*) *adj* similar

similitude (see-mee-lee-*tewd*) *f* similarity

simple (saṅgpl) *adj* simple; plain

simplement (saṅg-pler-*mahṅg*) *adv* simply

simuler (see-mew-*lay*) *v* simulate

simultané (see-mewl-tah-*nay*) *adj* simultaneous

sincère (saṅg-*sair*) *adj* honest, sincere

singe (saṅgzh) *m* monkey

singulier (saṅg-gew-*l*ʸay) *m* singular; *adj* peculiar, singular, queer

sinistre (see-*neestr*) *adj* sinister, ominous; *m* catastrophe

sinon (see-*nawṅg*) *conj* otherwise

siphon (see-*fawṅg*) *m* siphon, syphon

sirène (see-*rehn*) *f* siren; mermaid

sirop (see-*roa*) *m* syrup

site (seet) *m* site

situation (see-twah-sʸ*awṅg*) *f* situation; position, location

situé (see-*tway*) *adj* situated

six (seess) *num* six

sixième (see-zʸ*ehm*) *num* sixth

ski (skee) *m* ski; skiing; ~ **nautique** water ski

skier (skee-*ay*) *v* ski

skieur (skee-*ūr*) *m* skier

slip (sleep) *m* knickers *pl*, briefs *pl*

slogan (slogahṅg) *m* slogan

smoking (smo-*keeng*) *m* dinner-jacket; tuxedo *nAm*

snob (snob) *adj* snooty

sobre (sobr) *adj* sober

social (so-sʸ*ahl*) *adj* social

socialisme (so-sʸah-*leesm*) *m* socialism

socialiste (so-sʸah-*leest*) *adj* socialist; *m* socialist

société (so-sʸay-*tay*) *f* community, society; company

sœur (sūr) *f* sister

oi (swah) *pron* oneself; **soi-même**

pron oneself

soi-disant (swah-dee-*zahṅg*) *adj* so-called

soie (swah) *f* silk

soif (swahf) *f* thirst

soigné (swah-*ñay*) *adj* neat; thorough

soigner (swah-*ñay*) *v* tend; nurse

soigneux (swah-*ñur*) *adj* careful

soin (swaṅg) *m* care; ***prendre ~ de** *take care of; **soins de beauté** beauty treatment

soir (swaar) *m* night, evening; **ce ~** tonight

soirée (swah-*ray*) *f* evening

soit ... soit (swah) either ... or

soixante (swah-*sahṅgt*) *num* sixty

soixante-dix (swah-sahṅgt-*deess*) *num* seventy

sol (sol) *m* floor; soil, earth, ground

soldat (sol-*dah*) *m* soldier

solde (sold) *m* balance; **soldes** sales, clearance sale

sole (sol) *f* sole

soleil (so-*lay*) *m* sun; sunshine; **coucher du ~** sunset; **coup de ~** sunburn; **lever du ~** sunrise

solennel (so-lah-*nehl*) *adj* solemn

solide (so-*leed*) *adj* solid; firm, sound; *m* solid

solitaire (so-lee-*tair*) *adj* lonely

solitude (so-lee-*tewd*) *f* loneliness

soluble (so-*lewbl*) *adj* soluble

solution (so-lew-sʸ*awṅg*) *f* solution

sombre (sawṅgbr) *adj* sombre, obscure; gloomy

sommaire (so-*mair*) *m* summary

somme (som) *f* sum; amount; *m* nap; ~ **globale** lump sum

sommeil (so-*may*) *m* sleep

sommelier (so-mer-*l*ʸay) *m* wine-waiter

sommet (so-*may*) *m* summit; top, peak, height; ~ **de colline** hilltop

somnifère (som-nee-*fair*) *m* sleeping-pill

somnolent (som-no-*lahng*) *adj* sleepy

son[1] (sawng) *adj* (f sa, pl ses) his; her

son[2] (sawng) *m* sound

songer (sawng-*zhay*) *v* *dream; ~ à *think of

sonner (so-*nay*) *v* sound; *ring

sonnette (so-*neht*) *f* bell; doorbell

sorcière (sor-*s*ʸ*air*) *f* witch

sort (sawr) *m* fortune, lot, destiny

sorte (sort) *f* sort; **toutes sortes de** all sorts of

sortie (sor-*tee*) *f* way out, exit; ~ **de secours** emergency exit

sortir (sor-*teer*) *v* *go out

sot (soa) *adj* (f sotte) foolish, silly

sottise (so-*teez*) *f* nonsense, rubbish

souche (soosh) *f* stub

souci (soo-*see*) *m* concern, worry; care

se soucier de (soo-s*ʸay*) care about

soucieux (soo-s*ʸur*) *adj* concerned, worried

soucoupe (soo-*koop*) *f* saucer

soudain (soo-*dang*) *adj* sudden; *adv* suddenly

souder (soo-*day*) *v* solder; weld

soudure (soo-*dewr*) *f* joint

souffle (soofl) *m* breath

souffler (soo-*flay*) *v* *blow

souffrance (soo-*frahngss*) *f* suffering

souffrir (soo-*freer*) *v* suffer

souhait (sweh) *m* wish

souhaiter (sway-*tay*) *v* wish

souillé (soo-ʸ*ay*) *adj* soiled, dirty

souillure (soo-ʸ*ewr*) *f* blot

soulagement (soo-lahzh-*mahng*) *m* relief

soulager (soo-lah-*zhay*) *v* relieve

soulever (sool-*vay*) *v* lift; *bring up

soulier (soo-*l*ʸ*ay*) *m* shoe

souligner (soo-lee-*ñay*) *v* underline; stress, emphasize

soumettre (soo-*mehtr*) *v* subject; se

~ submit

soupape (soo-*pahp*) *f* valve

soupçon (soop-*sawng*) *m* suspicion

soupçonner (soop-so-*nay*) *v* suspect

soupçonneux (soop-so-*nur*) *adj* suspicious

soupe (soop) *f* soup

souper (soo-*pay*) *m* supper

souple (soopl) *adj* supple; flexible

source (soors) *f* well; fountain, source, spring

sourcil (soor-*see*) *m* eyebrow

sourd (soor) *adj* deaf

sourire (soo-*reer*) *m* smile; ~ **forcé** grin

sourire (soo-*reer*) *v* smile

souris (soo-*ree*) *f* mouse

sous (soo) *prep* under

sous-estimer (soo-zeh-stee-*may*) *v* underestimate

sous-locataire (soo-lo-kah-*tair*) *m* lodger

sous-marin (soo-mah-*rang*) *adj* underwater

soussigné (soo-see-*ñay*) *m* undersigned

sous-sol (soo-*sol*) *m* basement

sous-titre (soo-*teetr*) *m* subtitle

soustraire (soo-*strair*) *v* subtract

sous-vêtements (soo-veht-*mahng*) *mpl* underwear

soutenir (soot-*neer*) *v* support; *hold up

souterrain (soo-teh-*rang*) *adj* underground

soutien (soo-t*ʸang*) *m* support; relief

soutien-gorge (soo-t*ʸang*-*gorzh*) *m* brassiere, bra

souvenir (soo-*vneer*) *m* memory, remembrance; souvenir; se *souvenir recollect

souvent (soo-*vahng*) *adv* often; **le plus** ~ mostly

souverain (soo-*vrang*) *m* sovereign

soyeux (swah-*Yur*) *adj* silken

spacieux (spah-*sYur*) *adj* spacious, roomy, large

sparadrap (spah-rah-*drah*) *m* plaster, adhesive tape

spécial (spay-s*Yahl*) *adj* special; peculiar, particular

spécialement (spay-sYahl-*mahng*) *adv* especially

se spécialiser (spay-sYah-lee-*zay*) specialize

spécialiste (spay-sYah-*leest*) *m* specialist, expert

spécialité (spay-sYah-lee-*tay*) *f* speciality

spécifique (spay-see-*feek*) *adj* specific

spécimen (spay-see-*mehn*) *m* specimen

spectacle (spehk-*tahkl*) *m* spectacle; show; sight; ~ **de variétés** floor show, variety show

spectaculaire (spehk-tah-kew-*lair*) *adj* sensational

spectateur (spehk-tah-*tūr*) *m* spectator

spectre (spehktr) *m* spook

spéculer (spay-kew-*lay*) *v* speculate

sphère (sfair) *f* sphere

spirituel (spee-ree-*twehl*) *adj* spiritual; witty, humorous

spiritueux (spee-ree-*twur*) *mpl* liquor, spirits

splendeur (splahng-*dūr*) *f* splendour

splendide (splahng-*deed*) *adj* splendid; wonderful, glorious, enchanting, magnificent

sport (spawr) *m* sport; **sports d'hiver** winter sports

sportif (spor-*teef*) *m* sportsman

square (skwaar) *m* square

squelette (sker-*leht*) *m* skeleton

stable (stahbl) *adj* permanent, stable; solid, fixed

stade (stahd) *m* stadium

stand (stahng) *m* stand; ~ **de livres** bookstand

standard (stahng-*daar*) *adj* standard

standardiste (stahng-dahr-*deest*) *f* telephone operator, operator

starter (stahr-*tair*) *m* choke

station (stah-s*Yawng*) *f* station; ~ **balnéaire** seaside resort; ~ **de taxis** taxi rank; taxi stand *Am*; **station-service** *f* filling station, service station; gas station *Am*; ~ **thermale** spa

stationnaire (stah-sYo-*nair*) *adj* stationary

stationnement (stah-sYon-*mahng*) *m* parking; ~ **interdit** no parking

statistique (stah-tee-*steek*) *f* statistics *pl*

statue (stah-*tew*) *f* statue

stature (stah-*tēwr*) *f* figure

sténographe (stay-noa-*grahf*) *m* stenographer

sténographie (stay-noa-grah-*fee*) *f* shorthand

stéréo (*stay*-ray-oa) *f* stereo

stérile (stay-*reel*) *adj* sterile

stériliser (stay-ree-lee-*zay*) *v* sterilize

stimulant (stee-mew-*lahng*) *m* impulse; stimulant

stimuler (stee-mew-*lay*) *v* stimulate

stipulation (stee-pew-lah-s*Yawng*) *f* stipulation

stipuler (stee-pew-*lay*) *v* stipulate

stock (stok) *m* stock; supply; *avoir en* ~ stock

stop! (stop) stop!

stops (stop) *mpl* brake lights

store (stawr) *m* blind

strophe (strof) *f* stanza

structure (strewk-*tēwr*) *f* structure; fabric

stupide (stew-*peed*) *adj* foolish, stupid

style (steel) *m* style

stylo (stee-*loa*) *m* fountain-pen; ~ **à**

bille ballpoint-pen

subalterne (sew-bahl-*tehrn*) *adj* minor

subir (sew-*beer*) *v* suffer

sublime (sew-*bleem*) *adj* grand

subordonné (sew-bor-do-*nay*) *adj* subordinate

subsistance (sewb-zee-*stahngss*) *f* livelihood

substance (sewb-*stahngss*) *f* substance

substantiel (sewb-stahng-s*y*ehl) *adj* substantial

substantif (sewb-stahng-*teef*) *m* noun

substituer (sewb-stee-*tway*) *v* substitute

substitut (sewb-stee-*tew*) *m* substitute; deputy

subtil (sewb-*teel*) *adj* subtle

suburbain (sew-bewr-*bang*) *adj* suburban

subvention (sewb-vahng-s*y*awng) *f* subsidy; grant

succéder (sewk-say-*day*) *v* succeed

succès (sewk-*say*) *m* success; hit

succession (sewk-seh-s*y*awng) *f* sequence

succomber (sew-kawng-*bay*) *v* succumb

succulent (sew-kew-*lahng*) *adj* tasty

succursale (sew-kewr-*sahl*) *f* branch

sucer (sew-*say*) *v* suck

sucre (sewkr) *m* sugar

sucrer (sew-*kray*) *v* sweeten; **sucré** sweet

sud (sewd) *m* south

sud-américain (sew-dah-may-ree-*kang*) *adj* Latin-American

sud-est (sew-*dehst*) *m* south-east

sud-ouest (sew-*dwehst*) *m* south-west

Suède (swehd) *f* Sweden

Suédois (sway-*dwah*) *m* Swede

suédois (sway-*dwah*) *adj* Swedish

suer (sway) *v* perspire, sweat

sueur (swurr) *f* perspiration, sweat

** **suffire** (sew-*feer*) *v* *do, suffice

suffisant (sew-fee-*zahng*) *adj* enough, sufficient

suffoquer (sew-fo-*kay*) *v* choke

suffrage (sew-*fraazh*) *m* suffrage

suggérer (sewg-zhay-*ray*) *v* suggest

suggestion (sewg-zheh-st*y*awng) *f* suggestion

suicide (swee-*seed*) *m* suicide

Suisse (sweess) *f* Switzerland; *m* Swiss

suisse (sweess) *adj* Swiss

suite (sweet) *f* sequel; series; **et ainsi de ~** and so on; **par la ~** afterwards; **tout de ~** at once, instantly

suivant (swee-*vahng*) *adj* following, next

** **suivre** (sweevr) *v* follow; ***faire ~** forward

sujet (sew-*zhay*) *m* subject; issue, topic, theme; **~ à** liable to, subject to

superbe (sew-*pehrb*) *adj* superb

superficiel (sew-pehr-fee-s*y*ehl) *adj* superficial

superflu (sew-pehr-*flew*) *adj* superfluous; unnecessary, redundant

supérieur (sew-pay-r*y*urr) *adj* superior; top, upper; excellent

superlatif (sew-pehr-lah-*teef*) *adj* superlative; *m* superlative

supermarché (sew-pehr-mahr-*shay*) *m* supermarket

superstition (sew-pehr-stee-s*y*awng) *f* superstition

superviser (sew-pehr-vee-*zay*) *v* supervise

supervision (sew-pehr-vee-z*y*awng) *f* supervision

supplément (sew-play-*mahng*) *m* supplement; surcharge

supplémentaire (sew-play-mahng-*tair*) *adj* additional; extra

supplier (sew-plee-*ay*) *v* beg

supporter[1] (sew-por-*tay*) *v* *bear;

support

supporter² (sew-por-*tair*) *m* supporter

supposer (sew-poa-*zay*) *v* suppose; guess, assume, reckon

suppositoire (sew-poa-zee-*twaar*) *m* suppository

supprimer (sew-pree-*may*) *v* *do away with

suprême (sew-*prehm*) *adj* supreme

sur (sewr) *prep* upon, on; in; about

sûr (sewr) *adj* sure; safe, secure; **bien** ~ naturally

surcharge (sewr-*shahrzh*) *f* overweight

sûrement (sewr-*mahng*) *adv* surely

surface (sewr-*fahss*) *f* surface; area

surgir (sewr-*zheer*) *v* *arise

surmené (sewr-mer-*nay*) *adj* overtired, overstrung

se surmener (sewr-mer-*nay*) overwork

surnom (sewr-*nawng*) *m* nickname

surpasser (sewr-pah-*say*) *v* *outdo, exceed

surplus (sewr-*plew*) *m* surplus

***surprendre** (sewr-*prahngdr*) *v* surprise; amaze; *catch

surprise (sewr-*preez*) *f* surprise

surprise-partie (sewr-preez-pahr-*tee*) *f* party

surtout (sewr-*too*) *adv* most of all

surveillance (sewr-veh-*Yahngss*) *f* supervision

surveillant (sewr-veh-*Yahng*) *m* warden, supervisor

surveiller (sewr-vay-*Yay*) *v* watch; guard, patrol

***survenir** (sewr-ver-*neer*) *v* occur

survie (sewr-*vee*) *f* survival

***survivre** (sewr-*veevr*) *v* survive

suspect (sew-*spehkt*) *adj* suspicious; *m* suspect

suspecter (sew-spehk-*tay*) *v* suspect

suspendre (sew-*spahngdr*) *v* *hang; discontinue, suspend

suspension (sew-spahng-*sYawng*) *f* suspension

suture (sew-*tewr*) *f* stitch

suturer (sew-tew-*ray*) *v* sew up

svelte (svehlt) *adj* slender

Swahili (swah-ee-*lee*) *m* Swahili

syllabe (see-*lahb*) *f* syllable

symbole (sang-*bol*) *m* symbol

sympathie (sang-pah-*tee*) *f* sympathy

sympathique (sang-pah-*teek*) *adj* nice; pleasant

symphonie (sang-fo-*nee*) *f* symphony

symptôme (sangp-*tōam*) *m* symptom

synagogue (see-nah-*gog*) *f* synagogue

syndicat (sang-dee-*kah*) *m* trade-union; ~ **d'initiative** tourist office

synonyme (see-no-*neem*) *m* synonym

synthétique (sang-tay-*teek*) *adj* synthetic

Syrie (see-*ree*) *f* Syria

Syrien (see-*rYang*) *m* Syrian

syrien (see-*rYang*) *adj* Syrian

systématique (see-stay-mah-*teek*) *adj* systematic

système (see-*stehm*) *m* system; ~ **décimal** decimal system; ~ **de lubrification** lubrication system; ~ **de refroidissement** cooling system

T

tabac (tah-*bah*) *m* tobacco; **bureau de** ~ tobacconist's; **débitant de** ~ tobacconist; ~ **à rouler** cigarette tobacco; **tabac pour pipe** pipe tobacco

table (tahbl) *f* table; ~ **des matières** table of contents

tableau (tah-*bloa*) *m* chart; board; ~ **de bord** dashboard; ~ **de conversions** conversion chart; ~ **de distribution** switchboard; ~ **noir** blackboard

tablette (tah-*bleht*) f tablet

tablier (tah-blee-*ay*) m apron

tabou (tah-*boo*) m taboo

tache (tahsh) f speck, stain, spot, blot

tâche (taash) f duty, task

tacher (tah-*shay*) v stain

tâcher (tah-*shay*) v try

tacheté (tahsh-*tay*) adj spotted

tactique (tahk-*teek*) f tactics pl

taille (tigh) f waist; size

taille-crayon (tigh-kreh-*Yawng*) m pencil-sharpener

tailler (tah-*Yay*) v trim, chip; carve

tailleur (tah-*Yūrr*) m tailor

se *taire (tair) v *keep quiet, *be silent

talc (tahlk) m talc powder

talent (tah-*lahng*) m talent; faculty, gift

talon (tah-*lawng*) m heel; counterfoil

tambour (tahng-*bōōr*) m drum; **~ de frein** brake drum

tamiser (tah-mee-*zay*) v sift, sieve

tampon (tahng-*pawng*) m tampon

tamponner (tahng-po-*nay*) v bump

tandis que (tahng-dee ker) while; whilst

tangible (tahng-*zheebl*) adj tangible

tanière (tah-*n'air*) f den

tante (tahngt) f aunt

tapageur (tah-pah-*zhūrr*) adj rowdy

taper (tah-*pay*) v *strike; **~ à la machine** type

tapis (tah-*pee*) m carpet; rug, mat

tapisserie (tah-pee-*sree*) f tapestry

taquiner (tah-kee-*nay*) v kid, tease

tard (taar) adj late

tarif (tah-*reef*) m rate

tartine (tahr-*teen*) f sandwich

tas (tah) m pile, lot, heap

tasse (tahss) f cup; **~ à thé** teacup

taureau (toa-*roa*) m bull

taux (toa) m tariff; **~ d'escompte** bank-rate

taverne (tah-*vehrn*) f tavern

taxation (tahk-sah-*s'awng*) f taxation

taxe (tahks) f tax

taxi (tahk-*see*) m taxi; cab; **chauffeur de ~** taxi-driver

taximètre (tahk-see-*mehtr*) m taximeter

Tchèque (chehk) m Czech

tchèque (chehk) adj Czech

te (ter) pron you; yourself

technicien (tehk-nee-s'*ang*) m technician

technique (tehk-*neek*) f technique; adj technical

technologie (tehk-no-lo-*zhee*) f technology

*teindre (tangdr) v dye

teint (tang) m complexion; **grand ~** fast-dyed

teinture (tang-*tewr*) f dye

teinturerie (tang-tewr-*ree*) f dry-cleaner's

tel (tehl) adj such; **~ que** such as

télégramme (tay-lay-*grahm*) m cable, telegram

télégraphier (tay-lay-grah-*f'ay*) v cable, telegraph

télémètre (tay-lay-*mehtr*) m range-finder

télé-objectif (tay-lay-ob-zhehk-*teef*) m telephoto lens

télépathie (tay-lay-pah-*tee*) f telepathy

téléphone (tay-lay-*fon*) m telephone; phone; **coup de ~** telephone call

téléphoner (tay-lay-fo-*nay*) v phone; call, ring up; call up Am

téléphoniste (tay-lay-fo-*neest*) f telephonist

téléski (tay-lay-*skee*) m ski-lift

télévision (tay-lay-vee-z'*awng*) f television; television set; **~ par câble** cable television; **~ par satellite** satellite television

télex (tay-*lehks*) m telex

tellement (tehl-*mahng*) adv such; so

téméraire (tay-may-*rair*) *adj* daring

témoignage (tay-mwah-n^y*aazh*) *m* testimony

témoigner (tay-mwah-*ñay*) *v* testify

témoin (tay-*mwang*) *m* witness; ~ **oculaire** eye-witness

tempe (tahngp) *f* temple

température (tahng-pay-rah-*tewr*) *f* temperature; ~ **ambiante** room temperature

tempête (tahng-*peht*) *f* storm; tempest, gale; ~ **de neige** snowstorm, blizzard

temple (tahngpl) *m* temple

temporaire (tahng-po-*rair*) *adj* temporary

temps (tahng) *m* time; weather; **à** ~ in time; **ces derniers** ~ lately; **de temps en** ~ now and then, occasionally; ~ **libre** spare time

tenailles (ter-*nigh*) *fpl* pincers *pl*

tendance (tahng-*dahngss*) *f* tendency; ***avoir** ~ *be inclined to, tend

tendon (tahng-*dawng*) *m* sinew, tendon

tendre¹ (tahngdr) *adj* delicate, tender

tendre² (tahngdr) *v* stretch; ~ **à** tend to; **tendu** tense

tendresse (tahng-*drehss*} *f* tenderness

ténèbres (tay-*nehbr*) *fpl* dark; gloom

***tenir** (ter-*neer*) *v* *hold; *keep; **se** ~ **debout** *stand; ~ **à** care for

tennis (tay-*neess*) *m* tennis; ~ **de table** ping-pong

tension (tahng-s^y*awng*) *f* tension; stress, strain; pressure; ~ **artérielle** blood pressure

tentation (tahng-tah-s^y*awng*) *f* temptation

tentative (tahng-tah-*teev*) *f* try, attempt

tente (tahngt) *f* tent

tenter (tahng-*tay*) *v* try; attempt; tempt

tenue (ter-*new*) *f* conduct; dress; ~ **de soirée** evening dress

térébenthine (tay-ray-bahng-*teen*) *f* turpentine

terme (tehrm) *m* term

terminer (tehr-mee-*nay*) *v* finish; **se** ~ expire

terminus (tehr-mee-*newss*) *m* terminal

terne (tehrn) *adj* dim; dull, mat

terrain (teh-*rang*) *m* terrain; grounds; ~ **d'aviation** airfield; ~ **de camping** camping site; ~ **de golf** golf-course; ~ **de jeux** recreation ground

terrasse (teh-*rahss*) *f* terrace

terre (tair) *f* earth; soil, land; **à** ~ ashore; **hautes terres** uplands *pl*; **par** ~ down; ~ **cuite** ceramics *pl*; ~ **ferme** mainland

terre-à-terre (teh-rah-*tair*) *adj* down-to-earth

terreur (teh-*rūrr*) *f* terror; terrorism

terrible (tay-*reebl*) *adj* terrible; awful, dreadful, frightful

terrifiant (teh-ree-f^y*ahng*) *adj* terrifying; horrible, creepy

terrifier (tehk-ree-f^y*ay*) *v* terrify

territoire (teh-ree-*twaar*) *m* territory

terroir (teh-*rwaar*) *m* soil

terrorisme (teh-ro-*reesm*) *m* terrorism

terroriste (teh-ro-*reest*) *m* terrorist

Térylène (tay-ree-*lehn*) *m* terylene

test (tehst) *m* test

testament (teh-stah-*mahng*) *m* will

tête (teht) *f* head

têtu (tay-*tew*) *adj* head-strong, stubborn

texte (tehkst) *m* text

textile (tehk-*steel*) *m* textile

texture (tehk-*stewr*) *f* texture

Thaïlandais (tah-ee-lahng-*day*) *m* Thai

thaïlandais (tah-ee-lahng-*day*) *adj* Thai

Thaïlande (tah-ee-*lahngd*) *f* Thailand

thé (tay) *m* tea

théâtre (tay-*aatr*) *m* theatre; drama; ~ **de marionnettes** puppet-show; ~ **de variétés** variety theatre

théière (tay-*Yair*) *f* teapot

thème (tehm) *m* theme

théologie (tay-o-lo-*zhee*) *f* theology

théorie (tay-o-*ree*) *f* theory

théorique (tay-o-*reek*) *adj* theoretical

thérapie (tay-rah-*pee*) *f* therapy

thermomètre (tehr-mo-*mehtr*) *m* thermometer

thermoplongeur (tehr-moa-plawng-*zhŭr*) *m* immersion heater

thermos (tehr-*moss*) *m* thermos flask, vacuum flask

thermostat (tehr-mo-*stah*) *m* thermostat

thèse (taiz) *f* thesis

thon (tawng) *m* tuna

thym (tang) *m* thyme

ticket (tee-*kay*) *m* coupon

tiède (tYehd) *adj* lukewarm, tepid

le tien (ler tYang) yours

tiers (tYair) *adj* (f tierce) third

tige (teezh) *f* stem; rod

tigre (teegr) *m* tiger

tilleul (tee-Yurl) *m* limetree, lime

timbre (tangbr) *m* stamp; tone

timbre-poste (tang-brer-*post*) *m* postage stamp

timide (tee-*meed*) *adj* timid, shy

timidité (tee-mee-dee-*tay*) *f* timidity, shyness

timonier (tee-mo-nYay) *m* helmsman; steersman

tirage (tee-*raazh*) *m* draw; issue

tire-bouchon (teer-boo-shawng) *m* corkscrew

tirer (tee-*ray*) *v* *draw, pull; fire, *shoot

tiret (tee-*ray*) *m* dash

tiroir (tee-*rwaar*) *m* drawer

tisser (tee-*say*) *v* *weave

tisserand (tee-*srahng*) *m* weaver

tissu (tee-*sew*) *m* tissue; fabric, cloth, material

tissu-éponge (tee-sew-ay-*pawngz*) *m* towelling

titre (teetr) *m* title; heading

toast (toast) *m* toast

toboggan (to-bo-*gahng*) *m* slide

toi (twah) *pron* you

toile (twahl) *f* linen; **grosse** ~ canvas; ~ **d'araignée** cobweb

toilettes (twah-*leht*) *fpl* toilet, bathroom; washroom *nAm*; ~ **pour dames** ladies' room; powder-room; -- **pour hommes** men's room

toi-même (twah-*mehm*) *pron* yourself

toit (twah) *m* roof; ~ **de chaume** *m* thatched roof

tolérable (to-lay-*rahbl*) *adj* tolerable

tolérer (to-lay-*ray*) *v* *bear

tomate (to-*maht*) *f* tomato

tombe (tawngb) *f* tomb, grave

tomber (tawng-*bay*) *v* *fall

tome (tom) *m* volume

ton[1] (tawng) *adj* (f ta, pl tes) your

ton[2] (tawng) *m* note, tone

tonique (to-*neek*) *m* tonic; ~ **capillaire** hair tonic

tonne (ton) *f* ton

tonneau (to-*noa*) *m* barrel; cask

tonnerre (to-*nair*) *m* thunder

torche (torsh) *f* torch

torchon (tor-*shawng*) *m* tea-cloth

tordre (tordr) *v* twist; wrench

tordu (tor-*dew*) *adj* crooked

torsion (tor-sYawng) *f* twist

tort (tawr) *m* wrong; harm; *avoir ~ *be wrong; *faire du ~ wrong

tortue (tor-*tew*) *f* turtle

torture (tor-*tewr*) *f* torture

torturer (tor-tew-*ray*) *v* torture

tôt (toa) *adv* early

total (to-*tahl*) *adj* total; utter, overall; *m* total

totalement (to-tahl-*mahng*) *adv* completely

totalisateur (to-tah-lee-zah-*tŭrr*) *m* totalizator

totalitaire (to-tah-lee-*tair*) *adj* totalitarian

touchant (too-*shahng*) *adj* touching

toucher (too-*shay*) *v* touch; affect; *hit; cash; *m* touch

toujours (too-*zhŏŏr*) *adv* always; ever; ~ **et encore** again and again

tour (tŏŏr) *m* turn; move; *f* tower

tourisme (too-*reesm*) *m* tourism

touriste (too-*reest*) *m* tourist

tourment (toor-*mahng*) *m* torment

tourmenter (toor-mahng-*tay*) *v* torment

tournant (toor-*nahng*) *m* turn, curve; turning-point

tourne-disque (toor-ner-*deesk*) *m* record-player

tourner (toor-*nay*) *v* turn; *spin

tournevis (toor-ner-*veess*) *m* screwdriver

tournoi (toor-*nwah*) *m* tournament

tousser (too-*say*) *v* cough

tout (too) *adj* all; every; entire; *pron* everything; **du** ~ at all; **en** ~ altogether; ~ **à fait** quite; ~ **à l'heure** presently; ~ **au plus** at most; ~ **ce que** whatever; ~ **de suite** immediately, straight away; ~ **droit** straight on; ~ **le monde** everybody

toutefois (toot-*fwah*) *adv* still

toux (too) *f* cough

toxique (tok-*seek*) *adj* toxic

tracas (trah-*kah*) *m* bother

tracasser (trah-kah-*say*) *v* bother

trace (trahss) *f* trace

tracer (trah-*say*) *v* trace

tracteur (trahk-*tŭrr*) *m* tractor

tradition (trah-dee-s*Y*awng) *f* tradition

traditionnel (trah-dee-s*Y*o-*nehl*) *adj* traditional

traducteur (trah-dewk-*tŭrr*) *m* translator

traduction (trah-dewk-s*Y*awng) *f* translation

*****traduire** (trah-*dweer*) *v* translate

trafic (trah-*feek*) *m* traffic

tragédie (trah-zhay-*dee*) *f* tragedy; drama

tragique (trah-*zheek*) *adj* tragic

trahir (trah-*eer*) *v* betray

trahison (trah-ee-*zawng*) *f* treason

train (trang) *m* train; ~ **de marchandises** goods train; freight-train *nAm*; ~ **de nuit** night train; ~ **de voyageurs** passenger train; ~ **direct** through train; ~ **express** express train; ~ **local** local train

traîneau (treh-*noa*) *m* sledge; sleigh

traîner (tray-*nay*) *v* drag, haul

trait (tray) *m* line; trait; ~ **de caractère** characteristic; ~ **d'union** hyphen; ~ **du visage** feature

traite (treht) *f* draft

traité (tray-*tay*) *m* treaty

traitement (treht-*mahng*) *m* treatment

traiter (tray-*tay*) *v* treat; handle

traître (traitr) *m* traitor

trajet (trah-*zhay*) *m* way

tram (trahm) *m* tram; streetcar *nAm*

tranche (trahngsh) *f* slice

trancher (trahng-*shay*) *v* *cut off; settle

tranquille (trahng-*keel*) *adj* calm; tranquil, quiet, still

tranquillité (trahng-kee-lee-*tay*) *f* quiet

transaction (trahng-zahk-s*Y*awng) *f* transaction, deal

transatlantique (trahng-zaht-lahng-*teek*) *adj* transatlantic

transférer (trahng-sfay-*ray*) *v* transfer

transformateur (trahng-sfor-mah-*tŭrr*) *m* transformer

transformer (trahng-sfor-*may*) *v* transform

transition (trahng-zee-sᵞawng) f transition

transparent (trahng-spah-rahng) adj transparent; sheer

transpiration (trahng-spee-rah-sᵞawng) f perspiration

transpirer (trahng-spee-ray) v perspire

transport (trahng-spawr) m transportation, transport

transporter (trahng-spor-tay) v transport

trappe (trahp) f hatch

travail (trah-vigh) m (pl travaux) work, labour, job; ~ **artisanal** handwork; ~ **manuel** handicraft; **travaux ménagers** housekeeping, housework

travailler (trah-vah-ᵞay) v work

travailleur (trah-vah-ᵞūrr) m labourer

à travers (ah trah-vair) through; across

traversée (trah-vehr-say) f passage, crossing

traverser (trah-vehr-say) v cross; pass through

trébucher (tray-bew-shay) v stumble

trèfle (trehfl) m clover; shamrock

treize (traiz) num thirteen

treizième (treh-zᵞehm) num thirteenth

trembler (trahng-blay) v tremble; shiver

tremper (trahng-pay) v soak

trente (trahngt) num thirty

trentième (trahng-tᵞehm) num thirtieth

trépasser (tray-pah-say) v depart

très (tray) adv very; quite

trésor (tray-zawr) m treasure; darling; **Trésor** treasury

trésorier (tray-zo-rᵞay) m treasurer

triangle (tree-ahnggl) m triangle

triangulaire (tree-ahng-gew-lair) adj triangular

tribord (tree-bawr) m starboard

tribu (tree-bew) f tribe

tribunal (tree-bew-nahl) m court, law court

tribune (tree-bewn) f stand

tricher (tree-shay) v cheat

tricot (tree-koa) m knitted wear; jersey; ~ **de corps** undershirt

tricoter (tree-ko-tay) v *knit

trier (tree-ay) v sort

trimestre (tree-mehstr) m quarter

trimestriel (tree-meh-stree-ehl) adj quarterly

triomphant (tree-awng-fahng) adj triumphant

triomphe (tree-awngf) m triumph

triompher (tree-awng-fay) v triumph

triste (treest) adj sad

tristesse (tree-stehss) f sorrow, sadness

trivial (tree-vᵞahl) adj vulgar

troc (trok) m exchange

trognon (tro-ñawng) m core

trois (trwah) num three; ~ **quarts** three-quarter

troisième (trwah-zᵞehm) num third

trolleybus (tro-lay-bewss) m trolley-bus

tromper (trawng-pay) v deceive; **se** ~ *be mistaken; err

tromperie (trawng-pree) f deceit

trompette (trawng-peht) f trumpet

tronc (trawng) m trunk

trône (trōan) m throne

trop (troa) adv too

tropical (tro-pee-kahl) adj tropical

tropiques (tro-peek) mpl tropics pl

troquer (tro-kay) v swap

trottoir (tro-twaar) m pavement; sidewalk nAm

trou (troo) m hole

trouble (troobl) adj turbid; obscure; m perturbation

troubler (troo-blay) v disturb

troupeau (troo-poa) m herd; flock

troupes (troop) fpl troops pl

trousseau (troo-*soa*) *m* kit
trousse de secours (trooss der ser-*koor*) first-aid kit
trouver (troo-*vay*) *v* *find; *come across; consider
truc (trewk) *m* trick
truite (trweet) *f* trout
tu (tew) *pron* you
tube (tewb) *m* tube; ~ **de plongée** snorkel
tuberculose (tew-behr-kew-*lōaz*) *f* tuberculosis
tuer (tway) *v* kill
tuile (tweel) *f* tile
tulipe (tew-*leep*) *f* tulip
tumeur (tew-*mūrr*) *f* tumour; growth
tunique (tew-*neek*) *f* tunic
Tunisie (tew-nee-*zee*) *f* Tunisia
Tunisien (tew-nee-*zYang*) *m* Tunisian
tunisien (tew-nee-*zYang*) *adj* Tunisian
tunnel (tew-*nehl*) *m* tunnel
turbine (tewr-*been*) *f* turbine
turboréacteur (tewr-bo-ray-ahk-*tūrr*) *m* turbojet
Turc (tewrk) *m* Turk
turc (tewrk) *adj* Turkish
Turquie (tewr-*kee*) *f* Turkey
tutelle (tew-*tehl*) *f* custody
tuteur (tew-*tūrr*) *m* guardian, tutor
tuyau (twee-*Yoa*) *m* tube, pipe; ~ **d'échappement** exhaust
tympan (tang-*pahng*) *m* ear-drum
type (teep) *m* type; guy, chap
typhoïde (tee-fo-*eed*) *f* typhoid
typique (tee-*peek*) *adj* typical
tyran (tee-*rahng*) *m* tyrant

U

ulcère (ewl-*sair*) *m* sore, ulcer; ~ **à l'estomac** gastric ulcer

ultime (ewl-*teem*) *adj* ultimate
ultra-violet (ewl-trah-vYo-*lay*) *adj* ultraviolet
un (urng) *art* (f une) *a art*; *num* one; **l'un l'autre** each other; **l'un ou l'autre** either; **ni l'un ni l'autre** neither
unanime (ew-nah-*neem*) *adj* unanimous; like-minded
uni (ew-*nee*) *adj* joint; smooth
uniforme (ew-nee-*form*) *m* uniform; *adj* uniform
unilatéral (ew-nee-lah-tay-*rahl*) *adj* one-sided
union (ew-*nYawng*) *f* union
unique (ew-*neek*) *adj* unique; sole
uniquement (ew-neek-*mahng*) *adv* exclusively
unir (ew-*neer*) *v* unite
unité (ew-nee-*tay*) *f* unity; unit; ~ **monétaire** monetary unit
univers (ew-nee-*vair*) *m* universe
universel (ew-nee-vehr-*sehl*) *adj* universal; all-round
université (ew-nee-vehr-see-*tay*) *f* university
urbain (ewr-*bang*) *adj* urban
urgence (ewr-*zhahngss*) *f* urgency; emergency
urgent (ewr-*zhahng*) *adj* pressing, urgent
urine (ew-*reen*) *f* urine
Uruguay (ew-rew-*gay*) *m* Uruguay
Uruguayen (ew-rew-gay-*Yang*) *m* Uruguayan
uruguayen (ew-rew-gay-*Yang*) *adj* Uruguayan
usage (ew-*zaazh*) *m* usage
usager (ew-zah-*zhay*) *m* user
user (ew-*zay*) *v* use up; wear out; **usé** worn; threadbare, worn-out
usine (ew-*zeen*) *f* factory; mill, plant, works *pl*; ~ **à gaz** gasworks
ustensile (ew-stahng-*seel*) *m* utensil

usuel (ew-*zwehl*) *adj* customary

utérus (ew-tay-*rewss*) *m* womb

utile (ew-*teel*) *adj* useful

utilisable (ew-tee-lee-*zahbl*) *adj* usable

utilisateur (ew-tee-lee-zah-*tŭrr*) *m* consumer

utilisation (ew-tee-lee-zah-s*Yawng*) *f* utilization

utiliser (ew-tee-lee-*zay*) *v* utilize, employ

utilité (ew-tee-lee-*tay*) *f* utility, use

V

vacance (vah-*kahngss*) *f* vacancy; **vacances** holiday

vacant (vah-*kahng*) *adj* vacant, unoccupied

vacarme (vah-*kahrm*) *m* noise, racket

vaccination (vahk-see-nah-s*Yawng*) *f* vaccination

vacciner (vahk-see-*nay*) *v* vaccinate

vache (vahsh) *f* cow

vacillant (vah-see-*Yahng*) *adj* unsteady; shaky

vaciller (vah-see-*Yay*) *v* falter

vagabond (vah-gah-*bawng*) *m* tramp

vagabondage (vah-gah-bawng-*daazh*) *m* vagrancy

vagabonder (vah-gah-bawng-*day*) *v* tramp, roam

vague (vahg) *f* wave; *adj* vague; faint, obscure

vaillance (vah-*Yahngss*) *f* courage

vain (vang) *adj* vain; **en ~** in vain

***vaincre** (vangkr) *v* *overcome; conquer, defeat

vainqueur (vang-*kŭrr*) *m* winner

vaisseau (vay-*soa*) *m* vessel; **~ sanguin** blood-vessel

vaisselle (veh-*sehl*) *f* pottery; ***faire la ~** wash up

valable (vah-*lahbl*) *adj* valid

valet (vah-*lay*) *m* valet; knave

valeur (vah-*lŭrr*) *f* value, worth; **sans ~** worthless

valise (vah-*leez*) *f* case, bag, suitcase

vallée (vah-*lay*) *f* valley

***valoir** (vah-*lwaar*) *v* *be worth; **~ la peine** *be worth-while

valse (vahls) *f* waltz

vanille (vah-*neey*) *f* vanilla

vaniteux (vah-nee-*tur*) *adj* vain

vanneau (vah-*noa*) *m* pewit

se vanter (vahng-*tay*) boast

vapeur (vah *pŭrr*) *f* steam; vapour

vaporisateur (vah-po-ree-zah-*tŭrr*) *m* atomizer

variable (vah-r*Yahbl*) *adj* variable

variation (vah-r*Y*ah-s*Yawng*) *f* variation

varice (vah-*reess*) *f* varicose vein

varicelle (vah-ree-*sehl*) *f* chickenpox

varier (vah-r*Yay*) *v* vary

variété (vah-r*Y*ay-*tay*) *f* variety

variole (vah-r*Yol*) *f* smallpox

vase (vaaz) *m* vase; *f* mud *m*

vaseline (vah-*zleen*) *f* vaseline

vaste (vahst) *adj* large; wide, broad, vast; extensive

vautour (voa-*tōōr*) *m* vulture

veau (voa) *m* calf; veal; calf skin

végétarien (vay-zhay-tah-r*Yang*) *m* vegetarian

végétation (vay-zhay-tah-s*Yawng*) *f* vegetation

véhicule (vay-ee-*kewl*) *m* vehicle

veille (vāŷ*Y*) *f* day before

veiller (vay-*Yay*) *v* stay awake; **~ sur** look after

veine (vain) *f* vein

vélo (vay-*loa*) *m* bicycle, cycle

vélomoteur (vay-loa-mo-*tŭrr*) *m* motorbike *nAm*, moped

velours (ver-*lōōr*) *m* velvet; **~ côtelé** corduroy; **~ de coton** velveteen

vendable (vahng-*dahbl*) *adj* saleable

vendange (vahng-*dahngzh*) *f* vintage

vendeur (vahng-*dūr*) *m* salesman; shop assistant

vendeuse (vahng-*dūz*) *f* salesgirl

vendre (vahngdr) *v* *sell; **à** ~ for sale

vendredi (vahng-drer-*dee*) *m* Friday

vénéneux (vay-nay-*nur*) *adj* poisonous

vénérable (vay-nay-*rahbl*) *adj* venerable

Venezuela (vay-nay-zway-*lah*) *m* Venezuela

Vénézuélien (vay-nay-zway-*lYang*) *m* Venezuelan

vénézuélien (vay-nay-zway-*lYang*) *adj* Venezuelan

vengeance (vahng-*zhahngss*) *f* revenge

venger (vahng-*zhay*) *v* avenge

***venir** (ver-*neer*) *v* *come; ***faire** ~ *send for

vent (vahng) *m* wind; **coup de** ~ blow

vente (vahngt) *f* sale; ~ **aux enchères** auction; ~ **en gros** wholesale

venteux (vahng-*tur*) *adj* windy, gusty

ventilateur (vahng-tee-lah-*tūr*) *m* fan, ventilator

ventilation (vahng-tee-lah-*sYawng*) *f* ventilation

ventiler (vahng-tee-*lay*) *v* ventilate

ventre (vahngtr) *m* belly

venue (ver-*new*) *f* arrival

ver (vair) *m* worm

véranda (vay-rahng-*dah*) *f* veranda

verbal (vehr-*bahl*) *adj* verbal

verbe (vehrb) *m* verb

verdict (vehr-*deekt*) *m* verdict

verger (vehr-*zhay*) *m* orchard

véridique (vay-ree-*deek*) *adj* truthful

vérifier (vay-ree-*fYay*) *v* verify; check

véritable (vay-ree-*tahbl*) *adj* actual; very

vérité (vay-ree-*tay*) *f* truth

vernir (vehr-*neer*) *v* varnish; glaze

vernis (vehr-*nee*) *m* varnish; lacquer; ~ **à ongle** nail-polish

verre (vair) *m* glass; ~ **de couleur** stained glass; ~ **grossissant** magnifying glass; **verres de contact** contact lenses

verrou (veh-*roo*) *m* bolt

vers (vair) *m* verse; *prep* towards, at; ~ **le bas** downwards; ~ **le haut** up

versant (vehr-*sahng*) *m* slope

versement (vehr-ser-*mahng*) *m* deposit, remittance

verser (vehr-*say*) *v* pour; *shed

version (vehr-*sYawng*) *f* version

vert (vair) *adj* green

vertical (vehr-tee-*kahl*) *adj* vertical

vertige (vehr-*teezh*) *m* vertigo; dizziness, giddiness

vertu (vehr-*tew*) *f* virtue

vessie (vay-*see*) *f* bladder

veste (vehst) *f* jacket; ~ **de sport** blazer

vestiaire (veh-*stYair*) *m* cloakroom; checkroom *nAm*

vestibule (veh-stee-*bewl*) *m* hall, lobby

veston (veh-*stawng*) *m* jacket; ~ **sport** sports-jacket

vêtements (veht-*mahng*) *mpl* clothes *pl*; ~ **de sport** sportswear

vétérinaire (vay-tay-ree-*nair*) *m* veterinary surgeon

***vêtir** (vay-*teer*) *v* dress

veuf (vurf) *m* widower

veuve (vūrv) *f* widow

via (vee-*ah*) *prep* via

viaduc (vYah-*dewk*) *m* viaduct

viande (vYahngd) *f* meat

vibration (vee-brah-*sYawng*) *f* vibration

vibrer (vee-*bray*) *v* vibrate; tremble

vicaire (vee-*kair*) *m* vicar

vice-président (vee-spray-zee-*dahng*)

m vice-president

vicieux (vee-s^yur) *adj* vicious

victime (veek-*teem*) *f* victim; casualty

victoire (veek-*twaar*) *f* victory

vide (veed) *adj* empty; *m* vacuum

vider (vee-*day*) *v* empty

vie (vee) *f* life; lifetime; **en ~** alive; **~ privée** privacy

vieillard (v^yeh-*^yaar*) *m* old man

vieillesse (v^yeh-*^yehss*) *f* age, old age

vieilli (v^yay-*^yee*) *adj* ancient

vieillot (v^yeh-*^yoa*) *adj* quaint

vierge (v^yehrzh) *f* virgin

vieux (v^yur) *adj* (vieil; f vieille) old; aged, ancient

vif (veef) *adj* vivid; intense, brisk, lively

vigilant (vee-zhee-*lahng*) *adj* vigilant

vigne (veeñ) *f* vine

vignoble (vee-*ñobl*) *m* vineyard

vigoureux (vee-goo-*rur*) *adj* vigorous

vigueur (vee-*gūrr*) *f* strength

vilain (vee-*lang*) *adj* bad

vilebrequin (veel-brer-*kang*) *m* crankshaft

villa (vee-*lah*) *f* villa; cottage

village (vee-*laazh*) *m* village

ville (veel) *f* town

villégiature (vee-lay-zhah-*tewr*) *f* holiday resort

vin (vang) *m* wine

vinaigre (vee-*naigr*) *m* vinegar

vingt (vang) *num* twenty

vingtième (vang-*t^yehm*) *num* twentieth

violation (v^yo-lah-s^y*awng*) *f* violation

violence (v^yo-*lahngss*) *f* violence

violent (v^yo-*lahng*) *adj* violent; fierce, severe

violer (v^yo-*lay*) *v* assault, rape

violet (v^yo-*lay*) *adj* violet

violette (v^yo-*leht*) *f* violet

violon (v^yo-*lawng*) *m* violin

virage (vee-*raazh*) *m* turning, bend

virer (vee-*ray*) *v* turn

virgule (veer-*gewl*) *f* comma

vis (veess) *f* screw

visa (vee-*zah*) *m* visa

visage (vee-*zaazh*) *m* face

viser (vee-*zay*) *v* aim at

viseur (vee-*zūrr*) *m* view-finder

visibilité (vee-zee-bee-lee-*tay*) *f* visibility

visible (vee-*zeebl*) *adj* visible

vision (vee-z^y*awng*) *f* vision

visite (vee-*zeet*) *f* visit; call; **rendre ~ à** call on

visiter (vee-zee-*tay*) *v* visit

visiteur (vee-zee-*tūrr*) *m* visitor

vison (vee-*zawng*) *m* mink

visser (vee-*say*) *v* screw

vital (vee-*tahl*) *adj* vital

vitamine (vee-tah-*meen*) *f* vitamin

vite (veet) *adv* quickly

vitesse (vee-*tehss*) *f* speed; rate; gear; **en ~** in a hurry; **indicateur de ~** speedometer; **limitation de ~** speed limit; **~ de croisière** cruising speed

vitre (veetr) *f* window-pane

vitrine (vee-*treen*) *f* show-case, shop-window

vivant (vee-*vahng*) *adj* alive; live

*vivre (veevr) *v* live; experience

vocabulaire (vo-kah-bew-*lair*) *m* vocabulary

vocal (vo-*kahl*) *adj* vocal

vœu (vur) *m* desire; vow

voici (vwah-*see*) here is

voie (vwah) *f* way; track; lane; **~ d'eau** waterway; **~ ferrée** railway; railroad *nAm*

voilà (vwah-*lah*) *adv* there is; here you are

voile (vwahl) *f* sail; *m* veil

*voir (vwaar) *v* *see

voisin (vwah-*zang*) *m* neighbour

voisinage (vwah-zee-*naazh*) *m* vicinity,

neighbourhood

voiture (vwah-*tewr*) f car; carriage; ~ **d'enfant** pram; ~ **de sport** sports-car; ~ **Pullman** Pullman

voix (vwah) f voice; **à haute** ~ aloud

vol (vol) m flight; robbery, theft; ~ **charter** charter flight; ~ **de nuit** night flight; ~ **de retour** return flight

volaille (vo-*ligh*) f poultry, fowl

volant (vo-*lahng*) m steering-wheel

volcan (vol-*kahng*) m volcano

voler (vo-*lay*) v *fly; *steal; rob

volet (vo-*lay*) m shutter

voleur (vo-*lūrr*) m thief; robber

volontaire (vo-lawng-*tair*) adj voluntary; m volunteer

volonté (vo-lawng-*tay*) f will; will-power

volontiers (vo-lawng-*t*ʸay) adv willingly, gladly

volt (volt) m volt

voltage (vol-*taazh*) m voltage

volume (vo-*lewm*) m volume

volumineux (voa-lew-mee-*nur*) adj bulky, big

vomir (vo-*meer*) v vomit

vote (vot) m vote; **droit de** ~ franchise

voter (vo-*tay*) v vote

votre (votr) adj (pl vos) your

***vouloir** (voo-*lwaar*) v want; *will; **en** ~ **à** resent; ~ **dire** *mean

vous (voo) pron you; yourselves; **vous-même** pron yourself; **vous-mêmes** pron yourselves

voûte (voot) f vault, arch

voyage (vwah-ʸ*aazh*) m journey; trip, voyage; ~ **d'affaires** business trip; ~ **de retour** return journey

voyager (vwah-ʸah-*zhay*) v travel; ~ **en auto** motor

voyageur (vwah-ʸah-*zhūrr*) m traveller

voyelle (vwah-ʸ*ehl*) f vowel

vrai (vray) adj true; very

vraiment (vray-*mahng*) adv really

vraisemblable (vray-sahng-*blahbl*) adj probable

vu (vew) prep considering

vue (vew) f sight; view; **point de** ~ point of view

vulgaire (vewl-*gair*) adj vulgar

vulnérable (vewl-nay-*rahbl*) adj vulnerable

W

wagon (vah-*gawng*) m carriage; waggon, coach; passenger car Am; **wagon-lit** sleeping-car; **wagon-restaurant** dining-car

Y

y (ee) pron there; to it

yacht (ʸot) m yacht

Z

zèbre (zaibr) m zebra

zélé (zay-*lay*) adj zealous; diligent

zèle (zehl) m zeal

zénith (zay-*neet*) m zenith

zéro (zay-*roa*) m zero; nought

zinc (zangg) m zinc

zodiaque (zo-dʸ*ahk*) m zodiac

zone (zoān) f zone; area; ~ **de stationnement** parking zone; ~ **industrielle** industrial area

zoo (zoa) m zoo

zoologie (zoa-o-lo-*zhee*) f zoology

zoom (zoom) m zoom lens

Menu Reader

Food

à la, à l', au, aux in the manner of, as in, with

abats, abattis giblets, innards

abricot apricot

agneau lamb

aiglefin haddock

ail garlic

ailloli garlic mayonnaise

airelle a kind of cranberry

alouette sans tête slice of veal rolled and generally stuffed with minced meat, garlic and parsley

(à l')alsacienne usually garnished with sauerkraut, ham and sausages

amande almond

amuse-gueule appetizer

ananas pineapple

anchois anchovy

(à l')ancienne old style; usually with wine-flavoured cream sauce of mushrooms, onions or shallots

(à l')andalouse usually with green peppers, aubergines and tomatoes

andouille a kind of tripe sausage

andouillette smaller kind of tripe sausage

(à l')anglaise 1) usually boiled or steamed vegetables, especially potatoes 2) breaded and fried vegetables, meat, fish or fowl

anguille eel

~ **au vert** eel braised in a white sauce served with minced parsley and other greens

anis aniseed

artichaut (globe) artichoke

asperge asparagus

assiette plate

~ **anglaise** cold meat (US cold cuts)

~ **de charcuterie** assorted pork and other meat products

assorti assorted

aubergine aubergine (US eggplant)

ballottine (de volaille) boned fowl which is stuffed, rolled, cooked and served in gelatine

banane banana

bar bass

barbue brill

basilic basil

béarnaise sauce of egg-yolk, butter, vinegar, shallots, tarragon and white wine

bécasse woodcock

béchamel white sauce

beignet fritter generally filled with fruit, vegetables or meat

(à la) Bercy butter sauce of white wine and shallots

betterave beetroot

beurre butter

~ **blanc** white butter sauce of shallots, vinegar and white wine

~ **maître d'hôtel** butter with chopped parsley and lemon juice

~ **noir** browned butter sauce of vinegar and parsley

bifteck beef steak

(à la) bigarade brown sauce generally with oranges, sugar and vinegar

biscotte rusk (US zwieback)

biscuit biscuit (US cookie)

bisque cream soup of lobster or crayfish (US chowder)

blanc de volaille boned breast of fowl

blanchaille whitebait

blanquette de veau veal stew in white sauce

(au) bleu 1) of fish (usually trout), boiled very fresh 2) of cheese, blue-veined 3) of meat, very underdone (US rare)

bœuf beef

~ **bourguignon** chunks of beef stewed in red wine with onions, bacon and mushrooms

~ **en daube** larded chunks of beef marinated in red wine with vegetables and stewed

~ **miro(n)ton** cold boiled beef or beef stew with onion sauce

~ **mode** larded chunks of beef braised in red wine with carrots and onions

~ **salé** corned beef

bolet boletus mushroom

bombe glacée moulded ice-cream dessert

(à la) bordelaise red wine sauce with shallots, beef marrow and boletus mushrooms

bouchée à la reine vol-au-vent; puff-pastry shell filled with meat, sweetbreads or seafood and sometimes mushrooms

boudin black pudding (US blood sausage)

bouillabaisse assorted fish and shellfish stewed in white wine, garlic, saffron and olive oil

bouilli 1) boiled 2) boiled beef

bouillon bouillon, broth, stock

(à la) bourguignonne button mushrooms, pearl onions or shallots braised in rich red wine

braisé braised

brandade (de morue) prepared cod with cream, oil and garlic

brie white, mellow cheese

brioche small roll or cake

(à la) broche (on a) spit

brochet pike

(en) brochette (cooked on a) skewer

cabillaud fresh cod

café glacé coffee-flavoured ice-cream dessert

caille quail

camembert soft cheese with pungent flavour

canard (caneton) duck (duckling)

~ **à l'orange** roast duck braised with oranges and orange liqueur

cannelle cinnamon

cantal smooth, firm cheese not unlike Cheddar

câpre caper

carbonnade charcoal-grilled meat
  ~ **flamande** beef slices, onions and herbs braised in beer
cardon cardoon (vegetable)
carotte carrot
carottes Vichy steamed carrots
carpe carp
carré loin, rack
  ~ **de l'Est** usually square-shaped cheese of pungent flavour
carrelet plaice
carte des vins wine list
cassis blackcurrant
cassoulet toulousain butter-bean stew of goose or with mutton, pork and sometimes sausage
céleri celery (usually celery root)
  ~ **en branche** branch celery
  ~ **-rave** celeriac, celery root
cèpe boletus mushroom
cerfeuil chervil
cerise cherry
cervelle brains
champignon mushroom
  ~ **de Paris** button mushroom
chanterelle chanterelle mushroom
charbonnade charcoal-grilled meat
charcuterie various kinds of cold pork products
charlotte fruit dessert (usually apples) made in a deep, round mould
chasse venison
chasseur hunter's style; sauce of mushrooms, tomatoes, wine and garlic herbs
chateaubriand thick slice of beef taken from the fillet
chaud warm
chaudrée fish and seafood stew, often with garlic, herbs, onions and white wine

chausson aux pommes apple dumpling (US turnover)
chevreuil deer
chicorée endive (US chicory)
chou cabbage
  ~ **de Bruxelles** brussels sprouts
  ~ **à la crème** cream puff
  ~ **-fleur** cauliflower
  ~ **rouge** red cabbage
choucroute sauerkraut
  ~ **garnie** usually with ham, bacon and sausage
ciboulette chive
citron lemon
civet de lapin (lièvre) jugged rabbit (hare)
clafoutis fruit baked in pancake batter, brandy often added
clémentine pipless (US seedless) tangerine
cochon de lait suck(l)ing pig
(en) cocotte casserole
cœur heart
  ~ **d'artichaut** artichoke heart
(à la) Colbert dipped in egg batter and breadcrumbs, fried
colin hake
concombre cucumber
confit d'oie pieces of goose preserved in its own fat
confiture jam
consommation general word for drinks
consommé clear soup served hot or cold
  ~ **Célestine** with chicken and noodles
  ~ **aux cheveux d'ange** with thin noodles
  ~ **Colbert** with poached eggs, spring vegetables
  ~ **julienne** with shredded vegetables
  ~ **madrilène** cold and fla-

voured with tomatoes

~ **princesse** with diced chicken and asparagus tips

~ **aux vermicelles** with thin noodles

contre-filet sirloin

coq au vin chicken stewed in red wine with mushrooms, bacon, onions and herbs

coquelet cockerel

coquillage shellfish

coquille Saint-Jacques scallop gratinéed in its shell

corbeille de fruits basket of assorted fruit

cornichon small gherkin (US pickle)

côte chop or rib

~ **de bœuf** rib of beef

~ **de veau** veal chop

côtelette cutlet, chop

~ **d'agneau** lamb chop

~ **de porc** pork chop

coupe a metal or glass dish usually for individual desserts

~ **glacée** ice-cream dessert

courgette vegetable marrow (US zucchini)

couvert cover charge

~, **vin et service compris** price includes wine, service and cover charges

crabe crab

crème 1) a dessert with cream or a creamy dessert

~ **anglaise** custard

~ **caramel** caramel custard

~ **Chantilly** whipped cream

~ **glacée** ice-cream

crème 2) a creamy soup

crêpe large, paper-thin pancake

~ **Suzette** pancake with orange sauce, flamed with brandy and often orange liqueur

cresson (water)cress

crevette shrimp

croissant crescent-shaped flaky roll (usually served for breakfast)

croque-monsieur grilled or baked ham-and-cheese sandwich

croustade pie, pastry shell filled with fish, seafood, meat or vegetables

(en) croûte (in a) pastry crust

croûton small piece of bread, toasted or fried

cru raw

crudités raw vegetables usually served sliced, grated or diced as an hors d'oeuvre

crustacé shellfish

cuisse leg or thigh

cuisses de grenouilles frogs' legs

cuit cooked

bien ~ well-done

cumin caraway, cumin

darne thick fillet of fish, usually of salmon

datte date

daurade gilt-head

déjeuner lunch

délice often used to describe a dessert speciality of the chef

demi half

~**-sel** soft cream cheese, slightly salty

demoiselle de Cherbourg small rock lobster

(à la) dieppoise garnish of mussels and shrimp served in white-wine sauce

dinde, dindon turkey

dindonneau young turkey

dîner dinner

diplomate moulded custard dessert with crystallized fruit and lined with sponge fingers

steeped in liqueur

dodine de canard boned duck, rolled, stuffed, sometimes served cold in gelatine

(à la) du Barry garnish of cauliflower and cheese sauce, gratinéed

(aux) duxelles with minced mushrooms sautéed with butter, white wine and herbs

échalote shallot

écrevisse (freshwater) crayfish

~ **à la nage** simmered in white wine, aromatic vegetables and herbs

églefin haddock

émincé slices of cooked meat in gravy or thick cream sauce

endive chicory (US endive)

~ **à la bruxelloise** steamed chicory rolled in a slice of ham

entrecôte rib-eye steak

entrée dish served between the hors d'oeuvre or soup and the main course; the first course in a smaller dinner (US starter)

entremets small dish served before cheese; today it often means dessert

épaule shoulder

éperlan smelt

épice spice

épicé hot, peppered

épinard spinach

escalope de veau veal scallop, thin slice of veal

escalope viennoise wiener schnitzel; breaded veal cutlet

escargot snail

estouffade braised or steamed in tightly sealed vessel with minimum of cooking liquid

estragon tarragon

étuvé steamed, stewed with minimum of cooking liquid

faisan pheasant

farci stuffed

fenouil fennel

féra dace (fish)

fève broad bean

filet meat or fish fillet

~ **de bœuf** fillet of beef (US tenderloin)

~ **mignon** small round veal or pork fillet

~ **de sole** fillet of sole

(à la) financière rich sauce of pike dumplings, truffles, mushrooms, Madeira wine, sometimes with olives and crayfish

(aux) fines herbes with herbs

(à la) flamande Flemish style; usually a garnish of braised potatoes, carrots, cabbage, turnips, bacon and sausage (sometimes simmered in beer)

flambé dish flamed usually with brandy

flétan halibut

foie liver

~ **gras** goose or duck liver

fond d'artichaut artichocke heart (US bottom)

fondue (au fromage) melted-cheese mixture in a pot into which pieces of bread are dipped

fondue bourguignonne bite-size pieces of meat dipped into boiling oil at the table and eaten with a variety of sauces

fondue chinoise paper-thin slices of beef dipped into boiling bouillon and eaten with a variety of sauces

(à la) forestière forester's style; generally sautéed in butter with morel mushrooms, potatoes

and bacon

(au) four baked

frais, fraîche fresh

fraise strawberry

~ **des bois** wild

framboise raspberry

frappé chilled, iced

friand patty with meat filling

fricandeau braised, larded veal

fricassée browned pieces of meat braised with seasonings and vegetables and served in a thick sauce

frit fried

frites chips (US french fries)

friture (de poisson) fried fish

fromage cheese

~ **frais** fresh curd cheese

~ **de tête** brawn (US headcheese)

fruit confit candied fruit

fruits de mer mussels, oysters, clams

fumé smoked

galette flat, plain cake

garbure thick cabbage soup made of salted pork, spices and *confit d'oie*

garni garnished

(avec) garniture (with) vegetables

gâteau cake, flan, tart

gaufre waffle

gaufrette small, crisp, sweet wafer

(en) gelée jellied

gélinotte hazel-hen, hazel-grouse (US prairie chicken)

gibelotte de lapin rabbit stew in wine sauce

gibier game

~ **de saison** game in season

gigot d'agneau leg of lamb

girolle chanterelle mushroom

glace ice-cream

~ **(à la) napolitaine** ice-cream

layers of different flavours

glacé iced, glazed

goujon gudgeon

gras-double tripe simmered in wine and onions

(au) gratin browned with breadcrumbs or cheese

gratin dauphinois sliced potatoes gratinéed in the oven with eggs, cream and cheese

gratin de fruits de mer shellfish in heavy cream sauce and gratinéed

grillade grilled meat

grillé grilled

grive thrush

groseille à maquereau gooseberry

groseille rouge redcurrant

gruyère a hard cheese rich in flavour

haché minced, hashed

hachis mince, hash

hareng herring

haricot bean

~ **de mouton** stew of mutton with beans and potatoes

~ **vert** French bean (US green bean)

Henri IV artichoke hearts garnished with béarnaise sauce

hollandaise sauce of egg-yolks, butter and lemon juice or vinegar

homard lobster

~ **à l'américaine** (or **à l'armoricaine**) lobster flamed in brandy, simmered in white wine with garlic, tomatoes and herbs

~ **cardinal** flamed in brandy, diced, served in its shell with truffles and chopped mushrooms and gratinéed

~ **Newburg** cut into sections, cooked in brandy and fish stock

~ **Thermidor** simmered in white wine, sautéed in butter with mushrooms, herbs, spices, mustard, flamed in brandy and gratinéed with cheese

huile oil

huître oyster

~ **belon** flat, pinkish oyster

~ **de claire** similar to bluepoint oyster

~ **portugaise** small, fat oyster

jambon ham

~ **de Bayonne** raw, with a slightly salty flavour

~ **cru** raw, cured

~ **à l'os** baked ham

jardinière cooked assorted vegetables

jarret shank, shin

julienne vegetables cut into fine strips

jus gravy, juice

lamproie lamprey

langouste spiny lobster

langoustine Norway lobster, prawn, crawfish

langue tongue

lapin rabbit

lard bacon

légume vegetable

lentille lentil

levraut young hare, leveret

lièvre hare

limande dab

livarot small, round cheese from Normandy

longe de veau loin of veal

(à la) lorraine usually braised in red wine with red cabbage

loup (de mer) (sea) bass

(à la) lyonnaise generally sautéed with onions

macédoine mixed, diced vegetables or fruit

(au) madère with Madeira wine

maigre lean

maïs maize (US corn)

maître d'hôtel sautéed in butter with chopped parsley and lemon juice

maquereau mackerel

marcassin young boar

marchand de vin red wine sauce seasoned with shallots

mariné marinated

marinière sailor's style; garnish of mussels with other seafood simmered in white wine and spices

marjolaine marjoram

maroilles strong, semi-hard cheese from Picardy

marron chestnut

matelote freshwater-fish stew (especially of eel) with wine, onions, mushrooms

médaillon small, round cut of meat

menthe mint

menu in France, generally means *menu à prix fixe*, set meal at a fixed price

merguez very spicy sausage

merlan whiting

merluche dried hake

meunière floured and sautéed in butter with lemon juice and chopped parsley

miel honey

mijoté simmered

millefeuille flaky pastry with cream filling (US napoleon)

(à la) Mirabeau with anchovies, olives, tarragon

mirabelle small yellow plum

(à la) mode in the style (of); often means made according to a local recipe

moelle marrow (bone)

morille morel mushroom

Mornay *béchamel* sauce with cheese

moule mussel

moules marinière mussels simmered in white wine with shallots, thyme and parsley

mousse 1) any frothy cream dish 2) chopped or pounded meat or fish with eggs and cream

mousseline 1) frothy mixture containing cream, usually whipped 2) variation of hollandaise sauce with whipped cream

moutarde mustard

mouton mutton

munster soft cheese with a pungent flavour

mûre mulberry or blackberry

myrtille bilberry (US blueberry)

nature/au naturel plain, without dressing, sauce or stuffing

navarin mutton stew with turnips

navet turnip

(à la/en) neige snow-like; i.e. with beaten egg-whites

(à la) niçoise Riviera style; usually with garlic, anchovies, olives, onions, tomatoes

(à la) nivernaise a garnish of carrots, onions, potatoes

noisette 1) hazelnut 2) boneless round piece of meat usually taken from loin or rib

noix walnut

~ **de coco** coconut

~ **(de) muscade** nutmeg

~ **de veau** pope's eye of veal

(à la) normande usually cooked with gudgeon, shrimps, mushrooms, cream and sometimes truffles

nouilles noodles

œuf egg

~ **brouillé** scrambled

~ **à la coque** soft-boiled

~ **dur** hard-boiled

~ **farci** stuffed

~ **en gelée** lightly poached and served in gelatine

~ **au jambon** ham and eggs

~ **au/sur le plat** fried

~ **poché** poached

~ **Rossini** with truffles and Madeira wine

oie goose

oignon onion

omble-chevalier freshwater fish of the char family

omelette omelet

~ **norvégienne** ice-cream dessert covered with beaten egg-whites, quickly browned in oven and served flaming (US baked Alaska)

ortolan small game bird like a finch

os bone

~ **à moelle** marrow bone

oseille sorrel

oursin sea urchin

pain bread

palourde clam

pamplemousse grapefruit

panaché mixed; two or more kinds of something

pané breaded, rolled in breadcrumbs

(en) papillote encased in greased paper and baked

parfait ice-cream dessert

Parmentier containing potatoes

pastèque watermelon

pâté 1) a moulded pastry case which holds meat or fish 2) a thickish paste often of liver (contained in an earthenware dish)

~ **ardennais** a purée of pork and seasonings encased in a loaf of bread, served in slices

~ **de campagne** strongly flavoured with a variety of meat

~ **en croûte** in a pastry crust

~ **de foie gras** goose (or duck) liver paste

pâtes noodles, macaroni, spaghetti

paupiette (de veau) veal bird, thin slice of veal rolled around stuffing

(à la) paysanne country style; usually containing various vegetables

pêche peach

perche perch

perdreau young partridge

perdrix partridge

(à la) périgourdine preparation with truffles

persil parsley

petit small

~ **déjeuner** breakfast

~ **four** small, fancy cake (US fancy cookie)

~ **pain** roll

~ **pois** green pea

~ **salé (au chou)** salt pork (with cabbage)

~-**suisse** a mild-flavoured, double-cream cheese

pied de porc pig's trotter (US pig's foot)

pigeonneau squab

piment pimento

pintade guinea hen

piperade omelet with green peppers, garlic, tomatoes, ham

piquant sharp-tasting, spicy (e.g. of a sauce)

pissaladière onion and anchovy tart with black olives

plat plate

~ **du jour** speciality of the day

~ **principal** main dish

plateau de fromages cheese board

plie plaice

poché poached

(à la) poêle fried

(à) point medium

pointe d'asperge asparagus tip

poire pear

~ **à la Condé** served hot on a bed of vanilla-flavoured rice

~ **Belle Hélène** with vanilla ice-cream and chocolate sauce

poireau leek

pois pea

~ **chiche** chick pea

poisson fish

~ **d'eau douce** freshwater

~ **de mer** saltwater

poitrine breast, brisket

(au) poivre (with) pepper

poivron sweet pepper

pomme apple

pommes (de terre) potatoes

~ **allumettes** matchsticks

~ **chips** crisps (US potato chips)

~ **dauphine** mashed in butter and egg-yolks, mixed in seasoned flour and deep-fried

~ **duchesse** mashed with butter and egg-yolks

~ **en robe des champs** in their jackets

~ **frites** chips (US french fries)

~ **mousseline** mashed

~ **nature** boiled, steamed

~ **nouvelles** new

~ **vapeur** steamed, boiled

pont-l'évêque soft cheese, strong and pungent in flavour

porc pork

port-salut soft cheese, yellow in colour, mild in taste

potage soup

~ **bonne femme** potato, leek, mushroom, onion, rice and sometimes bacon

~ **cancalais** fish consommé (often with oysters or other seafood)

~ **Condé** mashed red beans

~ **Crécy** carrots

~ **cultivateur** mixed vegetables and bacon or pork

~ **du Barry** cream of cauliflower

~ **julienne** vegetables

~ **Longchamp** peas, sorrel and chervil

~ **Saint-Germain** split-pea, leek and onion

~ **soissonnais** haricot bean

pot-au-feu 1) stockpot of beef, potatoes and aromatic vegetables 2) stew

potée boiled pork or beef with vegetables, especially cabbage

potiron pumpkin

poularde fat pullet

~ **de Bresse** grain-fed; reputedly the finest available

~ **demi-deuil** with truffles inserted under the skin and simmered in broth

poule hen

~ **au pot** stewed with vegetables

~ **au riz** stewed in bouillon and served with rice

poulet chicken

~ **Marengo** sautéed in olive oil, cooked with white wine, tomatoes, garlic, shallots and mushrooms

pourboire tip (but *service* is the percentage added to the bill)

praire clam

pré-salé lamb pastured in the salt meadows on the Atlantic seashore

(à la) printanière with spring vegetables

prix price

~ **fixe** at a fixed price

profiterole au chocolat puff pastry filled with whipped cream or custard and covered with hot chocolate

(à la) provençale often with garlic, onions, herbs, olives, oil and tomatoes

prune plum

pruneau (blue) plum

~ **sec** prune

pudding blancmange, custard

puits d'amour pastry shell filled with liqueur-flavoured custard

purée pulped and strained fruit or vegetables

~ **de pommes de terre** mashed potatoes

quenelle light dumpling made of fish, fowl or meat

queue tail

quiche flan, open tart with meat or vegetable filling, eggs and cream

~ **lorraine** tart with cheese, bacon, eggs and cream

râble de lièvre saddle of hare

raclette hot, melted cheese scraped from a block of cheese; accompanied with boiled potatoes and gherkins

radis radish

(en) ragoût stew(ed)

raie skate, ray

raisin grape

~ **sec** raisin, sultana

ramequin small cheese tart

rascasse a Mediterranean fish, an

essential ingredient of *bouilla-baisse*

ratatouille Mediterranean stew of tomatoes, peppers, onions, garlic and aubergines, served hot or cold

ravigote vinegar sauce with chopped hard-boiled eggs, capers and peas

reblochon soft, mild cheese, pale cream colour (Savoy)

(à la) reine with mince meat or fowl

reine-claude greengage

repas meal

rhubarbe rhubarb

(à la) Richelieu garnish of tomatoes, peas, bacon and potatoes

rillettes usually minced pork (sometimes goose or duck) baked in its own fat

ris de veau sweetbread

rissole fritter, pasty

riz rice

~ **pilaf** rice boiled in a bouillon, sometimes with onions

rognon kidney

romarin rosemary

roquefort blue-veined cheese made from ewe's milk; strong, salty with piquant flavour

rosbif roast beef

rôti roast(ed)

rouelle de veau shank of veal (usually a round cut)

roulade 1) a rolled slice of meat or fish with stuffing 2) dessert with cream or jam stuffing (Swiss roll)

sabayon creamy dessert of egg-yolks, sugar and white wine flavoured with a citrus fruit, served warm

safran saffron

saignant underdone (US rare)

saint-pierre John Dory (fish)

salade salad

~ **chiffonnade** shredded lettuce and sorrel in melted butter, served with a dressing

~ **de fruits** fruit salad (US fruit cocktail)

~ **niçoise** lettuce, tomatoes, green beans, hard-boiled eggs, tunny, olives, green pepper, potatoes and anchovies

~ **russe** cooked vegetables in mayonnaise

~ **verte** green

salé salted

salmis game or fowl partially roasted, then simmered in wine and vegetable *purée*

salpicon garnish or stuffing of one or various elements held together by sauce

salsifis salsify

sandre pike perch

sanglier wild boar

sarcelle teal, small freshwater duck

sauce sauce

~ **béarnaise** vinegar, egg-yolks, butter, shallots and tarragon

~ **béchamel** white sauce

~ **au beurre blanc** butter, shallots, vinegar or lemon juice

~ **au beurre noir** browned butter

~ **bordelaise** brown sauce with boletus mushrooms, red wine, shallots and beef marrow

~ **bourguignonne** red wine sauce with herbs, onions and spices (sometimes tarragon)

~ **café de Paris** cream, mustard and herbs

~ **chasseur** brown sauce with

wine, mushrooms, onions, shallots and herbs

~ **diable** hot, spicy sauce with white wine, herbs, vinegar and cayenne pepper

~ **financière** cream, Madeira wine, herbs, spices, mushrooms, truffles and olives

~ **hollandaise** butter, egg-yolks and vinegar or lemon juice

~ **lyonnaise** onions, white wine and butter

~ **madère** brown sauce with Madeira wine base

~ **Mornay** *béchamel* sauce with cheese

~ **ravigote** vinegar sauce with chopped hardboiled eggs, capers and herbs; served cold

~ **rémoulade** mayonnaise enriched with mustard and herbs

~ **suprême** chicken-stock base, thick and bland, served with fowl

~ **tartare** mayonnaise base with gherkins, chives, capers and olives

~ **vinaigrette** oil, vinegar and herbs (sometimes mustard)

saucisse sausage

~ **de Francfort** frankfurter

saucisson a large sausage

saumon salmon

sauté lightly browned in hot butter, oil or fat, sautéed

savarin sponge cake steeped in rum and usually topped with cream

sel salt

selle saddle

selon grosseur (or **grandeur**) price according to size, e.g. of a lobster, often abbreviated **s.g.**

service (non) compris service (not)

included

sorbet water ice (US sherbet)

soufflé à la reine soufflé with finely chopped poultry or meat

soufflé Rothschild vanilla-flavoured soufflé with candied fruit

soupe soup

~ **au pistou** vegetables, noodles, garlic, basil and cheese

~ **à l'oignon** onion

~ **à l'oignon gratinée** onion soup topped with toast and grated cheese; gratinéed

spécialité (du chef) (chef's) speciality

steak steak

~ **haché** hamburger

~ **au poivre** broiled with crushed peppercorns (often flamed in brandy)

~ **tartare** minced beef, eaten raw, with sauce of egg-yolks, mustard, capers, onions, oil and parsley

sucre sugar

suprême de volaille boned chicken breast with creamy sauce

sur commande to your special order

(en) sus in addition, additional charge

tarte open(-faced) flan, tart

~ **Tatin** upside-down tart of caramelized apples

tartelette small tart

tendrons de veau breast of veal

(en) terrine a preparation of meat, fish, fowl or game baked in an earthenware dish called a *terrine*, served cold

tête head

thon tunny (US tuna)

(en) timbale meat, fish, seafood,

fruit or vegetables cooked in a pastry case or mould

tomate tomato

tomme a mild soft cheese

topinambour Jerusalem artichoke

tortue turtle

tournedos round cut of prime beef
~ **Rossini** garnished with foie gras and truffles, served with Madeira wine sauce

tout compris all-inclusive (price of a meal)

tranche slice
~ **napolitaine** cassata; slice of layered ice-cream and crystallized fruit

tripes tripe
~ **à la mode de Caen** baked with calf's trotters (US calf's feet), vegetables, apple brandy or cider

truffe truffle

truite trout

vacherin a mellow cheese
~ **glacé** an ice-cream dessert with meringue

vanille vanilla

(à la) vapeur steamed

varié assorted

veau veal

velouté a creamy soup (of vegetables or poultry), thickened with butter and flour

vert-pré a garnish of cress

viande meat
~ **séchée** dried beef served as hors d'oeuvre in paper-thin slices

viandes froides various cold slices of meat and ham (US cold cuts)

vinaigre vinegar

vinaigrette salad sauce of vinegar, oil, herbs and mustard

volaille fowl

vol-au-vent puff-pastry shell filled with meat, sweetbreads or fish and sometimes mushrooms

waterzooi de poulet chicken poached in white wine and shredded vegetables, cream and egg-yolks

yaourt yoghurt

Drinks

Alsace (93 communes situated on the River Rhine) produces virtually only dry white wine, notably *Gewurztraminer, Riesling, Sylvaner, Traminer;* the terms *grand vin* and *grand cru* are sometimes employed to indicate a wine of exceptional quality

Amer Picon an aperitif with wine and brandy base and quinine flavouring

Anjou a region of the Loire district producing fine rosé and white wine

apéritif often bittersweet, some aperitifs have a wine and brandy base with herbs and bitters (like *Amer Picon, Byrrh, Dubonnet*), others, called *pastis,* have an aniseed base (like *Pernod* or *Ricard*); an aperitif may also be simply vermouth (like *Noilly Prat*) or a liqueur drink like *blanc-cassis*

appellation d'origine contrôlée (A.O.C.) officially recognized wines of which there are over 250 in France; standards of quality are rigidly checked by government inspectors

armagnac a wine-distilled brandy from the Armagnac region, west of Toulouse

Beaujolais Burgundy's most southerly and extensive vineyards which produce mainly red wine, e.g., *Brouilly, Chénas, Chiroubles, Côte de Brouilly, Fleurie, Juliénas, Morgon, Moulin-à-Vent*

Belgique Belgium; though the Romans introduced wine-making to Belgium, the kingdom today only incidentally produces wine, primarily white, sometimes rosé and sparkling wine

bénédictine forest-green liqueur; brandy base, herbs and orange peel, reputedly secret formula

Berry a region of the Loire district producing red, white and rosé wine; e.g., *Châteaumeillant, Menetou-Salon, Quincy, Reuilly, Sancerre, Sauvignon*

bière beer

~ **blonde** light

~ **(en) bouteille** bottled

~ **brune** dark

~ **pression** draught (US draft)

~ **des Trappistes** malt beer brewed by Trappist monks

blanc-cassis white wine mixed with blackcurrant liqueur

Blayais a region of Bordeaux producing mainly red and white wine

boisson drink

Bordeaux divided into several regions: Blayais, Bourgeais, Entre-Deux-Mers, Fronsac, Graves, Médoc, Pomerol, St-Emilion, Sauternais; among the officially recognized wines are 34 reds, 23 whites and two rosés divided into three categories: general (e.g., *Bordeaux* or *Bordeaux supérieur*), regional (e.g., *Entre-Deux-Mers, Graves, Médoc*) and communal (e.g., *Margaux, Pauillac, Sauternes*); Bordeaux red wine is known as claret in America and Britain

Bourgeais a region of Bordeaux producing red and white table wine

Bourgogne Burgundy, divided into five regions: Beaujolais, Chablis, Côte Chalonnaise, Côte d'Or (which comprises the Côte de Beaune and the Côte de Nuits) and Mâconnais; Burgundy counts the largest number of officially recognized wines of France's wine-growing districts; there are four categories of wine: generic or regional (e.g., *Bourgogne* red, white or rosé), subregional (e.g., *Beaujolais, Beaujolais supérieur, Beaujolais-Villages, Côte de Beaune-Villages, Mâcon, Mâcon supérieur, Mâcon-Villages*), communal (e.g., *Beaune, Chablis, Fleurie, Meursault, Nuits-St-Georges, Volnay*) and vineyard *(climat)* (e.g., *Chambertin, Clos de Vougeot, Musigny*)

brut extra dry, refers to *Champagne*

Byrrh an aperitif with wine base and quinine, fortified with brandy

cacao cocoa

café coffee

~ **complet** with bread, roll, butter and jam; the Continental breakfast

~ **crème** with cream

~ **espresso** espresso

~ **filtre** percolated or dripped through a filter

~ **frappé** iced

~ **au lait** white (with milk)

~ **liégeois** cold with ice-cream, topped with whipped cream

~ **nature, noir** simple, black

~ **sans caféine** caffeine-free

calvados an apple brandy from Normandy

cassis blackcurrant liqueur

Chablis a region of Burgundy noted for its white wine

chambrer to bring wine gently to room *(chambre)* temperature

Champagne district divided into three large regions: Côte des Blancs, Montagne de Reims and Vallée de la Marne with some 200 kilometres (120 miles) of underground caves where the wine ferments; there are ordinary red, white and rosé wines but the production is overwhelmingly centered upon the sparkling white and rosé (usually referred to in English as pink Champagne) for which the region is universally known; vineyards are of little importance in classifying wines from Champagne since, according

to tradition, certain varieties of Champagne are produced by blending wine from different vineyards in proportions which are carefully-guarded secrets; sparkling Champagne is sold according to the amount of sugar added: *brut* (extra dry) contains up to 1.5 per cent sugar additive, *extra-sec* (very dry), 1.5–2.5 per cent, *sec* (dry), 2.5–5 per cent, *demi-sec* (slightly sweet), 5–8 per cent and *doux* (sweet), 8–15 per cent

Chartreuse a yellow or green liqueur of herbs and spices produced by monks of Grande Chartreuse in the French Alps

château castle; term employed traditionally in the district of Bordeaux to indicate a wine of exceptional quality; synonyms: *clos, domaine*

chocolat chocolate

cidre cider

citron pressé freshly squeezed lemon juice

citronnade lemon squash (US lemon drink)

claret see *Bordeaux*

clos vineyard; generally indicates a wine of exceptional quality

cognac cognac; the famed wine-distilled brandy from the Charente and Charente-Maritime regions

Cointreau orange liqueur

Corse Corsica; this Mediterranean island, a French department, produces fine wine, particularly from the hilly areas and Cape Corsica; red, white and rosé wine is characterized by a rich, full-bodied taste; the best wine, grown near Bastia, is the rosé *Patrimonio*

Côte de Beaune the southern half of Burgundy's celebrated Côte d'Or producing chiefly red wine; e.g., the prestigious *Aloxe-Corton* as well as *Beaune, Blagny, Chassagne-Montrachet, Meursault, Pernand-Vergelesses, Puligny-Montrachet, Santenay, Savigny-lès-Beaune, Volnay*

Côte de Nuits a region of Burgundy especially noted for its red wine, e.g., *Chambolle-Musigny, Fixin, Gevrey-Chambertin, Morey-St-Denis, Nuits-St-Georges, Vosne-Romanée*

Côte d'Or a famed region of Burgundy composed of the Côte de Beaune and de Nuits which is noted for its red and white wine

Côtes du Rhône extend from Vienne to Avignon along the banks of the River Rhone between the Burgundy and Provence wine districts; over a hundred communes offer a wide diversity in white, red and rosé wine of varying character; divided into a northern and southern region with notable wine: *Château-Grillet, Châteauneuf-du-Pape, Condrieu, Cornas, Côte-Rôtie, Crozes-Hermitage, Hermitage, Lirac, St-Joseph, St-Péray, Tavel*

crème 1) cream 2) sweetened liqueur like *crème de menthe, crème de cacao*

cru growth 1) refers to a particular vineyard and its wine 2) a system of grading wine; *premier cru, grand cru, cru classé*

curaçao originally from the name of the island of the Dutch Antilles, now applied to liqueur made from orange peel

cuvée a blend of wine from various vineyards, especially, according to tradition, in the making of Champagne

domaine used on a wine label it indicates a wine of exceptional quality

eau water

~ **gazeuse** fizzy (US carbonated)

~ **minérale** mineral

Entre-Deux-Mers a vast Bordeaux region called "between two seas"—actually it's between two rivers—which produces white wine

extra-sec very dry (of Champagne)

framboise raspberry liqueur or brandy

frappé 1) iced 2) milk shake

Fronsac a Bordeaux region producing chiefly red wine

Gueuzelambic a strong Flemish bitter beer brewed from wheat and barley

grand cru, grand vin indicates a wine of exceptional quality

Grand Marnier an orange liqueur

Graves a Bordeaux region especially noted for its white wine but also its red

Jura a six-kilometre- (four-mile-) wide strip which runs 80 kilometres (50 miles) parallel to the western Swiss border and Burgundy; offers white, red, rosé, golden and sparkling wine; there are four formally recognized wines: *Arbois, Château-*

Chalon, Côtes du Jura and *l'Etoile*

kirsch spirit distilled from cherries

Kriekenlambic a strong Brussels bitter beer flavoured with morello cherries

lait milk

~ **écrémé** skimmed

Languedoc district, formerly a French province, to the southwest of the Rhone delta; its ordinary table wine is often referred to as *vin du Midi* but other officially recognized wines, mostly white, are produced, including *Blanquette de Limoux* (sparkling), *Clairette du Languedoc*, *Fitou* and the *Muscats* from Frontignan, Lunel, Mireval and St-Jean-de-Minervois

limonade 1) lemonade 2) soft drink

Loire a district of 200,000 hectares (80,000 acres) sprawled over the vicinity of France's longest river, the Loire; produces much fine red, white and rosé wine in four regions: Anjou (e.g., *Coteaux-de-l'Aubance*, *Coteaux-du-Layon*, *Coteaux-de-la-Loire*, *Saumur*), Berry and Nivernais *(Menetou-Salon, Pouilly-sur-Loire, Quincy, Reuilly, Sancerre)*, Nantais *(Muscadet)* and Touraine *(Bourgueil, Chinon, Montlouis, Vouvray)*

Lorraine a flourishing and renowned wine district up to the 18th century, today it is of minor importance; good red, white and rosé wine continue to be produced (e.g., *Vins de la Moselle, Côtes-de-Toul*)

Mâcon a region of Burgundy producing basically red wine

marc spirit distilled from grape residue

Médoc a Bordeaux region producing highly reputed red wine including *Listrac, Margaux, Moulis, Pauillac, St-Estèphe, St-Julien*

mirabelle a brandy made from small yellow plums, particularly produced in the Alsace-Lorraine area

Muscadet a white wine from the Nantes area (Loire)

muscat 1) a type of grape 2) name given to dessert wine; especially renowned is the muscat from Frontignan (Languedoc)

Nantais a region of the Loire chiefly renowned for its *Muscadet* white wine but offers other wine, e.g., *Coteaux d'Ancenis, Gros-Plant*

Neuchâtel a Swiss region producing primarily white wine (e.g., *Auvernier, Cormondrèche, Cortaillod, Hauterive*)

Noilly Prat a French vermouth

orange pressée freshly squeezed orange juice

pastis aniseed-flavoured aperitif

Pernod an aniseed-flavoured aperitif

pétillant slightly sparkling

Pomerol a Bordeaux region producing red wine (e.g., *Château Pétrus, Lalande-de-Pomerol, Néac*)

Provence France's most ancient wine-producing district; it traces its history back over two-and-a-half milleniums when Greek colonists planted the first vineyards on the Mediterranean coast of Gaul; red, white and rosé wine is produced, e.g., *Bandol, Bellet, Cassis, Coteaux-d'Aix-en-Provence, Coteaux-des-Baux, Coteaux-de-Pierrevert, Côtes-de-Provence, Palette*

quetsche spirit distilled from plums

rancio dessert wine, especially from Roussillon, which is aged in oak casks under the Midi sun

Ricard an aniseed-flavoured aperitif

Roussillon district which was a French province with Perpignan as its capital; its wine is similar in character to that of the Languedoc to the immediate north; good red, white and rosé table wine, e.g., *Corbières du Roussillon* and *Roussillon Dels Aspres;* this region produces three quarters of France's naturally sweet wine, usually referred to as *rancio*, which is aged in oak casks under the Midi sun; notable examples among them are *Banyuls, Côtes-d'Agly, Côtes-du-Haut-Roussillon; Grand-Roussillon, Muscat de Rivesaltes, Rivesaltes*

St-Emilion a Bordeaux region producing red wine including *Lussac, Montagne, Parsac, Puisseguin, St-Georges*

St-Raphaël a quinine-flavoured aperitif

Sauternais a Bordeaux region noted for its white wine *(Sauternes)*, notably the prestigious *Château d'Yquem*

Savoie Savoy; the Alpine district

producing primarily dry, light and often slightly acid white wine (e.g., *Crépy, Seyssel*) but also good red, rosé and sparkling wine which is chiefly produced around Chambéry

Sud-Ouest a district in southwestern France producing quite varying types of wine, mostly white but some red and even rosé; the district includes the former province of Aquitaine, Béarn, Basque Country and Languedoc; wines of particular note are *Bergerac, Côtes-de-Duras, Gaillac, Jurançon, Madiran, Monbazillac, Montravel*

Suisse Switzerland; two-thirds of the nation's wine production consists of white wine; some 230 different vineyards are scattered over a dozen of Switzerland's 23 cantons though only four have a special significance: Neuchâtel, Tessin, Valais and Vaud

Suze an aperitif based on gentian

thé tea

Touraine for 14 centuries a celebrated wine district of the Loire producing red, white and rosé wine (e.g., *Bourgueil, Chinon, Montlouis, St-Nicolas-de-Bourgueil, Vouvray*)

Triple Sec an orange liqueur

Valais sometimes referred to as the California of Switzerland, this Swiss region produces nearly a quarter of the nation's wine; the region in the Rhone Valley is noted for providing Switzerland's best red wine (e.g., *Dôle*) and much of its finest white wine (e.g., *Arvine,*

Ermitage, Fendant, Johannisberg, Malvoisie)

Vaud a Swiss region producing primarily white wine (e.g., *Aigle, Dézaley, Mont-sur-Rolle, Lavaux, Yvorne*)

V.D.Q.S. (vin délimité de qualité supérieure) regional wine of exceptional quality, produced according to carefully defined specifications and checked by government inspectors

Vieille Cure a wine-distilled liqueur

vin wine

~ **blanc** white

~ **chambré** wine at room temperature

~ **doux** sweet, dessert

~ **gris** pinkish

~ **mousseux** sparkling

~ **ordinaire** table

~ **du pays** local

~ **rosé** rosé (pink in reference to Champagne)

~ **rouge** red

~ **sec** dry

V.S.O.P. (very special old pale) in reference to cognac, indicates that it has been aged at least 5 years

(vin de) xérès sherry

Mini French Grammar

Articles

All nouns in French are either masculine or feminine.

1. Definite article (the):

masc. le **train**   the train   *fem. la* **voiture**   the car

Le and la are contracted to **l'** when followed by a vowel or a silent **h***.

l'avion   the plane   **l'hôtel**   the hotel

Plural (masc. and fem.):

les **trains**   *les* **voitures**   *les* **avions**

2. Indefinite article (a/an):

masc. *un* **timbre**   a stamp   fem. *une* **lettre**   a letter

Plural (masc. and fem.):

des **timbres**   stamps   *des* **lettres**   letters

3. Some/any (partitive)

Expressed by **de, du, de la, de l', des** as follows:

masc. **du** (= de + le)   **de l'** when followed by a vowel
fem. **de la**   or a silent **h***

Plural (masc. and fem.): **des** (= de + les)

du **sel**   some salt   *de la* **moutarde**   some mustard
de l' **ail**   some garlic   *des* **oranges**   some oranges

In negatives sentences, **de** is generally used.

Il n'y a pas *de* **taxis.**   There aren't any taxis.
Je n'ai pas *d'* **argent.**   I haven't any money.

Note the contraction **d'** before a vowel.

Nouns

1. As already noted, nouns are either masculine or feminine. There are no short cuts for determining gender (though, note that most nouns ending in **-e, -té, -tion** are feminine). So always learn a noun together with its accompanying article.

2. The plural of the majority of nouns is formed by adding s to the singular. (The final **s** is not pronounced.)

3. To show possession, use the preposition **de** (of).

la fin *de* **la semaine**   the end of the week
le début *du* **mois**   the beginning of the month
le patron *de* **l'hôtel**   the owner of the hotel
les valises *des* **voyageurs**   the travellers' luggage

---

* In French the letter *h* at the beginning of a word is not pronounced. However, in several words the *h* is what is called "aspirate", i.e., no liaison is made with the word preceding it. E.g., *le héros*. See also Guide to Pronunciation, p. 12.

Adjectives

1. Adjectives agree with the noun in gender and number. Most of them form the feminine by adding **e** to the masculine (unless the word already ends in **e**). For the plural, add **s**.

a. **un grand magasin**   a big shop   **des grands magasins**
b. **une auto anglaise**   an English car   **des autos anglaises**

2. As can be seen from the above, adjectives can come (a) before the noun or (b) after the noun. Since it is basically a question of sound and idiom, rules are difficult to formulate briefly; but adjectives more often follow nouns.

3. **Demonstrative adjectives:**

this/that   **ce** *(masc.)*   these/those   **ces** *(masc. and fem.)*
             cet *(masc. before a vowel or silent h)*
             cette *(fem.)*

4. **Possessive adjectives:** These agree in number and gender with *the noun they modify,* i.e., with the thing possessed and not the possessor.

	masc.	fem.	plur.
my	**mon**	**ma**	**mes**
your	**ton**	**ta**	**tes**
his/her/its	**son**	**sa**	**ses**
our	**notre**	**notre**	**nos**
your	**votre**	**votre**	**vos**
their	**leur**	**leur**	**leurs**

Thus, depending on the context:

son fils   can mean *his* son or *her* son
sa chambre   can mean *his* room or *her* room
ses vêtements   can mean *his* clothes or *her* clothes

Personal pronouns

	Subject	Direct object	Indirect object	After a preposition
I	**je**	**me**	**me**	**moi**
you	**tu**	**te**	**te**	**toi**
he/it (masc.)	**il**	**le**	**lui**	**lui**
she/it (fem.)	**elle**	**la**	**lui**	**elle**
we	**nous**	**nous**	**nous**	**nous**
you	**vous**	**vous**	**vous**	**vous**
they (masc.)	**ils**	**les**	**leur**	**eux**
they (fem.)	**elles**	**les**	**leur**	**elles**

Note: There are two forms for "you" in French: **tu** is used when talking to relatives, close friends and children (and between young people); **vous** is used in all other cases, and is also the plural form of **tu**.

Adverbs

Adverbs are generally formed by adding **-ment** to the feminine form of the adjective.

masc.:	fem.:	adverb:
lent (slow)	**lente**	**lentement**
sérieux (serious)	**sérieuse**	**sérieusement**

Verbs

Three regular conjugations appear below, grouped by families according to their infinitive endings, -er, -ir and -re. Verbs with the ending -er are considered as the true regular conjugation in French. Verbs which do not follow the conjugations below are considered irregular (see irregular verb list). Note that there are some verbs which follow the regular conjugation of the category they belong to, but present some minor changes in the spelling of the stem. Example: *acheter, j'achète; broyer, je broie.*

		1st conj.	2nd conj.	3rd conj.
Infinitive		**chant er** *(sing)*	**fin ir** *(finish)*	**vend re**[1] *(sell)*
Present	je	chant **e**	fin **is**	vend **s**
	tu	chant **es**	fin **is**	vend **s**
	il	chant **e**	fin **it**	vend –
	nous	chant **ons**	fin **issons**	vend **ons**
	vous	chant **ez**	fin **issez**	vend **ez**
	ils	chant **ent**	fin **issent**	vend **ent**
Imperfect	je	chant **ais**	fin **issais**	vend **ais**
	tu	chant **ais**	fin **issais**	vend **ais**
	il	chant **ait**	fin **issait**	vend **ait**
	nous	chant **ions**	fin **issions**	vend **ions**
	vous	chant **iez**	fin **issiez**	vend **iez**
	ils	chant **aient**	fin **issaient**	vend **aient**
Future	je	chant **erai**	fin **irai**	vend **rai**
	tu	chant **eras**	fin **iras**	vend **ras**
	il	chant **era**	fin **ira**	vend **ra**
	nous	chant **erons**	fin **irons**	vend **rons**
	vous	chant **erez**	fin **irez**	vend **rez**
	ils	chant **eront**	fin **iront**	vend **ront**
Conditional	je	chant **erais**	fin **irais**	vend **rais**
	tu	chant **erais**	fin **irais**	vend **rais**
	il	chant **erait**	fin **irait**	vend **rait**
	nous	chant **erions**	fin **irions**	vend **rions**
	vous	chant **eriez**	fin **iriez**	vend **riez**
	ils	chant **eraient**	fin **iraient**	vend **raient**
Pres. subj.[2]	je	chant **e**	fin **isse**	vend **e**
	tu	chant **es**	fin **isses**	vend **es**
	il	chant **e**	fin **isse**	vend **e**
	nous	chant **ions**	fin **issions**	vend **ions**
	vous	chant **iez**	fin **issiez**	vend **iez**
	ils	chant **ent**	fin **issent**	vend **ent**
Past part.		chant **é(e)**	fin **i(e)**	vend **u(e)**

[1] conjugated in the same way: all verbs ending in *-andre, -endre, -ondre, -erdre, -ordre* (except *prendre* and its compounds).

[2] French verbs are always preceded by *que* when conjugated in all tenses of subjonctive. Examples: *que je chante, que nous finissions, qu'ils aient.*

Auxiliary verbs

	avoir *(to have)*		**être** *(to be)*	
	Present	*Imperfect*	*Present*	*Imperfect*
j', je	ai	avais	suis	étais
tu	as	avais	es	étais
il	a	avait	est	était
nous	avons	avions	sommes	étions
vous	avez	aviez	êtes	étiez
ils	ont	avaient	sont	étaient
	Future	*Conditional*	*Future*	*Conditional*
j', je	aurai	aurais	serai	serais
tu	auras	aurais	seras	serais
il	aura	aurait	sera	serait
nous	aurons	aurions	serons	serions
vous	aurez	auriez	serez	seriez
ils	auront	auraient	seront	seraient
	Pres. subj. [1]	*Pres. perf*	*Pres. subj.* [1]	*Pres. perf.*
j', je	aie	ai eu	sois	ai été
tu	aies	as eu	sois	as été
il	ait	a eu	soit	a été
nous	ayons	avons eu	soyons	avons été
vous	ayez	avez eu	soyez	avez été
ils	aient	ont eu	soient	ont été

[1] French verbs are always preceded by *que* when conjugated in all tenses of subjonctive. Examples: *que je chante, que nous finissions, qu'ils aient.*

Irregular verbs

Below is a list of the verbs and tenses commonly used in spoken French. In the listing a) stands for the present tense, b) for the imperfect, c) for the future, d) for the conditional, e) for the present subjective and f) for the past participle. In the present tense we have given the whole conjugation, for the other tenses the first person singular, as the conjugations for tenses other than present are similar to those used in the regular verbs. Unless otherwise indicated, verbs with prefixes *(ab-, ac-, com-, con-, contre-, de-, dé-, dis-, é-, en-, entr(e)-, ex-, in-, o-, par-, pré-, pour-, re-, ré-, sous-,* etc.) are conjugated like the stem verb.

absoudre
absolve
a) absous, absous, absout, absolvons, absolvez, absolvent;
b) absolvais; c) absoudrai; d) absoudrais; e) absolve;
f) absous, absoute

accroître
increase
a) accrois, accrois, accroît, accroissons, accroissez,
accroissent; b) accroissais; c) accroîtrai; d) accroîtrais;
e) accroisse; f) accru(e)

acquérir	a) acquiers, acquiers, acquiert, acquérons, acquérez, acquièrent;
acquire	b) acquérais; c) acquerrai; d) acquerrais; e) acquière; f) acquis(e)
aller	a) vais, vas, va, allons, allez, vont; b) allais; c) irai; d) irais;
go	e) aille; f) allé(e)
apercevoir	→recevoir
perceive	
apparaître	→connaître
appear	
assaillir	a) assaille, assailles, assaille, assaillons, assaillez, assaillent;
assail	b) assaillais; c) assaillirai; d) assaillirais; e) assaille; f) assailli(e)
asseoir	a) assieds, assieds, assied, asseyons, asseyez, asseyent; b) asseyais;
set	c) assiérai; d) assiérais; e) asseye; f) assis(e)
astreindre	→peindre
compel	
battre	a) bats, bats, bat, battons, battez, battent; b) battais; c) battrai;
beat	d) battrais; e) batte; f) battu(e)
boire	a) bois, bois, boit, buvons, buvez, boivent; b) buvais;
drink	c) boirai; d) boirais; e) boive; f) bu(e)
bouillir	a) bous, bous, bout, bouillons, bouillez, bouillent; b) bouillais;
boil	c) bouillirai; d) bouillirais; e) bouille; f) bouilli(e)
ceindre	→peindre
gird	
circoncire	→suffire
circumcise	
circonscrire	→écrire
limit	
clore	a) je clos, tu clos, il clôt, ils closent; b) —; c) clorai;
close	d) clorais; e) close; f) clos(e)
concevoir	→recevoir
conceive	
conclure	a) conclus, conclus, conclut, concluons, concluez, concluent;
conclude	b) concluais; c) conclurai; d) conclurais; e) conclue; f) conclu(e)
conduire	→cuire
drive	
connaître	a) connais, connais, connaît, connaissons, connaissez,
know	connaissent; b) connaissais; c) connaîtrai; d) connaîtrais;
	e) connaisse; f) connu(e)
conquérir	→acquérir
conquer	
construire	→cuire
build	
contraindre	→craindre
constrain	
contredire	→médire
contradict	

coudre *sew*	a) couds, couds, coud, cousons, cousez, cousent; b) cousais; c) coudrai; d) coudrais; e) couse; f) cousu(e)
courir *run*	a) cours, cours, court, courons, courez, courent; b) courais; c) courrai; d) courrais; e) coure; f) couru(e)
couvrir *cover*	a) couvre, couvres, couvre, couvrons, couvrez, couvrent; b) couvrais; c) couvrirai; d) couvrirais; e) couvre; f) couvert(e)
craindre *fear*	a) crains, crains, craint, craignons, craignez, craignent; b) craignais; c) craindrai; d) craindrais; e) craigne; f) craint(e)
croire *believe*	a) crois, crois, croit, croyons, croyez, croient; b) croyais; c) croirai; d) croirais; e) croie; f) cru(e)
croître *grow*	a) croîs, croîs, croît, croissons, croissez, croissent; b) croissais; c) croîtrai; d) croîtrais; e) croisse; f) crû, crue
cueillir *pick*	a) cueille, cueilles, cueille, cueillons, cueillez, cueillent; b) cueillais; c) cueillerai; d) cueillerais; e) cueille; f) cueilli(e)
cuire *cook*	a) cuis, cuis, cuit, cuisons, cuisez, cuisent; b) cuisais; c) cuirai; d) cuirais; e) cuise; f) cuit(e)
décevoir *deceive*	→recevoir
décrire *describe*	→écrire
déduire *deduct*	→cuire
détruire *destroy*	→cuire
devoir *have to*	a) dois, dois, doit, devons, devez, doivent; b) devais; c) devrai; d) devrais; e) doive; f) dû, due
dire *say*	a) dis, dis, dit, disons, dites, disent; b) disais; c) dirai; d) diràis; e) dise; f) dit(e)
dissoudre *dissolve*	→absoudre
dormir *sleep*	a) dors, dors, dort, dormons, dormez, dorment; b) dormais; c) dormirai; d) dormirais; e) dorme; f) dormi
échoir *fall to*	a) il échoit; b) —; c) il échoira; d) il échoirait; e) qu'il échoie; f) échu(e)
écrire *write*	a) écris, écris, écrit, écrivons, écrivez, écrivent; b) écrivais; c) écrirai; d) écrirais; e) écrive; f) écrit(e)
élire *elect*	→lire
émettre *emit*	→mettre
émouvoir *affect*	→mouvoir; f) ému(e)
empreindre *imprint*	→peindre

enduire *coat*	→cuire
enfreindre *infringe*	→craindre
envoyer *send*	a) envoie, envoies, envoie, envoyons, envoyez, envoient; b) envoyais; c) enverrai; d) enverrais; e) envoie; f) envoyé(e)
éteindre *switch off*	→peindre
étreindre *embrace*	→peindre
exclure *exclude*	→conclure
faillir *fail*	a) —; b) —; c) faillirai; d) faillirais; e) faille; f) failli
faire *do, make*	a) fais, fais, fait, faisons, faites, font; b) faisais; c) ferai; d) ferais; e) fasse; f) fait(e)
falloir *have to*	a) il faut; b) il fallait; c) il faudra; d) il faudrait; e) qu'il faille; f) il a fallu
feindre *feign*	→peindre
frire *fry*	→confire
fuir *escape*	a) fuis, fuis, fuit, fuyons, fuyez, fuient; b) fuyais; c) fuirai; d) fuirais; e) fuie; f) fui
geindre *whine*	→craindre
haïr *hate*	a) hais, hais, hait, haïssons, haïssez, haïssent; b) haïssais; c) haïrai; d) haïrais; e) haïsse; f) haï(e)
inclure *include*	→conclure
induire *induce*	→cuire
inscrire *register*	→écrire
instruire *instruct*	→cuire
interdire *forbid*	→médire
introduire *introduce*	→cuire
joindre *join*	a) joins, joins, joint, joignons, joignez, joignent; b) joignais; c) joindrai; d) joindrais; e) joigne; f) joint(e)
lire *read*	a) lis, lis, lit, lisons, lisez, lisent; b) lisais; c) lirai; d) lirais; e) lise; f) lu(e)

luire *shine*	a) luis, luis, luit, luisons, luisez, luisent; b) luisais; c) luirai; d) luirais; e) luise; f) lui
maudire *curse*	a) maudis, maudis, maudit, maudissons, maudissez, maudissent; b) maudissais; c) maudirai; d) maudirais; e) maudisse; f) maudit(e)
médire *speak ill of*	a) médis, médis, médit, médisons, médisez, médisent; b) médisais; c) médirai; d) médirais; e) médise; f) médit(e)
mentir *lie*	a) mens, mens, ment, mentons, mentez, mentent; b) mentais; c) mentirai; d) mentirais; e) mente; f) menti
mettre *put*	a) mets, mets, met, mettons, mettez, mettent; b) mettais; c) mettrai; d) mettrais; e) mette; f) mis(e)
moudre *grind*	a) mouds, mouds, moud, moulons, moulez, moulent; b) moulais; c) moudrai; d) moudrais; e) moule; f) moulu(e)
mourir *die*	a) meurs, meurs, meurt, mourons, mourez, meurent; b) mourais; c) mourrai; d) mourrais; e) meure; f) mort(e)
mouvoir *set in motion*	a) meus, meus, meut, mouvons, mouvez, meuvent; b) mouvais; c) mouvrai; d) mouvrais; e) meuve; f) mû, mue
naître *be born*	a) nais, nais, naît, naissons, naissez, naissent; b) naissais; c) naîtrai; d) naîtrais; e) naisse; f) né(e)
nuire *harm*	→cuire; f) nui
offrir *offer*	→couvrir
ouvrir *open*	→couvrir
paître *graze*	a) pais, pais, paît, paissons, paissez, paissent; b) paissais; c) paîtrai; d) paîtrais; e) paisse; f) —
paraître *appear*	→connaître
partir *leave*	→mentir; f) parti(e)
peindre *paint*	a) peins, peins, peint, peignons, peignez, peignent; b) peignais; c) peindrai; d) peindrais; e) peigne; f) peint(e)
percevoir *perceive*	→recevoir
plaindre *pity*	→craindre
plaire *please*	a) plais, plais, plaît, plaisons, plaisez, plaisent; b) plaisais; c) plairai; d) plairais; e) plaise; f) plu
pleuvoir *rain*	a) il pleut; b) il pleuvait; c) il pleuvra; d) il pleuvrait; e) qu'il pleuve; f) il a plu
pourvoir *provide*	a) pourvois, pourvois, pourvoit, pourvoyons, pourvoyez, pourvoient; b) pourvoyais; c) pourvoirai; d) pourvoirais; e) pourvoie; f) pourvu(e)

pouvoir *be able to*	a) peux (puis), peux, peut, pouvons, pouvez, peuvent; b) pouvais, c) pourrai; d) pourrais; e) puisse; f) pu
prédire *foretell*	a) prédis, prédis, prédit, prédisons, prédisez, prédisent; b) prédisais; c) prédirai; d) prédirais; e) prédise; f) prédit(e)
prendre *take*	a) prends, prends, prend, prenons, prenez, prennent; b) prenais; c) prendrai; d) prendrais; e) prenne; f) pris(e)
prescrire *prescribe*	→écrire
prévoir *foresee*	a) prévois, prévois, prévoit, prévoyons, prévoyez, prévoient; b) prévoyais; c) prévoirai; d) prévoirais; e) prévoie; f) prévu(e)
produire *produce*	→cuire
proscrire *outlaw*	→écrire
recevoir *receive*	a) reçois, reçois, reçoit, recevons, recevez, reçoivent; b) recevais; c) recevrai; d) recevrais; e) reçoive; f) reçu(e)
requérir *require*	→acquérir
restreindre *restrict*	→peindre
rire *laugh*	a) ris, ris, rit, rions, riez, rient; b) riais; c) rirai; d) rirais; e) rie; f) ri
savoir *know*	a) sais, sais, sait, savons, savez, savent; b) savais; c) saurai; d) saurais; e) sache; f) su(e)
séduire *seduce*	→cuire
sentir *feel*	→mentir; f) senti(e)
servir *serve*	a) sers, sers, sert, servons, servez, servent; b) servais; c) servirai; d) servirais; e) serve; f) servi(e)
sortir *go out*	→mentir; f) sorti(e)
souffrir *suffer*	→couvrir
souscrire *subscribe*	→écrire
suffire *be enough*	a) suffis, suffis, suffit, suffisons, suffisez, suffisent; b) suffisais; c) suffirai; d) suffirais; e) suffise; e) suffi
suivre *follow*	a) suis, suis, suit, suivons, suivez, suivent; b) suivais; c) suivrai; d) suivrais; e) suive; f) suivi(e)
taire *be silent*	a) tais, tais, tait, taisons, taisez, taisent; b) taisais; c) tairai; d) tairais; e) taise; f) tu(e)
teindre *dye*	→peindre

tenir
hold
a) tiens, tiens, tient, tenons, tenez, tiennent; b) tenais;
c) tiendrai; d) tiendrais; e) tienne; f) tenu(e)

traduire
translate
→cuire

traire
milk (cow)
a) trais, trais, trait, trayons, trayez, traient; b) trayais;
c) trairai; d) trairais; e) traie; f) trait(e)

transcrire
transcribe
→écrire

tressaillir
startle
→assaillir

vaincre
defeat
a) vaincs, vaincs, vainc, vainquons, vainquez, vainquent;
b) vainquais; c) vaincrai; d) vaincrais; e) vainque; f) vaincu(e)

valoir
be worth
a) vaux, vaux, vaut, valons, valez, valent; b) valais; c) vaudrai;
d) vaudrais; e) vaille; f) valu(e)

venir
come
→tenir

vêtir
dress
a) vêts, vêts, vêt, vêtons, vêtez, vêtent; b) vêtais; c) vêtirai;
d) vêtirais; e) vête; f) vêtu(e)

vivre
live
a) vis, vis, vit, vivons, vivez, vivent; b) vivais; c) vivrai;
d) vivrais; e) vive; f) vécu(e)

voir
see
a) vois, vois, voit, voyons, voyez, voient; b) voyais; c) verrai;
d) verrais; e) voie; f) vu(e)

vouloir
want
a) veux, veux, veut, voulons, voulez, veulent; b) voulais;
c) voudrai; d) voudrais; e) veuille; f) voulu(e)

French Abbreviations

ACF	*Automobile-Club de France*	Automobile Association of France
ACS	*Automobile-Club de Suisse*	Swiss Automobile Association
AELE	*Association européenne de libre-échange*	EFTA, European Free Trade Association
apr. J.-C.	*après Jésus-Christ*	A.D.
av. J.-C.	*avant Jésus-Christ*	B.C.
bd	*boulevard*	boulevard
c.-à-d.	*c'est-à-dire*	i.e.
c/c	*compte courant*	current account
CCP	*compte de chèques postaux*	postal account
CFF	*Chemins de fer fédéraux*	Swiss Federal Railways
ch	*chevaux-vapeur*	horsepower
Cie, Co.	*compagnie*	company
CRS	*Compagnies républicaines de sécurité*	French order and riot police
ct	*courant ; centime*	of the month; 1/100 of a franc
CV	*chevaux-vapeur*	horsepower
EU	*Etats-Unis*	United States
exp.	*expéditeur*	sender
F(F)	*franc français*	French franc
FB	*franc belge*	Belgian franc
Fs/Fr.s.	*franc suisse*	Swiss franc
h.	*heure*	hour, o'clock
hab.	*habitants*	inhabitants, population
M.	*Monsieur*	Mr.
Me	*Maître*	title for barrister or lawyer
Mgr	*Monseigneur*	ecclesiastic title for the rank of bishop
Mlle	*Mademoiselle*	Miss
MM.	*Messieurs*	gentlemen, Messrs.
Mme	*Madame*	Mrs.
n°	*numéro*	number
ONU	*Organisation des Nations Unies*	UN
OTAN	*Organisation du Traité de l'Atlantique Nord*	NATO, North Atlantic Treaty Organization
PCV	*payable chez vous*	transfer-charge call (collect call)

PDG	*président-directeur général*	chairman of the board
p.ex.	*par exemple*	e.g.
PJ	*police judiciaire*	criminal investigation department
p.p.	*port payé*	postage paid
P & T	*Postes et Télécommunications*	post and telecommunications (France)
PTT	*Postes, Télégraphes, Téléphones*	Post, Telegraph, Telephone (Belgium and Switzerland)
RATP	*Régie autonome des transports parisiens*	Parisian transport authority
RF	*République française*	the French Republic
RN	*route nationale*	national highway
RP	*Révérend Père*	Reverend Father
RSVP	*répondez, s'il vous plaît*	RSVP, please reply
s/	*sur*	on, at
SA	*société anonyme*	Ltd., Inc.
S.à r.l.	*société à responsabilité limitée*	limited liability company
SE	*Son Eminence; Son Excellence*	His Eminence; His/Her Excellency
SI	*Syndicat d'Initiative*	tourist office
SIDA	*syndrome immuno-déficitaire acquis*	AIDS
SM	*Sa Majesté*	His/Her Majesty
SNCB	*Société nationale des chemins de fer belges*	Belgian National Railways
SNCF	*Société nationale des chemins de fer français*	French National Railways
St, Ste	*saint, sainte*	saint
succ.	*successeur; succursale*	successor; branch office
s.v.p.	*s'il vous plaît*	please
TCB	*Touring-Club royal de Belgique*	Royal Touring Club of Belgium
TCF	*Touring-Club de France*	Touring Club of France
TCS	*Touring-Club Suisse*	Swiss Touring Club
TEE	*Trans Europ Express*	luxury train, first-class only
t.s.v.p.	*tournez, s'il vous plaît*	please turn over
TVA	*taxe à la valeur ajoutée*	VAT, value added tax
UE	*Union européenne*	European Union
Vve	*veuve*	widow

Numerals

Cardinal numbers		Ordinal numbers	
0	zéro	1er	premier
1	un	2^e	deuxième (second)
2	deux	3^e	troisième
3	trois	4^e	quatrième
4	quatre	5^e	cinquième
5	cinq	6^e	sixième
6	six	7^e	septième
7	sept	8^e	huitième
8	huit	9^e	neuvième
9	neuf	10^e	dixième
10	dix	11^e	onzième
11	onze	12^e	douzième
12	douze	13^e	treizième
13	treize	14^e	quatorzième
14	quatorze	15^e	quinzième
15	quinze	16^e	seizième
16	seize	17^e	dix-septième
17	dix-sept	18^e	dix-huitième
18	dix-huit	19^e	dix-neuvième
19	dix-neuf	20^e	vingtième
20	vingt	21^e	vingt et unième
21	vingt et un	22^e	vingt-deuxième
22	vingt-deux	23^e	vingt-troisième
30	trente	30^e	trentième
40	quarante	40^e	quarantième
50	cinquante	50^e	cinquantième
60	soixante	60^e	soixantième
70	soixante-dix	70^e	soixante-dixième
71	soixante et onze	71^e	soixante et onzième
72	soixante-douze	72^e	soixante-douzième
80	quatre-vingts	80^e	quatre-vingtième
81	quatre-vingt-un	81^e	quatre-vingt-unième
90	quatre-vingt-dix	90^e	quatre-vingt-dixième
100	cent	100^e	centième
101	cent un	101^e	cent unième
230	deux cent trente	200^e	deux centième
1 000	mille	330^e	trois cent trentième
1 107	onze cent sept	1 000^e	millième
2 000	deux mille	1 107^e	onze cent septième
000 000	un million	2 000^e	deux millième

Time

Although official time in France is based on the 24-hour clock, the 12-hour system is used in conversation.

If you have to indicate that it is a.m. or p.m., add *du matin, de l'après-midi* or *du soir*.

Thus:

huit heures du matin	8 a.m.
deux heures de l'après-midi	2 p.m.
huit heures du soir	8 p.m.

Days of the Week

dimanche	Sunday	*jeudi*	Thursday
lundi	Monday	*vendredi*	Friday
mardi	Tuesday	*samedi*	Saturday
mercredi	Wednesday		

Some Basic Phrases	Quelques expressions utiles
Please.	S'il vous plaît.
Thank you very much.	Merci beaucoup.
Don't mention it.	Il n'y a pas de quoi.
Good morning.	Bonjour *(matin)*.
Good afternoon.	Bonjour *(après-midi)*.
Good evening.	Bonsoir.
Good night.	Bonne nuit.
Good-bye.	Au revoir.
See you later.	A bientôt.
Where is/Where are...?	Où se trouve/Où se trouvent...?
What do you call this?	Comment appelez-vous ceci?
What does that mean?	Que veut dire cela?
Do you speak English?	Parlez-vous anglais?
Do you speak German?	Parlez-vous allemand?
Do you speak French?	Parlez-vous français?
Do you speak Spanish?	Parlez-vous espagnol?
Do you speak Italian?	Parlez-vous italien?
Could you speak more slowly, please?	Pourriez-vous parler plus lentement, s'il vous plaît?
I don't understand.	Je ne comprends pas.
Can I have...?	Puis-je avoir...?
Can you show me...?	Pouvez-vous m'indiquer...?
Can you tell me...?	Pouvez-vous me dire...?
Can you help me, please?	Pouvez-vous m'aider, s'il vous plaît?
I'd like...	Je voudrais...
We'd like...	Nous voudrions...
Please give me...	S'il vous plaît, donnez-moi...
Please bring me...	S'il vous plaît, apportez-moi...
I'm hungry.	J'ai faim.
I'm thirsty.	J'ai soif.
I'm lost.	Je me suis perdu.
Hurry up!	Dépêchez-vous!

| There is/There are… | Il y a… |
| There isn't/There aren't… | Il n'y a pas… |

Arrival

Arrivée

Your passport, please.	Votre passeport, s'il vous plaît.
Have you anything to declare?	Avez-vous quelque chose à déclarer?
No, nothing at all.	Non, rien du tout.
Can you help me with my luggage, please?	Pouvez-vous prendre mes bagages, s'il vous plaît?
Where's the bus to the centre of town, please?	Où est le bus pour le centre de la ville, s'il vous plaît?
This way, please.	Par ici, s'il vous plaît.
Where can I get a taxi?	Où puis-je trouver un taxi?
What's the fare to…?	Quel est le tarif pour…?
Take me to this address, please.	Conduisez-moi à cette adresse, s'il vous plaît.
I'm in a hurry.	Je suis pressé.

Hotel

Hôtel

My name is…	Je m'appelle…
Have you a reservation?	Avez-vous réservé?
I'd like a room with a bath.	J'aimerais une chambre avec bains.
What's the price per night?	Quel est le prix pour une nuit?
May I see the room?	Puis-je voir la chambre?
What's my room number, please?	Quel est le numéro de ma chambre, s'il vous plaît?
There's no hot water.	Il n'y a pas d'eau chaude.
May I see the manager, please?	Puis-je voir le directeur, s'il vous plaît?
Did anyone telephone me?	Y a-t-il eu des appels pour moi?
Is there any mail for me?	Y a-t-il du courrier pour moi?
May I have my bill (check), please?	Puis-je avoir ma note, s'il vous plaît?

Eating out

	Restaurant
Do you have a fixed-price menu?	Avez-vous un menu?
May I see the menu?	Puis-je voir la carte?
May we have an ashtray, please?	Pouvons-nous avoir un cendrier, s'il vous plaît?
Where's the toilet, please?	Où sont les toilettes, s'il vous plaît?
I'd like an hors-d'œuvre (starter).	Je voudrais un hors-d'œuvre.
Have you any soup?	Avez-vous du potage?
I'd like some fish.	J'aimerais du poisson.
What kind of fish do you have?	Qu'avez-vous comme poisson?
I'd like a steak.	Je voudrais un steak.
What vegetables have you got?	Quels légumes servez-vous?
Nothing more, thanks.	Je suis servi, merci.
What would you like to drink?	Qu'aimeriez-vous boire?
I'll have a beer, please.	J'aimerais une bière, s'il vous plaît.
I'd like a bottle of wine.	Je voudrais une bouteille de vin.
May I have the bill (check), please?	Puis-je avoir l'addition, s'il vous plaît?
Is service included?	Le service est-il compris?
Thank you, that was a very good meal.	Merci, c'était très bon.

Travelling

	Voyages
Where's the railway station, please?	Où se trouve la gare, s'il vous plaît?
Where's the ticket office, please?	Où est le guichet, s'il vous plaît?
I'd like a ticket to...	J'aimerais un billet pour...
First or second class?	Première ou deuxième classe?
First class, please.	Première classe, s'il vous plaît.
Single or return (one way or roundtrip)?	Aller simple ou aller et retour?
Do I have to change trains?	Est-ce que je dois changer de train?
What platform does the train for... leave from?	De quel quai part le train pour...?

Where's the nearest underground (subway) station?	Où est la station de métro la plus proche?
Where's the bus station, please?	Où est la gare routière, s'il vous plaît?
When's the first bus to…?	A quelle heure part le premier autobus pour…?
Please let me off at the next stop.	S'il vous plaît, déposez-moi au prochain arrêt.

Relaxing	**Distractions**
What's on at the cinema (movies)?	Que joue-t-on au cinéma?
What time does the film begin?	A quelle heure commence le film?
Are there any tickets for tonight?	Reste-t-il encore des places pour ce soir?
Where can we go dancing?	Où pouvons-nous aller danser?

Meeting people	**Rencontres**
How do you do.	Bonjour madame/mademoiselle/monsieur.
How are you?	Comment allez-vous?
Very well, thank you. And you?	Très bien, merci. Et vous?
May I introduce…?	Puis-je vous présenter…?
My name is…	Je m'appelle…
I'm very pleased to meet you.	Enchanté de faire votre connaissance.
How long have you been here?	Depuis combien de temps êtes-vous ici?
It was nice meeting you.	Enchanté d'avoir fait votre connaissance.
Do you mind if I smoke?	Est-ce que ça vous dérange que je fume?
Do you have a light, please?	Avez-vous du feu, s'il vous plaît?
May I get you a drink?	Puis-je vous offrir un verre?
May I invite you for dinner tonight?	Puis-je vous inviter à dîner ce soir?
Where shall we meet?	Où nous retrouverons-nous?

Shops, stores and services

Where's the nearest bank, please?

Where can I cash some travellers' cheques?

Can you give me some small change, please?

Where's the nearest chemist's (pharmacy)?

How do I get there?

Is it within walking distance?

Can you help me, please?

How much is this? And that?

It's not quite what I want.

I like it.

Can you recommend something for sunburn?

I'd like a haircut, please.

I'd like a manicure, please.

Magasins et services

Où se trouve la banque la plus proche, s'il vous plaît?

Où puis-je changer des chèques de voyage?

Pouvez-vous me donner de la monnaie, s'il vous plaît?

Où est la pharmacie la plus proche?

Comment puis-je m'y rendre?

Peut-on y aller à pied?

Pouvez-vous m'aider, s'il vous plaît?

Combien coûte ceci? Et cela?

Ce n'est pas exactement ce que je désire.

Cela me plaît.

Pouvez-vous me conseiller quelque chose contre les coups de soleil?

Je voudrais me faire couper les cheveux, s'il vous plaît.

Je voudrais une manucure, s'il vous plaît.

Street directions

Can you show me on the map where I am?

You are on the wrong road.

Go/Walk straight ahead.

It's on the left/on the right.

Directions

Pouvez-vous me montrer sur la carte où je me trouve?

Vous n'êtes pas sur la bonne route.

Continuez tout droit.

C'est à gauche/à droite.

Emergencies

Call a doctor quickly.

Call an ambulance.

Please call the police.

Urgences

Appelez vite un médecin.

Appelez une ambulance.

Appelez la police, s'il vous plaît.

anglais-français

english-french

Introduction

Ce dictionnaire a été conçu dans un but pratique. Vous n'y trouverez donc pas d'information linguistique inutile. Les adresses sont classées par ordre alphabétique, sans tenir compte du fait qu'un mot peut être simple ou composé, avec ou sans trait d'union. Seule exception à cette règle: quelques expressions idiomatiques qui ont été classées en fonction du terme le plus significatif.

Lorsqu'une adresse est suivie d'adresses secondaires (p. ex. expressions usuelles ou locutions), ces dernières sont également rangées par ordre alphabétique sous le mot vedette.

Chaque mot souche est suivi d'une transcription phonétique (voir le Guide de prononciation) et, s'il y a lieu, de l'indication de la catégorie grammaticale (substantif, verbe, adjectif, etc.). Lorsqu'un mot souche peut appartenir à plusieurs catégories grammaticales, les traductions qui s'y réfèrent sont groupées derrière chacune d'elles.

Les pluriels irréguliers des substantifs sont toujours donnés, de même que certains pluriels pouvant prêter à hésitation.

Pour éviter toute répétition, nous avons utilisé un tilde (~) en lieu et place de l'adresse principale.

Dans le pluriel des mots composés, le tiret (-) remplace la partie du mot qui demeure inchangée.

Un astérisque (*) signale les verbes irréguliers. Pour plus de détails, consulter la liste de ces verbes.

Ce dictionnaire tient compte de l'épellation anglaise. Les mots et les définitions des termes typiquement américains ont été indiqués comme tels (voir la liste des abréviations utilisées dans le texte).

Abréviations

adj	adjectif	*num*	numéral
adv	adverbe	*p*	imparfait
Am	américain	*pl*	pluriel
art	article	*plAm*	pluriel (américain)
conj	conjonction	*pp*	participe passé
f	féminin	*pr*	présent
fpl	féminin pluriel	*pref*	préfixe
m	masculin	*prep*	préposition
mpl	masculin pluriel	*pron*	pronom
n	nom	*v*	verbe
nAm	nom (américain)	*vAm*	verbe (américain)

Guide de prononciation

Chaque article de cette partie du dictionnaire est accompagné d'une transcription phonétique qui vous indique la prononciation des mots. Vous la lirez comme si chaque lettre ou groupe de lettres avait la même valeur qu'en français. Au-dessous figurent uniquement les lettres et les symboles ambigus ou particulièrement difficiles à comprendre. *Toutes* les consonnes, y compris celles placées à la fin d'une syllabe ou d'un mot, doivent être prononcées.

Les traits d'union séparent chaque syllabe. Celles que l'on doit accentuer sont imprimées en *italique*.

Les sons de deux langues ne coïncident jamais parfaitement; mais si vous suivez soigneusement nos indications, vous pourrez prononcer les mots étrangers de façon à vous faire comprendre. Pour faciliter votre tâche, nos transcriptions simplifient parfois légèrement le système phonétique de la langue, mais elles reflètent néanmoins les différences de son essentielles.

Consonnes

ð	le **th** anglais de **the**; **z** dit en zézayant
gh	comme **g** dans **gai**
h	doit être prononcé en expirant fortement; rappelle le **h** de l'interjection **h**ue!
ng/nng	comme dans campi**ng**; ou comme le dernier son de pai**n**, prononcé avec l'accent du Midi
s	toujours comme dans **s**i
θ	le **th** anglais de **th**ink; **s** dit en zézayant
y	toujours comme dans **y**eux

Au début ou à la fin d'un mot anglais, **b**, **d**, **v**, **z** sont moins sonores qu'en français. C'est également le cas avec **gh** et **ð**.

Voyelles et diphtongues

æ	entre **a** et **è**
i	entre **i** et **é**
ii	comme **i** dans l**i**re
o	proche du **o** de p**o**mme, mais avec la langue placée plus bas et plus retirée dans la bouche et avec les lèvres plus arrondies

1) Les voyelles longues sont indiquées par un dédoublement (p.ex. **oo**) ou par un accent circonflexe placé sur le second élément (p.ex. **eû**).

2) Nos transcriptions comprenant un **ï** doivent être lues comme des diphtongues; le **ï** ne doit pas être séparé de la voyelle qui le précède (comme dans tr**ahi**), mais doit se fondre dans celle-ci (comme dans **ail**).

3) Les lettres imprimées en petits caractères et dans une position surélevée doivent être prononcées d'une façon assez faible et rapide (p.ex. **ᵒᵘi, iᵉᵘ**).

Prononciation américaine

Notre transcription correspond à la prononciation anglaise habituelle. Si la langue américaine varie grandement d'une région à l'autre, elle présente tout de même quelques différences marquantes par rapport à l'anglais de Grande-Bretagne. Ainsi par exemple:

1) Le **r**, qu'il soit placé devant une consonne ou à la fin d'un mot, se prononce toujours (contrairement à l'habitude anglaise).

2) Le **ââ** devient **ææ** dans certains mots, tels que *ask*, *castle*, *laugh*, etc.

3) Le **o** anglais se prononce **a** ou souvent **oo**.

4) Placé devant **oû**, le son **y** est fréquemment omis (ainsi: *duty*, *tune*, *new*, etc.)

5) Enfin, l'accent tonique de certains mots peut varier considérablement.

A

a (éï,eu) *art* (an) un *art*

abbey (æ-bi) *n* abbaye *f*

abbreviation (eu-brii-vi-*éï*-cheunn) *n* abréviation *f*

aberration (æ-beu-*réï*-cheunn) *n* aberration *f*

ability (eu-*bi*-leu-ti) *n* capacité *f*

able (*éï*-beul) *adj* en mesure; capable; *be ~ to* *être capable de; *savoir, *pouvoir

abnormal (æb-*noo*-meul) *adj* anormal

aboard (eu-*bood*) *adv* à bord

abolish (eu-*bo*-lich) *v* abolir

abortion (eu-*boo*-cheunn) *n* avortement *m*

about (eu-*baout*) *prep* de; concernant, sur; autour de; *adv* à peu près; autour

above (eu-*bav*) *prep* au-dessus de; *adv* en haut

abroad (eu-*brood*) *adv* à l'étranger

abscess (æb-sèss) *n* abcès *m*

absence (æb-seunns) *n* absence *f*

absent (æb-seunnt) *adj* absent

absolutely (æb-seu-loût-li) *adv* absolument

abstain from (eub-*stéïn*) s'*abstenir de

abstract (æb-strækt) *adj* abstrait

absurd (eub-*seûd*) *adj* absurde

abundance (eu-*bann*-deunns) *n* abondance *f*

abundant (eu-*bann*-deunnt) *adj* abondant

abuse (eu-*byoûss*) *n* abus *m*

abyss (eu-*biss*) *n* abîme *m*

academy (eu-*kæ*-deu-mi) *n* académie *f*

accelerate (euk-*sè*-leu-réït) *v* accélérer

accelerator (euk-*sè*-leu-réï-teu) *n* accélérateur *m*

accent (æk-seunnt) *n* accent *m*

accept (euk-*sèpt*) *v* accepter

access (æk-sèss) *n* accès *m*

accessary (euk-*sè*-seu-ri) *n* complice *m*

accessible (euk-*sè*-seu-beul) *adj* accessible

accessories (euk-*sè*-seu-riz) *pl* accessoires *mpl*

accident (æk-si-deunnt) *n* accident *m*

accidental (æk-si-*dèn*-teul) *adj* accidentel

accommodate (eu-*ko*-meu-déït) *v* loger

accommodation (eu-ko-meu-*déï*-cheunn) *n* accommodation *f*, logement *m*

accompany (eu-*kamm*-peu-ni) *v* accompagner

accomplish (eu-*kamm*-plich) *v* achever; accomplir

in accordance with (inn eu-*koo*-deunns ^{ou}iδ) conformément à

according to (eu-*koo*-dinng toù) d'après, selon; conformément à

account (eu-*kaount*) n compte m; récit m; ~ **for** rendre compte de; **on** ~ **of** à cause de

accountable (eu-*kaoun*-teu-beul) adj explicable

accurate (æ-kyou-reut) adj précis

accuse (eu-*kyoûz*) v accuser

accused (eu-*kyoûzd*) n prévenu m

accustom (eu-*ka*-steumm) v familiariser; **accustomed** accoutumé, habitué

ache (éïk) v *faire mal; n douleur f

achieve (eu-*tchiiv*) v *parvenir à; accomplir

achievement (eu-*tchiiv*-meunnt) n performance f

acid (æ-sid) n acide m

acknowledge (euk-*no*-lidj) v *reconnaître; *admettre; confirmer

acne (æk-ni) n acné f

acorn (*éï*-koon) n gland m

acquaintance (eu-*kou^aéïn*-teunns) n connaissance f

acquire (eu-*k^{ou}aï^{eu}*) v *acquérir

acquisition (æ-k^{ou}i-*zi*-cheunn) n acquisition f

acquittal (eu-*k^{ou}i*-teul) v acquittement m

across (eu-*kross*) prep à travers; de l'autre côté de; adv de l'autre côté

act (ækt) n acte m; numéro m; v agir; se *conduire; jouer

action (æk-cheunn) n action f

active (æk-tiv) adj actif; animé

activity (æk-*ti*-veu-ti) n activité f

actor (æk-teu) n acteur m

actress (æk-triss) n actrice f

actual (æk-tchou-eul) adj véritable, réel

actually (æk-tchou-eu-li) adv en réalité

acute (eu-*kyoût*) adj aigu

adapt (eu-*dæpt*) v adapter

add (æd) v additionner; ajouter

addition (eu-*di*-cheunn) n addition f

additional (eu-*di*-cheu-neul) adj supplémentaire; accessoire

address (eu-*drèss*) n adresse f; v adresser; s'adresser à

addressee (æ-drè-*sii*) n destinataire m

adequate (æ-di-k^{ou}eut) adj adéquat; approprié

adjective (æ-djik-tiv) n adjectif m

adjourn (eu-*djeûnn*) v ajourner

adjust (eu-*djast*) v ajuster; rectifier; régler

administer (eud-*mi*-ni-steu) v administrer

administration (eud-mi-ni-*stréï*-cheunn) n administration f; gestion f

administrative (eud-*mi*-ni-streu-tiv) adj administratif; ~ **law** droit administratif

admiral (æd-meu-reul) n amiral m

admiration (æd-meu-*réï*-cheunn) n admiration f

admire (eud-*maï^{eu}*) v admirer

admission (eud-*mi*-cheunn) n admission f

admit (eud-*mit*) v *admettre; *reconnaître

admittance (eud-*mi*-teunns) n accès m; **no** ~ entrée interdite

adopt (eu-*dopt*) v adopter

adoption (eu-*dop*-cheunn) n adoption f

adorable (eu-*doo*-reu-beul) adj adorable

adult (æ-dalt) n adulte m; adj adulte

advance (eud-*vââns*) n avancement m; avance f; v avancer; **in** ~ à l'avance, d'avance

advanced (eud-*vâânst*) adj avancé

advantage (eud-*vâân*-tidj) *n* avantage *m*

advantageous (æd-veunn-*téi*-djeuss) *adj* avantageux

adventure (eud-*vèn*-tcheu) *n* aventure *f*

adverb (*æd*-veûb) *n* adverbe *m*

advertisement (eud-*veû*-tiss-meunnt) *n* annonce *f*; publicité *f*

advertising (*æd*-veu-taï-zinng) *n* publicité *f*

advice (eud-*vaïss*) *n* avis *m*, conseil *m*

advise (eud-*vaïz*) *v* donner des conseils, conseiller

advocate (*æd*-veu-keut) *n* partisan *m*

aerial (*è*^{eu}-ri-eul) *n* antenne *f*

aeroplane (*è*^{eu}-reu-pléïn) *n* avion *m*

affair (eu-*fè*^{eu}) *n* affaire *f*; liaison *f*, affaire de cœur

affect (eu-*fèkt*) *v* affecter; toucher

affected (eu-*fèk*-tid) *adj* affecté

affection (eu-*fèk*-cheunn) *n* affection *f*

affectionate (eu-*fèk*-cheu-nit) *adj* affectueux

affiliated (eu-*fi*-li-éï-tid) *adj* affilié

affirmative (eu-*feû*-meu-tiv) *adj* affirmatif

affliction (eu-*flik*-cheunn) *n* affliction *f*

afford (eu-*food*) *v* se *permettre

afraid (eu-*fréïd*) *adj* apeuré, effrayé; *be ~ *avoir peur

Africa (*æ*-fri-keu) Afrique *f*

African (*æ*-fri-keunn) *adj* africain; *n* Africain *m*

after (*ââf*-teu) *prep* après; derrière; *conj* après que

afternoon (ââf-teu-*noûn*) *n* après-midi *m/f*

afterwards (*ââf*-teu-^{ou}eudz) *adv* après; par la suite, ensuite

again (eu-*ghèn*) *adv* encore; de nouveau; *~ and again* toujours et encore

against (eu-*ghènst*) *prep* contre

age (éïdj) *n* âge *m*; vieillesse *f*; *of ~* majeur; *under ~* mineur

aged (*éï*-djid) *adj* âgé; vieux

agency (*éï*-djeunn-si) *n* agence *f*; bureau *m*

agenda (eu-*djèn*-deu) *n* ordre du jour

agent (*éï*-djeunnt) *n* agent *m*, représentant *m*

aggressive (eu-*ghrè*-siv) *adj* agressif

ago (eu-*ghô*^{ou}) *adv* il y a

agrarian (eu-*ghrè*^{eu}-ri-eunn) *adj* agraire

agree (eu-*ghrii*) *v* *être d'accord; *consentir; concorder

agreeable (eu-*ghrii*-eu-beul) *adj* agréable

agreement (eu-*ghrii*-meunnt) *n* contrat *m*; accord *m*; entente *f*

agriculture (*æ*-ghri-kal-tcheu) *n* agriculture *f*

ahead (eu-*hèd*) *adv* en avant; *~ of* devant; *go ~* continuer; *straight ~* tout droit

aid (éïd) *n* aide *f*; *v* assister, aider

ailment (*éïl*-meunnt) *n* affection *f*; maladie *f*

aim (éïm) *n* but *m*; *~ at* viser; rechercher, aspirer à

air (è^{eu}) *n* air *m*; *v* aérer

air-conditioning (*è*^{eu}-keunn-di-cheu-ninng) *n* climatisation *f*; **air-conditioned** *adj* climatisé

aircraft (*è*^{eu}-krââft) *n* (pl ~) avion *m*; appareil *m*

airfield (*è*^{eu}-fiild) *n* terrain d'aviation

air-filter (*è*^{eu}-fil-teu) *n* filtre à air

airline (*è*^{eu}-laïn) *n* ligne aérienne

airmail (*è*^{eu}-méïl) *n* poste aérienne

airplane (*è*^{eu}-pléïn) *nAm* avion *m*

airport (*è*^{eu}-poot) *n* aéroport *m*

air-sickness (*è*^{eu}-sik-neuss) *n* mal de l'air

airtight (*è*^{eu}-taït) *adj* hermétique

airy (*è^eu*-ri) *adj* aéré

aisle (aïl) *n* bas-côté *m* ; passage *m*

alarm (eu-*lââm*) *n* alerte *f* ; *v* alarmer

alarm-clock (eu-*lââm*-klok) *n* réveil *m*

album (*æl*-beumm) *n* album *m*

alcohol (*æl*-keu-hol) *n* alcool *m*

alcoholic (*æl*-keu-*ho*-lik) *adj* alcoolique

ale (éïl) *n* bière *f*

algebra (*æl*-dji-breu) *n* algèbre *f*

Algeria (*æl*-*dji^eu*-ri-eu) Algérie *f*

Algerian (*æl*-*dji^eu*-ri-eunn) *adj* algérien ; *n* Algérien *m*

alien (*éï*-li-eunn) *n* étranger *m* ; *adj* étranger

alike (eu-*laïk*) *adj* pareil, semblable ; *adv* de la même façon

alimony (*æ*-li-meu-ni) *n* pension alimentaire

alive (eu-*laïv*) *adj* en vie, vivant

all (ool) *adj* tout ; ~ **in** tout compris ; ~ **right!** bien! ; **at** ~ du tout

allergy (*æ*-leu-dji) *n* allergie *f*

alley (*æ*-li) *n* ruelle *f*

alliance (eu-*laï*-eunns) *n* alliance *f*

Allies (*æ*-laïz) *pl* Alliés

allot (eu-*lot*) *v* assigner

allow (eu-*laou*) *v* autoriser, *permettre ; ~ **to** autoriser à ; *be allowed *être autorisé

allowance (eu-*laou*-eunns) *n* allocation *f*

all-round (ool-*raound*) *adj* universel

almanac (*ool*-meu-næk) *n* almanach *m*

almond (*ââ*-meunnd) *n* amande *f*

almost (*ool*-mô^ou st) *adv* presque ; à peu près

alone (eu-*lô^ou n*) *adv* seul

along (eu-*lonng*) *prep* le long de

aloud (eu-*laoud*) *adv* à haute voix

alphabet (*æl*-feu-bèt) *n* alphabet *m*

already (ool-*rè*-di) *adv* déjà

also (*ool*-sô^ou) *adv* aussi ; de même, également

altar (*ool*-teu) *n* autel *m*

alter (*ool*-teu) *v* changer, modifier

alteration (ool-teu-*réï*-cheunn) *n* changement *m*, modification *f*

alternate (ool-*teû*-neut) *adj* alternatif

alternative (ool-*teû*-neu-tiv) *n* alternative *f*

although (ool-*ð^ou*) *conj* quoique, bien que

altitude (*æl*-ti-tyoüd) *n* altitude *f*

alto (*æl*-tô^ou) *n* (pl ~s) contralto *m*

altogether (ool-teu-*ghè*-ðeu) *adv* entièrement ; en tout

always (*ool*-^ou éïz) *adv* toujours

am (æm) *v* (pr be)

amaze (eu-*méïz*) *v* étonner, *surprendre

amazement (eu-*méïz*-meunnt) *n* étonnement *m*

ambassador (æm-*bæ*-seu-deu) *n* ambassadeur *m*

amber (*æm*-beu) *n* ambre *m*

ambiguous (æm-*bi*-ghyou-euss) *adj* ambigu ; équivoque

ambitious (æm-*bi*-cheuss) *adj* ambitieux

ambulance (*æm*-byou-leunns) *n* ambulance *f*

ambush (*æm*-bouch) *n* embuscade *f*

America (eu-*mè*-ri-keu) Amérique *f*

American (eu-*mè*-ri-keunn) *adj* américain ; *n* Américain *m*

amethyst (*æ*-mi-θïst) *n* améthyste *f*

amid (eu-*mid*) *prep* entre ; parmi, au milieu de

ammonia (eu-*mô^ou*-ni-eu) *n* ammoniaque *f*

amnesty (*æm*-ni-sti) *n* amnistie *f*

among (eu-*manng*) *prep* parmi ; au milieu de, entre ; ~ **other things** entre autres

amount (eu-*maount*) *n* quantité *f* ; montant *m*, somme *f* ; ~ **to** se monter à

amuse (eu-*myoûz*) *v* divertir, amuser

amusement (eu-*myoûz*-meunnt) *n* amusement *m*, divertissement *m*

amusing (eu-*myoû*-zinng) *adj* plaisant

anaemia (eu-*nii*-mi-eu) *n* anémie *f*

anaesthesia (æ-niss-*θii*-zi-eu) *n* anesthésie *f*

anaesthetic (æ-niss-*θè*-tik) *n* anesthésique *m*

analyse (æ-neu-laïz) *v* analyser

analysis (eu-*næ*-leu-siss) *n* (pl -ses) analyse *f*

analyst (æ-neu-list) *n* analyste *m*; psychanalyste *m*

anarchy (æ-neu-ki) *n* anarchie *f*

anatomy (eu-*næ*-teu-mi) *n* anatomie *f*

ancestor (æn-sè-steu) *n* ancêtre *m*

anchor (æng-keu) *n* ancre *f*

anchovy (æn-tcheu-vi) *n* anchois *m*

ancient (*éin*-cheunnt) *adj* vieux, ancien; démodé, vieilli; antique

and (ænd, eunnd) *conj* et

angel (*éin*-djeul) *n* ange *m*

anger (æng-gheu) *n* colère *f*; fureur *f*

angle (æng-gheul) *v* pêcher à la ligne; *n* angle *m*

angry (æng-ghri) *adj* en colère

animal (æ-ni-meul) *n* animal *m*

ankle (æng-keul) *n* cheville *f*

annex[1] (æ-nèks) *n* annexe *f*

annex[2] (eu-*nèks*) *v* annexer

anniversary (æ-ni-*veû*-seu-ri) *n* anniversaire *m*

announce (eu-*naouns*) *v* annoncer

announcement (eu-*naouns*-meunnt) *n* annonce *f*

annoy (eu-*noï*) *v* agacer, fâcher; ennuyer

annoyance (eu-*noï*-eunns) *n* ennui *m*

annoying (eu-*noï*-inng) *adj* fastidieux, ennuyeux

annual (æ-nyou-eul) *adj* annuel; *n* annuaire *m*

per annum (peur æ-neumm) par année

anonymous (eu-*no*-ni-meuss) *adj* anonyme

another (eu-*na*-ðeu) *adj* encore un; un autre

answer (*âân*-seu) *v* répondre à; *n* réponse *f*

ant (ænt) *n* fourmi *f*

anthology (æn-*θo*-leu-dji) *n* anthologie *f*

antibiotic (æn-ti-baï-*o*-tik) *n* antibiotique *m*

anticipate (æn-*ti*-si-péït) *v* *prévoir, anticiper; *prévenir

antifreeze (æn-ti-friiz) *n* antigel *m*

antipathy (æn-*ti*-peu-θi) *n* antipathie *f*

antique (æn-*tiik*) *adj* antique; *n* antiquité *f*; ~ **dealer** antiquaire *m*

antiquity (æn-*ti*-k^(ou)eu-ti) *n* Antiquité; **antiquities** *pl* antiquités

antiseptic (æn-ti-*sèp*-tik) *n* antiseptique *m*

antlers (ænt-leuz) *pl* andouiller *m*

anxiety (æng-*zaï*-eu-ti) *n* anxiété *f*

anxious (ængk-cheuss) *adj* désireux; inquiet

any (è-ni) *adj* n'importe quel

anybody (è-ni-bo-di) *pron* n'importe qui

anyhow (è-ni-haou) *adv* n'importe comment

anyone (è-ni-^(ou)ann) *pron* chacun

anything (è-ni-θinng) *pron* n'importe quoi

anyway (è-ni-^(ou)éï) *adv* de toute façon

anywhere (è-ni-^(ou)è^(eu)) *adv* n'importe où

apart (eu-*pâât*) *adv* à part, séparément; ~ **from** abstraction faite de

apartment (eu-*pâât*-meunnt) *n*Am appartement *m*; étage *m*; ~ **house** Am immeuble d'habitation

aperitif (eu-*pè*-reu-tiv) *n* apéritif *m*

apologize (eu-*po*-leu-djaïz) v s'excuser

apology (eu-*po*-leu-dji) n excuse f

apparatus (æ-peu-*réï*-teuss) n dispositif m, appareil m

apparent (eu-*pæ*-reunnt) adj apparent

apparently (eu-*pæ*-reunnt-li) adv apparemment ; manifestement

apparition (æ-peu-*ri*-cheunn) n apparition f

appeal (eu-*piil*) n appel m

appear (eu-*pi*ᵉᵘ) v sembler, *paraître ; *apparaître ; se présenter

appearance (eu-*pi*ᵉᵘ-reunns) n apparence f ; aspect m ; entrée f

appendicitis (eu-pèn-di-*saï*-tiss) n appendicite f

appendix (eu-*pèn*-diks) n (pl -dices, -dixes) appendice m

appetite (æ-peu-taït) n appétit m

appetizer (æ-peu-taï-zeu) n amuse-gueule m

appetizing (æ-peu-taï-zinng) adj appétissant

applause (eu-*plooz*) n applaudissements mpl

apple (æ-peul) n pomme f

appliance (eu-*plaï*-eunns) n appareil m

application (æ-pli-*kéï*-cheunn) n application f ; demande f ; candidature f

apply (eu-*plaï*) v appliquer ; se *servir de ; solliciter un emploi ; s'appliquer à

appoint (eu-*poïnt*) v désigner, nommer

appointment (eu-*poïnt*-meunnt) n rendez-vous m ; nomination f

appreciate (eu-*prii*-chi-éït) v évaluer ; apprécier

appreciation (eu-prii-chi-*éï*-cheunn) n appréciation f

approach (eu-*prô*ᵒᵘtch) v approcher ; n approche f ; accès m

appropriate (eu-*prô*ᵒᵘ-pri-eut) adj juste, approprié, adéquat

approval (eu-*proû*-veul) n approbation f ; consentement m, accord m ; **on** ~ à l'essai

approve (eu-*proûv*) v approuver ; ~ **of** *être d'accord avec

approximate (eu-*prok*-si-meut) adj approximatif

approximately (eu-*prok*-si-meut-li) adv à peu près, approximativement

apricot (*éï*-pri-kot) n abricot m

April (*éï*-preul) avril

apron (*éï*-preunn) n tablier m

Arab (æ roub) adj arabe ; n Arabe m

arbitrary (*ââ*-bi-treu-ri) adj arbitraire

arcade (ââ-*kéïd*) n arcade f

arch (ââtch) n arche f ; voûte f

archaeologist (ââ-ki-*o*-leu-djist) n archéologue m

archaeology (ââ-ki-*o*-leu-dji) n archéologie f

archbishop (ââtch-*bi*-cheup) n archevêque m

arched (ââtcht) adj arqué

architect (*ââ*-ki-tèkt) n architecte m

architecture (*ââ*-ki-tèk-tcheu) n architecture f

archives (*ââ*-kaïvz) pl archives fpl

are (ââ) v (pr be)

area (*è*ᵉᵘ-ri-eu) n région f ; zone f ; surface f ; ~ **code** indicatif m

Argentina (ââ-djeunn-*tii*-neu) Argentine f

Argentinian (ââ-djeunn-*ti*-ni-eunn) adj argentin ; n Argentin m

argue (*ââ*-ghyoû) v argumenter, discuter ; disputer

argument (*ââ*-ghyou-meunnt) n argument m ; discussion f ; dispute f

arid (æ-rid) adj aride

*arise (eu-*raïz*) v surgir

arithmetic (eu-*riθ*-meu-tik) n arithmétique f

arm (ââm) n bras m ; arme f ; v armer

armchair (ââm-tchè^{eu}) *n* fauteuil *m*

armed (ââmd) *adj* armé; ~ **forces** forces armées

armour (ââ-meu) *n* armure *f*

army (ââ-mi) *n* armée *f*

aroma (eu-rô^{ou}-meu) *n* arôme *m*

around (eu-*raound*) *prep* autour de; *adv* autour

arrange (eu-*réïndj*) *v* classer, arranger; préparer

arrangement (eu-*réïndj*-meunnt) *n* règlement *m*

arrest (eu-*rèst*) *v* arrêter; *n* arrestation *f*

arrival (eu-*raï*-veul) *n* arrivée *f*; venue *f*

arrive (eu-*raïv*) *v* arriver

arrow (æ-rô^{ou}) *n* flèche *f*

art (âât) *n* art *m*; habileté *f*; ~ **collection** collection d'art; ~ **exhibition** exposition d'art; ~ **gallery** galerie d'art; ~ **history** histoire de l'art; **arts and crafts** arts et métiers; ~ **school** académie des beaux-arts

artery (ââ-teu-ri) *n* artère *f*

artichoke (ââ-ti-tchô^{ou}k) *n* artichaut *m*

article (ââ-ti-keul) *n* article *m*

artifice (ââ-ti-fiss) *n* ruse *f*

artificial (ââ-ti-*fi*-cheul) *adj* artificiel

artist (ââ-tist) *n* artiste *m/f*

artistic (ââ-ti-stik) *adj* artistique

as (æz) *conj* comme; aussi; que; puisque, parce que; ~ **from** à partir de; ~ **if** comme si

asbestos (æz-bè-stoss) *n* amiante *m*

ascend (eu-*sènd*) *v* monter; *faire l'ascension de

ascent (eu-*sènt*) *n* montée *f*

ascertain (æ-seu-*téïn*) *v* constater; s'assurer de

ash (æch) *n* cendre *f*

ashamed (eu-*chéïmd*) *adj* honteux;

*be ~ *avoir honte

ashore (eu-*choo*) *adv* à terre

ashtray (æch-tréï) *n* cendrier *m*

Asia (*éï*-cheu) Asie *f*

Asian (*éï*-cheunn) *adj* asiatique; *n* Asiatique *m*

aside (eu-*saïd*) *adv* de côté, à part

ask (ââsk) *v* demander; prier

asleep (eu-*sliip*) *adj* endormi

asparagus (eu-*spæ*-reu-gheuss) *n* asperge *f*

aspect (æ-spèkt) *n* aspect *m*

asphalt (æss-fælt) *n* asphalte *m*

aspire (eu-*spai*^{eu}) *v* aspirer

aspirin (æ-speu-rinn) *n* aspirine *f*

ass (æss) *n* âne *m*

assassination (eu-sæ-si-*néï*-cheunn) *n* assassinat *m*

assault (eu-*soolt*) *v* attaquer; violer

assemble (eu-*sèm*-beul) *v* rassembler; monter, assembler

assembly (eu-*sèm*-bli) *n* réunion *f*, assemblée *f*

assignment (eu-*saïn*-meunnt) *n* tâche assignée

assign to (eu-*saïn*) assigner à; attribuer à

assist (eu-*sist*) *v* assister

assistance (eu-*si*-steunns) *n* secours *m*; aide *f*, assistance *f*

assistant (eu-*si*-steunnt) *n* assistant *m*

associate (eu-sô^{ou}-chi-eut) *n* partenaire *m*, associé *m*; allié *m*; membre *m*; *v* associer; ~ **with** fréquenter

association (eu-sô^{ou}-si-*éï*-cheunn) *n* association *f*

assort (eu-*soot*) *v* classer

assortment (eu-*soot*-meunnt) *n* assortiment *m*

assume (eu-*syoûm*) *v* supposer, présumer

assure (eu-*chou*^{eu}) *v* assurer

asthma (æss-meu) *n* asthme *m*

astonish (eu-*sto*-nich) *v* étonner

astonishing (eu-*sto*-ni-chinng) *adj* étonnant

astonishment (eu-*sto*-nich-meunnt) *n* étonnement *m*

astronomy (eu-*stro*-neu-mi) *n* astronomie *f*

asylum (eu-*saï*-leumm) *n* asile *m*; hospice *m*

at (æt) *prep* à, chez; vers

ate (èt) *v* (p eat)

atheist (*éï*-θi-ist) *n* athée *m*

athlete (*æθ*-liit) *n* athlète *m*

athletics (æθ-*lè*-tiks) *pl* athlétisme *m*

Atlantic (eut-*læn*-tik) Océan Atlantique

atmosphere (*æt*-meuss-fi^eu) *n* atmosphère *f*; ambiance *f*

atom (*æ*-teumm) *n* atome *m*

atomic (eu-*to*-mik) *adj* atomique; nucléaire

atomizer (*æ*-teu-maï-zeu) *n* vaporisateur *m*; aérosol *m*, pulvérisateur *m*

attach (eu-*tætch*) *v* attacher; fixer; *joindre

attack (eu-*tæk*) *v* attaquer; *n* attaque *f*

attain (eu-*téïn*) *v* *atteindre

attainable (eu-*téï*-neu-beul) *adj* faisable; accessible

attempt (eu-*tèmpt*) *v* tenter; essayer; *n* tentative *f*

attend (eu-*tènd*) *v* assister à; ~ **on** *servir; ~ **to** s'occuper de; *faire attention à, prêter attention à

attendance (eu-*tèn*-deunns) *n* assistance *f*

attendant (eu-*tèn*-deunnt) *n* gardien *m*

attention (eu-*tèn*-cheunn) *n* attention *f*; *pay ~ *faire attention

attentive (eu-*tèn*-tiv) *adj* attentif

attic (*æ*-tik) *n* grenier *m*

attitude (*æ*-ti-tyoûd) *n* attitude *f*

attorney (eu-*teû*-ni) *n* avocat *m*

attract (eu-*trækt*) *v* attirer

attraction (eu-*træk*-cheunn) *n* attraction *f*; attrait *m*

attractive (eu-*træk*-tiv) *adj* séduisant

auburn (*oo*-beunn) *adj* châtain

auction (*ook*-cheunn) *n* vente aux enchères

audible (*oo*-di-beul) *adj* audible

audience (*oo*-di-eunns) *n* public *m*

auditor (*oo*-di-teu) *n* auditeur *m*

auditorium (oo-di-*too*-ri-eumm) *n* auditorium *m*

August (*oo*-gheust) août

aunt (âânt) *n* tante *f*

Australia (o-*stréï*-li-eu) Australie *f*

Australian (o-*stréï*-li-eunn) *adj* australien; *n* Australien *m*

Austria (*o*-stri-eu) Autriche *f*

Austrian (*o*-stri-eunn) *adj* autrichien; *n* Autrichien *m*

authentic (oo-*θèn*-tik) *adj* authentique

author (*oo*-θeu) *n* auteur *m*

authoritarian (oo-θo-ri-*tè*^eu-ri-eunn) *adj* autoritaire

authority (oo-*θo*-reu-ti) *n* autorité *f*; pouvoir *m*

authorization (oo-θeu-raï-*zéï*-cheunn) *n* autorisation *f*; permission *f*

automatic (oo-teu-*mæ*-tik) *adj* automatique

automation (oo-teu-*méï*-cheunn) *n* automatisation *f*

automobile (*oo*-teu-meu-biil) *n* auto *f*; ~ **club** club automobile

autonomous (oo-*to*-neu-meuss) *adj* autonome

autopsy (*oo*-to-psi) *n* autopsie *f*

autumn (*oo*-teumm) *n* automne *m*

available (eu-*véï*-leu-beul) *adj* disponible

avalanche (*æ*-veu-lâânch) *n* avalanche *f*

avaricious (æ-veu-*ri*-cheuss) *adj* avare

avenue (æ-veu-nyoû) n avenue f

average (æ-veu-ridj) adj moyen; n moyenne f; **on the ~** en moyenne

averse (eu-veûss) adj opposé

aversion (eu-veû-cheunn) n aversion f

avert (eu-veût) v détourner

avoid (eu-voïd) v éviter

await (eu-ouéït) v attendre

awake (eu-ouéïk) adj réveillé

***awake** (eu-ouéïk) v réveiller

award (eu-ouood) n prix m; v décerner

aware (eu-ouèeu) adj conscient

away (eu-ouéï) adv loin; ***go ~** s'en *aller

awful (oo-feul) adj terrible

awkward (oo-koueud) adj embarrassant; maladroit

awning (oo-ninng) n marquise f

axe (æks) n hache f

axle (æk-seul) n essieu m

B

baby (béï-bi) n bébé m; **~ carriage** Am poussette f

babysitter (béï-bi-si-teu) n baby-sitter m

bachelor (bæ-tcheu-leu) n célibataire m

back (bæk) n dos m; adv en arrière; ***go ~** retourner

backache (bæ-kéïk) n mal au dos

backbone (bæk-bôoun) n épine dorsale

background (bæk-ghraound) n fond m; formation f

backwards (bæk-oueudz) adv en arrière

bacon (béï-keunn) n lard m

bacterium (bæk-tii-ri-eumm) n (pl -ria) bactérie f

bad (bæd) adj mauvais; grave; vilain

bag (bægh) n sac m; sac à main; valise f

baggage (bæ-ghidj) n bagage m; **~ deposit office** Am consigne f; **hand ~** Am bagage à main

bail (béïl) n caution f

bailiff (béï-lif) n huissier m

bait (béït) n amorce f

bake (béïk) v *cuire au four

baker (béï-keu) n boulanger m

bakery (béï-keu-ri) n boulangerie f

balance (bæ-leunns) n équilibre m; bilan m; solde m

balcony (bæl-keu-ni) n balcon m

bald (boold) adj chauve

ball (bool) n ballon m, balle f; bal m

ballet (bæ-léï) n ballet m

balloon (beu-loûn) n ballon m

ballpoint-pen (bool-poïnt-pèn) n stylo à bille

ballroom (bool-roûm) n salle de bal

bamboo (bæm-boû) n (pl ~s) bambou m

banana (beu-nââ-neu) n banane f

band (bænd) n orchestre m; lien m

bandage (bæn-didj) n pansement m

bandit (bæn-dit) n bandit m

bangle (bæng-gheul) n bracelet m

banisters (bæ-ni-steuz) pl rampe f

bank (bængk) n rive f; banque f; v déposer; **~ account** compte en banque

banknote (bængk-nôout) n billet de banque

bank-rate (bængk-réït) n taux d'escompte

bankrupt (bængk-rapt) adj en faillite

banner (bæ-neu) n bannière f

banquet (bæng-kouit) n banquet m

banqueting-hall (bæng-koui-tinng-hool) n salle de banquet

baptism (bæp-ti-zeumm) n baptême m

baptize (bæp-taïz) v baptiser

bar (bââ) *n* bar *m*; barre *f*; barreau *m*

barber (*bââ*-beu) *n* coiffeur *m*

bare (bè^{eu}) *adj* nu

barely (*bè^{eu}*-li) *adv* à peine

bargain (*bââ*-ghinn) *n* bonne affaire; *v* marchander

baritone (*bæ*-ri-tô^{ou}n) *n* bariton *m*

bark (bââk) *n* écorce *f*; *v* aboyer

barley (*bââ*-li) *n* orge *f*

barmaid (*bââ*-méïd) *n* barmaid *f*

barman (*bââ*-meunn) *n* (pl -men) barman *m*

barn (bâân) *n* grange *f*

barometer (beu-*ro*-mi-teu) *n* baromètre *m*

baroque (beu-*rok*) *adj* baroque

barracks (*bæ*-reuks) *pl* caserne *f*

barrel (*bæ*-reul) *n* tonneau *m*, baril *m*

barrier (*bæ*-ri-eu) *n* barrière *f*

barrister (*bæ*-ri-steu) *n* avocat *m*

bartender (*bââ*-tèn-deu) *n* barman *m*

base (béïss) *n* base *f*; fondement *m*; *v* baser

baseball (*béïss*-bool) *n* base-ball *m*

basement (*béïss*-meunnt) *n* sous-sol *m*

basic (*béï*-sik) *adj* fondamental

basilica (beu-*zi*-li-keu) *n* basilique *f*

basin (*béï*-seunn) *n* bol *m*, bassin *m*

basis (*béï*-siss) *n* (pl bases) base *f*

basket (*bââ*-skit) *n* panier *m*

bass¹ (béïss) *n* basse *f*

bass² (bæss) *n* (pl ~) perche *f*

bastard (*bââ*-steud) *n* bâtard *m*; salaud *m*

batch (bætch) *n* lot *m*

bath (bââθ) *n* bain *m*; ~ **salts** sels de bain; ~ **towel** serviette de bain

bathe (béïð) *v* se baigner

bathing-cap (*béï*-ðinng-kæp) *n* bonnet de bain

bathing-suit (*béï*-ðinng-soût) *n* maillot de bain

bathing-trunks (*béï*-ðinng-tranngks) *n* caleçon de bain

bathrobe (*bââθ*-rô^{ou}b) *n* peignoir *m*

bathroom (*bââθ*-roûm) *n* salle de bain; toilettes *fpl*

batter (*bæ*-teu) *n* pâte *f*

battery (*bæ*-teu-ri) *n* pile *f*; accumulateur *m*

battle (*bæ*-teul) *n* bataille *f*; lutte, combat *m*; *v* *combattre

bay (béï) *n* baie *f*; *v* aboyer

*****be** (bii) *v* *être

beach (biitch) *n* plage *f*; **nudist** ~ plage pour nudistes

bead (biid) *n* perle *f*; **beads** *pl* collier *m*; chapelet *m*

beak (biik) *n* bec *m*

beam (biim) *n* rayon *m*; poutre *f*

bean (biin) *n* haricot *m*

bear (bè^{eu}) *n* ours *m*

*****bear** (bè^{eu}) *v* porter; tolérer; supporter

beard (bi^{eu}d) *n* barbe *f*

bearer (*bè^{eu}*-reu) *n* porteur *m*

beast (biist) *n* bête *f*; ~ **of prey** bête de proie

*****beat** (biit) *v* frapper; *battre

beautiful (*byoû*-ti-feul) *adj* beau

beauty (*byoû*-ti) *n* beauté *f*; ~ **parlour** institut de beauté; ~ **salon** salon de beauté; ~ **treatment** soins de beauté

beaver (*bii*-veu) *n* castor *m*

because (bi-*koz*) *conj* parce que; étant donné que; ~ **of** en raison de, à cause de

*****become** (bi-*kamm*) *v* *devenir; bien *aller

bed (bèd) *n* lit *m*; ~ **and board** pension complète; ~ **and breakfast** chambre et petit déjeuner

bedding (*bè*-dinng) *n* literie *f*

bedroom (*bèd*-roûm) *n* chambre à coucher

bee (bii) *n* abeille *f*

beech (bii-tch) *n* hêtre *m*

beef (biif) *n* bœuf *m*

beehive (*bii*-haïv) *n* ruche *f*

been (biin) *v* (pp be)

beer (bi^{eu}) *n* bière *f*

beet (biit) *n* betterave *f*

beetle (*bii*-teul) *n* scarabée *m*

beetroot (*biit*-roût) *n* betterave *f*

before (bi-*foo*) *prep* avant; devant; *conj* avant que; *adv* d'avance; précédemment, avant

beg (bègh) *v* mendier; supplier; demander

beggar (*bè*-gheu) *n* mendiant *m*

*begin (bi-*ghinn*) *v* commencer; débuter

beginner (bi-*ghi*-neu) *n* débutant *m*

beginning (bi-*ghi*-ninng) *n* commencement *m*; début *m*

on behalf of (onn bi-*hââf* ov) au nom de; en faveur de

behave (bi-*héïv*) *v* se comporter

behaviour (bi-*héï*-vyeu) *n* comportement *m*

behind (bi-*haïnd*) *prep* derrière; *adv* en arrière

beige (béïj) *adj* beige

being (*bii*-inng) *n* être *m*

Belgian (*bèl*-djeunn) *adj* belge; *n* Belge *m*

Belgium (*bèl*-djeumm) Belgique *f*

belief (bi-*liif*) *n* croyance *f*

believe (bi-*liiv*) *v* *croire

bell (bèl) *n* cloche *f*; sonnette *f*

bellboy (*bèl*-boï) *n* chasseur *m*

belly (*bè*-li) *n* ventre *m*

belong (bi-*lonng*) *v* *appartenir

belongings (bi-*lonng*-inngz) *pl* affaires *fpl*

beloved (bi-*lavd*) *adj* aimé

below (bi-*lô^{ou}*) *prep* au-dessous de; en bas de; *adv* en dessous

belt (bèlt) *n* ceinture *f*; **garter ~** *Am*

porte-jarretelles *m*

bench (bèntch) *n* banc *m*

bend (bènd) *n* virage *m*, courbe *f*

*bend (bènd) *v* courber; ~ **down** se pencher

beneath (bi-*niiθ*) *prep* en dessous de; *adv* au-dessous

benefit (*bè*-ni-fit) *n* profit *m*, bénéfice *m*; avantage *m*; *v* profiter

bent (bènt) *adj* (pp bend) courbe

beret (*bè*-réï) *n* béret *m*

berry (*bè*-ri) *n* baie *f*

berth (beûθ) *n* couchette *f*

beside (bi-*saïd*) *prep* à côté de

besides (bi-*saïdz*) *adv* en outre; d'ailleurs; *prep* outre

best (bèst) *adj* le meilleur

bet (bèt) *n* pari *m*; enjeu *m*

*bet (bèt) *v* parier

betray (bi-*tréï*) *v* trahir

better (*bè*-teu) *adj* meilleur

between (bi-*t^{ou}iin*) *prep* entre

beverage (*bè*-veu-ridj) *n* boisson *f*

beware (bi-*^{ou}è^{eu}*) *v* *prendre garde, *faire attention

bewitch (bi-*^{ou}itch*) *v* ensorceler, enchanter

beyond (bi-*yonnd*) *prep* au delà de; outre; *adv* au delà

bible (*baï*-beul) *n* Bible *f*

bicycle (*baï*-si-keul) *n* bicyclette *f*; vélo *m*

big (bigh) *adj* grand; volumineux; gros; important

bile (baïl) *n* bile *f*

bilingual (baï-*linng*-gh^{ou}eul) *adj* bilingue

bill (bil) *n* facture *f*; addition *f*, note *f*; *v* facturer

billiards (*bil*-yeudz) *pl* billard *m*

*bind (baïnd) *v* lier

binding (*baïn*-dinng) *n* reliure *f*

binoculars (bi-*no*-kyeu-leuz) *pl* jumelles *fpl*

biology (baï-*o*-leu-dji) *n* biologie *f*

birch (beûtch) *n* bouleau *m*

bird (beûd) *n* oiseau *m*

Biro (*baï*-rô^{ou}) *n* crayon à bille

birth (beûθ) *n* naissance *f*

birthday (*beûθ*-déï) *n* anniversaire *m*

biscuit (*biss*-kit) *n* biscuit *m*

bishop (*bi*-cheup) *n* évêque *m*

bit (bit) *n* morceau *m*; peu *m*

bitch (bitch) *n* chienne *f*

bite (baït) *n* bouchée *f*; morsure *f*; piqûre *f*

***bite** (baït) *v* mordre

bitter (*bi*-teu) *adj* amer

black (blæk) *adj* noir; ~ **market** marché noir

blackberry (*blæk*-beu-ri) *n* mûre *f*

blackbird (*blæk*-beûd) *n* merle *m*

blackboard (*blæk*-bood) *n* tableau noir

black-currant (blæk-*ka*-reunnt) *n* cassis *m*

blackmail (*blæk*-méïl) *n* chantage *m*; *v* *faire chanter

blacksmith (*blæk*-smiθ) *n* forgeron *m*

bladder (*blæ*-deu) *n* vessie *f*

blade (bléïd) *n* lame *f*; ~ **of grass** brin d'herbe

blame (bléïm) *n* blâme *m*; *v* donner la faute à, blâmer

blank (blængk) *adj* blanc

blanket (*blæng*-kit) *n* couverture *f*

blast (blââst) *n* explosion *f*

blazer (*bléï*-zeu) *n* veste de sport, blazer *m*

bleach (bliitch) *v* décolorer

bleak (bliik) *adj* rude

***bleed** (bliid) *v* saigner

bless (blèss) *v* bénir

blessing (*blè*-sinng) *n* bénédiction *f*

blind (blaïnd) *n* store *m*, persienne *f*; *adj* aveugle; *v* aveugler

blister (*bli*-steu) *n* ampoule *f*, cloque *f*

blizzard (*bli*-zeud) *n* tempête de neige

block (blok) *v* obstruer, bloquer; *n* bloc *m*; ~ **of flats** immeuble d'habitation

blonde (blonnd) *n* blonde *f*

blood (blad) *n* sang *m*; ~ **pressure** tension artérielle

blood-poisoning (*blad*-poï-zeu-ninng) *n* septicémie *f*

blood-vessel (*blad*-vè-seul) *n* vaisseau sanguin

blot (blot) *n* tache *f*; souillure *f*; **blotting paper** papier buvard

blouse (blaouz) *n* chemisier *m*

blow (blô^{ou}) *n* claque *f*, coup *m*; coup de vent

***blow** (blô^{ou}) *v* souffler

blow-out (*blô^{ou}*-aout) *n* crevaison *f*

blue (blou) *adj* bleu; déprimé

blunt (blannt) *adj* émoussé

blush (blach) *v* rougir

board (bood) *n* planche *f*; tableau *m*; pension *f*; conseil *m*; ~ **and lodging** pension complète

boarder (*boo*-deu) *n* pensionnaire *m*

boarding-house (*boo*-dinng-haouss) *n* pension *f*

boarding-school (*boo*-dinng-skoûl) *n* internat *m*

boast (bô^{ou}st) *v* se vanter

boat (bô^{ou}t) *n* navire *m*, bateau *m*

body (*bo*-di) *n* corps *m*

bodyguard (*bo*-di-ghââd) *n* garde du corps

bog (bogh) *n* marais *m*

boil (boïl) *v* *bouillir; *n* furoncle *m*

bold (bô^{ou}ld) *adj* audacieux; effronté, hardi

Bolivia (beu-*li*-vi-eu) Bolivie *f*

Bolivian (beu-*li*-vi-eunn) *adj* bolivien; *n* Bolivien *m*

bolt (bô^{ou}lt) *n* verrou *m*; boulon *m*

bomb (bomm) *n* bombe *f*; *v* bombarder

bond (bonnd) *n* obligation *f*

bone (bôᵘn) *n* os *m*; arête *f*; *v* désosser

bonnet (*bo*-nit) *n* capot *m*

book (bouk) *n* livre *m*; *v* *retenir, réserver; *inscrire, enregistrer

booking (*bou*-kinng) *n* réservation *f*

bookseller (*bouk*-sè-leu) *n* libraire *m*

bookstand (*bouk*-stænd) *n* stand de livres

bookstore (*bouk*-stoo) *n* librairie *f*

boot (boût) *n* botte *f*; coffre *m*

booth (boûð) *n* échoppe *f*; cabine *f*

border (*boo*-deu) *n* frontière *f*; bord *m*

bore¹ (boo) *v* ennuyer; forer; *n* raseur *m*

bore² (boo) *v* (p bear)

boring (*boo*-rinng) *adj* ennuyeux

born (boon) *adj* né

borrow (*bo*-rôᵘ) *v* emprunter

bosom (*bou*-zeumm) *n* poitrine *f*; sein *m*

boss (boss) *n* chef *m*, patron *m*

botany (*bo*-teu-ni) *n* botanique *f*

both (bôᵘθ) *adj* les deux; **both ... and** aussi bien que

bother (*bo*-ðeu) *v* gêner, tracasser; s'efforcer; *n* tracas *m*

bottle (*bo*-teul) *n* bouteille *f*; ~ **opener** ouvre-bouteille *m*; **hot-water** ~ bouillotte *f*

bottleneck (*bo*-teul-nèk) *n* goulot d'étranglement

bottom (*bo*-teumm) *n* fond *m*; postérieur *m*, derrière *m*; *adj* inférieur

bough (baou) *n* branche *f*

bought (boot) *v* (p, pp buy)

boulder (*bôᵘl*-deu) *n* rocher *m*

bound (baound) *n* limite *f*; *be ~ to* *devoir; ~ **for** en route pour

boundary (*baoun*-deu-ri) *n* limite *f*; frontière *f*

bouquet (bou-*kéï*) *n* bouquet *m*

bourgeois (*bou*ᵉᵘ-j ᵒᵘ*ââ*) *adj* bourgeois

boutique (bou-*tiik*) *n* boutique *f*

bow¹ (baou) *v* courber

bow² (bôᵘ) *n* arc *m*; ~ **tie** nœud papillon

bowels (baouᵉᵘlz) *pl* intestins

bowl (bôᵘl) *n* bol *m*

bowling (*bôᵘ*-linng) *n* bowling *m*, jeu de quilles; ~ **alley** bowling *m*

box¹ (boks) *v* boxer; **boxing match** match dc boxe

box² (boks) *n* boîte *f*

box-office (*boks*-o-fiss) *n* guichet de location, guichet *m*

boy (boï) *n* garçon *m*; gamin *m*, gosse *m*; serviteur *m*; ~ **scout** scout *m*

bra (brââ) *n* soutien-gorge *m*

bracelet (*bréïss*-lit) *n* bracelet *m*

braces (*bréï*-siz) *pl* bretelles *fpl*

brain (bréïn) *n* cerveau *m*; intelligence *f*

brain-wave (*bréïn*-ᵒᵘéïv) *n* idée lumineuse

brake (bréïk) *n* frein *m*; ~ **drum** tambour de frein; ~ **lights** stops *mpl*

branch (brâântch) *n* branche *f*; succursale *f*

brand (brænd) *n* marque *f*

brand-new (brænd-*nyoû*) *adj* flambant neuf

brass (brââss) *n* laiton *m*; cuivre *m*, cuivre jaune; ~ **band** *n* fanfare *f*

brassiere (*bræ*-ziᵉᵘ) *n* soutien-gorge *m*

brassware (*brââss*-ᵒᵘèᵉᵘ) *n* cuivres *m*

brave (bréïv) *adj* courageux, brave

Brazil (breu-*zil*) Brésil *m*

Brazilian (breu-*zil*-yeunn) *adj* brésilien; *n* Brésilien *m*

breach (briitch) *n* brèche *f*

bread (brèd) *n* pain *m*; **wholemeal** ~ pain complet

breadth (brèdθ) *n* largeur *f*

break (bréïk) *n* fracture *f*; pause *f*

*break (bréïk) v rompre, casser; ~ **down** tomber en panne; analyser

breakdown (bréïk-daoun) n panne f

breakfast (brèk-feust) n petit déjeuner

bream (briim) n (pl ~) brème f

breast (brèst) n sein m

breaststroke (brèst-strôᵘk) n brasse f

breath (brèθ) n souffle m

breathe (briið) v respirer

breathing (brii-ðinng) n respiration f

breed (briid) n race f; espèce f

*breed (briid) v élever

breeze (briiz) n brise f

brew (broû) v brasser

brewery (broû-eu-ri) n brasserie f

bribe (braïb) v *corrompre

bribery (braï-beu-ri) n corruption f

brick (brik) n brique f

bricklayer (brik-léï ᵉᵘ) n maçon m

bride (braïd) n fiancée f

bridegroom (braïd-ghroûm) n marié m

bridge (bridj) n pont m; bridge m

brief (briif) adj bref

briefcase (briif-kéïss) n serviette f

briefs (briifs) pl slip m, caleçon m

bright (braït) adj brillant; malin, intelligent

brill (bril) n barbue f

brilliant (bril-yeunnt) adj brillant

brim (brimm) n bord m

*bring (brinng) v apporter; amener; ~ **back** rapporter, ramener; ~ **up** élever; soulever

brisk (brisk) adj vif

Britain (bri-teunn) Angleterre f

British (bri-tich) adj britannique

Briton (bri-teunn) n Britannique m; Anglais m

broad (brood) adj large; vaste, étendu; global

broadcast (brood-kââst) n émission f

*broadcast (brood-kââst) v *émettre

brochure (brôᵘ-chou ᵉᵘ) n brochure f

broke¹ (brôᵘk) v (p break)

broke² (brôᵘk) adj fauché

broken (brôᵘ-keunn) adj (pp break) cassé, brisé; en dérangement

broker (brôᵘ-keu) n courtier m

bronchitis (bronng-kaï-tiss) n bronchite f

bronze (bronnz) n bronze m; adj en bronze

brooch (brôᵘtch) n broche f

brook (brouk) n ruisseau m

broom (broûm) n balai m

brothel (bro-θeul) n bordel m

brother (bra-ðeu) n frère m

brother-in-law (bra-ðeu-rinn-loo) n (pl brothers-) beau-frère m

brought (broot) v (p, pp bring)

brown (braoun) adj brun

bruise (broûz) n bleu m, contusion f; v contusionner

brunette (broû-nèt) n brunette f

brush (brach) n brosse f; pinceau m; v lustrer, brosser

brutal (broû-teul) adj brutal

bubble (ba-beul) n bulle f

bucket (ba-kit) n seau m

buckle (ba-keul) n boucle f

bud (bad) n bourgeon m

budget (ba-djit) n budget m

buffet (bou-féï) n buffet m

bug (bagh) n punaise f; coléoptère m; nAm insecte m

*build (bild) v bâtir

building (bil-dinng) n construction f

bulb (balb) n bulbe m; oignon m; **light** ~ ampoule f

Bulgaria (bal-ghè ᵉᵘ-ri-eu) Bulgarie f

Bulgarian (bal-ghè ᵉᵘ-ri-eunn) adj bulgare; n Bulgare m

bulk (balk) n masse f; majorité f

bulky (bal-ki) adj volumineux

bull (boul) n taureau m

bullet (bou-lit) n balle f

bullfight (boul-faït) n corrida f

bullring (boul-rinng) n arène f

bump (bammp) v cogner; tamponner; frapper; n coup m

bumper (bamm-peu) n pare-choc m

bumpy (bamm-pi) adj cahoteux

bun (bann) n brioche f

bunch (banntch) n bouquet m; bande f

bundle (bann-deul) n paquet m; v relier, lier ensemble

bunk (banngk) n couchette f

buoy (boï) n bouée f

burden (beû-deunn) n fardeau m

bureau (byou^{eu}-rô^{ou}) n (pl ~x, ~s) bureau m; nAm commode f

bureaucracy (byou^{eu}-ro-kreu-si) n bureaucratie f

burglar (beû-ghleu) n cambrioleur m

burgle (beû-gheul) v cambrioler

burial (bè-ri-eul) n sépulture f, enterrement m

burn (beûnn) n brûlure f

***burn** (beûnn) v brûler

***burst** (beûst) v éclater

bury (bè-ri) v enterrer

bus (bass) n autobus m

bush (bouch) n buisson m

business (biz-neuss) n affaires fpl, commerce m; entreprise f, affaire f; occupation f; ~ **hours** heures d'ouverture, heures de bureau; ~ **trip** voyage d'affaires; **on** ~ pour affaires

businessman (biz-neuss-meunn) n (pl -men) homme d'affaires

bust (bast) n buste m

bustle (ba-seul) n remue-ménage m

busy (bi-zi) adj occupé; animé, affairé

but (bat) conj mais; cependant; prep sauf

butcher (bou-tcheu) n boucher m

butter (ba-teu) n beurre m

butterfly (ba-teu-flaï) n papillon m; ~ **stroke** brasse papillon

buttock (ba-teuk) n fesse f

button (ba-teunn) n bouton m; v boutonner

buttonhole (ba-teunn-hô^{ou}l) n boutonnière f

***buy** (baï) v acheter; *acquérir

buyer (baï-eu) n acheteur m

by (baï) prep par; en; près de

by-pass (baï-pââss) n route d'évitement; v contourner

C

cab (kæb) n taxi m

cabaret (kæ-beu-réï) n cabaret m; boîte de nuit

cabbage (kæ-bidj) n chou m

cab-driver (kæb-draï-veu) n chauffeur de taxi

cabin (kæ-binn) n cabine f; cabane f

cabinet (kæ-bi-neut) n cabinet m

cable (kéï-beul) n câble m; télégramme m; v télégraphier

café (kæ-féï) n café m

cafeteria (kæ-feu-ti^{eu}-ri-eu) n cafétéria f

caffeine (kæ-fiin) n caféine f

cage (kéïdj) n cage f

cake (kéïk) n gâteau m; pâtisserie f

calamity (keu-læ-meu-ti) n calamité f, catastrophe f

calcium (kæl-si-eumm) n calcium m

calculate (kæl-kyou-léït) v calculer

calculation (kæl-kyou-léï-cheunn) n calcul m

calculator (kæl-kyou-léï-teu) n calculatrice f

calendar (kæ-leunn-deu) n calendrier m

calf (kââf) n (pl calves) veau m; mollet m; ~ **skin** veau m

call (kool) v appeler; téléphoner; n appel m; visite f; coup de télépho-

ne; *be called s'appeler; ~ **names**
injurier; ~ **on** rendre visite à; ~ **up**
Am téléphoner

callus (kæ-leuss) n cal m

calm (kââm) adj tranquille, calme; ~
down calmer

calorie (kæ-leu-ri) n calorie f

Calvinism (kæl-vi-ni-zeumm) n calvi-
nisme m

came (kéïm) v (p come)

camel (kæ-meul) n chameau m

cameo (kæ-mi-ô^ou) n (pl ~s) camée
m

camera (kæ-meu-reu) n appareil photographique; caméra f; ~ **shop** magasin de photographe

camp (kæmp) n camp m; v camper

campaign (kæm-péïn) n campagne f

camp-bed (kæmp-bèd) n lit de camp

camper (kæm-peu) n campeur m

camping (kæm-pinng) n camping m;
~ **site** terrain de camping

camshaft (kæm-chââft) n arbre à cames

can (kæn) n boîte f; ~ **opener** ouvre-
boîte m

*can (kæn) v *pouvoir

Canada (kæ-neu-deu) Canada m

Canadian (keu-néï-di-eunn) adj canadien; n Canadien m

canal (keu-næl) n canal m

canary (keu-nè^eu-ri) n canari m

cancel (kæn-seul) v annuler

cancellation (kæn-seu-léï-cheunn) n
annulation f

cancer (kæn-seu) n cancer m

candelabrum (kæn-deu-lââ-breumm) n
(pl -bra) candélabre m

candidate (kæn-di-deut) n candidat m

candle (kæn-deul) n bougie f

candy (kæn-di) nAm bonbon m; confiserie f; ~ **store** Am confiserie f

cane (kéïn) n canne f

canister (kæ-ni-steu) n boîte métalli-

que

canoe (keu-noú) n canot m

canteen (kæn-tiin) n cantine f

canvas (kæn-veuss) n grosse toile

cap (kæp) n casquette f

capable (kéï-peu-beul) adj capable

capacity (keu-pæ-seu-ti) n capacité f;
puissance f; compétence f

cape (kéïp) n cape f; cap m

capital (kæ-pi-teul) n capitale f; capital m; adj capital, essentiel; ~ **letter** majuscule f

capitalism (kæ-pi-teu-li-zeumm) n capitalisme m

capitulation (keu-pi-tyou-léï-cheunn) n
capitulation f

capsule (kæp-syoûl) n capsule f

captain (kæp-tinn) n capitaine m;
commandant m

capture (kæp-tcheu) v *faire prisonnier, capturer; *prendre; n capture
f; prise f

car (kââ) n voiture f; ~ **hire** location
de voitures; ~ **park** parc de stationnement; ~ **rental** Am location de
voitures

carafe (keu-ræf) n carafe f

caramel (kæ-reu-meul) n caramel m

carat (kæ-reut) n carat m

caravan (kæ-reu-væn) n caravane f;
roulotte f

carburettor (kââ-byou-rè-teu) n carburateur m

card (kââd) n carte f; carte postale

cardboard (kââd-bood) n carton m;
adj en carton

cardigan (kââ-di-gheunn) n cardigan
m

cardinal (kââ-di-neul) n cardinal m;
adj cardinal, principal

care (kè^eu) n soin m; souci m; ~
about se soucier de; ~ **for** *tenir à;
*take ~ **of** *prendre soin de, s'occuper de

career (keu-*ri^{eu}*) *n* carrière *f*

carefree (*kè^{eu}*-frii) *adj* insouciant

careful (*kè^{eu}*-feul) *adj* prudent; soigneux, attentif

careless (*kè^{eu}*-leuss) *adj* inattentif, négligent

caretaker (*kè^{eu}*-téï-keu) *n* gardien *m*

cargo (*kââ*-ghô^{ou}) *n* (pl ~es) chargement *m*, cargaison *f*

carnival (*kââ*-ni-veul) *n* carnaval *m*

carp (kââp) *n* (pl ~) carpe *f*

carpenter (*kââ*-pinn-teu) *n* menuisier *m*

carpet (*kââ*-pit) *n* tapis *m*

carriage (*kæ*-ridj) *n* wagon *m*; carrosse *m*, voiture *f*

carrot (*kæ*-reut) *n* carotte *f*

carry (*kæ*-ri) *v* porter; *conduire; ~ on* continuer; *poursuivre; ~ out* réaliser

carry-cot (*kæ*-ri-kot) *n* berceau de voyage

cart (kâât) *n* charrette *f*

cartilage (*kââ*-ti-lidj) *n* cartilage *m*

carton (*kââ*-teunn) *n* carton *m*; cartouche *f*

cartoon (kââ-*toûn*) *n* dessins animés

cartridge (*kââ*-tridj) *n* cartouche *f*

carve (kââv) *v* découper; entailler, tailler

carving (*kââ*-vinng) *n* gravure *f*

case (kéïss) *n* cas *m*; affaire *f*; valise *f*; étui *m*; **attaché ~ porte-documents** *m*; **in ~** au cas où; **in ~ of** en cas de

cash (kæch) *n* argent liquide, argent comptant; *v* toucher, encaisser; ~ **dispenser** distributeur automatique *m*

cashier (kæ-*chi^{eu}*) *n* caissier *m*; caissière *f*

cashmere (*kæch*-mi^{eu}) *n* cachemire *m*

casino (keu-*sii*-nô^{ou}) *n* (pl ~s) casino *m*

cask (kââsk) *n* baril *m*, tonneau *m*

cast (kââst) *n* jet *m*

***cast** (kââst) *v* lancer, jeter; **cast iron** fonte *f*

castle (*kââ*-seul) *n* château *m*

casual (*kæ*-jou-eul) *adj* sans façons; en passant, fortuit

casualty (*kæ*-jou-eul-ti) *n* victime *f*

cat (kæt) *n* chat *m*

catacomb (*kæ*-teu-kô^{ou}m) *n* catacombe *f*

catalogue (*kæ*-teu-logh) *n* catalogue *m*

catarrh (keu-*tââ*) *n* catarrhe *m*

catastrophe (keu-*tæ*-streu-fi) *n* sinistre *m*

***catch** (kætch) *v* attraper; saisir; *surprendre; *prendre

category (*kæ*-ti-gheu-ri) *n* catégorie *f*

cathedral (keu-*θii*-dreul) *n* cathédrale *f*

catholic (*kæ*-θeu-lik) *adj* catholique

cattle (*kæ*-teul) *pl* bétail *m*

caught (koot) *v* (p, pp catch)

cauliflower (*ko*-li-flaou^{eu}) *n* chou-fleur

cause (kooz) *v* causer; provoquer; *n* cause *f*; raison *f*, motif *m*; ~ **to** *faire

causeway (*kooz*-^{ou}éï) *n* chaussée *f*

caution (*koo*-cheunn) *n* prudence *f*; *v* avertir

cautious (*koo*-cheuss) *adj* prudent

cave (kéïv) *n* grotte *f*; crevasse *f*

cavern (*kæ*-veunn) *n* caverne *f*

caviar (*kæ*-vi-ââ) *n* caviar *m*

cavity (*kæ*-veu-ti) *n* cavité *f*

cease (siiss) *v* cesser

ceiling (*sii*-linng) *n* plafond *m*

celebrate (*sè*-li-bréït) *v* célébrer

celebration (sè-li-*bréï*-cheunn) *n* célébration *f*

celebrity (si-*lè*-breu-ti) *n* célébrité *f*

celery (*sè*-leu-ri) *n* céleri *m*

celibacy (*sè-li-beu-si*) *n* célibat *m*

cell (sèl) *n* cellule *f*

cellar (*sè-leu*) *n* cave *f*

cellophane (*sè-leu-féïn*) *n* cellophane *f*

cement (si-*mènt*) *n* ciment *m*

cemetery (*sè-mi-tri*) *n* cimetière *m*

censorship (*sèn-seu-chip*) *n* censure *f*

centigrade (*sèn-ti-ghréïd*) *adj* centigrade

centimetre (*sèn-ti-mii-teu*) *n* centimètre *m*

central (*sèn-treul*) *adj* central; ~ **heating** chauffage central; ~ **station** gare centrale

centralize (*sèn-treu-laïz*) *v* centraliser

centre (*sèn-teu*) *n* centre *m*

century (*sèn-tcheu-ri*) *n* siècle *m*

ceramics (si-*ræ*-miks) *pl* terre cuite, céramique *f*

ceremony (*sè-reu-meu-ni*) *n* cérémonie *f*

certain (*seû*-teunn) *adj* certain

certificate (seu-ti-fi-keut) *n* certificat *m*; attestation *f*, document *m*, diplôme *f*

chain (tchéïn) *n* chaîne *f*

chair (tchè ᵉᵘ) *n* chaise *f*; siège *m*

chairman (*tchè* ᵉᵘ*-meunn*) *n* (pl -men) président *m*

chalet (*chæ-léï*) *n* chalet *m*

chalk (tchook) *n* craie *f*

challenge (*tchæ*-leunndj) *v* défier; *n* défi *m*

chamber (*tchéïm*-beu) *n* pièce *f*

chambermaid (*tchéïm*-beu-méïd) *n* femme de chambre

champagne (chæm-*péïn*) *n* champagne *m*

champion (*tchæm*-pyeunn) *n* champion *m*; défenseur *m*

chance (tchââns) *n* hasard *m*; chance *f*, occasion *f*; risque *m*; **by** ~ par hasard

change (tchéïndj) *v* modifier, changer; se changer; *n* modification *f*, changement *m*; petite monnaie, change *m*

channel (*tchæ*-neul) *n* canal *m*; **English Channel** La Manche

chaos (*kéï*-oss) *n* chaos *m*

chaotic (kéï-*o*-tik) *adj* chaotique

chap (tchæp) *n* type *m*

chapel (*tchæ*-peul) *n* église *f*, chapelle *f*

chaplain (*tchæ*-plinn) *n* chapelain *m*

character (*kæ*-reuk-teu) *n* caractère *m*

characteristic (kæ-reuk-teu-*ri*-stik) *adj* caractéristique; *n* caractéristique *f*; trait de caractère

characterize (*kæ*-reuk-teu-raïz) *v* caractériser

charcoal (*tchââ*-kô ᵒᵘl) *n* charbon de bois

charge (tchââdj) *v* demander; charger; accuser; *n* prix *m*; charge *f*, chargement *m*; accusation *f*; ~ **plate** *Am* carte de crédit; **free of** ~ à titre gracieux; **in** ~ **of** chargé de; *take* ~ **of** se charger de

charity (*tchæ*-reu-ti) *n* charité *f*

charm (tchââm) *n* attraits, charme *m*; amulette *f*

charming (*tchââ*-minng) *adj* séduisant

chart (tchâât) *n* tableau *m*; graphique *m*; carte marine; **conversion** ~ tableau de conversions

chase (tchéïss) *v* pourchasser; expulser, chasser; *n* chasse *f*

chasm (*kæ*-zeumm) *n* crevasse *f*

chassis (*chæ*-si) *n* (pl ~) châssis *m*

chaste (tchéïst) *adj* chaste

chat (tchæt) *v* bavarder, causer; *n* causette *f*, bavardage *m*

chatterbox (*tchæ*-teu-boks) *n* moulin à paroles

cheap (tchiip) *adj* bon marché; avantageux

cheat (tchiit) v tricher; duper
check (tchèk) v contrôler, vérifier; n damier m; nAm note f; chèque m; **check!** échec!; ~ **in** s'*inscrire; ~ **out** *partir
check-book (tchèk-bouk) nAm carnet de chèques
checkerboard (tchè-keu-bood) nAm échiquier m
checkers (tchè-keuz) plAm jeu de dames
checkroom (tchèk-roûm) nAm vestiaire m
check-up (tchè-kap) n examen m
cheek (tchiik) n joue f
cheek-bone (tchiik-bô°un) n pommette f
cheer (tchi°u) v acclamer; ~ **up** égayer
cheerful (tchi°u-feul) adj joyeux, gai
cheese (tchiiz) n fromage m
chef (chèf) n chef cuisinier
chemical (kè-mi-keul) adj chimique
chemist (kè-mist) n pharmacien m; **chemist's** pharmacie f; droguerie f
chemistry (kè-mi-stri) n chimie f
cheque (tchèk) n chèque m
cheque-book (tchèk-bouk) n carnet de chèques
chequered (tchè-keud) adj à carreaux, à damiers
cherry (tchè-ri) n cerise f
chess (tchèss) n échecs
chest (tchèst) n poitrine f; coffre m; ~ **of drawers** commode f
chestnut (tchèss-nat) n marron m
chew (tchoû) v mâcher
chewing-gum (tchoû-inng-ghamm) n chewing-gum m
chicken (tchi-kinn) n poulet m
chickenpox (tchi-kinn-poks) n varicelle f
chief (tchiif) n chef m; adj principal
chieftain (tchiif-teunn) n chef m

chilblain (tchil-bléïn) n engelure f
child (tchaïld) n (pl children) enfant m
childbirth (tchaïld-beûθ) n accouchement m
childhood (tchaïld-houd) n enfance f
Chile (tchi-li) Chili m
Chilean (tchi-li-eunn) adj chilien; n Chilien m
chill (tchil) n frisson m
chilly (tchi-li) adj frais
chimes (tchaïmz) pl carillon m
chimney (tchimm-ni) n cheminée f
chin (tchinn) n menton m
China (tchaï-neu) Chine f
china (tchaï-neu) n porcelaine f
Chinese (tchaï-niiz) adj chinois; n Chinois m
chink (tchinngk) n fissure f
chip (tchip) n éclat m; jeton m; v tailler, ébrécher; **chips** pommes frites
chiropodist (ki-ro-peu-dist) n pédicure m
chisel (tchi-zeul) n burin m
chives (tchaïvz) pl ciboulette f
chlorine (kloo-riin) n chlore m
chock-full (tchok-foul) adj plein à craquer, bourré
chocolate (tcho-kleut) n chocolat m; praline f
choice (tchoïss) n choix m; sélection f
choir (k°uaï°u) n chœur m
choke (tchô°uk) v suffoquer; étrangler, étouffer; n starter m
*****choose** (tchoûz) v choisir
chop (tchop) n côte f, côtelette f; v hacher
Christ (kraïst) Christ m
christen (kri-seunn) v baptiser
christening (kri-seu-ninng) n baptême m
Christian (kriss-tcheunn) adj chrétien;

~ **name** prénom *m*

Christmas (*kriss*-meuss) Noël

chromium (*krôᵒᵘ*-mi-eumm) *n* chrome *m*

chronic (*kro*-nik) *adj* chronique

chronological (kro-neu-*lo*-dji-keul) *adj* chronologique

chuckle (*tcha*-keul) *v* glousser

chunk (tchanngk) *n* gros morceau

church (tcheûtch) *n* église *f*

churchyard (*tcheûtch*-yââd) *n* cimetière *m*

cigar (si-*ghââ*) *n* cigare *m*; ~ **shop** bureau de tabac

cigarette (si-gheu-*rèt*) *n* cigarette *f*

cigarette-case (si-gheu-*rèt*-kéïss) *n* étui à cigarettes

cigarette-holder (si-gheu-*rèt*-hôᵒᵘl-deu) *n* fume-cigarettes *m*

cigarette-lighter (si-gheu-*rèt*-laï-teu) *n* briquet *m*

cinema (*si*-neu-meu) *n* cinéma *m*

cinnamon (*si*-neu-meunn) *n* cannelle *f*

circle (*seû*-keul) *n* cercle *m*; balcon *m*; *v* encercler, entourer

circulation (seû-kyou-*léï*-cheunn) *n* circulation *f*

circumstance (*seû*-keumm-stæns) *n* circonstance *f*

circus (*seû*-keuss) *n* cirque *m*

citizen (*si*-ti-zeunn) *n* citoyen *m*

citizenship (*si*-ti-zeunn-chip) *n* citoyenneté *f*

city (*si*-ti) *n* cité *f*

civic (*si*-vik) *adj* civique

civil (*si*-veul) *adj* civil; poli; ~ **law** droit civil; ~ **servant** fonctionnaire *m*

civilian (si-*vil*-yeunn) *adj* civil; *n* civil *m*

civilization (si-veu-laï-*zéï*-cheunn) *n* civilisation *f*

civilized (*si*-veu-laïzd) *adj* civilisé

claim (kléïm) *v* revendiquer, récla-

mer; prétendre; *n* revendication *f*, prétention *f*

clamp (klæmp) *n* mordache *f*; crampon *m*

clap (klæp) *v* applaudir

clarify (*klæ*-ri-faï) *v* éclaircir, clarifier

class (klââss) *n* classe *f*

classical (*klæ*-si-keul) *adj* classique

classify (*klæ*-si-faï) *v* classer

class-mate (*klââss*-méit) *n* camarade de classe

classroom (*klââss*-roûm) *n* salle de classe

clause (klooz) *n* clause *f*

claw (kloo) *n* griffe *f*

clay (kléï) *n* argile *f*

clean (kliin) *adj* pur, propre; *v* nettoyer

cleaning (*klii*-ninng) *n* nettoyage *m*; ~ **fluid** détachant *m*

clear (kliᵉᵘ) *adj* clair; *v* nettoyer

clearing (*kliᵉᵘ*-rinng) *n* clairière *f*

cleft (klèft) *n* fente *f*

clergyman (*kleû*-dji-meunn) *n* (pl -men) pasteur *m*; ecclésiastique *m*

clerk (klââk) *n* employé de bureau; greffier *m*; secrétaire *m*

clever (*klè*-veu) *adj* intelligent; astucieux, éveillé

client (*klaï*-eunnt) *n* client *m*

cliff (klif) *n* falaise *f*

climate (*klaï*-mit) *n* climat *m*

climb (klaïm) *v* grimper; *n* ascension *f*

clinic (*kli*-nik) *n* clinique *f*

cloak (klôᵒᵘk) *n* manteau *m*

cloakroom (*klôᵒᵘk*-roûm) *n* vestiaire *m*

clock (klok) *n* horloge *f*; **at ... o'-clock** à ... heures

cloister (*kloï*-steu) *n* cloître *m*

close[1] (klôᵒᵘz) *v* fermer; **closed** *adj* fermé, clos

close[2] (klôᵒᵘss) *adj* proche

closet (*klo*-zit) *n* placard *m*; *nAm* garde-robe *f*

cloth (kloθ) *n* tissu *m*; chiffon *m*

clothes (klô^{ou}ðz) *pl* habits *mpl*, vêtements *mpl*

clothes-brush (*klô^{ou}ðz*-brach) *n* brosse à habits

clothing (*klô^{ou}*-ðinng) *n* habillement *m*

cloud (klaoud) *n* nuage *m*

cloud-burst (*klaoud*-beûst) *n* rafale de pluie

cloudy (*klaou*-di) *adj* couvert, nuageux

clover (*klô^{ou}*-veu) *n* trèfle *m*

clown (klaoun) *n* clown *m*

club (klab) *n* club *m*; cercle *m*, association *f*; gourdin *m*, massue *f*

clumsy (*klamm*-zi) *adj* maladroit

clutch (klatch) *n* embrayage *m*; prise *f*

coach (kô^{ou}tch) *n* car *m*; wagon *m*; carrosse *m*; entraîneur *m*

coachwork (*kô^{ou}tch*-^{ou}eûk) *n* carrosserie *f*

coagulate (kô^{ou}-æ-ghyou-léït) *v* coaguler

coal (kô^{ou}l) *n* charbon *m*

coarse (kooss) *adj* grossier

coast (kô^{ou}st) *n* côte *f*

coat (kô^{ou}t) *n* pardessus *m*, manteau *m*

coat-hanger (*kô^{ou}t*-hæng-eu) *n* cintre *m*

cobweb (*kob*-^{ou}èb) *n* toile d'araignée

cocaine (kô^{ou}-*kéïn*) *n* cocaïne *f*

cock (kok) *n* coq *m*

cocktail (*kok*-téïl) *n* cocktail *m*

coconut (*kô^{ou}*-keu-nat) *n* noix de coco

cod (kod) *n* (pl ~) morue *f*

code (kô^{ou}d) *n* code *m*

coffee (*ko*-fi) *n* café *m*

coherence (kô^{ou}-*hi^{eu}*-reunns) *n* cohérence *f*

coin (koïn) *n* pièce de monnaie

coincide (kô^{ou}-inn-*saïd*) *v* coïncider

cold (kô^{ou}ld) *adj* froid; *n* froid *m*; rhume *m*; **catch a** ~ s'enrhumer

collapse (keu-*læps*) *v* s'effondrer, s'écrouler

collar (*ko*-leu) *n* collier *m*; col *m*; ~ **stud** bouton de col

collarbone (*ko*-leu-bô^{ou}n) *n* clavicule *f*

colleague (*ko* liigh) *n* collègue *m*

collect (keu-*lèkt*) *v* rassembler; *prendre, *aller chercher; quêter

collection (keu-*lèk*-cheunn) *n* collection *f*; levée *f*

collective (keu-*lèk*-tiv) *adj* collectif

collector (keu-*lèk*-teu) *n* collectionneur *m*; quêteur *m*

college (*ko*-lidj) *n* collège *m*

collide (keu-*laïd*) *v* entrer en collision

collision (keu-*li*-jeunn) *n* collision *f*; abordage *m*

Colombia (keu-*lomm*-bi-eu) Colombie *f*

Colombian (keu-*lomm*-bi-eunn) *adj* colombien; *n* Colombien *m*

colonel (*keû*-neul) *n* colonel *m*

colony (*ko*-leu-ni) *n* colonie *f*

colour (*ka*-leu) *n* couleur *f*; *v* colorer; ~ **film** film en couleurs

colourant (*ka*-leu-reunnt) *n* colorant *m*

colour-blind (*ka*-leu-blaïnd) *adj* daltonien

coloured (*ka*-leud) *adj* de couleur

colourful (*ka*-leu-feul) *adj* coloré

column (*ko*-leumm) *n* colonne *f*; rubrique *f*

coma (*kô^{ou}*-meu) *n* coma *m*

comb (kô^{ou}m) *v* peigner; *n* peigne *m*

combat (*komm*-bæt) *n* lutte *f*, combat *m*; *v* *combattre, lutter

combination (komm-bi-*néï*-cheunn) *n* combinaison *f*

combine (keumm-*baïn*) *v* combiner

*come (kamm) *v* *venir; ~ **across** rencontrer; trouver

comedian (keu-*mii*-di-eunn) *n* comédien *m*; comique *m*

comedy (*ko*-me-di) *n* comédie *f*; musical ~ comédie musicale

comfort (*kamm*-feut) *n* bien-être *m*, commodité *f*, confort *m*; réconfort *m*; *v* consoler

comfortable (*kamm*-feu-teu-beul) *adj* confortable

comic (*ko*-mik) *adj* comique

comics (*ko*-miks) *pl* bandes dessinées

coming (*ka*-minng) *n* arrivée *f*

comma (*ko*-meu) *n* virgule *f*

command (keu-*mâând*) *v* commander; *n* ordre *m*

commander (keu-*mâân*-deu) *n* commandant *m*

commemoration (keu-mè-meu-*réï*-cheunn) *n* commémoration *f*

commence (keu-*mèns*) *v* commencer

comment (*ko*-mènt) *n* commentaire *m*; *v* commenter

commerce (*ko*-meuss) *n* commerce *m*

commercial (keu-*meû*-cheul) *adj* commercial; *n* annonce publicitaire; ~ law droit commercial

commission (keu-*mi*-cheunn) *n* commission *f*

commit (keu-*mit*) *v* *remettre, confier; *commettre

committee (keu-*mi*-ti) *n* commission *f*, comité *m*

common (*ko*-meunn) *adj* commun; habituel; ordinaire

communicate (keu-*myoû*-ni-kéït) *v* communiquer

communication (keu-myoû-ni-*kéï*-cheunn) *n* communication *f*

communism (*ko*-myou-ni-zeumm) *n* communisme *m*

community (keu-*myoû*-neu-ti) *n* société *f*, communauté *f*

commuter (keu-*myoû*-teu) *n* navetteur *m*

compact (*komm*-pækt) *adj* compact

compact disc (*komm*-pækt disk) *n* compact disc *m*; ~ **player** lecteur de compact disc *m*

companion (keumm-*pæ*-nyeunn) *n* compagnon *m*

company (*kamm*-peu-ni) *n* compagnie *f*; entreprise *f*, société *f*

comparative (keumm-*pæ*-reu-tiv) *adj* relatif

compare (keumm-*pè*^{eu}) *v* comparer

comparison (keumm-*pæ*-ri-seunn) *n* comparaison *f*

compartment (keumm-*pâât*-meunnt) *n* compartiment *m*

compass (*kamm*-peuss) *n* boussole *f*

compel (keumm-*pèl*) *v* *contraindre

compensate (*komm*-peunn-séït) *v* compenser

compensation (komm-peunn-*séï*-cheunn) *n* compensation *f*; indemnité *f*

compete (keumm-*piit*) *v* *concourir

competition (komm-peu-*ti*-cheunn) *n* compétition *f*

competitor (keumm-*pè*-ti-teur) *n* concurrent *m*

compile (keumm-*païl*) *v* compiler

complain (keumm-*pléïn*) *v* se *plaindre

complaint (keumm-*pléïnt*) *n* plainte *f*; **complaints book** cahier de doléances

complete (keumm-*pliit*) *adj* entier, complet; *v* achever

completely (keumm-*pliit*-li) *adv* entièrement, totalement, complètement

complex (*komm*-plèks) *n* complexe *m*; *adj* complexe

complexion (keumm-*plèk*-cheunn) *n* teint *m*

complicated (*komm*-pli-kéï-tid) *adj*

compliqué

compliment (*komm*-pli-meunnt) *n* compliment *m*; *v* complimenter, féliciter

compose (keumm-*pô^{ou}z*) *v* composer

composer (keumm-*pô^{ou}*-zeu) *n* compositeur *m*

comprehensive (komm-pri-*hèn*-siv) *adj* étendu

comprise (keumm-*praïz*) *v* *comprendre, *inclure

compromise (*komm*-preu-maïz) *n* compromis *m*

compulsory (keumm-*pal*-seu-ri) *adj* obligatoire

computer (komm-*pyou*-teu) *n* ordinateur *m*; **lap-top** ~ ordinateur portable

comrade (*komm*-réïd) *n* camarade *m*

conceal (keunn-*siil*) *v* dissimuler

conceited (keunn-*sii*-tid) *adj* prétentieux

conceive (keunn-*siiv*) *v* *concevoir, *comprendre

concentrate (*konn*-seunn-tréït) *v* concentrer

concentration (konn-seunn-*tréï*-cheunn) *n* concentration *f*

conception (keunn-*sèp*-cheunn) *n* conception *f*

concern (keunn-*seûnn*) *v* regarder, concerner; *n* souci *m*; affaire *f*; entreprise *f*

concerned (keunn-*seûnnd*) *adj* soucieux; concerné

concerning (keunn-*seû*-ninng) *prep* relatif à, concernant

concert (*konn*-seut) *n* concert *m*; ~ **hall** salle de concert

concession (keunn-*sè*-cheunn) *n* concession *f*

concierge (kon-si-*è^{eu}j*) *n* concierge *m*

concise (keunn-*saïss*) *adj* concis

conclusion (keunng-*kloù*-jeunn) *n* con-

clusion *f*

concrete (*konng*-kriit) *adj* concret; *n* béton *m*

concussion (keunng-*ka*-cheunn) *n* commotion *f*

condition (keunn-*di*-cheunn) *n* condition *f*; état *m*, forme *f*; circonstance *f*

conditional (keunn-*di*-cheu-neul) *adj* conditionnel

condom (*konn*-dom) *n* préservatif *m*

conduct¹ (*konn*-dakt) *n* conduite *f*

conduct² (keunn-*dakt*) *v* *conduire; accompagner; diriger

conductor (keunn-*dak*-teu) *n* conducteur *m*; chef d'orchestre

confectioner (keunn-*fèk*-cheu-neu) *n* confiseur *m*

conference (*konn*-feu-reunns) *n* conférence *f*

confess (keunn-*fèss*) *v* *reconnaître; confesser; professer

confession (keunn-*fè*-cheunn) *n* confession *f*

confidence (*konn*-fi-deunns) *n* confiance *f*

confident (*konn*-fi-deunnt) *adj* confiant

confidential (konn-fi-*dèn*-cheul) *adj* confidentiel

confirm (keunn-*feûmm*) *v* confirmer

confirmation (konn-feu-*méï*-cheunn) *n* confirmation *f*

confiscate (*konn*-fi-skéït) *v* confisquer

conflict (*konn*-flikt) *n* conflit *m*

confuse (keunn-*fyoûz*) *v* confondre; **confused** *adj* confus

confusion (keunn-*fyoû*-jeunn) *n* confusion *f*

congratulate (keunng-*ghræ*-tchou-léït) *v* congratuler, féliciter

congratulation (keunng-ghræ-tchou-*léï*-cheunn) *n* félicitation *f*, félicitation *m*

congregation (konng-ghri-*ghéï*-cheunn) *n* communauté *f*, congrégation *f*

congress (*konng*-ghrèss) *n* congrès *m*

connect (keu-*nèkt*) *v* *joindre; *mettre en communication; brancher

connection (keu-*nèk*-cheunn) *n* relation *f*; rapport *m*; communication *f*, correspondance *f*

connoisseur (ko-neu-*seû*) *n* connaisseur *m*

connotation (ko-neu-*téï*-cheunn) *n* connotation *f*

conquer (*konng*-keu) *v* *conquérir; *vaincre

conqueror (*konng*-keu-reu) *n* conquérant *m*

conquest (*konng*-kᵒᵘèst) *n* conquête *f*

conscience (*konn*-cheunns) *n* conscience *f*

conscious (*konn*-cheuss) *adj* conscient

consciousness (*konn*-cheuss-neuss) *n* conscience *f*

conscript (*konn*-skript) *n* conscrit *m*

consent (keunn-*sènt*) *v* *consentir; approuver; *n* assentiment *m*, consentement *m*

consequence (*konn*-si-kᵒᵘeunns) *n* effet *m*, conséquence *f*

consequently (*konn*-si-kᵒᵘeunnt-li) *adv* par conséquent

conservative (keunn-*seû*-veu-tiv) *adj* conservateur

consider (keunn-*si*-deu) *v* considérer; envisager; trouver, estimer

considerable (keunn-*si*-deu-reu-beul) *adj* considérable; important, sensible

considerate (keunn-*si*-deu-reut) *adj* prévenant

consideration (keunn-si-deu-*réï*-cheunn) *n* considération *f*; égard *m*, attention *f*

considering (keunn-*si*-deu-rinng) *prep* vu

consignment (keunn-*saïn*-meunnt) *n* expédition *f*

consist of (keunn-*sist*) consister en

conspire (keunn-*spai*ᵉᵘ) *v* conspirer

constant (*konn*-steunnt) *adj* constant

constipated (*konn*-sti-péï-tid) *adj* constipé

constipation (konn-sti-*péï*-cheunn) *n* constipation *f*

constituency (keunn-*sti*-tchou-eunn-si) *n* circonscription électorale

constitution (konn-sti-*tyoû*-cheunn) *n* constitution *f*

construct (keunn-*strakt*) *v* *construire; bâtir, édifier

construction (keunn-*strak*-cheunn) *n* construction *f*; édification *f*; édifice *m*

consul (*konn*-seul) *n* consul *m*

consulate (*konn*-syou-leut) *n* consulat *m*

consult (keunn-*salt*) *v* consulter

consultation (konn-seul-*téï*-cheunn) *n* consultation *f*; ~ **hours** *n* heures de consultation

consumer (keunn-*syoû*-meu) *n* utilisateur *m*, consommateur *m*

contact (*konn*-tækt) *n* contact *m*; *v* contacter; ~ **lenses** verres de contact

contagious (keunn-*téï*-djeuss) *adj* contagieux

contain (keunn-*téïn*) *v* *contenir; *comprendre

container (keunn-*téï*-neu) *n* récipient *m*; conteneur *m*

contemporary (keunn-*tèm*-peu-reu-ri) *adj* contemporain; de l'époque; *n* contemporain *m*

contempt (keunn-*tèmpt*) *n* dédain *m*, mépris *m*

content (keunn-*tènt*) *adj* satisfait

contents (*konn*-tènts) *pl* contenu *m*

contest (*konn*-tèst) *n* combat *m*; concours *m*

continent (*konn*-ti-neunnt) *n* continent *m*

continental (konn-ti-*nèn*-teul) *adj* continental

continual (keunn-*ti*-nyou-eul) *adj* continuel

continue (keunn-*ti*-nyoû) *v* continuer; *poursuivre, durer

continuous (keunn-*ti*-nyou-euss) *adj* continuel, continu, ininterrompu

contour (*konn*-tou^eu) *n* contour *m*

contraceptive (konn-treu-*sèp*-tiv) *n* contraceptif *m*

contract[1] (*konn*-trækt) *n* contrat *m*

contract[2] (keunn-*trækt*) *v* attraper

contractor (keunn-*træk*-teu) *n* entrepreneur *m*

contradict (konn-treu-*dikt*) *v* *contredire

contradictory (konn-treu-*dik*-teu-ri) *adj* contradictoire

contrary (*konn*-treu-ri) *n* contraire *m*; *adj* opposé; **on the ~** au contraire

contrast (*konn*-trââst) *n* contraste *m*; différence *f*

contribution (konn-tri-*byoû*-cheunn) *n* contribution *f*

control (keunn-*trô^ou*l) *n* contrôle *m*; *v* contrôler

controversial (konn-treu-*veû*-cheul) *adj* discuté, controversé

convenience (keunn-*vii*-nyeunns) *n* commodité *f*

convenient (keunn-*vii*-nyeunnt) *adj* pratique; approprié, qui convient, commode

convent (*konn*-veunnt) *n* couvent *m*

conversation (konn-veu-*séi*-cheunn) *n* entretien *m*, conversation *f*

convert (keunn-*veût*) *v* convertir

convict[1] (keunn-*vikt*) *v* déclarer coupable

convict[2] (*konn*-vikt) *n* condamné *m*

conviction (keunn-*vik*-cheunn) *n* conviction *f*; condamnation *f*

convince (keunn-*vinns*) *v* *convaincre

convulsion (keunn-*val*-cheunn) *n* convulsion *f*

cook (kouk) *n* cuisinier *m*; *v* *cuire; préparer

cookbook (*kouk*-bouk) *nAm* livre de cuisine

cooker (*kou* keu) *n* cuisinière *f*; **gas ~** cuisinière à gaz

cookery-book (*kou*-keu-ri-bouk) *n* livre de cuisine

cookie (*kou*-ki) *nAm* biscuit *m*

cool (koûl) *adj* frais; **cooling system** système de refroidissement

co-operation (kô^ou-o-peu-*réi*-cheunn) *n* coopération *f*; collaboration *f*

co-operative (kô^ou-o-peu-reu-tiv) *adj* coopératif; coopérant; *n* coopérative *f*

co-ordinate (kô^ou-*oo*-di-néït) *v* coordonner

co-ordination (kô^ou-oo-di-*néi*-cheunn) *n* coordination *f*

copper (*ko*-peu) *n* cuivre *m*

copy (*ko*-pi) *n* copie *f*; exemplaire *m*; *v* copier; imiter; **carbon ~** copie *f*

coral (*ko*-reul) *n* corail *m*

cord (kood) *n* corde *f*; cordon *m*

cordial (*koo*-di-eul) *adj* cordial

corduroy (*koo*-deu-roï) *n* velours côtelé

core (koo) *n* cœur *m*; trognon *m*

cork (kook) *n* bouchon *m*

corkscrew (*kook*-skroû) *n* tire-bouchon *m*

corn (koon) *n* grain *m*; céréale *f*, blé *m*; durillon *m*, cor au pied; **~ on the cob** maïs en épi

corner (*koo*-neu) *n* coin *m*

cornfield (*koon*-fiild) *n* champ de blé

corpse (koops) *n* cadavre *m*

corpulent (*koo*-pyou-leunnt) *adj* corpulent; gros, obèse

correct (keu-*rèkt*) *adj* juste, correct; *v* corriger

correction (keu-*rèk*-cheunn) *n* correction *f*; rectification *f*

correctness (keu-*rèkt*-neuss) *n* exactitude *f*

correspond (ko-ri-*sponnd*) *v* correspondre; *être conforme

correspondence (ko-ri-*sponn*-deunns) *n* correspondance *f*

correspondent (ko-ri-*sponn*-deunnt) *n* correspondant *m*

corridor (*ko*-ri-doo) *n* corridor *m*

corrupt (keu-*rapt*) *adj* corrompu; *v* *corrompre

corruption (keu-*rap*-cheunn) *n* corruption *f*

corset (*koo*-sit) *n* corset *m*

cosmetics (koz-*mè*-tiks) *pl* cosmétiques *mpl*, produits de beauté

cost (kost) *n* coût *m*; prix *m*

*cost (kost) *v* coûter

cosy (*kôô*-zi) *adj* intime, confortable

cot (kot) *nAm* lit de camp

cottage (*ko*-tidj) *n* villa *f*

cotton (*ko*-teunn) *n* coton *m*; en coton

cotton-wool (*ko*-teunn-*ou*oul) *n* ouate *f*

couch (kaoutch) *n* canapé *m*

cough (kof) *n* toux *f*; *v* tousser

could (koud) *v* (p can)

council (*kaoun*-seul) *n* conseil *m*

councillor (*kaoun*-seu-leu) *n* conseiller *m*

counsel (*kaoun*-seul) *n* conseil *m*

counsellor (*kaoun*-seu-leu) *n* conseiller *m*

count (kaount) *v* compter; additionner; *inclure; considérer; *n* comte *m*

counter (*kaoun*-teu) *n* comptoir *m*; barre *f*

counterfeit (*kaoun*-teu-fiit) *v* *contrefaire

counterfoil (*kaoun*-teu-foïl) *n* talon *m*

counterpane (*kaoun*-teu-péïn) *n* couvre-lit *m*

countess (*kaoun*-tiss) *n* comtesse *f*

country (*kann*-tri) *n* pays *m*; campagne *f*; région *f*; ~ **house** maison de campagne

countryman (*kann*-tri-meunn) *n* (pl -men) compatriote *m*

countryside (*kann*-tri-saïd) *n* campagne *f*

county (*kaoun* ti) *n* comté *m*

couple (*ka*-peul) *n* couple *m*

coupon (*koû*-ponn) *n* ticket *m*, coupon *m*

courage (*ka*-ridj) *n* vaillance *f*, courage *m*

courageous (keu-*réï*-djeuss) *adj* brave, courageux

course (kooss) *n* cap *m*; plat *m*; cours *m*; **intensive** ~ cours accéléré; **of** ~ évidemment

court (koot) *n* tribunal *m*; cour *f*

courteous (*keû*-ti-euss) *adj* courtois

cousin (*ka*-zeunn) *n* cousine *f*, cousin *m*

cover (*ka*-veu) *v* *couvrir; *n* refuge *m*, abri *m*; couvercle *m*; couverture *f*

cow (kaou) *n* vache *f*

coward (*kaou*-eud) *n* lâche *m*

cowardly (*kaou*-eud-li) *adj* lâche

cow-hide (*kaou*-haïd) *n* peau de vache *f*

crab (kræb) *n* crabe *m*

crack (kræk) *n* craquement *m*; fissure *f*; *v* craquer; fendre

cracker (*kræ*-keu) *nAm* biscuit *m*

cradle (*kréï*-deul) *n* berceau *m*

cramp (kræmp) *n* crampe *f*

crane (kréïn) *n* grue *f*

crankcase (*krængk*-kéïss) *n* carter *m*

crankshaft (*krængk*-chââft) *n* vilebrequin *m*

crash (kræch) *n* collision *f*; *v* entrer en collision; s'écraser; ~ **barrier** glissière de sécurité

crate (kréit) *n* caisse *f*

crater (*kréï*-teu) *n* cratère *m*

crawl (krool) *v* ramper; *n* crawl *m*

craze (kréiz) *n* rage *f*

crazy (*kréï*-zi) *adj* fou; insensé

creak (kriik) *v* grincer

cream (kriim) *n* crème *f*; crème fraîche; *adj* crème

creamy (*krii*-mi) *adj* crémeux

crease (kriiss) *v* froisser; *n* pli *m*; faux pli

create (kri-*éit*) *v* créer

creature (*krii*-tcheu) *n* créature *f*; être *m*

credible (*krè*-di-beul) *adj* croyable

credit (*krè*-dit) *n* crédit *m*; *v* créditer; ~ **card** carte de crédit

creditor (*krè*-di-teu) *n* créditeur *m*

credulous (*krè*-dyou-leuss) *adj* crédule

creek (kriik) *n* baie *f*, crique *f*

***creep** (kriip) *v* ramper

creepy (*krii*-pi) *adj* lugubre, terrifiant

cremate (kri-*méit*) *v* incinérer

cremation (kri-*méï*-cheunn) *n* crémation *f*

crew (kroû) *n* équipage *m*

cricket (*kri*-kit) *n* cricket *m*; grillon *m*

crime (kraïm) *n* crime *m*

criminal (*kri*-mi-neul) *n* délinquant *m*, criminel *m*; *adj* criminel; ~ **law** droit pénal

criminality (kri-mi-*næ*-leu-ti) *n* criminalité *f*

crimson (*krimm*-zeunn) *adj* cramoisi

crippled (*kri*-peuld) *adj* estropié

crisis (*kraï*-siss) *n* (pl crises) crise *f*

crisp (krisp) *adj* croustillant

critic (*kri*-tik) *n* critique *m*

critical (*kri*-ti-keul) *adj* critique; précaire, délicat

criticism (*kri*-ti-si-zeumm) *n* critique *f*

criticize (*kri*-ti-saïz) *v* critiquer

crochet (*krô*ou-chéï) *v* *faire du crochet

crockery (*kro*-keu-ri) *n* poterie *f*, faïence *f*

crocodile (*kro*-keu-daïl) *n* crocodile *m*

crooked (*krou*-kid) *adj* tordu, courbe; malhonnête

crop (krop) *n* récolte *f*

cross (kross) *v* traverser; *adj* irrité, fâché; *n* croix *f*

cross-eyed (*kross*-aïd) *adj* louche

crossing (*kro*-sinng) *n* traversée *f*; croisement *m*; passage *m*; passage à niveau

crossroads (*kross*-rô*ou*dz) *n* carrefour *m*

crosswalk (*kross*-ouook) *nAm* passage pour piétons

crow (krô*ou*) *n* corneille *f*

crowbar (*krô*ou-bââ) *n* bec-de-corbin *m*

crowd (kraoud) *n* masse *f*, foule *f*

crowded (*kraou*-did) *adj* animé; bondé

crown (kraoun) *n* couronne *f*; *v* couronner

crucifix (*kroû*-si-fiks) *n* crucifix *m*

crucifixion (kroû-si-*fik*-cheunn) *n* crucifixion *f*

crucify (*kroû*-si-faï) *v* crucifier

cruel (krou*eu*l) *adj* cruel

cruise (kroûz) *n* croisière *f*

crumb (kramm) *n* miette *f*

crusade (kroû-*séïd*) *n* croisade *f*

crust (krast) *n* croûte *f*

crutch (kratch) *n* béquille *f*

cry (kraï) *v* pleurer; crier; appeler; *n* cri *m*; appel *m*

crystal (*kri*-steul) *n* cristal *m*; *adj* en cristal

Cuba (*kyoû*-beu) Cuba *m*

Cuban (*kyoû*-beunn) *adj* cubain; *n*

Cubain m

cube (kyoûb) n cube m

cuckoo (kou-koû) n coucou m

cucumber (kyoû-keumm-beu) n concombre m

cuddle (ka-deul) v câliner

cudgel (ka-djeul) n gourdin m

cuff (kaf) n manchette f

cuff-links (kaf-linngks) pl boutons de manchettes

cultivate (kal-ti-véït) v cultiver

culture (kal-tcheu) n culture f

cultured (kal-tcheud) adj cultivé

cunning (ka-ninng) adj rusé

cup (kap) n tasse f; coupe f

cupboard (ka-beud) n placard m

curb (keûb) n bord du trottoir; v freiner

cure (kyou^{eu}) v guérir; n cure f; guérison f

curio (kyou^{eu}-ri-ô^{ou}) n (pl ~s) curiosité f

curiosity (kyou^{eu}-ri-o-seu-ti) n curiosité f

curious (kyou^{eu}-ri-euss) adj curieux; étrange

curl (keûl) v boucler; friser; n boucle f

curler (keû-leu) n bigoudi m

curling-tongs (keû-linng-tonngz) pl fer à friser

curly (keû-li) adj bouclé

currant (ka-reunnt) n raisin sec; groseille f

currency (ka-reunn-si) n monnaie f; **foreign** ~ monnaie étrangère

current (ka-reunnt) n courant m; adj courant; **alternating** ~ courant alternatif; **direct** ~ courant continu

curry (ka-ri) n curry m

curse (keûss) v jurer; *maudire; n juron m

curtain (keû-teunn) n rideau m

curve (keûv) n courbe f; tournant m

curved (keûvd) adj courbe, courbé

cushion (kou-cheunn) n coussin m

custodian (ka-stô^{ou}-di-eunn) n gardien m

custody (ka-steu-di) n détention f; garde f; tutelle f

custom (ka-steumm) n coutume f; habitude f

customary (ka-steu-meu-ri) adj usuel, coutumier, ordinaire

customer (ka-steu-meu) n client m

Customs (ka-steummz) pl douane f; ~ **duty** droit de douane; ~ **officer** douanier m

cut (kat) n incision f; coupure f

*cut (kat) v couper; *réduire; ~ off découper; couper

cutlery (kat-leu-ri) n couvert m

cutlet (kat-leut) n côtelette f

cycle (saï-keul) n vélo m; bicyclette f; cycle m

cyclist (saï-klist) n cycliste m

cylinder (si-linn-deu) n cylindre m; ~ **head** tête de cylindre

cystitis (si-stai-tiss) n cystite f

Czech (tchèk) adj tchèque; n Tchèque m

Czech Republic (tchèk ri-pa-blik) République Tchèque

D

dad (dæd) n père m

daddy (dæ-di) n papa m

daffodil (dæ-feu-dil) n jonquille f

daily (déï-li) adj journalier, quotidien; n quotidien m

dairy (dè^{eu}-ri) n laiterie f

dam (dæm) n barrage m; digue f

damage (dæ-midj) n dommage m; v endommager

damp (dæmp) adj humide; moite; n

humidité f; v humidifier

dance (dââns) v danser; n danse f

dandelion (dæn-di-laï-eunn) n pissen-lit m

dandruff (dæn-dreuf) n pellicules

Dane (déïn) n Danois m

danger (déïn-djeu) n danger m

dangerous (déïn-djeu-reuss) adj dan-gereux

Danish (déï-nich) adj danois

dare (dè^{eu}) v oser; défier

daring (dè^{eu}-rinng) adj téméraire

dark (dââk) adj obscur; n obscurité f, ténèbres fpl

darling (dââ-linng) n trésor m, chéri m

darn (dâân) v repriser

dash (dæch) v se précipiter; n tiret m

dashboard (dæch-bood) n tableau de bord

data (déï-teu) pl donnée f

date[1] (déït) n date f; rendez-vous m; v dater; **out of** ~ démodé

date[2] (déït) n datte f

daughter (doo-teu) n fille f

dawn (doon) n aube f; aurore f

day (déï) n jour m; **by** ~ de jour; ~ **trip** excursion f; **per** ~ par jour; **the** ~ **before yesterday** avant-hier

daybreak (déï-bréïk) n lever du jour

daylight (déï-laït) n lumière du jour

dead (dèd) adj mort; décédé

deaf (dèf) adj sourd

deal (diil) n transaction f, affaire f

*****deal** (diil) v distribuer; ~ **with** v s'occuper de; *faire des affaires avec

dealer (dii-leu) n négociant m, mar-chand m

dear (di^{eu}) adj cher

death (dèθ) n mort f; ~ **penalty** pei-ne de mort

debate (di-béït) n débat m

debit (dè-bit) n débit m

debt (dèt) n dette f

decaffeinated (dii-kæ-fi-néï-tid) adj décaféiné

deceit (di-siit) n tromperie f

deceive (di-siiv) v tromper

December (di-sèm-beu) décembre

decency (dii-seunn-si) n décence f

decent (dii-seunnt) adj décent

decide (di-saïd) v décider

decision (di-si-jeunn) n décision f

deck (dèk) n pont m; ~ **cabin** cabine de pont; ~ **chair** chaise longue

declaration (dè-kleu-réï-cheunn) n dé-claration f

declare (di-klè^{eu}) v déclarer; indiquer

decoration (dè-keu-réï-cheunn) n dé-coration f

decrease (dii-kriiss) v *réduire; dimi-nuer; n diminution f

dedicate (dè-di-kéït) v dédier

deduce (di-dyoûss) v *déduire

deduct (di-dakt) v *déduire

deed (diid) n action f, acte m

deep (diip) adj profond

deep-freeze (diip-friiz) n congélateur m

deer (di^{eu}) n (pl ~) daim m

defeat (di-fiit) v *vaincre; n défaite f

defective (di-fèk-tiv) adj défectueux

defence (di-fèns) n défense f

defend (di-fènd) v défendre

deficiency (di-fi-cheunn-si) n déficien-ce f

deficit (dè-fi-sit) n déficit m

define (di-faïn) v définir; déterminer

definite (dè-fi-nit) adj déterminé; ex-plicite

definition (dè-fi-ni-cheunn) n défini-tion f

deformed (di-foomd) adj contrefait, difforme

degree (di-ghrii) n degré m; grade m

delay (di-léï) v retarder; différer; n retard m; ajournement m

delegate (*dè*-li-gheut) *n* délégué *m*

delegation (dè-li-*ghéï*-cheunn) *n* délégation *f*

deliberate[1] (di-*li*-beu-réït) *v* discuter, délibérer

deliberate[2] (di-*li*-beu-reut) *adj* délibéré

deliberation (di-li-beu-*réï*-cheunn) *n* discussion *f*, délibération *f*

delicacy (*dè*-li-keu-si) *n* délicatesse *f*

delicate (*dè*-li-keut) *adj* délicat; tendre

delicatessen (dè-li-keu-*tè*-seunn) *n* épicerie fine

delicious (di-*li*-cheuss) *adj* exquis, délicieux

delight (di-*laït*) *n* délice *m*, plaisir *m*; *v* enchanter

delightful (di-*laït*-feul) *adj* délicieux, ravissant

deliver (di-*li*-veu) *v* *remettre, livrer; délivrer

delivery (di-*li*-veu-ri) *n* remise *f*, livraison *f*; accouchement *m*; délivrance *f*; ~ **van** camion de livraison

demand (di-*mâând*) *v* nécessiter, exiger; *n* demande *f*

democracy (di-*mo*-kreu-si) *n* démocratie *f*

democratic (dè-meu-*kræ*-tik) *adj* démocratique

demolish (di-*mo*-lich) *v* démolir

demolition (dè-meu-*li*-cheunn) *n* démolition *f*

demonstrate (*dè*-meunn-stréït) *v* démontrer; manifester

demonstration (dè-meunn-*stréï*-cheunn) *n* démonstration *f*; manifestation *f*

den (dèn) *n* tanière *f*

Denmark (*dèn*-mââk) Danemark *m*

denomination (di-no-mi-*néï*-cheunn) *n* dénomination *f*

dense (dèns) *adj* dense

dent (dènt) *n* bosse *f*

dentist (*dèn*-tist) *n* dentiste *m*

denture (*dèn*-tcheu) *n* dentier *m*

deny (di-*naï*) *v* nier; dénier, refuser

deodorant (dii-*ô*ᵒᵘ-deu-reunnt) *n* désodorisant *m*

depart (di-*pâât*) *v* s'en *aller, *partir; trépasser

department (di-*pâât*-meunnt) *n* division *f*, département *m*; ~ **store** grand magasin

departure (di-*pââ*-tcheu) *n* départ *m*

dependant (di-*pèn*-deunnt) *adj* dépendant

depend on (di-*pènd*) dépendre de

deposit (di-*po*-zit) *n* versement *m*; consigne *f*; sédiment *m*, dépôt *m*; *v* déposer

depository (di-*po*-zi-teu-ri) *n* entrepôt *m*

depot (*dè*-pô ᵒᵘ) *n* dépôt *m*; *nAm* gare *f*

depress (di-*près*) *v* déprimer

depression (di-*prè*-cheunn) *n* dépression *f*

deprive of (di-*praïv*) priver de

depth (dèpθ) *n* profondeur *f*

deputy (*dè*-pyou-ti) *n* député *m*; substitut *m*

descend (di-*sènd*) *v* descendre

descendant (di-*sèn*-deunnt) *n* descendant *m*

descent (di-*sènt*) *n* descente *f*

describe (di-*skraïb*) *v* *décrire

description (di-*skrip*-cheunn) *n* description *f*; signalement *m*

desert[1] (*dè*-zeut) *n* désert *m*; *adj* sauvage, désert

desert[2] (di-*zeût*) *v* déserter; abandonner

deserve (di-*zeûv*) *v* mériter

design (di-*zaïn*) *v* créer; *n* dessein *m*

designate (*dè*-zigh-néït) *v* désigner

desirable (di-*zaï*ᵉᵘ-reu-beul) *adj* désirable

desire (di-*zaï^eu*) n vœu m; envie f, désir m; v *avoir envie de, désirer

desk (dèsk) n bureau m; pupitre m; banc d'école

despair (di-*spé^eu*) n désespoir m; v désespérer

despatch (di-*spætch*) v expédier

desperate (*dè*-speu-reut) adj désespéré

despise (di-*spaïz*) v mépriser

despite (di-*spaït*) prep malgré

dessert (di-*zeût*) n dessert m

destination (dè-sti-*néï*-cheunn) n destination f

destine (*dè*-stinn) v destiner

destiny (*dè*-sti-ni) n destin m, sort m

destroy (di-*stroï*) v dévaster, *détruire

destruction (di-*strak*-cheunn) n destruction f; anéantissement m

detach (di-*tætch*) v détacher

detail (*dii*-téïl) n particularité f, détail m

detailed (*dii*-téïld) adj détaillé

detect (di-*tèkt*) v détecter

detective (di-*tèk*-tiv) n détective m; ~ story roman policier

detergent (di-*teû*-djeunnt) n détergent m

determine (di-*teû*-minn) v définir, déterminer

determined (di-*teû*-minnd) adj résolu

detour (*dii*-tou^eu) n détour m; déviation f

devaluation (dii-væl-you-*éï*-cheunn) n dévaluation f

devalue (dii-*væl*-yoû) v dévaluer

develop (di-*vè*-leup) v développer

development (di-*vè*-leup-meunnt) n développement m

deviate (*dii*-vi-éït) v dévier

devil (*dè*-veul) n diable m

devise (di-*vaïz*) v *concevoir

devote (di-*vô^ou*t) v consacrer

dew (dyoû) n rosée f

diabetes (daï-eu-*bii*-tiiz) n diabète m

diabetic (daï-eu-*bè*-tik) n diabétique m

diagnose (daï-eugh-*nô^ou*z) v diagnostiquer; constater

diagnosis (daï-eugh-*nô^ou*-siss) n (pl -ses) diagnostic m

diagonal (daï-*æ*-gheu-neul) n diagonale f; adj diagonale

diagram (*daï*-eu-græm) n diagramme m; schéma m, graphique m

dialect (*daï*-eu-lèkt) n dialecte m

diamond (*daï*-eu-meunnd) n diamant m

diaper (*daï*-eu-peu) nAm couche f

diaphragm (*daï*-eu-fræm) n membrane f

diarrhoea (daï-eu-*ri*-eu) n diarrhée f

diary (*daï*-eu-ri) n agenda m; journal m

dictaphone (*dik*-teu-fô^ou n) n dictaphone m

dictate (dik-*téït*) v dicter

dictation (dik-*téï*-cheunn) n dictée f

dictator (dik-*téï*-teu) n dictateur m

dictionary (*dik*-cheu-neu-ri) n dictionnaire m

did (did) v (p do)

die (daï) v *mourir

diesel (*dii*-zeul) n diesel m

diet (*daï*-eut) n régime m

differ (*di*-feu) v différer

difference (*di*-feu-reunns) n différence f; distinction f

different (*di*-feu-reunnt) adj différent; autre

difficult (*di*-fi-keult) adj difficile; fastidieux

difficulty (*di*-fi-keul-ti) n difficulté f; peine f

*dig (digh) v creuser; fouiller

digest (di-*djèst*) v digérer

digestible (di-*djè*-steu-beul) adj digestible

digestion (di-*djèss*-tcheunn) *n* digestion *f*

digit (*di*-djit) *n* chiffre *m*

dignified (*digh*-ni-faïd) *adj* digne

dike (daïk) *n* digue *f*

dilapidated (di-*læ*-pi-déï-tid) *adj* délabré

diligence (*di*-li-djeunns) *n* élan *m*, application *f*

diligent (*di*-li-djeunnt) *adj* zélé, assidu

dilute (daï-*lyoût*) *v* allonger, diluer

dim (dimm) *adj* terne, mat; obscur, indistinct

dine (daïn) *v* dîner

dinghy (dinng-ghi) *n* canot *m*

dining-car (*daï*-ninng-kââ) *n* wagon-restaurant

dining-room (*daï*-ninng-roûm) *n* salle à manger

dinner (*di*-neu) *n* dîner *m*; déjeuner *m*

dinner-jacket (*di*-neu-djæ-kit) *n* smoking *m*

dinner-service (*di*-neu-seû-viss) *n* service de table

diphtheria (dif-*θi*^{eu}-ri-eu) *n* diphtérie *f*

diploma (di-*plô*^{ou}-meu) *n* diplôme *m*

diplomat (*di*-pleu-mæt) *n* diplomate *m*

direct (di-*rèkt*) *adj* direct; *v* diriger; administrer; *mettre en scène

direction (di-*rèk*-cheunn) *n* direction *f*; instruction *f*; réalisation *f*; administration *f*; **directional signal** Am indicateur de direction; **directions for use** mode d'emploi

directive (di-*rèk*-tiv) *n* directive *f*

director (di-*rèk*-teu) *n* directeur *m*; metteur en scène

dirt (deût) *n* saleté *f*

dirty (*deû*-ti) *adj* sale, souillé

disabled (di-*séï*-beuld) *adj* handicapé, invalide

disadvantage (di-seud-*vâân*-tidj) *n* désavantage *m*

disagree (di-seu-*ghrii*) *v* *être en désaccord

disagreeable (di-seu-*ghrii*-eu-beul) *adj* désagréable

disappear (di-seu-*pi*^{eu}) *v* *disparaître

disappoint (di-seu-*poïnt*) *v* *décevoir

disappointment (di-seu-*poïnt*-meunnt) *n* déception *f*

disapprove (di-seu-*proûv*) *v* désapprouver

disaster (di-*zââ*-steu) *n* désastre *m*; catastrophe *f*, calamité *f*

disastrous (di-*zââ*-streuss) *adj* désastreux

disc (disk) *n* disque *m*; **slipped ~** hernie *f*

discard (di-*skââd*) *v* se débarrasser de

discharge (diss-*tchââdj*) *v* décharger; **~ of** dispenser de

discipline (*di*-si-plinn) *n* discipline *f*

discolour (di-*ska*-leu) *v* décolorer

disconnect (di-skeu-*nèkt*) *v* *disjoindre; débrancher

discontented (di-skeunn-*tèn*-tid) *adj* mécontent

discontinue (di-skeunn-*ti*-nyoû) *v* suspendre, cesser

discount (*di*-skaount) *n* réduction *f*, rabais *m*

discover (di-*ska*-veu) *v* *découvrir

discovery (di-*ska*-veu-ri) *n* découverte *f*

discuss (di-*skass*) *v* discuter; *débattre

discussion (di-*ska*-cheunn) *n* discussion *f*; conversation *f*, délibération *f*, débat *m*

disease (di-*ziiz*) *n* maladie *f*

disembark (di-simm-*bââk*) *v* débarquer

disgrace (diss-*ghréïss*) *n* déshonneur

m

disguise (diss-*ghaïz*) *v* se déguiser ; *n* déguisement *m*

disgusting (diss-*gha*-stinng) *adj* répugnant, dégoûtant

dish (dich) *n* assiette *f* ; plat *m*

dishonest (di-*so*-nist) *adj* malhonnête

disinfect (di-sinn-*fèkt*) *v* désinfecter

disinfectant (di-sinn-*fèk*-teunnt) *n* désinfectant *m*

dislike (di-*slaïk*) *v* détester, ne pas aimer ; *n* répugnance *f*, aversion *f*, antipathie *f*

dislocated (*di*-sleu-kéï-tid) *adj* disloqué

dismiss (diss-*miss*) *v* *renvoyer

disorder (di-*soo*-deu) *n* désordre *m* ; confusion *f*

dispatch (di-*spætch*) *v* *envoyer, expédier

display (di-*spléï*) *v* étaler ; montrer ; *n* exposition *f*

displease (di-*spliiz*) *v* *déplaire

disposable (di-*spôᵒᵘ*-zeu-beul) *adj* à jeter

disposal (di-*spôᵒᵘ*-zeul) *n* disposition *f*

dispose of (di-*spôᵒᵘz*) disposer de

dispute (di-*spyoût*) *n* discussion *f* ; querelle *f*, litige *m* ; *v* se disputer, contester

dissatisfied (di-*sæ*-tiss-faïd) *adj* insatisfait

dissolve (di-*zolv*) *v* *dissoudre, diluer

dissuade from (di-s*ᵒᵘéïd*) dissuader

distance (*di*-steunns) *n* distance *f* ; ~ **in kilometres** kilométrage *m*

distant (*di*-steunnt) *adj* éloigné

distinct (di-*stinngkt*) *adj* net ; distinct

distinction (di-*stinngk*-cheunn) *n* distinction *f*, différence *f*

distinguish (di-*stinng*-ghᵒᵘich) *v* distinguer, discerner

distinguished (di-*stinng*-ghᵒᵘicht) *adj* distingué

distress (di-*strèss*) *n* détresse *f* ; ~ **signal** signal de détresse

distribute (di-*stri*-byoût) *v* distribuer

distributor (di-*stri*-byou-teu) *n* concessionnaire *m* ; distributeur *m*

district (*di*-strikt) *n* district *m* ; région *f* ; quartier *m*

disturb (di-*steûb*) *v* déranger

disturbance (di-*steû*-beunns) *n* dérangement *m* ; agitation *f*

ditch (ditch) *n* fossé *m*

dive (daïv) *v* plonger

diversion (daï-*veû*-cheunn) *n* déviation *f* ; diversion *f*

divide (di-*vaïd*) *v* diviser ; répartir ; séparer

divine (di-*vaïn*) *adj* divin

division (di-*vi*-jeunn) *n* division *f* ; séparation *f* ; département *m*

divorce (di-*vooss*) *n* divorce *m* ; *v* divorcer

dizziness (*di*-zi-neuss) *n* vertige *m*

dizzy (*di*-zi) *adj* étourdi

***do** (doù) *v* *faire ; *suffire

dock (dok) *n* dock *m* ; quai *m* ; *v* accoster

docker (*do*-keu) *n* docker *m*

doctor (*dok*-teu) *n* médecin *m*, docteur *m*

document (*do*-kyou-meunnt) *n* document *m*

dog (dogh) *n* chien *m*

dogged (*do*-ghid) *adj* obstiné

doll (dol) *n* poupée *f*

dome (dôᵒᵘm) *n* dôme *m*

domestic (deu-*mè*-stik) *adj* domestique ; intérieur ; *n* domestique *m*

domicile (*do*-mi-saïl) *n* domicile *m*

domination (do-mi-*néï*-cheunn) *n* domination *f*

dominion (deu-*mi*-nyeunn) *n* règne *m*

donate (dô ᵒᵘ-*néït*) *v* donner

donation (dôᵒᵘ-*néï*-cheunn) *n* don *m*,

donation f

done (dann) v (pp do)

donkey (donng-ki) n âne m

donor (dô^{ou}-neu) n donateur m

door (doo) n porte f; **revolving ~** porte tournante; **sliding ~** porte coulissante

doorbell (doo-bèl) n sonnette f

door-keeper (doo-kii-peu) n portier m

doorman (doo-meunn) n (pl -men) portier m

dormitory (doo-mi-tri) n dortoir m

dose (dô^{ou}ss) n dose f

dot (dot) n point m

double (da-beul) adj double

doubt (daout) v douter de, douter; n doute m; **without ~** sans doute

doubtful (daout-feul) adj douteux; incertain

dough (dô^{ou}) n pâte f

down[1] (daoun) adv en bas; vers le bas, par terre; adj déprimé; prep le long de, en bas de; **~ payment** acompte m

down[2] (daoun) n duvet m

downpour (daoun-poo) n averse f

downstairs (daoun-stè^{eu}z) adv en bas

downstream (daoun-striim) adv en aval

down-to-earth (daoun-tou-eûθ) adj terre-à-terre

downwards (daoun-^{ou}eudz) adv vers le bas

dozen (da-zeunn) n (pl ~, ~s) douzaine f

draft (drââft) n traite f

drag (drægh) v traîner

dragon (dræ-gheunn) n dragon m

drain (dréïn) v assécher; drainer; n égout m

drama (drââ-meu) n drame m; tragédie f; théâtre m

dramatic (dreu-mæ-tik) adj dramatique

dramatist (dræ-meu-tist) n dramaturge m

drank (drængk) v (p drink)

draper (dréi-peu) n drapier m

drapery (dréï-peu-ri) n étoffes fpl

draught (drââft) n courant d'air; **draughts** jeu de dames

draught-board (drââft-bood) n damier m

draw (droo) n tirage m

draw (droo) v dessiner; tirer; retirer; **~ up** rédiger

drawbridge (droo-bridj) n pont-levis m

drawer (droo-eu) n tiroir m; **drawers** caleçon m

drawing (droo-inng) n dessin m

drawing-pin (droo-inng-pinn) n punaise f

drawing-room (droo-inng-roûm) n salon m

dread (drèd) v *craindre; n crainte f

dreadful (drèd-feul) adj terrible, affreux

dream (driim) n rêve m

dream (driim) v rêver, songer

dress (drèss) v habiller; se *vêtir, s'habiller; *vêtir; panser; n robe f

dressing-gown (drè-sinng-ghaoun) n robe de chambre

dressing-room (drè-sinng-roûm) n loge f

dressing-table (drè-sinng-téï-beul) n coiffeuse f

dressmaker (drèss-méï-keu) n couturière f

drill (dril) v forer; entraîner; n foreuse f

drink (drinngk) n apéritif m, boisson f

drink (drinngk) v *boire

drinking-water (drinng-kinng-^{ou}oo-teu) n eau potable

drip-dry (drip-draï) adj repassage permanent, sans repassage

drive (draïv) *n* route *f*; promenade en voiture

*drive** (draïv) *v* *conduire

driver (*draï*-veu) *n* conducteur *m*

drizzle (*dri*-zeul) *n* crachin *m*

drop (drop) *v* laisser tomber; *n* goutte *f*

drought (draout) *n* sécheresse *f*

drown (draoun) *v* noyer; *be drowned** se noyer

drug (dragh) *n* drogue *f*; médicament *m*

drugstore (*dragh*-stoo) *nAm* droguerie *f*, pharmacie *f*; bazar *m*

drum (dramm) *n* tambour *m*

drunk (dranngk) *adj* (pp drink) ivre

dry (draï) *adj* sec; *v* sécher; essuyer

dry-clean (draï-*kliin*) *v* nettoyer à sec

dry-cleaner's (draï-*klii*-neuz) *n* teinturerie *f*

dryer (*draï*-eu) *n* séchoir *m*

duchess (da-tchiss) *n* duchesse *f*

duck (dak) *n* canard *m*

due (dyoû) *adj* attendu; payable; dû

dues (dyoûz) *pl* droits

dug (dagh) *v* (p, pp dig)

duke (dyoûk) *n* duc *m*

dull (dal) *adj* ennuyeux; terne, mat; émoussé

dumb (damm) *adj* muet; bête

dune (dyoûn) *n* dune *f*

dung (danng) *n* fumier *m*

dunghill (*danng*-hil) *n* tas de fumier

duration (dyou-*réï*-cheunn) *n* durée *f*

during (*dyou*eu-rinng) *prep* durant, pendant

dusk (dask) *n* crépuscule *m*

dust (dast) *n* poussière *f*

dustbin (*dast*-binn) *n* boîte à ordures

dusty (*da*-sti) *adj* poussiéreux

Dutch (datch) *adj* néerlandais, hollandais

Dutchman (*datch*-meunn) *n* (pl -men) Néerlandais *m*, Hollandais *m*

dutiable (*dyoû*-ti-eu-beul) *adj* imposable

duty (*dyoû*-ti) *n* devoir *m*; tâche *f*; droit d'importation; **Customs ~** droit de douane

duty-free (dyoû-ti-*frii*) *adj* exempt de droits

dwarf (d^{ou}oof) *n* nain *m*

dye (daï) *v* *teindre; *n* teinture *f*

dynamo (*daï*-neu-mô^{ou}) *n* (pl ~s) dynamo *f*

dysentery (*di*-seunn-tri) *n* dysenterie *f*

E

each (iitch) *adj* chaque; **~ other** l'un l'autre

eager (*ii*-gheu) *adj* désireux, impatient

eagle (*ii*-gheul) *n* aigle *m*

ear (i^{eu}) *n* oreille *f*

earache (*i*^{eu}-réïk) *n* mal d'oreille

ear-drum (*i*^{eu}-dramm) *n* tympan *m*

earl (eûl) *n* comte *m*

early (*eû*-li) *adj* tôt

earn (eûnn) *v* gagner

earnest (*eû*-nist) *n* sérieux *m*

earnings (*eû*-ninngz) *pl* revenu *m*, gains

earring (*i*^{eu}-rinng) *n* boucle d'oreille

earth (eûθ) *n* terre *f*; sol *m*

earthenware (*eû*-θeunn-^{ou}è^{eu}) *n* poterie *f*

earthquake (*eû*θ-k^{ou}éïk) *n* tremblement de terre

ease (iiz) *n* aisance *f*; aise *f*

east (iist) *n* est *m*

Easter (*ii*-steu) Pâques

easterly (*ii*-steu-li) *adj* oriental

eastern (*ii*-steunn) *adj* oriental

easy (*ii*-zi) *adj* facile; commode; **~ chair** fauteuil *m*

easy-going (*ii*-zi-ghô^ou^-inng) *adj* décontracté

*eat (iit) *v* manger; dîner

eavesdrop (*iivz*-drop) *v* écouter aux portes

ebony (*è*-beu-ni) *n* ébène *f*

eccentric (ik-*sèn*-trik) *adj* excentrique

echo (*è*-kô^ou^) *n* (pl ~es) écho *m*

eclipse (i-*klips*) *n* éclipse *f*

economic (ii-keu-*no*-mik) *adj* économique

economical (ii-keu-*no*-mi-keul) *adj* parcimonieux, économe

economist (i-*ko*-neu-mist) *n* économiste *m*

economize (i-*ko*-neu-maïz) *v* économiser

economy (i-*ko*-neu-mi) *n* économie *f*

ecstasy (*èk*-steu-zi) *n* extase *m*

Ecuador (*è*-k^ou^eu-doo) Equateur *m*

Ecuadorian (è-k^ou^eu-*doo*-ri-eunn) *n* Ecuadorien *m*

eczema (*èk*-si-meu) *n* eczéma *m*

edge (èdj) *n* rebord *m*, bord *m*

edible (*è*-di-beul) *adj* comestible

edition (i-*di*-cheunn) *n* édition *f*; **morning ~** édition du matin

editor (*è*-di-teu) *n* rédacteur *m*

educate (*è*-djou-kéït) *v* former, éduquer

education (è-djou-*kéï*-cheunn) *n* éducation *f*

eel (iil) *n* anguille *f*

effect (i-*fèkt*) *n* résultat *m*, effet *m*; *v* effectuer; **in ~** en fait

effective (i-*fèk*-tiv) *adj* efficace, effectif

efficient (i-*fi*-cheunnt) *adj* efficace

effort (*è*-feut) *n* effort *m*

egg (ègh) *n* œuf *m*

egg-cup (*ègh*-kap) *n* coquetier *m*

eggplant (*ègh*-plâânt) *n* aubergine *f*

egg-yolk (*ègh*-yô^ou^k) *n* jaune d'œuf *m*

egoistic (è-ghô^ou^-*i*-stik) *adj* égoïste

Egypt (*ii*-djipt) Egypte *f*

Egyptian (i-*djip*-cheunn) *adj* égyptien; *n* Egyptien *m*

eiderdown (*aï*-deu-daoun) *n* édredon *m*

eight (éït) *num* huit

eighteen (éï-*tiin*) *num* dix-huit

eighteenth (éï-*tiin*θ) *num* dix-huitième

eighth (éïtθ) *num* huitième

eighty (*éï*-ti) *num* quatre-vingts

either (*aï*-ðeu) *pron* l'un ou l'autre; **either ... or** ou ... ou, soit ... soit

elaborate (i-*læ*-beu-réït) *v* élaborer

elastic (i-*læ*-stik) *adj* élastique; flexible; élastique *m*

elasticity (è-læ-*sti*-seu-ti) *n* élasticité *f*

elbow (*èl*-bô^ou^) *n* coude *m*

elder (*èl*-deu) *adj* plus âgé

elderly (*èl*-deu-li) *adj* âgé

eldest (*èl*-dist) *adj* le plus âgé

elect (i-*lèkt*) *v* *élire

election (i-*lèk*-cheunn) *n* élection *f*

electric (i-*lèk*-trik) *adj* électrique; **~ razor** rasoir électrique; **~ cord** fil électrique

electrician (i-lèk-*tri*-cheunn) *n* électricien *m*

electricity (i-lèk-*tri*-seu-ti) *n* électricité *f*

electronic (i-lèk-*tro*-nik) *adj* électronique

elegance (*è*-li-gheunns) *n* élégance *f*

elegant (*è*-li-gheunnt) *adj* élégant

element (*è*-li-meunnt) *n* élément *m*

elephant (*è*-li-feunnt) *n* éléphant *m*

elevator (*è*-li-véï-teu) *nAm* ascenseur *m*

eleven (i-*lè*-veunn) *num* onze

eleventh (i-*lè*-veunnθ) *num* onzième

elf (èlf) *n* (pl elves) elfe *m*

eliminate (i-*li*-mi-néït) *v* éliminer

elm (èlm) *n* orme *m*

else (èls) *adv* autrement

elsewhere (èl-s*ou*è*eu*) *adv* ailleurs

elucidate (i-*loú*-si-déït) *v* élucider

emancipation (i-mæn-si-*péï*-cheunn) *n* émancipation *f*

embankment (imm-*bængk*-meunnt) *n* berge *f*

embargo (èm-*bââ*-ghô*ou*) *n* (pl ~es) embargo *m*

embark (imm-*bââk*) *v* embarquer

embarkation (èm-bââ-*kéï*-cheunn) *n* embarquement *m*

embarrass (imm-*bæ*-reuss) *v* embarrasser; déconcerter; gêner; **embarrassed** confus

embassy (*èm*-beu-si) *n* ambassade *f*

emblem (*èm*-bleumm) *n* emblème *m*

embrace (imm-*bréïss*) *v* *étreindre; *n* enlacement *m*

embroider (imm-*broï*-deu) *v* broder

embroidery (imm-*broï*-deu-ri) *n* broderie *f*

emerald (*è*-meu-reuld) *n* émeraude *f*

emergency (i-*meú*-djeunn-si) *n* cas d'urgence, urgence *f*; état d'urgence; ~ **exit** sortie de secours

emigrant (*è*-mi-ghreunnt) *n* émigrant *m*

emigrate (*è*-mi-ghréït) *v* émigrer

emigration (è-mi-*ghréï*-cheunn) *n* émigration *f*

emotion (i-*mô*ou-cheunn) *n* émoi *m*, émotion *f*

emperor (*èm*-peu-reu) *n* empereur *m*

emphasize (*èm*-feu-saïz) *v* souligner

empire (*èm*-paï*eu*) *n* empire *m*

employ (imm-*ploï*) *v* employer; utiliser

employee (èm-ploï-*ii*) *n* employé *m*

employer (imm-*ploï*-eu) *n* employeur *m*

employment (imm-*ploï*-meunnt) *n* emploi *m*; ~ **exchange** bureau de l'emploi

empress (*èm*-priss) *n* impératrice *f*

empty (*èmp*-ti) *adj* vide; *v* vider

enable (i-*néï*-beul) *v* *permettre

enamel (i-*næ*-meul) *n* émail *m*

enamelled (i-*næ*-meuld) *adj* émaillé

enchanting (inn-*tchâân*-tinng) *adj* splendide, ravissant

encircle (inn-*seû*-keul) *v* encercler, entourer

enclose (inng-*klô*ou*z*) *v* *inclure, *joindre

enclosure (inng-*klô*ou-jeu) *n* pièce jointe

encounter (inng-*kaoun*-teu) *v* rencontrer; *n* rencontre *f*

encourage (inng-*ka*-ridj) *v* encourager

encyclopaedia (èn-saï-kleu-*pii*-di-eu) *n* encyclopédie *f*

end (ènd) *n* fin *f*, bout *m*; conclusion *f*; *v* finir

ending (*èn*-dinng) *n* fin *f*

endless (*ènd*-leuss) *adj* infini

endorse (inn-*dooss*) *v* endosser

endure (inn-*dyou*eu) *v* endurer

enemy (*è*-neu-mi) *n* ennemi *m*

energetic (è-neu-*djè*-tik) *adj* énergique

energy (*è*-neu-dji) *n* énergie *f*; puissance *f*

engage (inng-*ghéïdj*) *v* engager; louer; s'engager; **engaged** fiancé; occupé

engagement (inng-*ghéïdj*-meunnt) *n* fiançailles *fpl*; engagement *m*; ~ **ring** bague de fiançailles

engine (*èn*-djinn) *n* machine *f*, moteur *m*; locomotive *f*

engineer (èn-dji-*ni*eu) *n* ingénieur *m*

England (*inng*-ghleunnd) Angleterre *f*

English (*inng*-ghlich) *adj* anglais

Englishman (*inng*-ghlich-meunn) *n* (pl -men) Anglais *m*

engrave (inng-*ghréïv*) *v* graver

engraver (inng-*ghréï*-veu) *n* graveur *m*

engraving (inng-*ghréï*-vinng) *n* estampe *f*; gravure *f*

enigma (i-*nigh*-meu) *n* énigme *f*

enjoy (inn-*djoï*) *v* jouir de, *prendre plaisir

enjoyable (inn-*djoï*-eu-beul) *adj* agréable, plaisant; bon

enjoyment (inn-*djoï*-meunnt) *n* plaisir *m*

enlarge (inn-*lââdj*) *v* agrandir; étendre

enlargement (inn-*lââdj*-meunnt) *n* agrandissement *m*

enormous (i-*noo*-meuss) *adj* gigantesque, énorme

enough (i-*naf*) *adv* assez; *adj* suffisant

enquire (inng-*k*^{ou}*aï*^{eu}) *v* s'informer; enquêter

enquiry (inng-*k*^{ou}*aï*^{eu}-ri) *n* information *f*; investigation *f*; enquête *f*

enter (*èn*-teu) *v* entrer; *inscrire

enterprise (*èn*-teu-praïz) *n* entreprise *f*

entertain (èn-teu-*téïn*) *v* divertir, amuser; *recevoir

entertainer (èn-teu-*téï*-neu) *n* animateur *m*

entertaining (èn-teu-*téï*-ninng) *adj* amusant, divertissant

entertainment (èn-teu-*téïn*-meunnt) *n* amusement *m*, divertissement *m*

enthusiasm (inn-θyoû-zi-æ-zeumm) *n* enthousiasme *m*

enthusiastic (inn-θyoû-zi-æ-stik) *adj* enthousiaste

entire (inn-*taï*^{eu}) *adj* tout, entier

entirely (inn-*taï*^{eu}-li) *adv* entièrement

entrance (*èn*-treunns) *n* entrée *f*; accès *m*

entrance-fee (*èn*-treunns-fii) *n* prix d'entrée

entry (*èn*-tri) *n* entrée *f*; admission *f*; inscription *f*; **no ~** défense d'entrer

envelope (*èn*-veu-lô^{ou}p) *n* enveloppe

f

envious (*èn*-vi-euss) *adj* envieux, jaloux

environment (inn-*vaï*^{eu}-reunn-meunnt) *n* environnement *m*; environs *mpl*

envoy (*èn*-voï) *n* envoyé *m*

envy (*èn*-vi) *n* envie *f*; *v* envier

epic (*è*-pik) *n* poème épique; *adj* épique

epidemic (è-pi-*dè*-mik) *n* épidémie *f*

epilepsy (*è*-pi-lèp-si) *n* épilepsie *f*

epilogue (*è*-pi-logh) *n* épilogue *m*

episode (*è*-pi-sô^{ou}d) *n* épisode *m*

equal (*ii*-k^{ou}eul) *adj* égal; *v* égaler

equality (i-*k*^{ou}*o*-leu-ti) *n* égalité *f*

equalize (*ii*-k^{ou}eu-laïz) *v* égaliser

equally (*ii*-k^{ou}eu-li) *adv* également

equator (i-*k*^{ou}*éï*-teu) *n* équateur *m*

equip (i-*k*^{ou}*ip*) *v* équiper

equipment (i-*k*^{ou}*ip*-meunnt) *n* équipement *m*

equivalent (i-*k*^{ou}*i*-veu-leunnt) *adj* équivalent

eraser (i-*réï*-zeu) *n* gomme *f*

erect (i-*rèkt*) *v* ériger; *adj* debout, droit

err (eû) *v* se tromper, errer

errand (*è*-reunnd) *n* commission *f*

error (*è*-reu) *n* faute *f*, erreur *f*

escalator (*è*-skeu-léï-teu) *n* escalier roulant

escape (i-*skéïp*) *v* échapper; *fuir; *n* évasion *f*

escort¹ (*è*-skoot) *n* escorte *f*

escort² (i-*skoot*) *v* escorter

especially (i-*spè*-cheu-li) *adv* principalement, spécialement

esplanade (è-spleu-*néïd*) *n* esplanade *f*

essay (*è*-séï) *n* essai *m*; dissertation *f*, composition *f*

essence (*è*-seunns) *n* essence *f*; fond *m*, nature *f*

essential (i-*sèn*-cheul) *adj* indispensable; fondamental, essentiel

essentially (i-*sèn*-cheu-li) *adv* essentiellement

establish (i-*stæ*-blich) *v* établir

estate (i-*stéit*) *n* propriété *f*

esteem (i-*stiim*) *n* respect *m*, estime *f*; *v* estimer

estimate¹ (è-sti-méit) *v* évaluer, estimer

estimate² (è-sti-meut) *n* estimation *f*

estuary (*èss*-tchou-eu-ri) *n* estuaire *m*

etcetera (èt-*sè*-teu-reu) et cætera

etching (è-tchinng) *n* eau-forte *f*

eternal (i-*teû*-neul) *adj* éternel

eternity (i-*teû*-nu-ti) *n* éternité *f*

ether (*ii*-θeu) *n* éther *m*

Ethiopia (i-θi-*ô*ᵒᵘ-pi-eu) Ethiopie *f*

Ethiopian (i-θi-*ô*ᵒᵘ-pi-eunn) *adj* éthiopien; *n* Ethiopien *m*

Europe (*you*ᵉᵘ-reup) Europe *f*

European (youᵉᵘ-reu-*pii*-eunn) *adj* européen; *n* Européen *m*

evacuate (i-*væ*-kyou-éit) *v* évacuer

evaluate (i-*væl*-you-éit) *v* évaluer

evaporate (i-*væ*-peu-réit) *v* évaporer

even (*ii*-veunn) *adj* lisse, plan, égal; constant; pair; *adv* même

evening (*iiv*-ninng) *n* soir *m*; ~ **dress** tenue de soirée

event (i-*vènt*) *n* événement *m*; cas *m*

eventual (i-*vèn*-tchou-eul) *adj* éventuel; final

ever (*è*-veu) *adv* jamais; toujours

every (*èv*-ri) *adj* tout, chaque

everybody (*èv*-ri-bo-di) *pron* tout le monde

everyday (*èv*-ri-déi) *adj* quotidien

everyone (*èv*-ri-ᵒᵘann) *pron* chacun, tout le monde

everything (*èv*-ri-θinng) *pron* tout

everywhere (*èv*-ri-ᵒᵘèᵉᵘ) *adv* partout

evidence (*è*-vi-deunns) *n* preuve *f*

evident (*è*-vi-deunnt) *adj* évident

evil (*ii*-veul) *n* mal *m*; *adj* méchant, mauvais

evolution (ii-veu-*loû*-cheunn) *n* évolution *f*

exact (igh-*zækt*) *adj* juste, exact

exactly (igh-*zækt*-li) *adv* exactement

exaggerate (igh-*zæ*-djeu-réit) *v* exagérer

examination (igh-zæ-mi-*néi*-cheunn) *n* examen *m*; interrogatoire *m*

examine (igh-*zæ*-minn) *v* examiner

example (igh-*zââm*-peul) *n* exemple *m*; **for** ~ par exemple

excavation (èks-keu-*véi*-cheunn) *n* excavation *f*

exceed (ik-*siid*) *v* excéder; surpasser

excel (ik-*sèl*) *v* exceller

excellent (*èk*-seu-leunnt) *adj* excellent

except (ik-*sèpt*) *prep* excepté

exception (ik-*sèp*-cheunn) *n* exception *f*

exceptional (ik-*sèp*-cheu-neul) *adj* extraordinaire, exceptionnel

excerpt (*èk*-seûpt) *n* extrait *m*

excess (ik-*sèss*) *n* excès *m*

excessive (ik-*sè*-siv) *adj* excessif

exchange (iks-*tchéindj*) *v* échanger, changer; *n* troc *m*; bourse *f*; ~ **office** bureau de change; ~ **rate** cours du change

excite (ik-*sait*) *v* exciter

excitement (ik-*sait*-meunnt) *n* agitation *f*, excitation *f*

exciting (ik-*saï*-tinng) *adj* passionnant

exclaim (ik-*skléim*) *v* exclamer

exclamation (èk-skleu-*méi*-cheunn) *n* exclamation *f*

exclude (ik-*skloûd*) *v* *exclure

exclusive (ik-*skloû*-siv) *adj* exclusif

exclusively (ik-*skloû*-siv-li) *adv* exclusivement, uniquement

excursion (ik-*skeû*-cheunn) *n* excursion *f*

excuse¹ (ik-*skyoûss*) *n* excuse *f*

excuse² (ik-*skyoûz*) *v* excuser

execute (*è*k-si-kyoût) *v* exécuter

execution (èk-si-*kyoû*-cheunn) *n* exécution *f*

executioner (èk-si-*kyoû*-cheu-neu) *n* bourreau *m*

executive (igh-*zè*-kyou-tiv) *adj* exécutif; *n* pouvoir exécutif; exécutif *m*

exempt (igh-*jèmpt*) *v* dispenser, exempter; *adj* exempt

exemption (igh-*zèmp*-cheunn) *n* exemption *f*

exercise (*è*k-seu-saïz) *n* exercice *m*; *v* exercer

exhale (èks-*héïl*) *v* expirer

exhaust (igh-*zoost*) *n* tuyau d'échappement, échappement *m*; *v* exténuer; ~ **gases** gaz d'échappement

exhibit (ig-*zi*-bit) *v* exposer; exhiber

exhibition (èk-si-*bi*-cheunn) *n* exhibition *f*, exposition *f*

exile (*è*k-saïl) *n* exile *m*; exilé *m*

exist (igh-*zist*) *v* exister

existence (igh-*zi*-steunns) *n* existence *f*

exit (*è*k-sit) *n* sortie *f*

exotic (igh-*zo*-tik) *adj* exotique

expand (ik-*spænd*) *v* étendre; déployer

expect (ik-*spèkt*) *v* attendre

expectation (èk-spèk-*téï*-cheunn) *n* espérance *f*

expedition (èk-speu-*di*-cheunn) *n* expédition *f*

expel (ik-*spèl*) *v* expulser

expenditure (ik-*spèn*-di-tcheu) *n* dépense *f*

expense (ik-*spèns*) *n* dépense *f*; **expenses** *pl* frais *mpl*

expensive (ik-*spèn*-siv) *adj* cher; coûteux

experience (ik-*spi*ᵉ*u*-ri-eunns) *n* expérience *f*; *v* éprouver, *vivre, *faire l'expérience de; **experienced** expérimenté

experiment (ik-*spè*-ri-meunnt) *n* épreuve *f*, expérience *f*; *v* expérimenter

expert (*è*k-speût) *n* spécialiste *m*, expert *m*; *adj* compétent

expire (ik-*spaï*ᵉ*u*-ri) *v* *venir à échéance, se terminer, expirer; **expired** périmé

expiry (ik-*spaï*ᵉ*u*-ri) *n* expiration *f*

explain (ik-*spléïn*) *v* expliquer

explanation (èk-spleu-*néï*-cheunn) *n* éclaircissement *m*, explication *f*

explicit (ik-*spli*-sit) *adj* formel, explicite

explode (ik-*splô*ᵒ*u*d) *v* exploser

exploit (ik-*sploït*) *v* exploiter

explore (ik-*sploo*) *v* explorer

explosion (ik-*splô*ᵒ*u*-jeunn) *n* explosion *f*

explosive (ik-*splô*ᵒ*u*-siv) *adj* explosif; *n* explosif *m*

export[1] (ik-*spoot*) *v* exporter

export[2] (*è*k-spoot) *n* exportation *f*

exportation (èk-spoo-*téï*-cheunn) *n* exportation *f*

exports (*è*k-spoots) *pl* exportation *f*

exposition (èk-speu-*zi*-cheunn) *n* exposition *f*

exposure (ik-*spô*ᵒ*u*-jeu) *n* privation *f*; exposition *f*; ~ **meter** photomètre *m*

express (ik-*sprèss*) *v* exprimer; manifester; *adj* exprès; explicite; ~ **train** train express

expression (ik-*sprè*-cheunn) *n* expression *f*

exquisite (ik-*sk*ᵒ*u*i-zit) *adj* exquis

extend (ik-*stènd*) *v* étendre; agrandir; accorder

extension (ik-*stèn*-cheunn) *n* prolongation *f*; agrandissement *m*; ligne intérieure; ~ **cord** rallonge *f*

extensive (ik-*stèn*-siv) *adj* considérable; vaste, étendu

extent (ik-*stènt*) *n* dimension *f*

exterior (èk-*sti*ᵉᵘ-ri-eu) *adj* extérieur; *n* extérieur *m*

external (èk-*steù*-neul) *adj* extérieur

extinguish (ik-*stinng*-ghᵒᵘich) *v* *éteindre

extort (ik-*stoot*) *v* extorquer

extortion (ik-*stoo*-cheunn) *n* extorsion *f*

extra (*èk*-streu) *adj* supplémentaire

extract¹ (ik-*strækt*) *v* arracher, *extraire

extract² (*èk*-strækt) *n* fragment *m*

extradite (*èk*-streu-daït) *v* extrader

extraordinary (ik-*stroo*-deunn-ri) *adj* extraordinaire

extravagant (ik-*stræ*-veu-gheunnt) *adj* exagéré, extravagant

extreme (ik-*striim*) *adj* extrême; *n* extrême *m*

exuberant (igh-*zyoû*-beu-reunnt) *adj* exubérant

eye (aï) *n* œil *m*

eyebrow (*aï*-braou) *n* sourcil *m*

eyelash (*aï*-læch) *n* cil *m*

eyelid (*aï*-lid) *n* paupière *f*

eye-pencil (*aï*-pèn-seul) *n* crayon pour les yeux

eye-shadow (*aï*-chæ-dôᵒᵘ) *n* ombre à paupières

eye-witness (*aï*-ᵒᵘit-neuss) *n* témoin oculaire

F

fable (*féï*-beul) *n* fable *f*

fabric (*fæ*-brik) *n* tissu *m*; structure *f*

façade (feu-*sââd*) *n* façade *f*

face (féïss) *n* visage *m*; *v* affronter; ~ **massage** massage facial; **facing** en face de

face-cream (*féïss*-kriim) *n* crème de beauté

face-pack (*féïss*-pæk) *n* masque de beauté

face-powder (*féïss*-paou-deu) *n* poudre de riz

facility (feu-*si*-li-ti) *n* facilité *f*

fact (fækt) *n* fait *m*; **in** ~ de fait

factor (*fæk*-teu) *n* facteur *m*

factory (*fæk*-teu-ri) *n* usine *f*

factual (*fæk*-tchou-eul) *adj* réel

faculty (*fæ*-keul-ti) *n* faculté *f*; don *m*, talent *m*, aptitude *f*

fad (fæd) *n* lubie *f*

fade (féïd) *v* se faner, *déteindre

faience (faï-*anss*) *n* faïence *f*

fail (féïl) *v* échouer; manquer; *omettre; **without** ~ sans faute

failure (*féïl*-yeu) *n* échec *m*

faint (féïnt) *v* s'évanouir; *adj* faible, vague, défaillant

fair (fè ᵉᵘ) *n* foire *f*; *adj* honnête, juste; blond; beau

fairly (*fè*ᵉᵘ-li) *adv* assez, plutôt

fairy (*fè*ᵉᵘ-ri) *n* fée *f*

fairytale (*fè*ᵉᵘ-ri-téïl) *n* conte de fées

faith (féïθ) *n* foi *f*; confiance *f*

faithful (*féïθ*-foul) *adj* fidèle

fake (féïk) *n* falsification *f*

fall (fool) *n* chute *f*; *nAm* automne *m*
*fall (fool) *v* tomber

false (foolss) *adj* faux; inexact; ~ **teeth** dentier *m*

falter (*fool*-teu) *v* vaciller; balbutier

fame (féïm) *n* renommée *f*, célébrité *f*; réputation *f*

familiar (feu-*mil*-yeu) *adj* familier

family (*fæ*-meu-li) *n* famille *f*; ~ **name** nom de famille

famous (*féï*-meuss) *adj* fameux

fan (fæn) *n* ventilateur *m*; éventail *m*; fan *m*; ~ **belt** courroie de ventilateur

fanatical (feu-*næ*-ti-keul) *adj* fanatique

fancy (*fæn*-si) *v* aimer, *avoir envie

de; s'imaginer, imaginer; n caprice m; imagination f

fantastic (fæn-*tæ*-stik) adj fantastique

fantasy (*fæn*-teu-zi) n fantaisie f

far (fââ) adj loin; adv beaucoup; **by ~** de beaucoup; **so ~** jusqu'à maintenant

far-away (*fââ*-reu-⁰⁴éi) adj éloigné

farce (fââss) n farce f

fare (fè⁰⁴) n prix du voyage; chère f, nourriture f

farm (fââm) n ferme f

farmer (*fââ*-meu) n fermier m; **farmer's wife** fermière f

farmhouse (*fââm*-haouss) n ferme f

far-off (*fââ*-rof) adj lointain

fascinate (*fæ*-si-néït) v fasciner

fascism (*fæ*-chi-zeumm) n fascisme m

fascist (*fæ*-chist) adj fasciste

fashion (*fæ*-cheunn) n mode f; mode m

fashionable (*fæ*-cheu-neu-beul) adj à la mode

fast (fââst) adj prompt, rapide; ferme

fast-dyed (fââst-*daïd*) adj lavable, grand teint

fasten (*fââ*-seunn) v attacher; fermer

fastener (*fââ*-seu-neu) n fermeture f

fat (fæt) adj gras, gros; n graisse f

fatal (*féï*-teul) adj néfaste, mortel, fatal

fate (féït) n destin m

father (*fââ*-ðeu) n père m

father-in-law (*fââ*-ðeu-rinn-loo) n (pl fathers-) beau-père m

fatherland (*fââ*-ðeu-leunnd) n patrie f

fatness (*fæt*-neuss) n obésité f

fatty (*fæ*-ti) adj gras

faucet (*foo*-sit) nAm robinet m

fault (foolt) n faute f; imperfection f, défaut m

faultless (*foolt*-leuss) adj impeccable; parfait

faulty (*fool*-ti) adj imparfait, défec-

tueux

favour (*féï*-veu) n faveur f; v favoriser

favourable (*féï*-veu-reu-beul) adj favorable

favourite (*féï*-veu-rit) n favori m; adj préféré

fax (faks) n fax m; **send a ~** envoyer un fax

fear (fi⁰⁴) n crainte f, peur f; v *craindre

feasible (*fii*-zeu-beul) adj faisable

feast (fiist) n fête f

feat (fiit) n accomplissement m

feather (*fè*-ðeu) n plume f

feature (*fii*-tcheu) n caractéristique f; trait du visage

February (*fè*-brou-eu-ri) février

federal (*fè*-deu-reul) adj fédéral

federation (fè-deu-*réï*-cheunn) n fédération f; confédération f

fee (fii) n honoraires mpl

feeble (*fii*-beul) adj faible

*feed** (fiid) v nourrir; **fed up with** dégoûté

*feel** (fiil) v *sentir; palper; **~ like** *avoir envie de

feeling (*fii*-linng) n sensation f

fell (fèl) v (p fall)

fellow (*fè*-lô⁰⁴) n gars m

felt¹ (fèlt) n feutre m

felt² (fèlt) v (p, pp feel)

female (*fii*-méïl) adj féminin

feminine (*fè*-mi-ninn) adj féminin

fence (fèns) n clôture f; barrière f; v *faire de l'escrime

fender (*fèn*-deu) n pare-choc m

ferment (feu-*mènt*) v fermenter

ferry-boat (*fè*-ri-bô⁰⁴t) n ferry-boat m

fertile (*feû*-taïl) adj fertile

festival (*fè*-sti-veul) n festival m

festive (*fè*-stiv) adj de fête

fetch (fètch) v apporter; *aller chercher

fever (*fii*-veu) *n* fièvre *f*

feverish (*fii*-veu-rich) *adj* fiévreux

few (fyoû) *adj* peu de

fiancé (fi-*an*-séi) *n* fiancé *m*

fiancée (fi-*an*-séi) *n* fiancée *f*

fibre (*faï*-beu) *n* fibre *f*

fiction (*fik*-cheunn) *n* fiction *f*

field (fiild) *n* champ *m*; domaine *m*; ~ **glasses** jumelles *fpl*

fierce (fi^{eu}ss) *adj* féroce; sauvage, violent

fifteen (fif-*tiin*) *num* quinze

fifteenth (fif-*tiin*θ) *num* quinzième

fifth (fifθ) *num* cinquième

fifty (*fif*-ti) *num* cinquante

fig (figh) *n* figue *f*

fight (faït) *n* lutte *f*, combat *m*

***fight** (faït) *v* se *battre, *combattre

figure (*fi*-gheu) *n* stature *f*, forme *f*; chiffre *m*

file (faïl) *n* lime *f*; dossier *m*; file *f*

Filipino (fi-li-*pii*-nò^{ou}) *n* Philippin *m*

fill (fil) *v* remplir; ~ **in** remplir; **filling station** station-service *f*; ~ **out** *Am* remplir; ~ **up** *faire le plein

filling (*fi*-linng) *n* plombage *m*; farce *f*

film (film) *n* film *m*; pellicule *f*; *v* filmer

filter (*fil*-teu) *n* filtre *m*

filthy (*fil*-θi) *adj* répugnant, sale

final (*faï*-neul) *adj* final

finance (faï-*næns*) *v* financer

finances (faï-*næn*-siz) *pl* finances *fpl*

financial (faï-*næn*-cheul) *adj* financier

finch (finntch) *n* pinson *m*

***find** (faïnd) *v* trouver

fine (faïn) *n* amende *f*; *adj* fin; joli; formidable, merveilleux; ~ **arts** beaux-arts *mpl*

finger (*finng*-gheu) *n* doigt *m*; **little** ~ auriculaire *m*

fingerprint (*finng*-gheu-prinnt) *n* empreinte digitale

finish (*fi*-nich) *v* achever, finir; terminer; *n* fin *f*; ligne d'arrivée

Finland (*finn*-leunnd) Finlande *f*

Finn (finn) *n* Finlandais *m*

Finnish (*fi*-nich) *adj* finlandais

fire (faï^{eu}) *n* feu *m*; incendie *m*; *v* tirer; licencier

fire-alarm (*faï^{eu}*-reu-lââm) *n* alarme d'incendie

fire-brigade (*faï^{eu}*-bri ghéïd) *n* pompiers

fire-escape (*faï^{eu}*-ri-skéïp) *n* escalier de secours

fire-extinguisher (*faï^{eu}*-rik-stinng-gh^{ou}i-cheu) *n* extincteur *m*

fireplace (*faï^{eu}*-pléïss) *n* cheminée *f*

fireproof (*faï^{eu}*-proûf) *adj* ignifuge; qui va au four

firm (feûmm) *adj* ferme; solide; *n* firme *f*

first (feûst) *num* premier; **at** ~ d'abord; au début; ~ **name** prénom *m*

first-aid (feûst-*éïd*) *n* premier secours; ~ **kit** trousse de secours; ~ **post** poste de secours

first-class (feûst-*klââss*) *adj* de première qualité

first-rate (feûst-*réït*) *adj* de premier ordre, de première qualité

fir-tree (*feû*-trii) *n* conifère *m*, sapin *m*

fish¹ (fich) *n* (pl ~, ~es) poisson *m*; ~ **shop** poissonnerie *f*

fish² (fich) *v* pêcher; **fishing gear** attirail de pêche; **fishing hook** hameçon *m*; **fishing industry** pêche *f*; **fishing licence** permis de pêche; **fishing line** ligne de pêche; **fishing net** filet de pêche; **fishing rod** canne à pêche; **fishing tackle** attirail de pêche

fishbone (*fich*-bô^{ou}n) *n* arête *f*

fisherman (*fi*-cheu-meunn) *n* (pl -men)

pêcheur *m*

fist (fist) *n* poing *m*

fit (fit) *adj* convenable; *n* attaque *f*; *v* *convenir; **fitting room** cabine d'essayage

five (faïv) *num* cinq

fix (fiks) *v* réparer

fixed (fikst) *adj* fixe

fizz (fiz) *n* pétillement *m*

fjord (fyood) *n* fjord *m*

flag (flægh) *n* drapeau *m*

flame (fléïm) *n* flamme *f*

flamingo (fleu-*minng*-ghô ᵒᵘ) *n* (pl ~s, ~es) flamant *m*

flannel (*flæ*-neul) *n* flanelle *f*

flash (flæch) *n* éclair *m*

flash-bulb (*flæch*-balb) *n* ampoule de flash

flash-light (*flæch*-laït) *n* lampe de poche

flask (flââsk) *n* flacon *m*; **thermos ~** thermos *m*

flat (flæt) *adj* plan, plat; *n* appartement *m*; ~ **tyre** pneu crevé

flavour (*fléï*-veu) *n* saveur *f*; *v* assaisonner

fleet (fliit) *n* flotte *f*

flesh (flèch) *n* chair *f*

flew (floù) *v* (p fly)

flex (flèks) *n* fil électrique

flexible (*flèk*-si-beul) *adj* flexible; souple

flight (flaït) *n* vol *m*; **charter ~** vol charter

flint (flinnt) *n* pierre à briquet

float (flô ᵒᵘ t) *v* flotter; *n* flotteur *m*

flock (flok) *n* troupeau *m*

flood (flad) *n* inondation *f*; marée haute

floor (floo) *n* sol *m*; étage *m*; ~ **show** spectacle de variétés

florist (*flo*-rist) *n* fleuriste *m*

flour (flaou ᵉᵘ) *n* farine *f*

flow (flô ᵒᵘ) *v* s'écouler, couler

flower (flaou ᵉᵘ) *n* fleur *f*

flowerbed (*flaou* ᵉᵘ -bèd) *n* plate-bande *f*

flower-shop (*flaou* ᵉᵘ -chop) *n* fleuriste *m*

flown (flô ᵒᵘ n) *v* (pp fly)

flu (floù) *n* grippe *f*

fluent (*floû*-eunnt) *adj* couramment

fluid (*floû*-id) *adj* fluide; *n* liquide *m*

flute (floût) *n* flûte *f*

fly (flaï) *n* mouche *f*; braguette *f*

*****fly** (flaï) *v* voler

foam (fô ᵒᵘ m) *n* mousse *f*; *v* mousser

foam-rubber (*fô* ᵒᵘ m-ra-beu) *n* caoutchouc mousse

focus (*fô* ᵒᵘ -keuss) *n* foyer *m*

fog (fogh) *n* brouillard *m*

foggy (*fo*-ghi) *adj* brumeux

foglamp (*fogh*-læmp) *n* phare anti-brouillard

fold (fô ᵒᵘ ld) *v* plier; *n* pli *m*

folk (fô ᵒᵘ k) *n* peuple *m*; ~ **song** chanson populaire

folk-dance (*fô* ᵒᵘ k-dââns) *n* danse folklorique

folklore (*fô* ᵒᵘ k-loo) *n* folklore *m*

follow (*fo*-lô ᵒᵘ) *v* *suivre; **following** *adj* prochain, suivant

*****be fond of** (bii fonnd ov) aimer

food (foûd) *n* nourriture *f*; manger *m*; ~ **poisoning** intoxication alimentaire

foodstuffs (*foûd*-stafs) *pl* aliments *mpl*

fool (foûl) *n* idiot *m*, fou *m*; *v* *faire marcher

foolish (*foû*-lich) *adj* sot, stupide; absurde

foot (fout) *n* (pl feet) pied *m*; ~ **powder** poudre pour les pieds; **on ~** à pied

football (*fout*-bool) *n* ballon *m*; ~ **match** match de football

foot-brake (*fout*-bréïk) *n* frein à pédale

footpath (*fout*-pââθ) *n* sentier pour piétons

footwear (*fout*-ᵒᵘèᵉᵘ) *n* chaussures

for (foo, feu) *prep* pour; pendant; à cause de, en raison de, par; *conj* car

***forbid** (feu-*bid*) *v* *interdire

force (fooss) *v* obliger, forcer; *n* puissance *f*, force *f*; **by ~** forcément; **driving ~** force motrice

ford (food) *n* gué *m*

forecast (*foo*-kââst) *n* prévision *f*; *v* *prévoir

foreground (*foo*-ghraound) *n* premier plan

forehead (*fo*-rèd) *n* front *m*

foreign (*fo*-rinn) *adj* étranger

foreigner (*fo*-ri-neu) *n* étranger *m*

foreman (*foo*-meunn) *n* (pl -men) contremaître *m*

foremost (*foo*-môᵒᵘst) *adj* premier

foresail (*foo*-séil) *n* misaine *f*

forest (*fo*-rist) *n* bois *m*, forêt *f*

forester (*fo*-ri-steu) *n* forestier *m*

forge (foodj) *v* falsifier

***forget** (feu-*ghèt*) *v* oublier

forgetful (feu-*ghèt*-feul) *adj* oublieux

***forgive** (feu-*ghiv*) *v* pardonner

fork (fook) *n* fourchette *f*; bifurcation *f*; *v* bifurquer

form (foom) *n* forme *f*; formulaire *m*; classe *f*; *v* former

formal (*foo*-meul) *adj* cérémonieux

formality (foo-*mæ*-leu-ti) *n* formalité *f*

former (*foo*-meu) *adj* ancien; précédent; **formerly** antérieurement, auparavant

formula (*foo*-myou-leu) *n* (pl ~e, ~s) formule *f*

fort (foot) *n* fort *m*

fortnight (*foot*-naït) *n* quinze jours

fortress (*foo*-triss) *n* forteresse *f*

fortunate (*foo*-tcheu-neut) *adj* heureux

fortune (*foo*-tchoûn) *n* fortune *f*; sort *m*, chance *f*

forty (*foo*-ti) *num* quarante

forward (*foo*-ᵒᵘeud) *adv* en avant; *v* *faire suivre

foster-parents (*fo*-steu-pèᵉᵘ-reunnts) *pl* parents nourriciers

fought (foot) *v* (p, pp fight)

foul (faoul) *adj* malpropre; infâme

found¹ (faound) *v* (p, pp find)

found² (faound) *v* fonder, établir

foundation (faoun-*déï*-cheunn) *n* fondation *f*; **~ cream** fond de teint

fountain (*faoun*-tinn) *n* fontaine *f*; source *f*

fountain-pen (*faoun*-tinn-pèn) *n* stylo *m*

four (foo) *num* quatre

fourteen (foo-*tiin*) *num* quatorze

fourteenth (foo-*tiin*θ) *num* quatorzième

fourth (fooθ) *num* quatrième

fowl (faoul) *n* (pl ~s, ~) volaille *f*

fox (foks) *n* renard *m*

fraction (*fræk*-cheunn) *n* fraction *f*

fracture (*fræk*-tcheu) *v* fracturer; *n* fracture *f*

fragile (*fræ*-djaïl) *adj* fragile

fragment (*frægh*-meunnt) *n* fragment *m*; morceau *m*

frame (fréïm) *n* cadre *m*; monture *f*

France (frââns) France *f*

franchise (*fræn*-tchaïz) *n* droit de vote

fraternity (freu-*teû*-neu-ti) *n* fraternité *f*

fraud (frood) *n* fraude *f*

fray (fréï) *v* s'effilocher

free (frii) *adj* libre; gratuit; **~ of charge** gratuit; **~ ticket** billet gratuit

freedom (*frii*-deumm) *n* liberté *f*

***freeze** (friiz) *v* geler

freezing (*frii*-zinng) *adj* glacial

freezing-point (*frii*-zinng-poïnt) *n* point de congélation

freight (fréït) n fret m, chargement m

freight-train (fréït-tréïn) nAm train de marchandises

French (frèntch) adj français

Frenchman (frèntch-meunn) n (pl -men) Français m

frequency (frii-kᵒᵘeunn-si) n fréquence f

frequent (frii-kᵒᵘeunnt) adj courant, fréquent

fresh (frèch) adj frais; ~ **water** eau douce

friction (frik-cheunn) n friction f

Friday (fraï-di) vendredi m

fridge (fridj) n réfrigérateur m, frigo m

friend (frènd) n ami m; amie f

friendly (frènd-li) adj gentil; amical

friendship (frènd-chip) n amitié f

fright (fraït) n peur f, frayeur f

frighten (fraï-teunn) v effrayer

frightened (fraï-teunnd) adj effrayé; *be ~ *être effrayé

frightful (fraït-feul) adj terrible, affreux

fringe (frinndj) n frange f

frock (frok) n robe f

frog (frogh) n grenouille f

from (fromm) prep de; à partir de

front (frannt) n face f; in ~ of devant

frontier (frann-tiᵉᵘ) n frontière f

frost (frost) n gel m

froth (froθ) n écume f

frozen (frôᵒᵘ-zeunn) adj congelé; ~ **food** aliments surgelés

fruit (froût) n fruits; fruit m

fry (fraï) v *faire sauter; *frire

frying-pan (fraï-inng-pæn) n poêle à frire

fuel (fyoû-eul) n combustible m; essence f; ~ **pump** Am distributeur d'essence

full (foul) adj plein; ~ **board** pension complète; ~ **stop** point m; ~ **up** complet

fun (fann) n divertissement m, plaisir m

function (fanngk-cheunn) n fonction f

fund (fannd) n fonds mpl

fundamental (fann-deu-mèn-teul) adj fondamental

funeral (fyoû-neu-reul) n funérailles fpl

funnel (fa-neul) n entonnoir m

funny (fa-ni) adj drôle, amusant; bizarre

fur (feû) n fourrure f; ~ **coat** manteau de fourrure; **furs** pelage m

furious (fyouᵉᵘ-ri-euss) adj furibond, furieux

furnace (feû-niss) n fournaise f

furnish (feû-nich) v fournir, procurer; installer, meubler; ~ **with** approvisionner en

furniture (feû-ni-tcheu) n meubles

furrier (fa-ri-eu) n fourreur m

further (feû-ðeu) adj plus loin; complémentaire

furthermore (feû-ðeu-moo) adv en outre

furthest (feû-ðist) adj le plus éloigné

fuse (fyoûz) n fusible m; mèche f

fuss (fass) n agitation f; embarras m, chichi m

future (fyoû-tcheu) n avenir m; adj futur

G

gable (ghéï-beul) n pignon m

gadget (ghæ-djit) n gadget m

gaiety (ghéï-eu-ti) n gaîté f

gain (ghéïn) v gagner; n gain m

gait (ghéït) n allure f, démarche f

gale (ghéïl) n tempête f

gall (ghool) n bile f; ~ **bladder** vésicule biliaire

gallery (*ghæ*-leu-ri) *n* galerie *f*

gallop (*ghæ*-leup) *n* galop *m*

gallows (*ghæ*-lô⁰ᵘz) *pl* gibet *m*

gallstone (*ghool*-stô⁰ᵘn) *n* calcul biliaire

game (ghéïm) *n* jeu *m*; gibier *m*; ~ **reserve** réserve zoologique

gang (ghæng) *n* bande *f*; équipe *f*

gangway (*ghæng*-⁰ᵘéï) *n* passerelle *f*

gaol (djéïl) *n* prison *f*

gap (ghæp) *n* brèche *f*

garage (*ghæ*-râãj) *n* garage *m*; *v* garer

garbage (*ghâã*-bidj) *n* détritus *m*, ordures *fpl*

garden (*ghâã*-deunn) *n* jardin *m*; **public** ~ jardin public; **zoological gardens** jardin zoologique

gardener (*ghâã*-deu-neu) *n* jardinier *m*

gargle (*ghâã*-gheul) *v* se gargariser

garlic (*ghâã*-lik) *n* ail *m*

gas (ghæss) *n* gaz *m*; *nAm* essence *f*; ~ **cooker** cuisinière à gaz; ~ **pump** *Am* pompe à essence; ~ **station** *Am* station-service *f*; ~ **stove** fourneau à gaz

gasoline (*ghæ*-seu-liin) *nAm* essence *f*

gastric (*ghæ*-strik) *adj* gastrique; ~ **ulcer** ulcère à l'estomac

gasworks (*ghæss*-⁰ᵘeûks) *n* usine à gaz

gate (ghéït) *n* porte *f*; grille *f*

gather (*ghæ*-ðeu) *v* collectionner; se réunir; rentrer

gauge (ghéïdj) *n* jauge *f*

gauze (ghooz) *n* gaze *f*

gave (ghéïv) *v* (p give)

gay (ghéï) *adj* gai; éclatant

gaze (ghéïz) *v* fixer

gear (ghi⁰ᵘ) *n* vitesse *f*; équipement *m*; **change** ~ changer de vitesse; ~ **lever** levier de vitesse

gear-box (*ghi⁰ᵘ*-boks) *n* boîte de vitesse

gem (djèm) *n* joyau *m*, pierre précieuse; bijou *m*

gender (*djèn*-deu) *n* genre *m*

general (*djè*-neu-reul) *adj* général; en général *m*; ~ **practitioner** médecin généraliste; **in** ~ en général

generate (*djè*-neu-réït) *v* *produire

generation (djè-neu-*réï*-chounn) *n* génération *f*

generator (*djè*-neu-réï-teur) *n* générateur *m*

generosity (djè-neu-*ro*-seu-ti) *n* générosité *f*

generous (*djè*-neu-reuss) *adj* large, généreux

genital (*djè*-ni-teul) *adj* génital

genius (*djii*-ni-euss) *n* génie *m*

gentle (*djèn*-teul) *adj* doux; léger; délicat

gentleman (*djèn*-teul-meunn) *n* (pl -men) monsieur *m*

genuine (*djè*-nyou-inn) *adj* authentique

geography (dji-*o*-ghreu-fi) *n* géographie *f*

geology (dji-*o*-leu-dji) *n* géologie *f*

geometry (dji-*o*-meu-tri) *n* géométrie *f*

germ (djeûmm) *n* microbe *m*; germe *m*

German (*djeû*-meunn) *adj* allemand; *n* Allemand *m*

Germany (*djeû*-meu-ni) Allemagne *f*

gesticulate (dji-*sti*-kyou-léït) *v* gesticuler

*get (ghèt) *v* *obtenir; *aller prendre; *devenir; ~ **back** retourner; ~ **off** descendre; ~ **on** monter; progresser; ~ **up** se lever

ghost (ghô⁰ᵘst) *n* fantôme *m*; esprit *m*

giant (*djaï*-eunnt) *n* géant *m*

giddiness (*ghi*-di-neuss) *n* vertige *m*

giddy (*ghi*-di) *adj* étourdi

gift (ghift) *n* don *m*, cadeau *m*; talent *m*

gifted (*ghif*-tid) *adj* doué

gigantic (djaï-*ghæn*-tik) *adj* gigantesque

giggle (*ghi*-gheul) *v* glousser

gill (ghil) *n* branchie *f*

gilt (ghilt) *adj* doré

ginger (*djin*-djeu) *n* gingembre *m*

gipsy (*djip*-si) *n* bohémien *m*

girdle (*gheû*-deul) *n* gaine *f*

girl (gheûl) *n* fille *f*; ~ **guide** scout *m*

*give (ghiv) *v* donner; passer; ~ **away** révéler; ~ **in** céder; ~ **up** renoncer

glacier (*ghlæ*-si-eu) *n* glacier *m*

glad (ghlæd) *adj* joyeux, content; **gladly** avec plaisir, volontiers

gladness (*ghlæd*-neuss) *n* joie *f*

glamorous (*ghlæ*-meu-reuss) *adj* enchanteur, charmant

glamour (*ghlæ*-meu) *n* charme *m*

glance (ghlâânss) *n* coup d'œil; *v* jeter un coup d'œil

gland (ghlænd) *n* glande *f*

glare (ghlè\ eu) *n* éclat *m*; éblouissement *m*

glaring (*ghlè\ eu*-rinng) *adj* éblouissant

glass (ghlââss) *n* verre *m*; de verre; **glasses** lunettes *fpl*; **magnifying** ~ verre grossissant

glaze (ghléïz) *v* vernir

glen (ghlèn) *n* gorge *f*

glide (ghlaïd) *v* glisser

glider (*ghlaï*-deu) *n* planeur *m*

glimpse (ghlimmpss) *n* aperçu *m*; coup d'œil; *v* *entrevoir

global (*ghlô\ ou*-beul) *adj* mondial

globe (ghlô\ oub) *n* globe *m*

gloom (ghloûm) *n* ténèbres *fpl*

gloomy (*ghloû*-mi) *adj* sombre

glorious (*ghloo*-ri-euss) *adj* splendide

glory (*ghloo*-ri) *n* gloire *f*; honneur *m*, louange *f*

gloss (ghloss) *n* lustre *m*

glossy (*ghlo*-si) *adj* luisant

glove (ghlav) *n* gant *m*

glow (ghlô\ ou) *v* briller; *n* éclat *m*

glue (ghloû) *n* colle *f*

*go (ghô\ ou) *v* se rendre, *aller; marcher; *devenir; ~ **ahead** continuer; ~ **away** *partir; ~ **back** retourner; ~ **home** rentrer; ~ **in** entrer; ~ **on** continuer; ~ **out** *sortir; ~ **through** endurer

goal (ghô\ oul) *n* objectif *m*, but *m*

goalkeeper (*ghô\ oul*-kii-peu) *n* gardien de but

goat (ghô\ out) *n* bouc *m*, chèvre *f*

god (ghod) *n* dieu *m*

goddess (*gho*-diss) *n* déesse *f*

godfather (*ghod*-fââ-ðeu) *n* parrain *m*

goggles (*gho*-gheulz) *pl* lunettes de plongée

gold (ghô\ ould) *n* or *m*; ~ **leaf** or en feuille

golden (*ghô\ oul*-deunn) *adj* en or

goldmine (*ghô\ ould*-maïn) *n* mine d'or

goldsmith (*ghô\ ould*-smiθ) *n* orfèvre *m*

golf (gholf) *n* golf *m*

golf-club (*gholf*-klab) *n* club de golf

golf-course (*gholf*-kooss) *n* terrain de golf

golf-links (*gholf*-linngks) *n* terrain de golf

gondola (*ghonn*-deu-leu) *n* gondole *f*

gone (ghonn) *adv* (pp go) parti

good (ghoud) *adj* bon; sage, brave

good-bye! (ghoud-*baï*) au revoir!

good-humoured (ghoud-*hyoû*-meud) *adj* de bonne humeur

good-looking (ghoud-*lou*-kinng) *adj* joli

good-natured (ghoud-*néï*-tcheud) *adj* de bon caractère

goods (ghoudz) *pl* marchandise *f*, biens *mpl*; ~ **train** train de marchandises

good-tempered (*ghoud-tèm-peud*) *adj* de bonne humeur

goodwill (*ghoud-*ou*il*) *n* bienveillance *f*

goose (*ghoûss*) *n* (pl geese) oie *f*

gooseberry (*ghouz-beu-ri*) *n* groseille à maquereau

goose-flesh (*ghoûss-flèch*) *n* chair de poule

gorge (*ghoodj*) *n* gorge *f*

gorgeous (*ghoo-djeuss*) *adj* magnifique

gospel (*gho-speul*) *n* évangile *m*

gossip (*gho-sip*) *n* commérage *m*; *v* *faire des commérages

got (*ghot*) *v* (p, pp get)

gout (*ghaout*) *n* goutte *f*

govern (*gha-veunn*) *v* gouverner

governess (*gha-veu-niss*) *n* gouvernante *f*

government (*gha-veunn-meunnt*) *n* régime *m*, gouvernement *m*

governor (*gha-veu-neu*) *n* gouverneur *m*

gown (*ghaoun*) *n* robe *f*

grace (*ghréiss*) *n* grâce *f*; clémence *f*

graceful (*ghréïss-feul*) *adj* charmant, gracieux

grade (*ghréïd*) *n* grade *m*; *v* classer

gradient (*ghréï-di-eunnt*) *n* inclinaison *f*

gradual (*ghræ-djou-eul*) *adj* graduel

graduate (*ghræ-djou-éït*) *v* *obtenir un diplôme

grain (*ghréïn*) *n* grain *m*, blé *m*, céréale *f*

gram (*ghræm*) *n* gramme *m*

grammar (*ghræ-meu*) *n* grammaire *f*

grammatical (*ghreu-mæ-ti-keul*) *adj* grammatical

gramophone (*ghræ-meu-fô*ou*n*) *n* phonographe *m*

grand (*ghrænd*) *adj* sublime

granddad (*ghræn-dæd*) *n* grand-papa *m*

granddaughter (*ghræn-doo-teu*) *n* petite-fille *f*

grandfather (*ghræn-fââ-ðeu*) *n* grand-père *m*; pépé *m*; bon-papa *m*

grandmother (*ghræn-ma-ðeu*) *n* grand-mère *f*; mémé *f*, bonne-maman *f*

grandparents (*ghræn-pè*eu*-reunnts*) *pl* grands-parents *mpl*

grandson (*ghræn-sann*) *n* petit-fils *m*

granite (*ghræ-nit*) *n* granit *m*

grant (*ghrâânt*) *v* accorder; concéder; *n* subvention *f*, bourse *f*

grapefruit (*ghréïp-froût*) *n* pamplemousse *m*

grapes (*ghréïps*) *pl* raisin *m*

graph (*ghræf*) *n* diagramme *m*

graphic (*ghræ-fik*) *adj* graphique

grasp (*ghrââsp*) *v* saisir; *n* prise *f*

grass (*ghrââss*) *n* herbe *f*

grasshopper (*ghrââss-ho-peu*) *n* sauterelle *f*

grate (*ghréït*) *n* grille *f*; *v* râper

grateful (*ghréït-feul*) *adj* reconnaissant

grater (*ghréï-teu*) *n* râpe *f*

gratis (*ghræ-tiss*) *adj* gratuit

gratitude (*ghræ-ti-tyoûd*) *n* gratitude *f*

gratuity (*ghreu-tyoû-eu-ti*) *n* pourboire *m*

grave (*ghréïv*) *n* tombe *f*; *adj* grave

gravel (*ghræ-veul*) *n* gravier *m*

gravestone (*ghréïv-stô*ou*n*) *n* pierre tombale

graveyard (*ghréïv-yââd*) *n* cimetière *m*

gravity (*ghræ-veu-ti*) *n* gravité *f*

gravy (*ghréï-vi*) *n* jus *m*

graze (*ghréïz*) *v* *paître; *n* égratignure *f*

grease (*ghriiss*) *n* graisse *f*; *v* graisser

greasy (*ghrii-si*) *adj* graisseux

great (ghréït) *adj* grand; **Great Britain** Grande-Bretagne *f*

Greece (ghriiss) Grèce *f*

greed (ghriid) *n* cupidité *f*

greedy (*ghrii*-di) *adj* cupide; gourmand

Greek (ghriik) *adj* grec; *n* Grec *m*

green (ghriin) *adj* vert; ~ **card** carte verte

greengrocer (*ghriin*-ghrô^{ou}-seu) *n* marchand de légumes

greenhouse (*ghriin*-haouss) *n* serre *f*

greens (ghriinz) *pl* légumes *mpl*

greet (ghriit) *v* saluer

greeting (*ghrii*-tinng) *n* salutation *f*

grey (ghréï) *adj* gris

greyhound (*ghréï*-haound) *n* lévrier *m*

grief (ghriif) *n* chagrin *m*; affliction *f*, douleur *f*

grieve (ghriiv) *v* *avoir de la peine

grill (ghril) *n* grill *m*; *v* griller

grill-room (*ghril*-roûm) *n* rôtisserie *f*

grin (ghrinn) *n* sourire forcé

***grind** (ghraïnd) *v* *moudre; pulvériser

grip (ghrip) *v* saisir; *n* prise *f*, étreinte *f*; *nAm* mallette *f*

grit (ghrit) *n* gravillon *m*

groan (ghrô^{ou}n) *v* gémir

grocer (*ghrô^{ou}*-seu) *n* épicier *m*; **grocer's** épicerie *f*

groceries (*ghrô^{ou}*-seu-riz) *pl* articles d'épicerie

groin (ghroïn) *n* aine *f*

groove (ghroûv) *n* sillon *m*

gross[1] (ghrô^{ou}ss) *n* (pl ~) grosse *f*

gross[2] (ghrô^{ou}ss) *adj* grossier; brut

grotto (*ghro*-tô^{ou}) *n* (pl ~es, ~s) grotte *f*

ground[1] (ghraound) *n* fond *m*, sol *m*; ~ **floor** rez-de-chaussée *m*; **grounds** terrain *m*

ground[2] (ghraound) *v* (p, pp grind)

group (ghroûp) *n* groupe *m*

grouse (ghraouss) *n* (pl ~) coq de bruyère

grove (ghrô^{ou}v) *n* bosquet *m*

***grow** (ghrô^{ou}) *v* grandir; cultiver; *devenir

growl (ghraoul) *v* grogner

grown-up (*ghrô^{ou}n*-ap) *adj* adulte; *n* adulte *m*

growth (ghrô^{ou}θ) *n* croissance *f*; tumeur *f*

grudge (ghradj) *v* envier

grumble (*ghramm*-beul) *v* grogner

guarantee (ghæ-reunn-*tii*) *n* garantie *f*; caution *f*; *v* garantir

guarantor (ghæ-reunn-*too*) *n* garant *m*

guard (ghââd) *n* garde *m*; *v* surveiller

guardian (*ghââ*-di-eunn) *n* tuteur *m*

guess (ghèss) *v* deviner; *croire, supposer; *n* conjecture *f*

guest (ghèst) *n* hôte *m*, invité *m*

guest-house (*ghèst*-haouss) *n* pension *f*

guest-room (*ghèst*-roûm) *n* chambre d'ami

guide (ghaïd) *n* guide *m*; *v* *conduire

guidebook (*ghaïd*-bouk) *n* guide *m*

guide-dog (*ghaïd*-dogh) *n* chien d'aveugle

guilt (ghilt) *n* culpabilité *f*

guilty (*ghil*-ti) *adj* coupable

guinea-pig (*ghi*-ni-pigh) *n* cochon d'Inde

guitar (ghi-*tââ*) *n* guitare *f*

gulf (ghalf) *n* golfe *m*

gull (ghal) *n* mouette *f*

gum (ghamm) *n* gencive *f*; gomme *f*; colle *f*

gun (ghann) *n* fusil *m*, revolver *m*; canon *m*

gunpowder (*ghann*-paou-deu) *n* poudre à canon

gust (ghast) *n* rafale *f*

gusty (*gha*-sti) *adj* venteux

gut (ghat) *n* intestin *m*; **guts** cran *m*

gutter (*gha*-teu) *n* caniveau *m*

guy (ghaï) *n* type *m*

gymnasium (djimm-*néï*-zi-eumm) *n* (pl ~s, -sia) gymnase *m*

gymnast (*djimm*-næst) *n* gymnaste *m*

gymnastics (djimm-*næ*-stiks) *pl* gymnastique *f*

gynaecologist (ghaï-neu-*ko*-leu-djist) *n* gynécologue *m*

H

haberdashery (*hæ*-beu-dæ-cheu-ri) *n* mercerie *f*

habit (*hæ*-bit) *n* habitude *f*

habitable (*hæ*-bi-teu-beul) *adj* habitable

habitual (heu-*bi*-tchou-eul) *adj* habituel

had (hæd) *v* (p, pp have)

haddock (*hæ*-deuk) *n* (pl ~) aiglefin *m*

haemorrhage (*hè*-meu-ridj) *n* hémorragie *f*

haemorrhoids (*hè*-meu-roïdz) *pl* hémorroïdes *fpl*

hail (héïl) *n* grêle *f*

hair (hè*eu*) *n* cheveu *m*; ~ **cream** crème capillaire; ~ **gel** gel pour les cheveux *m*; ~ **piece** postiche *m*; ~ **rollers** bigoudis *mpl*

hairbrush (*hè**eu*-brach) *n* brosse à cheveux

haircut (*hè**eu*-kat) *n* coupe de cheveux

hair-do (*hè**eu*-doù) *n* coiffure *f*

hairdresser (*hè**eu*-drè-seu) *n* coiffeur *m*

hair-dryer (*hè**eu*-draï-eu) *n* sèche-cheveux *m*

hair-grip (*hè**eu*-ghrip) *n* pince à cheveux

hair-net (*hè**eu*-nèt) *n* résille *f*

hair-oil (*hè**eu*-roïl) *n* huile capillaire

hairpin (*hè**eu*-pinn) *n* épingle à cheveux

hair-spray (*hè**eu*-spréï) *n* laque capillaire

hairy (*hè**eu*-ri) *adj* chevelu

half¹ (hââf) *adj* demi; *adv* à moitié

half² (hââf) *n* (pl halves) moitié *f*

half-time (hââf-*taïm*) *n* mi-temps *f*

halfway (hââf-*ou*éï) *adv* à mi-chemin

halibut (*hæ*-li-beut) *n* (pl ~) flétan *m*

hall (hool) *n* vestibule *m*; salle *f*

halt (hoolt) *v* s'arrêter

halve (hââv) *v* diviser en deux

ham (hæm) *n* jambon *m*

hamlet (*hæm*-leut) *n* hameau *m*

hammer (*hæ*-meu) *n* marteau *m*

hammock (*hæ*-meuk) *n* hamac *m*

hamper (*hæm*-peu) *n* panier *m*

hand (hænd) *n* main *f*; *v* *remettre; ~ **cream** crème pour les mains

handbag (*hænd*-bægh) *n* sac à main

handbook (*hænd*-bouk) *n* manuel *m*

hand-brake (*hænd*-bréïk) *n* frein à main

handcuffs (*hænd*-kafs) *pl* menottes *fpl*

handful (*hænd*-foul) *n* poignée *f*

handicraft (*hæn*-di-krââft) *n* travail manuel; artisanat *m*

handkerchief (*hæng*-keu-tchif) *n* mouchoir *m*

handle (*hæn*-deul) *n* manche *m*, poignée *f*; *v* manipuler; traiter

hand-made (hænd-*méïd*) *adj* fait à la main

handshake (*hænd*-chéïk) *n* poignée de main

handsome (*hæn*-seumm) *adj* beau

handwork (*hænd*-*ou*eûk) *n* travail artisanal

handwriting (*hænd*-raï-tinng) *n* écriture *f*

handy (*hæn*-di) *adj* commode

*hang (hæng) *v* suspendre; pendre

hanger (*hæng*-eu) *n* cintre *m*

hangover (*hæng*-ô^{ou}-veu) *n* gueule de bois

happen (*hæ*-peunn) *v* se *produire, arriver

happening (*hæ*-peu-ninng) *n* événement *m*

happiness (*hæ*-pi-neuss) *n* bonheur *m*

happy (*hæ*-pi) *adj* content, heureux

harbour (*hââ*-beu) *n* port *m*

hard (hââd) *adj* dur; difficile; **hardly** à peine

hardware (*hââd*-^{ou}è^{eu}) *n* quincaillerie *f*; ~ **store** quincaillerie *f*

hare (hè^{eu}) *n* lièvre *m*

harm (hââm) *n* mal *m*; tort *m*; *v* *faire du mal

harmful (*hââm*-feul) *adj* préjudiciable, nuisible

harmless (*hââm*-leuss) *adj* inoffensif

harmony (*hââ*-meu-ni) *n* harmonie *f*

harp (hââp) *n* harpe *f*

harpsichord (*hââp*-si-kood) *n* clavecin *m*

harsh (hââch) *adj* âpre; sévère; cruel

harvest (*hââ*-vist) *n* moisson *f*

has (hæz) *v* (pr have)

haste (héïst) *n* promptitude *f*, hâte *f*

hasten (*héï*-seunn) *v* se hâter

hasty (*héï*-sti) *adj* précipité

hat (hæt) *n* chapeau *m*; ~ **rack** porte-manteau *m*

hatch (hætch) *n* trappe *f*

hate (héït) *v* détester; *haïr; *n* haine *f*

hatred (*héï*-trid) *n* haine *f*

haughty (*hoo*-ti) *adj* hautain

haul (hool) *v* traîner

*have (hæv) *v* *avoir; *faire; ~ **to** *devoir

haversack (*hæ*-veu-sæk) *n* havresac *m*

hawk (hook) *n* faucon *m*

hay (héï) *n* foin *m*; ~ **fever** rhume des foins

hazard (*hæ*-zeud) *n* hasard *m*

haze (héïz) *n* brume *f*

hazelnut (*héï*-zeul-nat) *n* noisette *f*

hazy (*héï*-zi) *adj* brumeux; nébuleux

he (hii) *pron* il

head (hèd) *n* tête *f*; *v* diriger; ~ **of state** chef d'Etat; ~ **teacher** directeur d'école

headache (*hè*-déïk) *n* mal de tête

heading (*hè*-dinng) *n* titre *m*

headlamp (*hèd*-læmp) *n* phare *m*

headland (*hèd*-leunnd) *n* promontoire *m*

headlight (*hèd*-laït) *n* phare *m*

headline (*hèd*-laïn) *n* manchette *f*

headmaster (hèd-*mââ*-steu) *n* directeur d'école

headquarters (hèd-*k^{ou}oo*-teuz) *pl* quartier général

head-strong (*hèd*-stronng) *adj* têtu

head-waiter (hèd-^{ou}*éï*-teu) *n* maître d'hôtel

heal (hiil) *v* guérir

health (hèlθ) *n* santé *f*; ~ **centre** dispensaire *m*; ~ **certificate** certificat médical

healthy (*hèl*-θi) *adj* sain

heap (hiip) *n* amoncellement *m*, tas *m*

*hear (hi^{eu}) *v* entendre

hearing (*hi^{eu}*-rinng) *n* ouïe *f*

heart (hâât) *n* cœur *m*; **by** ~ par cœur; ~ **attack** crise cardiaque

heartburn (*hâât*-beunn) *n* brûlures d'estomac

hearth (hââθ) *n* cheminée *f*

heartless (*hâât*-leuss) *adj* insensible

hearty (*hââ*-ti) *adj* cordial

heat (hiit) *n* chaleur *f*; *v* chauffer; **heating pad** coussin chauffant

heater (*hii*-teu) *n* appareil de chauffage; **immersion** ~ thermoplongeur *m*

heath (hiiθ) *n* lande *f*

heathen (*hii*-ðeunn) *n* païen *m*

heather (*hè*-ðeu) *n* bruyère *f*

heating (*hii*-tinng) *n* chauffage *m*

heaven (*hè*-veunn) *n* ciel *m*

heavy (*hè*-vi) *adj* lourd

Hebrew (*hii*-brou) *n* hébreu *m*

hedge (hèdj) *n* haie *f*

hedgehog (*hèdj*-hogh) *n* hérisson *m*

heel (hiil) *n* talon *m*

height (haït) *n* hauteur *f*; sommet *m*, apogée *m*

hell (hèl) *n* enfer *m*

hello! (hè-*lôou*) bonjour!

helm (hèlm) *n* barre *f*

helmet (*hèl*-mit) *n* casque *m*

helmsman (*hèlmz*-meunn) *n* timonier *m*

help (hèlp) *v* aider; *n* aide *f*

helper (*hèl*-peu) *n* aide *m*

helpful (*hèlp*-feul) *adj* serviable

helping (*hèl*-pinng) *n* portion *f*

hem (hèm) *n* ourlet *m*

hemp (hèmp) *n* chanvre *m*

hen (hèn) *n* poule *f*

henceforth (hèns-*fooθ*) *adv* dorénavant

her (heû) *pron* la *art/pron*, lui; *adj* son

herb (heûb) *n* herbe *f*

herd (heûd) *n* troupeau *m*

here (hieu) *adv* ici; ~ **you are** voilà

hereditary (hi-*rè*-di-teu-ri) *adj* héréditaire

hernia (*heû*-ni-eu) *n* hernie *f*

hero (*hieu*-rôou) *n* (pl ~es) héros *m*

heron (*hè*-reunn) *n* héron *m*

herring (*hè*-rinng) *n* (pl ~, ~s) hareng *m*

herself (heû-*sèlf*) *pron* se; elle-même

hesitate (*hè*-zi-téït) *v* hésiter

heterosexual (hè-teu-reu-*sèk*-chou-eul)

adj hétérosexuel

hiccup (*hi*-kap) *n* hoquet *m*

hide (haïd) *n* peau *f*

** **hide** (haïd) *v* cacher; dissimuler

hideous (*hi*-di-euss) *adj* hideux

hierarchy (*haïeu*-râ-ki) *n* hiérarchie *f*

high (haï) *adj* haut

highway (*haï*-ouéï) *n* route principale; *nAm* autoroute *f*

hijack (*haï*-djæk) *v* détourner

hike (haïk) *v* faire des randonnées

hill (hil) *n* colline *f*

hillock (*hi*-leuk) *n* monticule *m*

hillside (*hil*-saïd) *n* coteau *m*

hilltop (*hil*-top) *n* sommet de colline

hilly (*hi*-li) *adj* accidenté

him (himm) *pron* le, lui

himself (himm-*sèlf*) *pron* se; lui-même

hinder (*hinn*-deu) *v* gêner

hinge (hinndj) *n* charnière *f*

hip (hip) *n* hanche *f*

hire (haïeu) *v* louer; **for** ~ à louer

hire-purchase (haïeu-*peû*-tcheuss) *n* achat à tempérament

his (hiz) *adj* son

historian (hi-*stoo*-ri-eunn) *n* historien *m*

historic (hi-*sto*-rik) *adj* historique

historical (hi-*sto*-ri-keul) *adj* historique

history (*hi*-steu-ri) *n* histoire *f*

hit (hit) *n* succès *m*

** **hit** (hit) *v* frapper; toucher

hitchhike (*hitch*-haïk) *v* *faire de l'auto-stop

hitchhiker (*hitch*-haï-keu) *n* auto-stoppeur *m*

hoarse (hooss) *adj* rauque, enroué

hobby (*ho*-bi) *n* hobby *m*, passe-temps *m*

hobby-horse (*ho*-bi-hooss) *n* dada *m*

hockey (*ho*-ki) *n* hockey *m*

hoist (hoïst) *v* hisser

hold (hô^{ou}ld) *n* cale *f*

***hold** (hô^{ou}ld) *v* *tenir; garder; ~ **on** s'accrocher; ~ **up** *soutenir

hold-up (hô^{ou}l-dap) *n* attaque *f*

hole (hô^{ou}l) *n* trou *m*

holiday (ho-leu-di) *n* vacances; jour de fête; ~ **camp** camp de vacances; ~ **resort** villégiature *f*; **on** ~ en vacances

Holland (ho-leunnd) Hollande *f*

hollow (ho-lô^{ou}) *adj* creux

holy (hô^{ou}-li) *adj* sacré

homage (ho-midj) *n* hommage *m*

home (hô^{ou}m) *n* maison *f*; foyer *m*, demeure *f*; *adv* chez soi; **at** ~ à la maison

home-made (hô^{ou}m-*méïd*) *adj* fait à la maison

homesickness (hô^{ou}m-sik-neuss) *n* mal du pays

homosexual (hô^{ou}-meu-*sèk*-chou-eul) *adj* homosexuel

honest (o-nist) *adj* honnête; sincère

honesty (o-ni-sti) *n* honnêteté *f*

honey (ha-ni) *n* miel *m*

honeymoon (ha-ni-moûn) *n* lune de miel

honk (hanngk) *vAm* klaxonner

honour (o-neu) *n* honneur *m*; *v* honorer, rendre hommage

honourable (o-neu-reu-beul) *adj* honorable; honnête

hood (houd) *n* capuchon *m*; *nAm* capot *m*

hoof (hoûf) *n* sabot *m*

hook (houk) *n* crochet *m*

hoot (hoût) *v* klaxonner

hooter (hoû-teu) *n* klaxon *m*

hoover (hoû-veu) *v* passer l'aspirateur

hop¹ (hop) *v* sautiller; *n* saut *m*

hop² (hop) *n* houblon *m*

hope (hô^{ou}p) *n* espoir *m*; *v* espérer

hopeful (hô^{ou}p-feul) *adj* plein d'espoir

hopeless (hô^{ou}p-leuss) *adj* désespéré

horizon (heu-*raï*-zeunn) *n* horizon *m*

horizontal (ho-ri-*zonn*-teul) *adj* horizontal

horn (hoon) *n* corne *f*; cor *m*; klaxon *m*

horrible (ho-ri-beul) *adj* horrible; terrifiant, atroce, horrifiant

horror (ho-reu) *n* épouvante *f*, horreur *f*

horse (hooss) *n* cheval *m*

horseman (hooss-meunn) *n* (pl -men) cavalier *m*

horsepower (hooss-paou^{eu}) *n* cheval-vapeur *m*

horserace (hooss-réïss) *n* course de chevaux

horseradish (hooss-ræ-dich) *n* raifort *m*

horseshoe (hooss-choû) *n* fer à cheval

horticulture (hoo-ti-kal-tcheu) *n* horticulture *f*

hosiery (hô^{ou}-jeu-ri) *n* bonneterie *f*

hospitable (ho-spi-teu-beul) *adj* hospitalier

hospital (ho-spi-teul) *n* hôpital *m*

hospitality (ho-spi-*tæ*-leu-ti) *n* hospitalité *f*

host (hô^{ou}st) *n* hôte *m*

hostage (ho-stidj) *n* otage *m*

hostel (ho-steul) *n* auberge *f*

hostess (hô^{ou}-stiss) *n* hôtesse *f*

hostile (ho-staïl) *adj* hostile

hot (hot) *adj* chaud

hotel (hô^{ou}-*tèl*) *n* hôtel *m*

hot-tempered (hot-*tèm*-peud) *adj* coléreux

hour (aou^{eu}) *n* heure *f*

hourly (aou^{eu}-li) *adj* toutes les heures

house (haouss) *n* maison *f*; habitation *f*; immeuble *m*; ~ **agent** agent immobilier; ~ **block** *Am* pâté de maisons; **public** ~ café *m*

houseboat (haouss-bô^{ou}t) *n* maison-bateau

household (*haouss*-hô^{ou}ld) *n* ménage *m*

housekeeper (*haouss*-kii-peu) *n* gouvernante *f*

housekeeping (*haouss*-kii-pinng) *n* travaux ménagers, ménage *m*

housemaid (*haouss*-méïd) *n* bonne *f*

housewife (*haouss*-^{ou}aïf) *n* ménagère *f*

housework (*haouss*-^{ou}eûk) *n* travaux ménagers

how (haou) *adv* comment; que; ~ **many** combien; ~ **much** combien

however (haou-è-veu) *conj* pourtant, cependant

hug (hagh) *v* *étreindre; *n* étreinte *f*

huge (hyoûdj) *adj* immense, énorme

hum (hamm) *v* fredonner

human (*hyoû*-meunn) *adj* humain; ~ **being** être humain

humanity (hyou-*mæ*-neu-ti) *n* humanité *f*

humble (*hamm*-beul) *adj* humble

humid (*hyoû*-mid) *adj* humide

humidity (hyou-*mi*-deu-ti) *n* humidité *f*

humorous (*hyoû*-meu-reuss) *adj* comique, spirituel, drôle

humour (*hyoû*-meu) *n* humour *m*

hundred (*hann*-dreud) *n* cent

Hungarian (hanng-*ghè^{eu}*-ri-eunn) *adj* hongrois; *n* Hongrois *m*

Hungary (*hanng*-gheu-ri) Hongrie *f*

hunger (*hanng*-gheu) *n* faim *f*

hungry (*hanng*-ghri) *adj* affamé

hunt (hannt) *v* chasser; *n* chasse *f*; ~ **for** chercher

hunter (*hann*-teu) *n* chasseur *m*

hurricane (*ha*-ri-keunn) *n* ouragan *m*; ~ **lamp** lampe-tempête *f*

hurry (*ha*-ri) *v* se dépêcher, se presser; *n* hâte *f*; **in a** ~ en vitesse

*hurt (heût) *v* *faire mal, blesser; offenser

hurtful (*heût*-feul) *adj* nuisible

husband (*haz*-beunnd) *n* époux *m*, mari *m*

hut (hat) *n* hutte *f*

hydrogen (*haï*-dreu-djeunn) *n* hydrogène *m*

hygiene (*haï*-djiin) *n* hygiène *f*

hygienic (haï-*djii*-nik) *adj* hygiénique

hymn (himm) *n* hymne *m*

hyphen (*haï*-feunn) *n* trait d'union

hypocrisy (hi-*po*-kreu-si) *n* hypocrisie *f*

hypocrite (*hi*-peu-krit) *n* hypocrite *m*

hypocritical (hi-peu-*kri*-ti-keul) *adj* hypocrite, fourbe

hysterical (hi-*stè*-ri-keul) *adj* hystérique

I

I (aï) *pron* je

ice (aïss) *n* glace *f*

ice-bag (*aïss*-bægh) *n* sac à glace

ice-cream (*aïss*-kriim) *n* crème glacée, glace *f*

Iceland (*aïss*-leunnd) Islande *f*

Icelander (*aïss*-leunn-deu) *n* Islandais *m*

Icelandic (aïss-*læn*-dik) *adj* islandais

icon (*aï*-konn) *n* icône *f*

idea (aï-*di^{eu}*) *n* idée *f*; pensée *f*; notion *f*, concept *m*

ideal (aï-*di^{eu}*) *adj* idéal; *n* idéal *m*

identical (aï-*dèn*-ti-keul) *adj* identique

identification (aï-dèn-ti-fi-*kéï*-cheunn) *n* identification *f*

identify (aï-*dèn*-ti-faï) *v* identifier

identity (aï-*dèn*-teu-ti) *n* identité *f*; ~ **card** carte d'identité

idiom (*i*-di-eumm) *n* idiome *m*

idiomatic (i-di-eu-*mæ*-tik) *adj* idiomatique

idiot (*i*-di-eut) *n* idiot *m*

idiotic (i-di-*o*-tik) *adj* idiot

idle (aï-deul) *adj* oisif; futile

idol (aï-deul) *n* idole *f*

if (if) *conj* si

ignition (igh-*ni*-cheunn) *n* allumage *m*; ~ **coil** bobine d'allumage

ignorant (*igh*-neu-reunnt) *adj* ignorant

ignore (igh-*noo*) *v* ignorer

ill (il) *adj* malade; mauvais; méchant

illegal (i-*lii*-gheul) *adj* illégal

illegible (i-*lè*-djeu-beul) *adj* illisible

illiterate (i-*li*-teu-reut) *n* illettré *m*

illness (*il*-neuss) *n* maladie *f*

illuminate (i-*loú*-mi-néït) *v* illuminer

illumination (i-loú-mi-*néï*-cheunn) *n* illumination *f*

illusion (i-*loú*-jeunn) *n* illusion *f*

illustrate (*i*-leu-stréït) *v* illustrer

illustration (i-leu-*stréï*-cheunn) *n* illustration *f*

image (*i*-midj) *n* image *f*

imaginary (i-*mæ*-dji-neu-ri) *adj* imaginaire

imagination (i-mæ-dji-*néï*-cheunn) *n* imagination *f*

imagine (i-*mæ*-djinn) *v* imaginer; s'imaginer; se figurer

imitate (*i*-mi-téït) *v* imiter

imitation (i-mi-*téï*-cheunn) *n* imitation *f*

immediate (i-*mii*-dyeut) *adj* immédiat

immediately (i-*mii*-dyeut-li) *adv* sur-le-champ, tout de suite, immédiatement

immense (i-*mèns*) *adj* immense, énorme

immigrant (*i*-mi-ghreunnt) *n* immigrant *m*

immigrate (*i*-mi-ghréït) *v* immigrer

immigration (i-mi-*ghréï*-cheunn) *n* immigration *f*

immodest (i-*mo*-dist) *adj* immodeste

immunity (i-*myoú*-neu-ti) *n* immunité *f*

immunize (*i*-myou-naïz) *v* immuniser

impartial (imm-*pââ*-cheul) *adj* impartial

impassable (imm-*pââ*-seu-beul) *adj* impraticable

impatient (imm-*péï*-cheunnt) *adj* impatient

impede (imm-*piid*) *v* entraver

impediment (imm-*pè*-di-meunnt) *n* entrave *f*

imperfect (imm-*peû*-fikt) *adj* imparfait

imperial (imm-*pi*^{eu}-ri-eul) *adj* impérial

impersonal (imm-*peû*-seu-neul) *adj* impersonnel

impertinence (imm-*peû*-ti-neunns) *n* impertinence *f*

impertinent (imm-*peû*-ti-neunnt) *adj* insolent, effronté, impertinent

implement[1] (*imm*-pli-meunnt) *n* instrument *m*, outil *m*

implement[2] (*imm*-pli-mènt) *v* réaliser

imply (imm-*plaï*) *v* impliquer; comporter

impolite (imm-peu-*laït*) *adj* impoli

import[1] (imm-*poot*) *v* importer

import[2] (*imm*-poot) *n* importation *f*; ~ **duty** taxe d'importation

importance (imm-*poo*-teunns) *n* importance *f*

important (imm-*poo*-teunnt) *adj* important

importer (imm-*poo*-teu) *n* importateur *m*

imposing (imm-*pô*^{ou}-zinng) *adj* imposant

impossible (imm-*po*-seu-beul) *adj* impossible

impotence (*imm*-peu-teunns) *n* impotence *f*

impotent (*imm*-peu-teunnt) *adj* impotent

impound (imm-*paound*) *v* confisquer

impress (imm-*prèss*) *v* *faire impression sur, impressionner

impression (imm-*prè*-cheunn) *n* impression *f*

impressive (imm-*prè*-siv) *adj* impressionnant

imprison (imm-*pri*-zeunn) *v* emprisonner

imprisonment (imm-*pri*-zeunn-meunnt) *n* emprisonnement *m*

improbable (imm-*pro*-beu-beul) *adj* improbable

improper (imm-*pro*-peu) *adj* impropre

improve (imm-*proûv*) *v* améliorer

improvement (imm-*proûv*-meunnt) *n* amélioration *f*

improvise (*imm*-preu-vaïz) *v* improviser

impudent (*imm*-pyou-deunnt) *adj* insolent

impulse (*imm*-pals) *n* impulsion *f*; stimulant *m*

impulsive (imm-*pal*-siv) *adj* impulsif

in (inn) *prep* en; dans, sur; *adv* dedans

inaccessible (i-næk-*sè*-seu-beul) *adj* inaccessible

inaccurate (i-*næ*-kyou-reut) *adj* incorrect

inadequate (i-*næ*-di-k^{ou}eut) *adj* inadéquat

incapable (inng-*kéï*-peu-beul) *adj* incapable

incense (*inn*-sèns) *n* encens *m*

incident (*inn*-si-deunnt) *n* incident *m*

incidental (inn-si-*dèn*-teul) *adj* fortuit

incite (inn-*saït*) *v* inciter

inclination (inng-kli-*néï*-cheunn) *n* penchant *m*

incline (inng-*klaïn*) *n* pente *f*

inclined (inng-*klaïnd*) *adj* disposé, enclin; *be ~ to *v* *avoir tendance

include (inng-*kloûd*) *v* *comprendre, *inclure

inclusive (inng-*kloû*-siv) *adj* compris

income (*inng*-keumm) *n* revenu *m*

income-tax (*inng*-keumm-tæks) *n* impôt sur le revenu

incompetent (inng-*komm*-peu-teunnt) *adj* incompétent

incomplete (inn-keumm-*pliit*) *adj* incomplet

inconceivable (inng-keunn-*sii*-veu-beul) *adj* inconcevable

inconspicuous (inng-keunn-*spi*-kyou-euss) *adj* discret

inconvenience (inng-keunn-*vii*-nyeunns) *n* désagrément *m*, inconvénient *m*

inconvenient (inng-keunn-*vii*-nyeunnt) *adj* inopportun; gênant

incorrect (inng-keu-*rèkt*) *adj* inexact, incorrect

increase[1] (inng-*kriiss*) *v* augmenter; s'accumuler, *croître

increase[2] (*inng*-kriiss) *n* augmentation *f*; relèvement *m*

incredible (inng-*krè*-deu-beul) *adj* incroyable

incurable (inng-*kyou^{eu}*-reu-beul) *adj* incurable

indecent (inn-*dii*-seunnt) *adj* indécent

indeed (inn-*diid*) *adv* en effet

indefinite (inn-*dè*-fi-nit) *adj* indéfini

indemnity (inn-*dèm*-neu-ti) *n* dédommagement *m*, indemnité *f*

independence (inn-di-*pèn*-deunns) *n* indépendance *f*

independent (inn-di-*pèn*-deunnt) *adj* indépendant; autonome

index (*inn*-dèks) *n* index *m*; ~ **finger** index *m*

India (*inn*-di-eu) Inde *f*

Indian (*inn*-di-eunn) *adj* indien; *n* Indien *m*

indicate (*inn*-di-kéït) *v* signaler, indiquer

indication (inn-di-*kéï*-cheunn) *n* signe *m*, indication *f*

indicator (*inn*-di-kéï-teu) *n* clignotant *m*

indifferent (inn-*di*-feu-reunnt) *adj* indifférent

indigestion (inn-di-*djèss*-tcheunn) *n* indigestion *f*

indignation (inn-digh-*néï*-cheunn) *n* indignation *f*

indirect (inn-di-*rèkt*) *adj* indirect

individual (inn-di-*vi*-djou-eul) *adj* particulier, individuel; *n* individu *m*

Indonesia (inn-deu-*nii*-zi-eu) Indonésie *f*

Indonesian (inn-deu-*nii*-zi-eunn) *adj* indonésien; *n* Indonésien *m*

indoor (*inn*-doo) *adj* intérieur

indoors (inn-*dooz*) *adv* à l'intérieur

indulge (inn-*daldj*) *v* céder

industrial (inn-*da*-stri-eul) *adj* industriel; ~ **area** zone industrielle

industrious (inn-*da*-stri-euss) *adj* industrieux

industry (*inn*-deu-stri) *n* industrie *f*

inedible (i-*nè*-di-beul) *adj* immangeable

inefficient (i-ni-*fi*-cheunnt) *adj* inefficace

inevitable (i-*nè*-vi-teu-beul) *adj* inévitable

inexpensive (i-nik-*spèn*-siv) *adj* bon marché

inexperienced (i-nik-*spiᵉᵘ*-ri-eunnst) *adj* inexpérimenté

infant (*inn*-feunnt) *n* nourrisson *m*

infantry (*inn*-feunn-tri) *n* infanterie *f*

infect (inn-*fèkt*) *v* infecter

infection (inn-*fèk*-cheunn) *n* infection *f*

infectious (inn-*fèk*-cheuss) *adj* infectieux

infer (inn-*feû*) *v* *déduire

inferior (inn-*fiᵉᵘ*-ri-eu) *adj* moindre, inférieur

infinite (*inn*-fi-neut) *adj* infini

infinitive (inn-*fi*-ni-tiv) *n* infinitif *m*

infirmary (inn-*feû*-meu-ri) *n* infirmerie *f*

inflammable (inn-*flæ*-meu-beul) *adj* inflammable

inflammation (inn-fleu-*méï*-cheunn) *n* inflammation *f*

inflatable (inn-*fléï*-teu-beul) *adj* gonflable

inflate (inn-*fléït*) *v* gonfler

inflation (inn-*fléï*-cheunn) *n* inflation *f*

influence (*inn*-flou-eunns) *n* influence *f*; *v* influencer

influential (inn-flou-*èn*-cheul) *adj* influent

influenza (inn-flou-*èn*-zeu) *n* grippe *f*

inform (inn-*foom*) *v* informer; *mettre au courant, communiquer

informal (inn-*foo*-meul) *adj* sans cérémonie

information (inn-feu-*méï*-cheunn) *n* information *f*; renseignement *m*, communication *f*; ~ **bureau** bureau de renseignements

infra-red (inn-freu-*rèd*) *adj* infrarouge

infrequent (inn-*frii*-kᵒᵘeunnt) *adj* peu fréquent

ingredient (inng-*ghrii*-di-eunnt) *n* ingrédient *m*

inhabit (inn-*hæ*-bit) *v* habiter

inhabitable (inn-*hæ*-bi-teu-beul) *adj* habitable

inhabitant (inn-*hæ*-bi-teunnt) *n* habitant *m*

inhale (inn-*héïl*) *v* inhaler

inherit (inn-*hè*-rit) *v* hériter

inheritance (inn-*hè*-ri-teunns) *n* héritage *m*

initial (i-*ni*-cheul) *adj* initial; *n* initiale *f*; *v* parapher

initiative (i-*ni*-cheu-tiv) *n* initiative *f*

inject (inn-*djèkt*) *v* injecter

injection (inn-*djèk*-cheunn) *n* injection *f*

injure (*inn*-djeu) *v* blesser; offenser

injury (*inn*-djeu-ri) *n* blessure *f*; lésion *f*

injustice (inn-*dja*-stiss) *n* injustice *f*

ink (inngk) *n* encre *f*

inlet (*inn*-lèt) *n* crique *f*

inn (inn) *n* auberge *f*

inner (*i*-neu) *adj* intérieur; ~ **tube** chambre à air

inn-keeper (*inn*-kii-pcu) *n* aubergiste *m*

innocence (*i*-neu-seunns) *n* innocence *f*

innocent (*i*-neu-seunnt) *adj* innocent

inoculate (i-*no*-kyou-léit) *v* inoculer

inoculation (i-no-kyou-*léi*-cheunn) *n* inoculation *f*

inquire (inng-k^ou_ai^eu) *v* se renseigner, s'informer

inquiry (inng-k^ou_ai^eu-ri) *n* question *f*, enquête *f*; ~ **office** bureau de renseignements

inquisitive (inng-k^ou_i-zeu-tiv) *adj* curieux

insane (inn-*séin*) *adj* fou

inscription (inn-*skrip*-cheunn) *n* inscription *f* ·

insect (*inn*-sèkt) *n* insecte *m*; ~ **repellent** insectifuge *m*

insecticide (inn-*sèk*-ti-saïd) *n* insecticide *m*

insensitive (inn-*sèn*-seu-tiv) *adj* insensible

insert (inn-*seût*) *v* insérer

inside (inn-*saïd*) *n* intérieur *m*; *adj* intérieur; *adv* à l'intérieur; dedans; *prep* dans, à l'intérieur de; ~ **out** à l'envers; **insides** entrailles *fpl*

insight (*inn*-saït) *n* compréhension *f*

insignificant (inn-sigh-*ni*-fi-keunnt) *adj* insignifiant; sans importance; futile

insist (inn-*sist*) *v* insister; persister

insolence (*inn*-seu-leunns) *n* insolence *f*

insolent (*inn*-seu-leunnt) *adj* insolent

insomnia (inn-*somm*-ni-eu) *n* insomnie *f*

inspect (inn-*spèkt*) *v* inspecter

inspection (inn-*spèk*-cheunn) *n* inspection *f*; contrôle *m*

inspector (inn-*spèk*-teu) *n* inspecteur *m*

inspire (inn-*spaï^eu*) *v* inspirer

install (inn-*stool*) *v* installer

installation (inn-steu-*léi*-cheunn) *n* installation *f*

instalment (inn-*stool*-meunnt) *n* paiement à tempérament

instance (*inn*-steunns) *n* exemple *m*; cas *m*; **for** ~ par exemple

instant (*inn*-steunnt) *n* instant *m*

instantly (*inn*-steunnt-li) *adv* instantanément, tout de suite, immédiatement

instead of (inn-*stèd* ov) au lieu de

instinct (*inn*-stinngkt) *n* instinct *m*

institute (*inn*-sti-tyoût) *n* institut *m*; institution *f*; *v* instituer

institution (inn-sti-*tyoû*-cheunn) *n* institution *f*

instruct (inn-*strakt*) *v* *instruire

instruction (inn-*strak*-cheunn) *n* instruction *f*

instructive (inn-*strak*-tiv) *adj* instructif

instructor (inn-*strak*-teu) *n* instructeur *m*

instrument (*inn*-strou-meunnt) *n* instrument *m*; **musical** ~ instrument de musique

insufficient (inn-seu-*fi*-cheunnt) *adj* insuffisant

insulate (*inn*-syou-léit) *v* isoler

insulation (inn-syou-*léi*-cheunn) *n* isolation *f*

insulator (*inn*-syou-léï-teu) *n* isolateur *m*

insult[1] (inn-*salt*) *v* insulter

insult² (*inn*-salt) *n* insulte *f*

insurance (inn-*chou^eu*-reunns) *n* assurance *f*; ~ **policy** police d'assurance

insure (inn-*chou^eu*) *v* assurer

intact (inn-tækt) *adj* intact

intellect (*inn*-teu-lèkt) *n* intellect *m*, intelligence *f*

intellectual (inn-teu-*lèk*-tchou-eul) *adj* intellectuel

intelligence (inn-*tè*-li-djeunns) *n* intelligence *f*

intelligent (inn-*tè*-li-djeunnt) *adj* intelligent

intend (inn-tènd) *v* *avoir l'intention de

intense (inn-tèns) *adj* intense; vif

intention (inn-tèn-cheunn) *n* intention *f*

intentional (inn-*tèn*-cheu-neul) *adj* intentionnel

intercourse (*inn*-teu-kooss) *n* rapport *m*

interest (*inn*-treust) *n* intérêt *m*; *v* intéresser

interesting (*inn*-treu-stinng) *adj* intéressant

interfere (inn-teu-*fi^eu*) *v* *intervenir; ~ **with** se mêler de

interference (inn-teu-*fi^eu*-reunns) *n* ingérence *f*

interim (*inn*-teu-rimm) *n* intérim *m*

interior (inn-*ti^eu*-ri-eu) *n* intérieur *m*

interlude (*inn*-teu-loûd) *n* interlude *m*

intermediary (inn-teu-*mii*-dyeu-ri) *n* intermédiaire *m*

intermission (inn-teu-*mi*-cheunn) *n* entracte *m*

internal (inn-*teû*-neul) *adj* intérieur, interne

international (inn-teu-*næ*-cheu-neul) *adj* international

interpret (inn-*teû*-prit) *v* interpréter

interpreter (inn-*teû*-pri-teu) *n* interprète *m*

interrogate (inn-*tè*-reu-ghéït) *v* interroger

interrogation (inn-tè-reu-*ghéï*-cheunn) *n* interrogatoire *m*

interrogative (inn-teu-*ro*-gheu-tiv) *adj* interrogatif

interrupt (inn-teu-rapt) *v* *interrompre

interruption (inn-teu-*rap*-cheunn) *n* interruption *f*

intersection (inn-teu-*sèk*-cheunn) *n* intersection *f*

interval (*inn*-teu-veul) *n* entracte *m*; intervalle *m*

intervene (inn-teu-viin) *v* *intervenir

interview (*inn*-teu-vyoû) *n* entrevue *f*, interview *f*

intestine (inn-*tè*-stinn) *n* intestin *m*

intimate (*inn*-ti-meut) *adj* intime

into (*inn*-tou) *prep* dans

intolerable (inn-*to*-leu-reu-beul) *adj* intolérable

intoxicated (inn-*tok*-si-kéï-tid) *adj* ivre

intrigue (inn-triigh) *n* intrigue *f*

introduce (inn-treu-*dyoûss*) *v* présenter; *introduire

introduction (inn-treu-*dak*-cheunn) *n* présentation *f*; introduction *f*

invade (inn-véïd) *v* envahir

invalid¹ (*inn*-veu-liid) *n* infirme *m*; *adj* infirme

invalid² (inn-*væ*-lid) *adj* nul

invasion (inn-*véï*-jeunn) *n* invasion *f*

invent (inn-vènt) *v* inventer

invention (inn-*vèn*-cheunn) *n* invention *f*

inventive (inn-*vèn*-tiv) *adj* inventif

inventor (inn-*vèn*-teu) *n* inventeur *m*

inventory (*inn*-veunn-tri) *n* inventaire *m*

invert (inn-veût) *v* intervertir

invest (inn-vèst) *v* investir; placer

investigate (inn-*vè*-sti-ghéït) *v* enquêter

investigation (inn-vè-sti-*ghéï*-cheunn) *n* investigation *f*

investment (inn-*vèst*-meunnt) *n* investissement *m*; placement *m*

investor (inn-*vè*-steu) *n* investisseur *m*

invisible (inn-*vi*-zeu-beul) *adj* invisible

invitation (inn-vi-*téï*-cheunn) *n* invitation *f*

invite (inn-*vaït*) *v* inviter

invoice (*inn*-voïss) *n* facture *f*

involve (inn-*volv*) *v* impliquer

inwards (*inn*-ᵒᵘeudz) *adv* vers l'intérieur

iodine (*aï*-eu-diin) *n* iode *m*

Iran (i-*râân*) Iran *m*

Iranian (i-*réï*-ni-eunn) *adj* iranien; *n* Iranien *m*

Iraq (i-*râak*) Irak *m*

Iraqi (i-*rââ*-ki) *adj* irakien; *n* Irakien *m*

irascible (i-*ræ*-si-beul) *adj* irascible

Ireland (*aï*ᵉᵘ-leunnd) Irlande *f*

Irish (*aï*ᵉᵘ-rich) *adj* irlandais

Irishman (*aï*ᵉᵘ-rich-meunn) *n* (pl -men) Irlandais *m*

iron (*aï*-eunn) *n* fer *m*; fer à repasser; en fer; *v* repasser

ironical (aï-*ro*-ni-keul) *adj* ironique

ironworks (*aï*-eunn-ᵒᵘeûks) *n* fonderie *f*

irony (*aï*ᵉᵘ-reu-ni) *n* ironie *f*

irregular (i-*rè*-ghyou-leu) *adj* irrégulier

irreparable (i-*rè*-peu-reu-beul) *adj* irréparable

irrevocable (i-*rè*-veu-keu-beul) *adj* irrévocable

irritable (*i*-ri-teu-beul) *adj* irritable

irritate (*i*-ri-téït) *v* agacer, irriter

is (iz) *v* (pr be)

island (*aï*-leunnd) *n* île *f*

isolate (*aï*-seu-léït) *v* isoler

isolation (aï-seu-*léï*-cheunn) *n* isolement *m*; isolation *f*

Israel (*iz*-réïl) Israël *m*

Israeli (iz-*réï*-li) *adj* israélien; *n* Israélien *m*

issue (*i*-choû) *v* distribuer; *n* émission *f*, tirage *m*, édition *f*; question *f*, sujet *m*; conséquence *f*, issue *f*, résultat *m*, conclusion *f*, fin *f*

isthmus (*iss*-meuss) *n* isthme *m*

it (it) *pron* le

Italian (i-*tæl*-yeunn) *adj* italien; *n* Italien *m*

italics (i-*tæ*-liks) *pl* italiques *mpl*

Italy (*i*-teu-li) Italie *f*

itch (itch) *n* démangeaison *f*; prurit *m*; *v* démanger

item (*aï*-teumm) *n* article *m*; point *m*

itinerant (aï-*ti*-neu-reunnt) *adj* ambulant

itinerary (aï-*ti*-neu-reu-ri) *n* itinéraire *m*

ivory (*aï*-veu-ri) *n* ivoire *m*

ivy (*aï*-vi) *n* lierre *m*

J

jack (djæk) *n* cric *m*

jacket (*djæ*-kit) *n* veste *f*, veston *m*; jaquette *f*

jade (djéïd) *n* jade *m*

jail (djéïl) *n* prison *f*

jailer (*djéï*-leu) *n* geôlier *m*

jam (djæm) *n* confiture *f*; embouteillage *m*

janitor (*djæ*-ni-teu) *n* concierge *m*

January (*djæ*-nyou-eu-ri) janvier

Japan (djeu-*pæn*) Japon *m*

Japanese (djæ-peu-*niiz*) *adj* japonais; *n* Japonais *m*

jar (djââ) *n* jarre *f*

jaundice (*djoon*-diss) *n* jaunisse *f*

jaw (djoo) *n* mâchoire *f*

jealous (*djè*-leuss) *adj* jaloux

jealousy (*djè*-leu-si) *n* jalousie *f*

jeans (djiinz) *pl* blue-jean *m*

jelly (*djè*-li) *n* gelée *f*

jelly-fish (*djè*-li-fich) *n* méduse *f*

jersey (*djeû*-zi) *n* jersey *m*; chandail *m*

jet (djèt) *n* jet *m*; avion à réaction

jetty (*djè*-ti) *n* jetée *f*

Jew (djoû) *n* juif *m*

jewel (*djoû*-eul) *n* bijou *m*

jeweller (*djoû*-eu-leu) *n* bijoutier *m*

jewellery (*djoû*-eul-ri) *n* bijoux; joaillerie *f*

Jewish (*djoû*-ich) *adj* juif

job (djob) *n* boulot *m*; emploi *m*, travail *m*

jockey (*djo*-ki) *n* jockey *m*

join (djoïn) *v* *joindre; s'affilier à, adhérer à; assembler, réunir

joint (djoïnt) *n* articulation *f*; soudure *f*; *adj* uni, conjoint

jointly (*djoïnt*-li) *adv* conjointement

joke (djô^{ou}k) *n* blague *f*, plaisanterie *f*

jolly (*djo*-li) *adj* gai

Jordan (*djoo*-deunn) Jordanie *f*

Jordanian (djoo-*déï*-ni-eunn) *adj* jordanien; *n* Jordanien *m*

journal (*djeû*-neul) *n* périodique *m*

journalism (*djeû*-neu-li-zeumm) *n* journalisme *m*

journalist (*djeû*-neu-list) *n* journaliste *m*

journey (*djeû*-ni) *n* voyage *m*

joy (djoï) *n* plaisir *m*, joie *f*

joyful (*djoï*-feul) *adj* content, joyeux

jubilee (*djoû*-bi-lii) *n* anniversaire *m*

judge (djadj) *n* juge *m*; *v* juger; apprécier

judgment (*djadj*-meunnt) *n* jugement *m*

jug (djagh) *n* cruche *f*

Jugoslav (youø-gheu-*slââv*) *adj* yougoslave; *n* Yougoslave *m*

Jugoslavia (youø-gheu-*slââ*-vi-eu) You-goslavie *f*

juice (djoûss) *n* jus *m*

juicy (*djoû*-si) *adj* juteux

July (djou-*laï*) juillet

jump (djammp) *v* sauter; *n* bond *m*, saut *m*

jumper (*djamm*-peu) *n* chandail *m*

junction (*djanngk*-cheunn) *n* carrefour *m*; jonction *f*

June (djoûn) juin

jungle (*djanng*-gheul) *n* jungle *f*

junior (*djoû*-nyeu) *adj* cadet

junk (djanngk) *n* rebut *m*

jury (*djou*^{eu}-ri) *n* jury *m*

just (djast) *adj* légitime, juste; exact; *adv* à peine; juste

justice (*dja*-stiss) *n* droit *m*; justice *f*

juvenile (*djoû*-veu-naïl) *adj* juvénile

K

kangaroo (kæng-gheu-*roû*) *n* kangourou *m*

keel (kiil) *n* quille *f*

keen (kiin) *adj* passionné; aigu

*keep (kiip) *v* *tenir; garder; continuer; ~ **away from** se *tenir éloigné de; ~ **off** ne pas toucher; ~ **on** continuer; ~ **quiet** se *taire; ~ **up** persévérer; ~ **up with** *être à la hauteur de

keg (kègh) *n* baril *m*

kennel (*kè*-neul) *n* chenil *m*

Kenya (*kè*-nyeu) Kenya *m*

kerosene (*kè*-reu-siin) *n* pétrole *m*

kettle (*kè*-teul) *n* bouilloire *f*

key (kii) *n* clé *f*

keyhole (*kii*-hô^{ou}l) *n* trou de la serrure

khaki (*kââ*-ki) *n* kaki *m*

kick (kik) *v* donner des coups de pied; *n* coup de pied

kick-off (ki-*kof*) *n* coup d'envoi

kid (kid) *n* enfant *m*, gosse *m*; chevreau *m*; *v* taquiner

kidney (*kid*-ni) *n* rein *m*

kill (kil) *v* tuer

kilogram (*ki*-leu-ghræm) *n* kilo *m*

kilometre (*ki*-leu-mii-teu) *n* kilomètre *m*

kind (kaïnd) *adj* gentil, aimable; bon; *n* genre *m*

kindergarten (*kinn*-deu-ghââ-teunn) *n* école maternelle

king (kinng) *n* roi *m*

kingdom (*kinng*-deumm) *n* royaume *m*

kiosk (*kii*-osk) *n* kiosque *m*

kiss (kiss) *n* baiser *m*; *v* embrasser

kit (kit) *n* trousseau *m*

kitchen (*ki*-tchînn) *n* cuisine *f*; ~ **garden** jardin potager

knapsack (*næp*-sæk) *n* havresac *m*

knave (néïv) *n* valet *m*

knee (nii) *n* genou *m*

kneecap (*nii*-kæp) *n* rotule *f*

* **kneel** (niil) *v* s'agenouiller

knew (nyoû) *v* (p know)

knickers (*ni*-keuz) *pl* slip *m*

knife (naïf) *n* (pl knives) couteau *m*

knight (naït) *n* chevalier *m*

knit (nit) *v* tricoter

knob (nob) *n* bouton *m*

knock (nok) *v* frapper; *n* coup *m*; ~ **against** cogner contre; ~ **down** renverser

knot (not) *n* nœud *m*; *v* nouer

* **know** (nô^ou) *v* *savoir, *connaître

knowledge (*no*-lidj) *n* connaissance *f*

knuckle (*na*-keul) *n* jointure *f*

L

label (*léï*-beul) *n* étiquette *f*; *v* étiqueter

laboratory (leu-*bo*-reu-teu-ri) *n* laboratoire *m*

labour (*léï*-beu) *n* travail *m*, labeur *m*; douleurs; *v* bûcher, peiner; **labor permit** *Am* permis de travail

labourer (*léï*-beu-reu) *n* travailleur *m*

labour-saving (*léï*-beu-séï-vinng) *adj* qui économise du travail

labyrinth (*læ*-beu-rinnθ) *n* labyrinthe *m*

lace (léïss) *n* dentelle *f*; lacet *m*

lack (læk) *n* manque *m*; *v* manquer

lacquer (*læ*-keu) *n* vernis *m*

lad (læd) *n* garçon *m*

ladder (*læ*-deu) *n* échelle *f*

lady (*léï*-di) *n* dame *f*; **ladies' room** toilettes pour dames

lagoon (leu-*ghoûn*) *n* lagune *f*

lake (léïk) *n* lac *m*

lamb (læm) *n* agneau *m*

lame (léïm) *adj* paralysé, boiteux

lamentable (*læ*-meunn-teu-beul) *adj* lamentable

lamp (læmp) *n* lampe *f*

lamp-post (*læmp*-pô^oust) *n* lampadaire *m*

lampshade (*læmp*-chéïd) *n* abat-jour *m*

land (lænd) *n* pays *m*, terre *f*; *v* atterrir; débarquer

landlady (*lænd*-léï-di) *n* logeuse *f*

landlord (*lænd*-lood) *n* propriétaire *m*; logeur *m*

landmark (*lænd*-mââk) *n* point de repère; jalon *m*

landscape (*lænd*-skéïp) *n* paysage *m*

lane (léïn) *n* ruelle *f*, chemin *m*; voie *f*

language (*læng*-gh^{ou}idj) *n* langue *f*; ~ **laboratory** laboratoire de langues

lantern (*læn*-teunn) *n* lanterne *f*

lapel (leu-*pèl*) *n* revers *m*

larder (*lââ*-deu) *n* garde-manger *m*

large (lââdj) *adj* vaste; spacieux

lark (lââk) *n* alouette *f*

laryngitis (læ-rinn-*djaï*-tiss) *n* laryngite *f*

last (lââst) *adj* dernier; précédent; *v* durer; **at** ~ enfin; en fin de compte

lasting (*lââ*-stinng) *adj* durable

latchkey (*lætch*-kii) *n* clé de la maison

late (léït) *adj* tard; en retard

lately (*léït*-li) *adv* ces derniers temps, dernièrement, récemment

lather (*lââ*-ðeu) *n* écume *f*

Latin America (*læ*-tinn eu-*mè*-ri-keu) Amérique latine

Latin-American (læ-tinn-eu-*mè*-ri-keunn) *adj* sud-américain

latitude (*læ*-ti-tyoûd) *n* latitude *f*

laugh (lââf) *v* *rire; *n* rire *m*

laughter (*lââf*-teu) *n* rire *m*

launch (loontch) *v* lancer; *n* bateau *à* moteur

launching (*loon*-tchinng) *n* lancement *m*

launderette (loon-deu-*rèt*) *n* laverie automatique

laundry (*loon*-dri) *n* blanchisserie *f*; lessive *f*

lavatory (*læ*-veu-teu-ri) *n* cabinet *m*

lavish (*læ*-vich) *adj* prodigue

law (loo) *n* loi *f*; droit *m*; ~ **court** tribunal *m*

lawful (*loo*-feul) *adj* légal

lawn (loon) *n* gazon *m*, pelouse *f*

lawsuit (*loo*-soût) *n* procès *m*

lawyer (*loo*-yeu) *n* avocat *m*; juriste *m*

laxative (*læk*-seu-tiv) *n* laxatif *m*

*lay (léï) *v* placer, poser; ~ **bricks** maçonner

layer (*léï*^{eu}) *n* couche *f*

layman (*léï*-meunn) *n* profane *m*

lazy (*léï*-zi) *adj* paresseux

lead[1] (liid) *n* avance *f*; conduite *f*; laisse *f*

lead[2] (lèd) *n* plomb *m*

*lead (liid) *v* diriger

leader (*lii*-deu) *n* leader *m*, dirigeant *m*

leadership (*lii*-deu-chip) *n* direction *f*

leading (*lii*-dinng) *adj* dominant, principal

leaf (liif) *n* (pl leaves) feuille *f*

league (liigh) *n* ligue *f*

leak (liik) *v* *fuir; *n* fuite *f*

leaky (*lii*-ki) *adj* ayant une fuite

lean (liin) *adj* maigre

*lean (liin) *v* s'appuyer

leap (liip) *n* saut *m*

*leap (liip) *v* bondir

leap-year (*liip*-yi^{eu}) *n* année bissextile

*learn (leûnn) *v* *apprendre

learner (*leû*-neu) *n* débutant *m*

lease (liiss) *n* location *f*; bail *m*; *v* donner en location, louer

leash (liich) *n* laisse *f*

least (liist) *adj* moindre; **at** ~ au moins

leather (*lè*-ðeu) *n* cuir *m*; en cuir

leave (liiv) *n* permission *f*

*leave (liiv) *v* *partir, quitter; laisser; ~ **out** *omettre

Lebanese (lè-beu-*niiz*) *adj* libanais; *n* Libanais *m*

Lebanon (*lè*-beu-neunn) Liban *m*

lecture (*lèk*-tcheu) *n* cours *m*, conférence *f*

left[1] (lèft) *adj* gauche

left[2] (lèft) *v* (p, pp leave)

left-hand (*lèft*-hænd) *adj* à gauche, de gauche

left-handed (lèft-*hæn*-did) *adj* gaucher

leg (lègh) *n* pied *m*, jambe *f*

legacy (*lè*-gheu-si) *n* legs *m*

legal (*lii*-gheul) *adj* légitime, légal; juridique

legalization (lii-gheu-laï-*zéi*-cheunn) *n* légalisation *f*

legation (li-*ghéi*-cheunn) *n* légation *f*

legible (*lè*-dji-beul) *adj* lisible

legitimate (li-*dji*-ti-meut) *adj* légitime

leisure (*lè*-jeu) *n* loisir *m*; aise *f*

lemon (*lè*-meunn) *n* citron *m*

lemonade (lè-meu-*néid*) *n* limonade *f*

lend (lènd) *v* prêter

length (lèngθ) *n* longueur *f*

lengthen (*lèng*-θeunn) *v* allonger

lengthways (*lèng*θ-ᵒᵘéïz) *adv* en long

lens (lènz) *n* lentille *f*; **telephoto ~** télé-objectif *m*; **zoom ~** zoom *m*

leprosy (*lè*-preu-si) *n* lèpre *f*

less (lèss) *adv* moins

lessen (*lè*-seunn) *v* diminuer

lesson (*lè*-seunn) *n* leçon *f*

let (lèt) *v* laisser; louer; **~ down** désenchanter

letter (*lè*-teu) *n* lettre *f*; **~ of credit** lettre de crédit; **~ of recommandation** lettre de recommandation

letter-box (*lè*-teu-boks) *n* boîte aux lettres

lettuce (*lè*-tiss) *n* laitue *f*

level (*lè*-veul) *adj* égal; plat, lisse, plan; *n* niveau *m*; *v* égaliser, niveler; **~ crossing** passage à niveau

lever (*lii*-veu) *n* levier *m*

Levis (*lii*-vaïz) *pl* blue-jean *m*

liability (laï-eu-*bi*-leu-ti) *n* responsabilité *f*

liable (*laï*-eu-beul) *adj* responsable; **~ to** sujet à

liberal (*li*-beu-reul) *adj* libéral; généreux, large

liberation (li-beu-*réi*-cheunn) *n* libération *f*

Liberia (laï-*biᵉᵘ*-ri-eu) Libéria *m*

Liberian (laï-*biᵉᵘ*-ri-eunn) *adj* libérien; *n* Libérien *m*

liberty (*li*-beu-ti) *n* liberté *f*

library (*laï*-breu-ri) *n* bibliothèque *f*

licence (*laï*-seunns) *n* licence *f*; permis *m*; **driving ~** permis de conduire; **~ number** *Am* numéro d'immatriculation; **~ plate** *Am* plaque d'immatriculation

license (*laï*-seunns) *v* autoriser

lick (lik) *v* lécher

lid (lid) *n* couvercle *m*

lie (laï) *v* *mentir; *n* mensonge *m*

lie (laï) *v* *être couché; **~ down** se coucher

life (laïf) *n* (pl lives) vie *f*; **~ insurance** assurance-vie *f*

lifebelt (*laïf*-bèlt) *n* bouée de sauvetage

lifetime (*laïf*-taïm) *n* vie *f*

lift (lift) *v* soulever, lever; *n* ascenseur *m*

light (laït) *n* lumière *f*; *adj* léger; clair; **~ bulb** ampoule *f*

light (laït) *v* allumer

lighter (*laï*-teu) *n* briquet *m*

lighthouse (*laït*-haouss) *n* phare *m*

lighting (*laï*-tinng) *n* éclairage *m*

lightning (*laït*-ninng) *n* éclair *m*

like (laïk) *v* aimer; bien aimer; *adj* pareil; *conj* comme

likely (*laï*-kli) *adj* probable

like-minded (laïk-*maïn*-did) *adj* unanime

likewise (*laïk*-ᵒᵘaïz) *adv* de la même manière, également

lily (*li*-li) *n* lis *m*

limb (limm) *n* membre *m*

lime (laïm) *n* chaux *f*; tilleul *m*; limette *f*

limetree (*laïm*-trii) *n* tilleul *m*

limit (*li*-mit) *n* limite *f*; *v* limiter

limp (limmp) *v* boiter; *adj* flasque

line (laïn) *n* ligne *f*; trait *m*; fil *m*; rangée *f*; **stand in ~** *Am* *faire la queue

linen (*li*-ninn) *n* toile *f*; linge *m*

liner (*laï*-neu) *n* paquebot *m*

lining (*laï*-ninng) *n* doublure *f*

link (linngk) *v* relier; *n* lien *m*; maillon *m*

lion (*laï*-eunn) *n* lion *m*

lip (lip) *n* lèvre *f*

lipsalve (*lip*-sââv) *n* pommade pour les lèvres

lipstick (*lip*-stik) *n* rouge à lèvres

liqueur (li-*kyou^{eu}*) *n* liqueur *f*

liquid (*li*-k^{ou}id) *adj* liquide; *n* liquide *m*

liquor (*li*-keu) *n* spiritueux *mpl*

liquorice (*li*-keu-riss) *n* réglisse *f*

list (list) *n* liste *f*; *v* *inscrire

listen (*li*-seunn) *v* écouter

listener (*liss*-neu) *n* auditeur *m*

literary (*li*-treu-ri) *adj* littéraire

literature (*li*-treu-tcheu) *n* littérature *f*

litre (*lii*-teu) *n* litre *m*

litter (*li*-teu) *n* détritus *m*; immondices *fpl*; portée *f*

little (*li*-teul) *adj* petit; peu

live¹ (liv) *v* *vivre; habiter

live² (laïv) *adj* vivant

livelihood (*laïv*-li-houd) *n* subsistance *f*

lively (*laïv*-li) *adj* vif

liver (*li*-veu) *n* foie *m*

living-room (*li*-vinng-roûm) *n* pièce de séjour, salle de séjour

load (lô^{ou}d) *n* chargement *m*; fardeau *m*; *v* charger

loaf (lô^{ou}f) *n* (pl loaves) miche *f*

loan (lô^{ou}n) *n* prêt *m*

lobby (*lo*-bi) *n* vestibule *m*

lobster (*lob*-steu) *n* homard *m*

local (*lô^{ou}*-keul) *adj* local; ~ **call** communication locale; ~ **train** train local

locality (lô^{ou}-*kæ*-leu-ti) *n* localité *f*

locate (lô^{ou}-*kéit*) *v* localiser

location (lô^{ou}-*kéï*-cheunn) *n* situation

lock (lok) *v* fermer à clé; *n* serrure *f*; écluse *f*; ~ **up** enfermer

locomotive (lô^{ou}-keu-*mô^{ou}*-tiv) *n* locomotive *f*

lodge (lodj) *v* loger; *n* pavillon de chasse

lodger (*lo*-djeu) *n* sous-locataire *m*

lodgings (*lo*-djinngz) *pl* logement *m*

log (logh) *n* bûche *f*

logic (*lo*-djik) *n* logique *f*

logical (*lo*-dji-keul) *adj* logique

lonely (*lô^{ou}n*-li) *adj* solitaire

long (lonng) *adj* long; ~ **for** désirer; **no longer** ne ... plus

longing (*lonng*-inng) *n* envie *f*

longitude (*lonn*-dji-tyoûd) *n* longitude *f*

look (louk) *v* regarder; sembler, *avoir l'air; *n* coup d'œil, regard *m*; apparence *f*, aspect *m*; ~ **after** s'occuper de, *prendre soin de, veiller sur; ~ **at** regarder; ~ **for** chercher; ~ **out** *prendre garde, *faire attention; ~ **up** chercher

looking-glass (*lou*-kinng-ghlââss) *n* miroir *m*

loop (loûp) *n* boucle *f*

loose (loûss) *adj* lâche

loosen (*loû*-seunn) *v* desserrer

lord (lood) *n* lord *m*

lorry (*lo*-ri) *n* camion *m*

***lose** (loûz) *v* perdre

loss (loss) *n* perte *f*

lost (lost) *adj* égaré; disparu; ~ **and found** objets trouvés; ~ **property office** bureau des objets trouvés

lot (lot) *n* sort *m*; tas *m*, quantité *f*

lotion (*lô^{ou}*-cheunn) *n* lotion *f*; **after-shave** ~ after-shave *m*

lottery (*lo*-teu-ri) *n* loterie *f*

loud (laoud) *adj* fort

loud-speaker (laoud-*spii*-keu) *n* haut-parleur *m*

lounge (laoundj) n foyer m

louse (laouss) n (pl lice) pou m

love (lav) v aimer; n amour m; **in ~** amoureux

lovely (lav-li) adj délicieux, ravissant, beau

lover (la-veu) n amant m

love-story (lav-stoo-ri) n histoire d'amour

low (lô^{ou}) adj bas; profond; déprimé; ~ **tide** marée basse

lower (lô^{ou}-eu) v baisser; amener; adj inférieur, bas

lowlands (lô^{ou}-leunndz) pl plaine f

loyal (loï-eul) adj loyal

lubricate (loû-bri-kéït) v huiler, lubrifier

lubrication (loû-bri-kéï-cheunn) n lubrification f; ~ **oil** lubrifiant m; ~ **system** système de lubrification

luck (lak) n chance f; hasard m; **bad ~** malchance f

lucky (la-ki) adj chanceux; ~ **charm** porte-bonheur m

ludicrous (loû-di-kreuss) adj ridicule, grotesque

luggage (la-ghidj) n bagage m; **hand ~** bagage à main; **left ~ office** consigne f; ~ **rack** porte-bagages m, filet à bagage; ~ **van** fourgon m

lukewarm (loûk-^{ou}oom) adj tiède

lumbago (lamm-béï-ghô^{ou}) n lumbago m

luminous (loû-mi-neuss) adj lumineux

lump (lammp) n morceau m, grumeau m; bosse f; ~ **of sugar** morceau de sucre; ~ **sum** somme globale

lumpy (lamm-pi) adj grumeleux

lunacy (loû-neu-si) n folie f

lunatic (loû-neu-tik) adj fou; n aliéné mental

lunch (lanntch) n lunch m, déjeuner m

luncheon (lann-tcheunn) n déjeuner m

lung (lanng) n poumon m

lust (last) n concupiscence f

luxurious (lagh-jou^{eu}-ri-euss) adj luxueux

luxury (lak-cheu-ri) n luxe m

M

machine (meu-chiin) n appareil m, machine f

machinery (meu-chii-neu-ri) n machinerie f; mécanisme m

mackerel (mæ-kreul) n (pl ~) maquereau m

mackintosh (mæ-kinn-toch) n imperméable m

mad (mæd) adj dément, insensé, fou; enragé

madam (mæ-deumm) n madame f

madness (mæd-neuss) n démence f

magazine (mæ-gheu-ziin) n revue f

magic (mæ-djik) n magie f; adj magique

magician (meu-dji-cheunn) n prestidigitateur m

magistrate (mæ-dji-stréït) n magistrat m

magnetic (mægh-nè-tik) adj magnétique

magneto (mægh-nii-tô^{ou}) n (pl ~s) magnéto f

magnificent (mægh-ni-fi-seunnt) adj magnifique; grandiose, splendide

magpie (mægh-païe) n pie f

maid (méïd) n bonne f

maiden name (méï-deunn néïm) nom de jeune fille

mail (méïl) n courrier m; v *mettre à la poste; ~ **order** Am mandat-poste m

mailbox (méïl-boks) nAm boîte aux lettres

main (méïn) *adj* principal; majeur; ~ **deck** pont principal; ~ **line** ligne principale; ~ **road** route principale; ~ **street** rue principale

mainland (*méïn*-leunnd) *n* terre ferme

mainly (*méïn*-li) *adv* principalement

mains (méïnz) *pl* secteur *m*

maintain (méïn-*téïn*) *v* *maintenir

maintenance (*méïn*-teu-neunns) *n* entretien *m*

maize (méïz) *n* maïs *m*

major (*méï*-djeu) *adj* grand; majeur

majority (meu-*djo*-reu-ti) *n* majorité *f*

***make** (méïk) *v* *faire, rendre; gagner; réussir; ~ **do with** se débrouiller avec; ~ **good** compenser; ~ **up** dresser

make-up (*méï*-kap) *n* maquillage *m*

malaria (meu-*lê* eu-ri-eu) *n* malaria *f*

Malay (meu-*léï*) *n* Malais *m*

Malaysia (meu-*léï*-zi-eu) Malaysia *m*

Malaysian (meu-*léï*-zi-eunn) *adj* malaisien

male (méïl) *adj* mâle

malicious (meu-*li*-cheuss) *adj* malveillant

malignant (meu-*ligh*-neunnt) *adj* malin

mallet (*mæ*-lit) *n* maillet *m*

malnutrition (mæl-nyou-*tri*-cheunn) *n* dénutrition *f*

mammal (*mæ*-meul) *n* mammifère *m*

mammoth (*mæ*-meuθ) *n* mammouth *m*

man (mæn) *n* (pl men) homme *m*; **men's room** toilettes pour hommes

manage (*mæ*-nidj) *v* diriger; réussir

manageable (*mæ*-ni-djeu-beul) *adj* maniable

management (*mæ*-nidj-meunnt) *n* direction *f*; gestion *f*

manager (*mæ*-ni-djeu) *n* chef *m*, directeur *m*

mandarin (*mæn*-deu-rinn) *n* mandarine *f*

mandate (*mæn*-déït) *n* mandat *m*

manger (*méïn*-djeu) *n* mangeoire *f*

manicure (*mæ*-ni-kyou eu) *n* manucure *f*; *v* soigner les ongles

mankind (mæn-*kaïnd*) *n* humanité *f*

mannequin (*mæ*-neu-kinn) *n* mannequin *m*

manner (*mæ*-neu) *n* mode *m*, manière *f*; **manners** *pl* savoir-vivre *m*

man-of-war (mæ-neuv- ou oo) *n* navire de guerre

manor-house (*mæ*-neu-haouss) *n* manoir *m*

mansion (*mæn*-cheunn) *n* manoir *m*

manual (*mæ*-nyou-eul) *adj* manuel

manufacture (mæ-nyou-*fæk*-tcheu) *v* fabriquer

manufacturer (mæ-nyou-*fæk*-tcheu-reu) *n* fabricant *m*

manure (meu-*nyou* eu) *n* fumier *m*

manuscript (*mæ*-nyou-skript) *n* manuscrit *m*

many (*mè*-ni) *adj* beaucoup de

map (mæp) *n* carte *f*; plan *m*

maple (*méï*-peul) *n* érable *m*

marble (*mââ*-beul) *n* marbre *m*; bille *f*

March (mââtch) mars

march (mââtch) *v* marcher; *n* marche *f*

mare (mè eu) *n* jument *f*

margarine (mââ-djeu-*riin*) *n* margarine *f*

margin (*mââ*-djinn) *n* marge *f*

maritime (*mæ*-ri-taïm) *adj* maritime

mark (mââk) *v* marquer; caractériser; *n* marque *f*; note *f*; cible *f*

market (*mââ*-kit) *n* marché *m*

market-place (*mââ*-kit-pléïss) *n* place du marché

marmalade (*mââ*-meu-léïd) *n* marmelade *f*

marriage (*mæ*-ridj) *n* mariage *m*

marrow (mæ-rôᵒᵘ) *n* moelle *f*

marry (mæ-ri) *v* épouser, se marier

marsh (mââch) *n* marais *m*

marshy (mââ-chi) *adj* marécageux

martyr (mââ-teu) *n* martyr *m*

marvel (mââ-veul) *n* merveille *f*; *v* s'émerveiller

marvellous (mââ-veu-leuss) *adj* merveilleux

mascara (mæ-*skââ*-reu) *n* cosmétique pour les cils

masculine (*mæ*-skyou-linn) *adj* masculin

mash (mæch) *v* écraser

mask (mââsk) *n* masque *m*

Mass (mæss) *n* messe *f*

mass (mæss) *n* masse *f*; ~ **production** production en série

massage (mæ-sââj) *n* massage *m*; *v* masser

masseur (mæ-*seû*) *n* masseur *m*

massive (*mæ*-siv) *adj* massif

mast (mââst) *n* mât *m*

master (*mââ*-steu) *n* maître *m*; patron *m*; professeur *m*, instituteur *m*; *v* maîtriser

masterpiece (*mââ*-steu-piiss) *n* chef-d'œuvre *m*

mat (mæt) *n* tapis *m*; *adj* mat, terne

match (mætch) *n* allumette *f*; match *m*; *v* s'accorder avec

match-box (*mætch*-boks) *n* boîte d'allumettes

material (meu-*tiᵉᵘ*-ri-eul) *n* matériel *m*; tissu *m*; *adj* physique, matériel

mathematical (mæ-θeu-*mæ*-ti-keul) *adj* mathématique

mathematics (mæ-θeu-*mæ*-tiks) *n* mathématiques *fpl*

matrimonial (mæ-tri-*môᵒᵘ*-ni-eul) *adj* matrimonial

matrimony (*mæ*-tri-meu-ni) *n* mariage *m*

matter (*mæ*-teu) *n* matière *f*; affaire *f*, question *f*; *v* *avoir de l'importance; **as a ~ of fact** effectivement, en fait

matter-of-fact (mæ-teu-reuv-*fækt*) *adj* réaliste

mattress (*mæ*-treuss) *n* matelas *m*

mature (meu-*tyouᵉᵘ*) *adj* mûr

maturity (meu-*tyouᵉᵘ*-reu-ti) *n* maturité *f*

mausoleum (moo-seu-*lii*-eumm) *n* mausolée *m*

mauve (môᵒᵘv) *adj* mauve

May (méï) mai

*may (méï) *v* *pouvoir

maybe (*méï*-bii) *adv* peut-être

mayor (mèᵉᵘ) *n* maire *m*

maze (méïz) *n* labyrinthe *m*

me (mii) *pron* moi; me

meadow (mè-dôᵒᵘ) *n* pré *m*

meal (miil) *n* repas *m*

mean (miin) *adj* mesquin; *n* moyenne *f*

*mean (miin) *v* signifier; *vouloir dire

meaning (*mii*-ninng) *n* signification *f*

meaningless (*mii*-ninng-leuss) *adj* dénué de sens

means (miinz) *n* moyen *m*; **by no ~** aucunement, en aucun cas

in the meantime (inn ðeu *miin*-taïm) en attendant, entre-temps

meanwhile (*miin*-ᵒᵘaïl) *adv* entre-temps

measles (*mii*-zeulz) *n* rougeole *f*

measure (*mè*-jeu) *v* mesurer; *n* mesure *f*

meat (miit) *n* viande *f*

mechanic (mi-*kæ*-nik) *n* monteur *m*, mécanicien *m*

mechanical (mi-*kæ*-ni-keul) *adj* mécanique

mechanism (*mè*-keu-ni-zeumm) *n* mécanisme *m*

medal (*mè*-deul) *n* médaille *f*

mediaeval (mè-di-*ii*-veul) *adj* médiéval

mediate (mii-di-éit) *v* *servir d'intermédiaire

mediator (mii-di-éï-teu) *n* médiateur *m*

medical (mè-di-keul) *adj* médical

medicine (mèd-sinn) *n* médicament *m*; médecine *f*

meditate (mè-di-téït) *v* méditer

Mediterranean (mè-di-teu-*réï*-ni-eunn) Méditerranée *f*

medium (mii-di-eumm) *adj* moyen

*meet (miit) *v* rencontrer

meeting (mii-tinng) *n* assemblée *f*, réunion *f*; rencontre *f*

meeting-place (mii-tinng-pléïss) *n* lieu de rencontre

melancholy (mè-leunng-keu-li) *n* mélancolie *f*

mellow (mè-lô°u) *adj* moelleux

melodrama (mè-leu-drââ-meu) *n* mélodrame *m*

melody (mè-leu-di) *n* mélodie *f*

melon (mè-leunn) *n* melon *m*

melt (mèlt) *v* fondre

member (mèm-beu) *n* membre *m*; **Member of Parliament** député *m*

membership (mèm-beu-chip) *n* affiliation *f*

memo (mè-mô°u) *n* (pl ~s) mémorandum *m*

memorable (mè-meu-reu-beul) *adj* mémorable

memorial (meu-*moo*-ri-eul) *n* mémorial *m*

memorize (mè-meu-raïz) *v* *apprendre par cœur

memory (mè-meu-ri) *n* mémoire *f*; souvenir *m*

mend (mènd) *v* réparer

menstruation (mèn-strou-*éï*-cheunn) *n* menstruation *f*

mental (mèn-teul) *adj* mental

mention (*mèn*-cheunn) *v* mentionner; *n* mention *f*

menu (mè-nyou) *n* carte *f*, menu *m*

merchandise (meû-tcheunn-daïz) *n* marchandise *f*

merchant (meû-tcheunnt) *n* commerçant *m*, marchand *m*

merciful (meû-si-feul) *adj* miséricordieux

mercury (meû-kyou-ri) *n* mercure *m*

mercy (meû-si) *n* miséricorde *f*, clémence *f*

mere (mi°u) *adj* pur

merely (*mi*°u-li) *adv* seulement

merger (meû-djeu) *n* fusion *f*

merit (mè-rit) *v* mériter; *n* mérite *m*

mermaid (meû-méïd) *n* sirène *f*

merry (mè-ri) *adj* joyeux

merry-go-round (mè-ri-ghô°u-raound) *n* chevaux de bois

mesh (mèch) *n* maille *f*

mess (mèss) *n* désordre *m*, gâchis *m*; ~ **up** gâcher

message (mè-sidj) *n* commission *f*, message *m*

messenger (mè-sinn-djeu) *n* messager *m*

metal (mè-teul) *n* métal *m*; métallique

meter (mii-teu) *n* compteur *m*

method (mè-θeud) *n* méthode *f*; ordre *m*

methodical (meu-θo-di-keul) *adj* méthodique

methylated spirits (mè-θeu-léï-tid *spi*-rits) alcool à brûler

metre (mii-teu) *n* mètre *m*

metric (mè-trik) *adj* métrique

Mexican (mèk-si-keunn) *adj* mexicain; *n* Mexicain *m*

Mexico (mèk-si-kô°u) Mexique *m*

mezzanine (mè-zeu-niin) *n* entresol *m*

microphone (maï-kreu-fô°un) *n* microphone *m*

microwave oven (*maï*-kreu-^{ou}éïv *a*-veunn) *n* four à micro-ondes *m*

midday (*mid*-déï) *n* midi *m*

middle (*mi*-deul) *n* milieu *m*; *adj* du milieu; **Middle Ages** moyen-âge *m*; ~ **class** classe moyenne; **middle-class** *adj* bourgeois

midnight (*mid*-naït) *n* minuit *m*

midsummer (*mid*-sa-meu) *n* plein été *m*

midwife (*mid*-^{ou}aïf) *n* (pl -wives) sagefemme *f*

might (maït) *n* puissance *f*

*might (maït) *v* *pouvoir

mighty (*maï*-ti) *adj* puissant

mild (maïld) *adj* doux

mildew (*mil*-dyou) *n* moisissure *f*

mile (maïl) *n* mille *m*

mileage (*maï*-lidj) *n* nombre de milles

milepost (*maïl*-pô^{ou}st) *n* poteau indicateur

milestone (*maïl*-stô^{ou}n) *n* borne routière

milieu (*mii*-lyeû) *n* milieu *m*

military (*mi*-li-teu-ri) *adj* militaire; ~ **force** force armée

milk (milk) *n* lait *m*

milkman (*milk*-meunn) *n* (pl -men) laitier *m*

milk-shake (*milk*-chéïk) *n* frappé *m*

milky (*mil*-ki) *adj* laiteux

mill (mil) *n* moulin *m*; usine *f*

miller (*mi*-leu) *n* meunier *m*

milliner (*mi*-li-neu) *n* modiste *f*

million (*mil*-yeunn) *n* million *m*

millionaire (mil-yeu-*nè^{eu}*) *n* millionnaire *m*

mince (minns) *v* hacher

mind (maïnd) *n* esprit *m*; *v* *faire objection à; prêter attention à

mine (maïn) *n* mine *f*

miner (*maï*-neu) *n* mineur *m*

mineral (*mi*-neu-reul) *n* minéral *m*; ~ **water** eau minérale

miniature (*minn*-yeu-tcheu) *n* miniatu-re *f*

minimum (*mi*-ni-meumm) *n* minimum *m*

mining (*maï*-ninng) *n* exploitation minière

minister (*mi*-ni-steu) *n* ministre *m*; pasteur *m*; **Prime Minister** premier ministre

ministry (*mi*-ni-stri) *n* ministère *m*

mink (minngk) *n* vison *m*

minor (*maï*-neu) *adj* petit, menu, mineur; subalterne; *n* mineur *m*

minority (maï-*no*-reu-ti) *n* minorité *f*

mint (minnt) *n* menthe *f*

minus (*maï*-neuss) *prep* moins

minute¹ (*mi*-nit) *n* minute *f*; **minutes** compte rendu

minute² (maï-*nyoût*) *adj* minuscule

miracle (*mi*-reu-keul) *n* miracle *m*

miraculous (mi-*ræ*-kyou-leuss) *adj* miraculeux

mirror (*mi*-reu) *n* miroir *m*

misbehave (miss-bi-*héïv*) *v* se *conduire mal

miscarriage (miss-*kæ*-ridj) *n* fausse couche

miscellaneous (mi-seu-*léï*-ni-euss) *adj* divers

mischief (*miss*-tchif) *n* espièglerie *f*; mal *m*, dommage *m*, malice *f*

mischievous (*miss*-tchi-veuss) *adj* malicieux

miserable (*mi*-zeu-reu-beul) *adj* misérable, malheureux

misery (*mi*-zeu-ri) *n* détresse *f*, misère *f*

misfortune (miss-*foo*-tchèn) *n* infortune *f*, malheur *m*

*mislay (miss-*léï*) *v* égarer

misplaced (miss-*pléïst*) *adj* inopportun; mal placé

mispronounce (miss-preu-*naouns*) *v* mal prononcer

miss¹ (miss) mademoiselle, demoiselle

f

miss² (miss) v manquer

missing (*mi*-sinng) adj manquant; ~ **person** disparu m

mist (mist) n brume f, brouillard m

mistake (mi-*stéïk*) n méprise f, faute f, erreur f

*mistake (mi-*stéïk*) v confondre

mistaken (mi-*stéï*-keunn) adj erroné; ***be ~** se tromper

mister (*mi*-steu) n monsieur m

mistress (*mi*-streuss) n maîtresse de maison; patronne f; maîtresse f

mistrust (miss-*trast*) v se méfier de

misty (*mi*-sti) adj brumeux

*misunderstand (mi-sann-deu-*stænd*) v mal *comprendre

misunderstanding (mi-sann-deu-*stæn*-dinng) n malentendu m

misuse (miss-*youss*) n abus m

mittens (*mi*-teunnz) pl moufles fpl

mix (miks) v mélanger, mêler; ~ **with** fréquenter

mixed (mikst) adj mêlé, mélangé

mixer (*mik*-seu) n mixeur m

mixture (*miks*-tcheu) n mélange m

moan (môᵘn) v gémir

moat (môᵘt) n douve f

mobile (*môᵘ*-baïl) adj mobile

mock (mok) v se moquer de

mockery (*mo*-keu-ri) n moquerie f

model (*mo*-deul) n modèle m; mannequin m; v façonner, modeler

moderate (*mo*-deu-reut) adj modéré

modern (*mo*-deunn) adj moderne

modest (*mo*-dist) adj modeste

modesty (*mo*-di-sti) n modestie f

modify (*mo*-di-faï) v modifier

mohair (*môᵘ*-hèᵘ) n mohair m

moist (moïst) adj mouillé, moite

moisten (*moï*-seunn) v humecter

moisture (*moïss*-tcheu) n humidité f; **moisturizing cream** crème hydratante

molar (*môᵘ*-leu) n molaire f

moment (*môᵘ*-meunnt) n instant m, moment m

momentary (*môᵘ*-meunn-teu-ri) adj momentané

monarch (*mo*-neuk) n monarque m

monarchy (*mo*-neu-ki) n monarchie f

monastery (*mo*-neu-stri) n monastère m

Monday (*mann*-di) lundi m

monetary (*ma*-ni-teu-ri) adj monétaire; ~ **unit** unité monétaire

money (*ma*-ni) n argent m; ~ **exchange** bureau de change; ~ **order** mandat-poste m

monk (manngk) n moine m

monkey (*manng*-ki) n singe m

monologue (*mo*-no-logh) n monologue m

monopoly (meu-*no*-peu-li) n monopole m

monotonous (meu-*no*-teu-neuss) adj monotone

month (mannθ) n mois m

monthly (*mann*θ-li) adj mensuel; ~ **magazine** revue mensuelle

monument (*mo*-nyou-meunnt) n monument m

mood (moûd) n humeur f

moon (moûn) n lune f

moonlight (*moûn*-laït) n clair de lune

moor (mouᵘ) n bruyère f, lande f

moose (moûss) n (pl ~, ~s) élan m

moped (*môᵘ*-pèd) n vélomoteur m

moral (*mo*-reul) n morale f; adj moral; **morals** mœurs fpl

morality (meu-*ræ*-leu-ti) n moralité f

more (moo) adj plus; **once ~** une fois de plus

moreover (moo-*rôᵘ*-veu) adv d'ailleurs, de plus

morning (*moo*-ninng) n matin m; ~ **paper** journal du matin

Moroccan (meu-*ro*-keunn) adj marocain; *n* Marocain *m*

Morocco (meu-*ro*-kô^{ou}) Maroc *m*

morphia (*moo*-fi-eu) *n* morphine *f*

morphine (*moo*-fiin) *n* morphine *f*

morsel (*moo*-seul) *n* morceau *m*

mortal (*moo*-teul) *adj* fatal, mortel

mortgage (*moo*-ghidj) *n* hypothèque *f*

mosaic (meu-*zëï*-ik) *n* mosaïque *f*

mosque (mosk) *n* mosquée *f*

mosquito (meu-*skii*-tô^{ou}) *n* (pl ~es) moustique *m*

mosquito-net (meu-*skii*-tô^{ou}-nèt) *n* moustiquaire *f*

moss (moss) *n* mousse *f*

most (mô^{ou}st) *adj* le plus; **at** ~ au maximum, tout au plus; ~ **of all** surtout

mostly (*mô^{ou}*st-li) *adv* le plus souvent

motel (mô^{ou}-*tèl*) *n* motel *m*

moth (moθ) *n* mite *f*

mother (*ma*-ðeu) *n* mère *f*; ~ **tongue** langue maternelle

mother-in-law (*ma*-ðeu-rinn-loo) *n* (pl mothers-) belle-mère *f*

mother-of-pearl (ma-ðeu-reuv-*peûl*) *n* nacre *f*

motion (*mô^{ou}*-cheunn) *n* mouvement *m*; motion *f*

motive (*mô^{ou}*-tiv) *n* motif *m*

motor (*mô^{ou}*-teu) *n* moteur *m*; *v* voyager en auto; ~ **body** *Am* carrosserie *f*; **starter** ~ démarreur *m*

motorbike (*mô^{ou}*-teu-baïk) *nAm* vélomoteur *m*

motor-boat (*mô^{ou}*-teu-bô^{ou}t) *n* canot automobile

motor-car (*mô^{ou}*-teu-kââ) *n* automobile *f*

motor-cycle (*mô^{ou}*-teu-saï-keul) *n* motocyclette *f*

motoring (*mô^{ou}*-teu-rinng) *n* automobilisme *m*

motorist (*mô^{ou}*-teu-rist) *n* automobiliste *m*

motorway (*mô^{ou}*-teu-^{ou}éï) *n* autoroute *f*

motto (mo-tô^{ou}) *n* (pl ~es, ~s) devise *f*

mouldy (*mô^{ou}l*-di) *adj* moisi

mound (maound) *n* butte *f*

mount (maount) *v* monter; *n* mont *m*

mountain (*maoun*-tinn) *n* montagne *f*; ~ **pass** col *m*; ~ **range** chaîne de montagnes

mountaineering (maoun-ti-*ni^{eu}*-rinng) *n* alpinisme *m*

mountainous (*maoun*-ti-neuss) *adj* montagneux

mourning (*moo*-ninng) *n* deuil *m*

mouse (maouss) *n* (pl mice) souris *f*

moustache (meu-*stââch*) *n* moustache *f*

mouth (maouθ) *n* bouche *f*; gueule *f*; embouchure *f*

mouthwash (*maouθ*-^{ou}och) *n* eau dentifrice

movable (*moû*-veu-beul) *adj* mobile

move (moûv) *v* bouger; déplacer; se *mouvoir; déménager; *émouvoir; *n* tour *m*, pas *m*; déménagement *m*

movement (*moûv*-meunnt) *n* mouvement *m*

movie (*moû*-vi) *n* film *m*; **movies** *Am* cinéma *m*; ~ **theater** *Am* cinéma *m*

much (match) *adj* beaucoup de; *adv* beaucoup; **as** ~ autant

muck (mak) *n* gadoue *f*

mud (mad) *n* boue *f*

muddle (*ma*-deul) *n* fouillis *m*, pagaille *f*, confusion *f*; *v* embrouiller

muddy (*ma*-di) *adj* boueux

mud-guard (*mad*-ghââd) *n* garde-boue *m*

muffler (*maf*-leu) *nAm* silencieux *m*

mug (magh) *n* gobelet *m*, chope *f*

mulberry (*mal*-beu-ri) *n* mûre *f*

mule (myoûl) *n* mulet *m*, mule *f*

mullet (*ma*-lit) *n* mulet *m*

multiplication (mal-ti-pli-*kéï*-cheunn) *n* multiplication *f*

multiply (*mal*-ti-plaï) *v* multiplier

mumps (mammps) *n* oreillons *mpl*

municipal (myoû-*ni*-si-peul) *adj* municipal

municipality (myoû-ni-si-*pæ*-leu-ti) *n* municipalité *f*

murder (*meû*-deu) *n* assassinat *m*; *v* assassiner

murderer (*meû*-deu-reu) *n* meurtrier *m*

muscle (*ma*-seul) *n* muscle *m*

muscular (*ma*-skyou-leu) *adj* musclé

museum (myoû-*zii*-eumm) *n* musée *m*

mushroom (*mach*-roûm) *n* champignon *m*

music (*myoû*-zik) *n* musique *f*; ~ **academy** conservatoire *m*

musical (*myoû*-zi-keul) *adj* musical; *n* comédie musicale

music-hall (*myoû*-zik-hool) *n* musichall *m*

musician (myoû-*zi*-cheunn) *n* musicien *m*

muslin (*maz*-linn) *n* mousseline *f*

mussel (*ma*-seul) *n* moule *f*

*must (mast) *v* *falloir

mustard (*ma*-steud) *n* moutarde *f*

mute (myoût) *adj* muet

mutiny (*myoû*-ti-ni) *n* mutinerie *f*

mutton (*ma*-teunn) *n* mouton *m*

mutual (*myoû*-tchou-eul) *adj* mutuel, réciproque

my (maï) *adj* mon

myself (maï-*sèlf*) *pron* me; moi-même

mysterious (mi-*sti*[eu]-ri-euss) *adj* mystérieux

mystery (*mi*-steu-ri) *n* énigme *f*, mystère *m*

myth (miθ) *n* mythe *m*

N

nail (néïl) *n* ongle *m*; clou *m*

nailbrush (*néïl*-brach) *n* brosse à ongles

nail-file (*néïl*-faïl) *n* lime à ongles

nail-polish (*néïl*-po-lich) *n* vernis à ongle

nail-scissors (*néïl*-si-zeuz) *pl* ciseaux à ongles

naïve (*néï*-*iiv*) *adj* naïf

naked (*néï*-kid) *adj* nu; dénudé

name (néïm) *n* nom *m*; *v* nommer; **in the ~ of** au nom de

namely (*néïm*-li) *adv* notamment

nap (næp) *n* somme *m*

napkin (*næp*-kinn) *n* serviette *f*

nappy (*næ*-pi) *n* couche *f*

narcosis (nââ-*kô*[ou]-siss) *n* (pl -ses) narcose *f*

narcotic (nââ-*ko*-tik) *n* narcotique *m*

narrow (næ-rô[ou]) *adj* serré, étroit

narrow-minded (næ-rô[ou]-*maïn*-did) *adj* borné

nasty (*nââ*-sti) *adj* antipathique, désagréable; méchant

nation (*néï*-cheunn) *n* nation *f*; peuple *m*

national (*næ*-cheu-neul) *adj* national; de l'Etat; ~ **anthem** hymne national; ~ **dress** costume national; ~ **park** parc national

nationality (næ-cheu-*næ*-leu-ti) *n* nationalité *f*

nationalize (*næ*-cheu-neu-laïz) *v* nationaliser

native (*néï*-tiv) *n* indigène *m*; *adj* indigène; ~ **country** patrie *f*, pays natal; ~ **language** langue maternelle

natural (*næ*-tcheu-reul) *adj* naturel; inné

naturally (*næ*-tcheu-reu-li) *adv* bien sûr, naturellement

nature (*néi*-tcheu) *n* nature *f*

naughty (*noo*-ti) *adj* polisson, méchant

nausea (*noo*-si-eu) *n* nausée *f*

naval (*néi*-veul) *adj* naval

navel (*néi*-veul) *n* nombril *m*

navigable (*næ*-vi-gheu-beul) *adj* navigable

navigate (*næ*-vi-ghéit) *v* naviguer

navigation (næ-vi-*ghéi*-cheunn) *n* navigation *f*

navy (*néi*-vi) *n* marine *f*

near (ni*eu*) *prep* près de; *adj* proche, près

nearby (*ni*eu-baï) *adj* proche

nearly (*ni*eu-li) *adv* presque

neat (niit) *adj* soigné; pur

necessary (*nè*-seu-seu-ri) *adj* nécessaire

necessity (neu-*sè*-seu-ti) *n* nécessité *f*

neck (nèk) *n* cou *m*; **nape of the ~** nuque *f*

necklace (*nèk*-leuss) *n* collier *m*

necktie (*nèk*-taï) *n* cravate *f*

need (niid) *v* *falloir, *avoir besoin de; *n* besoin *m*; nécessité *f*; **~ to** *devoir

needle (*nii*-deul) *n* aiguille *f*

needlework (*nii*-deul-eu*euk*) *n* travail à l'aiguille

negative (*nè*-gheu-tiv) *adj* négatif; *n* négatif *m*

neglect (ni-*ghlèkt*) *v* négliger; *n* négligence *f*

neglectful (ni-*ghlèkt*-feul) *adj* négligent

negligee (*nè*-ghli-jéi) *n* négligé *m*

negotiate (ni-*ghô*ou-chi-éit) *v* négocier

negotiation (ni-ghô*ou*-chi-éi-cheunn) *n* négociation *f*

Negro (*nii*-ghrô*ou*) *n* (pl ~es) noir *m*

neighbour (*néi*-beu) *n* voisin *m*

neighbourhood (*néi*-beu-houd) *n* voisinage *m*

neighbouring (*néi*-beu-rinng) *adj* contigu, avoisinant

neither (*naï*-ðeu) *pron* ni l'un ni l'autre; **neither ... nor** ni ... ni

neon (*nii*-onn) *n* néon *m*

nephew (*nè*-fyou) *n* neveu *m*

nerve (neûv) *n* nerf *m*; audace *f*

nervous (*neû*-veuss) *adj* nerveux

nest (nèst) *n* nid *m*

net (nèt) *n* filet *m*; *adj* net

the Netherlands (*nè*-ðeu-leunndz) Pays-Bas *mpl*

network (*nèt*-ou*euk*) *n* réseau *m*

neuralgia (nyou*eu*-*ræl*-djeu) *n* névralgie *f*

neurosis (nyou*eu*-*rô*ou-siss) *n* névrose *f*

neuter (*nyoû*-teu) *adj* neutre

neutral (*nyoû*-treul) *adj* neutre

never (*nè*-veu) *adv* ne ... jamais

nevertheless (nè-veu-ðeu-*lèss*) *adv* néanmoins

new (nyou) *adj* nouveau; **New Year** Nouvel An

news (nyouz) *n* nouvelles, nouvelle *f*; actualités

newsagent (*nyou*-zéi-djeunnt) *n* marchand de journaux

newspaper (*nyou*z-péi-peu) *n* journal *m*

newsreel (*nyou*z-riil) *n* actualités

newsstand (*nyou*z-stænd) *n* kiosque à journaux

New Zealand (nyou *zii*-leunnd) Nouvelle-Zélande *f*

next (nèkst) *adj* prochain, suivant; **~ to** à côté de

next-door (nèkst-*doo*) *adv* à côté

nice (naïss) *adj* gentil, joli, plaisant; bon; sympathique

nickel (*ni*-keul) *n* nickel *m*

nickname (*nik*-néim) *n* surnom *m*

nicotine (*ni*-keu-tiin) *n* nicotine *f*

niece (niiss) *n* nièce *f*

Nigeria (naï-*djï*^{eu}-ri-eu) Nigeria *m*

Nigerian (naï-*djï*^{eu}-ri-eunn) *adj* nigérien; *n* Nigérien *m*

night (naït) *n* nuit *f*; soir *m*; **by ~** de nuit; **~ flight** vol de nuit; **~ rate** tarif de nuit; **~ train** train de nuit

nightclub (*naït*-klab) *n* boîte de nuit

night-cream (*naït*-kriim) *n* crème de nuit

nightdress (*naït*-drèss) *n* chemise de nuit

nightingale (*naï*-tinng-ghéïl) *n* rossignol *m*

nightly (*naït*-li) *adj* nocturne

nil (nil) rien

nine (naïn) *num* neuf

nineteen (naïn-*tiin*) *num* dix-neuf

nineteenth (naïn-*tiin*θ) *num* dix-neuvième

ninety (*naïn*-ti) *num* quatre-vingt-dix

ninth (naïnθ) *num* neuvième

nitrogen (*naï*-treu-djeunn) *n* azote *m*

no (nô^{ou}) *non*; *adj* aucun; **~ one** ne ... personne

nobility (nô^{ou}-*bi*-leu-ti) *n* noblesse *f*

noble (*nô^{ou}*-beul) *adj* noble

nobody (*nô^{ou}*-bo-di) *pron* ne ... personne

nod (nod) *n* inclination de la tête; *v* opiner de la tête

noise (noïz) *n* bruit *m*; fracas *m*, vacarme *m*

noisy (*noï*-zi) *adj* bruyant; sonore

nominal (*no*-mi-neul) *adj* nominal

nominate (*no*-mi-néït) *v* nommer

nomination (no-mi-*néï*-cheunn) *n* nomination *f*

none (nann) *pron* aucun

nonsense (*nonn*-seunns) *n* sottise *f*

noon (noûn) *n* midi *m*

normal (*noo*-meul) *adj* normal

north (nooθ) *n* nord *m*; *adj* septen-

trional; **North Pole** pôle nord

north-east (nooθ-*iist*) *n* nord-est *m*

northerly (noo-*đeu*-li) *adj* du nord

northern (noo-đeunn) *adj* septentrional

north-west (nooθ-^{ou}*èst*) *n* nord-ouest *m*

Norway (*noo*-^{ou}éï) Norvège *f*

Norwegian (noo-^{ou}*ii*-djeunn) *adj* norvégien; *n* Norvégien *m*

nose (nô^{ou}z) *n* nez *m*

nosebleed (*nô^{ou}*z-bliid) *n* saignement de nez

nostril (*no*-stril) *n* narine *f*

not (not) *adv* ne ... pas

notary (*nô^{ou}*-teu-ri) *n* notaire *m*

note (nô^{ou}t) *n* note *f*; ton *m*; *v* noter; observer, constater

notebook (*nô^{ou}t*-bouk) *n* carnet *m*

noted (*nô^{ou}*-tid) *adj* illustre

notepaper (*nô^{ou}t*-péï-peu) *n* papier à écrire, papier à lettres

nothing (*na*-θinng) *n* rien, ne ... rien

notice (*nô^{ou}*-tiss) *v* observer, noter, remarquer; *n* avis *m*, nouvelle *f*; attention *f*

noticeable (*nô^{ou}*-ti-seu-beul) *adj* perceptible; remarquable

notify (*nô^{ou}*-ti-faï) *v* notifier; avertir

notion (*nô^{ou}*-cheunn) *n* notion *f*

notorious (nô^{ou}-*too*-ri-euss) *adj* notoire

nougat (noû-ghââ) *n* nougat *m*

nought (noot) *n* zéro *m*

noun (naoun) *n* nom *m*, substantif *m*

nourishing (*na*-ri-chinng) *adj* nourrissant

novel (*no*-veul) *n* roman *m*

novelist (*no*-veu-list) *n* romancier *m*

November (nô^{ou}-*vèm*-beu) novembre *m*

now (naou) *adv* maintenant; à l'heure actuelle; **~ and then** de temps en temps

nowadays (*naou*-eu-déïz) *adv* actuellement

nowhere (*nô*ᵒᵘ-*ou*èᵉᵘ) *adv* nulle part

nozzle (*no*-zeul) *n* bec *m*

nuance (nyoû-*anss*) *n* nuance *f*

nuclear (*nyoû*-kli-eu) *adj* nucléaire; ~ energy énergie nucléaire

nucleus (*nyoû*-kli-euss) *n* noyau *m*

nude (nyoûd) *adj* nu; *n* nu *m*

nuisance (*nyoû*-seunns) *n* ennui *m*

numb (namm) *adj* engourdi

number (*namm*-beu) *n* numéro *m*; chiffre *m*, nombre *m*

numeral (*nyoû*-meu-reul) *n* nombre *m*

numerous (*nyoû*-meu-reuss) *adj* nombreux

nun (nann) *n* religieuse *f*

nunnery (*na*-neu-ri) *n* couvent *m*

nurse (neûss) *n* infirmière *f*; bonne d'enfants; *v* soigner; allaiter

nursery (*neû*-seu-ri) *n* chambre d'enfants; crèche *f*; pépinière *f*

nut (nat) *n* noix *f*; écrou *m*

nutcrackers (*nat*-kræ-keuz) *pl* casse-noix *m*

nutmeg (*nat*-mègh) *n* muscade *f*

nutritious (nyoû-*tri*-cheuss) *adj* nutritif

nutshell (*nat*-chèl) *n* coquille de noix

nylon (*naï*-lonn) *n* nylon *m*

O

oak (ô°ᵘk) *n* chêne *m*

oar (oo) *n* rame *f*

oasis (ô°ᵘ-*éï*-siss) *n* (pl oases) oasis *f*

oath (ô°ᵘθ) *n* serment *m*

oats (ô°ᵘts) *pl* avoine *f*

obedience (eu-*bii*-di-eunns) *n* obéissance *f*

obedient (eu-*bii*-di-eunnt) *adj* obéissant

obey (eu-*béï*) *v* obéir

object¹ (*ob*-djikt) *n* objet *m*; objectif *m*

object² (eub-*djèkt*) *v* objecter; ~ to *faire objection à

objection (eub-*djèk*-cheunn) *n* objection *f*

objective (eub-*djèk*-tiv) *adj* objectif; *n* objectif *m*

obligatory (eu-*bli*-gheu-teu-ri) *adj* obligatoire

oblige (eu-*blaïdj*) *v* obliger; *be obliged to *être obligé de; *devoir

obliging (eu-*blaï*-djinng) *adj* obligeant

oblong (*ob*-lonng) *adj* oblong; *n* rectangle *m*

obscene (eub-*siin*) *adj* obscène

obscure (eub-*skyou*ᵉᵘ) *adj* confus, vague, sombre, obscur

observation (ob-zeu-*véï*-cheunn) *n* observation *f*

observatory (eub-*zeû*-veu-tri) *n* observatoire *m*

observe (eub-*zeûv*) *v* observer

obsession (eub-*sè*-cheunn) *n* obsession *f*

obstacle (*ob*-steu-keul) *n* obstacle *m*

obstinate (*ob*-sti-neut) *adj* obstiné; opiniâtre

obtain (eub-*téïn*) *v* se procurer, *obtenir

obtainable (eub-*téï*-neu-beul) *adj* disponible

obvious (*ob*-vi-euss) *adj* évident

occasion (eu-*kéï*-jeunn) *n* occasion *f*; motif *m*

occasionally (eu-*kéï*-jeu-neu-li) *adv* de temps en temps

occupant (*o*-kyou-peunnt) *n* occupant *m*

occupation (o-kyou-*péï*-cheunn) *n* occupation *f*

occupy (*o*-kyou-paï) *v* occuper

occur (eu-*keû*) *v* se passer, se *produire, *survenir

occurrence (eu-*ka*-reunns) *n* événement *m*

ocean (ô^{ou}-cheunn) *n* océan *m*

October (ok-tô^{ou}-beu) octobre

octopus (*ok*-teu-peuss) *n* pieuvre *f*

oculist (*o*-kyou-kst) *n* oculiste *m*

odd (od) *adj* bizarre; impair

odour (ô^{ou}-deu) *n* odeur *f*

of (ov, euv) *prep* de

off (of) *prep* de

offence (eu-*fèns*) *n* infraction *f*; offense *f*, outrage *m*

offend (eu-*fènd*) *v* blesser, offenser; outrager

offensive (eu-*fèn*-siv) *adj* offensif; désobligeant; *n* offensive *f*

offer (*o*-feu) *v* *offrir; *n* offre *f*

office (*o*-fiss) *n* bureau *m*; fonction *f*; ~ **hours** heures de bureau

officer (*o*-fi-seu) *n* officier *m*

official (eu-*fi*-cheul) *adj* officiel

off-licence (*of*-laï-seunns) *n* magasin de spiritueux

often (*o*-feunn) *adv* souvent

oil (oïl) *n* huile *f*; pétrole *m*; **fuel** ~ mazout *m*; ~ **filter** filtre à huile; ~ **pressure** pression d'huile

oil-painting (oïl-*péin*-tinng) *n* peinture à l'huile

oil-refinery (*oïl*-ri-faï-neu-ri) *n* raffinerie de pétrole

oil-well (*oïl*-^{ou}èl) *n* gisement de pétrole, puits de pétrole

oily (*oï*-li) *adj* huileux

ointment (*oïnt*-meunnt) *n* onguent *m*

okay! (ô^{ou}-*kéi*) d'accord!

old (ô^{ou}ld) *adj* vieux; ~ **age** vieillesse *f*

old-fashioned (ô^{ou}ld-*fæ*-cheunnd) *adj* démodé

olive (*o*-liv) *n* olive *f*; ~ **oil** huile d'olive

omelette (*omm*-leut) *n* omelette *f*

ominous (*o*-mi-neuss) *adj* sinistre

omit (eu-*mit*) *v* *omettre

omnipotent (omm-*ni*-peu-teunnt) *adj* omnipotent

on (onn) *prep* sur; à

once (^{ou}anns) *adv* une fois; **at** ~ immédiatement, tout de suite; ~ **more** une fois de plus

oncoming (onn-ka-minng) *adj* venant à la rencontre, proche

one (^{ou}ann) *num* un; *pron* on

oneself (^{ou}ann-*sèlf*) *pron* soi-même

onion (*a*-nyeunn) *n* oignon *m*

only (ô^{ou}n-li) *adj* seul; *adv* rien que, seulement; *conj* cependant

onwards (onn-^{ou}eudz) *adv* en avant

onyx (*o*-niks) *n* onyx *m*

opal (ô^{ou}-peul) *n* opale *f*

open (ô^{ou}-peunn) *v* *ouvrir; *adj* ouvert; franc

opening (ô^{ou}-peu-ninng) *n* ouverture *f*

opera (*o*-peu-reu) *n* opéra *m*; ~ **house** opéra *m*

operate (*o*-peu-réit) *v* opérer, fonctionner

operation (o-peu-*réï*-cheunn) *n* fonctionnement *m*; opération *f*

operator (*o*-peu-réï-teu) *n* standardiste *f*

operetta (o-peu-rè-teu) *n* opérette *f*

opinion (eu-*pi*-nyeunn) *n* idée *f*, opinion *f*

opponent (eu-*pô*^{ou}-neunnt) *n* adversaire *m*

opportunity (o-peu-*tyoû*-neu-ti) *n* occasion *f*

oppose (eu-*pô*^{ou}z) *v* s'opposer

opposite (*o*-peu-zit) *prep* en face de; *adj* opposé, contraire

opposition (o-peu-*zi*-cheunn) *n* opposition *f*

oppress (eu-*près*) *v* oppresser, opprimer

optician (op-*ti*-cheunn) *n* opticien *m*

optimism (*op*-ti-mi-zeumm) *n* optimisme *m*

optimist (*op*-ti-mist) *n* optimiste *m*

optimistic (op-ti-*mi*-stik) *adj* optimiste

optional (*op*-cheu-neul) *adj* facultatif

or (oo) *conj* ou

oral (*oe*-reul) *adj* oral

orange (*o*-rinndj) *n* orange *f*; *adj* orange

orchard (*oo*-tcheud) *n* verger *m*

orchestra (*oo*-ki-streu) *n* orchestre *m*; ~ **seat** *Am* fauteuil d'orchestre

order (*oo*-deu) *v* commander; *n* ordre *m*; commandement *m*; commande *f*; **in** ~ en règle; **in** ~ **to** afin de; **made to** ~ fait sur commande; **out of** ~ en dérangement; **postal** ~ mandat-poste *m*

order-form (*oo*-deu-foom) *n* bon de commande

ordinary (*oo*-deunn-ri) *adj* commun, habituel

ore (oo) *n* minerai *m*

organ (*oo*-gheunn) *n* organe *m*; orgue *m*

organic (oo-*ghæ*-nik) *adj* organique

organization (oo-gheu-naï-*zéï*-cheunn) *n* organisation *f*

organize (*oo*-gheu-naïz) *v* organiser

Orient (*oo*-ri-eunnt) *n* orient *m*

oriental (oo-ri-*èn*-teul) *adj* oriental

orientate (*oo*-ri-eunn-téït) *v* s'orienter

origin (*o*-ri-djinn) *n* origine *f*; descendance *f*, provenance *f*

original (eu-*ri*-dji-neul) *adj* authentique, original

originally (eu-*ri*-dji-neu-li) *adv* originairement

orlon (*oo*-lonn) *n* orlon *m*

ornament (*oo*-neu-meunnt) *n* ornement *m*

ornamental (oo-neu-*mèn*-teul) *adj* ornemental

orphan (*oo*-feunn) *n* orphelin *m*

orthodox (*oo*-θeu-doks) *adj* orthodoxe

ostrich (*o*-stritch) *n* autruche *f*

other (*a*-ðeu) *adj* autre

otherwise (*a*-ðeu-ᵒᵘaïz) *conj* sinon; *adv* autrement

****ought to** (oot) ***devoir

our (aouᵉᵘ) *adj* notre

ourselves (aouᵉᵘ-*sèlvz*) *pron* nous; nous-mêmes

out (aout) *adv* dehors, hors; ~ **of** en dehors de, de

outbreak (*aout*-bréïk) *n* déchaînement *m*

outcome (*aout*-kamm) *n* résultat *m*

****outdo** (aout-*doú*) *v* surpasser

outdoors (aout-*dooz*) *adv* dehors

outer (*aou*-teu) *adj* extérieur

outfit (*aout*-fit) *n* équipement *m*

outline (*aout*-laïn) *n* contour *m*; *v* esquisser

outlook (*aout*-louk) *n* prévision *f*; point de vue

output (*aout*-pout) *n* production *f*

outrage (*aout*-réïdj) *n* outrage *m*

outside (aout-*saïd*) *adv* dehors; *prep* hors de; *n* extérieur *m*

outsize (*aout*-saïz) *n* hors série

outskirts (*aout*-skeûts) *pl* faubourg *m*

outstanding (aout-*stæn*-dinng) *adj* éminent

outward (*aout*-ᵒᵘeud) *adj* externe

outwards (*aout*-ᵒᵘeudz) *adv* vers l'extérieur

oval (*ôᵒᵘ*-veul) *adj* ovale

oven (*a*-veunn) *n* four *m*

over (*ôᵒᵘ*-veu) *prep* au-dessus de, par-dessus; passé; *adv* au-dessus; *adj* fini; ~ **there** là-bas

overall (*ôᵒᵘ*-veu-rool) *adj* total

overalls (*ôᵒᵘ*-veu-roolz) *pl* salopette *f*

overcast (*ôᵒᵘ*-veu-kâst) *adj* nuageux

overcoat (*ôᵒᵘ*-veu-kôᵒᵘt) *n* pardessus *m*

****overcome** (ôᵒᵘ-veu-*kamm*) *v* ***vaincre

overdue (ô^{ou}-veu-*dyoû*) *adj* en retard ; arriéré

overgrown (ô^{ou}-veu-*ghrô^{ou}n*) *adj* couvert de verdure

overhaul (ô^{ou}-veu-*hool*) *v* reviser

overhead (ô^{ou}-veu-*hèd*) *adv* en haut

overlook (ô^{ou}-veu-*louk*) *v* ignorer

overnight (ô^{ou}-veu-*naït*) *adv* de nuit

overseas (ô^{ou}-veu-*siiz*) *adj* d'outre-mer

oversight (ô^{ou}-veu-saït) *n* inadvertance *f*

*****oversleep** (ô^{ou}-veu-*sliip*) *v* *dormir trop longtemps

overstrung (ô^{ou}-veu-*stranng*) *adj* surmené

*****overtake** (ô^{ou}-veu-*téïk*) *v* dépasser ; **no overtaking** défense de doubler

over-tired (ô^{ou}-veu-*taï^{eu}d*) *adj* surmené

overture (ô^{ou}-veu-tcheu) *n* ouverture *f*

overweight (ô^{ou}-veu-^{ou}éït) *n* surcharge *f*

overwhelm (ô^{ou}-veu-^{ou}èlm) *v* déconcerter, écraser

overwork (ô^{ou}-veu-^{ou}eûk) *v* se surmener

owe (ô^{ou}) *v* *devoir ; **owing to** en raison de

owl (aoul) *n* hibou *m*

own (ô^{ou}n) *v* posséder ; *adj* propre

owner (ô^{ou}-neu) *n* propriétaire *m*

ox (oks) *n* (pl oxen) bœuf *m*

oxygen (*ok*-si-djeunn) *n* oxygène *m*

oyster (*oï*-steu) *n* huître *f*

P

pace (péïss) *n* allure *f* ; démarche *f*, pas *m* ; rythme *m*

Pacific Ocean (peu-*si*-fik ô^{ou}-cheunn) Océan Pacifique

pacifism (*pæ*-si-fi-zeumm) *n* pacifisme *m*

pacifist (*pæ*-si-fist) *n* pacifiste *m*

pack (pæk) *v* emballer ; ~ **up** emballer

package (*pæ*-kidj) *n* colis *m*

packet (*pæ*-kit) *n* paquet *m*

packing (*pæ*-kinng) *n* emballage *m*

pad (pæd) *n* coussinet *m* ; bloc-notes *m*

paddle (*pæ*-deul) *n* pagaie *f*

padlock (*pæd*-lok) *n* cadenas *m*

pagan (*péï*-gheunn) *adj* païen ; *n* païen *m*

page (péïdj) *n* page *f*

page-boy (*péïdj*-boï) *n* page *m*

pail (péïl) *n* seau *m*

pain (péïn) *n* douleur *f* ; **pains** peine *f*

painful (*péïn*-feul) *adj* douloureux

painless (*péïn*-leuss) *adj* sans douleur

paint (péïnt) *n* peinture *f* ; *v* *peindre

paint-box (*péïnt*-boks) *n* boîte de couleurs

paint-brush (*péïnt*-brach) *n* pinceau *m*

painter (*péïn*-teu) *n* peintre *m*

painting (*péïn*-tinng) *n* peinture *f*

pair (pè^{eu}) *n* paire *f*

Pakistan (pââ-ki-*stâân*) Pakistan *m*

Pakistani (pââ-ki-*stââ*-ni) *adj* pakistanais ; *n* Pakistanais *m*

palace (*pæ*-leuss) *n* palais *m*

pale (péïl) *adj* pâle

palm (pââm) *n* palme *f* ; paume *f*

palpable (*pæl*-peu-beul) *adj* palpable

palpitation (pæl-pi-*téï*-cheunn) *n* palpitation *f*

pan (pæn) *n* casserole *f*

pane (péïn) *n* carreau *m*

panel (*pæ*-neul) *n* panneau *m*

panelling (*pæ*-neu-linng) *n* lambrissage *m*

panic (*pæ*-nik) *n* panique *f*

pant (pænt) *v* haleter

panties (*pæn*-tiz) *pl* culotte *f*

pants (pænts) *pl* caleçon *m*; *plAm* pantalon *m*

pant-suit (pænt-soût) *n* ensemble-pantalon

panty-hose (pæn-ti-hôᵒᵘz) *n* collants *mpl*

paper (péï-peu) *n* papier *m*; journal *m*; en papier; **carbon ~** papier carbone; **~ bag** sac en papier; **~ napkin** serviette de papier; **typing ~** papier à machine; **wrapping ~** papier d'emballage

paperback (péï-peu-bæk) *n* livre de poche

paper-knife (péï-peu-naïf) *n* coupe-papier *m*

parade (peu-réïd) *n* parade *f*

paraffin (pæ-reu-finn) *n* pétrole *m*

paragraph (pæ-reu-ghrââf) *n* paragraphe *m*

parakeet (pæ-reu-kiit) *n* perruche *f*

paralise (pæ-reu-laïz) *v* paralyser

parallel (pæ-reu-lèl) *adj* parallèle; *n* parallèle *m*

parcel (pââ-seul) *n* colis *m*, paquet *m*

pardon (pââ-deunn) *n* pardon *m*; grâce *f*

parents (pèᵉᵘ-reunnts) *pl* parents *m*

parents-in-law (pèᵉᵘ-reunnts-inn-loo) *pl* beaux-parents *mpl*

parish (pæ-rich) *n* paroisse *f*

park (pââk) *n* parc *m*; *v* se garer

parking (pââ-king) *n* stationnement *m*; **no ~** stationnement interdit; **~ fee** droit de stationnement; **~ light** feu de position; **~ lot** *Am* parking *m*; **~ meter** parcomètre *m*; **~ zone** zone de stationnement

parliament (pââ-leu-meunnt) *n* parlement *m*

parliamentary (pââ-leu-mèn-teu-ri) *adj* parlementaire

parrot (pæ-reut) *n* perroquet *m*

parsley (pââ-sli) *n* persil *m*

parson (pââ-seunn) *n* pasteur *m*

parsonage (pââ-seu-nidj) *n* presbytère *m*

part (pâât) *n* part *f*, partie *f*; morceau *m*; *v* séparer; **spare ~** pièce de rechange

partial (pââ-cheul) *adj* partiel; partial

participant (pââ-ti-si-peunnt) *n* participant *m*

participate (pââ-ti-si-péït) *v* participer

particular (peu-ti-kyou-leu) *adj* spécial, particulier; exigeant; **in ~** en particulier

parting (pââ-tinng) *n* adieu *m*; raie *f*

partition (pââ-ti-cheunn) *n* cloison *f*

partly (pâât-li) *adv* en partie, partiellement

partner (pâât-neu) *n* partenaire *m*; associé *m*

partridge (pââ-tridj) *n* perdrix *f*

party (pââ-ti) *n* parti *m*; surprise-partie *f*; groupe *m*

pass (pââss) *v* passer, dépasser; réussir; *vAm* doubler; **no passing** *Am* défense de doubler; **~ by** passer à côté; **~ through** traverser

passage (pæ-sidj) *n* passage *m*; traversée *f*

passenger (pæ-seunn-djeu) *n* passager *m*; **~ car** *Am* wagon *m*; **~ train** train de voyageurs

passer-by (pââ-seu-baï) *n* passant *m*

passion (pæ-cheunn) *n* passion *f*; colère *f*

passionate (pæ-cheu-neut) *adj* passionné

passive (pæ-siv) *adj* passif

passport (pââss-poot) *n* passeport *m*; **~ control** contrôle des passeports; **~ photograph** photo d'identité

password (pââss-ᵒᵘeûd) *n* mot de passe

past (pââst) *n* passé *m*; *adj* passé, dernier; *prep* le long de, au delà de

paste (péïst) *n* pâte *f*; *v* coller

pastry (péï-stri) *n* pâtisserie *f*; ~ **shop** pâtisserie *f*

pasture (pââss-tcheu) *n* pâture *f*

patch (pætch) *v* rapiécer

patent (péï-teunnt) *n* brevet *m*

path (pââθ) *n* sentier *m*

patience (péï-cheunns) *n* patience *f*

patient (péï-cheunnt) *adj* patient; *n* patient *m*

patriot (péï-tri-eut) *n* patriote *m*

patrol (peu-trô^{ou}l) *n* patrouille *f*; *v* patrouiller; surveiller

pattern (pæ-teunn) *n* motif *m*, dessin *m*

pause (pooz) *n* pause *f*; *v* s'*interrompre

pave (péïv) *v* paver

pavement (péïv-meunnt) *n* trottoir *m*; pavage *m*

pavilion (peu-vil-yeunn) *n* pavillon *m*

paw (poo) *n* patte *f*

pawn (poon) *v* donner en gage, *mettre en gage; *n* pion *m*

pawnbroker (poon-brô^{ou}-keu) *n* prêteur sur gage

pay (péï) *n* salaire *m*, paye *f*

***pay** (péï) *v* payer; ~ **attention to** *faire attention à; **paying** rentable; ~ **off** amortir; ~ **on account** payer à tempérament

pay-desk (péï-dèsk) *n* caisse *f*

payee (péï-ii) *n* bénéficiaire *m*

payment (péï-meunnt) *n* paiement *m*

pea (pii) *n* pois *m*

peace (piiss) *n* paix *f*

peaceful (piiss-feul) *adj* paisible

peach (piitch) *n* pêche *f*

peacock (pii-kok) *n* paon *m*

peak (piik) *n* sommet *m*; apogée *m*; ~ **hour** heure de pointe; ~ **season** pleine saison

peanut (pii-nat) *n* cacahuète *f*

pear (pè^{eu}) *n* poire *f*

pearl (peûl) *n* perle *f*

peasant (pè-zeunnt) *n* paysan *m*

pebble (pè-beul) *n* galet *m*

peculiar (pi-kyoûl-yeu) *adj* singulier; spécial, particulier

peculiarity (pi-kyoû-li-æ-reu-ti) *n* particularité *f*

pedal (pè-deul) *n* pédale *f*

pedestrian (pi-dè-stri-eunn) *n* piéton *m*; **no pedestrians** interdit aux piétons; ~ **crossing** passage clouté

pedicure (pè-di-kyou^{eu}) *n* pédicure *m*

peel (piil) *v* peler; *n* pelure *f*

peep (piip) *v* épier

peg (pègh) *n* patère *f*

pelican (pè-li-keunn) *n* pélican *m*

pelvis (pèl-viss) *n* bassin *m*

pen (pèn) *n* plume *f*

penalty (pè-neul-ti) *n* amende *f*; peine *f*; ~ **kick** penalty *m*

pencil (pèn-seul) *n* crayon *m*

pencil-sharpener (pèn-seul-chââp-neu) *n* taille-crayon *m*

pendant (pèn-deunnt) *n* pendentif *m*

penetrate (pè-ni-tréït) *v* pénétrer

penguin (pèng-gh^{ou}inn) *n* pingouin *m*

penicillin (pè-ni-si-linn) *n* pénicilline *f*

peninsula (peu-ninn-syou-leu) *n* péninsule *f*

penknife (pèn-naïf) *n* (pl -knives) canif *m*

pension¹ (pan-si-on) *n* pension *f*

pension² (pèn-cheunn) *n* pension *f*

people (pii-peul) *pl* gens *mpl/fpl*; *n* peuple *m*

pepper (pè-peu) *n* poivre *m*

peppermint (pè-peu-minnt) *n* menthe *f*

perceive (peu-siiv) *v* *percevoir

percent (peu-sènt) *n* pour cent

percentage (peu-sèn-tidj) *n* pourcentage *m*

perceptible (peu-sèp-ti-beul) *adj* perceptible

perception (peu-*sèp*-cheunn) *n* perception *f*

perch (peûtch) (pl ~) perche *f*

percolator (*peû*-keu-léï-teu) *n* percolateur *m*

perfect (*peû*-fikt) *adj* parfait

perfection (peu-*fèk*-cheunn) *n* perfection *f*

perform (peu-*foom*) *v* accomplir

performance (peu-*foo*-meunns) *n* performance *f*

perfume (*peû*-fyoûm) *n* parfum *m*

perhaps (peu-*hæps*) *adv* peut-être

peril (*pè*-ril) *n* péril *m*

perilous (*pè*-ri-leuss) *adj* périlleux

period (*pi*eu-ri-eud) *n* époque *f*, période *f*; point *m*

periodical (pieu-ri-*o*-di-keul) *n* périodique *m*; *adj* périodique

perish (*pè*-rich) *v* périr

perishable (*pè*-ri-cheu-beul) *adj* périssable

perjury (*peû*-djeu-ri) *n* faux serment *m*

permanent (*peû*-meu-neunnt) *adj* durable, permanent; stable, fixe; ~ **press** pli permanent; ~ **wave** permanente *f*

permission (peu-*mi*-cheunn) *n* permission *f*, autorisation *f*; permis *m*, licence *f*

permit[1] (peu-*mit*) *v* *permettre

permit[2] (*peû*-mit) *n* permis *m*

peroxide (peu-*rok*-saïd) *n* eau oxygénée

perpendicular (peû-peunn-*di*-kyou-leu) *adj* perpendiculaire

Persia (*peû*-cheu) Perse *f*

Persian (*peû*-cheunn) *adj* persan; *n* Persan *m*

person (*peû*-seunn) *n* personne *f*; per ~ par personne

personal (*peû*-seu-neul) *adj* personnel

personality (peû-seu-*næ*-leu-ti) *n* personnalité *f*

personnel (peû-seu-*nèl*) *n* personnel *m*

perspective (peu-*spèk*-tiv) *n* perspective *f*

perspiration (peû-speu-*réï*-cheunn) *n* transpiration *f*, sueur *f*

perspire (peu-*spai*eu) *v* transpirer, suer

persuade (peu-*s*ouéïd) *v* persuader; *convaincre

persuasion (peu-*s*ouéï-jeunn) *n* conviction *f*

pessimism (*pè*-si-mi-zeumm) *n* pessimisme *m*

pessimist (*pè*-si-mist) *n* pessimiste *m*

pessimistic (pè-si-*mi*-stik) *adj* pessimiste

pet (pèt) *n* animal familier; chouchou *m*; favori

petal (*pè*-teul) *n* pétale *m*

petition (pi-*ti*-cheunn) *n* pétition *f*

petrol (*pè*-treul) *n* essence *f*; ~ **pump** pompe à essence; ~ **station** poste d'essence; ~ **tank** réservoir d'essence

petroleum (pi-*trô*ou-li-eumm) *n* pétrole *m*

petty (*pè*-ti) *adj* petit, futile, insignifiant; ~ **cash** petite monnaie

pewit (*pii*-ouit) *n* vanneau *m*

pewter (*pyoû*-teu) *n* étain *m*

phantom (*fæn*-teumm) *n* fantôme *m*

pharmacology (fââ-meu-*ko*-leu-dji) *n* pharmacologie *f*

pharmacy (*fââ*-meu-si) *n* pharmacie *f*; droguerie *f*

phase (féïz) *n* phase *f*

pheasant (*fè*-zeunnt) *n* faisan *m*

Philippine (*fi*-li-païn) *adj* philippin

Philippines (*fi*-li-piinz) *pl* Philippines *fpl*

philosopher (fi-*lo*-seu-feu) *n* philosophe *m*

philosophy (fi-*lo*-seu-fi) *n* philosophie

f

phone (fô^{ou}n) *n* téléphone *m*; *v* téléphoner

phonetic (feu-*nè*-tik) *adj* phonétique

photo (fô^{ou}-tô^{ou}) *n* (pl ~s) photo *f*

photocopy (fô^{ou}-teu-ko-pi) *n* photocopie *f*; *v* photocopier

photograph (fô^{ou}-teu-ghrââf) *n* photographie *f*; *v* photographier

photographer (feu-*to*-ghreu-feu) *n* photographe *m*

photography (feu-*to*-ghreu-fi) *n* photographie *f*

phrase (fréïz) *n* locution *f*

phrase-book (*fréïz*-bouk) *n* manuel de conversation

physical (*fi*-zi-keul) *adj* physique

physician (fi-*zi*-cheunn) *n* médecin *m*

physicist (*fi*-zi-sist) *n* physicien *m*

physics (*fi*-ziks) *n* physique *f*

physiology (fi-zi-*o*-leu-dji) *n* physiologie *f*

pianist (*pii*-eu-nist) *n* pianiste *m*

piano (pi-*æ*-nô^{ou}) *n* piano *m*; **grand** ~ piano à queue

pick (pik) *v* *cueillir; choisir; *n* choix *m*; ~ **up** ramasser; *aller chercher; **pick-up van** camionnette *f*

pick-axe (*pik*-kæks) *n* pioche *f*

pickles (*pi*-keulz) *pl* conserves au vinaigre, marinade *f*

picnic (*pik*-nik) *n* pique-nique *m*; *v* pique-niquer

picture (*pik*-tcheu) *n* peinture *f*; illustration *f*, gravure *f*; image *f*; ~ **postcard** carte postale, carte postale illustrée; **pictures** cinéma *m*

picturesque (pik-tcheu-*rèsk*) *adj* pittoresque

piece (piiss) *n* morceau *m*, pièce *f*

pier (pi^{eu}) *n* jetée *f*

pierce (pi^{eu}ss) *v* percer

pig (pigh) *n* cochon *m*

pigeon (*pi*-djeunn) *n* pigeon *m*

pig-headed (pigh-*hè*-did) *adj* obstiné

piglet (*pigh*-leut) *n* cochon de lait

pigskin (*pigh*-skinn) *n* peau de porc

pike (païk) (pl ~) brochet *m*

pile (païl) *n* tas *m*; *v* entasser; **piles** *pl* hémorroïdes *fpl*

pilgrim (*pil*-ghrimm) *n* pèlerin *m*

pilgrimage (*pil*-ghri-midj) *n* pèlerinage *m*

pill (pil) *n* pilule *f*

pillar (*pi*-leu) *n* colonne *f*, pilier *m*

pillar-box (*pi*-leu-boks) *n* boîte aux lettres

pillow (*pi*-lô^{ou}) *n* oreiller *m*

pillow-case (*pi*-lô^{ou}-kéïss) *n* taie d'oreiller

pilot (*paï*-leut) *n* pilote *m*

pimple (*pimm*-peul) *n* pustule *f*

pin (pinn) *n* épingle *f*; *v* épingler; **bobby** ~ *Am* pince à cheveux

pincers (*pinn*-seuz) *pl* tenailles *fpl*

pinch (pinntch) *v* pincer

pineapple (*païn*-næ-peul) *n* ananas *m*

ping-pong (*pinng*-ponng) *n* tennis de table

pink (pinngk) *adj* rose

pioneer (paï-eu-*ni^{eu}*) *n* pionnier *m*

pious (*païn*-euss) *adj* pieux

pip (pip) *n* pépin *m*

pipe (païp) *n* pipe *f*; tuyau *m*; ~ **cleaner** cure-pipe *m*; ~ **tobacco** tabac pour pipe

pirate (*païn^{eu}*-reut) *n* pirate *m*

pistol (*pi*-steul) *n* pistolet *m*

piston (*pi*-steunn) *n* piston *m*; ~ **ring** segment de piston

piston-rod (*pi*-steunn-rod) *n* tige de piston

pit (pit) *n* fosse *f*; mine *f*

pitcher (*pi*-tcheu) *n* cruche *f*

pity (*pi*-ti) *n* pitié *f*; *v* *avoir pitié de, compatir; **what a pity!** dommage!

placard (*plæ*-kââd) *n* affiche *f*

place (pléïss) *n* place *f*; *v* poser, pla-

cer; ~ **of birth** lieu de naissance;
*take ~ *avoir lieu

plague (pléïgh) n fléau m

plaice (pléïss) (pl ~) plie f

plain (pléïn) adj clair; ordinaire, simple; n plaine f

plan (plæn) n plan m; v planifier

plane (pléïn) adj plat; n avion m; ~
crash accident d'avion

planet (plæ-nit) n planète f

planetarium (plæ-ni-tè⁴⁻ri-eumm) n
planétarium m

plank (plængk) n planche f

plant (plâânt) n plante f; usine f; v
planter

plantation (plæn-téï-cheunn) n plantation f

plaster (plââ-steu) n crépi m, plâtre
m; sparadrap m

plastic (plæ-stik) adj plastique; n
plastique m

plate (pléit) n assiette f; plaque f

plateau (plæ-tô⁰ᵘ) n (pl ~x, ~s) plateau m

platform (plæt-foom) n quai m; ~
ticket billet de quai

platinum (plæ-ti-neumm) n platine m

play (pléï) v jouer; n jeu m; pièce de
théâtre; **one-act** ~ pièce en un acte; ~ **truant** *faire l'école buissonnière

player (pléï⁴ᵘ) n joueur m

playground (pléï-ghraound) n terrain
de jeux

playing-card (pléï-inng-kââd) n carte
de jeu

playwright (pléï-raït) n dramaturge m

plea (plii) n plaidoyer m

plead (pliid) v plaider

pleasant (plè-zeunnt) adj plaisant,
sympathique, agréable

please (pliiz) s'il vous plaît; v *plaire;
pleased content; **pleasing** agréable

pleasure (plè-jeu) n agrément m, divertissement m, plaisir m

plentiful (plèn-ti-feul) adj abondant

plenty (plèn-ti) n abondance f

pliers (plaï⁴ᵘz) pl pince f

plimsolls (plimm-seulz) pl chaussures
de basket

plot (plot) n conspiration f, complot
m; intrigue f; lopin m

plough (plaou) n charrue f; v labourer

plucky (pla-ki) adj courageux

plug (plagh) n fiche f; ~ **in** brancher

plum (plamm) n prune f

plumber (pla-meu) n plombier m

plump (plammp) adj potelé

plural (plou⁴ᵘ-reul) n pluriel m

plus (plass) prep plus

pneumatic (nyoû-mæ-tik) adj pneumatique

pneumonia (nyoû-mô⁰ᵘ-ni-eu) n pneumonie f

poach (pô⁰ᵘtch) v braconner

pocket (po-kit) n poche f

pocket-book (po-kit-bouk) n portefeuille m

pocket-comb (po-kit-kô⁰ᵘm) n peigne
de poche

pocket-knife (po-kit-naïf) n (pl
-knives) couteau de poche

pocket-watch (po-kit-⁰ᵘotch) n montre de gousset

poem (pô⁰ᵘ-imm) n poème m

poet (pô⁰ᵘ-it) n poète m

poetry (pô⁰ᵘ-i-tri) n poésie f

point (poïnt) n point m; pointe f; v
montrer du doigt; ~ **of view** point
de vue; ~ **out** indiquer

pointed (poïn-tid) adj pointu

poison (poï-zeunn) n poison m; v empoisonner

poisonous (poï-zeu-neuss) adj vénéneux

Poland (pô⁰ᵘ-leunnd) Pologne f

Pole (pô⁰ᵘl) n Polonais m

pole (pô^{ou}l) *n* poteau *m*

police (peu-*liiss*) *pl* police *f*

policeman (peu-*liiss*-meunn) *n* (pl -men) agent de police, policier *m*

police-station (peu-*liiss*-stéï-cheunn) *n* commissariat de police

policy (*po*-li-si) *n* politique *f*; police *f*

polio (*pô^{ou}*-li-ô^{ou}) *n* poliomyélite *f*

Polish (*pô^{ou}*-lich) *adj* polonais

polish (*po*-lich) *v* polir

polite (peu-*laït*) *adj* poli

political (peu-*li*-ti-keul) *adj* politique

politician (po-li-*ti*-cheunn) *n* politicien *m*

politics (*po*-li-tiks) *n* politique *f*

pollution (peu-*loû*-cheunn) *n* pollution *f*

pond (ponnd) *n* étang *m*

pony (*pô^{ou}*-ni) *n* poney *m*

poor (pou^{eu}) *adj* pauvre; indigent; piètre

pope (pô^{ou}p) *n* pape *m*

poplin (*po*-plinn) *n* popeline *f*

pop music (pop *myoû*-zik) musique pop

poppy (*po*-pi) *n* coquelicot *m*; pavot *m*

popular (*po*-pyou-leu) *adj* populaire

population (po-pyou-*léï*-cheunn) *n* population *f*

populous (*po*-pyou-leuss) *adj* populeux

porcelain (*poo*-seu-linn) *n* porcelaine *f*

porcupine (*poo*-kyou-païn) *n* porc-épic *m*

pork (pook) *n* porc *m*

port (poot) *n* port *m*; bâbord *m*

portable (*poo*-teu-beul) *adj* portatif

porter (*poo*-teu) *n* porteur *m*; portier *m*

porthole (*poot*-hô^{ou}l) *n* hublot *m*

portion (*poo*-cheunn) *n* portion *f*

portrait (*poo*-trit) *n* portrait *m*

Portugal (*poo*-tyou-gheul) Portugal *m*

Portuguese (poo-tyou-*ghiiz*) *adj* portugais; *n* Portugais *m*

position (peu-*zi*-cheunn) *n* position *f*; situation *f*; attitude *f*

positive (*po*-zeu-tiv) *adj* positif; *n* positif *m*

possess (peu-*zèss*) *v* posséder; **possessed** *adj* possédé

possession (peu-*zè*-cheunn) *n* possession *f*; **possessions** biens *mpl*

possibility (po-seu-*bi*-leu-ti) *n* possibilité *f*

possible (*po*-seu-beul) *adj* possible; éventuel

post (pô^{ou}st) *n* poteau *m*; poste *m*; poste *f*; *v* poster; **post-office** bureau de poste

postage (*pô^{ou}*-stidj) *n* port *m*; ~ **paid** port payé; ~ **stamp** timbre-poste *m*

postcard (*pô^{ou}st*-kââd) *n* carte postale

poster (*pô^{ou}*-steu) *n* affiche *f*

poste restante (pô^{ou}st rè-*stant*) poste restante

postman (*pô^{ou}st*-meunn) *n* (pl -men) facteur *m*

post-paid (pô^{ou}st-*péïd*) *adj* port payé

postpone (peu-*spô^{ou}n*) *v* ajourner, *renvoyer à

pot (pot) *n* pot *m*

potato (peu-*téï*-tô^{ou}) *n* (pl ~es) pomme de terre

pottery (*po*-teu-ri) *n* poterie *f*; vaisselle *f*

pouch (paoutch) *n* pochette *f*

poulterer (*pô^{ou}l*-teu-reu) *n* marchand de volaille

poultry (*pô^{ou}l*-tri) *n* volaille *f*

pound (paound) *n* livre *f*

pour (poo) *v* verser

poverty (*po*-veu-ti) *n* pauvreté *f*

powder (*paou*-deu) *n* poudre *f*; ~ **compact** poudrier *m*; **talc** ~ talc *m*

powder-puff (*paou*-deu-paf) *n* houppette *f*

powder-room (*paou*-deu-roûm) *n* toilettes pour dames

power (*paou^eu*) *n* force *f*, puissance *f*; énergie *f*; pouvoir *m*

powerful (*paou^eu*-feul) *adj* puissant; fort

powerless (*paou^eu*-leuss) *adj* impuissant

power-station (*paou^eu*-stéï-cheunn) *n* centrale *f*

practical (*præk*-ti-keul) *adj* pratique

practically (*præk*-ti-kli) *adv* pratiquement

practice (*præk*-tiss) *n* pratique *f*

practise (*præk*-tiss) *v* pratiquer; s'exercer

praise (préïz) *v* louer; *n* éloge *m*

pram (præm) *n* voiture d'enfant

prawn (proon) *n* crevette *f*, crevette rose

pray (préï) *v* prier

prayer (*prè*^eu) *n* prière *f*

preach (priitch) *v* prêcher

precarious (pri-*ké*^eu-ri-euss) *adj* précaire

precaution (pri-*koo*-cheunn) *n* précaution *f*

precede (pri-*siid*) *v* précéder

preceding (pri-*sii*-dinng) *adj* précédent

precious (*prè*-cheuss) *adj* précieux

precipice (*prè*-si-piss) *n* précipice *m*

precipitation (pri-si-pi-*téï*-cheunn) *n* précipitation *f*

precise (pri-*saïss*) *adj* précis, exact; méticuleux

predecessor (*prii*-di-sè-seu) *n* prédécesseur *m*

predict (pri-*dikt*) *v* *prédire

prefer (pri-*feû*) *v* aimer mieux, préférer

preferable (*prè*-feu-reu-beul) *adj* préférable

preference (*prè*-feu-reunns) *n* préférence *f*

prefix (*prii*-fiks) *n* préfixe *m*

pregnant (*prègh*-neunnt) *adj* enceinte

prejudice (*prè*-djeu-diss) *n* préjugé *m*

preliminary (pri-*li*-mi-neu-ri) *adj* préliminaire

premature (*prè*-meu-tchou^eu) *adj* prématuré

premier (*prèm*-i^eu) *n* premier ministre

premises (*prè*-mi-siz) *pl* locaux *mpl*

premium (*prii*-mi-eumm) *n* prime *f*

prepaid (prii-*péïd*) *adj* payé d'avance

preparation (prè-peu-*réï*-cheunn) *n* préparation *f*

prepare (pri-*pè*^eu) *v* préparer

prepared (pri-*pè*^eu d) *adj* prêt

preposition (prè-peu-*zi*-cheunn) *n* préposition *f*

prescribe (pri-*skraïb*) *v* *prescrire

prescription (pri-*skrip*-cheunn) *n* prescription *f*

presence (*prè*-zeunns) *n* présence *f*

present[1] (*prè*-zeunnt) *n* cadeau *m*; présent *m*; *adj* actuel; présent

present[2] (pri-*zènt*) *v* présenter

presently (*prè*-zeunnt-li) *adv* tout à l'heure

preservation (prè-zeu-*véï*-cheunn) *n* conservation *f*

preserve (pri-*zeûv*) *v* conserver; *mettre en conserve

president (*prè*-zi-deunnt) *n* président *m*

press (prèss) *n* presse *f*; *v* appuyer, presser; repasser; ~ **conference** conférence de presse

pressing (*prè*-sinng) *adj* pressant, urgent

pressure (*prè*-cheu) *n* pression *f*; tension *f*; **atmospheric** ~ pression atmosphérique

pressure-cooker (*prè*-cheu-kou-keu) *n* cocotte à pression

prestige (prè-*stiij*) *n* prestige *m*

presumable (pri-*zyoŭ*-meu-beul) *adj* probable

presumptuous (pri-*zammp*-cheuss) *adj* présomptueux

pretence (pri-*tèns*) *n* prétexte *m*

pretend (pri-*tènd*) *v* *feindre, prétendre

pretext (*prii*-tèkst) *n* prétexte *m*

pretty (*pri*-ti) *adj* beau, joli; *adv* assez, plutôt, passablement

prevent (pri-*vènt*) *v* empêcher; *prévenir

preventive (pri-*vèn*-tiv) *adj* préventif

previous (*prii*-vi-euss) *adj* précédent, antérieur, préalable

pre-war (prii-*ŏŏoo*) *adj* d'avant-guerre

price (praïss) *v* fixer le prix; ~ list prix-courant *m*

priceless (*praïss*-leuss) *adj* inestimable

price-list (*praïss*-list) *n* prix *m*

prick (prik) *v* piquer

pride (praïd) *n* orgueil *m*

priest (priist) *n* prêtre *m*

primary (*praï*-meu-ri) *adj* primaire; premier, primordial; élémentaire

prince (prinns) *n* prince *m*

princess (prinn-*sèss*) *n* princesse *f*

principal (*prinn*-seu-peul) *adj* principal; *n* proviseur *m*, directeur *m*

principle (*prinn*-seu-peul) *n* principe *m*

print (prinnt) *v* imprimer; *n* épreuve *f*; estampe *f*; **printed matter** imprimé *m*

prior (praï*eu*) *adj* antérieur

priority (praï-*o*-reu-ti) *n* priorité *f*

prison (*pri*-zeunn) *n* prison *f*

prisoner (*pri*-zeu-neu) *n* détenu *m*, prisonnier *m*; ~ **of war** prisonnier de guerre

privacy (*praï*-veu-si) *n* intimité *f*, vie privée

private (*praï*-vit) *adj* particulier, privé; personnel

privilege (*pri*-vi-lidj) *n* privilège *m*

prize (praïz) *n* prix *m*; récompense *f*

probable (*pro*-beu-beul) *adj* vraisemblable, probable

probably (*pro*-beu-bli) *adv* probablement

problem (*pro*-bleumm) *n* problème *m*; question *f*

procedure (preu-*sii*-djeu) *n* procédure *f*

proceed (preu-*siid*) *v* procéder

process (*prô*ŏŭ-sèss) *n* processus *m*, procédé *m*; procès *m*

procession (preu-*sè*-cheunn) *n* procession *f*, cortège *m*

proclaim (preu-*kléïm*) *v* proclamer

produce[1] (preu-*dyoŭss*) *v* *produire

produce[2] (*prod*-yoŭss) *n* produit *m*

producer (preu-*dyoŭ*-seu) *n* producteur *m*

product (*pro*-dakt) *n* produit *m*

production (preu-*dak*-cheunn) *n* production *f*

profession (preu-*fè*-cheunn) *n* métier *m*, profession *f*

professional (preu-*fè*-cheu-neul) *adj* professionnel

professor (preu-*fè*-seu) *n* professeur *m*

profit (*pro*-fit) *n* bénéfice *m*, profit *m*; avantage *m*; *v* profiter

profitable (*pro*-fi-teu-beul) *adj* profitable

profound (preu-*faound*) *adj* profond

programme (*prô*ŏŭ-ghræm) *n* programme *m*

progress[1] (*prô*ŏŭ-ghrèss) *n* progrès *m*

progress[2] (preu-*ghrèss*) *v* avancer

progressive (preu-*ghrè*-siv) *adj* progressiste; progressif

prohibit (preu-*hi*-bit) *v* *interdire

prohibition (prô*ŏŭ*-i-*bi*-cheunn) *n* interdiction *f*

prohibitive (preu-*hi*-bi-tiv) *adj* inabordable

project (*pro*-djèkt) *n* plan *m*, projet *m*

promenade (pro-meu-*nââd*) *n* promenade *f*

promise (*pro*-miss) *n* promesse *f*; *v* *promettre

promote (preu-*môou*t) *v* *promouvoir

promotion (preu-*môou*-cheunn) *n* promotion *f*

prompt (prommpt) *adj* instantané, prompt

pronoun (*prôou*-naoun) *n* pronom *m*

pronounce (preu-*naouns*) *v* prononcer

pronunciation (preu-nann-si-*éí*-cheunn) *n* prononciation *f*

proof (proûf) *n* preuve *f*

propaganda (pro-peu-*ghæn*-deu) *n* propagande *f*

propel (preu-*pèl*) *v* propulser

propeller (preu-*pè*-leu) *n* hélice *f*

proper (*pro*-peu) *adj* juste; convenable, pertinent, adéquat, approprié

property (*pro*-peu-ti) *n* propriété *f*

prophet (*pro*-fit) *n* prophète *m*

proportion (preu-*poo*-cheunn) *n* proportion *f*

proportional (preu-*poo*-cheu-neul) *adj* proportionnel

proposal (preu-*pôou*-zeul) *n* proposition *f*

propose (preu-*pôou*z) *v* proposer

proposition (pro-peu-*zi*-cheunn) *n* proposition *f*

proprietor (preu-*praï*-eu-teu) *n* propriétaire *m*

prospect (*pro*-spèkt) *n* perspective *f*

prospectus (preu-*spèk*-teuss) *n* prospectus *m*

prosperity (pro-*spè*-reu-ti) *n* prospérité *f*

prosperous (*pro*-speu-reuss) *adj* prospère

prostitute (*pro*-sti-tyoût) *n* prostituée *f*

protect (preu-*tèkt*) *v* protéger

protection (preu-*tèk*-cheunn) *n* protection *f*

protein (*prôou*-tiin) *n* protéine *f*

protest[1] (*prôou*-tèst) *n* protestation *f*

protest[2] (preu-*tèst*) *v* protester

Protestant (*pro*-ti-steunnt) *adj* protestant

proud (praoud) *adj* fier; orgueilleux

prove (proûv) *v* démontrer, prouver; se révéler

proverb (*pro*-veûb) *n* proverbe *m*

provide (preu-*vaïd*) *v* fournir; **provided that** pourvu que

province (*pro*-vinns) *n* province *f*

provincial (preu-*vinn*-cheul) *adj* provincial

provisional (preu-*vi*-jeu-neul) *adj* provisoire

provisions (preu-*vi*-jeunnz) *pl* provision *f*

prune (proûn) *n* pruneau *m*

psychiatrist (saï-*kaï*-eu-trist) *n* psychiatre *m*

psychic (*saï*-kik) *adj* psychique

psychoanalyst (saï-kô^{ou}-æ-neu-list) *n* psychanalyste *m*

psychological (saï-ko-*lo*-dji-keul) *adj* psychologique

psychologist (saï-*ko*-leu-djist) *n* psychologue *m*

psychology (saï-*ko*-leu-dji) *n* psychologie *f*

pub (pab) *n* bistrot *m*

public (*pa*-blik) *adj* public; général; *n* public *m*; ~ **garden** jardin public; ~ **house** café *m*

publication (pa-bli-*kéí*-cheunn) *n* publication *f*

publicity (pa-*bli*-seu-ti) *n* publicité *f*

publish (*pa*-blich) *v* publier

publisher (*pa*-bli-cheu) *n* éditeur *m*

puddle (*pa*-deul) *n* flaque *f*

pull (poul) *v* tirer; ~ **out** *partir; ~ **up** s'arrêter

pulley (*pou*-li) *n* (pl ~s) poulie *f*

Pullman (*poul*-meunn) *n* voiture Pullman

pullover (*pou*-lô^ou-veu) *n* pull-over *m*

pulpit (*poul*-pit) *n* pupitre *m*, chaire *f*

pulse (pals) *n* pouls *m*

pump (pammp) *n* pompe *f*; *v* pomper

punch (panntch) *v* donner des coups de poing; *n* coup de poing

punctual (*panngk*-tchou-eul) *adj* ponctuel

puncture (*panngk*-tcheu) *n* crevaison *f*

punctured (*panngk*-tcheud) *adj* crevé

punish (*pa*-nich) *v* punir

punishment (*pa*-nich-meunnt) *n* punition *f*

pupil (*pyoû*-peul) *n* élève *m*

puppet-show (*pa*-pit-chô^ou) *n* théâtre de marionnettes

purchase (*peû*-tcheuss) *v* acheter; *n* acquisition *f*, achat *m*; ~ **price** prix d'achat

purchaser (*peû*-tcheu-seu) *n* acheteur *m*

pure (pyou^eu) *adj* pur

purple (*peû*-peul) *adj* pourpre

purpose (*peû*-peuss) *n* intention *f*, but *m*; **on** ~ intentionnel

purse (peûss) *n* bourse *f*, porte-monnaie *m*

pursue (peu-*syoû*) *v* *poursuivre; aspirer à

pus (pass) *n* pus *m*

push (pouch) *n* poussée *f*, coup *m*; *v* pousser

push-button (*pouch*-ba-teunn) *n* poussoir *m*

***put** (pout) *v* placer, poser, *mettre; ~ **away** ranger; ~ **off** ajourner; ~ **on** *mettre; ~ **out** *éteindre

puzzle (*pa*-zeul) *n* casse-tête *m*; énigme *f*; *v* embarrasser; **jigsaw** ~

puzzle *m*

puzzling (*paz*-linng) *adj* embarrassant

pyjamas (peu-*djââ*-meuz) *pl* pyjama *m*

Q

quack (k^ouæk) *n* guérisseur *m*, charlatan *m*

quail (k^ou*éïl*) *n* (pl ~, ~s) caille *f*

quaint (k^ou*éïnt*) *adj* étrange; vieillot

qualification (k^ou*o*-li-fi-*kéï*-cheunn) *n* qualification *f*; réserve *f*, restriction *f*

qualified (k^ou*o*-li-faïd) *adj* qualifié; compétent

qualify (k^ou*o*-li-faï) *v* *être qualifié

quality (k^ou*o*-leu-ti) *n* qualité *f*; caractéristique *f*

quantity (k^ou*onn*-teu-ti) *n* quantité *f*; nombre *m*

quarantine (k^ou*o*-reunn-tiin) *n* quarantaine *f*

quarrel (k^ou*o*-reul) *v* se quereller, se disputer; *n* querelle *f*

quarry (k^ou*o*-ri) *n* carrière *f*

quarter (k^ou*oo*-teu) *n* quart *m*; trimestre *m*; quartier *m*; ~ **of an hour** quart d'heure

quarterly (k^ou*oo*-teu-li) *adj* trimestriel

quay (kii) *n* quai *m*

queen (k^ou*iin*) *n* reine *f*

queer (k^ou*i*^eu) *adj* singulier, étrange; drôle

query (k^ou*i*^eu-ri) *n* question *f*; *v* s'informer; *mettre en doute

question (k^ou*èss*-tcheunn) *n* question *f*; problème *m*; *v* interroger; *mettre en doute; ~ **mark** point d'interrogation

queue (kyoû) *n* queue *f*; *v* *faire la queue

quick (k^ou*ik*) *adj* rapide

quick-tempered (kᵒᵘik-*tèm*-peud) *adj* irascible

quiet (kᵒᵘai-eut) *adj* paisible, calme, tranquille; *n* silence *m*, tranquillité *f*

quilt (kᵒᵘilt) *n* courtepointe *f*

quinine (kᵒᵘi-*niin*) *n* quinine *f*

quit (kᵒᵘit) *v* cesser

quite (kᵒᵘaït) *adv* entièrement, tout à fait; passablement, assez, plutôt; très

quiz (kᵒᵘiz) *n* (pl ~zes) jeu concours *m*

quota (kᵒᵘô*-teu) *n* quote-part *f*

quotation (kᵒᵘôᵘ- *téï*-cheunn) *n* citation *f*; **~ marks** guillemets *mpl*

quote (kᵒᵘôᵘt) *v* citer

R

rabbit (*ræ*-bit) *n* lapin *m*

rabies (*réï*-biz) *n* rage *f*

race (réïss) *n* course *f*; race *f*

race-course (*réïss*-kooss) *n* champ de courses, hippodrome *m*

race-horse (*réïss*-hooss) *n* cheval de course

race-track (*réïss*-træk) *n* piste de courses

racial (*réï*-cheul) *adj* racial

racket (*ræ*-kit) *n* vacarme *m*

racquet (*ræ*-kit) *n* raquette *f*

radiator (*réï*-di-éï-teu) *n* radiateur *m*

radical (*ræ*-di-keul) *adj* radical

radio (*réï*-di-ôᵘ) *n* radio *f*

radish (*ræ*-dich) *n* radis *m*

radius (*réï*-di-euss) *n* (pl radii) rayon *m*

raft (rââft) *n* radeau *m*

rag (rægh) *n* chiffon *m*

rage (réïdj) *n* fureur *f*, rage *f*; *v* rager, sévir

raid (réïd) *n* raid *m*

rail (réïl) *n* balustrade *f*, barre *f*

railing (*réï*-linng) *n* rampe *f*

railroad (*réïl*-rôᵘd) *nAm* voie ferrée, chemin de fer

railway (*réïl*-ᵘéï) *n* chemin de fer, voie ferrée

rain (réïn) *n* pluie *f*; *v* *pleuvoir

rainbow (*réïn*-bôᵘ) *n* arc-en-ciel *m*

raincoat (*réïn*-kôᵘt) *n* imperméable *m*

rainproof (*réïn*-prôûf) *adj* imperméable

rainy (*réï*-ni) *adj* pluvieux

raise (réïz) *v* élever; relever; cultiver; prélever; *nAm* augmentation de salaire

raisin (*réï*-zeunn) *n* raisin sec

rake (réïk) *n* râteau *m*

rally (*ræ*-li) *n* rassemblement *m*

ramp (ræmp) *n* pente *f*

ramshackle (*ræm*-chæ-keul) *adj* croulant

rancid (*ræn*-sid) *adj* rance

rang (ræng) *v* (p ring)

range (réïndj) *n* gamme *f*

range-finder (*réïndj*-faïn-deu) *n* télémètre *m*

rank (rængk) *n* grade *m*; rang *m*

ransom (*ræn*-seumm) *n* rançon *f*

rape (réïp) *v* violer

rapid (*ræ*-pid) *adj* rapide

rapids (*ræ*-pidz) *pl* rapide *m*

rare (rèᵘ) *adj* rare

rarely (*rèᵘ*-li) *adv* rarement

rascal (*rââ*-skeul) *n* coquin *m*, fripon *m*

rash (ræch) *n* éruption *f*; *adj* impétueux, inconsidéré

raspberry (*rââz*-beu-ri) *n* framboise *f*

rat (ræt) *n* rat *m*

rate (réït) *n* tarif *m*; vitesse *f*; **at any ~** de toute façon, quoiqu'il en soit; **~ of exchange** cours du change

rather (*rââ*-ðeu) *adv* assez, passablement, plutôt

ration (*ræ*-cheunn) *n* ration *f*

rattan (ræ-*tæn*) *n* rotin *m*

raven (*réï*-veunn) *n* corbeau *m*

raw (roo) *adj* cru; ~ **material** matière première

ray (réï) *n* rayon *m*

rayon (*réï*-onn) *n* rayonne *f*

razor (*réï*-zeu) *n* rasoir *m*

razor-blade (*réï*-zeu-bléïd) *n* lame de rasoir

reach (riitch) *v* *atteindre; *n* portée *f*

reaction (ri-*æk*-cheunn) *n* réaction *f*

***read** (riid) *v* *lire

reading (*rii*-dinng) *n* lecture *f*

reading-lamp (*rii*-dinng-læmp) *n* lampe de travail

reading-room (*rii*-dinng-roûm) *n* salle de lecture

ready (*rè*-di) *adj* prêt

ready-made (*rè*-di-*méïd*) *adj* de confection

real (ri*eu*l) *adj* réel

reality (ri-*æ*-leu-ti) *n* réalité *f*

realizable (*ri*eu-laï-zeu-beul) *adj* réalisable

realize (*ri*eu-laïz) *v* se rendre compte; réaliser

really (*ri*eu-li) *adv* vraiment, réellement; en réalité

rear (ri*eu*) *n* arrière *m*; *v* élever

rear-light (ri*eu*-laït) *n* feu arrière

reason (*rii*-zeunn) *n* cause *f*, raison *f*; sens *m*; *v* raisonner

reasonable (*rii*-zeu-neu-beul) *adj* raisonnable; équitable

reassure (rii-eu-*chou*eu) *v* rassurer

rebate (*rii*-béït) *n* réduction *f*, rabais *m*

rebellion (ri-*bèl*-yeunn) *n* révolte *f*, rébellion *f*

recall (ri-*kool*) *v* se rappeler; rappeler; révoquer

receipt (ri-*siit*) *n* reçu *m*; réception *f*

receive (ri-*siiv*) *v* *recevoir

receiver (ri-*sii*-veu) *n* écouteur *m*

recent (*rii*-seunnt) *adj* récent

recently (*rii*-seunnt-li) *adv* l'autre jour, récemment

reception (ri-*sèp*-cheunn) *n* réception *f*; accueil *m*; ~ **office** réception *f*

receptionist (ri-*sèp*-cheu-nist) *n* hôtesse *f*

recession (ri-*sè*-cheunn) *n* récession *f*

recipe (*rè*-si-pi) *n* recette *f*

recital (ri-*saï*-teul) *n* récital *m*

reckon (*rè*-keunn) *v* calculer; estimer; supposer

recognition (rè-keugh-*ni*-cheunn) *n* reconnaissance *f*

recognize (*rè*-keugh-naïz) *v* *reconnaître

recollect (rè-keu-*lèkt*) *v* se *souvenir

recommence (rii-keu-*mèns*) *v* recommencer

recommend (rè-keu-*mènd*) *v* recommander; conseiller

recommendation (rè-keu-mèn-*déï*-cheunn) *n* recommandation *f*

reconciliation (rè-keunn-si-li-*éï*-cheunn) *n* réconciliation *f*

record[1] (*rè*-kood) *n* disque *m*; record *m*; dossier *m*; **long-playing** ~ microsillon *m*

record[2] (ri-*kood*) *v* enregistrer

recorder (ri-*koo*-deu) *n* magnétophone *m*

recording (ri-*koo*-dinng) *n* enregistrement *m*

record-player (*rè*-kood-pléï*eu*) *n* tourne-disque *m*

recover (ri-*ka*-veu) *v* récupérer; se *remettre, guérir

recovery (ri-*ka*-veu-ri) *n* guérison *f*

recreation (rè-kri-*éï*-cheunn) *n* récréation *f*; ~ **centre** centre de loisirs; ~ **ground** terrain de jeux

recruit (ri-*krôut*) *n* recrue *f*

rectangle (rèk-tæng-gheul) n rectangle m

rectangular (rèk-tæng-ghyou-leu) adj rectangulaire

rector (rèk-teu) n pasteur m, recteur m

rectory (rèk-teu-ri) n presbytère m

rectum (rèk-teumm) n rectum m

red (rèd) adj rouge

redeem (ri-diim) v délivrer

reduce (ri-dyoûss) v *réduire, diminuer

reduction (ri-dak-cheunn) n rabais m, réduction f

redundant (ri-dann-deunnt) adj superflu

reed (riid) n roseau m

reef (riif) n récif m

reference (rèf-reunns) n référence f; rapport m; **with ~ to** relatif à

refer to (ri-feû) *renvoyer à

refill (rii-fil) n recharge f

refinery (ri-faï-neu-ri) n raffinerie f

reflect (ri-flèkt) v refléter

reflection (ri-flèk-cheunn) n reflet m

reflector (ri-flèk-teu) n réflecteur m

reformation (rè-feu-méï-cheunn) n réforme f

refresh (ri-frèch) v rafraîchir

refreshment (ri-frèch-meunnt) n rafraîchissement m

refrigerator (ri-fri-djeu-réï-teu) n frigidaire m, réfrigérateur m

refund¹ (ri-fannd) v rendre, rembourser

refund² (rii-fannd) n remboursement m

refusal (ri-fyoû-zeul) n refus m

refuse¹ (ri-fyoûz) v refuser

refuse² (rè-fyoûss) n rebut m

regard (ri-ghââd) v considérer; n respect m; **as regards** quant à, concernant, en ce qui concerne

regarding (ri-ghââ-dinng) prep en ce

qui concerne, concernant; à propos de

regatta (ri-ghæ-teu) n régate f

régime (réï-jiim) n régime m

region (rii-djeunn) n région f

regional (rii-djeu-neul) adj régional

register (rè-dji-steu) v s'*inscrire; recommander; **registered letter** lettre recommandée

registration (rè-dji-stréï-cheunn) n inscription f; **~ form** formulaire d'inscription; **~ number** numéro d'immatriculation; **~ plate** plaque d'immatriculation

regret (ri-ghrèt) v regretter; n regret m

regular (rè-ghyou-leu) adj régulier; ordinaire, normal

regulate (rè-ghyou-léït) v régler

regulation (rè-ghyou-léï-cheunn) n règlement m

rehabilitation (rii-heu-bi-li-téï-cheunn) n rééducation f

rehearsal (ri-heû-seul) n répétition f

rehearse (ri-heûss) v répéter

reign (réïn) n règne m; v régner

reimburse (rii-imm-beûss) v restituer, rembourser

reindeer (réïn-di^eu) n (pl ~) renne m

reject (ri-djèkt) v refuser, rejeter

relate (ri-léït) v relater

related (ri-léï-tid) adj apparenté

relation (ri-léï-cheunn) n rapport m, relation f; parent m

relative (rè-leu-tiv) n parent m; adj relatif

relax (ri-læks) v se détendre

relaxation (ri-læk-séï-cheunn) n détente f

reliable (ri-laï-eu-beul) adj digne de confiance

relic (rè-lik) n relique f

relief (ri-liif) n soulagement m; soutien m; relief m

relieve (ri-*liiv*) v soulager; relayer

religion (ri-*li*-djeunn) n religion f

religious (ri-*li*-djeuss) adj religieux

rely on (ri-*lai*) compter sur

remain (ri-*méïn*) v rester

remainder (ri-*méïn*-deu) n restant m, reste m

remaining (ri-*méï*-ninng) adj restant

remark (ri-*mââk*) n remarque f; v remarquer

remarkable (ri-*mââ*-keu-beul) adj remarquable

remedy (*rè*-meu-di) n remède m

remember (ri-*mèm*-beu) v se rappeler; *retenir

remembrance (ri-*mèm*-breunns) n souvenir m

remind (ri-*maïnd*) v rappeler

remit (ri-*mit*) v *remettre

remittance (ri-*mi*-teunns) n versement m

remnant (*rèm*-neunnt) n reste m, restant m

remote (ri-*môout*) adj éloigné, lointain

removal (ri-*moû*-veul) n déplacement m

remove (ri-*moûv*) v enlever

remunerate (ri-*myoû*-neu-réït) v rémunérer

remuneration (ri-myoû-neu-*réï*-cheunn) n rémunération f

renew (ri-*nyoû*) v renouveler; prolonger

rent (rènt) v louer; n loyer m

repair (ri-*pèeu*) v réparer; n réparation f

reparation (rè-peu-*réï*-cheunn) n réparation f

***repay** (ri-*péï*) v rembourser

repayment (ri-*péï*-meunnt) n remboursement m

repeat (ri-*piit*) v répéter

repellent (ri-*pè*-leunnt) adj écœurant, répugnant

repentance (ri-*pèn*-teunns) n repentir m

repertory (*rè*-peu-teu-ri) n répertoire m

repetition (rè-peu-*ti*-cheunn) n répétition f

replace (ri-*pléïss*) v remplacer

reply (ri-*plaï*) v répondre; n réponse f; in ~ en réponse

report (ri-*poot*) v relater; rapporter; se présenter; n compte rendu, rapport m

reporter (ri-*poo*-teu) n reporter m

represent (rè-pri-*zènt*) v représenter

representation (rè-pri-zèn-*téï*-cheunn) n représentation f

representative (rè-pri-*zèn*-teu-tiv) adj représentatif

reprimand (*rè*-pri-mâând) v réprimander

reproach (ri-*prôou*tch) n reproche m; v reprocher

reproduce (rii-preu-*dyoûss*) v *reproduire

reproduction (rii-preu-*dak*-cheunn) n reproduction f

reptile (*rèp*-taïl) n reptile m

republic (ri-*pa*-blik) n république f

republican (ri-*pa*-bli-keunn) adj républicain

repulsive (ri-*pal*-siv) adj repoussant

reputation (rè-pyou-*téï*-cheunn) n réputation f; renom m

request (ri-*kouèst*) n requête f; demande f; v *requérir

require (ri-*kouaïeu*) v exiger

requirement (ri-*kouaïeu*-meunnt) n exigence f

requisite (*rè*-koui-zit) adj requis

rescue (*rè*-skyoû) v sauver; n sauvetage m

research (ri-*seûtch*) n recherche f

resemblance (ri-*zèm*-bleunns) n ressemblance f

resemble (ri-*zèm*-beul) v ressembler à

resent (ri-*zènt*) v s'offenser de, en *vouloir à

reservation (rè-zeu-*véï*-cheunn) n réservation f

reserve (ri-*zeûv*) v réserver; *retenir; n réserve f

reserved (ri-*zeûvd*) adj réservé

reservoir (*rè*-zeu-v°uâà) n réservoir m

reside (ri-*zaïd*) v résider

residence (*rè*-zi-deunns) n résidence f; ~ **permit** permis de séjour

resident (*rè*-zi-deunnt) n résident m; adj domicilié; interne

resign (ri-*zaïn*) v démissionner

resignation (rè-zigh-*néï*-cheunn) n démission f

resin (*rè*-zinn) n résine f

resist (ri-*zist*) v résister

resistance (ri-*zi*-steunns) n résistance f

resolute (*rè*-zeu-loût) adj résolu, déterminé

respect (ri-*spèkt*) n respect m; estime f, considération f; v respecter

respectable (ri-*spèk*-teu-beul) adj honorable, respectable

respectful (ri-*spèkt*-feul) adj respectueux

respective (ri-*spèk*-tiv) adj respectif

respiration (rè-speu-*réï*-cheunn) n respiration f

respite (*rè*-spaït) n répit m

responsibility (ri-sponn-seu-*bi*-leu-ti) n responsabilité f

responsible (ri-*sponn*-seu-beul) adj responsable

rest (rèst) n repos m; reste m; v se reposer

restaurant (*rè*-steu-ron) n restaurant m

restful (*rèst*-feul) adj reposant

rest-home (*rèst*-hô°um) n maison de repos

restless (*rèst*-leuss) adj agité; inquiet

restrain (ri-*stréïn*) v *contenir, *retenir

restriction (ri-*strik*-cheunn) n restriction f

result (ri-*zalt*) n résultat m; effet m; v résulter

resume (ri-*zyoûm*) v *reprendre

résumé (*rè*-zyou-méï) n résumé m

retail (*rii*-téïl) v détailler; ~ **trade** commerce de détail

retailer (*rii*-téï-leu) n détaillant m; revendeur m

retina (*rè*-ti-neu) n rétine f

retired (ri-*taï*°ud) adj retraité

return (ri-*teûnn*) v *revenir, retourner; n retour m; ~ **flight** vol de retour; ~ **journey** voyage de retour

reunite (rii-yoû-*naït*) v réunir

reveal (ri-*viil*) v révéler

revelation (rè-veu-*léï*-cheunn) n révélation f

revenge (ri-*vèndj*) n vengeance f

revenue (*rè*-veu-nyoû) n recettes, revenu m

reverse (ri-*veûss*) n contraire m; revers m; marche arrière; revirement m; adj inverse; v *faire marche arrière

review (ri-*vyoû*) n critique f; revue f

revise (ri-*vaïz*) v reviser

revision (ri-*vi*-jeunn) n révision f

revival (ri-*vaï*-veul) n reprise f

revolt (ri-*vô°ult*) v se révolter; n rébellion f, révolte f

revolting (ri-*vô°ul*-tinng) adj dégoûtant, révoltant, répugnant

revolution (rè-veu-*loû*-cheunn) n révolution f; rotation f

revolutionary (rè-veu-*loû*-cheu-neu-ri) adj révolutionnaire

revolver (ri-*vol*-veu) n revolver m

revue (ri-*vyoû*) n revue f

reward (ri-°u*ood*) n récompense f; v

récompenser

rheumatism (*roû*-meu-ti-zeumm) *n* rhumatisme *m*

rhinoceros (raï-*no*-seu-reuss) *n* (pl ~, ~es) rhinocéros *m*

rhubarb (*roû*-bââb) *n* rhubarbe *f*

rhyme (raïm) *n* rime *f*

rhythm (*ri*-ðeumm) *n* rythme *m*

rib (rib) *n* côte *f*

ribbon (*ri*-beunn) *n* ruban *m*

rice (raïss) *n* riz *m*

rich (ritch) *adj* riche

riches (*ri*-tchiz) *pl* richesse *f*

riddle (*ri*-deul) *n* énigme *f*

ride (raïd) *n* course *f*

*****ride** (raïd) *v* rouler; monter à cheval

rider (raï-deu) *n* cavalier *m*

ridge (ridj) *n* arête *f*

ridicule (*ri*-di-kyoûl) *v* ridiculiser

ridiculous (ri-*di*-kyou-leuss) *adj* ridicule

riding (*raï*-dinng) *n* équitation *f*

riding-school (*raï*-dinng-skoûl) *n* manège *m*

rifle (*raï*-feul) *v* fusil *m*

right (raït) *n* droit *m*; *adj* correct, juste; droit; équitable; **all right!** d'accord!; ***be ~** *avoir raison; **~ of way** priorité de passage

righteous (*raï*-tcheuss) *adj* juste

right-hand (*raït*-hænd) *adj* à droite, de droite

rightly (*raït*-li) *adv* justement

rim (rimm) *n* jante *f*; rebord *m*

ring (rinng) *n* bague *f*; cercle *m*; piste *f*

*****ring** (rinng) *v* sonner; **~ up** téléphoner

rinse (rinns) *v* rincer; *n* rinçage *m*

riot (*raï*-eut) *n* émeute *f*

rip (rip) *v* déchirer

ripe (raïp) *adj* mûr

rise (raïz) *n* augmentation de salaire, augmentation *f*; élévation *f*; mon-

tée *f*; essor *m*

*****rise** (raïz) *v* se lever; monter

rising (*raï*-zinng) *n* insurrection *f*

risk (risk) *n* risque *m*; danger *m*; *v* risquer

risky (*ri*-ski) *adj* dangereux, risqué

rival (*raï*-veul) *n* rival *m*; concurrent *m*; *v* rivaliser

rivalry (*raï*-veul-ri) *n* rivalité *f*; concurrence *f*

river (*ri*-veu) *n* fleuve *m*; **~ bank** rive *f*

riverside (*ri*-veu-saïd) *n* bord de la rivière

roach (rôᵘtch) *n* (pl ~) gardon *m*

road (rôᵘd) *n* rue *f*, route *f*; **~ fork** *n* bifurcation *f*; **~ map** carte routière; **~ system** réseau routier; **~ up** route en réfection

roadhouse (*rôᵘd*-haousse) *n* auberge *f*

roadside (*rôᵘd*-saïd) *n* bord de la route; **~ restaurant** auberge *f*

roadway (*rôᵘd*-ᵒᵘéï) *nAm* chaussée *f*

roam (rôᵘm) *v* vagabonder

roar (roo) *v* mugir, rugir; *n* rugissement *m*, grondement *m*

roast (rôᵘst) *v* griller, rôtir

rob (rob) *v* voler

robber (*ro*-beu) *n* voleur *m*

robbery (*ro*-beu-ri) *n* vol *m*

robe (rôᵘb) *n* robe *f*

robin (*ro*-binn) *n* rouge-gorge *m*

robust (rôᵘ-*bast*) *adj* robuste

rock (rok) *n* rocher *m*; *v* balancer

rocket (*ro*-kit) *n* fusée *f*

rocky (*ro*-ki) *adj* rocheux

rod (rod) *n* barre *f*, tige *f*

roe (rôᵘ) *n* œufs de poisson, laitance *f*

roll (rôᵘl) *v* rouler; *n* rouleau *m*; petit pain

roller-skating (*rôᵘ*-leu-skéï-tinng) *n* patinage à roulettes

Roman Catholic (*rôᵘ*-meunn *kæ*-θeu-lik) catholique

romance (reu-*mæns*) *n* idylle *f*

romantic (reu-*mæn*-tik) *adj* romantique

roof (roûf) *n* toit *m*; **thatched** ~ toit de chaume *m*

room (roûm) *n* pièce *f*, chambre *f*; espace *m*, place *f*; ~ **and board** pension complète; ~ **service** service d'étage; ~ **temperature** température ambiante

roomy (*roû*-mi) *adj* spacieux

root (roût) *n* racine *f*

rope (rô°up) *n* corde *f*

rosary (*rô°u*-zeu-ri) *n* rosaire *m*

rose (rô°uz) *n* rose *f*; *adj* rose

rotten (*ro*-teunn) *adj* pourri

rouge (roûj) *n* rouge *m*

rough (raf) *adj* rugueux

roulette (roû-*lèt*) *n* roulette *f*

round (raound) *adj* rond; *prep* autour de; *n* reprise *f*; ~ **trip** *Am* aller et retour

roundabout (*raoun*-deu-baout) *n* rond-point *m*

rounded (*raoun*-did) *adj* arrondi

route (roût) *n* route *f*

routine (roû-*tiin*) *n* routine *f*

row¹ (rô°u) *n* rang *m*; *v* ramer

row² (raou) *n* querelle *f*

rowdy (*raou*-di) *adj* tapageur

rowing-boat (*rô°u*-inng-bô°ut) *n* bateau à rames

royal (*roï*-eul) *adj* royal

rub (rab) *v* frotter

rubber (*ra*-beu) *n* caoutchouc *m*; gomme *f*; ~ **band** élastique *m*

rubbish (*ra*-bich) *n* détritus *m*; radotage *m*, sottise *f*; **talk** ~ baratiner

rubbish-bin (*ra*-bich-binn) *n* poubelle *f*

ruby (*roû*-bi) *n* rubis *m*

rucksack (*rak*-sæk) *n* sac à dos

rudder (*ra*-deu) *n* gouvernail *m*

rude (roûd) *adj* grossier

rug (ragh) *n* tapis *m*

ruin (*roû*-inn) *v* ruiner; *n* ruine *f*

ruination (roû-i-*néï*-cheunn) *n* effondrement *m*

rule (roûl) *n* règle *f*; régime *m*, gouvernement *m*, règne *m*; *v* régner, gouverner; **as a** ~ généralement, en général

ruler (*roû*-leu) *n* monarque *m*, dirigeant *m*; règle *f*

Rumania (roû-*méï*-ni-eu) Roumanie *f*

Rumanian (roû-*méï*-ni-eunn) *adj* roumain; *n* Roumain *m*

rumour (*roû*-meu) *n* rumeur *f*

*****run** (rann) *v* *courir; ~ **into** rencontrer

runaway (*ra*-neu-°uéï) *n* fugitif *m*

rung (rann) *v* (pp ring)

runway (*rann*-°uéï) *n* piste de décollage

rural (*rou°u*-reul) *adj* rural

ruse (roûz) *n* ruse *f*

rush (rach) *v* se presser; *n* jonc *m*

rush-hour (*rach*-aou°u) *n* heure de pointe

Russia (*ra*-cheu) Russie *f*

Russian (*ra*-cheunn) *adj* russe; *n* Russe *m*

rust (rast) *n* rouille *f*

rustic (*ra*-stik) *adj* rustique

rusty (*ra*-sti) *adj* rouillé

S

saccharin (*sæ*-keu-rinn) *n* saccharine *f*

sack (sæk) *n* sac *m*

sacred (*séï*-krid) *adj* sacré

sacrifice (*sæ*-kri-faïss) *n* sacrifice *m*; *v* sacrifier

sacrilege (*sæ*-kri-lidj) *n* sacrilège *m*

sad (sæd) *adj* triste; malheureux, affligé, mélancolique

saddle (*sæ*-deul) *n* selle *f*

sadness (*sæd*-neuss) *n* tristesse *f*

safe (séïf) *adj* sûr ; *n* coffre-fort

safety (*séïf*-ti) *n* sécurité *f*

safety-belt (*séïf*-ti-bèlt) *n* ceinture de sécurité

safety-pin (*séïf*-ti-pinn) *n* épingle de sûreté

safety-razor (*séïf*-ti-réï-zeu) *n* rasoir *m*

sail (séïl) *v* naviguer ; *n* voile *f*

sailing-boat (*séï*-linng-bô⁰ut) *n* bateau à voiles

sailor (*séï*-leu) *n* marin *m*

saint (séïnt) *n* saint *m*

salad (*sæ*-leud) *n* salade *f*

salad-oil (*sæ*-leud-oïl) *n* huile de table

salary (*sæ*-leu-ri) *n* paie *f*, salaire *m*

sale (séïl) *n* vente *f* ; clearance ~ soldes ; **for** ~ à vendre ; **sales** soldes

saleable (*séï*-leu-beul) *adj* vendable

salesgirl (*séïlz*-gheul) *n* vendeuse *f*

salesman (*séïlz*-meunn) *n* (pl -men) vendeur *m*

salmon (*sæ*-meunn) *n* (pl ~) saumon *m*

salon (*sæ*-lon) *n* salon *m*

saloon (seu-*loûn*) *n* café *m*

salt (soolt) *n* sel *m*

salt-cellar (*soolt*-sè-leu) *n* salière *f*

salty (*sool*-ti) *adj* salé

salute (seu-*loût*) *v* saluer

salve (sââv) *n* onguent *m*

same (séïm) *adj* même

sample (*sââm*-peul) *n* échantillon *m*

sanatorium (sæ-neu-*too*-ri-eumm) *n* (pl ~s, -ria) sanatorium *m*

sand (sænd) *n* sable *m*

sandal (*sæn*-deul) *n* sandale *f*

sandpaper (*sænd*-péï-peu) *n* papier de verre

sandwich (*sæn*-⁰uidj) *n* sandwich *m* ; tartine *f*

sandy (*sæn*-di) *adj* sableux

sanitary (*sæ*-ni-teu-ri) *adj* sanitaire ; ~ **towel** serviette hygiénique

sapphire (*sæ*-faï⁰u) *n* saphir *m*

sardine (sââ-*diin*) *n* sardine *f*

satchel (*sæ*-tcheul) *n* cartable *m*

satellite (*sæ*-teu-laït) *n* satellite *m*

satin (*sæ*-tinn) *n* satin *m*

satisfaction (sæ-tiss-*fæk*-cheunn) *n* satisfaction *f*

satisfy (*sæ*-tiss-faï) *v* *satisfaire

Saturday (*sæ*-teu-di) samedi *m*

sauce (sooss) *n* sauce *f*

saucepan (*sooss*-peunn) *n* poêle *f*

saucer (*soo*-seu) *n* soucoupe *f*

Saudi Arabia (saou-di-eu-*réï*-bi-eu) Arabie Séoudite

sauna (*soo*-neu) *n* sauna *m*

sausage (*so*-sidj) *n* saucisse *f*

savage (*sæ*-vidj) *adj* sauvage

save (séïv) *v* sauver ; épargner

savings (*séï*-vinngz) *pl* économies ; ~ **bank** caisse d'épargne

saviour (*séï*-vyeu) *n* sauveur *m*

savoury (*séï*-veu-ri) *adj* savoureux ; piquant

saw¹ (soo) *v* (p see)

saw² (soo) *n* scie *f*

sawdust (*soo*-dast) *n* sciure *f*

saw-mill (*soo*-mil) *n* scierie *f*

***say** (séï) *v* *dire

scaffolding (*skæ*-feul-dinng) *n* échafaudage *m*

scale (skéïl) *n* échelle *f* ; gamme *f* ; écaille *f* ; **scales** *pl* balance *f*

scandal (*skæn*-deul) *n* scandale *m*

Scandinavia (skæn-di-*néï*-vi-eu) Scandinavie *f*

Scandinavian (skæn-di-*néï*-vi-eunn) *adj* scandinave ; *n* Scandinave *m*

scapegoat (*skéïp*-ghô⁰ut) *n* bouc émissaire

scar (skââ) *n* cicatrice *f*

scarce (ske⁰uss) *adj* rare

scarcely (*skè⁰u*-sli) *adv* à peine

scarcity (*skè^{eu}*-seu-ti) *n* pénurie *f*

scare (*skè^{eu}*) *v* effrayer; *n* panique *f*

scarf (*skââf*) *n* (pl ~s, scarves) écharpe *f*

scarlet (*skââ*-leut) *adj* écarlate

scary (*skè^{eu}*-ri) *adj* inquiétant

scatter (*skæ*-teu) *v* disperser

scene (siin) *n* scène *f*

scenery (*sii*-neu-ri) *n* paysage *m*

scenic (*sii*-nik) *adj* pittoresque

scent (sènt) *n* parfum *m*

schedule (*chè*-dyoûl) *n* horaire *m*

scheme (skiim) *n* plan *m*; projet *m*

scholar (*sko*-leu) *n* érudit *m*; élève *m*

scholarship (*sko*-leu-chip) *n* bourse d'études

school (skoûl) *n* école *f*

schoolboy (*skoûl*-boï) *n* écolier *m*

schoolgirl (*skoûl*-gheûl) *n* écolière *f*

schoolmaster (*skoûl*-mââ-steu) *n* instituteur *m*, maître d'école

schoolteacher (*skoûl*-tii-tcheu) *n* instituteur *m*

science (*saï*-eunns) *n* science *f*

scientific (saï-eunn-*ti*-fik) *adj* scientifique

scientist (*saï*-eunn-tist) *n* savant *m*

scissors (*si*-zeuz) *pl* ciseaux *mpl*

scold (skô^{ou}ld) *v* gronder; insulter

scooter (*skoû*-teu) *n* scooter *m*; patinette *f*

score (skoo) *n* nombre de points; *v* marquer

scorn (skoon) *n* dédain *m*, mépris *m*; *v* mépriser

Scot (skot) *n* Ecossais *m*

Scotch (skotch) *adj* écossais; **scotch tape** ruban adhésif

Scotland (*skot*-leunnd) Ecosse *f*

Scottish (*sko*-tich) *adj* écossais

scout (skaout) *n* scout *m*

scrap (skræp) *n* morceau *m*

scrap-book (*skræp*-bouk) *n* album de collage

scrape (skréïp) *v* racler

scrap-iron (*skræ*-paï^{eu}n) *n* ferraille *f*

scratch (skrætch) *v* érafler, gratter; *n* rayure *f*, égratignure *f*

scream (skriim) *v* hurler, crier; *n* cri *m*

screen (skriin) *n* écran *m*

screw (skroû) *n* vis *f*; *v* visser

screw-driver (*skroû*-draï-veu) *n* tournevis *m*

scrub (skrab) *v* frotter; *n* buisson *m*

sculptor (*skalp*-teu) *n* sculpteur *m*

sculpture (*skalp*-tcheu) *n* sculpture *f*

sea (sii) *n* mer *f*

sea-bird (*sii*-beûd) *n* oiseau de mer

sea-coast (*sii*-kô^{ou}st) *n* littoral *m*

seagull (*sii*-ghal) *n* mouette *f*, goéland *m*

seal (siil) *n* sceau *m*; phoque *m*

seam (siim) *n* couture *f*

seaman (*sii*-meunn) *n* (pl -men) marin *m*

seamless (*siim*-leuss) *adj* sans couture

seaport (*sii*-poot) *n* port de mer

search (seûtch) *v* chercher; fouiller; *n* fouille *f*

searchlight (*seûtch*-laït) *n* projecteur *m*

seascape (*sii*-skéïp) *n* marine *f*

sea-shell (*sii*-chèl) *n* coquillage *m*

seashore (*sii*-choo) *n* bord de la mer

seasick (*sii*-sik) *adj* souffrant du mal de mer

seasickness (*sii*-sik-neuss) *n* mal de mer

seaside (*sii*-saïd) *n* bord de la mer; ~ **resort** station balnéaire

season (*sii*-zeunn) *n* saison *f*; **high ~** pleine saison; **low ~** morte-saison *f*; **off ~** hors saison

season-ticket (*sii*-zeunn-ti-kit) *n* carte d'abonnement

seat (siit) *n* siège *m*; place *f*

seat-belt (*siit*-bèlt) *n* ceinture de sécurité

sea-urchin (*sii*-eû-tchinn) n oursin m

sea-water (*sii*-ᵒᵘoo-teu) n eau de mer

second (sè-keunnd) num deuxième; n seconde f; instant m

secondary (sè-keunn-deu-ri) adj secondaire; ~ **school** école secondaire

second-hand (sè-keunnd-*hænd*) adj d'occasion

secret (*sii*-kreut) n secret m; adj secret

secretary (sè-kreu-tri) n secrétaire f; secrétaire m

section (*sèk*-cheunn) n section f; case f, service m

secure (si-*kyou*ᵉᵘ) adj sûr; v s'assurer de

security (si-*kyou*ᵉᵘ-reu-ti) n sécurité f; caution f

sedate (si-*déit*) adj posé

sedative (*sè*-deu-tiv) n sédatif m

seduce (si-*dyoûss*) v *séduire

* **see** (sii) v *voir; *comprendre, se rendre compte; ~ **to** s'occuper de

seed (siid) n semence f

* **seek** (siik) v chercher

seem (siim) v *paraître, sembler

seen (siin) v (pp see)

seesaw (*sii*-soo) n balançoire f

seize (siiz) v saisir

seldom (*sèl*-deumm) adv rarement

select (si-*lèkt*) v sélectionner, choisir; adj exquis, choisi

selection (si-*lèk*-cheunn) n choix m, sélection f

self-centred (sèlf-*sèn*-teud) adj égocentrique

self-employed (sèl-fimm-*ploïd*) adj indépendant

self-evident (sèl-*fè*-vi-deunnt) adj évident

self-government (sèlf-*gha*-veu-meunnt) n autonomie f

selfish (*sèl*-fich) adj égoïste

selfishness (*sèl*-fich-neuss) n égoïsme m

self-service (sèlf-*seû*-viss) n libre-service m

* **sell** (sèl) v vendre

semblance (*sèm*-bleunns) n apparence f

semi- (*sè*-mi) semi-

semicircle (*sè*-mi-seû-keul) n demi-cercle m

semi-colon (sè-mi-*kô*ᵒᵘ-leunn) n point-virgule m

senate (*sè*-neut) n sénat m

senator (*sè*-neu-teu) n sénateur m

* **send** (sènd) v expédier, *envoyer; ~ **back** *renvoyer; ~ **for** *faire venir; ~ **off** expédier

senile (*sii*-naïl) adj sénile

sensation (sèn-*séï*-cheunn) n sensation f; impression f

sensational (sèn-*séï*-cheu-neul) adj spectaculaire, sensationnel

sense (sèns) n sens m; bon sens, raison f; signification f; v *percevoir; ~ **of honour** sens de l'honneur

senseless (*sèns*-leuss) adj insensé

sensible (*sèn*-seu-beul) adj raisonnable

sensitive (*sèn*-si-tiv) adj sensible

sentence (*sèn*-teunns) n phrase f; jugement m; v condamner

sentimental (sèn-ti-*mèn*-teul) adj sentimental

separate¹ (*sè*-peu-réït) v séparer

separate² (*sè*-peu-reut) adj distinct, séparé

separately (*sè*-peu-reut-li) adv à part

September (sèp-*tèm*-beu) septembre

septic (*sèp*-tik) adj septique; * **become** ~ s'infecter

sequel (*sii*-kᵒᵘeul) n suite f

sequence (*sii*-kᵒᵘeunns) n succession f; série f

serene (seu-*riin*) *adj* serein; clair

serial (*si^{eu}*-ri-eul) *n* feuilleton *m*

series (*si^{eu}*-riiz) *n* (pl ~) suite *f*, série *f*

serious (*si^{eu}*-ri-euss) *adj* sérieux

seriousness (*si^{eu}*-ri-euss-neuss) *n* sérieux *m*

sermon (*seû*-meunn) *n* sermon *m*

serum (*si^{eu}*-reumm) *n* sérum *m*

servant (*seû*-veunnt) *n* domestique *m*

serve (seûv) *v* *servir

service (*seû*-viss) *n* service *m*; ~ **charge** service *m*; ~ **station** station-service *f*

serviette (seû-vi-èt) *n* serviette *f*

session (*sè*-cheunn) *n* séance *f*

set (sèt) *n* jeu *m*, groupe *m*

*set (sèt) *v* poser; ~ **menu** menu fixe; ~ **out** *partir

setting (*sè*-tinng) *n* cadre *m*; ~ **lotion** fixateur *m*

settle (*sè*-teul) *v* régler, arranger; ~ **down** s'établir

settlement (*sè*-teul-meunnt) *n* règlement *m*, arrangement *m*, accord *m*

seven (*sè*-veunn) *num* sept

seventeen (sè-veunn-*tiin*) *num* dix-sept

seventeenth (sè-veunn-*tiinθ*) *num* dix-septième

seventh (*sè*-veunnθ) *num* septième

seventy (*sè*-veunn-ti) *num* soixante-dix

several (*sè*-veu-reul) *adj* divers, plusieurs

severe (si-*vi^{eu}*) *adj* violent, sévère, grave

sew (sô^{ou}) *v* *coudre; ~ **up** suturer

sewer (*soû*-eu) *n* égout *m*

sewing-machine (*sô^{ou}*-inng-meu-chiin) *n* machine à coudre

sex (sèks) *n* sexe *m*

sexton (*sèk*-steunn) *n* sacristain *m*

sexual (*sèk*-chou-eul) *adj* sexuel

sexuality (sèk-chou-æ-leu-ti) *n* sexualité *f*

shade (chéïd) *n* ombre *f*; nuance *f*

shadow (*chæ*-dô^{ou}) *n* ombre *f*

shady (*chéï*-di) *adj* ombragé

*shake (chéïk) *v* secouer

shaky (*chéï*-ki) *adj* vacillant

*shall (chæl) *v* *devoir

shallow (*chæ*-lô^{ou}) *adj* peu profond

shame (chéïm) *n* honte *f*; déshonneur *m*; **shame!** quelle honte!

shampoo (chæm-*poú*) *n* shampooing *m*

shamrock (*chæm*-rok) *n* trèfle *m*

shape (chéïp) *n* forme *f*; *v* former

share (chè^{eu}) *v* partager; *n* part *f*; action *f*

shark (chââk) *n* requin *m*

sharp (chââp) *adj* aigu

sharpen (*chââ*-peunn) *v* affiler, aiguiser

shave (chéïv) *v* se raser

shaver (*chéï*-veu) *n* rasoir électrique

shaving-brush (*chéï*-vinng-brach) *n* blaireau *m*

shaving-cream (*chéï*-vinng-kriim) *n* crème à raser

shaving-soap (*chéï*-vinng-sô^{ou}p) *n* savon à barbe

shawl (chool) *n* châle *m*

she (chii) *pron* elle

shed (chèd) *n* réduit *m*

*shed (chèd) *v* verser; répandre

sheep (chiip) *n* (pl ~) mouton *m*

sheer (chi^{eu}) *adj* absolu, pur; fin, transparent

sheet (chiit) *n* drap *m*; feuille *f*; plaque *f*

shelf (chèlf) *n* (pl shelves) étagère *f*

shell (chèl) *n* coquille *f*

shellfish (*chèl*-fich) *n* crustacé *m*

shelter (*chèl*-teu) *n* abri *m*; *v* abriter

shepherd (*chè*-peud) *n* berger *m*

shift (chift) *n* équipe *f*

*shine (chaïn) *v* briller; resplendir

ship (chip) *n* navire *m*; *v* expédier;
   shipping line compagnie de navigation

shipowner (*chi*-pô^{ou}-neu) *n* armateur
   m

shipyard (*chip*-yââd) *n* chantier naval

shirt (cheût) *n* chemise *f*

shiver (*chi*-veu) *v* trembler, frissonner; *n* frisson *m*

shivery (*chi*-veu-ri) *adj* frissonnant

shock (chok) *n* choc *m*; *v* choquer;
   ~ absorber amortisseur *m*

shocking (*cho*-kinng) *adj* choquant

shoe (choû) *n* chaussure *f*; **gym
   shoes** chaussures de gymnastique;
   ~ polish cirage *m*

shoe-lace (*choû*-léiss) *n* lacet *m*

shoemaker (*choû*-méï-keu) *n* cordonnier *m*

shoe-shop (*choû*-chop) *n* magasin de
   chaussures

shook (chouk) *v* (p shake)

*shoot (choût) *v* tirer

shop (chop) *n* boutique *f*; *v* *faire
   des achats; **~ assistant** vendeur *m*;
   shopping bag sac à provisions;
   shopping centre centre commercial

shopkeeper (*chop*-kii-peu) *n* commerçant *m*

shop-window (chop-^{ou}*inn*-dô^{ou}) *n* vitrine *f*

shore (choo) *n* rive *f*, rivage *m*

short (choot) *adj* court; petit; **~ circuit** court-circuit *m*

shortage (*choo*-tidj) *n* carence *f*, manque *m*

shortcoming (*choot*-ka-minng) *n* imperfection *f*

shorten (*choo*-teunn) *v* raccourcir

shorthand (*choot*-hænd) *n* sténographie *f*

shortly (*choot*-li) *adv* sous peu, prochainement, bientôt

shorts (choots) *pl* short *m*; *plAm* caleçon *m*

short-sighted (choot-*saï*-tid) *adj* myope

shot (chot) *n* coup de feu; piqûre *f*;
   prise de vue

*should (choud) *v* *devoir

shoulder (*chô^{ou}l*-deu) *n* épaule *f*

shout (chaout) *v* crier; *n* cri *m*

shovel (*cha*-veul) *n* pelle *f*

show (chô^{ou}) *n* représentation *f*,
   spectacle *m*; exposition *f*

*show (chô^{ou}) *v* montrer; exposer;
   démontrer

show-case (*chô^{ou}*-kéiss) *n* vitrine *f*

shower (chaou^{eu}) *n* douche *f*; averse
   f

showroom (*chô^{ou}*-roûm) *n* salle d'exposition

shriek (chriik) *v* pousser des cris; *n*
   cri aigu

shrimp (chrimmp) *n* crevette *f*

shrine (chraïn) *n* sanctuaire *m*

*shrink (chrinngk) *v* rétrécir

shrinkproof (*chrinngk*-proûf) *adj* irrétrécissable

shrub (chrab) *n* arbuste *m*

shudder (*cha*-deu) *n* frisson *m*

shuffle (*cha*-feul) *v* *battre

*shut (chat) *v* fermer; **shut** clos, fermé; **~ in** enfermer

shutter (*cha*-teu) *n* persienne *f*, volet
   m

shy (chaï) *adj* farouche, timide

shyness (*chaï*-neuss) *n* timidité *f*

Siam (saï-*æm*) Siam *m*

Siamese (saï-eu-*miiz*) *adj* siamois; *n*
   Siamois *m*

sick (sik) *adj* malade; ayant mal au
   cœur

sickness (*sik*-neuss) *n* maladie *f*; mal
   au cœur

side (saïd) *n* côté *m*; parti *m*; **one-
   sided** *adj* unilatéral

sideburns (*saïd*-beûnnz) *pl* favoris

sidelight (*saïd*-laït) *n* lumière latérale

side-street (*saïd*-striit) *n* rue transversale

sidewalk (*saïd*-^{ou}ook) *nAm* trottoir *m*

sideways (*saïd*-^{ou}éiz) *adv* de côté

siege (siidj) *n* siège *m*

sieve (siv) *n* passoire *f*; *v* tamiser

sift (sift) *v* tamiser

sight (saït) *n* vue *f*; spectacle *m*; curiosité *f*

sign (saïn) *n* marque *f*, signe *m*; geste *m*; *v* signer

signal (*sigh*-neul) *n* signal *m*; signe *m*; *v* signaler

signature (*sigh*-neu-tcheu) *n* signature *f*

significant (sigh-*ni*-fi-keunnt) *adj* significatif

signpost (*saïn*-pô^{ou}st) *n* poteau indicateur

silence (*saï*-leunns) *n* silence *m*; *v* *faire taire

silencer (*saï*-leunn-seu) *n* silencieux *m*

silent (*saï*-leunnt) *adj* silencieux; ***be ~** se *taire

silk (silk) *n* soie *f*

silken (*sil*-keunn) *adj* soyeux

silly (*si*-li) *adj* bête, sot

silver (*sil*-veu) *n* argent *m*; en argent

silversmith (*sil*-veu-smiθ) *n* orfèvre *m*

silverware (*sil*-veu-^{ou}è^{eu}) *n* argenterie *f*

similar (*si*-mi-leu) *adj* analogue, similaire

similarity (si-mi-*læ*-reu-ti) *n* similitude *f*

simple (*simm*-peul) *adj* ingénu, simple; ordinaire

simply (*simm*-pli) *adv* simplement

simulate (*si*-myou-léït) *v* simuler

simultaneous (si-meul-*téï*-ni-euss) *adj* simultané

sin (sinn) *n* péché *m*

since (sinns) *prep* depuis; *adv* depuis; *conj* depuis que; comme

sincere (sinn-*si*^{eu}) *adj* sincère

sinew (*si*-nyoû) *n* tendon *m*

***sing** (sinng) *v* chanter

singer (*sinng*-eu) *n* chanteur *m*; chanteuse *f*

single (*sinng*-gheul) *adj* seul; célibataire

singular (*sinng*-ghyou-leu) *n* singulier *m*; *adj* singulier

sinister (*si*-ni-steu) *adj* sinistre

sink (sinngk) *n* évier *m*

***sink** (sinngk) *v* s'enfoncer

sip (sip) *n* gorgée *f*

siphon (*saï*-feunn) *n* siphon *m*

sir (seû) monsieur *m*

siren (*saï*^{eu}-reunn) *n* sirène *f*

sister (*si*-steu) *n* sœur *f*

sister-in-law (*si*-steu-rinn-loo) *n* (*pl* sisters-) belle-sœur *f*

***sit** (sit) *v* *être assis; **~ down** s'*asseoir

site (saït) *n* site *m*; position *f*

sitting-room (*si*-tinng-roûm) *n* salon *m*

situated (*si*-tchou-éï-tid) *adj* situé

situation (si-tchou-*éï*-cheunn) *n* situation *f*

six (siks) *num* six

sixteen (siks-*tiin*) *num* seize

sixteenth (siks-*tiinθ*) *num* seizième

sixth (siksθ) *num* sixième

sixty (*siks*-ti) *num* soixante

size (saïz) *n* taille *f*, mesure *f*; dimension *f*, grandeur *f*; format *m*

skate (skéït) *v* patiner; *n* patin *m*

skating (*skéï*-tinng) *n* patinage *m*

skating-rink (*skéï*-tinng-rinngk) *n* patinoire *f*

skeleton (*skè*-li-teunn) *n* squelette *m*

sketch (skètch) *n* dessin *m*, esquisse *f*; *v* dessiner, esquisser

sketch-book (*skètch*-bouk) *n* cahier de

croquis

ski[1] (skii) v skier

ski[2] (skii) n (pl ~, ~s) ski m; ~ **boots** chaussures de ski; ~ **pants** pantalon de ski; ~ **poles** Am bâtons de ski; ~ **sticks** bâtons de ski

skid (skid) v déraper

skier (skii-eu) n skieur m

skiing (skii-inng) n ski m

ski-jump (skii-djammp) n saut à ski

skilful (skil-feul) adj habile, adroit

ski-lift (skii-lift) n téléski m

skill (skil) n habileté f

skilled (skild) adj habile; expert

skin (skinn) n peau f; ~ **cream** crème de beauté

skip (skip) v sautiller; sauter

skirt (skeût) n jupe f

skull (skal) n crâne m

sky (skaï) n ciel m; air m

skyscraper (skaï-skréï-peu) n gratte-ciel m

slack (slæk) adj lent

slacks (slæks) pl pantalon m

slam (slæm) v claquer

slander (slâân-deu) n calomnie f

slant (slâânt) v s'incliner

slanting (slâân-tinng) adj oblique, en pente, incliné

slap (slæp) v *battre; n claque f

slate (sléït) n ardoise f

slave (sléïv) n esclave m

sledge (slèdj) n luge f, traîneau m

sleep (sliip) n sommeil m

*****sleep** (sliip) v *dormir

sleeping-bag (slii-pinng-bægh) n sac de couchage

sleeping-car (slii-pinng-kââ) n wagon-lit

sleeping-pill (slii-pinng-pil) n somnifère m

sleepless (sliip-leuss) adj sans sommeil

sleepy (slii-pi) adj somnolent

sleeve (sliiv) n manche f; housse f

sleigh (sléï) n luge f, traîneau m

slender (slèn-deu) adj svelte

slice (slaïss) n tranche f

slide (slaïd) n glissade f; toboggan m; diapositive f

*****slide** (slaïd) v glisser

slight (slaït) adj léger; faible

slim (slimm) adj mince; v maigrir

slip (slip) v déraper, glisser; s'échapper; n faux pas; combinaison f

slipper (sli-peu) n pantoufle f

slippery (sli-peu-ri) adj glissant

slogan (slô^{ou}-gheunn) n devise f, slogan m

slope (slô^{ou}p) n versant m; v décliner

sloping (slô^{ou}-pinng) adj en pente

sloppy (slo-pi) adj désordonné

slot (slot) n fente f

slot-machine (slot-meu-chiin) n appareil à jetons

slovenly (sla-veunn-li) adj mal soigné

slow (slô^{ou}) adj lent; ~ **down** ralentir; freiner

sluice (sloûss) n écluse f

slum (slamm) n bas quartier

slump (slammp) n baisse des prix

slush (slach) n boue f

sly (slaï) adj malin

smack (smæk) v donner une claque; n claque f

small (smool) adj petit; faible

smallpox (smool-poks) n variole f

smart (smâât) adj élégant; adroit, alerte

smell (smèl) n odeur f

*****smell** (smèl) v *sentir; *sentir mauvais

smelly (smè-li) adj malodorant

smile (smaïl) v *sourire; n sourire m

smith (smiθ) n forgeron m

smoke (smô^{ou}k) v fumer; n fumée f; **no smoking** défense de fumer

smoker (smô^{ou}-keu) n fumeur m;

compartiment fumeurs

smoking-compartment (*smô^ou*-kinng-keumm-pâât-meunnt) *n* compartiment fumeurs

smoking-room (*smô^ou*-kinng-roûm) *n* fumoir *m*

smooth (smoûð) *adj* uni, plat, lisse; doux

smuggle (*sma*-gheul) *v* passer en contrebande

snack (snæk) *n* casse-croûte *m*

snack-bar (*snæk*-bââ) *n* snack-bar *m*

snail (snéïl) *n* escargot *m*

snake (snéïk) *n* serpent *m*

snapshot (*snæp*-chot) *n* instantané *m*

sneakers (*snii*-keuz) *plAm* chaussures de gymnastique

sneeze (sniiz) *v* éternuer

sniper (*snaï*-peu) *n* franc-tireur *m*

snooty (*snoû*-ti) *adj* snob

snore (snoo) *v* ronfler

snorkel (*snoo*-keul) *n* tube de plongée

snout (snaout) *n* museau *m*

snow (snô^ou) *n* neige *f*; *v* neiger

snowstorm (*snô^ou*-stoom) *n* tempête de neige

snowy (*snô^ou*-i) *adj* neigeux

so (sô^ou) *conj* donc; *adv* ainsi, tellement, si; **and ~ on** et ainsi de suite; **~ far** jusqu'à présent; **~ that** de manière que, pour que, afin que

soak (sô^ouk) *v* tremper

soap (sô^up) *n* savon *m*; **~ powder** savon en poudre

sober (*sô^ou*-beu) *adj* sobre; pondéré

so-called (sô^ou-*koold*) *adj* soi-disant

soccer (*so*-keu) *n* football *m*; **~ team** équipe *f*

social (*sô^ou*-cheul) *adj* social

socialism (*sô^ou*-cheu-li-zeumm) *n* socialisme *m*

socialist (*sô^ou*-cheu-list) *adj* socialiste; *n* socialiste *m*

society (seu-*saï*-eu-ti) *n* société *f*; as-

sociation *f*; compagnie *f*

sock (sok) *n* chaussette *f*

socket (*so*-kit) *n* douille *f*

soda-water (*sô^ou*-deu-^ou oo-teu) *n* eau de Seltz, eau gazeuse

sofa (*sô^ou*-feu) *n* canapé *m*

soft (soft) *adj* mou; **~ drink** boisson non alcoolisée

soften (*so*-feunn) *v* adoucir

soil (soïl) *n* sol *m*; terroir *m*, tcrrc *f*

soiled (soïld) *adj* souillé

sold (sô^ould) *v* (p, pp sell); **~ out** épuisé

solder (*sol*-deu) *v* souder

soldering-iron (*sol*-deu-rinng-aï^eu n) *n* fer à souder

soldier (*sô^ou l*-djeu) *n* soldat *m*

sole¹ (sô^oul) *adj* unique

sole² (sô^oul) *n* semelle *f*; sole *f*

solely (*sô^ou l*-li) *adv* exclusivement

solemn (*so*-leumm) *adj* solennel

solicitor (seu-*li*-si-teu) *n* avoué *m*, avocat *m*

solid (*so*-lid) *adj* robuste, solide; massif; *n* solide *m*

soluble (*so*-lyou-beul) *adj* soluble

solution (seu-*loû*-cheunn) *n* solution *f*

solve (solv) *v* *résoudre

sombre (*somm*-beu) *adj* sombre

some (samm) *adj* quelques; *pron* certains, quelques; un peu; **~ day** un jour ou l'autre; **~ more** encore un peu; **~ time** une fois

somebody (*samm*-beu-di) *pron* quelqu'un

somehow (*samm*-haou) *adv* d'une manière ou d'une autre

someone (*samm*-^ou ann) *pron* quelqu'un

something (*samm*-θinng) *pron* quelque chose

sometimes (*samm*-taïmz) *adv* parfois

somewhat (*samm*-^ou ot) *adv* quelque peu

somewhere (*samm-*ᵒᵘè*ᵉᵘ*) *adv* quelque part

son (sann) *n* fils *m*

song (sonng) *n* chanson *f*

son-in-law (*sa*-ninn-loo) *n* (pl sons-) gendre *m*

soon (soûn) *adv* rapidement, sous peu, prochainement, bientôt; **as ~ as** dès que

sooner (*soû*-neu) *adv* plutôt

sore (soo) *adj* douloureux; *n* douleur *f*; ulcère *m*; **~ throat** mal de gorge

sorrow (*so*-rôᵘ) *n* tristesse *f*, douleur *f*, chagrin *m*

sorry (*so*-ri) *adj* désolé; **sorry!** excusez-moi!, pardon!

sort (soot) *v* classer, ranger; *n* catégorie *f*, sorte *f*; **all sorts of** toutes sortes de

soul (sôᵘl) *n* âme *f*; esprit *m*

sound (saound) *n* son *m*; *v* sonner; *adj* solide

soundproof (*saound*-proûf) *adj* insonorisé

soup (soûp) *n* soupe *f*

soup-plate (*soûp*-pléit) *n* assiette à soupe

soup-spoon (*soûp*-spoûn) *n* cuillère à soupe

sour (saouᵉᵘ) *adj* aigre

source (sooss) *n* source *f*

south (saouθ) *n* sud *m*; **South Pole** pôle sud

South Africa (saouθ æ-fri-keu) Afrique du Sud

South America (saouθ eu-mè-ri-keu) Amérique du Sud

south-east (saouθ-*iist*) *n* sud-est *m*

southerly (*sa*-ðeu-li) *adj* méridional

southern (*sa*-ðeunn) *adj* méridional

south-west (saouθ-ᵒᵘèst) *n* sud-ouest *m*

souvenir (*soû*-veu-niᵉᵘ) *n* souvenir *m*

sovereign (*sov*-rinn) *n* souverain *m*

*sow (sôᵒᵘ) *v* semer

spa (spââ) *n* station thermale

space (spéïss) *n* espace *m*; distance *f*, intervalle *m*; *v* espacer

spacious (*spéï*-cheuss) *adj* spacieux

spade (spéïd) *n* bêche *f*, pelle *f*

Spain (spéïn) Espagne *f*

Spaniard (*spæ*-nyeud) *n* Espagnol *m*

Spanish (*spæ*-nich) *adj* espagnol

spanking (*spæng*-kinng) *n* fessée *f*

spanner (*spæ*-neu) *n* clé à écrous

spare (spèᵉᵘ) *adj* de réserve, disponible; *v* se passer de; **~ part** pièce détachée; **~ room** chambre d'ami; **~ time** temps libre; **~ tyre** pneu de rechange; **~ wheel** roue de secours

spark (spââk) *n* étincelle *f*

sparking-plug (*spââ*-kinng-plagh) *n* bougie d'allumage

sparkle (*spââ*-keul) *v* briller

sparkling (*spââ*-klinng) *adj* scintillant; mousseux

sparrow (*spæ*-rôᵘ) *n* moineau *m*

*speak (spiik) *v* parler

spear (spiᵉᵘ) *n* lance *f*

special (*spè*-cheul) *adj* particulier, spécial; **~ delivery** exprès

specialist (*spè*-cheu-list) *n* spécialiste *m*

speciality (spè-chi-æ-leu-ti) *n* spécialité *f*

specialize (*spè*-cheu-laïz) *v* se spécialiser

specially (*spè*-cheu-li) *adv* particulièrement

species (*spii*-chiiz) *n* (pl ~) espèce *f*

specific (speu-*si*-fik) *adj* spécifique

specimen (*spè*-si-meunn) *n* spécimen *m*

speck (spèk) *n* tache *f*

spectacle (*spèk*-teu-keul) *n* spectacle *m*; **spectacles** lunettes *fpl*

spectator (spèk-*téï*-teu) *n* spectateur *m*

speculate (*spè*-kyou-léit) *v* spéculer

speech (spiitch) *n* parole *f*; allocution *f*, discours *m*; langage *m*

speechless (*spiitch*-leuss) *adj* interloqué

speed (spiid) *n* vitesse *f*; rapidité *f*, hâte *f*; cruising ~ vitesse de croisière; ~ limit limite de vitesse, limitation de vitesse

* speed (spiid) *v* foncer; rouler trop vite

speeding (*spii*-dinng) *n* excès de vitesse

speedometer (spii-*do*-mi-teu) *n* indicateur de vitesse

spell (spèl) *n* enchantement *m*

* spell (spèl) *v* épeler

spelling (*spè*-linng) *n* orthographe *f*

* spend (spènd) *v* dépenser; employer

sphere (sfi^{eu}) *n* sphère *f*

spice (spaïss) *n* épice *f*

spiced (spaïst) *adj* épicé

spicy (*spaï*-si) *adj* épicé

spider (*spaï*-deu) *n* araignée *f*; spider's web toile d'araignée

* spill (spil) *v* répandre

* spin (spinn) *v* filer; tourner

spinach (*spi*-nidj) *n* épinards *mpl*

spine (spaïn) *n* épine dorsale

spinster (*spinn*-steu) *n* vieille fille

spire (spaï^{eu}) *n* aiguille *f*

spirit (*spi*-rit) *n* esprit *m*; humeur *f*; spirits boissons alcoolisées, spiritueux *mpl*; moral *m*; ~ stove réchaud à alcool

spiritual (*spi*-ri-tchou-eul) *adj* spirituel

spit (spit) *n* crachat *m*, salive *f*; broche *f*

* spit (spit) *v* cracher

in spite of (inn spaït ov) en dépit de, malgré

spiteful (*spaït*-feul) *adj* malveillant

splash (splæch) *v* éclabousser

splendid (*splèn*-did) *adj* magnifique, splendide

splendour (*splèn*-deu) *n* splendeur *f*

splint (splinnt) *n* éclisse *f*

splinter (*splinn*-teu) *n* écharde *f*

* split (split) *v* fendre

* spoil (spoïl) *v* gâter

spoke¹ (spô^{ou}k) *v* (p speak)

spoke² (spô^{ou}k) *n* rayon *m*

sponge (spanndj) *n* éponge *f*

spook (spoúk) *n* spectre *m*, fantôme *m*

spool (spoúl) *n* bobine *f*

spoon (spoún) *n* cuillère *f*

spoonful (*spoún*-foul) *n* cuillerée *f*

sport (spoot) *n* sport *m*

sports-car (*spoots*-kââ) *n* voiture de sport

sports-jacket (*spoots*-djæ-kit) *n* veston sport

sportsman (*spoots*-meunn) *n* (pl -men) sportif *m*

sportswear (*spoots*-^{ou}è^{eu}) *n* vêtements de sport

spot (spot) *n* tache *f*; lieu *m*, endroit *m*

spotless (*spot*-leuss) *adj* immaculé

spotlight (*spot*-laït) *n* projecteur *m*

spotted (*spo*-tid) *adj* tacheté

spout (spaout) *n* jet *m*

sprain (spréïn) *v* fouler; *n* foulure *f*

* spread (sprèd) *v* étendre

spring (sprinng) *n* printemps *m*; ressort *m*; source *f*

springtime (*sprinng*-taïm) *n* printemps *m*

sprouts (spraouts) *pl* choux de Bruxelles

spy (spaï) *n* espion *m*

squadron (*skou*o-dreunn) *n* escadrille *f*

square (skou è^{eu}) *adj* carré; *n* carré *m*; square *m*, place *f*

squash (skou och) *n* jus de fruits

squirrel (*skou*i-reul) *n* écureuil *m*

squirt (skou eût) *n* jet *m*

stable (*stéï*-beul) *adj* stable ; *n* étable *f*

stack (stæk) *n* pile *f*

stadium (*stéï*-di-eumm) *n* stade *m*

staff (stââf) *n* personnel *m*

stage (stéïdj) *n* scène *f* ; phase *f*, étape *f*

stain (stéïn) *v* tacher ; *n* tache *f* ; **stained glass** verre de couleur ; ~ **remover** détachant *m*

stainless (*stéïn*-leuss) *adj* immaculé ; ~ **steel** acier inoxydable

staircase (*stèeu*-kéïss) *n* escalier *m*

stairs (stèeu z) *pl* escalier *m*

stale (stéïl) *adj* rassis

stall (stool) *n* étal *m* ; fauteuil d'orchestre

stamina (*stæ*-mi-neu) *n* endurance *f*

stamp (stæmp) *n* timbre *m* ; *v* affranchir ; piétiner ; ~ **machine** distributeur de timbres

stand (stænd) *n* stand *m* ; tribune *f*

***stand** (stænd) *v* se *tenir debout

standard (*stæn*-deud) *n* norme *f* ; standard ; ~ **of living** niveau de vie

stanza (*stæn*-zeu) *n* strophe *f*

staple (*stéï*-peul) *n* agrafe *f*

star (stââ) *n* étoile *f*

starboard (*stââ*-beud) *n* tribord *m*

starch (stââtch) *n* amidon *m* ; *v* amidonner

stare (stè*eu*) *v* fixer

starling (*stââ*-linng) *n* étourneau *m*

start (stâât) *v* commencer ; *n* début *m* ; **starter motor** démarreur *m*

starting-point (*stââ*-tinng-poïnt) *n* point de départ

state (stéït) *n* Etat *m* ; état *m* ; *v* déclarer

the States Etats-Unis

statement (*stéït*-meunnt) *n* déclaration *f*

statesman (*stéïts*-meunn) *n* (pl -men) homme d'Etat

station (*stéï*-cheunn) *n* gare *f* ; poste *m*

stationary (*stéï*-cheu-neu-ri) *adj* stationnaire

stationer's (*stéï*-cheu-neuz) *n* papeterie *f*

stationery (*stéï*-cheu-neu-ri) *n* papeterie *f*

station-master (*stéï*-cheunn-mââ-steu) *n* chef de gare

statistics (steu-*ti*-stiks) *pl* statistique *f*

statue (*stæ*-tchoù) *n* statue *f*

stay (stéï) *v* rester ; séjourner ; *n* séjour *m*

steadfast (*stèd*-fââst) *adj* ferme

steady (*stè*-di) *adj* ferme

steak (stéïk) *n* bifteck *m*

***steal** (stiil) *v* voler

steam (stiim) *n* vapeur *f*

steamer (*stii*-meu) *n* bateau à vapeur

steel (stiil) *n* acier *m*

steep (stiip) *adj* abrupt, escarpé

steeple (*stii*-peul) *n* clocher *m*

steering-column (*stieu*-rinng-koleumm) *n* colonne de direction

steering-wheel (*stieu*-rinng-*ou*ïl) *n* volant *m*

stem (stèm) *n* tige *f*

stenographer (stè-*no*-ghreu-feu) *n* sténographe *m*

step (stèp) *n* pas *m* ; marche *f* ; *v* marcher

stepchild (*stèp*-tchaïld) *n* (pl -children) enfant d'un autre lit

stepfather (*stèp*-fââ-ðeu) *n* beau-père *m*

stepmother (*stèp*-ma-ðeu) *n* belle-mère *f*

stereo (*stè*-ri-ô*ou*) *n* stéréo *f*

sterile (*stè*-raïl) *adj* stérile

sterilize (*stè*-ri-laïz) *v* stériliser

stern (steùn) *adj* sévère

steward (*styoù*-eud) *n* steward *m*

stewardess (*styoù*-eu-dèss) *n* hôtesse

de l'air

stick (stik) n bâton m

*****stick** (stik) v coller

sticky (sti-ki) adj gluant

stiff (stif) adj raide

still (stil) adv encore; toutefois; adj tranquille

stillness (stil-neuss) n silence m

stimulant (sti-myou-leunnt) n stimulant m

stimulate (sti-myou-léit) v stimuler

sting (stinng) n piqûre f

*****sting** (stinng) v piquer

stingy (stinn-dji) adj mesquin

*****stink** (stinngk) v puer

stipulate (sti-pyou-léit) v stipuler

stipulation (sti-pyou-léi-cheunn) n stipulation f

stir (steû) v bouger; remuer

stirrup (sti-reup) n étrier m

stitch (stitch) n point m, point de côté; suture f

stock (stok) n stock m; v *avoir en stock; ~ **exchange** bourse des valeurs, bourse f; ~ **market** marché des valeurs; **stocks and shares** actions

stocking (sto-kinng) n bas m

stole¹ (stô⁰ul) v (p steal)

stole² (stô⁰ul) n étole f

stomach (sta-meuk) n estomac m

stomach-ache (sta-meuk-kéïk) n mal au ventre, mal d'estomac

stone (stô⁰un) n pierre f; pierre précieuse; noyau m; en pierre; **pumice** ~ pierre ponce

stood (stoud) v (p, pp stand)

stop (stop) v arrêter; cesser; n arrêt m; **stop!** stop!

stopper (sto-peu) n bouchon m

storage (stoo-ridj) n emmagasinage m

store (stoo) n provision f; magasin m; v emmagasiner

store-house (stoo-haouss) n magasin

m

storey (stoo-ri) n étage m

stork (stook) n cigogne f

storm (stoom) n tempête f

stormy (stoo-mi) adj orageux

story (stoo-ri) n histoire f

stout (staout) adj gros, obèse, corpulent

stove (stô⁰v) n fourneau m; cuisinière f

straight (stréït) adj droit; adv directement; ~ **ahead** tout droit; ~ **away** directement, tout de suite; ~ **on** tout droit

strain (stréïn) n effort m; tension f; v forcer; filtrer

strainer (stréï-neu) n passoire f

strange (stréïndj) adj étrange; bizarre

stranger (stréïn-djeu) n étranger m; inconnu m

strangle (stræng-gheul) v étrangler

strap (stræp) n courroie f

straw (stroo) n paille f

strawberry (stroo-beu-ri) n fraise f

stream (striim) n ruisseau m; courant m; v couler

street (striit) n rue f

streetcar (striit-kââ) nAm tram m

street-organ (strii-too-gheunn) n orgue de Barbarie

strength (strèngθ) n vigueur f, force f

stress (strèss) n tension f; accent m; v souligner

stretch (strètch) v tendre; n section f

strict (strikt) adj sévère

strife (straïf) n lutte f

strike (straïk) n grève f

*****strike** (straïk) v frapper; *faire grève; amener

striking (straï-kinng) adj frappant, remarquable

string (strinng) n ficelle f; corde f

strip (strip) n bande f

stripe (straïp) n raie f

striped (straïpt) *adj* rayé

stroke (strô^{ou}k) *n* attaque *f*

stroll (strô^{ou}l) *v* flâner; *n* promenade *f*

strong (stronng) *adj* fort; puissant

stronghold (*stronng*-hô^{ou}ld) *n* place forte

structure (*strak*-tcheu) *n* structure *f*

struggle (*stra*-gheul) *n* combat *m*, lutte *f*; *v* lutter

stub (stab) *n* souche *f*

stubborn (*sta*-beunn) *adj* têtu

student (*styoû*-deunnt) *n* étudiant *m*; étudiante *f*

study (*sta*-di) *v* étudier; *n* étude *f*; cabinet *m*

stuff (staf) *n* substance *f*; fatras *m*

stuffed (staft) *adj* farci

stuffing (*sta*-finng) *n* farce *f*

stuffy (*sta*-fi) *adj* étouffant

stumble (*stamm*-beul) *v* trébucher

stung (stanng) *v* (p, pp sting)

stupid (*styoû*-pid) *adj* stupide

style (staïl) *n* style *m*

subject[1] (*sab*-djikt) *n* sujet *m*; ~ **to** sujet à

subject[2] (seub-*djèkt*) *v* *soumettre

submit (seub-*mit*) *v* se *soumettre

subordinate (seu-*boo*-di-neut) *adj* subordonné; secondaire

subscriber (seub-*skraï*-beu) *n* abonné *m*

subscription (seub-*skrip*-cheunn) *n* abonnement *m*

subsequent (*sab*-si-k^{ou}eunnt) *adj* postérieur

subsidy (*sab*-si-di) *n* subvention *f*

substance (*sab*-steunns) *n* substance *f*

substantial (seub-*stæn*-cheul) *adj* matériel; réel; substantiel

substitute (*sab*-sti-tyoût) *v* substituer; *n* substitut *m*

subtitle (*sab*-taï-teul) *n* sous-titre *m*

subtle (*sa*-teul) *adj* subtil

subtract (seub-*trækt*) *v* *soustraire

suburb (*sa*-beûb) *n* banlieue *f*, faubourg *m*

suburban (seu-*beû*-beunn) *adj* suburbain

subway (*sab*-^{ou}éï) *nAm* métro *m*

succeed (seuk-*siid*) *v* réussir; succéder

success (seuk-*sèss*) *n* succès *m*

successful (seuk-*sèss*-feul) *adj* réussi

succumb (seu-*kamm*) *v* succomber

such (satch) *adj* tel; *adv* tellement; ~ **as** tel que

suck (sak) *v* sucer

sudden (*sa*-deunn) *adj* soudain

suddenly (*sa*-deunn-li) *adv* soudain

suede (s^{ou}éïd) *n* daim *m*

suffer (*sa*-feu) *v* *souffrir; subir

suffering (*sa*-feu-rinng) *n* souffrance *f*

suffice (seu-*faïss*) *v* *suffire

sufficient (seu-*fi*-cheunnt) *adj* adéquat, suffisant

suffrage (*sa*-fridj) *n* droit de vote, suffrage *m*

sugar (*chou*-gheu) *n* sucre *m*

suggest (seu-*djèst*) *v* suggérer

suggestion (seu-*djèss*-tcheunn) *n* suggestion *f*

suicide (*soû*-i-saïd) *n* suicide *m*

suit (soût) *v* *convenir; adapter à; bien *aller; *n* complet *m*

suitable (*soû*-teu-beul) *adj* qui convient, approprié

suitcase (*soût*-kéïss) *n* valise *f*

suite (s^{ou}iit) *n* appartement *m*

sum (samm) *n* somme *f*

summary (*sa*-meu-ri) *n* sommaire *m*, résumé *m*

summer (*sa*-meu) *n* été *m*; ~ **time** heure d'été

summit (*sa*-mit) *n* sommet *m*

summons (*sa*-meunnz) *n* (pl ~es) convocation *f*

sun (sann) *n* soleil *m*

sunbathe (*sann*-béïð) *v* *prendre un bain de soleil

sunburn (*sann*-beunn) *n* coup de soleil

Sunday (*sann*-di) dimanche *m*

sun-glasses (*sann*-ghlââ-siz) *pl* lunettes de soleil

sunlight (*sann*-laït) *n* lumière du soleil

sunny (*sa*-ni) *adj* ensoleillé

sunrise (*sann*-raïz) *n* lever du soleil

sunset (*sann*-sèt) *n* coucher du soleil

sunshade (*sann*-chéïd) *n* parasol *m*

sunshine (*sann*-chaïn) *n* soleil *m*

sunstroke (*sann*-strôᵒuk) *n* insolation *f*

suntan oil (*sann*-tæn-oïl) huile solaire

superb (sou-*peûb*) *adj* grandiose, superbe

superficial (soû-peu-*fi*-cheul) *adj* superficiel

superfluous (sou-*peû*-flou-euss) *adj* superflu

superior (sou-*pi*ᵉu-ri-eu) *adj* supérieur, majeur

superlative (sou-*peû*-leu-tiv) *adj* superlatif; *n* superlatif *m*

supermarket (*soû*-peu-mââ-kit) *n* supermarché *m*

superstition (soû-peu-*sti*-cheunn) *n* superstition *f*

supervise (*soû*-peu-vaïz) *v* superviser

supervision (soû-peu-*vi*-jeunn) *n* supervision *f*, surveillance *f*

supervisor (*soû*-peu-vaï-zeu) *n* surveillant *m*

supper (*sa*-peu) *n* souper *m*

supple (*sa*-peul) *adj* souple, flexible

supplement (*sa*-pli-meunnt) *n* supplément *m*

supply (seu-*plaï*) *n* fourniture *f*; stock *m*; offre *f*; *v* fournir

support (seu-*poot*) *v* supporter, *soutenir; *n* soutien *m*; ~ **hose** bas élastiques

supporter (seu-*poo*-teu) *n* supporter *m*

suppose (seu-*pô*ᵒuz) *v* supposer; **supposing that** en admettant que

suppository (seu-*po*-zi-teu-ri) *n* suppositoire *m*

suppress (seu-*prèss*) *v* réprimer

surcharge (*seû*-tchââdj) *n* supplément *m*

sure (chouᵉu) *adj* sûr

surely (*chou*ᵉu-li) *adv* sûrement

surface (*seû*-fiss) *n* surface *f*

surgeon (*seû*-djeunn) *n* chirurgien *m*; **veterinary** ~ vétérinaire *m*

surgery (*seû*-djeu-ri) *n* opération *f*; cabinet de consultations

surname (*seû*-néïm) *n* nom de famille

surplus (*seû*-pleuss) *n* surplus *m*

surprise (seu-*praïz*) *n* surprise *f*; *v* *surprendre

surrender (seu-*rèn*-deu) *v* se rendre; *n* reddition *f*

surround (seu-*raound*) *v* entourer

surrounding (seu-*raoun*-dinng) *adj* environnant

surroundings (seu-*raoun*-dinngz) *pl* alentours *mpl*

survey (*seû*-véï) *n* résumé *m*

survival (seu-*vaï*-veul) *n* survie *f*

survive (seu-*vaïv*) *v* *survivre

suspect¹ (seu-*spèkt*) *v* soupçonner; suspecter

suspect² (*sa*-spèkt) *n* suspect *m*

suspend (seu-*spènd*) *v* suspendre

suspenders (seu-*spèn*-deuz) *plAm* bretelles *fpl*; **suspender belt** porte-jarretelles *m*

suspension (seu-*spèn*-cheunn) *n* suspension *f*; ~ **bridge** pont suspendu

suspicion (seu-*spi*-cheunn) *n* soupçon *m*; défiance *f*, méfiance *f*

suspicious (seu-*spi*-cheuss) *adj* suspect; soupçonneux, méfiant

sustain (seu-*stéïn*) *v* endurer

Swahili (sᵒueu-*hii*-li) *n* Swahili *m*

swallow ($s^{ou}o$-lô^{ou}) v avaler; n hirondelle f

swam (s^{ou}æm) v (p swim)

swamp (s^{ou}ommp) n marais m

swan (s^{ou}onn) n cygne m

swap (s^{ou}op) v troquer

*****swear** (s^{ou}è^{eu}) v jurer

sweat (s^{ou}èt) n sueur f; v suer

sweater (s^{ou}è-teu) n chandail m

Swede (s^{ou}iid) n Suédois m

Sweden (s^{ou}ii-deunn) Suède f

Swedish (s^{ou}ii-dich) adj suédois

sweet (s^{ou}iit) adj sucré; gentil; n bonbon m; dessert m; **sweets** douceurs fpl, bonbons

sweeten (s^{ou}ii-teunn) v sucrer

sweetheart (s^{ou}iit-hâât) n mon amour, chéri m

sweetshop (s^{ou}iit-chop) n confiserie f

swell (s^{ou}èl) adj formidable

*****swell** (s^{ou}èl) v enfler

swelling (s^{ou}è-linng) n enflure f

swift (s^{ou}ift) adj rapide

*****swim** (s^{ou}imm) v nager

swimmer (s^{ou}i-meu) n nageur m

swimming (s^{ou}i-minng) n natation f; ~ **pool** piscine f

swimming-trunks (s^{ou}i-minng-tranngks) n caleçon de bain

swim-suit (s^{ou}imm-soût) n maillot de bain

swindle (s^{ou}inn-deul) v escroquer; n escroquerie f

swindler (s^{ou}inn-dleu) n escroc m

swing (s^{ou}inng) n balançoire f

*****swing** (s^{ou}inng) v balancer

Swiss (s^{ou}iss) adj suisse; n Suisse m

switch (s^{ou}itch) n commutateur m; v changer; ~ **off** *éteindre; ~ **on** allumer

switchboard (s^{ou}itch-bood) n tableau de distribution

Switzerland (s^{ou}it-seu-leunnd) Suisse f

sword (sood) n épée f

swum (s^{ou}amm) v (pp swim)

syllable (si-leu-beul) n syllabe f

symbol (simm-beul) n symbole m

sympathetic (simm-peu-θè-tik) adj cordial, compatissant

sympathy (simm-peu-θi) n sympathie f; compassion f

symphony (simm-feu-ni) n symphonie f

symptom (simm-teumm) n symptôme m

synagogue (si-neu-ghogh) n synagogue f

synonym (si-neu-nimm) n synonyme m

synthetic (sinn-θè-tik) adj synthétique

syphon (saï-feunn) n siphon m

Syria (si-ri-eu) Syrie f

Syrian (si-ri-eunn) adj syrien; n Syrien m

syringe (si-rinndj) n seringue f

syrup (si-reup) n sirop m

system (si-steumm) n système m; **decimal** ~ système décimal

systematic (si-steu-mæ-tik) adj systématique

T

table (téï-beul) n table f; ~ **of contents** table des matières; ~ **tennis** ping-pong m

table-cloth (téï-beul-kloθ) n nappe f

tablespoon (téï-beul-spoûn) n cuillère f

tablet (tæ-blit) n tablette f

taboo (teu-boû) n tabou m

tactics (tæk-tiks) pl tactique f

tag (tægh) n étiquette f

tail (téïl) n queue f

tail-light (téïl-laït) n feu arrière

tailor (*téï*-leu) n tailleur m

tailor-made (*téï*-leu-méïd) adj fait sur mesure

***take** (téïk) v *prendre; saisir; *conduire; *concevoir, *comprendre; ~ **away** emporter; enlever; ~ **off** décoller; ~ **out** ôter; ~ **over** *reprendre; ~ **place** *avoir lieu; ~ **up** occuper

take-off (*téï*-kof) n décollage m

tale (téïl) n conte m, récit m

talent (*tæ*-leunnt) n don m, talent m

talented (*tæ*-leunn-tid) adj doué

talk (took) v parler; n conversation f

talkative (*too*-keu-tiv) adj bavard

tall (tool) adj haut; grand

tame (téïm) adj domestiqué, apprivoisé; v apprivoiser

tampon (*tæm*-peunn) n tampon m

tangerine (tæn-djeu-*riin*) n mandarine f

tangible (*tæn*-dji-beul) adj tangible

tank (tængk) n réservoir m

tanker (*tæng*-keu) n bateau-citerne m

tanned (tænd) adj hâlé

tap (tæp) n robinet m; coup m; v frapper

tape (téïp) n bande f; cordon m; **adhesive** ~ ruban adhésif; sparadrap m

tape-measure (*téïp*-mè-jeu) n centimètre m

tape-recorder (*téïp*-ri-koo-deu) n magnétophone m

tapestry (*tæ*-pi-stri) n tapisserie f

tar (tââ) n goudron m

target (*tââ*-ghit) n objectif m, cible f

tariff (*tæ*-rif) n taux m

tarpaulin (tââ-*poo*-linn) n bâche f

task (tââsk) n tâche f

taste (téïst) n goût m; v *avoir goût de; goûter

tasteless (*téïst*-leuss) adj insipide

tasty (*téï*-sti) adj succulent, savoureux

taught (toot) v (p, pp teach)

tavern (*tæ*-veunn) n taverne f

tax (tæks) n impôt m; v imposer

taxation (tæk-*séï*-cheunn) n taxation f

tax-free (*tæks*-frii) adj exempt d'impôts

taxi (*tæk*-si) n taxi m; ~ **rank** station de taxis; ~ **stand** Am station de taxis

taxi-driver (*tæk*-si-draï-veu) n chauffeur de taxi

taxi-meter (*tæk*-si-mii-teu) n taximètre m

tea (tii) n thé m

***teach** (tiitch) v *apprendre, enseigner

teacher (*tii*-tcheu) n professeur m, maître m; instituteur m, maître d'école

teachings (*tii*-tchinngz) pl enseignements

tea-cloth (*tii*-kloθ) n torchon m

teacup (*tii*-kap) n tasse à thé

team (tiim) n équipe f

teapot (*tii*-pot) n théière f

tear[1] (ti^{eu}) n larme f

tear[2] (tè^{eu}) n déchirure f; ***tear** v déchirer

tear-jerker (*ti^{eu}*-djeu-keu) n mélo m

tease (tiiz) v taquiner

tea-set (*tii*-sèt) n service à thé

tea-shop (*tii*-chop) n salon de thé

teaspoon (*tii*-spoun) n cuillère à thé

teaspoonful (*tii*-spoun-foul) n cuillerée à thé

technical (*tèk*-ni-keul) adj technique

technician (tèk-*ni*-cheunn) n technicien m

technique (tèk-*niik*) n technique f

technology (tèk-*no*-leu-dji) n technologie f

teenager (*tii*-néï-djeu) n adolescent m

teetotaller (tii-*tô^{ou}*-teu-leu) n antialcoolique m

telegram (*tè*-li-ghræm) *n* télégramme *m*

telegraph (*tè*-li-ghrââf) *v* télégraphier

telepathy (ti-*lè*-peu-θi) *n* télépathie *f*

telephone (*tè*-li-fô°u n) *n* téléphone *m* ; ~ **book** *Am* annuaire téléphonique ; ~ **booth** cabine téléphonique ; ~ **call** coup de téléphone, appel téléphonique ; ~ **directory** annuaire téléphonique, bottin *m* ; ~ **exchange** central téléphonique ; ~ **operator** standardiste *f*

television (*tè*-li-vi-jeunn) *n* télévision *f* ; ~ **set** télévision *f* ; **cable** ~ télévision par câble ; **satellite** ~ télévision par satellite

telex (*tè*-lèks) *n* télex *m*

*tell (tèl) *v* *dire ; raconter

temper (*tèm*-peu) *n* colère *f*

temperature (*tèm*-preu-tcheu) *n* température *f*

tempest (*tèm*-pist) *n* tempête *f*

temple (*tèm*-peul) *n* temple *m* ; tempe *f*

temporary (*tèm*-peu-reu-ri) *adj* provisoire, temporaire

tempt (tèmpt) *v* tenter

temptation (tèmp-*téï*-cheunn) *n* tentation *f*

ten (tèn) *num* dix

tenant (*tè*-neunnt) *n* locataire *m*

tend (tènd) *v* *avoir tendance ; soigner ; ~ **to** tendre à

tendency (*tèn*-deunn-si) *n* inclination *f*, tendance *f*

tender (*tèn*-deu) *adj* tendre, délicat

tendon (*tèn*-deunn) *n* tendon *m*

tennis (*tè*-niss) *n* tennis *m* ; ~ **shoes** chaussures de tennis

tennis-court (*tè*-niss-koot) *n* court de tennis

tense (tèns) *adj* tendu

tension (*tèn*-cheunn) *n* tension *f*

tent (tènt) *n* tente *f*

tenth (tènθ) *num* dixième

tepid (*tè*-pid) *adj* tiède

term (teûmm) *n* terme *m* ; période *f* ; condition *f*

terminal (*teû*-mi-neul) *n* terminus *m*

terrace (*tè*-reuss) *n* terrasse *f*

terrain (tè-*réïn*) *n* terrain *m*

terrible (*tè*-ri-beul) *adj* épouvantable, terrible

terrific (teu-*ri*-fik) *adj* formidable

terrify (*tè*-ri-faï) *v* terrifier

territory (*tè*-ri-teu-ri) *n* territoire *m*

terror (*tè*-reu) *n* terreur *f*

terrorism (*tè*-reu-ri-zeumm) *n* terrorisme *m*, terreur *f*

terrorist (*tè*-reu-rist) *n* terroriste *m*

terylene (*tè*-reu-liin) *n* Térylène *m*

test (tèst) *n* test *m*, épreuve *f* ; *v* essayer, éprouver

testify (*tè*-sti-faï) *v* témoigner

text (tèkst) *n* texte *m*

textbook (*tèks*-bouk) *n* manuel *m*

textile (*tèk*-staïl) *n* textile *m*

texture (*tèks*-tcheu) *n* texture *f*

Thai (taï) *adj* thaïlandais ; *n* Thaïlandais *m*

Thailand (*taï*-lænd) Thaïlande *f*

than (ðæn) *conj* que

thank (θængk) *v* remercier ; ~ **you** merci

thankful (*θængk*-feul) *adj* reconnaissant

that (ðæt) *adj* ce ; *pron* celui-là, cela ; qui ; *conj* que

thaw (θoo) *v* dégeler, fondre ; *n* dégel *m*

the (ðeu,ði) *art* le *art* ; **the ... the** plus ... plus

theatre (*θï*eu-teu) *n* théâtre *m*

theft (θèft) *n* vol *m*

their (ðè°u) *adj* leur

them (ðèm) *pron* les ; leur

theme (θiim) *n* thème *m*, sujet *m*

themselves (ðeumm-*sèlvz*) *pron* se ;

eux-mêmes

then (ðèn) *adv* alors; ensuite, puis

theology (θi-*o*-leu-dji) *n* théologie *f*

theoretical (θi*eu*-*rè*-ti-keul) *adj* théorique

theory (*θieu*-ri) *n* théorie *f*

therapy (θè-reu-pi) *n* thérapie *f*

there (ðè*eu*) *adv* là

therefore (ðè*eu*-foo) *conj* donc

thermometer (θeu-*mo*-mi-teu) *n* thermomètre *m*

thermostat (*θeû*-meu-stæt) *n* thermostat *m*

these (ðiiz) *adj* ces

thesis (*θii*-siss) *n* (pl theses) thèse *f*

they (ðéï) *pron* ils

thick (θik) *adj* gros; épais

thicken (*θi*-keunn) *v* épaissir

thickness (*θik*-neuss) *n* épaisseur *f*

thief (θiif) *n* (pl thieves) voleur *m*

thigh (θaï) *n* cuisse *f*

thimble (*θimm*-beul) *n* dé *m*

thin (θinn) *adj* mince; maigre

thing (θinng) *n* chose *f*

* **think** (θinngk) *v* penser; réfléchir; ~ **of** penser à; songer à; ~ **over** réfléchir

thinker (*θinng*-keu) *n* penseur *m*

third (θeûd) *num* troisième

thirst (θeûst) *n* soif *f*

thirsty (*θeû*-sti) *adj* assoiffé

thirteen (θeû-*tiin*) *num* treize

thirteenth (θeû-*tiinθ*) *num* treizième

thirtieth (*θeû*-ti-euθ) *num* trentième

thirty (*θeû*-ti) *num* trente

this (ðiss) *adj* ce; *pron* ceci

thistle (*θi*-seul) *n* chardon *m*

thorn (θoon) *n* épine *f*

thorough (*θa*-reu) *adj* minutieux, soigné

thoroughbred (*θa*-reu-brèd) *adj* pur sang

thoroughfare (*θa*-reu-fè*eu*) *n* route principale, artère *f*

those (ðô*ou*z) *adj* ces; *pron* ceux-là

though (ðô*ou*) *conj* bien que, encore que, quoique; *adv* pourtant

thought[1] (θoot) *v* (p, pp think)

thought[2] (θoot) *n* pensée *f*

thoughtful (*θoot*-feul) *adj* pensif; prévenant

thousand (*θaou*-zeunnd) *num* mille

thread (θrèd) *n* fil *m*; *v* enfiler

threadbare (*θrèd*-bè*eu*) *adj* usé

threat (θrèt) *n* menace *f*

threaten (*θrè*-teunn) *v* menacer; **threatening** menaçant

three (θrii) *num* trois

three-quarter (θrii-*kou*oo-teu) *adj* trois quarts

threshold (*θrè*-chô*ou*ld) *n* seuil *m*

threw (θroû) *v* (p throw)

thrifty (*θrif*-ti) *adj* parcimonieux

throat (θrô*ou*t) *n* gorge *f*

throne (θrô*ou*n) *n* trône *m*

through (θroû) *prep* à travers

throughout (θroû-*aout*) *adv* partout

throw (θrô*ou*) *n* lancement *m*

* **throw** (θrô*ou*) *v* jeter, lancer

thrush (θrach) *n* grive *f*

thumb (θamm) *n* pouce *m*

thumbtack (*θamm*-tæk) *nAm* punaise *f*

thump (θammp) *v* marteler

thunder (*θann*-deu) *n* tonnerre *m*; *v* gronder

thunderstorm (*θann*-deu-stoom) *n* orage *m*

thundery (*θann*-deu-ri) *adj* orageux

Thursday (*θeûz*-di) *n* jeudi *m*

thus (ðass) *adv* ainsi

thyme (taïm) *n* thym *m*

tick (tik) *n* marque *f*; ~ **off** pointer

ticket (*ti*-kit) *n* billet *m*; contravention *f*; ~ **collector** contrôleur *m*; ~ **machine** distributeur de billets

tickle (*ti*-keul) *v* chatouiller

tide (taïd) *n* marée *f*; **high** ~ marée

haute; **low** ~ marée basse

tidings (taï-dinngz) pl nouvelles

tidy (taï-di) adj ordonné; ~ **up** ranger

tie (taï) v nouer, attacher; n cravate f

tiger (taï-gheu) n tigre m

tight (taït) adj serré; étroit, juste; adv fortement

tighten (taï-teunn) v serrer; resserrer; se resserrer

tights (taïts) pl collants mpl

tile (taïl) n carreau m; tuile f

till (til) prep jusqu'à; conj jusqu'à ce que

timber (timm-beu) n bois d'œuvre

time (taïm) n temps m; fois f; **all the ~** continuellement; **in** ~ à temps; ~ **of arrival** heure d'arrivée; ~ **of departure** heure de départ

time-saving (taïm-séï-vinng) adj qui fait gagner du temps

timetable (taïm-téï-beul) n horaire m

timid (ti-mid) adj timide

timidity (ti-mi-deu-ti) n timidité f

tin (tinn) n étain m; boîte f; **tinned food** conserves fpl

tinfoil (tinn-foïl) n papier d'étain

tin-opener (ti-nôᵒᵘ-peu-neu) n ouvre-boîte m

tiny (taï-ni) adj minuscule

tip (tip) n bout m; pourboire m

tire[1] (taïᵉᵘ) n pneu m

tire[2] (taïᵉᵘ) v fatiguer

tired (taïᵉᵘd) adj fatigué; ~ **of** las de

tiring (taïᵉᵘ-rinng) adj fatigant

tissue (ti-chou) n tissu m; mouchoir de papier

title (taï-teul) n titre m

to (toù) prep jusque; à, pour, chez; afin de

toad (tôᵒᵘd) n crapaud m

toadstool (tôᵒᵘd-stoûl) n champignon m

toast (tôᵒᵘst) n toast m

tobacco (teu-bæ-kôᵒᵘ) n (pl ~s) tabac

m; ~ **pouch** blague à tabac

tobacconist (teu-bæ-keu-nist) n débitant de tabac; **tobacconist's** bureau de tabac

today (teu-déï) adv aujourd'hui

toddler (tod-leu) n bambin m

toe (tôᵒᵘ) n orteil m

toffee (to-fi) n caramel m

together (teu-ghè-ðeu) adv ensemble

toilet (toï-leut) n toilettes fpl; ~ **case** nécessaire de toilette

toilet-paper (toï-leut-péï-peu) n papier hygiénique

toiletry (toï-leu-tri) n articles de toilette

token (tôᵒᵘ-keunn) n signe m; preuve f; jeton m

told (tôᵒᵘld) v (p, pp tell)

tolerable (to-leu-reu-beul) adj tolérable

toll (tôᵒᵘl) n péage m

tomato (teu-mââ-tôᵒᵘ) n (pl ~es) tomate f

tomb (toûm) n tombe f

tombstone (toûm-stôᵒᵘn) n pierre tombale

tomorrow (teu-mo-rôᵒᵘ) adv demain

ton (tann) n tonne f

tone (tôᵒᵘn) n ton m; timbre m

tongs (tonngz) pl pince f

tongue (tanng) n langue f

tonic (to-nik) n tonique m

tonight (teu-naït) adv cette nuit, ce soir

tonsilitis (tonn-seu-laï-tiss) n amygdalite f

tonsils (tonn-seulz) pl amygdales fpl

too (toù) adv trop; aussi

took (touk) v (p take)

tool (toûl) n instrument m, outil m; ~ **kit** boîte à outils

toot (toût) vAm klaxonner

tooth (toûθ) n (pl teeth) dent f

toothache (toù-θéïk) n mal aux dents

toothbrush (*toûθ*-brach) *n* brosse à dents

toothpaste (*toûθ*-péïst) *n* pâte dentifrice

toothpick (*toûθ*-pik) *n* cure-dent *m*

toothpowder (*toûθ*-paou-deu) *n* poudre dentifrice

top (top) *n* sommet *m*; dessus *m*; couvercle *m*; supérieur; **on ~ of** au-dessus de; **~ side** haut *m*

topcoat (*top*-kô*ou*t) *n* pardessus *m*

topic (*to*-pik) *n* sujet *m*

topical (*to*-pi-keul) *adj* actuel

torch (tootch) *n* torche *f*; lampe de poche

torment¹ (too-*mènt*) *v* tourmenter

torment² (*too*-mènt) *n* tourment *m*

torture (*too*-tcheu) *n* torture *f*; *v* torturer

toss (toss) *v* lancer

tot (tot) *n* bambin *m*

total (*tô*ᵒᵘ-teul) *adj* total; complet, absolu; *n* total *m*

totalitarian (tôᵒᵘ-tæ-li-*tè*ᵉᵘ-ri-eunn) *adj* totalitaire

totalizator (*tô*ᵒᵘ-teu-laï-zéï-teu) *n* totalisateur *m*

touch (tatch) *v* toucher; *n* contact *m*, attouchement *m*; toucher *m*

touching (*ta*-tching) *adj* touchant

tough (taf) *adj* coriace

tour (touᵉᵘ) *n* excursion *f*

tourism (*tou*ᵉᵘ-ri-zeumm) *n* tourisme *m*

tourist (*tou*ᵉᵘ-rist) *n* touriste *m*; **~ class** classe touriste; **~ office** syndicat d'initiative

tournament (*tou*ᵉᵘ-neu-meunnt) *n* tournoi *m*

tow (tôᵒᵘ) *v* remorquer

towards (teu-ᵒᵘ*oodz*) *prep* vers; envers

towel (taouᵉᵘl) *n* serviette *f*

towelling (*taou*ᵉᵘ-linng) *n* tissu-éponge *m*

tower (taouᵉᵘ) *n* tour *f*

town (taoun) *n* ville *f*; **~ centre** centre de la ville; **~ hall** hôtel de ville

townspeople (*taounz*-pii-peul) *pl* citadins *mpl*

toxic (*tok*-sik) *adj* toxique

toy (toï) *n* jouet *m*

toyshop (*toï*-chop) *n* magasin de jouets

trace (tréïss) *n* trace *f*; *v* tracer, retracer

track (træk) *n* voie *f*; piste *f*

tractor (*træk*-teu) *n* tracteur *m*

trade (tréïd) *n* commerce *m*; métier *m*; *v* *faire du commerce

trademark (*tréïd*-mââk) *n* marque de fabrique

trader (*tréï*-deu) *n* commerçant *m*

tradesman (*tréïdz*-meunn) *n* (pl -men) marchand *m*

trade-union (tréïd-*yoû*-nyeunn) *n* syndicat *m*

tradition (treu-*di*-cheunn) *n* tradition *f*

traditional (treu-*di*-cheu-neul) *adj* traditionnel

traffic (*træ*-fik) *n* circulation *f*; **~ jam** embouteillage *m*; **~ light** feu de circulation

trafficator (*træ*-fi-kéï-teu) *n* indicateur de direction

tragedy (*træ*-djeu-di) *n* tragédie *f*

tragic (*træ*-djik) *adj* tragique

trail (tréïl) *n* piste *f*, sentier *m*

trailer (*tréï*-leu) *n* remorque *f*; *nAm* caravane *f*

train (tréïn) *n* train *m*; *v* dresser, former; **stopping ~** omnibus *m*; **through ~** train direct; **~ ferry** ferry-boat *m*

training (*tréï*-ninng) *n* entraînement *m*

trait (tréït) *n* trait *m*

traitor (*tréï*-teu) *n* traître *m*

tram (træm) *n* tram *m*

tramp (træmp) *n* chemineau *m*, vagabond *m*; *v* vagabonder

tranquil (*træng*-kᵒᵘil) *adj* tranquille

tranquillizer (*træng*-kᵒᵘi-laï-zeu) *n* calmant *m*

transaction (træn-*zæk*-cheunn) *n* transaction *f*

transatlantic (træn-zeut-*læn*-tik) *adj* transatlantique

transfer (træns-*feu*) *v* transférer

transform (træns-*foom*) *v* transformer

transformer (træns-*foo*-meu) *n* transformateur *m*

transition (træn-*si*-cheunn) *n* transition *f*

translate (træns-*léït*) *v* *traduire

translation (træns-*léi*-cheunn) *n* traduction *f*

translator (træns-*léi*-teu) *n* traducteur *m*

transmission (trænz-*mi*-cheunn) *n* émission *f*

transmit (trænz-*mit*) *v* *émettre

transmitter (trænz-*mi*-teu) *n* émetteur *m*

transparent (træn-*spè*ᵉᵘ-reunnt) *adj* transparent

transport[1] (*træn*-spoot) *n* transport *m*

transport[2] (træn-*spoot*) *v* transporter

transportation (træn-spoo-*téi*-cheunn) *n* transport *m*

trap (træp) *n* piège *m*

trash (træch) *n* déchets *mpl*; ~ **can** *Am* boîte à ordures

travel (*træ*-veul) *v* voyager; ~ **agency** bureau de voyages; ~ **agent** agent de voyages; ~ **insurance** assurance-voyages *f*; **travelling expenses** frais de voyage

traveller (*træ*-veu-leu) *n* voyageur *m*; **traveller's cheque** chèque de voyage

tray (tréi) *n* plateau *m*

treason (*trii*-zeunn) *n* trahison *f*

treasure (*trè*-jeu) *n* trésor *m*

treasurer (*trè*-jeu-reu) *n* trésorier *m*

treasury (*trè*-jeu-ri) *n* Trésor *m*

treat (triit) *v* traiter

treatment (*triit*-meunnt) *n* traitement *m*

treaty (*trii*-ti) *n* traité *m*

tree (trii) *n* arbre *m*

tremble (*trèm*-beul) *v* frissonner, trembler; vibrer

tremendous (tri-*mèn*-deuss) *adj* énorme

trespass (*trèss*-peuss) *v* empiéter

trespasser (*trèss*-peu-seu) *n* intrus *m*

trial (traïᵉᵘl) *n* procès *m*; essai *m*

triangle (*traï*-æng-gheul) *n* triangle *m*

triangular (traï-*æng*-ghyou-leu) *adj* triangulaire

tribe (traïb) *n* tribu *f*

tributary (*tri*-byou-teu-ri) *n* affluent *m*

tribute (*tri*-byoût) *n* hommage *m*

trick (trik) *n* truc *m*

trigger (*tri*-gheu) *n* gâchette *f*

trim (trimm) *v* tailler

trip (trip) *n* excursion *f*, voyage *m*

triumph (*traï*-eummf) *n* triomphe *m*; *v* triompher

triumphant (traï-*amm*-feunnt) *adj* triomphant

trolley-bus (*tro*-li-bass) *n* trolleybus *m*

troops (troûps) *pl* troupes *fpl*

tropical (*tro*-pi-keul) *adj* tropical

tropics (*tro*-piks) *pl* tropiques *mpl*

trouble (*tra*-beul) *n* ennui *m*, peine *f*, dérangement *m*; *v* déranger

troublesome (*tra*-beul-seumm) *adj* gênant

trousers (*traou*-zeuz) *pl* pantalon *m*

trout (traout) *n* (pl ~) truite *f*

truck (trak) *nAm* camion *m*

true (troû) *adj* vrai; réel; loyal, fidèle

trumpet (*tramm*-pit) *n* trompette *f*

trunk (tranngk) *n* malle *f*; tronc *m*;

nAm coffre *m*; **trunks** *pl* culotte de gymnastique

trunk-call (*tranngk-kool*) *n* appel interurbain

trust (*trast*) *v* *faire confiance; *n* confiance *f*

trustworthy (*trast-*ou*eû-ði*) *adj* digne de confiance

truth (*trouθ*) *n* vérité *f*

truthful (*trouθ-feul*) *adj* véridique

try (*traï*) *v* essayer; tenter, s'efforcer; *n* tentative *f*; ~ **on** essayer

tube (*tyoûb*) *n* tuyau *m*, tube *m*

tuberculosis (*tyoû-beû-kyou-lô*ou*-siss*) *n* tuberculose *f*

Tuesday (*tyoûz-di*) mardi *m*

tug (*tagh*) *v* remorquer; *n* remorqueur *m*; à-coup *m*

tuition (*tyoû-i-cheunn*) *n* enseignement *m*

tulip (*tyoû-lip*) *n* tulipe *f*

tumbler (*tamm-bleu*) *n* gobelet *m*

tumour (*tyoû-meu*) *n* tumeur *f*

tuna (*tyoû-neu*) *n* (*pl* ~, ~s) thon *m*

tune (*tyoûn*) *n* air *m*; ~ **in** accorder

tuneful (*tyoûn-feul*) *adj* harmonieux

tunic (*tyoû-nik*) *n* tunique *f*

Tunisia (*tyoû-ni-zi-eu*) Tunisie *f*

Tunisian (*tyoû-ni-zi-eunn*) *adj* tunisien; *n* Tunisien *m*

tunnel (*ta-neul*) *n* tunnel *m*

turbine (*teû-baïn*) *n* turbine *f*

turbojet (*teû-bô*ou*-djèt*) *n* turboréacteur *m*

Turk (*teûk*) *n* Turc *m*

Turkey (*teû-ki*) Turquie *f*

turkey (*teû-ki*) *n* dinde *f*

Turkish (*teû-kich*) *adj* turc; ~ **bath** bain turc

turn (*teûnn*) *v* tourner; retourner, virer; *n* revirement *m*, tour *m*; tournant *m*; ~ **back** retourner; ~ **down** rejeter; ~ **into** changer en; ~ **off** fermer; ~ **on** allumer; *ouvrir;

~ **over** retourner; ~ **round** retourner; se retourner

turning (*teû-ninng*) *n* virage *m*

turning-point (*teû-ninng-poïnt*) *n* tournant *m*

turnover (*teû-nô*ou*-veu*) *n* chiffre d'affaires; ~ **tax** impôt sur le chiffre d'affaires

turnpike (*teûnn-païk*) *nAm* route à péage

turpentine (*teû-peunn-taïn*) *n* térébenthine *f*

turtle (*teû-teul*) *n* tortue *f*

tutor (*tyoû-teu*) *n* précepteur *m*; tuteur *m*

tuxedo (*tak-sii-dô*ou) *nAm* (*pl* ~s, ~es) smoking *m*

tweed (*t*ou*iid*) *n* tweed *m*

tweezers (*t*ou*ii-zeuz*) *pl* pince *f*

twelfth (*t*ou*èlfθ*) *num* douzième

twelve (*t*ou*èlv*) *num* douze

twentieth (*t*ou*èn-ti-euθ*) *num* vingtième

twenty (*t*ou*èn-ti*) *num* vingt

twice (*t*ou*aïss*) *adv* deux fois

twig (*t*ou*igh*) *n* brindille *f*

twilight (*t*ou*aï-laït*) *n* crépuscule *m*

twine (*t*ou*aïn*) *n* ficelle *f*

twins (*t*ou*innz*) *pl* jumeaux *mpl*; **twin beds** lits jumeaux

twist (*t*ou*ist*) *v* tordre; *n* torsion *f*

two (*toû*) *num* deux

two-piece (*toû-piiss*) *adj* deux-pièces *m*

type (*taïp*) *v* taper à la machine, dactylographier; *n* type *m*

typewriter (*taïp-raï-teu*) *n* machine à écrire

typewritten (*taïp-ri-teunn*) dactylographié

typhoid (*taï-foïd*) *n* typhoïde *f*

typical (*ti-pi-keul*) *adj* caractéristique, typique

typist (*taï-pist*) *n* dactylo *f*

tyrant (*tai*^(eu)-reunnt) *n* tyran *m*

tyre (tai^(eu)) *n* pneu *m* ; ~ **pressure** pression des pneus

U

ugly (*a*-ghli) *adj* laid

ulcer (*al*-seu) *n* ulcère *m*

ultimate (*al*-ti-meut) *adj* ultime

ultraviolet (al-treu-*vai*^(eu)-leut) *adj* ultra-violet

umbrella (amm-*brè*-leu) *n* parapluie *m*

umpire (*amm*-paï^(eu)) *n* arbitre *m*

unable (a-*néï*-beul) *adj* incapable

unacceptable (a-neuk-*sèp*-teu-beul) *adj* inacceptable

unaccountable (a-neu-*kaoun*-teu-beul) *adj* inexplicable

unaccustomed (a-neu-*ka*-steummd) *adj* inhabitué

unanimous (youû-*næ*-ni-meuss) *adj* unanime

unanswered (a-*nâân*-seud) *adj* sans réponse

unauthorized (a-*noo*-θeu-raïzd) *adj* illicite

unavoidable (a-neu-*voï*-deu-beul) *adj* inévitable

unaware (a-neu-^(ou)*è*^(eu)) *adj* inconscient

unbearable (ann-*bè*^(eu)-reu-beul) *adj* insupportable

unbreakable (ann-*bréï*-keu-beul) *adj* incassable

unbroken (ann-*brô*^(ou)-keunn) *adj* intact

unbutton (ann-*ba*-teunn) *v* déboutonner

uncertain (ann-*seû*-teunn) *adj* incertain

uncle (*anng*-keul) *n* oncle *m*

unclean (ann-*kliin*) *adj* malpropre

uncomfortable (ann-*kamm*-feu-teu-beul) *adj* inconfortable

uncommon (ann-*ko*-meunn) *adj* inhabituel, rare

unconditional (ann-keunn-*di*-cheu-neul) *adj* inconditionnel

unconscious (ann-*konn*-cheuss) *adj* inconscient

uncork (ann-*kook*) *v* déboucher

uncover (ann-*ka*-veu) *v* *découvrir

uncultivated (ann-*kal*-ti-véï-tid) *adj* inculte

under (*ann*-deu) *prep* en bas de, sous

undercurrent (*ann*-deu-ka-reunnt) *n* courant *m*

underestimate (ann-deu-*rè*-sti-méït) *v* sous-estimer

underground (ann-deu-*ghraound*) *adj* souterrain ; *n* métro *m*

underline (ann-deu-*laïn*) *v* souligner

underneath (ann-deu-*niiθ*) *adv* dessous

underpants (*ann*-deu-pænts) *plAm* caleçon *m*

undershirt (*ann*-deu-cheût) *n* tricot de corps

undersigned (*ann*-deu-saïnd) *n* soussigné *m*

* **understand** (ann-deu-*stænd*) *v* *comprendre

understanding (ann-deu-*stæn*-dinng) *n* compréhension *f*

* **undertake** (ann-deu-*téïk*) *v* *entreprendre

undertaking (ann-deu-*téï*-kinng) *n* entreprise *f*

underwater (*ann*-deu-^(ou)oo-teu) *adj* sous-marin

underwear (*ann*-deu-^(ou)è^(eu)) *n* sous-vêtements *mpl*

undesirable (ann-di-*zaï*^(eu)-reu-beul) *adj* indésirable

* **undo** (ann-*doû*) *v* *défaire

undoubtedly (ann-*daou*-tid-li) *adv*

sans doute

undress (ann-*drèss*) *v* se déshabiller

undulating (*ann*-dyou-léï-tinng) *adj* ondulé

unearned (a-*neûnnd*) *adj* immérité

uneasy (a-*nii*-zi) *adj* mal à l'aise

uneducated (a-*nè*-dyou-*kéï*-tid) *adj* ignorant

unemployed (a-nimm-*ploïd*) *adj* en chômage

unemployment (a-nimm-*ploï*-meunnt) *n* chômage *m*

unequal (a-*nii*-k⁰ᵘeul) *adj* inégal

uneven (a-*nii*-veunn) *adj* inégal, accidenté; irrégulier

unexpected (a-nik-*spèk*-tid) *adj* imprévu, inattendu

unfair (ann-*fè*ᵉᵘ) *adj* inéquitable, injuste

unfaithful (ann-*féï*θ-feul) *adj* infidèle

unfamiliar (ann-feu-*mil*-yeu) *adj* inconnu

unfasten (ann-*fââ*-seunn) *v* détacher

unfavourable (ann-*féï*-veu-reu-beul) *adj* défavorable

unfit (ann-*fit*) *adj* impropre

unfold (ann-*fô*ᵒᵘ*ld*) *v* déplier

unfortunate (ann-*foo*-tcheu-neut) *adj* malheureux

unfortunately (ann-*foo*-tcheu-neut-li) *adv* hélas, malheureusement

unfriendly (ann-*frènd*-li) *adj* désobligeant

unfurnished (ann-*feû*-nicht) *adj* non meublé

ungrateful (ann-*ghréït*-feul) *adj* ingrat

unhappy (ann-*hæ*-pi) *adj* malheureux

unhealthy (ann-*hèl*-θi) *adj* malsain

unhurt (ann-*heût*) *adj* indemne

uniform (*you*-ni-foom) *n* uniforme *m*; *adj* uniforme

unimportant (a-nimm-*poo*-teunnt) *adj* insignifiant

uninhabitable (a-ninn-*hæ*-bi-teu-beul)

adj inhabitable

uninhabited (a-ninn-*hæ*-bi-tid) *adj* inhabité

unintentional (a-ninn-*tèn*-cheu-neul) *adj* involontaire

union (*you*-nyeunn) *n* union *f*; ligue *f*, confédération *f*

unique (you-*niik*) *adj* unique

unit (*you*-nit) *n* unité *f*

unite (you-*naït*) *v* unir

United States (you-*naï*-tid stéïts) Etats-Unis

unity (*you*-neu-ti) *n* unité *f*

universal (you-ni-*veû*-seul) *adj* général, universel

universe (*you*-ni-veûss) *n* univers *m*

university (you-ni-*veû*-seu-ti) *n* université *f*

unjust (ann-*djast*) *adj* injuste

unkind (ann-*kaïnd*) *adj* désagréable, peu aimable

unknown (ann-*nô*ᵒᵘ*n*) *adj* inconnu

unlawful (ann-*loo*-feul) *adj* illicite

unleaded (ann-*lèd*-id) *adj* sans plomb

unlearn (ann-*leûnn*) *v* désapprendre

unless (eunn-*lèss*) *conj* à moins que

unlike (ann-*laïk*) *adj* différent

unlikely (ann-*laï*-kli) *adj* improbable

unlimited (ann-*li*-mi-tid) *adj* illimité

unload (ann-*lô*ᵒᵘ*d*) *v* décharger

unlock (ann-*lok*) *v* *ouvrir

unlucky (ann-*la*-ki) *adj* infortuné

unnecessary (ann-*nè*-seu-seu-ri) *adj* superflu

unoccupied (a-*no*-kyou-païd) *adj* vacant

unpack (ann-*pæk*) *v* déballer

unpleasant (ann-*plè*-zeunnt) *adj* ennuyeux, déplaisant; désagréable, antipathique

unpopular (ann-*po*-pyou-leu) *adj* peu aimé, impopulaire

unprotected (ann-preu-*tèk*-tid) *adj* non protégé

unqualified (ann-*k^ou o*-li-faïd) *adj* incompétent

unreal (ann-*ri^eu*l) *adj* irréel

unreasonable (ann-*rii*-zeu-neu-beul) *adj* déraisonnable

unreliable (ann-ri-*laï*-eu-beul) *adj* douteux

unrest (ann-*rèst*) *n* agitation *f*; inquiétude *f*

unsafe (ann-*séïf*) *adj* dangereux

unsatisfactory (ann-sæ-tiss-*fæk*-teu-ri) *adj* insatisfaisant

unscrew (ann-*skroû*) *v* dévisser

unselfish (ann-*sèl*-fich) *adj* désintéressé

unskilled (ann-*skild*) *adj* non qualifié

unsound (ann-*saound*) *adj* malsain

unstable (ann-*stéï*-beul) *adj* instable

unsteady (ann-*stè*-di) *adj* branlant, instable; vacillant

unsuccessful (ann-seuk-*sèss*-feul) *adj* infructueux

unsuitable (ann-*soû*-teu-beul) *adj* inadéquat

unsurpassed (ann-seu-*pââst*) *adj* sans pareil

untidy (ann-*taï*-di) *adj* désordonné

untie (ann-*taï*) *v* dénouer

until (eunn-*til*) *prep* jusqu'à

untrue (ann-*troû*) *adj* faux

untrustworthy (ann-*trast*-^ou eû-ði) *adj* sujet à caution

unusual (ann-*you*-jou-eul) *adj* inhabituel, insolite

unwell (ann-^ou *èl*) *adj* indisposé

unwilling (ann-^ou *i*-linng) *adj* à contre-cœur

unwise (ann-^ou *aïz*) *adj* imprudent

unwrap (ann-*ræp*) *v* déballer

up (ap) *adv* vers le haut, en haut

upholster (ap-*hô^ou l*-steu) *v* capitonner, *recouvrir

upkeep (*ap*-kiip) *n* entretien *m*

uplands (*ap*-leunndz) *pl* hautes terres

upon (eu-*ponn*) *prep* sur

upper (*a*-peu) *adj* supérieur

upright (*ap*-raït) *adj* droit; *adv* debout

upset (ap-*sèt*) *v* déranger; *adj* bouleversé

upside-down (ap-saïd-*daoun*) *adv* sens dessus dessous

upstairs (ap-*stè^eu z*) *adv* en haut

upstream (ap-*striim*) *adv* en amont

upwards (*ap*-^ou eudz) *adv* vers le haut

urban (*e^u*-beunn) *adj* urbain

urge (eûdj) *v* exhorter; *n* impulsion *f*

urgency (*e^u*-djeunn-si) *n* urgence *f*

urgent (*e^u*-djeunnt) *adj* urgent

urine (*you^eu*-rinn) *n* urine *f*

Uruguay (*you^eu*-reu-gh^ou aï) Uruguay *m*

Uruguayan (you^eu-reu-*gh^ou aï*-eunn) *adj* uruguayen; *n* Uruguayen *m*

us (ass) *pron* nous

usable (*you*-zeu-beul) *adj* utilisable

usage (*you*-zidj) *n* usage *m*

use¹ (youz) *v* employer; *be used to *être habitué à; ~ up user

use² (youss) *n* emploi *m*; utilité *f*; *be of ~ *servir

useful (*youss*-feul) *adj* utile

useless (*youss*-leuss) *adj* inutile

user (*you*-zeu) *n* usager *m*

usher (*a*-cheu) *n* ouvreur *m*

usherette (a-cheu-*rèt*) *n* ouvreuse *f*

usual (*you*-jou-eul) *adj* ordinaire

usually (*you*-jou-eu-li) *adv* habituellement

utensil (you-*tèn*-seul) *n* outil *m*, ustensile *m*

utility (you-*ti*-leu-ti) *n* utilité *f*

utilize (*you*-ti-laïz) *v* utiliser

utmost (*at*-mô^ou st) *adj* extrême

utter (*a*-teu) *adj* complet, total; *v* *émettre

V

vacancy (*véi*-keunn-si) *n* vacance *f*

vacant (*véi*-keunnt) *adj* vacant

vacate (veu-*kéit*) *v* évacuer

vacation (veu-*kéi*-cheunn) *n* congé *m*

vaccinate (*væk*-si-néït) *v* vacciner

vaccination (væk-si-*néi*-cheunn) *n* vaccination *f*

vacuum (*væ*-kyou-eumm) *n* vide *m*; *vAm* passer l'aspirateur; ~ **cleaner** aspirateur *m*; ~ **flask** thermos *m*

vagrancy (*véi*-ghreunn-si) *n* vagabondage *m*

vague (véigh) *adj* vague

vain (véïn) *adj* vaniteux; vain; **in** ~ inutilement, en vain

valet (*væ*-lit) *n* valet *m*

valid (*væ*-lid) *adj* valable

valley (*væ*-li) *n* vallée *f*

valuable (*væ*-lyou-beul) *adj* de valeur, précieux; **valuables** *pl* objets de valeur

value (*væ*-lyoû) *n* valeur *f*; *v* estimer

valve (vælv) *n* soupape *f*

van (væn) *n* fourgon *m*

vanilla (veu-*ni*-leu) *n* vanille *f*

vanish (*væ*-nich) *v* *disparaître

vapour (*véi*-peu) *n* vapeur *f*

variable (*vè*^eu-ri-eu-beul) *adj* variable

variation (vè^eu-ri-*éi*-cheunn) *n* variation *f*; changement *m*

varied (*vè*^eu-rid) *adj* varié

variety (veu-*rai*-eu-ti) *n* variété *f*; ~ **show** spectacle de variétés; ~ **theatre** théâtre de variétés

various (*vè*^eu-ri-euss) *adj* divers

varnish (*vââ*-nich) *n* laque *f*, vernis *m*; *v* vernir

vary (*vè*^eu-ri) *v* varier; changer; différer

vase (vââz) *n* vase *m*

vaseline (*væ*-seu-liin) *n* vaseline *f*

vast (vââst) *adj* immense, vaste

vault (voolt) *n* voûte *f*; chambre forte

veal (viil) *n* veau *m*

vegetable (*vè*-djeu-teu-beul) *n* légume *m*; ~ **merchant** marchand de légumes

vegetarian (vè-dji-*tè*^eu-ri-eunn) *n* végétarien *m*

vegetation (vè-dji-*téi*-cheunn) *n* végétation *f*

vehicle (*vii*-eu-keul) *n* véhicule *m*

veil (véil) *n* voile *m*

vein (véïn) *n* veine *f*; **varicose** ~ varice *f*

velvet (*vèl*-vit) *n* velours *m*

velveteen (vèl-vi-*tiin*) *n* velours de coton

venerable (*vè*-neu-reu-beul) *adj* vénérable

venereal disease (vi-*ni*^eu-ri-eul di-*ziiz*) maladie vénérienne

Venezuela (vè-ni-*z*^ou*éi*-leu) Venezuela *m*

Venezuelan (vè-ni-*z*^ou*éi*-leunn) *adj* vénézuélien; *n* Vénézuélien *m*

ventilate (*vèn*-ti-léït) *v* ventiler; aérer

ventilation (vèn-ti-*léi*-cheunn) *n* ventilation *f*; aération *f*

ventilator (*vèn*-ti-léï-teu) *n* ventilateur *m*

venture (*vèn*-tcheu) *v* risquer

veranda (veu-*ræn*-deu) *n* véranda *f*

verb (veûb) *n* verbe *m*

verbal (*veû*-beul) *adj* verbal

verdict (*veû*-dikt) *n* sentence *f*, verdict *m*

verge (veûdj) *n* bord *m*

verify (*vè*-ri-faï) *v* vérifier

verse (veûss) *n* vers *m*

version (*veû*-cheunn) *n* version *f*

versus (*veû*-seuss) *prep* contre

vertical (*veû*-ti-keul) *adj* vertical

vertigo (*veû*-ti-ghô^ou) *n* vertige *m*

very (*vè*-ri) *adv* très; *adj* vrai, véritable, précis; extrême

vessel (*vè*-seul) *n* vaisseau *m*; récipient *m*

vest (vèst) *n* chemise *f*; *nAm* gilet *m*

veterinary surgeon (*vè*-tri-neu-ri *seû*-djeunn) vétérinaire *m*

via (vaï*eu*) *prep* via

vibrate (vaï-*bréit*) *v* vibrer

vibration (vaï-*bréi*-cheunn) *n* vibration *f*

vicar (*vi*-keu) *n* vicaire *m*

vice-president (vaïss-*prè*-zi-deunnt) *n* vice-président *m*

vicinity (vi-*si*-neu-ti) *n* alentours *mpl*, voisinage *m*

vicious (*vi*-cheuss) *adj* vicieux

victim (*vik*-timm) *n* victime *f*; dupe *f*

victory (*vik*-teu-ri) *n* victoire *f*

video camera (*vi*-di-ô*ou* *kæ*-meu-reu) *n* caméra vidéo *f*

video recorder (*vi*-di-ô*ou* ri-*koo*-deu) *n* magnétoscope *m*

view (vyoû) *n* vue *f*; point de vue, opinion *f*; *v* contempler

view-finder (*vyoû*-faïn-deu) *n* viseur *m*

vigilant (*vi*-dji-leunnt) *adj* vigilant

villa (*vi*-leu) *n* villa *f*

village (*vi*-lidj) *n* village *m*

villain (*vi*-leunn) *n* scélérat *m*

vine (vaïn) *n* vigne *f*

vinegar (*vi*-ni-gheu) *n* vinaigre *m*

vineyard (*vinn*-yeud) *n* vignoble *m*

vintage (*vinn*-tidj) *n* vendange *f*

violation (vaï*eu*-*léi*-cheunn) *n* violation *f*

violence (*vaï*eu*-leunns) *n* violence *f*

violent (*vaï*eu*-leunnt) *adj* violent; intense

violet (*vaï*eu*-leut) *n* violette *f*; *adj* violet

violin (vaï*eu*-*linn*) *n* violon *m*

virgin (*veû*-djinn) *n* vierge *f*

virtue (*veû*-tchoù) *n* vertu *f*

visa (*vii*-zeu) *n* visa *m*

visibility (vi-zeu-*bi*-leu-ti) *n* visibilité *f*

visible (*vi*-zeu-beul) *adj* visible

vision (*vi*-jeunn) *n* vision *f*

visit (*vi*-zit) *v* visiter; *n* visite *f*; **visiting hours** heures de visite

visiting-card (*vi*-zi-tinng-kââd) *n* carte de visite

visitor (*vi*-zi-teu) *n* visiteur *m*

vital (*vai*-teul) *adj* vital

vitamin (*vi*-teu-minn) *n* vitamine *f*

vivid (*vi*-vid) *adj* vif

vocabulary (veu-*kæ*-byou-leu-ri) *n* vocabulaire *m*

vocal (*vô*ou*-keul) *adj* vocal

vocalist (*vô*ou*-keu-list) *n* chanteur *m*

voice (voïss) *n* voix *f*

void (voïd) *adj* nul

volcano (vol-*kéï*-nô*ou*) *n* (pl ~es, ~s) volcan *m*

volt (vô*ou*lt) *n* volt *m*

voltage (*vô*ou*l-tidj) *n* voltage *m*

volume (*vo*-lyoum) *n* volume *m*; tome *m*

voluntary (*vo*-leunn-teu-ri) *adj* volontaire

volunteer (vo-leunn-*ti*eu) *n* volontaire *m*

vomit (*vo*-mit) *v* vomir

vote (vô*ou*t) *v* voter; *n* vote *m*

voucher (*vaou*-tcheu) *n* reçu *m*, bon *m*

vow (vaou) *n* vœu *m*, serment *m*; *v* jurer

vowel (vaou*eu*l) *n* voyelle *f*

voyage (*voï*-idj) *n* voyage *m*

vulgar (*val*-gheu) *adj* vulgaire; ordinaire, trivial

vulnerable (*val*-neu-reu-beul) *adj* vulnérable

vulture (*val*-tcheu) *n* vautour *m*

W

wade (^{ou}éïd) *v* patauger

wafer (^{ou}éï-feu) *n* gaufrette *f*

waffle (^{ou}o-feul) *n* gaufre *f*

wages (^{ou}éï-djiz) *pl* gages *mpl*

waggon (^{ou}æ-gheunn) *n* wagon *m*

waist (^{ou}éïst) *n* taille *f*

waistcoat (^{ou}éïss-kô^{ou}t) *n* gilet *m*

wait (^{ou}éït) *v* attendre; ~ **on** *servir

waiter (^{ou}éï-teu) *n* garçon *m*

waiting (^{ou}éï-tinng) *n* attente *f*

waiting-list (^{ou}éï-tinng-list) *n* liste d'attente

waiting-room (^{ou}éï-tinng-roûm) *n* salle d'attente

waitress (^{ou}éï-triss) *n* serveuse *f*

***wake** (^{ou}éïk) *v* réveiller; ~ **up** s'éveiller, se réveiller

walk (^{ou}ook) *v* marcher; se promener; *n* promenade *f*; démarche *f*; **walking** à pied

walker (^{ou}oo-keu) *n* promeneur *m*

walking-stick (^{ou}oo-kinng-stik) *n* canne *f*

wall (^{ou}ool) *n* mur *m*; cloison *f*

wallet (^{ou}o-lit) *n* portefeuille *m*

wallpaper (^{ou}ool-péï-peu) *n* papier peint

walnut (^{ou}ool-nat) *n* noix *f*

waltz (^{ou}ools) *n* valse *f*

wander (^{ou}onn-deu) *v* errer

want (^{ou}onnt) *v* *vouloir; désirer; *n* besoin *m*; carence *f*, manque *m*

war (^{ou}oo) *n* guerre *f*

warden (^{ou}oo-deunn) *n* surveillant *m*, gardien *m*

wardrobe (^{ou}oo-drô^{ou}b) *n* garde-robe *f*

warehouse (^{ou}è^{eu}-haouss) *n* magasin *m*, dépôt *m*

wares (^{ou}è^{eu}z) *pl* marchandise *f*

warm (^{ou}oom) *adj* chaud; *v* chauffer

warmth (^{ou}oomθ) *n* chaleur *f*

warn (^{ou}oon) *v* *prévenir, avertir

warning (^{ou}oo-ninng) *n* avertissement *m*

wary (^{ou}è^{eu}-ri) *adj* prudent

was (^{ou}oz) *v* (p be)

wash (^{ou}och) *v* laver; ~ **and wear** sans repassage; ~ **up** *faire la vaisselle

washable (^{ou}o-cheu-beul) *adj* lavable

wash-basin (^{ou}och-béï-seunn) *n* lavabo *m*

washing (^{ou}o-chinng) *n* lavage *m*; lessive *f*

washing-machine (^{ou}o-chinng-meuchiin) *n* machine à laver

washing-powder (^{ou}o-chinng-paoudeu) *n* savon en poudre

washroom (^{ou}och-roûm) *nAm* toilettes *fpl*

wash-stand (^{ou}och-stænd) *n* lavabo *m*

wasp (^{ou}osp) *n* guêpe *f*

waste (^{ou}éïst) *v* gaspiller; *n* gaspillage *m*; *adj* en friche

wasteful (^{ou}éïst-feul) *adj* gaspilleur

wastepaper-basket (^{ou}éïst-péï-peubââ-skit) *n* corbeille à papier

watch (^{ou}otch) *v* regarder, observer; surveiller; *n* montre *f*; ~ **for** guetter; ~ **out** *prendre garde

watch-maker (^{ou}otch-méï-keu) *n* horloger *m*

watch-strap (^{ou}otch-stræp) *n* bracelet pour montre

water (^{ou}oo-teu) *n* eau *f*; **iced** ~ eau glacée; **running** ~ eau courante; ~ **pump** pompe à eau; ~ **ski** ski nautique

water-colour (^{ou}oo-teu-ka-leu) *n* couleur à l'eau; aquarelle *f*

watercress (^{ou}oo-teu-krèss) *n* cresson *m*

waterfall (^{ou}oo-teu-fool) *n* cascade *f*

watermelon (^{ou}oo-teu-mè-leunn) *n* pastèque *f*

waterproof (^{ou}oo-teu-proûf) *adj* imperméable

water-softener (^{ou}oo-teu-sof-neu) *n* adoucisseur d'eau

waterway (^{ou}oo-teu-^{ou}éï) *n* voie d'eau

watt (^{ou}ot) *n* watt *m*

wave (^{ou}éïv) *n* ondulation *f*, vague *f*; *v* *faire signe

wave-length (^{ou}éïv-lèngθ) *n* longueur d'onde

wavy (^{ou}éï-vi) *adj* ondulé

wax (^{ou}æks) *n* cire *f*

waxworks (^{ou}æks-^{ou}eûks) *pl* musée des figures de cire

way (^{ou}éï) *n* manière *f*, façon *f*; voie *f*; côté *m*, direction *f*; distance *f*; **any ~** n'importe comment; **by the ~** à propos; **one-way traffic** sens unique; **out of the ~** écarté; **the other ~ round** en sens inverse; **~ back** chemin du retour; **~ in** entrée *f*; **~ out** sortie *f*

wayside (^{ou}éï-saïd) *n* bord de la route

we (^{ou}ii) *pron* nous

weak (^{ou}iik) *adj* faible; léger

weakness (^{ou}iik-neuss) *n* faiblesse *f*

wealth (^{ou}èlθ) *n* richesse *f*

wealthy (^{ou}èl-θi) *adj* riche

weapon (^{ou}è-peunn) *n* arme *f*

*wear (^{ou}è^{eu}) *v* porter; **~ out** user

weary (^{ou}ie^u-ri) *adj* las, fatigué

weather (^{ou}è-ðeu) *n* temps *m*; **~ forecast** bulletin météorologique

*weave (^{ou}iiv) *v* tisser

weaver (^{ou}ii-veu) *n* tisserand *m*

wedding (^{ou}è-dinng) *n* mariage *m*

wedding-ring (^{ou}è-dinng-rinng) *n* alliance *f*

wedge (^{ou}èdj) *n* cale *f*

Wednesday (^{ou}ènz-di) *n* mercredi *m*

weed (^{ou}iid) *n* mauvaise herbe *f*

week (^{ou}iik) *n* semaine *f*

weekday (^{ou}iik-déï) *n* jour de la semaine

weekly (^{ou}ii-kli) *adj* hebdomadaire

*weep (^{ou}iip) *v* pleurer

weigh (^{ou}éï) *v* peser

weighing-machine (^{ou}éï-inng-meu-chiin) *n* bascule *f*

weight (^{ou}éït) *n* poids *m*

welcome (^{ou}èl-keumm) *adj* bienvenu; *n* accueil *m*; *v* *accueillir

weld (^{ou}èld) *v* souder

welfare (^{ou}èl-fè^{eu}) *n* bien-être *m*

well[1] (^{ou}èl) *adv* sain; **as ~** également, aussi bien; **as ~ as** aussi bien que; **well!** bien!

well[2] (^{ou}èl) *n* source *f*, puits *m*

well-founded (^{ou}èl-*faoun*-did) *adj* bien fondé

well-known (^{ou}èl-*nô*^{ou}n) *adj* connu

well-to-do (^{ou}èl-teu-*doû*) *adj* aisé

went (^{ou}ènt) *v* (p go)

were (^{ou}eû) *v* (p be)

west (^{ou}èst) *n* occident *m*, ouest *m*

westerly (^{ou}è-steu-li) *adj* occidental

western (^{ou}è-steunn) *adj* occidental

wet (^{ou}èt) *adj* mouillé; humide

whale (^{ou}éïl) *n* baleine *f*

wharf (^{ou}oof) *n* (pl ~s, wharves) quai *m*

what (^{ou}ot) *pron* quoi; ce que; **~ for** pourquoi

whatever (^{ou}o-*tè*-veu) *pron* tout ce que

wheat (^{ou}iit) *n* blé *m*

wheel (^{ou}iil) *n* roue *f*

wheelbarrow (^{ou}iil-bæ-rô^{ou}) *n* brouette *f*

wheelchair (^{ou}iil-tchè^{eu}) *n* fauteuil roulant

when (^{ou}èn) *adv* quand; *conj* quand, lorsque

whenever (^{ou}è-*nè*-veu) *conj* n'importe quand

where (^{ou}è^{eu}) *adv* où; *conj* où

wherever (ᵒᵘè-ᵉᵘ-rè-veu) *conj* partout où

whether (ᵒᵘè-ðeu) *conj* si; **whether ... or** si ... ou

which (ᵒᵘitch) *pron* quel; qui

whichever (ᵒᵘi-tchè-veu) *adj* n'importe quel

while (ᵒᵘaïl) *conj* tandis que; *n* moment *m*

whilst (ᵒᵘaïlst) *conj* tandis que

whim (ᵒᵘimm) *n* lubie *f*, caprice *m*

whip (ᵒᵘip) *n* fouet *m*; *v* fouetter

whiskers (ᵒᵘi-skeuz) *pl* favoris

whisper (ᵒᵘi-speu) *v* chuchoter; *n* chuchotement *m*

whistle (ᵒᵘi-seul) *v* siffler; *n* sifflet *m*

white (ᵒᵘaït) *adj* blanc

whitebait (ᵒᵘaït-béit) *n* blanchaille *f*

whiting (ᵒᵘaï-tinng) *n* (pl ~) merlan *m*

Whitsun (ᵒᵘit-seunn) Pentecôte *f*

who (hoû) *pron* qui

whoever (hoû-è-veu) *pron* quiconque

whole (hôᵒᵘl) *adj* complet, entier; intact; *n* ensemble *m*

wholesale (hôᵒᵘl-séïl) *n* vente en gros; ~ **dealer** grossiste *m*

wholesome (hôᵒᵘl-seumm) *adj* sain

wholly (hôᵒᵘl-li) *adv* entièrement

whom (hoûm) *pron* à qui

whore (hoo) *n* putain *f*

whose (hoûz) *pron* dont; de qui

why (ᵒᵘaï) *adv* pourquoi

wicked (ᵒᵘi-kid) *adj* mauvais

wide (ᵒᵘaïd) *adj* vaste, large

widen (ᵒᵘaï-deunn) *v* élargir

widow (ᵒᵘi-dôᵒᵘ) *n* veuve *f*

widower (ᵒᵘi-dôᵒᵘ-eu) *n* veuf *m*

width (ᵒᵘidθ) *n* largeur *f*

wife (ᵒᵘaïf) *n* (pl wives) épouse *f*, femme *f*

wig (ᵒᵘigh) *n* perruque *f*

wild (ᵒᵘaïld) *adj* sauvage; féroce

will (ᵒᵘil) *n* volonté *f*; testament *m*

*will (ᵒᵘil) *v* *vouloir

willing (ᵒᵘi-linng) *adj* disposé

willingly (ᵒᵘi-linng-li) *adv* volontiers

will-power (ᵒᵘil-paouᵉᵘ) *n* volonté *f*

*win (ᵒᵘinn) *v* gagner

wind (ᵒᵘinnd) *n* vent *m*

*wind (ᵒᵘaïnd) *v* serpenter; remonter, enrouler

winding (ᵒᵘaïn-dinng) *adj* serpentant

windmill (ᵒᵘinnd-mil) *n* moulin à vent

window (ᵒᵘinn-dôᵒᵘ) *n* fenêtre *f*

window-sill (ᵒᵘinn-dôᵒᵘ-sil) *n* rebord de fenêtre

windscreen (ᵒᵘinnd-skriin) *n* pare-brise *m*; ~ **wiper** essuie-glace *m*

windshield (ᵒᵘinnd-chiild) *nAm* pare-brise *m*; ~ **wiper** *Am* essuie-glace *m*

windy (ᵒᵘinn-di) *adj* venteux

wine (ᵒᵘaïn) *n* vin *m*

wine-cellar (ᵒᵘaïn-sè-leu) *n* cave *f*

wine-list (ᵒᵘaïn-list) *n* carte des vins

wine-merchant (ᵒᵘaïn-meû-tcheunnt) *n* négociant en vins

wine-waiter (ᵒᵘaïn-ᵒᵘéi-teu) *n* sommelier *m*

wing (ᵒᵘinng) *n* aile *f*

winkle (ᵒᵘinng-keul) *n* bigorneau *m*

winner (ᵒᵘi-neu) *n* vainqueur *m*

winning (ᵒᵘi-ninng) *adj* gagnant; **winnings** *pl* gains

winter (ᵒᵘinn-teu) *n* hiver *m*; ~ **sports** sports d'hiver

wipe (ᵒᵘaïp) *v* ôter, essuyer

wire (ᵒᵘaïᵉᵘ) *n* fil *m*; fil de fer

wireless (ᵒᵘaïᵉᵘ-leuss) *n* radio *f*

wisdom (ᵒᵘiz-deumm) *n* sagesse *f*

wise (ᵒᵘaïz) *adj* sage

wish (ᵒᵘich) *v* désirer, souhaiter; *n* désir *m*, souhait *m*

witch (ᵒᵘitch) *n* sorcière *f*

with (ᵒᵘið) *prep* avec; chez; de

*withdraw (ᵒᵘið-droo) *v* retirer

within (ᵒᵘi-ðinn) *prep* dans; *adv* à

l'intérieur

without (ᵒᵘi-ðaout) *prep* sans

witness (ᵒᵘit-neuss) *n* témoin *m*

wits (ᵒᵘits) *pl* raison *f*

witty (ᵒᵘi-ti) *adj* spirituel

wolf (ᵒᵘoulf) *n* (pl wolves) loup *m*

woman (ᵒᵘou-meunn) *n* (pl women) femme *f*

womb (ᵒᵘoûm) *n* utérus *m*

won (ᵒᵘann) *v* (p, pp win)

wonder (ᵒᵘann-deu) *n* miracle *m*; étonnement *m*; *v* se demander

wonderful (ᵒᵘann-deu-feul) *adj* splendide, merveilleux; délicieux

wood (ᵒᵘoud) *n* bois *m*

wood-carving (ᵒᵘoud-kââ-vinng) *n* sculpture sur bois

wooded (ᵒᵘou-did) *adj* boisé

wooden (ᵒᵘou-deunn) *adj* en bois; ~ **shoe** sabot *m*

woodland (ᵒᵘoud-leunnd) *n* pays boisé

wool (ᵒᵘoul) *n* laine *f*; **darning ~** laine à repriser

woollen (ᵒᵘou-leunn) *adj* en laine

word (ᵒᵘeûd) *n* mot *m*

wore (ᵒᵘoo) *v* (p wear)

work (ᵒᵘeûk) *n* travail *m*; activité *f*; *v* travailler; fonctionner; **working day** jour ouvrable; ~ **of art** œuvre d'art; ~ **permit** permis de travail

worker (ᵒᵘeû-keu) *n* ouvrier *m*

working (ᵒᵘeû-kinng) *n* fonctionnement *m*

workman (ᵒᵘeûk-meunn) *n* (pl -men) ouvrier *m*

works (ᵒᵘeûks) *pl* usine *f*

workshop (ᵒᵘeûk-chop) *n* atelier *m*

world (ᵒᵘeûld) *n* monde *m*; ~ **war** guerre mondiale

world-famous (ᵒᵘeûld-féi-meuss) *adj* de renommée mondiale

world-wide (ᵒᵘeûld-ᵒᵘaïd) *adj* mondial

worm (ᵒᵘeûmm) *n* ver *m*

worn (ᵒᵘoon) *adj* (pp wear) usé

worn-out (ᵒᵘoon-aout) *adj* usé

worried (ᵒᵘa-rid) *adj* soucieux

worry (ᵒᵘa-ri) *v* s'inquiéter; *n* souci *m*, inquiétude *f*

worse (ᵒᵘeûss) *adj* pire; *adv* pire

worship (ᵒᵘeû-chip) *v* adorer; *n* culte *m*

worst (ᵒᵘeûst) *adj* le plus mauvais; *adv* le pire

worsted (ᵒᵘou-stid) *n* laine peignée

worth (ᵒᵘeûθ) *n* valeur *f*; ***be ~** *valoir; ***be worth-while** *valoir la peine

worthless (ᵒᵘeûθ-leuss) *adj* sans valeur

worthy of (ᵒᵘeû-ði euv) digne de

would (ᵒᵘoud) *v* (p will) *avoir l'habitude de

wound¹ (ᵒᵘoûnd) *n* blessure *f*; *v* offenser, blesser

wound² (ᵒᵘaound) *v* (p, pp wind)

wrap (ræp) *v* envelopper

wreck (rèk) *n* épave *f*; *v* *détruire

wrench (rèntch) *n* clé *f*; secousse *f*; *v* tordre

wrinkle (rinng-keul) *n* ride *f*

wrist (rist) *n* poignet *m*

wrist-watch (rist-ᵒᵘotch) *n* bracelet-montre *m*

*write (raït) *v* *écrire; **in writing** par écrit; ~ **down** noter

writer (raï-teu) *n* écrivain *m*

writing-pad (raï-tinng-pæd) *n* bloc-notes *m*

writing-paper (raï-tinng-péi-peu) *n* papier à lettres

written (ri-teunn) *adj* (pp write) par écrit

wrong (ronng) *adj* impropre, incorrect; *n* tort *m*; *v* *faire du tort; ***be ~** *avoir tort

wrote (rôᵒᵘt) *v* (p write)

X

Xmas (*kriss*-meuss) Noël

X-ray (*èks*-réï) *n* radiographie *f*; *v* radiographier

Y

yacht (yot) *n* yacht *m*

yacht-club (*yot*-klab) *n* yacht-club *m*

yachting (*yo*-tinng) *n* yachting *m*

yard (yââd) *n* cour *f*

yarn (yâân) *n* fil *m*

yawn (yoon) *v* bâiller

year (yi*eu*) *n* année *f*

yearly (*yi*eu-li) *adj* annuel

yeast (yiist) *n* levure *f*

yell (yèl) *v* hurler; *n* cri *m*

yellow (*yè*-lô ou) *adj* jaune

yes (yèss) oui

yesterday (*yè*-steu-di) *adv* hier

yet (yèt) *adv* encore; *conj* pourtant, cependant

yield (yiild) *v* rendre; céder

yoke (yô ou k) *n* joug *m*

yolk (yô ou k) *n* jaune d'œuf

you (yoû) *pron* tu; te; vous

young (yanng) *adj* jeune

your (yoo) *adj* votre; ton; vos

yourself (yoo-*sèlf*) *pron* te; toi-même; vous-même

yourselves (yoo-*sèlvz*) *pron* vous; vous-mêmes

youth (yoûθ) *n* jeunesse *f*; ~ **hostel** auberge de jeunesse

Z

zeal (ziil) *n* zèle *m*

zealous (*zè*-leuss) *adj* zélé

zebra (*zii*-breu) *n* zèbre *m*

zenith (*zè*-niθ) *n* zénith *m*; apogée *m*

zero (*zi*eu-rô ou) *n* (pl ~s) zéro *m*

zest (zèst) *n* entrain *m*

zinc (zinngk) *n* zinc *m*

zip (zip) *n* fermeture éclair; ~ **code** *Am* code postal

zipper (*zi*-peu) *n* fermeture éclair

zodiac (*zô*-di-æk) *n* zodiaque *m*

zone (zô ou n) *n* zone *f*; région *f*

zoo (zoû) *n* (pl ~s) zoo *m*

zoology (zô ou-*o*-leu-dji) *n* zoologie *f*

Lexique gastronomique

Mets

almond amande

anchovy anchois

angel food cake gâteau aux blancs d'œufs

angels on horseback huîtres enrobées de lard, grillées et servies sur toast

appetizer amuse-gueule

apple pomme
  ~ **dumpling** sorte de chausson aux pommes
  ~ **sauce** purée de pommes

Arbroath smoky églefin fumé

artichoke artichaut

asparagus asperge
  ~ **tip** pointe d'asperge

assorted varié

avocado (pear) avocat

bacon lard à griller
  ~ **and eggs** œufs au lard

bagel petit pain en forme de couronne

baked au four
  ~ **Alaska** omelette norvégienne
  ~ **beans** haricots blancs dans une sauce tomate
  ~ **potato** pomme de terre en robe des champs cuite au four

Bakewell tart gâteau aux amandes et à la confiture

baloney sorte de mortadelle

banana banane
  ~ **split** banane coupée en tranches, servie avec de la glace et des noix, arrosée de sirop ou de crème au chocolat

barbecue 1) hachis de bœuf dans une sauce relevée aux tomates, servi dans un petit pain 2) repas en plein air
  ~ **sauce** sauce aux tomates très relevée

barbecued grillé au charbon de bois

basil basilic

bass bar

bean haricot, fève

beef bœuf
  ~ **olive** paupiette de bœuf

beefburger bifteck haché, grillé et servi dans un petit pain

beet, beetroot betterave rouge

bilberry myrtille

bill addition
  ~ **of fare** carte des mets, menu

biscuit 1) gâteau sec, biscuit (GB) 2) petit pain (US)

black pudding boudin noir

blackberry mûre sauvage

blackcurrant cassis

bloater hareng saur
blood sausage boudin noir
blueberry myrtille
boiled bouilli
Bologna (sausage) sorte de mortadelle
bone os
boned désossé
Boston baked beans haricots blancs au lard et à la mélasse dans une sauce tomate
Boston cream pie tourte à la crème en couches superposées, glacée au chocolat
brains cervelle
braised braisé
bramble pudding pudding aux mûres (souvent servi avec des pommes)
braunschweiger saucisson au foie fumé
bread pain
breaded pané
breakfast petit déjeuner
bream brème (poisson)
breast poitrine, blanc de volaille
brisket poitrine de bœuf
broad bean grosse fève
broth bouillon
brown Betty sorte de charlotte aux pommes et aux épices recouverte de chapelure
brunch repas qui tient lieu de petit déjeuner et de déjeuner
brussels sprout chou de Bruxelles
bubble and squeak sorte de galette de pommes de terre et choux, parfois accompagnés de morceaux de bœuf
bun 1) petit pain au lait avec des fruits secs 2) sorte de petit pain (US)
butter beurre
buttered beurré

cabbage chou
Caesar salad salade verte, ail, anchois, croûtons et fromage râpé
cake gâteau, tourte
cakes biscuits, pâtisseries
calf veau
Canadian bacon carré de porc fumé, coupé en fines tranches
caper câpre
capercaillie, capercailzie coq de bruyère
carp carpe
carrot carotte
cashew noix de cajou
casserole en cocotte
catfish poisson-chat
catsup ketchup
cauliflower chou-fleur
celery céleri
cereal céréale, cornflakes
   hot ~ porridge
check addition
Cheddar (cheese) fromage à pâte dure au goût légèrement acide
cheese fromage
   ~ board plateau de fromages
   ~ cake gâteau au fromage double crème
cheeseburger bifteck haché, grillé avec une tranche de fromage, servi dans un petit pain
chef's salad salade de jambon, poulet, œufs durs, tomates, laitue et fromage
cherry cerise
chestnut marron
chicken poulet
chicory 1) endive (GB) 2) (e)scarole, chicorée (US)
chili con carne hachis de bœuf aux haricots rouges et aux piments rouges
chili pepper piment rouge
chips 1) pommes frites (GB) 2)

pommes chips (US)

chitt(er)lings tripes de porc

chive ciboulette

chocolate chocolat

choice premier choix

chop côtelette

~ **suey** émincé de porc ou de poulet, de riz et de légumes

chopped émincé, haché

chowder bisque

Christmas pudding cake anglais aux fruits secs, parfois flambé; très nourrissant et servi à Noël

chutney condiment indien épicé à saveur aigre-douce

cinnamon cannelle

clam palourde

club sandwich double sandwich au *bacon*, poulet, tomate, salade et mayonnaise

cobbler compote de fruits recouverte de pâte

cock-a-leekie soup crème de volaille et de poireaux

coconut noix de coco

cod cabillaud

Colchester oyster huître anglaise très renommée

cold cuts/meat assiette anglaise, viandes froides

coleslaw salade de chou

cooked cuit

cookie biscuit

corn 1) blé (GB) 2) maïs (US)

~ **on the cob** épi de maïs

cornflakes flocons de maïs

cottage cheese fromage frais

cottage pie hachis de viande aux oignons recouvert de purée de pommes de terre

course plat

cover charge prix du couvert

crab crabe

cracker biscuit salé, craquelin

cranberry canneberge

~ **sauce** confiture de canneberges

crawfish, crayfish 1) écrevisse 2) langouste (GB) 3) langoustine (US)

cream 1) crème 2) velouté (potage) 3) crème (dessert)

~ **cheese** fromage double crème

~ **puff** chou à la crème

creamed potatoes pommes de terre coupées en dés dans une sauce béchamel

creole mets très relevé, préparé avec des tomates, des poivrons et des oignons, servi avec du riz blanc

cress cresson

crisps pommes chips

crumpet sorte de petit pain rond, grillé et beurré

cucumber concombre

Cumberland ham jambon fumé très réputé

Cumberland sauce sauce aigredouce; vin, jus d'orange, zeste de citron, épices et gelée de groseilles

cupcake madeleine

cured salé et parfois fumé

currant 1) raisin de Corinthe 2) groseille

curried au curry

custard crème anglaise, flan

cutlet sorte d'escalope, fine tranche de viande, côtelette

dab limande

Danish pastry pâtisserie ou gâteau riche en levure

date datte

Derby cheese fromage à pâte molle et au goût piquant, de couleur jaune pâle

devilled à la diable; assaisonnement très relevé

devil's food cake tourte au chocolat

devils on horseback pruneaux cuits dans du vin rouge et farcis d'amandes et d'anchois, enrobés de lard et grillés

Devonshire cream double crème, très épaisse

diced coupé en dés

diet food aliment diététique

dill aneth

dinner dîner, repas du soir

dish plat, assiette, mets

donut, doughnut boule de Berlin, beignet en forme d'anneau

double cream double crème, crème entière

Dover sole sole de Douvres, très réputée

dressing 1) sauce à salade 2) farce pour la volaille (US)

Dublin Bay prawn langoustine

duck canard

duckling caneton

dumpling boulette de pâte

Dutch apple pie tarte aux pommes saupoudrée de cassonade ou nappée de mélasse

eel anguille

egg œuf
    boiled ~ à la coque
    fried ~ au plat
    hard-boiled ~ dur
    poached ~ poché
    scrambled ~ brouillé
    soft-boiled ~ mollet

eggplant aubergine

endive 1) (e)scarole, chicorée (GB) 2) endive (US)

entrée 1) entrée (GB) 2) plat principal (US)

fennel fenouil

fig figue

fillet filet de viande ou de poisson

finnan haddock églefin fumé

fish poisson
    ~ **and chips** filets de poisson frits et pommes frites
    ~ **cake** galette de poisson et de pommes de terre

flan tarte

flapjack matefaim, crêpe épaisse

flounder flet, plie

forcemeat farce, hachis

fowl volaille

frankfurter saucisse de Francfort

French bean haricot vert

French bread baguette

French dressing 1) vinaigrette (GB) 2) sauce à salade crémeuse assaisonnée de ketchup (US)

french fries pommes frites

French toast croûte dorée

fresh frais

fried frit, grillé

fritter beignet

frogs' legs cuisses de grenouilles

frosting glaçage

fry friture

game gibier

gammon jambon fumé

garfish aiguille de mer

garlic ail

garnish garniture

gherkin cornichon

giblets abats, abattis

ginger gingembre

goose oie
    ~ **berry** groseille à maquereau

grape raisin
    ~ **fruit** pamplemousse

grated râpé

gravy jus de viande épaissi

grayling omble

green bean haricot vert

green pepper poivron vert
green salad laitue, salade verte
greens garniture de légumes verts
grilled grillé
grilse saumoneau
grouse petit coq de bruyère
gumbo 1) gombo (légume d'origine africaine) 2) plat créole à base d'*okra*, de viande, de poisson ou de fruits de mer et de légumes
haddock églefin
haggis panse de mouton farcie aux flocons d'avoine
hake colin
half moitié, demi
halibut flétan
ham jambon
  ∼ **and eggs** œufs au jambon
hare lièvre
haricot bean haricot blanc
hash 1) émincé 2) hachis de bœuf recouvert de pommes de terre
hazelnut noisette
heart cœur
herb herbe aromatique
herring hareng
home-made fait maison
hominy grits bouillie de maïs, sorte de polenta
honey miel
  ∼**dew melon** variété de melon très doux à la chair vert-jaune
horse-radish raifort
hot 1) chaud 2) épicé
  ∼ **cross bun** brioche aux raisins (se mange pendant le Carême)
  ∼ **dog** hot-dog, saucisse chaude dans un pain
huckleberry myrtille
hush puppy beignet de farine de maïs
ice-cream glace
iced glacé

icing glaçage
Idaho baked potato pomme de terre en robe des champs cuite au four
Irish stew ragoût de mouton aux oignons et aux pommes de terre
Italian dressing vinaigrette
jam confiture
jellied en gelée
Jell-O dessert à la gélatine
jelly gelée de fruits
Jerusalem artichoke topinambour
John Dory Saint-Pierre (poisson)
jugged hare civet de lièvre
juice jus
juniper berry baie de genièvre
junket lait caillé sucré
kale chou frisé
kedgeree miettes de poisson au riz, aux œufs et au beurre
kidney rognon
kipper hareng fumé
lamb agneau
Lancashire hot pot ragoût de côtelettes, de rognons d'agneau, de pommes de terre et d'oignons
larded lardé
lean maigre
leek poireau
leg gigot, cuisse
lemon citron
  ∼ **sole** limande
lentil lentille
lettuce laitue, salade verte
lima bean fève
lime lime, citron vert
liver foie
loaf pain, miche
lobster homard
loin filet, carré
Long Island duck canard de Long Island, très réputé
low-calorie pauvre en calories
lox saumon fumé

lunch déjeuner, repas de midi
macaroon macaron
mackerel maquereau
maize maïs
mandarin mandarine
maple syrup sirop d'érable
marinated mariné
marjoram marjolaine
marmalade confiture d'orange ou d'autres agrumes, marmelade
marrow moelle
 ~ **bone** os à moelle
marshmallow bonbon à la guimauve
marzipan massepain, pâte d'amandes
mashed potatoes purée de pommes de terre
meal repas
meat viande
 ~ **ball** boulette de viande
 ~ **loaf** rôti haché
medium (done) à point
melted fondu
Melton Mowbray pie croustade de viande
milk lait
mince hachis
 ~ **pie** tartelette aux fruits confits et aux épices
minced haché
 ~ **meat** viande hachée
mint menthe
mixed mélangé, panaché
 ~ **grill** brochette de viande
molasses mélasse
morel morille
mulberry mûre
mullet mulet
mulligatawny soup potage au poulet, très épicé, d'origine indienne
mushroom champignon
muskmelon sorte de melon

mussel moule
mustard moutarde
mutton mouton
noodle nouille
nut noix
oatmeal (porridge) porridge, bouillie d'avoine
oil huile
okra pousse de *gumbo* généralement utilisée pour lier les potages et les ragoûts
omelet omelette
onion oignon
ox tongue langue de bœuf
oyster huître
pancake crêpe, matefaim
parsley persil
parsnip panais (racine comestible)
partridge perdrix
pastry pâtisserie
pasty pâté, chausson, rissole
pea petit pois
peach pêche
peanut cacahuète
 ~ **butter** beurre d'arachide
pear poire
pearl barley orge perlé
pepper poivre
 ~ **mint** menthe (poivrée)
perch perche
persimmon kaki
pheasant faisan
pickerel brocheton (poisson)
pickle 1) légume ou fruit au vinaigre 2) cornichon (US)
pickled en saumure, au vinaigre
pie tarte, recouverte le plus souvent d'une couche de pâte, farcie ou garnie de viande, de légumes, de fruits ou de crème anglaise
pig porc
pike brochet
pineapple ananas

plaice plie, carrelet

plain nature

plate plat, assiette

plum 1) prune 2) pruneau 3) raisin sec

~ **pudding** cake anglais aux fruits secs, parfois flambé; très nourrissant et servi à Noël

poached poché

popcorn grains de maïs éclatés

popover petit pain au lait

pork porc

porterhouse steak épaisse tranche de filet de bœuf

pot roast bœuf braisé aux légumes

potato pomme de terre

~ **chips** 1) pommes frites (GB) 2) pommes chips (US)

~ **in its jacket** pomme de terre en robe des champs

potted shrimps crevettes au beurre épicé (fondu et refroidi)

poultry volaille

prawn grosse crevette rose

prune pruneau

ptarmigan perdrix des neiges

pudding pudding (mou ou consistant) à base de farine, garni de viande, de poisson, de légumes ou de fruits

pumpernickel pain de seigle complet

pumpkin potiron, courge

quail caille

quince coing

rabbit lapin

radish radis

rainbow trout truite arc-en-ciel

raisin raisin sec

rare saignant

raspberry framboise

raw cru

red mullet rouget

red (sweet) pepper poivron rouge

redcurrant groseille rouge

relish condiment fait de légumes émincés au vinaigre

rhubarb rhubarbe

rib (of beef) côte (de bœuf)

rib-eye steak entrecôte

rice riz

rissole croquette de viande ou de poisson

river trout truite de rivière

roast(ed) rôti(e)

Rock Cornish hen variété de poulet de grain

roe œufs de poisson

roll petit pain

rollmop herring filet de hareng mariné au vin blanc, enroulé sur un cornichon

round steak quasi de bœuf

Rubens sandwich corned-beef sur toast, avec choucroute, emmenthal et sauce à salade, servi chaud

rump steak rumsteak

rusk biscotte

rye bread pain de seigle

saddle selle

saffron safran

sage sauge

salad salade

~ **bar** choix de salades

~ **cream** sauce à salade crémeuse, légèrement sucrée

~ **dressing** sauce à salade

salmon saumon

~ **trout** truite saumonée

salt sel

salted salé

sauerkraut choucroute

sausage saucisse, saucisson

sauté(ed) sauté

scallop 1) peigne (coquille Saint-Jacques) 2) escalope de veau

scone petit pain tendre à base de

farine de blé ou d'orge

Scotch broth soupe à base d'agneau ou de bœuf et de légumes

Scotch woodcock toast avec œufs brouillés et beurre d'anchois

sea bass loup de mer

sea kale chou marin

seafood poissons et fruits de mer

(in) season (en) saison

seasoning assaisonnement

service charge montant à payer pour le service

service (not) included service (non) compris

set menu menu fixe

shad alose (sorte de sardine)

shallot échalote

shellfish crustacé

sherbet sorbet

shoulder épaule

shredded wheat croquettes de froment (servies au petit déjeuner)

shrimp crevette

silverside (of beef) gîte (de bœuf)

sirloin steak steak d'aloyau

skewer brochette

slice tranche

sliced coupé en tranches

sloppy Joe hachis de bœuf dans une sauce relevée aux tomates, servi dans un petit pain

smelt éperlan

smoked fumé

snack repas léger, collation

soup potage, soupe

sour aigre

soused herring hareng au vinaigre et aux épices

spare rib côte de porc grillée

spice épice

spinach épinard

spiny lobster langouste

(on a) spit (à la) broche

sponge cake gâteau mousseline

sprat harenguet

squash courgette

starter hors-d'œuvre

steak and kidney pie croustade de viande de bœuf et de rognons

steamed cuit à la vapeur

stew ragoût

Stilton (cheese) fromage anglais réputé (blanc ou à moisissures bleues)

strawberry fraise

string bean haricot vert

stuffed farci, fourré

stuffing farce

suck(l)ing pig cochon de lait

sugar sucre

sugarless sans sucre

sundae coupe de glace aux fruits, noix, crème Chantilly et parfois sirop

supper souper, léger repas du soir

swede rutabaga

sweet 1) doux 2) dessert

~ **corn** maïs jaune

~ **potato** patate douce

sweetbread ris de veau

Swiss cheese emmenthal

Swiss roll biscuit roulé à la confiture

Swiss steak tranche de bœuf braisée avec des légumes et des épices

T-bone steak morceau de contrefilet et de filet séparés par un os en forme de T

table d'hôte menu fixe

tangerine orange-mandarine

tarragon estragon

tart tarte (généralement aux fruits)

tenderloin filet (de viande)

Thousand Island dressing mayonnaise aux piments ou au ketchup, avec des poivrons, des olives et des œufs durs

thyme thym

toad-in-the-hole morceaux de viande ou de saucisse briochés

toasted grillé

~ **cheese** toast au fromage

tomato tomate

tongue langue

treacle mélasse

trifle sorte de charlotte russe à l'eau-de-vie avec amandes, confiture, crème Chantilly et crème anglaise

trout truite

truffle truffe

tuna, tunny thon

turkey dinde

turnip navet

turnover chausson

turtle tortue

underdone saignant

vanilla vanille

veal veau

~ **bird** paupiette de veau

vegetable légume

~ **marrow** courgette

venison gros gibier

vichyssoise soupe froide aux poireaux, pommes de terre et crème

vinegar vinaigre

Virginia baked ham jambon cuit au four, piqué de clous de girofles, garni de tranches d'ananas, de cerises et glacé avec le jus des fruits

wafer gaufrette

waffle sorte de gaufre, chaude

walnut noix

water ice sorbet

watercress cresson de fontaine

watermelon pastèque

well-done bien cuit

Welsh rabbit/rarebit croûte au fromage

whelk buccin (mollusque)

whipped cream crème Chantilly

whitebait blanchaille

Wiener Schnitzel escalope viennoise

wine list carte des vins

woodcock bécasse

Worcestershire sauce condiment liquide piquant, à base de vinaigre, de soja et d'ail

yoghurt yaourt

York ham jambon (fumé) d'York

Yorkshire pudding sorte de pâte à choux cuite et servie avec le rosbif

zucchini courgette

zwieback biscotte

Boissons

ale bière brune, légèrement sucrée, fermentée à haute température

bitter ~ brune, amère et plutôt lourde

brown ~ brune en bouteille, légèrement sucrée

light ~ blonde en bouteille

mild ~ brune à la pression, au goût prononcé

pale ~ blonde en bouteille

angostura essence aromatique amère ajoutée aux cocktails

applejack eau-de-vie de pomme

Athol Brose boisson écossaise composée de whisky, de miel, d'eau et parfois de flocons d'avoine

Bacardi cocktail cocktail au rhum avec du gin, du sirop de grenadine et du jus de lime (citron vert)

barley water boisson rafraîchissante à base d'orge et aromatisée de citron

barley wine bière brune très alcoolisée

beer bière

bottled ~ en bouteille

draft, draught ~ à la pression

bitters apéritifs et digestifs à base de racines, d'écorces ou d'herbes

black velvet champagne additionné de *stout* (accompagne souvent les huîtres)

bloody Mary vodka, jus de tomate et épices

bourbon whisky américain, à base de maïs

brandy 1) appellation générique désignant les eaux-de-vie de vin ou de fruit 2) cognac

~ **Alexander** mélange d'eau-de-vie, de crème de cacao et de crème fraîche

British wines vins «anglais» faits de raisins (ou du jus de raisin) importés en Grande-Bretagne

cherry brandy liqueur de cerise

chocolate chocolat

cider cidre

~ **cup** mélange de cidre, d'épices, de sucre et de glace

claret vin rouge de Bordeaux

cobbler *long drink* glacé à base de fruits, auquel on ajoute du vin ou une liqueur

coffee café

~ **with cream** crème

black ~ noir

caffeine-free ~ décaféiné

white ~ au lait

cordial liqueur

cream crème

cup boisson rafraîchissante composée de vin glacé, d'eau gazeuse, d'un spiritueux et décorée d'une tranche d'orange, de citron ou de concombre

daiquiri cocktail au rhum, au jus de lime et d'ananas

double double dose

Drambuie liqueur à base de whisky et de miel

dry martini 1) vermouth sec (GB) 2) cocktail au gin avec un peu de vermouth sec (US)

egg-nog boisson faite de rhum ou d'un autre alcool fort avec des jaunes d'œufs battus et du sucre

gin and it mélange de gin et de

vermouth italien

gin-fizz gin avec jus de citron, sucre et soda

ginger ale boisson sans alcool, parfumée à l'essence de gingembre

ginger beer boisson légèrement alcoolisée, à base de gingembre et de sucre

grasshopper mélange de crème de menthe, de crème de cacao et de crème fraîche

Guinness (stout) bière brune légèrement sucrée, au goût très prononcé et à forte teneur en malt et houblon

half pint environ 3 décilitres

highball eau-de-vie ou whisky allongé d'eau gazeuse ou de *ginger ale*

iced glacé

Irish coffee café sucré, arrosé de whisky irlandais et nappé de crème Chantilly

Irish Mist liqueur irlandaise à base de whisky et de miel

Irish whiskey whisky irlandais, moins âpre que le *scotch;* outre l'orge, il contient du seigle, de l'avoine et du blé

juice jus

lager bière blonde légère, servie très fraîche

lemon squash citronnade

lemonade limonade

lime juice jus de lime (citron vert)

liquor spiritueux

long drink alcool allongé d'eau ou d'une boisson gazeuse, avec des glaçons

madeira madère

Manhattan whisky américain, vermouth et *angostura*

milk lait

~ shake frappé

mineral water eau minérale

mulled wine vin chaud aux épices

neat sans glace et sans eau, sec, pur

old-fashioned whisky, *angostura,* cerises au marasquin et sucre

on the rocks avec des glaçons

Ovaltine Ovomaltine

Pimm's cup(s) boisson alcoolisée mélangée à du jus de fruit ou du soda

~ No. 1 à base de gin

~ No. 2 à base de whisky

~ No. 3 à base de rhum

~ No. 4 à base d'eau-de-vie

pink champagne champagne rosé

pink lady mélange de blanc d'œuf, de Calvados, de jus de citron, de grenadine et de gin

pint environ 6 décilitres

port (wine) porto

porter bière brune et amère

quart 1,14 litre (US 0,95 litre)

root beer boisson gazeuse sucrée, aromatisée d'herbes et de racines

rum rhum

rye (whiskey) whisky de seigle, plus lourd et plus âpre que le *bourbon*

scotch (whisky) whisky écossais, généralement fait d'une combinaison de whisky d'orge et de whisky de blé

screwdriver vodka et jus d'orange

shandy *bitter ale* mélangée à une limonade ou une *ginger beer*

sherry xérès

short drink tout alcool non dilué

shot dose de spiritueux

sloe gin-fizz liqueur de prunelle avec soda et jus de citron

soda water eau gazeuse, soda

soft drink boisson sans alcool
spirits spiritueux
stinger cognac et crème de menthe
stout bière brune fortement houblonnée et alcoolisée
straight alcool bu sec, pur
tea thé
toddy grog
Tom Collins gin, jus de citron, sucre, eau gazeuse

tonic (water) eau gazéifiée, aromatisée de quinine
water eau
whisky sour whisky, jus de citron, sucre et soda
wine vin
   dry ~ sec
   red ~ rouge
   sparkling ~ mousseux
   sweet ~ doux (de dessert)
   white ~ blanc

Mini-grammaire anglaise

L'article

L'article défini (le, la, les) a une seule forme: *the*.

the room, the rooms	la chambre, les chambres

L'article indéfini (un, une, des) a deux formes: *a* s'emploie devant une consonne, *an* devant une voyelle ou un «h» muet.

a coat	un manteau
an umbrella	un parapluie
an hour	une heure

Some indique une quantité ou un nombre indéfini.

I'd like some water, please.	Je voudrais de l'eau, s.v.p.

Any s'emploie dans les phrases négatives et différents types d'interrogatives.

There isn't any soap.	Il n'y a pas de savon.
Do you have any stamps?	Avez-vous des timbres?

Le nom

Le pluriel de la plupart des noms se forme par l'addition de -*(e)s* au singulier.

cup — cups (tasse — tasses)	**dress — dresses** (robe — robes)

Note: Si un nom se termine par -*y* précédé d'une consonne, le pluriel se termine par -*ies;* si le -*y* est précédé d'une voyelle, il n'y a pas de changement.

lady — ladies (dame — dames)	**key — keys** (clef — clefs)

Quelques pluriels irréguliers:

man — men (homme — hommes)	**foot — feet** (pied — pieds)
woman — women (femme — femmes)	**tooth — teeth** (dent — dents)
child — children (enfant — enfants)	**mouse — mice** (souris — souris)

Le complément du nom (génitif)

1. Le possesseur est une personne: si le nom ne se termine pas par -*s*, on ajoute *'s*.

the boy's room	la chambre du garçon
the children's clothes	les vêtements des enfants

Si le nom se termine par *s*, on ajoute l'apostrophe (').

the boys' room	la chambre des garçons

2. Le possesseur n'est pas une personne: on utilise la préposition *of*:

the key of the door	la clef de la porte

L'adjectif

Les adjectifs se placent normalement avant le nom.

a large brown suitcase	une grande valise brune

Il y a deux façons de former le comparatif et le superlatif des adjectifs:

1. Les adjectifs d'une syllabe et de nombreux adjectifs de deux syllabes prennent la terminaison -*(e)r* et -*(e)st*.

small (petit) **— smaller — smallest**	**pretty** (joli) **— prettier — prettiest***

2. Les adjectifs de trois syllabes et plus, et certains de deux (en particulier ceux qui se terminent par -*ful* et -*less*) forment leurs comparatifs et superlatifs avec *more* et *most*.

expensive (cher) **— more expensive — most expensive**	

---

* L'«y» se change en «i» lorsqu'il est précédé d'une consonne.

Le pronom

	Sujet	Complément (dir./indir.)	Possessif 1	2
Singulier				
1re personne	I	me	my	mine
2e personne	you	you	your	yours
3e personne (m)	he	him	his	his
(f)	she	her	her	hers
(n)	it	it	its	–
Pluriel				
1re personne	we	us	our	ours
2e personne	you	you	your	yours
3e personne	they	them	their	their

Note: L'anglais ignore le tutoiement. La forme *you* signifie donc «tu» et «vous».

Le cas complément s'emploie aussi après les prépositions.

Give it to me. Donnez-le-moi.

La forme 1 du possessif correspond à «mon», «ton», etc., la forme 2 à «le mien», «le tien», etc.

Where's my key? Où est ma clef? **That's not mine.** Ce n'est pas la mienne.

Verbes auxiliaires

a. **to be** (être)

	Forme contractée	Négatif — formes contractées		
I am	I'm		I'm not	
you are	you're	you're not	ou	you aren't
he is	he's	he's not		he isn't
she is	she's	she's not		she isn't
it is	it's	it's not		it isn't
we are	we're	we're not		we aren't
they are	they're	they're not		they aren't

Interrogatif: **Am I? Are you? Is he?** etc.

b. **to have** (avoir)

	Contraction		Contraction
I have	I've	we have	we've
you have	you've	you have	you've
he/she/it has	he/she/it's	they have	they've

Négation: **I have not (I haven't)**
Interrogation: **Have you? — Has he?**

c. to do (faire)

	Négatif contracté		Négatif contracté
I do	**I don't**	**we do**	**we don't**
you do	**you don't**	**you do**	**you don't**
he/she/it does	**he/she/it doesn't**	**they do**	**they don't**

Interrogation: **Do you? Does he/she/it?**

Autres verbes

L'infinitif est utilisé pour toutes les personnes du présent; on ajoute simplement *-(e)s* à la 3ᵉ personne du singulier.

	(to) love (aimer)	**(to) come** (venir)	**(to) go** (aller)
I	love	come	go
you	love	come	go
he/she/it	loves	comes	goes
we	love	come	go
they	love	come	go

La négation se forme au moyen de l'auxiliaire *do/does* + *not* + infinitif du verbe.

We do not (don't) like this hotel.   Nous n'aimons pas cet hôtel.

L'interrogation se forme aussi avec l'auxiliaire *do* + sujet + infinitif.

Do you like her?   L'aimez-vous?

Verbes irréguliers

L'imparfait et le participe passé des verbes réguliers se forment en ajoutant *-(e)s* à l'infinitif. La liste suivante vous donne les verbes irréguliers anglais. Les verbes composés ou précédés d'un préfixe se conjuguent comme les verbes principaux: p.ex. *withdraw* se conjugue comme *draw* et *mistake* comme *take*.

Infinitif	Imparfait	Participe passé	
arise	arose	arisen	*(se) lever*
awake	awoke	awoken	*(se) réveiller*
be	was	been	*être*
bear	bore	borne	*porter*
beat	beat	beaten	*battre*
become	became	become	*devenir*
begin	began	begun	*commencer*
bend	bent	bent	*plier*
bet	bet	bet	*parier*
bid	bade/bid	bidden/bid	*ordonner*
bind	bound	bound	*attacher*
bite	bit	bitten	*mordre*
bleed	bled	bled	*saigner*
blow	blew	blown	*souffler*
break	broke	broken	*briser*
breed	bred	bred	*élever*

bring	brought	brought	*apporter*
build	built	built	*bâtir*
burn	burnt/burned	burnt/burned	*brûler*
burst	burst	burst	*éclater*
buy	bought	bought	*acheter*
can*	could	—	*pouvoir*
cast	cast	cast	*jeter*
catch	caught	caught	*attraper*
choose	chose	chosen	*choisir*
cling	clung	clung	*se cramponner*
clothe	clothed/clad	clothed/clad	*vêtir*
come	came	come	*venir*
cost	cost	cost	*coûter*
creep	crept	crept	*ramper*
cut	cut	cut	*couper*
deal	dealt	dealt	*conclure (marché)*
dig	dug	dug	*creuser*
do (he does)	did	done	*faire*
draw	drew	drawn	*dessiner*
dream	dreamt/dreamed	dreamt/dreamed	*rêver*
drink	drank	drunk	*boire*
drive	drove	driven	*conduire (auto)*
dwell	dwelt	dwelt	*habiter*
eat	ate	eaten	*manger*
fall	fell	fallen	*tomber*
feed	fed	fed	*nourrir*
feel	felt	felt	*ressentir*
fight	fought	fought	*combattre*
find	found	found	*trouver*
flee	fled	fled	*fuir*
fling	flung	flung	*lancer*
fly	flew	flown	*voler*
forsake	forsook	forsaken	*abandonner*
freeze	froze	frozen	*geler*
get	got	got	*obtenir*
give	gave	given	*donner*
go	went	gone	*aller*
grind	ground	ground	*moudre*
grow	grew	grown	*croître*
hang	hung	hung	*pendre*
have	had	had	*avoir*
hear	heard	heard	*entendre*
hew	hewed	hewed/hewn	*couper*
hide	hid	hidden	*cacher*
hit	hit	hit	*frapper*
hold	held	held	*tenir*
hurt	hurt	hurt	*blesser*
keep	kept	kept	*garder*
kneel	knelt	knelt	*s'agenouiller*

* présent de l'indicatif

knit	knitted/knit	knitted/knit	*tricoter/unir*
know	knew	known	*savoir*
lay	laid	laid	*étendre, placer*
lead	led	led	*guider*
lean	leant/leaned	leant/leaned	*s'appuyer*
leap	leapt/leaped	leapt/leaped	*sauter*
learn	learnt/learned	learnt/learned	*apprendre*
leave	left	left	*quitter*
lend	lent	lent	*prêter*
let	let	let	*permettre*
lie	lay	lain	*être couché*
light	lit/lighted	lit/lighted	*allumer*
lose	lost	lost	*perdre*
make	made	made	*faire*
may*	might	—	*pouvoir*
mean	meant	meant	*signifier*
meet	met	met	*rencontrer*
mow	mowed	mowed/mown	*faucher*
must*	—	—	*falloir*
ought (to)*	—	—	*devoir*
pay	paid	paid	*payer*
put	put	put	*mettre*
read	read	read	*lire*
rid	rid	rid	*débarrasser*
ride	rode	ridden	*monter (à cheval)*
ring	rang	rung	*sonner*
rise	rose	risen	*se lever*
run	ran	run	*courir*
saw	sawed	sawn	*scier*
say	said	said	*dire*
see	saw	seen	*voir*
seek	sought	sought	*chercher*
sell	sold	sold	*vendre*
send	sent	sent	*envoyer*
set	set	set	*poser*
sew	sewed	sewed/sewn	*coudre*
shake	shook	shaken	*secouer*
shall*	should	—	*devoir*
shed	shed	shed	*verser*
shine	shone	shone	*briller*
shoot	shot	shot	*tirer*
show	showed	shown	*montrer*
shrink	shrank	shrunk	*rétrécir*
shut	shut	shut	*fermer*
sing	sang	sung	*chanter*
sink	sank	sunk	*couler*
sit	sat	sat	*s'asseoir*
sleep	slept	slept	*dormir*
slide	slid	slid	*glisser*

* présent de l'indicatif

sling	slung	slung	*jeter*
slink	slunk	slunk	*s'esquiver*
slit	slit	slit	*fendre*
smell	smelled/smelt	smelled/smelt	*sentir (odeur)*
sow	sowed	sown/sowed	*semer*
speak	spoke	spoken	*parler*
speed	sped/speeded	sped/speeded	*accélérer*
spell	spelt/spelled	spelt/spelled	*épeler*
spend	spent	spent	*dépenser*
spill	spilt/spilled	spilt/spilled	*renverser*
spin	spun	spun	*filer*
spit	spat	spat	*cracher*
split	split	split	*fendre, séparer*
spoil	spoilt/spoiled	spoilt/spoiled	*gâter*
spread	spread	spread	*répandre, enduire*
spring	sprang	sprung	*jaillir*
stand	stood	stood	*se tenir debout*
steal	stole	stolen	*dérober*
stick	stuck	stuck	*coller*
sting	stung	stung	*piquer*
stink	stank/stunk	stunk	*empester*
strew	strewed	strewed/strewn	*joncher*
stride	strode	stridden	*marcher à grands pas*
strike	struck	struck/stricken	*frapper*
string	strung	strung	*ficeler*
strive	strove	striven	*s'efforcer*
swear	swore	sworn	*jurer*
sweep	swept	swept	*balayer*
swell	swelled	swollen	*enfler*
swim	swam	swum	*nager*
swing	swung	swung	*se balancer*
take	took	taken	*prendre*
teach	taught	taught	*enseigner*
tear	tore	torn	*déchirer*
tell	told	told	*dire*
think	thought	thought	*penser*
throw	threw	thrown	*jeter*
thrust	thrust	thrust	*pousser*
tread	trod	trodden	*piétiner*
wake	woke/waked	woken/waked	*(se) réveiller*
wear	wore	worn	*porter (habit)*
weave	wove	woven	*tisser*
weep	wept	wept	*pleurer*
will*	would	—	*vouloir*
win	won	won	*gagner*
wind	wound	wound	*enrouler*
wring	wrung	wrung	*tordre*
write	wrote	written	*écrire*

---

* présent de l'indicatif

Abréviations anglaises

AA	*Automobile Association*	Automobile Club de Grande-Bretagne
AAA	*American Automobile Association*	Automobile Club des Etats-Unis
ABC	*American Broadcasting Company*	société privée de radio-diffusion et de télévision (US)
A.D.	*anno Domini*	apr. J.-C.
AIDS	*acquired immune deficiency syndrome*	SIDA
Am.	*America ; American*	Amérique; américain
a.m.	*ante meridiem (before noon)*	avant midi (de minuit à midi)
Amtrak	*American railroad corporation*	société privée des chemins de fer américains
AT & T	*American Telephone and Telegraph Company*	compagnie privée des téléphones et télégraphes (US)
Ave.	*avenue*	avenue
BBC	*British Broadcasting Corporation*	société britannique de radio-diffusion et de télévision
B.C.	*before Christ*	av. J.-C.
bldg.	*building*	immeuble
Blvd.	*boulevard*	boulevard
B.R.	*British Rail*	chemins de fer britanniques
Brit.	*Britain ; British*	Grande-Bretagne ; britannique
Bros.	*brothers*	frères
¢	*cent*	1/100 de dollar
Can.	*Canada ; Canadian*	Canada ; canadien
CBS	*Columbia Broadcasting System*	société privée de radiodiffusion et de télévision (US)
CID	*Criminal Investigation Department*	police judiciaire (GB)
CNN	*Cable News Network*	société privée de télévision
CNR	*Canadian National Railway*	société nationale des chemins de fer canadiens
c/o	*(in) care of*	p.a., aux bons soins de
Co.	*company*	compagnie
Corp.	*corporation*	type de société
CPR	*Canadian Pacific Railways*	société privée des chemins de fer canadiens

D.C.	*District of Columbia*	District de Columbia (Washington, D.C.)
DDS	*Doctor of Dental Science*	dentiste
dept.	*department*	département
e.g.	*for instance*	par exemple
Eng.	*England; English*	Angleterre; anglais
EU	*European Union*	UE
excl.	*excluding; exclusive*	non compris, exclu
ft.	*foot/feet*	pied/pieds (30,5 cm)
GB	*Great Britain*	Grande-Bretagne
H.E.	*His/Her Excellency; His Eminence*	Son Excellence; Son Eminence
H.H.	*His Holiness*	Sa Sainteté
H.M.	*His/Her Majesty*	Sa Majesté
H.M.S.	*Her Majesty's ship*	bâtiment de la marine royale de Grande-Bretagne
hp	*horsepower*	chevaux-vapeur
Hwy	*highway*	route nationale
i.e.	*that is to say*	c'est-à-dire
in.	*inch*	pouce (2,54 cm)
Inc.	*incorporated*	type de société anonyme américaine
incl.	*including, inclusive*	compris, inclus
£	*pound sterling*	livre sterling
L.A.	*Los Angeles*	Los Angeles
Ltd.	*limited*	type de société anonyme britannique
M.D.	*Doctor of Medicine*	médecin
M.P.	*Member of Parliament*	membre du Parlement britannique
mph	*miles per hour*	miles à l'heure
Mr.	*Mister*	monsieur
Mrs.	*Missis*	madame
Ms.	*Missis/Miss*	madame/mademoiselle
nat.	*national*	national
NBC	*National Broadcasting Company*	société privée de radiodiffusion et de télévision (US)
No.	*number*	numéro
N.Y.C.	*New York City*	ville de New York
O.B.E.	*Officer (of the Order) of the British Empire*	Officier de l'Ordre de l'Empire britannique
p.	*page; penny/pence*	page; 1/100 de livre sterling
p.a.	*per annum*	par année, annuel
Ph.D.	*Doctor of Philosophy*	docteur en philosophie

p.m.	*post meridiem*	après midi
	(after noon)	(de midi à minuit)
PO	*Post Office*	bureau de poste
POO	*post office order*	mandat postal
P.T.O.	*please turn over*	tournez, s'il vous plaît
RAC	*Royal Automobile Club*	Automobile Club
		de Grande-Bretagne
RCMP	*Royal Canadian*	police royale montée
	Mounted Police	canadienne
Rd.	*road*	route, rue
ref.	*reference*	voir, comparer
Rev.	*reverend*	pasteur dans l'Eglise
		anglicane
RFD	*rural free delivery*	distribution du courrier
		à la campagne
RR	*railroad*	chemin de fer
RSVP	*please reply*	répondez, s'il vous plaît
$	*dollar*	dollar
Soc.	*society*	société
St.	*saint ; street*	saint ; rue
STD	*Subscriber Trunk Dialling*	téléphone automatique
UK	*United Kingdom*	Royaume-Uni
UN	*United Nations*	Nations Unies
UPS	*United Parcel Service*	service d'expédition
		de colis (US)
US	*United States*	Etats-Unis
USS	*United States Ship*	bâtiment de la marine de
		guerre américaine
VAT	*value added tax*	TVA
VIP	*very important person*	personne jouissant de
		privilèges particuliers
Xmas	*Christmas*	Noël
yd.	*yard*	yard (91,44 cm)
YMCA	*Young Men's Christian*	Union Chrétienne
	Association	de Jeunes Gens
YWCA	*Young Women's Christian*	Union Chrétienne
	Association	de Jeunes Filles
ZIP	*ZIP code*	numéro (code) postal

Nombres

Nombres cardinaux		Nombres ordinaux	
0	zero	1st	first
1	one	2nd	second
2	two	3rd	third
3	three	4th	fourth
4	four	5th	fifth
5	five	6th	sixth
6	six	7th	seventh
7	seven	8th	eighth
8	eight	9th	ninth
9	nine	10th	tenth
10	ten	11th	eleventh
11	eleven	12th	twelfth
12	twelve	13th	thirteenth
13	thirteen	14th	fourteenth
14	fourteen	15th	fifteenth
15	fifteen	16th	sixteenth
16	sixteen	17th	seventeenth
17	seventeen	18th	eighteenth
18	eighteen	19th	nineteenth
19	nineteen	20th	twentieth
20	twenty	21st	twenty-first
21	twenty-one	22nd	twenty-second
22	twenty-two	23rd	twenty-third
23	twenty-three	24th	twenty-fourth
24	twenty-four	25th	twenty-fifth
25	twenty-five	26th	twenty-sixth
30	thirty	27th	twenty-seventh
40	forty	28th	twenty-eighth
50	fifty	29th	twenty-ninth
60	sixty	30th	thirtieth
70	seventy	40th	fortieth
80	eighty	50th	fiftieth
90	ninety	60th	sixtieth
100	a/one hundred	70th	seventieth
230	two hundred and thirty	80th	eightieth
		90th	ninetieth
1,000	a/one thousand	100th	hundredth
10,000	ten thousand	230th	two hundred and thirtieth
100,000	a/one hundred thousand		
1,000,000	a/one million	1,000th	thousandth

L'heure

Les Britanniques et les Américains utilisent le système des douze heures. L'expression *a.m. (ante meridiem)* désigne les heures précédant midi, *p.m. (post meridiem)* celles de l'après-midi et du soir (jusqu'à minuit). Toutefois, en Grande-Bretagne, les horaires sont progressivement libellés sur le modèle continental.

I'll come at seven a.m. Je viendrai à 7 h. du matin.
I'll come at one p.m. Je viendrai à 1 h. de l'après-midi.
I'll come at eight p.m. Je viendrai à 8 h. du soir.

Les jours de la semaine

Sunday	dimanche	*Thursday*	jeudi
Monday	lundi	*Friday*	vendredi
Tuesday	mardi	*Saturday*	samedi
Wednesday	mercredi		

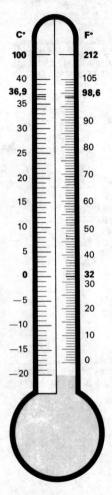

C°	F°
100	212
40	105
36,9	98,6
35	
30	90
25	80
20	70
15	60
10	50
5	40
0	32
	30
−5	20
−10	10
−15	0
−20	

Conversion tables/
Tables de conversion

Metres and feet
The figure in the middle stands for both metres and feet, e.g. 1 metre = 3.281 ft. and 1 foot = 0.30 m.

Mètres et pieds
Le chiffre du milieu représente à la fois des mètres et des pieds. Par ex.: 1 mètre = 3,281 pieds et 1 pied = 0,30 m.

Metres/Mètres		Feet/Pieds
0.30	1	3.281
0.61	2	6.563
0.91	3	9.843
1.22	4	13.124
1.52	5	16.403
1.83	6	19.686
2.13	7	22.967
2.44	8	26.248
2.74	9	29.529
3.05	10	32.810
3.66	12	39.372
4.27	14	45.934
6.10	20	65.620
7.62	25	82.023
15.24	50	164.046
22.86	75	246.069
30.48	100	328.092

Temperature
To convert Centigrade to Fahrenheit, multiply by 1.8 and add 32.
To convert Fahrenheit to Centigrade, subtract 32 from Fahrenheit and divide by 1.8.

Température
Pour convertir les degrés centigrades en degrés Fahrenheit, multipliez les premiers par 1,8 et ajoutez 32 au total obtenu.
Pour convertir les degrés Fahrenheit en degrés centigrades, soustrayez 32 et divisez le résultat par 1,8.